Lords of Finance

Liaquat Ahamed has been a professional investment manager for twenty-five years. He has worked at the World Bank in Washington, D.C., and the New York-based partnership of Fischer Francis Trees and Watts, where he served as chief executive. He is currently an adviser to several hedge fund groups, including the Rock Creek Group and the Rohatyn Group, is a director of Aspen Insurance Co., and is on the board of trustees of the Brookings Institution. He has degrees in economics from Harvard and Cambridge universities. *Lords of Finance*, which was shortlisted for the BBC Samuel Johnson Prize for Non-fiction and which won the *Financial Times*/Goldman Sachs Business Book of the Year Award, the Spear's Financial History Book of the Year Award, and the 2010 Pulitzer Prize for History, is Liaquat Ahamed's first book.

Praise for *Lords of Finance*

'Magisterial . . . A brilliantly readable history of an earlier era of economic implosion: the 1929 crash and those who caused it.'   *Observer*

'[Ahamed] provides a compelling and convincing narrative of bungling, tortured bankers vainly trying to reconcile their conflicting duties to their countries and to the global economy. The strength of his book is in humanising the world's descent into economic chaos.'
Robert Peston, *Sunday Times*

'A brilliant and timely book . . . Today's policy makers have learned from these dreadful mistakes, but they still have more to do to restore economic stability and bring down unemployment. They need to read this book.'   Richard Lambert, *Guardian*

'One of those rare books – authoritative, readable and relevant – that puts the "story" back into history . . . a spellbinding, richly human [and] cinematic narrative.'   Strobe Talbott

'[Ahamed's] book has immense importance to modern policymaking. It is voluminous history of the Great Depression seen through the actions of central bankers. The principal figures in the story are the governors of the central banks of the US, Great Britain, France and Germany. This is a fascinating and even a great book.'   *The Times*

'A major work of scholarship which offers vivid portraits of the central bankers of the day.'   *Daily Telegraph*

'A magisterial work . . . A grand, sweeping narrative of immense scope and power . . . A beautifully written book; Ahamed has a gift for phrase-making and storytelling that most full-time writers would envy – the decision to build *Lords of Finance* around these four men is a brilliant conceit . . . You read Ahamed's sections on reparations with a growing sense of horror, knowing how it all turns out. But you also read this book with a growing sense of recognition . . . you can't help thinking about the economic crisis we're living through now.'   *International Herald Tribune*

'A salutary warning from the past about the unexpected consequences of policy mistakes at the highest level. Historical but topical.'
Financial Times

'Highly readable . . . [Ahamed] cannot have foreseen how timely his book would be.'   Niall Ferguson

'Superlative . . . a subject of real fascination . . . *Lords of Finance* has the flair and wisdom to find a wide readership on the strength of its main ideas.'
New York Times

'The author of this timely insider's view of the crisis is a professional investment manager in New York who writes in plain English. He has a keen eye for detail.'   *Daily Mail*

'Fascinating . . . a brisk, original, incisive and entertaining account of a crucial time in the world's economic history that continues to affect us all today. Anyone who wants to understand the origins of the economic world we live in would do well to read this book.'   Michael Beschloss

Absorbing [and] provocative, not least because it is still relevant.'
The Economist

'A great read.'   George Soros

Lords of Finance

LIAQUAT AHAMED

WINDMILL BOOKS

Published by Windmill Books, 2010

6 8 10 9 7 5

Photograph credits – Page xii: J. Gaiger/Hulton Archive/Getty Images; pp. 34,
46, and 154: © Bettmann/Corbis; p. 62: Banque de France – Anonyme; pp.
242 and 290: Federal Reserve Bank of New York; p. 346: MPI/Hulton
Archive/Getty Images; p. 394: Hulton Archive/Getty Images; p. 478:
Bildarchiv Preussischer Kulturbesitz/Art Resource, N.Y.

First published in Great Britain in 2009 by William Heinemann

Windmill Books
Random House, 20 Vauxhall Bridge Road,
London SW1V 2SA

www.rbooks.co.uk

Addresses for companies within The Random House Group Limited can be
found at: www.randomhouse.co.uk/offices.htm

The Random House Group Limited Reg. No. 954009

A CIP catalogue record for this book
is available from the British Library

ISBN: 9780099493082

Designed by Marysarah Quinn

The Random House Group Limited supports The Forest Stewardship Council
(FSC), the leading international forest certification organisation. All our titles
that are printed on Greenpeace approved FSC certified paper carry
the FSC logo. Our paper procurement policy can be found at
www.rbooks.co.uk/environment

Typeset by SX Composing DTP, Rayleigh, Essex

Printed and bound in Great Britain by
CPI Cox & Wyman, Reading, RG1 8EX

TO MEENA

CONTENTS

FIGURES

Read no history—nothing but biography,
for that is life without theory.

—Benjamin Disraeli

Montagu Norman on the Duchess of York, *August 15, 1931*

INTRODUCTION

ON AUGUST 15, 1931, the following press statement was issued: "The Governor of the Bank of England has been indisposed as a result of the exceptional strain to which he has been subjected in recent months. Acting on medical advice he has abandoned all work and has gone abroad for rest and change." The governor was Montagu Collet Norman, D.S.O.—having repeatedly turned down a title, he was not, as so many people assumed, Sir Montagu Norman or Lord Norman. Nevertheless, he did take great pride in that D.S.O after his name—the Distinguished Service Order, the second highest decoration for bravery by a military officer.

Norman was generally wary of the press and was infamous for the lengths to which he would go to escape prying reporters—traveling under a false identity; skipping off trains; even once, slipping over the side of an ocean vessel by way of a rope ladder in rough seas. On this occasion, however, as he prepared to board the liner *Duchess of York* for Canada, he was unusually forthcoming. With that talent for understatement that came so naturally to his class and country, he declared to the reporters gathered at dockside, "I feel I want a rest because I have had a very hard time lately. I have not been quite as well as I would like and I think a trip on this fine boat will do me good."

The fragility of his mental constitution had long been an open secret within financial circles. Few members of the public knew the real truth— that for the last two weeks, as the world financial crisis had reached a crescendo and the European banking system teetered on the edge of collapse, the governor had been incapacitated by a nervous breakdown, brought on by extreme stress. The Bank press release, carried in newspapers from San Francisco to Shanghai, therefore came as a great shock to investors everywhere.

It is difficult so many years after these events to recapture the power and prestige of Montagu Norman in that period between the wars—his name carries little resonance now. But at the time, he was considered the most influential central banker in the world, according to the *New York Times*, the "monarch of [an] invisible empire." For Jean Monnet, godfather of the European Union, the Bank of England was then "the citadel of citadels" and "Montagu Norman was the man who governed the citadel. He was redoubtable."

Over the previous decade, he and the heads of the three other major central banks had been part of what the newspapers had dubbed "the most exclusive club in the world." Norman, Benjamin Strong of the New York Federal Reserve Bank, Hjalmar Schacht of the Reichsbank, and Émile Moreau of the Banque de France had formed a quartet of central bankers who had taken on the job of reconstructing the global financial machinery after the First World War.

But by the middle of 1931, Norman was the only remaining member of the original foursome. Strong had died in 1928 at the age of fifty-five, Moreau had retired in 1930, and Schacht had resigned in a dispute with his own government in 1930 and was flirting with Adolf Hitler and the Nazi Party. And so the mantle of leadership of the financial world had fallen on the shoulders of this colorful but enigmatic Englishman with his "waggish" smile, his theatrical air of mystery, his Van Dyke beard, and his conspiratorial costume: broad-brimmed hat, flowing cape, and sparkling emerald tie pin.

For the world's most important central banker to have a nervous breakdown as the global economy sank yet deeper into the second year of an unprecedented depression was truly unfortunate. Production in almost every country had collapsed—in the two worst hit, the United States and

Germany, it had fallen 40 percent. Factories throughout the industrial world—from the car plants of Detroit to the steel mills of the Ruhr, from the silk mills of Lyons to the shipyards of Tyneside—were shuttered or working at a fraction of capacity. Faced with shrinking demand, businesses had cut prices by 25 percent in the two years since the slump had begun.

Armies of the unemployed now haunted the towns and cities of the industrial nations. In the United States, the world's largest economy, some 8 million men and women, close to 15 percent of the labor force, were out of work. Another 2.5 million men in Britain and 5 million in Germany, the second and third largest economies in the world, had joined the unemployment lines. Of the four great economic powers, only France seemed to have been somewhat protected from the ravages of the storm sweeping the world, but even it was now beginning to slide downward.

Gangs of unemployed youths and men with nothing to do loitered aimlessly at street corners, in parks, in bars and cafés. As more and more people were thrown out of work and unable to afford a decent place to live, grim jerry-built shantytowns constructed of packing cases, scrap iron, grease drums, tarpaulins, and even of motor car bodies had sprung up in cities such as New York and Chicago—there was even an encampment in Central Park. Similar makeshift colonies littered the fringes of Berlin, Hamburg, and Dresden. In the United States, millions of vagrants, escaping the blight of inner-city poverty, had taken to the road in search of some kind—any kind—of work.

Unemployment led to violence and revolt. In the United States, food riots broke out in Arkansas, Oklahoma, and across the central and southwestern states. In Britain, the miners went out on strike, followed by the cotton mill workers and the weavers. Berlin was almost in a state of civil war. During the elections of September 1930, the Nazis, playing on the fears and frustrations of the unemployed and blaming everyone else—the Allies, the Communists, and the Jews—for the misery of Germany, gained close to 6.5 million votes, increasing their seats in the Reichstag from 12 to 107 and making them the second largest parliamentary party after the Social Democrats. Meanwhile in the streets, Nazi and Communist gangs clashed daily. There were coups in Portugal, Brazil, Argentina, Peru, and Spain.

The biggest economic threat now came from the collapsing banking system. In December 1930, the Bank of United States, which despite its name was a private bank with no official status, went down in the largest single bank failure in U.S. history, leaving frozen some $200 million in depositors' funds. In May 1931, the biggest bank in Austria, the Creditanstalt, owned by the Rothschilds no less, with $250 million in assets, closed its doors. On June 20, President Herbert Hoover announced a one-year moratorium on all payments of debts and reparations stemming from the war. In July, the Danatbank, the third largest in Germany, foundered, precipitating a run on the whole German banking system and a tidal wave of capital out of the country. The chancellor, Heinrich Brüning, declared a bank holiday, restricted how much German citizens could withdraw from their bank accounts, and suspended payments on Germany's short-term foreign debt. Later that month the crisis spread to the City of London, which, having lent heavily to Germany, found these claims now frozen. Suddenly, faced with the previously unthinkable prospect that Britain itself might be unable to meet its obligations, investors around the world started withdrawing funds from London. The Bank of England was forced to borrow $650 million from banks in France and the United States, including the Banque de France and the New York Federal Reserve Bank, to prevent its gold reserves from being completely depleted.

As the unemployment lines lengthened, banks shut their doors, farm prices collapsed, and factories closed, there was talk of apocalypse. On June 22, the noted economist John Maynard Keynes told a Chicago audience, "We are today in the middle of the greatest catastrophe—the greatest catastrophe due almost to entirely economic causes—of the modern world. I am told that the view is held in Moscow that this is the last, the culminating crisis of capitalism, and that our existing order of society will not survive it." The historian Arnold Toynbee, who knew a thing or two about the rise and fall of civilizations, wrote in his annual review of the year's events for the Royal Institute of International Affairs, "In 1931, men and women all over the world were seriously contemplating and frankly discussing the possibility that the Western system of Society might break down and cease to work."

During the summer a letter that Montagu Norman had written just a few months before to his counterpart at the Banque de France, Clément Moret, appeared in the press. "Unless drastic measures are taken to save it, the capitalist system throughout the civilized world will be wrecked within a year," declared Norman, adding in the waspish tone that he reserved for the French, "I should like this prediction to be filed for future reference." It was rumored that before he went off to convalesce in Canada, he had insisted that ration books be printed in case the country reverted to barter in the wake of a general currency collapse across Europe.

At times of crisis, central bankers generally believe that it is prudent to obey the admonition that mothers over the centuries have passed on to their children: "If you can't say anything nice, don't say anything at all." It avoids the recurring dilemma that confronts financial officials dealing with a panic—they can be honest in their public statements and thereby feed the frenzy or they can try to be reassuring, which usually entails resorting to outright untruths. That a man in Norman's position was willing to talk quite openly about the collapse of Western civilization signaled loud and clear that, in the face of the "economic blizzard," monetary leaders were running out of ideas and ready to declare defeat.

Not only was Norman the most eminent banker in the world, he was also admired as a man of character and judgment by financiers and officials of every shade of political opinion. Within that bastion of the plutocracy the partnership of the House of Morgan, for example, no one's advice or counsel was more highly valued—the firm's senior partner, Thomas Lamont, would later acclaim him as "the wisest man he had ever met." At the other end of the political spectrum, the British chancellor of the exchequer, Philip Snowden, a fervent Socialist who had himself frequently predicted the collapse of capitalism, could write gushingly that Norman "might have stepped out of the frame of the portrait of the most handsome courtier who ever graced the court of a queen," that "his sympathy with the suffering of nations is as tender as that of a woman for her child," and that he had "in abundant measure the quality of inspiring confidence."

Norman had acquired his reputation for economic and financial perspicacity because he had been so right on so many things. Ever since the end of the war, he had been a fervent opponent of exacting reparations from Germany. Throughout the 1920s, he had raised the alarm that the world was running short of gold reserves. From an early stage, he had warned about the dangers of the stock market bubble in the United States.

But a few lonely voices insisted that it was he and the policies he espoused, especially his rigid, almost theological, belief in the benefits of the gold standard, that were to blame for the economic catastrophe that was overtaking the West. One of them was that of John Maynard Keynes. Another was that of Winston Churchill. A few days before Norman left for Canada on his enforced holiday, Churchill, who had lost most of his savings in the Wall Street crash two years earlier, wrote from Biarritz to his friend and former secretary Eddie Marsh, "Everyone I meet seems vaguely alarmed that something terrible is going to happen financially. . . . I hope we shall hang Montagu Norman if it does. I will certainly turn King's evidence against him."

THE COLLAPSE OF the world economy from 1929 to 1933—now justly called the Great Depression—was the seminal economic event of the twentieth century. No country escaped its clutches; for more than ten years the malaise that it brought in its wake hung over the world, poisoning every aspect of social and material life and crippling the future of a whole generation. From it flowed the turmoil of Europe in the "low dishonest decade" of the 1930s, the rise of Hitler and Nazism, and the eventual slide of much of the globe into a Second World War even more terrible than the First.

The story of the descent from the roaring boom of the twenties into the Great Depression can be told in many different ways. In this book, I have chosen to tell it by looking over the shoulders of the men in charge of the four principal central banks of the world: the Bank of England, the Federal Reserve System, the Reichsbank, and the Banque de France.

When the First World War ended in 1918, among its innumerable casualties was the world's financial system. During the latter half of the nineteenth century, an elaborate machinery of international credit, centered in London, had been built upon the foundations of the gold standard and brought with it a remarkable expansion of trade and prosperity across the globe. In 1919, that machinery lay in ruins. Britain, France, and Germany were close to bankruptcy, their economies saddled with debt, their populations impoverished by rising prices, their currencies collapsing. Only the United States had emerged from the war economically stronger.

Governments then believed matters of finance were best left to bankers; and so the task of restoring the world's finances fell into the hands of the central banks of the four major surviving powers: Britain, France, Germany, and the United States.

This book traces the efforts of these central bankers to reconstruct the system of international finance after the First World War. It describes how, for a brief period in the mid-1920s, they appeared to succeed: the world's currencies were stabilized, capital began flowing freely across the globe, and economic growth resumed once again. But beneath the veneer of boomtown prosperity, cracks began to appear and the gold standard, which all had believed would provide an umbrella of stability, proved to be a straitjacket. The final chapters of the book describe the frantic and eventually futile attempts of central bankers as they struggled to prevent the whole world economy from plunging into the downward spiral of the Great Depression.

The 1920s were an era, like today's, when central bankers were invested with unusual power and extraordinary prestige. Four men in particular dominate this story: at the Bank of England was the neurotic and enigmatic Montagu Norman; at the Banque de France, Émile Moreau, xenophobic and suspicious; at the Reichsbank, the rigid and arrogant but also brilliant and cunning Hjalmar Schacht; and finally, at the Federal Reserve Bank of New York, Benjamin Strong, whose veneer of energy and drive masked a deeply wounded and overburdened man.

These four characters were, for much of the decade, at the center of events. Their lives and careers provide a distinctive window into this period of economic history, which helps to focus the complex history of the 1920s—the whole sorry and poisonous story of the failed peace, of war debts and reparations, of hyperinflation, of hard times in Europe and bonanza in America, of the boom and then the ensuing bust—to a more human, and manageable, scale.

Each in his own way illuminates the national psyche of his time. Montagu Norman, with his quixotic reliance on his faulty intuition, embodied a Britain stuck in the past and not yet reconciled to its newly diminished standing in the world. Émile Moreau, in his insularity and rancor, reflected all too accurately a France that had turned inward to lick the terrible wounds of war. Benjamin Strong, the man of action, represented a new generation in America, actively engaged in bringing its financial muscle to bear in world affairs. Only Hjalmar Schacht, in his angry arrogance, seemed out of tune with the weak and defeated Germany for which he spoke, although perhaps he was simply expressing a hidden truth about the nation's deeper mood.

There is also something very poignant in the contrast between the power these four men once exerted and their almost complete disappearance from the pages of history. Once styled by newspapers as the "World's Most Exclusive Club," these four once familiar names, lost under the rubble of time, now mean nothing to most people.

The 1920s were a time of transition. The curtain had come down on one age and a new age had yet to begin. Central banks were still privately owned, their key objectives to preserve the value of the currency and douse banking panics. They were only just beginning to espouse the notion that it was their responsibility to stabilize the economy.

During the nineteenth century, the governors of the Bank of England

and the Banque de France were shadowy figures, well known in financial circles but otherwise out of the public eye. By contrast, in the 1920s, very much like today, central bankers became a major focus of public attention. Rumors of their decisions and secret meetings filled the daily press as they confronted many of the same economic issues and problems that their successors do today: dramatic movements in stock markets, volatile currencies, and great tides of capital spilling from one financial center to another.

They had to operate, however, in old-fashioned ways with only primitive tools and sources of information at their disposal. Economic statistics had only just begun to be collected. The bankers communicated by mail—at a time when a letter from New York to London took a week to arrive—or, in situations of real urgency, by cable. It was only in the very last stages of the drama that they could even contact one another on the telephone, and then only with some difficulty.

The tempo of life was also different. No one flew from one city to another. It was the golden age of the ocean liner when a transatlantic crossing took five days, and one traveled with one's manservant, evening dress being de rigueur at dinner. It was an era when Benjamin Strong, head of the New York Federal Reserve, could disappear to Europe for four months without raising too many eyebrows—he would cross the Atlantic in May, spend the summer crisscrossing among the capitals of Europe consulting with his colleagues, take the occasional break at some of the more elegant spas and watering holes, and finally return to New York in September.

The world in which they operated was both cosmopolitan and curiously parochial. It was a society in which racial and national stereotypes were taken for granted as matters of fact rather than prejudice, a world in which Jack Morgan, son of the mighty Pierpont Morgan, might refuse to participate in a loan to Germany on the grounds that Germans were "second rate people" or oppose the appointment of Jews and Catholics to the Harvard Board of Overseers because "the Jew is always a Jew first and an American second, and the Roman Catholic, I fear, too often, a Papist first and an American second." In finance, during the late nineteenth century and early twentieth century, whether in London or New York, Berlin or Paris, there was one great divide. On one side stood the big Anglo-Saxon banking firms: J. P. Morgan, Brown Brothers, Barings; on the other the Jewish concerns: the four branches of the Rothschilds, Lazards, the great German Jewish banking houses of Warburgs and Kuhn Loeb, and mavericks such as Sir Ernest Cassel. Though the WASPs were, like so many people in those days, casually anti-Semitic, the two groups treated each other with a wary respect. They were all, however, snobs who looked down on interlopers. It was a society that could be smug and complacent, indifferent to the problems of unemployment or poverty. Only in Germany— and that is part of this story—did those undercurrents of prejudice eventually become truly malevolent.

As I began writing of these four central bankers and the role each played in setting the world on the path toward the Great Depression, another figure kept appearing, almost intruding into the scene: John Maynard Keynes, the greatest economist of his generation, though only thirty-six when he first appears in 1919. During every act of the drama so painfully being played out, he refused to keep quiet, insisting on at least one monologue even if it was from offstage. Unlike the others, he was not a decision maker. In those years, he was simply an independent observer, a commentator. But at every twist and turn of the plot, there he was holding forth from the wings, with his irreverent and playful wit, his luminous and constantly questioning intellect, and above all his remarkable ability to be right.

Keynes proved to be a useful counterpoint to the other four in the story that follows. They were all great lords of finance, standard-bearers of an orthodoxy that seemed to imprison them. By contrast, Keynes was a gadfly, a Cambridge don, a self-made millionaire, a publisher, journalist, and best-selling author who was breaking free from the paralyzing consensus that would lead to such disaster. Though only a decade younger than the four grandees, he might have been born into an entirely different generation.

To UNDERSTAND THE role of central bankers during the Great Depression, it is first necessary to understand what a central bank is and a little about how it operates. Central banks are mysterious institutions, the full details of their inner workings so arcane that very few outsiders, even economists, fully understand them. Boiled down to its essentials, a central bank is a bank that has been granted a monopoly over the issuance of currency.* This power gives it the ability to regulate the price of credit—interest rates—and hence to determine how much money flows through the economy.

Despite their role as national institutions determining credit policy for their entire countries, in 1914 most central banks were still privately owned. They therefore occupied a strange hybrid zone, accountable primarily to their directors, who were mainly bankers, paying dividends to their share-holders, but given extraordinary powers for entirely nonprofit purposes. Unlike today, however, when central banks are required by law to promote price stability and full employment, in 1914 the single most important, indeed overriding, objective of these institutions was to preserve the value of the currency.

At the time, all major currencies were on the gold standard, which tied a currency in value to a very specific quantity of gold. The pound sterling, for example, was defined as equivalent to 113 grains of pure gold, a grain being a unit of weight notionally equal to that of a typical grain taken from the middle of an ear of wheat. Similarly, the dollar was defined as 23.22 grains of gold of similar fineness. Since all currencies were fixed against gold, a corollary was that they were all fixed against one another. Thus there were 113/23.22 or $4.86 to the pound. All paper money was legally obligated to be freely convertible into its gold equivalent, and each of the

---

*The monopoly need not be complete. In Britain, while the Bank of England was granted a monopoly of currency in 1844, Scottish banks continued to issue currency and existing English banks with the authority to issue currency were grandfathered. The last private English banknotes were issued in 1921 by Fox, Fowler and Company, a Somerset bank.

major central banks stood ready to exchange gold bullion for any amount of their own currencies.

Gold had been used as a form of currency for millennia. As of 1913, a little over $3 billion, about a quarter of the currency actually circulating around the world, consisted of gold coins, another 15 percent of silver, and the remaining 60 percent of paper money. Gold coinage, however, was only a part, and not the most important part, of the picture.

Most of the monetary gold in the world, almost two-thirds, did not circulate but lay buried deep underground, stacked up in the form of ingots in the vaults of banks. In each country, though every bank held some bullion, the bulk of the nation's gold was concentrated in the vaults of the central bank. This hidden treasure provided the reserves for the banking system, determined the supply of money and credit within the economy, and served as the anchor for the gold standard.

While central banks had been granted the right to issue currency—in effect to print money—in order to ensure that that privilege was not abused, each one of them was required by law to maintain a certain quantity of bullion as backing for its paper money. These regulations varied from country to country. For example, at the Bank of England, the first $75 million equivalent of pounds that it printed were exempt, but any currency in excess of this amount had to be fully matched by gold. The Federal Reserve (the Fed), on the other hand, was required to have 40 percent of all the currency it issued on hand in gold—with no exemption floor. But varied as these regulations were, their ultimate effect was to tie the amount of each currency automatically and almost mechanically to its central banks' gold reserves.

In order to control the flow of currency into the economy, the central bank varied interest rates. It was like turning the dials up or down a notch on a giant monetary thermostat. When gold accumulated in its vaults, it would reduce the cost of credit, encouraging consumers and businesses to borrow and thus pump more money into the system. By contrast, when gold was scarce, interest rates were raised, consumers and businesses cut back, and the amount of currency in circulation contracted.

Because the value of a currency was tied, by law, to a specific quantity of gold and because the amount of currency that could be issued was tied to the quantity of gold reserves, governments had to live within their means, and when strapped for cash, could not manipulate the value of the currency. Inflation therefore remained low. Joining the gold standard became a "badge of honor," a signal that each subscribing government had pledged itself to a stable currency and orthodox financial policies. By 1914, fifty-nine countries had bound their currencies to gold.

Few people realized how fragile a system this was, built as it was on so narrow a base. The totality of gold ever mined in the whole world since the dawn of time was barely enough to fill a modest two-story town house. Moreover, new supplies were neither stable nor predictable, coming as they did in fits and starts and only by sheer coincidence arriving in sufficient quantities to meet the needs of the world economy. As a result, during periods when new gold finds were lean, such as between the California and Australian gold rushes of the 1850s and the discoveries in South Africa in the 1890s, prices of commodities fell across the world.

The gold standard was not without its critics. Many were simply cranks. Others, however, believed that allowing the growth of credit to be restricted by the amount of gold, especially during periods of falling prices, hurt producers and debtors—especially farmers, who were both.

The most famous spokesman for looser money and easier credit was Williams Jennings Bryan, the populist congressman from the farm state of Nebraska. He campaigned tirelessly to break the privileged status of gold and to expand the base upon which credit was created by including silver as a reserve metal. At the Democratic convention of 1896 he made one of the great speeches of American history—a wonderfully overripe flight of rhetoric delivered in that deep commanding voice of his—in which, addressing Eastern bankers, he declared, "You came to tell us that the great cities are in favor of the gold standard; we reply that the great cities rest upon our broad and fertile plains. Burn down your cities and leave our farms, and your cities will spring up again as if by magic. But destroy our farms and the grass will grow in the city. . . . You shall not press down upon the brow of labor this crown of thorns. You shall not crucify mankind upon a cross of gold."

It was a message whose time had come and gone. Ten years before he delivered that speech, two gold prospectors in South Africa, while out for a Sunday walk on a farm in the Witwatersrand, stumbled across a rocky formation that they recognized as gold-bearing reef. It proved to be an outcrop of the largest goldfield in the world. By the time of Bryan's speech, gold production had jumped 50 percent, South Africa had overtaken the United States as the world's largest producer, and the gold drought was over. Prices for all goods, including agricultural commodities, once again began to rise. Bryan won the Democratic nomination then and twice more, in 1900 and 1908, but he was never elected president.

Though prices rose and fell in great cycles under the gold standard due to ebbs and flows in the supply of the precious metal, the slope of these curves was gentle and at the end of the day prices returned to where they began. While it may have succeeded in controlling inflation, the gold standard was incapable of preventing the sort of financial booms and busts that were, and continue to be, such a feature of the economic landscape. These bubbles and crises seem to be deep-rooted in human nature and inherent to the capitalist system. By one count there have been sixty different crises since the early seventeenth century—the first documented bank panic can, however, be dated to A.D. 33 when the Emperor Tiberius had to inject one million gold pieces of public money into the Roman financial system to keep it from collapsing.

Each of these episodes differed in detail. Some originated in the stock market, some in the credit market, some in the foreign exchange market, occasionally even in the world of commodities. Sometimes they affected a single country, sometimes a group of countries, very occasionally the whole world. All, however, shared a common pattern: an eerily similar cycle from greed to fear.

Financial crises would generally begin innocently enough with a surge of healthy optimism among investors. Over time, reinforced by cavalier attitudes to risk among bankers, this optimism would transform itself into overconfidence, occasionally even into a mania. The accompanying boom would go on for much longer than anyone expected. Then would come a sudden shock—a bankruptcy, a surprisingly large loss, a financial scandal involving fraud. Whatever the event, it would provoke a sudden and dramatic shift in sentiment. Panic would ensue. As investors were forced to liquidate into a falling market, losses would mount, banks would cut back their loans, and frightened depositors would start pulling their money out of banks.

If all that happened during these periods of so-called distress was that foolish investors and lenders lost money, no one else would have cared. But a problem in one bank raised fears of problems at other banks. And because financial institutions were so interconnected, borrowing large amounts of money from one another even in the nineteenth century, difficulties in one area would transmit themselves through the entire system. It was precisely because crises had a way of spreading, threatening to undermine the integrity of the whole system, that central banks became involved. In addition to keeping their hands on the levers of the gold standard, they therefore acquired a second role—that of forestalling bank panics and other financial crises.

The central banks had powerful tools to deal with these outbursts—specifically their authority to print currency and their ability to marshal their large concentrated holdings of gold. But for all of this armory of instruments, ultimately the goal of a central bank in a financial crisis was both very simple and very elusive—to reestablish trust in banks.

Such breakdowns are not some historical curiosity. As I write this in October 2008, the world is in the middle of one such panic—the most severe for seventy-five years, since the bank runs of 1931–1933 that feature so prominently in the last few chapters of this book. The credit markets are frozen, financial institutions are hoarding cash, banks are going under or being taken over by the week, stock markets are crumbling. Nothing brings home the fragility of the banking system or the potency of a financial crisis more vividly than writing about these issues from the eye of the storm. Watching the world's central bankers and finance officials grappling with the current situation—trying one thing after another to restore confidence, throwing everything they can at the problem, coping daily with unexpected and startling shifts in market sentiment—reinforces the lesson that there is no magic bullet or simple formula for dealing with financial panics. In trying to calm anxious investors and soothe skittish markets, central bankers are called upon to wrestle with some of the most elemental and unpredictable forces of mass psychology. It is the skill that they display in navigating these storms through uncharted waters that ultimately makes or breaks their reputation.

PART ONE

✳

THE
UNEXPECTED
STORM

✳

AUGUST 1914

1. PROLOGUE

*What an extraordinary episode in the economic
progress of man that age was which came to an end
in August 1914!*

—JOHN MAYNARD KEYNES,
The Economic Consequences of the Peace

IN 1914, London stood at the center of an elaborate network of international credit, built upon the foundations of the gold standard. The system had brought with it a remarkable expansion of trade and prosperity across the globe. The previous forty years had seen no big wars or great revolutions. The technological advances of the mid-nineteenth century—railways, steamships, and the telegraph—had spread across the world, opening up vast territories to settlement and trade. International commerce boomed as European capital flowed freely around the globe, financing ports in India, rubber plantations in Malaya, cotton in Egypt, factories in Russia, wheat fields in Canada, gold and diamond mines in South Africa, cattle ranches in Argentina, the Berlin-to-Baghdad Railway, and both the Suez and the Panama canals. Although every so often the system was shaken by financial crises and banking panics, depressions in trade were short-lived and the world economy had always bounced back.

More than anything else, more even than the belief in free trade, or the ideology of low taxation and small government, the gold standard was the economic totem of the age. Gold was the lifeblood of the financial system.

It was the anchor for most currencies, it provided the foundation for banks, and in a time of war or panic, it served as a store of safety. For the growing middle classes of the world, who provided so much of the savings, the gold standard was more than simply an ingenious system for regulating the issue of currency. It served to reinforce all those Victorian virtues of economy and prudence in public policy. It had, in the words of H. G. Wells, "a magnificent stupid honesty" about it. Among bankers, whether in London or New York, Paris or Berlin, it was revered with an almost religious fervor, as a gift of providence, a code of behavior transcending time and place.

In 1909, the British journalist Norman Angell, then Paris editor of the French edition of the *Daily Mail,* published a pamphlet entitled *Europe's Optical Illusion.* The thesis of his slim volume was that the economic benefits of war were so illusory—hence the title—and the commercial and financial linkages between countries now so extensive that no rational country should contemplate starting a war. The economic chaos, especially the disruptions to international credit, that would ensue from a war among the Great Powers would harm all sides and the victor would lose as much as the vanquished. Even if war were to break out in Europe by accident, it would speedily be brought to an end.

Angell was well placed to write about global interdependence. All his life he had been something of a nomad. Born into a middle-class Lincolnshire family, he had been sent at an early age to a French lycée in St. Omer. At seventeen he became the editor of an English-language newspaper in Geneva, attending the university there, and then, despairing of the future of Europe, emigrated to the United States. Though only five feet tall and of slight build, he plunged into a life of manual labor, working in California for seven years variously as a vine planter, irrigation-ditch digger, cowpuncher, mail carrier, and prospector, before eventually settling down as a reporter for the *St. Louis Globe-Democrat* and the *San Francisco Chronicle.* Returning to Europe in 1898, he moved to Paris, where he joined the *Daily Mail.*

Angell's pamphlet was issued in book form in 1910 under the title *The*

Great Illusion. The argument that it was not so much the cruelty of war as its economic futility that made it unacceptable as an instrument of state power struck a chord in that materialistic era. The work became a cult. By 1913, it had sold more than a million copies and been translated into twenty-two languages, including Chinese, Japanese, Arabic, and Persian. More than forty organizations were formed to spread its message. It was quoted by Sir Edward Grey, the British foreign secretary; by Count von Metternich; and by Jean Jaurès, the French Socialist leader. Even Kaiser Wilhelm, better known for his bellicosity than his embrace of pacifism, was said to have expressed some interest in the theory.

Angell's most prominent disciple was Reginald Brett, second Viscount Esher, a liberally minded establishment figure, and close confidant of King Edward VII. Though Lord Esher had been offered numerous high positions in government, he preferred to remain merely deputy constable and lieutenant governor of Windsor Castle while exerting his considerable influence behind the scenes. Most important, he was a founding member of the Committee of Imperial Defense, an informal but powerful organization formed after the debacles of the Boer War to reflect and advise on the military strategy of the British Empire.

In February 1912, the committee conducted hearings on issues related to trade in time of war. Much of the German merchant marine was then insured through Lloyds of London, and the committee was dumbfounded to hear the chairman of Lloyds testify that in the event of war, were German ships to be sunk by the Royal Navy, Lloyds would be both honor-bound and, according to its lawyers, legally obliged to cover the losses. The possibility that while Britain and Germany were at war, British insurance companies would be required to compensate the Kaiser for his sunken tonnage made it hard even to conceive of a European conflict.

It was no wonder that during a series of lectures on *The Great Illusion* delivered at Cambridge and the Sorbonne, Lord Esher would declare that "new economic factors clearly prove the inanity of war," and that the "commercial disaster, financial ruin and individual suffering" of a European war would be so great as to make it unthinkable. Lord Esher and Angell were right about the meager benefits and the high costs of war. But trusting too much in the rationality of nations and seduced by the extraordinary economic achievements of the era—a period the French would later so evocatively call La Belle Époque—they totally misjudged the likelihood that a war involving all the major European powers would break out.

2. A STRANGE AND LONELY MAN

BRITAIN: 1914

Anybody who goes to see a psychiatrist ought to have his head examined.

—SAMUEL GOLDWYN

ON TUESDAY, July 28, 1914, Montagu Norman, then one of the partners in the Anglo-American merchant banking firm of Brown Shipley, came up to London for the day. It was the height of the holiday season, and like almost everyone else of his class in Britain, he had spent much of the previous week in the country. He was in the process of dissolving his partnership and was required briefly in the City. That same afternoon it was reported that Austria had declared war on Serbia and was already bombarding Belgrade. Despite this news, Norman, "feeling far from well" under the strain of the painful negotiations, decided to return to the country.

Neither he nor almost anyone else in Britain imagined that over the next few days the country would face the most severe banking crisis in its history; that the international financial system, which had brought so much prosperity to the world, would completely unravel; and that, within less than a week, most of Europe, Britain included, would have stumbled blindly into war.

Norman, indeed most of his countrymen, had paid only cursory attention to the brewing European crisis over the previous month. The assassination in Sarajevo of the archduke Franz Ferdinand, heir presumptive to the Austrian Empire, and his wife Sophie by a comic-opera band of bomb-throwing Serbian nationalists on June 28 had seemed at the time to be just another violent chapter in the disturbed history of the Balkans. It did finally capture the news headlines in Britain when Austria issued an ultimatum to Serbia on July 24, accusing it of being complicit in the assassination and threatening war. But even then, most people blithely continued with their relaxed summer schedule. It was hard to get too concerned about a crisis in Central Europe when the prime minister himself, H. H. Asquith, felt sufficiently at ease to insist upon his weekend of golfing in Berkshire, and the foreign secretary, Sir Edward Grey, had gone off, as he did every weekend in the summer, to his lodge in Hampshire for a spot of trout fishing.

It had been one of those glorious English summers, not a cloud in the sky for days on end, with temperatures in the 90s. Norman had taken an earlier extended two-month holiday in the United States, spending his time, as he usually did on his annual visits, in New York and Maine. He had sailed back to England at the end of June, to spend a leisurely July in London, enjoying the good weather, catching up with old friends from Eton, and passing the days at Lord's watching cricket, a family obsession. He had also finally settled with his partners about withdrawing his capital, and going his own way. It had been a painful decision. His grandfather had been the senior partner at Brown Shipley, an affiliate of the U.S. investment house of Brown Brothers, for more than thirty-five years. Norman himself had worked there since 1894. But a combination of ill health and recurring conflicts with the other members of the firm had seemed to leave him with little choice but to sever his connections.

Norman returned to Gloucestershire on the morning of Wednesday, July 29, to find an urgent telegram recalling him to London. Taking a train the same day, he arrived in the evening, too late to attend a frantic meeting of the "Court"—the board of directors—of the Bank of England. Norman had been a member of this exclusive club since 1905.

Though forty-three years old, Norman was still not married and lived alone in a large two-story stucco house, Thorpe Lodge, just off Holland Park in West London. The house and his staff of seven servants were his two great luxuries. When he had bought it in 1905, it was a wreck; over the next seven years, he had devoted his energies to a complete reconstruction. He had designed much of the interior himself, including the furniture. Influenced by the ideals of William Morris and the Arts and Crafts movement, he had hired the best craftsmen and employed the most expensive materials, even occasionally stopping by the workshops on his way home from the City to help with the carpentry.

His taste in decoration was, it has to be said, a little idiosyncratic, even odd. The house was paneled in exotic woods imported from Africa and the Americas, giving it the austere and gloomy air of a sort of millionaire's monastery. There was little ornamentation: an entrance hall of shimmering bricks, which looked like mother-of pearl but were in fact a type of industrial silicone; two giant embroidered Japanese panels depicting peacocks; and a gigantic seventeenth-century Italian fireplace. But it was his haven from the world. On one side, he had built a huge groin-vaulted music room, in which he held small concerts: string quartets playing chamber music by Brahms or Schubert, occasionally for Norman alone. And below the house, he had converted a small paddock into an exquisite little terraced garden shaded by fruit trees, overlooked by a pergola where he took his meals in summer.

Although he had some inherited wealth, the house aside, Norman lived quite simply. He had passed his father's estate at Much Hadham, in Hertfordshire, on to his younger brother, who was married and had a family, while he contented himself with a little farmyard cottage on the grounds.

NORMAN NEITHER LOOKED nor dressed like a banker. Tall, with a broad forehead and a pointed beard, already white, he had the long fine hands of an artist or a musician. He looked more like a grandee out of Velázquez or a courtier from the time of Charles II. But despite appearances, his professional pedigree was impeccable: his father and mother had come from two of the most established and well-known English banking families.

Born in 1871, Montagu Norman, from his early childhood, had never quite seemed to fit in. He was sickly from birth and as a boy suffered from terrible migraines. His emotional and highly strung mother, herself subject to depressions and imaginary illnesses, fussed over him excessively. Like his grandfather and father before him, he went to Eton. But unlike his grandfather, father, uncle, and eventually his brother, who had all been captains of the cricket XI, Montagu did not excel in the atmosphere of competition and athleticism, and was a misfit—lonely, isolated, and generally moody. In 1889 he went up to King's College, Cambridge, but again unhappy and out of place, he withdrew after a year.

Even as a young adult, he seemed to have a hard time finding himself. He spent a desultory couple of years traveling in Europe, living for a year in Dresden, where he picked up German and an interest in speculative philosophy, and a year in Switzerland. In 1892, he returned to England to join the family concern, Martins Bank, in which his father and an uncle were partners, as a trainee clerk in the Lombard Street branch. Unable to muster much enthusiasm or interest in the dull business of commercial banking, in 1894, he decided to try out his maternal grandfather's bank, Brown Shipley. Its main activity was financing trade between the United States and Britain, which at least got him out of London and enabled him to spend almost two years working at the offices of Brown Brothers in New York City. He found life in America, with its fewer social restrictions, more liberating and less hidebound than the constricted world of London banking and even began to contemplate settling in the United States.

Instead, he found his deliverance in war. In October 1899, the Boer War broke out. Norman, who had joined the militia in 1894, spending several weeks in training every summer, and by now a captain, immediately volunteered for active service. He was not a particularly fervent imperialist. Rather he seems to have been motivated by a romantic quest for adventure and a desire to escape his mundane existence.

By the time he arrived in South Africa in March 1900, the British occupying force of some 150,000 men was engaged in a bitter guerrilla war with a Boer insurgency of some 20,000 men. Placed in command of a counterinsurgency unit, whose job it was to hunt down Boer commandos, Norman became a changed man in the field. Despite the difficult conditions, poor food, oppressive heat, and lack of sleep, he relished the danger and discovered a newfound confidence. "I feel a different person now . . . ," he wrote to his parents. "One looks ahead with something of dismay to the time when one will again have to settle down to civilized life."

He was eventually awarded a D.S.O.—the Distinguished Service Order, the second highest decoration for bravery by an officer. It would remain one of his proudest achievements—for many years, even when he had attained worldwide prominence, it was the only distinction that he insisted on including in his entry in the British edition of *Who's Who*. But sheer physical hardship took its toll on his frail constitution, and in October 1901, he developed severe gastritis and was invalided home.

Back in civilian life, he spent the next two years rebuilding his health, including several months convalescing at his uncle's villa at Hyères on the Riviera, thus beginning a long affair with the Côte d'Azur. Not until 1905 was he able to resume full-time work at Brown Shipley, where for the next six years he was one of the four main partners—an especially dispiriting time marred by endless disagreements with his colleagues over business strategy.

But it was his personal life that weighed most on him. In 1906, a broken engagement drove him into the first of his nervous breakdowns. Thereafter he displayed the classic signs of manic depression: periods of euphoria followed by severe despondency. Normally one of the most charming of companions, when afflicted by one of his black moods, which could last for weeks, he would become extremely irritable, indulging in tantrums and lashing out irrationally at anyone and everyone around him. After 1909, these episodes intensified until in September 1911 he collapsed. Advised by his doctors to take a complete rest, he worked only intermittently for the next three years, becoming progressively more reclusive. As if searching for something, he traveled a great deal. He embarked on a three-month holiday through Egypt and the Sudan in December 1911, and set off, a year later, on another extended journey through the West Indies and South America.

In Panama, a friendly bank manager recommended that he consult the Swiss psychiatrist Dr. Carl Jung. He immediately returned to Europe and arranged for an appointment in Zurich. In April 1913, following a few days of tests, including blood and spinal fluid tests, the rising young psychiatrist informed Norman that he was suffering from "general paralysis of the insane" (GPI), a term then used to describe the onset of mental illness associated with tertiary syphilis, and that he would be dead in a few months. While some of the symptoms of GPI were in fact similar to those associated with manic depression—sudden shifts between euphoria and profound melancholy, bursts of creativity followed by suicidal tendencies, delusions of grandeur—this was an egregious misdiagnosis.

Profoundly shaken, Norman sought a second opinion from another Swiss doctor, Dr. Roger Vittoz, a specialist in nervous diseases, under whose care he spent the next three months in Zurich. Vittoz had developed a method of alleviating mental stress, using techniques similar to those used in meditation. His patients were taught to calm themselves by concentrating on a series of elaborate patterns, or sometimes on a single word. Vittoz would later become very popular in certain social circles in London, where his patients included Lady Ottoline Morrell, Julian Huxley, and T. S. Eliot.

For Norman it was the beginning of a lifelong history of experimenting with esoteric religions and spiritual practices. For a while, he was a practicing Theosophist. In the 1920s, he became a follower of Émile Coué, a French psychologist who preached the power of self-mastery through conscious autosuggestion, a sort of New Age positive-thinking cult very much in vogue during those years. He even dabbled in spiritualism. He would end up embracing all sorts of strange ideas, insisting to one of his colleagues, for example, that he could walk through walls. Because he also took a certain mischievous pleasure in twitting people with his more unconventional notions, it was always difficult to know how seriously to take him.

It was perhaps not surprising that Norman should have acquired a reputation as an oddity and an eccentric. He was viewed by his City acquaintances as a strange and lonely man who spent his evenings alone in his grand house immersed in Brahms, and who frequently quoted the Chinese sage Lao Tzu. He certainly made no attempt to fit into the clubby atmosphere of the City. His interests were primarily aesthetic and philosophical, and though he counted a few bankers among his close friends, he generally preferred to mix in a more eclectic circle of artists and designers.

BY THURSDAY, JULY 30, it had become apparent that what had initially appeared to be just a remote Balkan affair between a fading empire and one of its minor states was escalating toward a general European war. In response to Austria's attack on Serbia, Russia had now ordered a general mobilization. The international political crisis brought a financial crisis in its wake. The Berlin, Vienna, Budapest, Brussels, and St. Petersburg stock exchanges all had to suspend trading. With all the bourses of Europe except Paris's shut, the panic liquidation of securities concentrated on London.

On Friday, July 31, when Norman arrived at his City office, just north of the Bank of England, he found the financial community solidly against any British involvement in a Continental conflict. David Lloyd George, the chancellor of the exchequer, would later recount how Walter Cunliffe, the governor of the Bank of England, a man of few words not usually given to theatrical displays, came to plead "with tears in his eyes 'Keep us out of it. We shall be ruined if we are dragged in.'"

London was the financial capital of the world, and the City's livelihood depended much more on foreign finance than on providing capital to domestic industry. The merchant bankers housed in the warren of streets around the Bank of England, that select inner circle of household names— Rothschilds, Barings, Morgan Grenfell, Lazards, Hambros, Schroders, Kleinworts, and Brown Shipley, which gave the City of London its mystique—oversaw the greatest international lending operation the world had ever seen. Every year a billion dollars of foreign bonds were issued through

London bankers. In the previous year, Barings and the Hongkong and Shanghai Bank had syndicated a loan of $125 million to China; Hambros had brought a loan to the Kingdom of Denmark to market; Rothschilds had underwritten a $50 million issue for Brazil and was in the midst of negotiations for another loan; there had been bond issues for Rumania, for the cities of Stockholm, Montreal, and Vancouver. In April, Schroders had even led an $80 million bond issue for the imperial government of Austria, a country against which Britain might soon be at war. All of this financing and the profits that went with it would dry up in the event of war.

The closure of stock exchanges around Europe, and the risk that gold shipments would be prohibited, causing the entire gold standard to unravel, created a more immediate problem. It was now difficult, if not impossible, for Europeans to send money abroad to settle their trade debts. The merchant banks, which had guaranteed all this paper, were faced with bankruptcy.

Bankers were not the only ones terrified by the threat posed to world financial order by the prospect of war. Even the foreign secretary, Sir Edward Grey, who of all the cabinet had staked his career on the ambiguous "understanding" with France and was most committed to fighting, warned the French ambassador that "the coming conflict will plunge the finances of Europe into trouble, that Britain was facing an economic and financial crisis without precedent, and that British neutrality might be the only way of averting the complete collapse of European credit."

At ten o'clock on Friday morning, a notice was posted on the door of the stock exchange announcing that it was to be closed until further notice, for the first time since its founding in 1773.

Banks around the city began refusing to pay out gold sovereigns to customers. Soon a long queue assembled outside the Bank of England on Threadneedle Street, the one bank that remained legally obliged to convert five-pound notes into gold coins. There was no panic, just an atmosphere of "acute anxiety." While the crowd, many of them women who "stood nervously fingering their notes," was admitted into the Bank's inner courtyard, an even larger group of bemused onlookers gathered on the steps of the Royal Exchange opposite. The *Times* reported that "although many hundreds of people, a great many of them foreigners, must have been in the queue in the course of the day, there was no kind of disorder." This was in sharp contrast to the reports of panic coming from the cities of Europe and could be attributed, asserted the *Times* haughtily, to the "traditionally phlegmatic and cool" character of the English. On the next day, the crowd outside the Bank was even larger, but there was still no sense of real alarm. Nevertheless, just in case, the Bank's porters, in their distinctive salmon-pink tailcoats, red waistcoats, and top hats, were sworn in as special policemen, with the right to make arrests.

There may have been no riots in the streets, but fear was sweeping through the boardrooms of the great commercial banks. For the previous six months they had been engaged in a terrible controversy with the Bank of England over the adequacy of both their own and the Bank's gold reserves in the event of just such a crisis. In February, a memorandum circulated to a committee of bankers had warned that "in case of an outbreak of war, foreign nations would have the power, and would use it ruthlessly, of inflicting serious financial disturbance by demanding gold." Now faced with the prospect of large parts of the City of London going under, the commercial bankers in a panic had begun withdrawing gold from their accounts at the Bank of England. Its bullion reserves fell from over \$130 million on Wednesday, July 29, to less than \$50 million on Saturday, August 1, when the Bank, to attract deposits and conserve its rapidly diminishing stock of gold, announced that it had raised its interest rates to an unprecedented 10 percent.

Meanwhile on the Continent, the crisis was inexorably ratcheting up. Germany countered the Russian mobilization with a general mobilization of its own on Friday, July 31, and dispatched an ultimatum demanding that France declare its neutrality and turn over the fortresses of Toul and Verdun as a pledge of good faith. Next day, it declared war on Russia, and France ordered its own general mobilization. By Sunday, it was clear that in a matter of hours, France, committed to its alliance with Russia, would also be at war with Germany. That weekend Norman cabled his American partners at Brown Brothers in New York, "European prospects very gloomy."

Over the weekend, the mood of Britain shifted decisively in favor of war. It was the August Bank Holiday weekend and thousands of people, too excited to stay home and drawn outdoors by the sunshine, crammed into the center of London all the way from Trafalgar Square across White-hall to Buckingham Palace, blocking all car and bus traffic, cheering and singing patriotic songs—"La Marseillaise" as well as "God Save the King"—and clamoring for action.

On Monday, the City would normally have been completely deserted for the August Bank Holiday. Instead, Norman joined 150 other bankers gathered at the Bank of England. It was a stormy meeting. As Lloyd George, the chancellor of the exchequer, would later remark, "Financiers in a fright do not make a heroic picture." Many of the men participating did not know whether or not they had lost everything they had. Voices were raised and one banker even "shook his fist" at the governor himself. The meeting decided to recommend to the chancellor that the Bank Holiday should be extended for another three days to buy time for the panic to subside. The Treasury also announced that all trade debts would automatically be extended for an extra month while the Bank of England decided how best to go about bailing out the merchant banks threatened with insolvency or even bankruptcy.*

Norman's immediate concern in those first few days was simply to make sure that Brown Shipley would survive. Otherwise, he would have no hope of getting his capital out. Over the weekend, hundreds of the firm's American clients, stranded in Europe, gathered at the Pall Mall offices, trying to cash their letters of credit. But as the dust began to settle, it became apparent that with so much of the firm's business concentrated in the United States, which remained happily neutral, it would emerge relatively unscathed. As a member of the Court of the Bank of England,

---

*Eventually the government would end up assuming the risk on all this unpaid trade debt until the end of the war.

however, Norman found himself having to spend most of his time on the business of the Bank, particularly in trying to disentangle the labyrinth of unpaid trade debts.

Strangely, the enormous tensions of the time, the burden of the workload, which left him little time to brood, actually seemed to alleviate his mental incapacities. As he wrote to a friend in the United States, "I have been at work morning and night, and not an ache or pain have I had, nor even been better for years past." In an odd but very real way, the war was to be good for him.

Hjalmar Schacht

3. THE YOUNG WIZARD

GERMANY: 1914

'Tis a common proof
That lowliness is young ambition's ladder
—WILLIAM SHAKESPEARE, *Julius Caesar*

ACROSS EUROPE that week, people were left stunned by the speed of events. The crisis seemed to have come from nowhere. And even though most of the Continent had been half expecting a war for the last decade, few could have imagined, at the end of June, that it would be the assassination of an Austrian archduke that would set off the avalanche.

The continued complacency of most Germans during the month of July 1914, even after the assassination in Sarajevo, was very much the result of a deliberate campaign by their own government to project a surface of calm. Behind the scenes, Austria was being goaded on by the highest circles in Berlin to use the assassination as an excuse to bring Serbia to heel once and for all. Meanwhile, both the Austrian and German leaders took great pains in public to keep their intentions well disguised. All put on a great show of maintaining their usual summer holiday schedules. The emperor Franz Joseph made a point of staying at his hunting lodge at Bad Ischl for all of July. The kaiser departed on July 6 for his annual three-week holiday, aboard his yacht, *Hohenzollern*, in the Norwegian fjords. The chancellor, Theobald von Bethmann-Hollweg, came to Berlin for some emergency meetings in early July but rapidly resumed his holiday on his 7,500-acre estate at Hohenfinow, some thirty miles away, while the chief of the General Staff, General Helmuth von Moltke, remained in Karlsbad taking the waters, and Secretary of State Gottlieb von Jagow departed on his honeymoon.

Among those whom the crisis took by surprise was a thirty-six-year-old banker in Berlin with the uniquely improbable name of Horace Greeley Hjalmar Schacht. In spite of the authorities' elaborate charade, rumors of war had already begun to percolate early in July within the highest banking circles in Germany. One of those who seemed to take a particularly pessimistic view of the situation from the start was Max Warburg, scion of the prominent Hamburg banking family, who significantly was known to be close to the imperial court. The famously indiscreet kaiser himself contributed to the gossip from those circles by insisting that his friend Albert Ballin, head of the Hamburg-America Line, be informed in advance of a general mobilization. There was also talk that the crown prince had been breaking the strictest confidences to warn his friends in financial circles, including the managing director of the Dresdner Bank, Eugen Guttmann, that for all the surface calm, the optimism of the Berlin Stock Exchange was misplaced and war between Germany and Russia very likely.

But Hjalmar Schacht, only an assistant director and branch manager at Guttmann's Dresdner Bank, was still too far down the Berlin banking hierarchy to be party to these exalted hints from court. From his lowly point of view, he found it hard to believe that the situation had been allowed to spiral so far out of control—it seemed so profoundly irrational to let international rivalries threaten the German economic miracle.

THOUGH SCHACHT'S POSITION at the Dresdner, one of Germany's two largest banks, was still modest, for a young man in imperial Germany with no family connections, he had come a long way. He was certainly being noticed. In the months before the crisis began, he had been working on a loan for the city of Budapest, financed by a consortium of German, Swiss, and Dutch banks. The Swiss banker Felix Somary would later recount how Schacht even then "considerably outshone his fellow directors, all sons of rich fathers or mere time-servers."

With his clipped military mustache and brush-cut hair parted very precisely down the center, Schacht could easily have passed for a Prussian officer. He walked very erectly with a "curiously stiff gait," his rigid bearing, exaggerated by the starched, high, gleaming white celluloid collars that he favored. But he was neither a Prussian nor in any way connected to the military. He came from a lower-middle-class family, originating from the area of Germany bordering on Denmark, and had been brought up in Hamburg, the most cosmopolitan city in the whole empire.

Schacht would one day become famous for his boundless ambition and ferocious will to succeed. They were in part a reaction against a father with a long history of failure. Wilhelm Ludwig Leonhard Maximillian Schacht had been born on the western coast of North Schleswig, a narrow neck of land connecting Denmark to Germany. The Dithmarschen is a region of salt marshes and small isolated dairy farms, a bleak and wind-swept country protected by large dykes against the constantly encroaching North Sea. The people are reputedly independent and tough, laconic to the point of rudeness. Schleswig and the neighboring duchy of Holstein had historically been ruled by the Danish crown, although the population was split between German- and Danish-speakers and throughout the nineteenth century, sovereignty over the two states had been subject to a dispute between Prussia and the Kingdom of Denmark.* In 1866, following two short wars, Bismarck annexed Schleswig and Holstein, incorporating them into the Prussian empire. After the war, in 1920, the northern parts of Schleswig, including the region from which the Schacht family had come, reverted to Denmark as a result of a plebiscite.

Wilhelm Schacht was one of the eleven children of a country doctor.

---

*The origins of the dispute were so arcane that Lord Palmerston famously remarked that only three men in the world fully understood them: Prince Albert, who was dead; a clerk in the Foreign Office, whom it had driven mad; and Palmerston himself, who had forgotten.

In 1869, unhappy at the prospect of having become a Prussian subject liable to the Prussian military draft, five of the Schacht brothers emigrated to the United States, where Wilhelm spent seven years. But although he became a U.S. citizen, he never quite managed to find his feet, drifting from one job to another, working for a while in a German brewery in Brooklyn and in a typewriter factory in upstate New York. Finally, in 1876, he decided to return to Germany.

Arriving back just as the economic boom unleashed by the Franco-Prussian War was ending and a depression setting in, he continued to be plagued by the same bad luck. During the next six years, he tried his hand at various professions—schoolteacher, editor of a provincial newspaper, manager of a soap factory, bookkeeper for a firm of coffee importers—all unsuccessfully. Eventually he found a job as a clerk with the Equitable Insurance Company, where he would remain for the next thirty years. While Schacht was always a little defensive about his father, claiming that he was simply "a restless wanderer unable to remain for long in one place," the contrast between the father's fecklessness and the gigantic ambitions of the son could not have been greater. Even Schacht could not help observing in his autobiography that by the age of twenty-five, he was already earning more than his father.

In contrast to his awkward and retiring father, his mother, "sentimental, gay and full of feeling," always cheerful despite years of hardship, provided the center of affection for the family. Born the Honorable Constanze Justine Sophie von Eggers, the daughter of a Danish baron whose family had a long history of service to the crown, she had taken a large step down the social ladder by marrying Wilhelm Schacht. Her grandfather, a counselor to the king, had worked for the emancipation of serfs and had been responsible for a currency reform in Denmark in the late eighteenth century. But the family fortunes had declined over the years, leaving young Constanze von Eggers without any inheritance. She had met Wilhelm Schacht, then a penniless student, in 1869 and followed him to the United States, where they were married three years later.

Hjalmar Schacht himself was born in 1877, a few months after his family returned to Germany, in the small town of Tingleff in North Schleswig. He was christened with the unusual names Horace Greeley Hjalmar—in a typically impractical gesture, his father had chosen his first two names as a tribute to the founder and editor of the *New York Tribune*, whom he had admired while living in Brooklyn. His grandmother had insisted, however, that he have at least one conventional German or Danish name, and the young Schacht grew up as Hjalmar. Later in his life, though, some of his English friends and associates would use the name Horace.

During his early childhood, the family moved frequently as Wilhelm Schacht bounced from job to job, but in 1883, they finally settled in Hamburg. Germany in the last few years of the nineteenth century was a country of contradictions. Gripped by the most rigid class system in Europe—in fact almost a caste system—and governed by an autocratic constitution that still vested most of the power in the monarch and in the Junker military cadre surrounding him, it simultaneously offered Europe's most meritocratic educational system. But for that, Schacht might have been condemned to the narrow confines of lower-middle-class existence as a clerk or perhaps a teacher. Instead, in 1886, at the age of nine, he was accepted into the Johanneum, one of the finest gymnasia in Hamburg, where he received a rigorous classical education, emphasizing Latin, Greek, and mathematics.

He could not completely escape the constrictions of his class-ridden society. Life at school was full of petty humiliations stemming from his family's poverty: taunts at his living in a ratty tenement district, mockery of the cheap cloth of his trousers, sharing a graduation gown because he could not afford to buy one for himself. Cold-shouldered by the richer students, he was solitary, obsessively hardworking, and conscientious.

In 1895, Schacht graduated from the Johanneum and entered a university. Finally liberated, over the next few years he actually seemed to enjoy himself. He wrote poetry; joined a literary society; worked as a stringer for the *Kleines Journal*, a gossipy Berlin tabloid; and even composed the libretto for an operetta.* While he initially enrolled at the University of Kiel, he followed the German practice of transferring from one university to another, spending semesters in Berlin, Munich, Leipzig, and in 1897, the winter semester in Paris. He began as a medical student, tried his hand at literature and philology, and eventually graduated with a major in political economy, going on to write a doctoral thesis on the foundations of English mercantilism in the eighteenth century.

Doctorate in hand, Schacht began a career in public relations, initially at an export trade association, writing economic commentary for a Prussian journal on the side. Diligent and reliable, eager to impress the bankers and business magnates whom he was now beginning to meet, in 1902, he finally caught the attention of a board member of the Dresdner Bank and was offered a job. He rose quickly and, by 1914, was a well-established middle-level officer of one of the powerful banks in Berlin.

In imperial Germany, a man of Schacht's background would have found his opportunities for advancement in the military or the civil service limited. But in the years leading up to the war, Germany had gone from being an agrarian backwater at the edge of Western Europe, to becoming its leading industrial power, overtaking even Britain—an economic surge that had thrown open enormous opportunities in business to ambitious men. It was a particularly good time to be a banker, for in no other European country were banks quite so powerful. While Berlin still could not compete with either London or even Paris as an international financial center, the large German houses dominated the domestic economic landscape as the main suppliers of long-term capital to industry.

Disguising his social insecurities behind a stiffly formal exterior, Schacht seemed to possess a natural ability to get himself noticed. In 1905, his fluency in English got him sent with a member of the Dresdner's board to the United States, where they met with President Theodore Roosevelt, and

---

*Many years later, when he was a prominent official, the libretto was much to his embarrassment made public. Schacht sued the man responsible.

more important for a young banker, were invited to lunch in the partners' dining room at J. P. Morgan & Co.

He also married well—to the daughter of a Prussian police officer who had been assigned to the imperial court. By 1914, they had two children, the eleven-year-old Lisa and the four-year-old Jens, and were living in a small villa in the western garden suburb of Zehlendorf, from which Schacht commuted to and from work into the Potsdammerplatz station on one of the modern electric trains that now linked all of Berlin.

As Schacht watched the international crisis grow, he continued to hope, even until the end of July, for a last-minute diplomatic solution. Though he insisted that it would never come to war, this assertion stemmed primarily from wishful thinking. He had done well for himself in imperial Germany, had much to lose, and found it difficult to look at his own country dispassionately. For despite his liberal family background, he was a typical product of the Kaiserreich—conformist, unquestioningly nationalistic, and fiercely proud of his country and its material and intellectual achievements.

Like most other German bankers and businessmen, he believed that the villain of the piece was a fading Britain conspiring to deny Germany its rightful place among the Great Powers. As he later wrote, "Germany's steady advance in the world's markets had aroused the antagonism of those older industrial countries, who felt their chances in the markets were being threatened." England in particular had "engaged in creating a strong network of alliances and agreements directed against Germany," designed to encircle it.

That last few days of July 1914 constituted a whispering gallery of rumors and counterrumors. Berlin was gripped by alternating waves of war hysteria and anxiety. From the Dresdner Bank's headquarters next to the Opera House on the Bebelplatz, Schacht had a ringside seat at the epic drama being enacted in the streets below. Daily, huge crowds of people paraded under the great limes of Unter den Linden, singing "Deutschland, Deutschland, Über Alles" and other patriotic songs. Several times that week angry mobs attempted to storm the Russian embassy, only a few blocks away from his office.

Finally, on Friday, July 31, at 5:00 p.m. a lone lieutenant of the Grenadier Guards climbed up on the base of the giant equestrian statue of Frederick the Great, which divided Unter den Linden just outside the Dresdner's offices, to read a proclamation in the emperor's name. The Russians had ordered a general mobilization. A state of Drohende Kriegsfahr, imminent danger of war, was in force in Germany—still one step away from a declaration of war, but placing the city of Berlin under full military control.

The next day, when a general mobilization was announced, the streets went wild with excitement. Pubs and beer gardens stayed open all night. A craze of spy hunting swept over the city and the country. Anyone suspected of being a Russian agent, including a few German soldiers, was beaten to death. On August 3, Germany declared war on France, and to reach France, invaded Belgium the next morning. Britain, which had guaranteed Belgian neutrality since 1839, issued an ultimatum to Germany to withdraw. When this expired at midnight on August 4 and Germany found herself at war with Britain, a large "howling mob" stoned all the windows of the British embassy, then moved on to the Hotel Adlon next door to demand the heads of English journalists staying there. Bizarre rumors spread through the country. According to one police report, "The Paris banking house of Mendelssohn is trying to send a hundred million francs, in gold, across Germany to Russia." The hunt for "gold cars" became a curious obsession in the countryside; vehicles driven by innocent Germans were accosted by armed peasants and gamekeepers. A German countess and a duchess were even shot by accident.

Nevertheless, despite the public hysteria, those first few days of war proved to be relatively benign. Germany seemed to be weathering the financial storm that swept across Europe remarkably well—in Schacht's view, far better than was Britain. There were some minor debacles. The collapse of stock values in the last week of July put several banks in Germany in difficulties—the Norddeutsche Handelsbank, one of the largest banks in Hanover, had to close its doors—and was accompanied by the usual litany of suicides by overextended financiers. One of the best-known bankers in Thuringia shot himself on Wednesday, July 29, and the next day a private banker in Potsdam killed his wife, then took cyanide himself.

But for all this turmoil among the rich, the general public remained remarkably calm. There was a nationwide run on small savings institutions, and long lines of women, many of them domestic servants and factory workers, could be seen patiently waiting outside the city municipal savings banks to withdraw their deposits. But there was none of the usual panic demand for gold that in those days routinely accompanied entry into war, and the Reichsbank lost only about $25 million of its $500 million in gold reserves in the first few days.

It was no secret that the Reichsbank had been preparing against such an event for several years. The financial spadework had begun in earnest after the Agadir crisis of 1911 when Germany decided deliberately to provoke a confrontation with France over Morocco. In the middle of the crisis, Germany was hit by a financial panic. The stock market plunged by 30 percent in a single day, there was a run on banks across the country as the public lost its nerve and started cashing in currency notes for gold, and the Reichsbank lost a fifth of its gold reserves in the space of a month. Some of this was rumored to have been caused by a withdrawal of funds by French and Russian banks, supposedly orchestrated by the French finance minister. The Reichsbank came close to falling below the statutory minimum of gold backing against its currency notes. Faced with the potential humiliation of being driven off the gold standard, the kaiser backed down and had to watch impotently while the French ended up taking over most of Morocco.

A few months later, the emperor, still nursing his wounded pride, summoned a group of bankers, including the president of the Reichsbank, Rudolf von Havenstein, and demanded to know whether German banks were capable of financing a European war. When they hesitated, he reputedly told them, "The next time I ask that question, I expect a different answer from you gentlemen."

After that episode, the German government was determined that it would never again allow itself to be financially blackmailed. Banks were told to build up their gold reserves, the Reichsbank itself increasing its holdings from $200 million at the time of Agadir to $500 million in 1914—by comparison, the Bank of England held only some $200 million. The government even revived a plan originally conceived by Frederick the Great back in the eighteenth century for a war chest of bullion—$75 million in gold and silver—stored in the Julius Tower in the fortress of Spandau on the western outskirts of Berlin. Furthermore, to prevent the sort of raid on the mark that the French had allegedly orchestrated in the Moroccan crisis, the Reichsbank instructed banks to curb the amount of money taken on deposit from foreigners.

With all these measures under its belt, the Reichsbank entered August 1914 with large enough gold reserves on hand to feel confident about avoiding a replay of 1911 and was also quick, once the crisis became apparent, to take preemptive action by suspending the gold convertibility of the mark on July 31.

But as Schacht watched the long columns of soldiers in their field-grey uniforms marching through the cheering, weeping crowds of Berlin, he could not help thinking back to Prince Bismarck. The Iron Chancellor had spent his whole career making sure that Germany would not be so isolated within Europe that it would have to fight a war on two fronts against Russia and France. As a schoolboy of seventeen, Schacht had attended a torchlight procession staged in honor of the prince, then seventy-nine years old, in retirement at his estate at Friedrichsruh in the Saxon Forest, just outside Hamburg. The image of "a tremendous solemnity [emanating] from the old man as though he alone foresaw how onerous and dark the future would be" engraved itself on Schacht's memory. He liked to think that during the parade Bismarck had cast that piercing look directly at him in an attempt to warn the young man and the other schoolboys gathered there, not to "allow his work to be carelessly destroyed." Even in youth, Schacht had a vivid imagination and a grandiose vision of his own destiny.

4. A SAFE PAIR
OF HANDS

THE UNITED STATES: 1914

Show me a hero and I will write you a tragedy.
—F. Scott Fitzgerald

AMONG THE MANY thousands of Americans in Europe during that last summer of peace were Benjamin Strong, the forty-one-year-old president of the Bankers Trust Company, and his beautiful twenty-six-year-old wife, Katharine. Theirs was a leisurely trip, combining work and pleasure. Strong had been elected president of the bank in January, following the retirement of his father-in-law, Edmund Converse, and this was his first extended vacation since taking over. He had left the United States in the middle of May and, after visiting Paris on business, met up with Katharine in Berlin. They spent several weeks there with Katharine's older sister, the baroness Antoinette von Romberg, who had moved to Berlin in 1907 after a highly public divorce and child-custody battle in New York, and married Baron Maximilien von Romberg, a Prussian aristocrat and captain in the Eighteenth Fusiliers.* The Strongs then proceeded to London and were in England when news of the archduke's assassination arrived. However, the

---

*On September 22, 1914, Captain von Romberg was killed in action, one of the first German officers to die in the war. See "Baron Von Romberg Killed," *New York Times*, September 30, 1914.

Benjamin Strong in 1914

reaction of the financial markets was muted, and they felt no need to rush home. Instead, they remained in London for several weeks, not sailing back to America until late July.

They returned to a New York more concerned about the threats to business prosperity from the Democratic administration than about a European conflagration. By the last week of July, Strong was back at his office at 14 Wall Street. At thirty-seven stories high, the Bankers Trust headquarters was one of the great signature buildings of the financial district, the third tallest in the city, its crown a granite seven-story stepped pyramid, visible for miles around. Finished from floor to ceiling in the most delicate Tavernelle Clair cream-colored Italian marble, the bank's offices were among the most luxurious in the city.

In the mere twelve years since its founding, Bankers Trust had grown more than thirtyfold. With deposits of close to $200 million, it was the second largest trust company in the country and considered one of the dominant institutions on Wall Street. Nevertheless, it was still surrounded with a certain mystery. In 1912, during the Pujo Committee hearings on the power of New York banks and the "money trust," it came to light that though Bankers Trust had numerous stockholders, the entire voting power was vested in the hands of just three trustees: Henry Davison, a senior partner at J. P. Morgan & Co.; George Case of White and Case, Morgan's principal counsel; and Daniel Reid, a founder and executive of Morgan-controlled U.S. Steel. The fact that a penthouse apartment had been specially constructed on the thirty-first floor of the Bankers Trust building for Pierpont Morgan himself* only served to confirm the widely held view that Bankers Trust was simply one more manifestation of the power of the House of Morgan.

The summer had been very quiet on Wall Street. After a bull market that had stretched through the first few years of the century, stocks had been flat for almost four years, and the volume of trading was low. Mem-

---

*Pierpont Morgan died in 1913 without ever occupying the apartment. It was until very recently a restaurant.

bers of the exchange had taken advantage of the July lull in trading to move to their summer homes on Long Island or the Jersey shore. The first signs of crisis hit New York on Tuesday, July 28, when Austria declared war on Serbia. The Dow fell by 3 points from 79 to 76, a decline of 4 percent, but the next day seemed to recover its poise, despite the suspension of trading on the major markets across Europe, from Rome to Brussels, including the largest on the Continent, Berlin. On Thursday, July 30, the United States woke to news of a Russian general mobilization, and stocks experienced their single largest down day since the panic of 1907, falling 7 percent.

Although no one saw even a remote likelihood that the United States would become involved, it was widely feared that as the biggest importer of capital in the world, it would be badly hurt by a shutdown of international credit. Some $500 million in European loans to Americans was scheduled to fall due between the beginning of August and the end of the year. Under normal circumstances, it would have been taken for granted that these would be rolled over. But in the current situation, there was a risk that European investors would demand immediate repayment, while at the same time exports might be hit because of threats to shipping. Over the next few days, the dollar, normally fixed at $4.86 to the pound, fell dramatically as American borrowers scrambled to cover their debts falling due with gold and European currencies, especially sterling.

Late on Thursday, July 30, Strong was summoned to a meeting at the temporary offices of J. P. Morgan & Co. at 15 Broad Street—the headquarters at 23 Wall Street were being reconstructed. The city's inner circle of banking officials were there: Jack Morgan, the nominal head of the House of Morgan and son of the founder; Henry Davison, the senior partner; A. Barton Hepburn, chairman of the Chase National Bank; Francis L. Hine, president of the First National Bank; and Charles Sabin of the Guaranty Trust Company. The gathering broke up early. Anxious to avoid compounding the general alarm now tottering on the edge of panic, the participants adopted the time-honored tradition of captains of finance everywhere and issued a series of anodyne statements that were heavily economical with the truth: they "were so little worried that they were dispersing to go out of New York." Jack Morgan declared that he was returning to the yacht party from which he had been summoned; Henry Davison said that he was leaving for his summer home on Long Island.

But the following morning, once the news hit New York that even the London exchange had been forced to suspend trading, the same bankers met again—this time joined by Frank Vanderlip of the National City Bank and Dwight Morrow, one of the new Morgan partners—and decided to close the New York Stock Exchange.

AMONG THE EIGHT men gathered at the House of Morgan that Friday morning in August, the one who seemed to understand best the significance of the tempest of events was Henry Davison, Jack Morgan's right-hand man—he essentially ran the firm while Morgan, the largest capital partner, lived the life of an English squire. A few days after the meeting, Davison telegraphed his colleague, Thomas Lamont, who was trout fishing in Montana. "The credit of all Europe has broken down absolutely. Specie payments suspended and moratorium in force in France and practically in all countries, though not officially in England . . . it is as if we had had an earthquake, are as yet somewhat stunned, but will soon get to righting things." Even then, as the dollar plummeted, money flooded out of the United States, and borrowers struggled to remain solvent, Davison's intuition told him that this was to be a time of new openings for himself, for the House of Morgan, and for the country.

But then Henry Davison had a remarkable nose for opportunity. He was a self-made man. In this, he was not unusual. In fact, the only one of the eight barons of Wall Street meeting that day to have inherited his wealth was Jack Morgan. A. Barton Hepburn had been a professor of mathematics before entering the world of finance. Several had not even gone to college. Frank Vanderlip had grown up on a farm in Illinois and started his career as a journalist. Charles Sabin had begun as a flour sales-man, going into banking only when an Albany firm hired him because it needed a pitcher for its baseball team. Davison himself had grown up in the hardscrabble hills of north central Pennsylvania, the son of an itinerant plow salesman.

While Benjamin Strong, the youngest of the eight men at the Morgan meeting, had neither been born to wealth nor had attended college, he had most of the other advantages that a ruling-class background could provide. Tall and slim, good-looking but for a prematurely receding hairline and a large nose that spoke of ruthlessness, he exuded the confidence of the Ivy League athletic star. Born of good Yankee stock and able to trace his roots back to a Puritan family that had landed in Massachusetts from Taunton, England, in 1630, he came from a line of merchants and bankers. Benjamin's great-grandfather, also named Benjamin, had been Alexander Hamilton's clerk at the U.S. Treasury and one of the founders of the Seaman's Bank. Members of the family, all extremely conscious of their social obligations, were very active in church affairs. The first Benjamin Strong was on the Executive Committee of the American Bible Association and his son Oliver became president of the Society for the Reformation of Delinquents. Strong's mother's family had similar roots—her father was a minister and sat on the Presbyterian Board of Publications.

Benjamin was born in a small Hudson Valley town in 1872, the fourth child of five, and grew up in the New Jersey suburbs. When he graduated from Montclair High School in 1891, he had intended to follow his elder brother to Princeton, but his father, who helped manage the private finances and philanthropies of the railroad millionaire Morris K. Jesup, was going through a period of financial difficulty; so Benjamin had to skip college and instead joined a Wall Street brokerage firm, which he quit in 1900 to join a bank.

In 1895, Strong married Margaret Leboutillier; in 1898, the young couple moved to Englewood, New Jersey, and over the next few years had two boys and two girls, and established themselves as an up-and-coming young couple among the socially prominent of the town. Strong played golf and bridge, was a member of the Englewood tennis team, and became treasurer of the Englewood Hospital. It was there he met Davison.

In later years, when Davison had become one of the great figures in banking, it was part of the folk wisdom of the Street that the path to fame and fortune lay on the 8:22 a.m. train from Englewood that Harry Davison took into the city every morning. If you happened to strike up an acquaintance with him and he liked you, it was said, then you were made. As with all myths, there was some truth to this. Two of Davison's future partners, Thomas Lamont and Dwight Morrow, had been discovered and launched on their Wall Street careers because they were neighbors to Davison; and in 1904, Davison offered Strong a job as secretary of the Bankers Trust Company, which he had helped found the year before.

Strong owed Davison more than his career. In May 1905, while he was away at work, his wife, Margaret, apparently in the grip of postpartum depression after the birth of their fourth child, and recently released from a sanatorium in Atlantic City, chanced upon a revolver that the Strongs had just bought after a burglary scare in the neighborhood and shot herself. The next year Strong's eldest daughter died of scarlet fever. The Davisons immediately took Strong's three surviving children—Benjamin Jr., Philip, and Katherine—into their home.

In 1907, after less than two years of widowhood, Strong remarried—some thought with undue haste. His new wife, Katharine, a shy girl of eighteen, seventeen years his junior, was the daughter of Edmund Converse, the extremely rich president of Bankers Trust and a longtime associate of Pierpont Morgan. Henry Davison served as best man, and the new couple moved from Englewood to a house on the Converse estate in Greenwich, Connecticut, where Katharine could be close to her family.

A few months later, in October 1907, the United States was rocked by a severe financial crisis. The panic began, like so many before it, with the failure of a large speculative venture, this time an attempt by a couple of unscrupulous characters to corner the market in the stock of a copper company. When they failed and one of them, the president of a Brooklyn-based bank, was rumored to have lost $50 million, most of it borrowed, a run on his bank set in. By the end of October, the fear had infected the whole city and there were runs on a variety of banks across

New York, including the Knickerbocker Trust Company, the third largest in the city.

The United States was then the only major economic power without a central bank. Throughout its history, the country had displayed an unusually ambivalent attitude to the whole institution of central banking. While East Coast financiers, who were lenders of money, kept pressing the case for placing authority over the country's monetary system in a single overarching bank, there was much support for the argument, particularly from farmers, who typically borrowed money, that putting so much power in the hands of one institution was somehow un-American and undemocratic. Because of this fundamental disagreement, banking policy in the United States had careened from one extreme to another.

In 1791, Alexander Hamilton, the secretary of the treasury, had created the country's first central bank, the First Bank of the United States, although its domain was not very grand because there were only four other banks in the whole country at the time. In 1811, the First Bank's charter was allowed to expire. In 1816, the country tried again, setting up what came to be known as the Second Bank of the United States. In 1836, the republic had second thoughts once again and under President Andrew Jackson, the Second Bank's charter was also not renewed. For the next seventy-plus years, the United States survived and even prospered without a central bank, albeit at the price of having a primitive, fragmented, and unstable banking system especially prone to periodic panics and crises.

In 1907, as one New York bank after another fell victim to a run, the financial community, without any central bank to look to, turned to J. Pierpont Morgan, the preeminent financier of his generation. He had lived through more panics than had any other banker, in 1895 actually bailing out the United States government itself when it was within days of running out of gold and defaulting on its debts to Europe. Though J. P. Morgan & Co. was by no means the country's biggest bank, Pierpont Morgan himself had acquired an extraordinary aura of authority that gave him the right, indeed the obligation, to take command during financial crises. It helped that he was believed to be not simply rich, but extremely rich—like the Rockefellers or the Vanderbilts or Andrew Carnegie—and that with his fierce glowering stare and terrible temper, he intimidated most people, including his own partners. It would turn out that the first of these attributes was exaggerated, for he was not nearly as wealthy as most people thought—when he died in 1913, leaving an estate then valued at $80 million, John D. Rockefeller, who himself was worth $1 billion, is said to have shaken his head and said, "And to think that he wasn't even a rich man."

Morgan swiftly assembled the very best financiers to assist him with the rescue effort, drafting Davison and Strong to act as his principal lieutenants—they were exactly the type of young men with which he liked to surround himself: athletic, good-looking, decisive, and confident. The task force had two assignments. The first, on which Davison and Strong concentrated, was to decide which banks caught in the upheavals were to be bailed out and which left to go under. The second, which Morgan led, was to raise the money for the rescue effort. By early November, despite having injected $3 million of his own cash, raised over $8 million from the other banks collectively, secured a commitment from the secretary of the treasury to provide $25 million in deposits, and even managed to extract $10 million from John D. Rockefeller Sr., Morgan had been unable to check the panic. Depositors continued to withdraw their money and one of the largest trust companies in the country, with over $100 million in deposits, tottered on the edge of collapse.

Finally, on the night of Sunday, November 3, Morgan summoned the presidents of the major New York banks to his new library, at the corner of Madison Avenue and Thirty-sixth Street, an Italian Renaissance–style palace he had built next door to his house to showcase his collection of rare books, manuscripts, and other artwork. Its marble floors, frescoed ceilings, walls lined with tapestries and triple-tiered bookcases of Circassian walnut, crammed full of rare Bibles and illuminated medieval manuscripts, made it an incongruous setting for a meeting of the banking establishment. Once the moneymen had gathered, Morgan had the great ornamented bronze doors to the library locked and refused to let anyone leave until all had collectively agreed to commit a further $25 million to the rescue fund.

The 1907 panic exposed how fragile and vulnerable was the country's banking system. Though the panic had finally been contained by decisive action on Morgan's part, it became clear that the United States could not afford to keep relying on one man to guarantee its stability, especially since that man was now seventy years old, semiretired, and focused primarily on amassing an unsurpassed art collection and yachting to more congenial climes with his bevy of middle-aged mistresses.

Shaken by the crisis, the U.S. Congress decided to act. In 1908, it created the National Monetary Commission, consisting of nine senators and nine representatives, and chaired by Senator Nelson Aldrich, to undertake a comprehensive study of the banking system and to make recommendations for its reform. Over the next few years, the commission produced a voluminous set of studies on central banking in Europe but not much else. Memories of how close the system had come to imploding progressively dimmed and the momentum for reform stalled.

In 1912, Davison, now a Morgan partner, frustrated by the lack of progress and fearing that without changes the next panic would be even more catastrophic, set out to convene a meeting of experts to develop a formal plan to establish an American central bank—the third in the nation's history. Only five men were invited. Besides Davison himself, there was Senator Aldrich; Frank Vanderlip, the forty-eight-year-old president of the National City Bank, the largest in the country; Paul Warburg, of the well-known Hamburg banking family, a forty-two-year-old partner at Kuhn Loeb who, although he had only just moved to New York, was probably the greatest expert on central banking in the United States; A. Piatt Andrew Jr., the thirty-nine-year-old assistant secretary of the treasury, who had been a professor at Harvard and accompanied the original commission on its European study tour; and Benjamin Strong, then thirty-nine years old.

Davison was worried, and for good reason, that any plan put together by a group from Wall Street would immediately be suspect as the misbegotten product of a bankers' cabal. He therefore chose to hold the meeting in secret on a small private island off the coast of Georgia—in effect creating the very bankers' cabal that would have aroused so much public suspicion. The preparations were elaborate. Each guest was told to go to Hoboken Station in New Jersey on November 22 and board Senator Aldrich's private railroad car, which they would find hitched with its blinds drawn to the Florida train. They were not to dine together, nor to meet up beforehand, but to come aboard singly and as unobtrusively as possible, all under cover of going duck hunting. As an added precaution, they were to use only their first names. Strong was to be Mr. Benjamin, Warburg Mr. Paul. Davison and Vanderlip went a step further and adopted the ringingly obvious pseudonyms Wilbur and Orville. Later in life, the group used to refer to themselves as the "First Name Club."

Disembarking at Brunswick, Georgia, they were taken by boat to Jekyll Island, one of the small barrier islands off the Georgia coast, owned by the private Jekyll Island Club, which had opened in 1888 as a hunting and winter retreat for wealthy northerners. Described by one magazine as "the richest, the most exclusive and most inaccessible club in the world," it numbered only some fifty members, including J. P. Morgan, William Vanderbilt, William Rockefeller, Joseph Pulitzer, and various Astors and Goulds. Membership was now closed and had become hereditary.

For the next ten days, the little party had the club with its skeleton staff to themselves—it had been closed for the summer and would not be open to other members for several weeks. They worked every day from early morning to midnight, convening in the luxurious rambling clubhouse with its turret, fifteen-foot ceilings, and numerous verandas and bay windows overlooking the Atlantic Ocean. Davison and Strong rose at daybreak to go riding or swimming, before settling down to work after breakfast. They ate copiously—pans of fresh oysters, country hams, wild turkey—and celebrated Thanksgiving together. Vanderlip would later write that it had been "the highest pitch of intellectual awareness that I have ever experienced." The group dispersed under an oath of secrecy, a pledge that all faithfully kept. Although the fact of the meeting came to light in a magazine some four years later, none of the participants would publicly admit to having been there for another twenty years.

The plan they developed over those ten days, the final details of which were drafted by Vanderlip and Strong, was unveiled to the public on January 16, 1911. Known as the Aldrich Plan, it had at its center a single institution—the National Reserve Association—a central bank in everything but name that would have branches all over the country, with authority to issue currency and to lend to commercial banks. While the government was to be represented on the association's board, the association itself was to be owned and controlled by banks, a sort of bankers' cooperative.

Nelson Aldrich may have been the most knowledgeable member of the Senate about finance, but the cause of central banking in the United States could not have found a worse champion. In a Senate full of very rich men—it was becoming known as the "millionaires' club"—he was one of the richest, having supposedly sold his stake in the United Traction and Electric Company of Rhode Island for $10 million; he boasted a grand estate in Newport, Rhode Island, and his daughter Abby had married John D. Rockefeller Jr. He was a fervent supporter of big business, a bitter enemy of regulation, an advocate of high tariffs; rumors abounded, furthermore, that he traded political favors for financial contributions. In short, he was the living embodiment of everything that opponents of a central bank most feared.

Over the next few months, much to Strong's dismay, Progressives and midwestern Republicans joined forces to kill the plan; but in early 1913, the Democrats in Congress, led by Senator Carter Glass, salvaged the idea by modifying it. Rather than creating a single central bank, which would involve too great a concentration of power, the Glass Plan called for a number of autonomous regional institutions: Federal Reserve Banks, as they were to be named. While these individual entities were to be controlled and run by local bankers, a capstone—the Federal Reserve Board, a public agency whose members were to be appointed by the president—was placed in an oversight role over the whole structure.

Although Glass's bill copied many of the essentials of the Aldrich Plan, Strong actively campaigned against it, predicting that its decentralized structure would simply perpetuate the fragmentation and diffusion of authority that had so bedeviled American banking and would only lead to conflict and confusion. Eventually New York bankers—pragmatic as ever and recognizing that the Glass Plan at least offered something better than the status quo—came around and it was signed into law as the Federal Reserve Act by Woodrow Wilson on December 23, 1913.

DURING THE FIRST few days of August 1914, Strong was caught up in a flurry of meetings. On the morning of Saturday, August 1, he conferred with the other bankers of the Clearing Association at the Metropolitan Club of New York. That evening he was at the Vanderbilt Hotel for a large meeting of New York bankers with Treasury Secretary William McAdoo, who announced the issue of $100 million of emergency currency to meet the panic demand for cash. The following Monday he left for Washington.

Strong's most immediate concern was the problem of American tourists stuck in Europe. Banks and hotels, alarmed by the sharp fall in the dollar, and afraid that paper currency might lose its value, were refusing to cash travelers' checks or bank drafts. Thousands of Americans, most of them well off, found themselves marooned on the Continent without usable cash. Reports were rife of some being turned out of hotels and forced to sleep at railway stations, or walking the streets of Paris at night. Those who succeeded in cashing their checks were often able to do so only at the equivalent of 75 cents on the dollar.

Bankers Trust was then the main issuer of travelers' checks to Americans going to Europe. Luckily for Strong, Fred Kent, the man in charge of the bank's foreign exchange business, just happened to be on holiday in London. He immediately organized a two-thousand-strong mass meeting at the Waldorf Hotel on Aldwich, where he arranged to provide temporary funds to his stranded countrymen.

In the final outcome, should the Europeans not accept dollars, Americans always had the option of paying in gold. But how to get the gold into a Continent now at war? Insurance rates on private shipping had skyrocketed to prohibitive levels overnight. Strong persuaded the government to ship private gold over on a warship, and on August 6, the cruiser *Tennessee* left the Brooklyn Navy Yard with $7.5 million in gold aboard.

This was what Strong was good at: taking charge to address immediate and practical problems, even if it meant stepping on a few toes. Leadership came naturally to him. While he may not have had quite the polished, cosmopolitan grace of some Morgan partners, people liked him and responded well to his dominant personality; he was well known and admired on Wall Street. "Wherever he sat was the head of the table," said a contemporary. Few people, though, could claim to know him intimately, and signs of a darker side sometimes manifested themselves from behind that gregarious and sociable veneer. He was a "Jekyll and Hyde personality, usually polite but flying at times into terrible rages" remembered one colleague. Those flashes of intense and startling anger provided brief glimpses into the pain and sorrow that he otherwise kept well hidden.

It was during that August of commuting between New York and Washington that Strong was first approached about becoming governor of the newly created Federal Reserve Bank of New York. If the Aldrich Plan of a single central bank had gone through, leaders of the New York banking community, such as Davison and Vanderlip, had long singled out Strong as the potential head. Now, under the Federal Reserve System, with multiple reserve banks and a Board in Washington, they came to the conclusion that he would be most effective and useful to them as the head of the Federal Reserve Bank of New York. Of the twelve regional reserve banks created by the new act, that of New York would be the largest.*

---

*By the mid-1920s, the New York Fed was two and a half times as large as its nearest rival, Chicago, and some ten times greater than the smallest Federal Reserve bank, that of Minneapolis.

They correctly foresaw that the New York Fed—their reserve bank—would, by virtue of its size and its expertise, very likely come to dominate the system.

He was the perfect choice. His career as a banker had been distinguished; he had undergone his baptism by fire during the panic of 1907; after being party to the conception of an American central bank on that Georgia island, he had become one of the experts in the field; and finally, he was well known to the partners at J. P. Morgan. Lacking perhaps the flair of a Davison or the urbane savoir faire of Thomas Lamont, his was undoubtedly a safe pair of hands.

The offer put Strong in a real dilemma and initially he refused it. Although like other New York bankers he had reconciled himself to the new system, he still thought it fundamentally flawed, and had campaigned actively to block it. He insisted that personal financial considerations did not sway him, but it is hard to believe that they were not a factor. He had no inherited wealth; he had only just been made president of Bankers Trust at the comparatively young age of forty-one, and had not yet had the opportunity to accumulate a fortune of his own. In taking the job, he would have to resign every directorship he held. The salary he would receive, $30,000 per year, while very attractive, was a fraction of what he could make as the president of a large New York bank. His father-in-law was especially strongly opposed to his taking the job, saying, "Ben is not going to live on my money"—Converse was reputed to be worth over $20 million and Katharine stood to inherit a considerable fortune. The Strongs' current lifestyle would however be impossible to sustain on his diminished income. Only the year before, the family—husband, wife, his three children from his first marriage, and his two daughters from his second—had moved into a luxurious eight-thousand-square-foot apartment in one of the city's most prestigious buildings, 903 Park Avenue, where apartments covered a full floor and rented for $15,000 a year.

In early October, Strong was invited by Davison and Warburg for a weekend in the country. They both made the case to him that it was his duty to accept a post in which he could do more for the public good than anywhere else. Davison was a hard man to argue with, especially when Strong owed him so much. On October 5, 1914, the Federal Reserve Bank of New York formally announced that Benjamin Strong had been elected its first governor.

5. L'INSPECTEUR DES FINANCES

> *There isn't a bourgeois alive who in the ferment of*
> *his youth, if only for a day or for a minute, hasn't*
> *thought himself capable of . . . noble exploits . . . in a*
> *corner of every notary's heart lie the moldy remains*
> *of a poet.*
>
> —GUSTAVE FLAUBERT, *Madame Bovary*

IN PARIS that summer, Aimé Hilaire Émile Moreau, director general of the Banque d'Algérie et Tunisie, the central bank for the French colonies of Algeria and Tunisia, was absorbed like everyone else in France in L'Affaire Caillaux. It was the latest in a long chain of scandals that had done so much to embellish the politics of the Third Republic and provide such a wonderful source of entertainment for the French public. In early 1914, *Le Figaro*, a conservative newspaper, had launched a campaign against the introduction of an income tax by Joseph Caillaux, finance minister and leader of the Radical Party. On its front page, it ran some youthful love letters from Caillaux to a former mistress, the already married Berthe Gueydan, who had eventually divorced her husband, a high civil servant, to become the first Mme. Caillaux. Much had happened since this correspondence. After Caillaux had married Berthe, he started an affair with

Émile Moreau

yet another married woman, the tall ash-blonde Henriette Claretie, divorced Berthe, and married his new mistress.

In March 1914, the second Mme. Caillaux, outraged that her husband's affairs, even those prior to her arrival in his life, should be so scandalously publicized—and perhaps fearing that some of their own adulterous correspondence might also find its way into the press—took matters into her own hands. At 3:00 p.m. on March 16, she left her home, dressed in the most elegant clothes for a reception at the Italian embassy that evening. On the way she stopped off at Gastinne Renette, the elite gun shop on the Right Bank, bought a Browning automatic, proceeded to the offices of *Le Figaro*, waited an hour for Gaston Calmette, the editor, and confronting him, declared, "You know why I have come," and calmly pumped six shots into him at point-blank range from the pistol that was hidden in her expensive fur muffs, killing him instantly.

The scandal split France and even provoked riots in Paris between supporters of Caillaux and right-wing agitators protesting the declining standards of the country's ruling classes. The trial began on July 20, and the daily court proceedings dominated the headlines in every newspaper and captivated the city. Parisians, it seemed, were much more interested in the melodramatic mixture of adultery and moral corruption in high political circles, of Joseph Caillaux's extensive network of mistresses, of his seduction of the heretofore simple, shy, and retiring Henriette Caillaux, than in distant rumblings from the Balkans.

For Moreau, the trial carried especial significance. He had been a student of Caillaux's at the École Libre des Sciences Politiques in the early 1890s, when Caillaux had been an up-and-coming glamorous young man, rich, flamboyant, and as *inspecteur des finances,* a member of the elite administrative corps founded by Napoléon to conduct audits over the financial affairs of the state. The École Libre des Sciences Politiques—Sciences Po as it was and still is known—was an expensive private graduate school, established in 1872 after the Franco-Prussian War. Its founder had sought to create an up-to-date training ground for the new governing elite of France, capable of resisting the "democratic excesses" of the early years of the republic. The faculty was not composed of academics but was drawn from highly placed politicians, civil servants, and businessmen. In its short life, Sciences Po had become the primary recruiting ground for the upper reaches of the civil service.

While Moreau was at Sciences Po, all France, including the school, was split by the Dreyfus affair. In 1894 a young Jewish artillery officer, Captain Alfred Dreyfus, was wrongly convicted of treason when French intelligence officials conspired to fabricate evidence that he had worked as a spy for Germany. The ensuing scandal pitted an old France—insular, royalist, and Catholic—against a new France seeking to modernize itself, a France that was more cosmopolitan, liberal, and outward looking. The head of Sciences Po was a committed Dreyfusard and several anti-Dreyfusard professors eventually resigned in protest.

Unlike most his fellow students at Sciences Po, with their well-to-do, sophisticated Parisian backgrounds, Moreau was a provincial who had only arrived in Paris in 1893, at the age of twenty-five, to enroll at the school. Born in Poitiers, the son of a local magistrate, Moreau had attended the lycée there and then obtained a license in law from its university. His family, minor gentry from Poitou, the ancient countryside around Poitiers, had roots there that went far back into history. One of his ancestors, Dutron de Bornier, had represented the area in the provincial assembly during the eighteenth century. His great-grandfather, Joseph Marie-François Moreau, had been a representative of the Third Estate when the Estates-General gathered at Versailles in 1789 to launch what was to be the Revolution; he later sat in the convention that did so much to press the Revolution home. He had subsequently become an important figure in the local administration—even after the restoration of the monarchy—as *receveur général de finance*, responsible for collecting the taxes of the newly established department of Vienne.

In 1896, Moreau followed in Caillaux's footsteps and, after a brilliant performance in the ferociously competitive entrance exams for the upper civil service, had also become an *inspecteur des finances*. Although the examination system had made the inspectorate largely meritocratic, candidates still had to have a parental guarantee of a private income of 2,000 francs per year until they were promoted.* Moreau was now a member of the elite administrative class that exercised the true power in France during those years. The country was nominally governed by a clique of ministers who rotated in and out of office at the mercy of a vociferous and fractious national assembly. Governments had a typical life of less than seven months: there was a total of fifty different ministries in the forty-four years between the founding of the Third Republic in 1870 and 1914, some lasting a single day. But behind all the minor dramas of ministers resigning, governments falling, and the roundabout of the same old faces, France was run by this quiet, confident, extremely able, and well-trained college of mandarins.

Once inside the civil service, Moreau rose rapidly. In 1899, Caillaux became minister of finance, the first of his eventual seven terms in that position, and Moreau worked under him. In 1902, Moreau was handpicked by the new minister of finance, Maurice Rouvier, to be his *chef de cabinet*. The cabinet was the minister's private secretariat, generally made up of his protégés and unusually promising junior civil servants who managed the full range of the minister's activities, dealt with his correspondence, acted as a liaison with his constituency, and prepared his briefing papers. To be *chef de cabinet* was to be the minister's principal aide and chief of staff, a role as much political as administrative.

Rouvier, a moderate republican, by profession a banker, was one of the most competent ministers of finance that the Third Republic produced. He also had an unfortunate capacity for getting involved in scandals; indeed he had the distinction of being tainted by the two best-known *affaires* of that squalid era. In 1887, it was revealed that Daniel Wilson, son-in-law of President Jules Grévy, had been selling decorations, including nominations to the Légion d'Honneur, from his office in the Élysée Palace. Rouvier was prime minister at the time, and though not directly implicated in

---

*Then the equivalent of $400, 2,000 francs was well below the wage of a typical skilled American worker.

the trafficking, was, along with the bewildered old president, forced to resign.

Rouvier's exile was short-lived. Two years later he was back in government as minister of finance. In 1892, however, the Panama Canal Company went bankrupt and some 800,000 French investors lost $200 million. The investigation revealed a chain of corruption, slush funds, and influence peddling that wove through the high social and political circles of Paris. Rouvier was found to have had extensive dealings with two shadowy figures at the heart of the affair, the baron Jacques de Reinach, a German Jew with an Italian title, who then died in suspicious circumstances in what was implausibly declared to be suicide, and Cornelius Herz, a shady international adventurer and financier who promptly skipped the country. In the parliamentary inquiry that followed, Rouvier, accused along with 104 other deputies and countless journalists of accepting payoffs, defended himself by arguing that he had only accepted the money because he thought the project was in the national interest, and after all, his fortune had not "increased abnormally" in the process. Though insufficient evidence was produced to indict him, he was forced once more to resign and spent the next ten years in the political wilderness. He had only just been rehabilitated when Moreau first went to work for him in 1902.

Moreau never allowed Rouvier's strange conception of public ethics to get in the way of his admiration for the man. Willing though he was to concede that his "beloved" mentor had suffered from a curious incapacity to distinguish between private interests and public responsibilities, he brushed it off as no worse than that of any other politician of the time—an aspect of that general "moral collapse [which was] very common in political circles" and continued to express his undying gratitude and loyalty to Rouvier for the enormous generosity he had received as a young man.

In 1905, Rouvier became prime minister for the second time, with Moreau as his principal aide and right-hand man. Within two months, the government was faced with a major international crisis. That March, the kaiser, who had an unfortunate habit of speaking out of turn, paid a visit to Tangiers, and in a challenge to French ascendancy in North Africa proclaimed his support for Moroccan independence. Rouvier initially tried to negotiate with Germany, but the kaiser, sensing France's weakness, kept increasing his demands. As the tensions mounted, Germany mobilized its reserves and France moved troops to the frontier. Over the next few months, Rouvier skillfully defused the crisis, not only retaining France's special position in Morocco, but also engineering a graceful exit from a confrontation with Germany and setting in train the first conversations with the British that would lead to the Anglo-French entente. For Moreau, still only thirty-six, it was a heady experience to be at the center of a great international storm. But it was the fate of Third Republic ministries to last only a few months and the Rouvier government was soon voted out.

During his more than twenty years in and out of office, Rouvier had made many enemies, not least because of his own shady financial dealings. With Rouvier out of power, these enemies now targeted Moreau. On his presenting himself for reassignment, he was not sent back to the ministry of finance but seconded to the Banque d'Algérie, the central bank of Algeria and Tunisia, a minor financial institution compared to the Banque de France or the other great state banks. For a high-flying young official from the Ministry of Finance who had climbed his way to the center of things, it was a form of exile. It was not quite as onerous as it sounds, because Algeria had a special status among French possessions and the bank's headquarters were in the heart of political Paris, within a stone's throw of the National Assembly and the Ministry of Foreign Affairs at 207 Boulevard Saint Germain.

While privately owned, the Banque d'Algérie was one of the key organs of colonial policy. Over the next eight years, Moreau, who was promoted to director general in 1911, was instrumental in the development of the Algerian wine industry; was at the forefront of the fight against usury among the Tunisian Berbers; and worked closely with the military governor of Morocco, the future Maréchal Lyautey, to help finance public works during the military occupation and subsequent colonization of Morocco.

He was, and saw himself as, much more than just a banker; he was a servant of the state. In January 1914, he was made a Commandeur de la Légion d'Honneur, a distinction restricted to no more than 1,250 people.

But for all these achievements, the Banque d'Algérie was still a backwater for so ambitious and talented an official. His former contemporaries at the ministry were now running the finances not of a mere colony but of the whole country and its empire. When he thought back on what had happened to him, he could not help being bitter—he had been stuck in this dead-end job for the last eight years, apparently forgotten.

Perhaps Moreau had risen too far and too fast, arousing resentments among his peers. Perhaps it was that he was different from the others: a man of few words, blunt and almost rude, who had made no attempt to enter salon society and had none of the airs and graces of the Parisian higher civil servant. Very much a provincial, he proudly went out of his way to remain so. In 1908, he had been elected mayor of his home commune, Saint Léomer. It was a tiny place of only a few hundred residents, but he seized every opportunity he had to go back there. His property, La Frissonaire, had been in the family since 1600. It was there that he felt most comfortable, among the friends with whom he had grown up, his fellow squires, the local *notaires,* and magistrates.

IN ANY OTHER year, the last week of July would have found Moreau avidly awaiting the circular from the Minister of Agriculture, fixing the dates of the shooting season. He tried to make a point of being at La Frissonaire at the opening of hunting. As he liked to say, there were just enough quail, partridge, and rabbit on the estate "to keep it exciting, and not so much that one got bored." But as July ran into August, it became apparent that this year, though the weather was perfect, he was going to have to leave his guns in their racks.

By Monday, July 27, several straws in the wind suggested that the Balkan crisis was beginning to assume alarming proportions. Madame Cailux began to be progressively edged off the front pages of even the Parisian apers. Every evening, a crowd generally gathered on the Boulevard Poissonière outside the offices of *Le Matin,* most popular of the French yellow apers, in whose windows were posted the latest bulletins. There were the ievitable fights. But no longer was it simply the opponents of Caillaux gainst his supporters. Brawls were now breaking out over national secu-ty, between those who opposed the extension of military service and the artisans of the Réveil National, the new patriotic movement.

Also gold coins began mysteriously to vanish from circulation. Having een burned by disastrous experiments with paper money twice before—nce in the early eighteenth century during the ill-fated Mississippi Bub-le, and then again by the assignats issued during the Revolution—the 'rench had developed a healthy mistrust of banks and all but the hardest ietallic currency. At the first sign of trouble, gold coins disappeared into hose countless *bas de laine,* the proverbial long woolen stockings in which very French peasant was said to keep his little hoard of gold under the iattress or into those notaries' strongboxes where the bourgeoisie kept heir savings.

After eight days of court proceedings, at 9:30 p.m. on the night of July 8, the all-male jury voted 11 to 1 to acquit Mme. Caillaux. They concluded hat she had been so uncontrollably distraught over the revelations in *Le 'igaro* as to be driven to violence—the murder was therefore to be deemed *n crime passionel.* For all its drama, the verdict came as something of an nticlimax. Fighting did break out outside the Palais de Justice, and a large ontingent of policemen had to be deployed to disperse the royalist ultras f Action Française who hated Caillaux. But most Parisians were now nore concerned about how to pay for their groceries—gold or silver coins vere hard to come by; the shops, even the cafés, had stopped accepting anknotes, and even the food markets at Les Halles had come to a grind-ng halt.

By 4:00 the next morning, several hundred people gathered around the 3anque de France to convert notes into gold. That afternoon, the crowd

swelled to more than thirty thousand in a line that wove for over a mi
along the side streets surrounding the Hotel du Toulouse, where th
Banque was headquartered, along the Rue de Radziwill, past the Pala
Royale, and up the Rue de Rivoli to the Jardin des Tuileries. Two hundre
and fifty policemen kept order. The *Times*'s reporter was taken aback b
the scene. "All classes of society mingled in the interminable queue and
was significant of the universal thriftiness in France that numbers of quit
humble persons had evidently savings to withdraw from the guardianshi
of the National Bank."

The Banque announced that it was prepared to continue paying ou
gold for as long as was necessary. After all, it had the largest single hoar
of gold in the world. In 1897, its incoming governor, Georges Pallain, ha
gathered his staff to tell them that the Banque's duty was to prepare fc
"every eventuality," his code word for a war of revenge against German
to reverse the disaster of 1870. Under Pallain, the Banque de France ha
steadily begun to accumulate gold. Every time the Reichsbank's gold re
serves increased, the Banque was a step ahead—a sort of arms race wit
gold as the object. By July 1914, it had over $800 million in bullion.

The French central bank had not, however, painstakingly built up thi
mountain of precious metal just to see it dissipated into the hands of it
own nervous citizens. The treasure was there to support the state in
national endeavor. For more than a decade, every manager of the Banque
more than 250 branches had kept locked in his safe, in a place that wa
instructed should be "always easily accessible," a secret envelope, to b
opened only in the event of a general mobilization. Inside this envelop
was Le Circulaire Bleu.

Written on grayish blue paper over Governor Pallain's signature it con
tained each manager's instructions in the event of war. With general mo
bilization, he would face "immense and perilous duties." He was to mee
this "formidable test" with "calmness, vigilance, initiative, and firmness.
The first and immediate task would be to cease paying out gold immedi
ately. Should the branch's town fall into enemy hands, he was to defen
the assets in his care with "all [his] authority and . . . energy." Thus, whe

the order for general mobilization was issued at 4:00 p.m. on Saturday, August 1, French gold reserves were immediately immobilized.

An hour later, it was also impossible to get a taxi in Paris. All public transport—cars, wagons, and buses—was requisitioned to move troops. The only way to get about was on foot. Within twenty-four hours, public services came to a grinding halt as every able-bodied male headed for the railway stations, the Gare du Nord and the Gare de l'Est. Even the grandest hotels, such as the Ritz and the Crillon, lost their waiters; dinner was served by chambermaids.

Within days of the outbreak of war and for the next few weeks, an unnatural calm settled over the city as it basked gloriously in the August sunshine. The grand department stores for which Paris was famous were deserted; there was no traffic—the buses had disappeared to the front; and the *métro* ran only sporadically. Theaters and cinemas were closed; the cafés shut at 8:00 p.m., the restaurants at 9.30 p.m. Before the month was out, with all the foreigners gone, the big hotels lay empty.

At the end of August that silence was shattered. The German army swept through Belgium and across northern France in a great flanking movement around the French left wing, and by August 29 was just twenty-five miles from the city. Gunfire could be heard in Paris and there were reports that German soldiers had been seen on the outskirts. The next day, a Sunday, a lone German plane circled overhead and dropped three bombs, filled with lead bullets, near the Gare de l'Est. No one was injured. On Monday a second plane swooped across the rooftops and let go of its bombs near the Rue Quatre Septembre, intending them, it was said, for the Banque de France. Again only a few windows were broken.

Few people—certainly not the Germans—were yet aware that on August 18, with the invaders still two hundred miles away in Brussels, the Banque de France had already set in motion its emergency plan—Paris, after all, had fallen to foreigners three times in the previous hundred years. Its gold reserves—38,800 gold ingots and innumerable bags of coins valued at $800 million and weighing some 1,300 tons—had been shipped in the utmost secrecy by rail and truck to safety at prearranged sites in the Massif Central and the south of France. The massive logistical operation went off without a hitch until one of the trains carrying coins derailed at Clermont-Ferrand. Five hundred men had been required to get it back on the tracks, collect the money, and keep off curious spectators. By early September, the Banque's vaults in Paris were empty.

6. MONEY GENERALS

CENTRAL BANKS: 1914–19

Endless money forms the sinews of war.

—CICERO, *Philippics*

As THE LIGHTS started to go out over Europe that fateful first week of August, every banker and finance minister seemed to be fixated not on military preparations or the movements of armies but on the size and durability of his gold reserves. The obsession was almost medieval. This was, after all, 1914, not 1814. Paper money had been in wide use for more than two centuries, and merchants and traders had developed highly sophisticated systems of credit. The idea that the scope of the war might be limited by the amount of gold on hand seems anachronistic. Nevertheless, here was the London magazine *United Empire* declaring that it was "the amounts of coin and bullion in the hands of the Continental Great Powers at the outbreak of hostilities" that would largely determine "the intensity . . . and probable duration of the war."

The focus on the prosaic matter of bank reserves was a symptom of the general complacency that surrounded those first few months of the war. Despite the hysteria of the crowds on the streets of Berlin, Paris, and London, an odd atmosphere of unreality hung in the air. No one could quite understand what this war was about or why it had come, but no one expected it to last very long. While the soldiers on both sides marched off to war, each one expecting to give the enemy a good pasting, the generals were promising they would be home for Christmas. Buoyed by such optimism from the military professionals, financial officials calculated that because the war was bound to be short, the important thing was to be in good financial shape, with gold reserves intact at the end.

So smug were the bankers and economists that they even allowed themselves to be convinced that the discipline of "sound money" itself would bring everyone to their senses and force an end to the war. On August 30, 1914, barely a month into the fighting, Charles Conant of the *New York Times* reported that the international banking community was very confident that there would not be the sort of "unlimited issue of paper [money] and its steady depreciation," which had wrought such inflationary havoc in previous wars. "Monetary science is better understood at the present time than in those days," declared the bankers confidently.

Sir Felix Schuster, chairman of the Union of London and Smith's Bank, one of the City's most prominent bankers, went confidently around telling everyone that the fighting would grind to a halt within six months—the interruption of trade would be too great. John Maynard Keynes, then a thirty-one-year-old economics don at King's College, Cambridge, who had made himself something of an overnight expert on war finance, announced to his friends in September 1914 that "he was quite certain that war could not last more than a year" because by then the liquid wealth of Europe that could be utilized to finance the war would be "used up," and he became quite angry at the stupidity of anyone who thought otherwise. In November 1914, the *Economist* predicted that the war would be over in a few months. That same month, at a dinner party in Paris given in honor of the visiting British secretary of state for war, Field Marshal Lord Kitchener, the French finance minister confidently proclaimed that the fighting would have to be over by July 1915 because money would have run out. And it was not only the Allied experts who were so blinkered. The Hungarian finance minister, Baron Janos Teleszky, when questioned in the cabinet about how long his country could pay for the war, replied three weeks.

And so as the financiers of Europe watched their continent slip toward Armageddon, its credit system collapsing onto itself, world stock markets closing their doors, and the gold standard grinding to a halt,* they clung to the illusion that global commerce would be disrupted only briefly and the world would rapidly return to "business as usual." Few imagined that they might be witnessing the last and dying convulsions of an entire economic order.

The experts seemed to have forgotten that among the first casualties of war is not only truth but also sound finance. None of the big wars of the previous century—for example, the Napoleonic Wars or the American Civil War—had been held back by a mere lack of gold. These had been fights to the death in which the belligerents had been willing to resort to everything and anything—taxes, borrowing, the printing of ever larger quantities of money—to raise the cash to pay for the war.

By the end of 1915, eighteen million men were mobilized across Europe. On the Western Front, two gigantic armies—three million men from the Allied nations and two and a half million Germans—sat stalemated, bogged down in trenches along a five-hundred-mile front stretching from the Channel through Belgium and France to the Swiss border. Like a giant sleeping reptile stretched across the face of Western Europe, the front remained immobile. By a perverse sort of logic, as hundreds of thousands of men were led to the slaughter, their terrible sacrifice was called upon to justify pressing on, and the carnage generated its own momentum.

Still, the complacency of those first few months took a long time to evaporate. Even into 1916, the dogma that this would be a short war lingered as general after general predicted victory in another six months. By then the five major powers—Britain, France, Russia, Germany, Austria-

---

*The gold standard was officially suspended in Germany and France in August 1914. In Britain, the government maintained the legal fiction that the gold standard was still in operation. Theoretically, British citizens could demand gold for their Bank of England notes and were, until May 1917, free to export gold. In reality the threat posed by German submarines made insurance prohibitively high and gold exports were never feasible.

Hungary—were spending a massive $3 billion each month, nearly 50 percent of their collective GDP. No other war in history had absorbed so much of the wealth of so many nations at one time.

Countries varied in how they raised the funds. Nevertheless, there were certain common themes. To pay for such a gigantic effort by taxation alone would have entailed tax rates at confiscatory levels and was therefore impossible. Daunted by the task, none of the governments even tried, and taxes accounted for but a tiny fraction of the new money raised. Instead, the belligerents resorted principally to borrowing. Once they had exhausted every potential source of loans, they relied on a technique almost as old as war itself: inflation. Unlike medieval kings, however, who accomplished this either by shaving pieces of gold and silver off the outer edge of their coins—a practice known as clipping—or of issuing coinage made of cheaper alloys—currency debasement—governments in the Great War turned to their central banks, often relying on complex accounting ruses to disguise the process. Central banks in turn, abandoning their long-standing principle of only issuing currency backed by gold, simply printed the money.

VERY, VERY RELUCTANTLY

Of all the European countries at war, Britain, in an effort to live up to its long history of fiscal prudence, was the most responsible in its financial policies. In four years of fighting, the government spent a total of $43 billion on the war effort, including $11 billion in loans, which it funneled to its poorer Continental allies, principally France and Russia. To pay for all this, it raised about $9 billion, or 20 percent, through additional taxes and almost $27 billion by long-term borrowing, both domestically and in the United States. The remainder it borrowed from banks, including a large chunk from the Bank of England. As a result, the quantity of money in circulation within Britain doubled in four years, doubling prices with it.

Turning to the Bank of England for money was not as unprecedented a policy as City bankers reared on nineteenth-century principles of finance liked to think. For the Bank had been originally created, in fact, not to regulate the currency but to help pay for a war. In 1688, James II, the last Catholic king of England and Scotland, was driven from his throne, having alienated much of his people by attempting to restore Roman Catholicism as the official religion of the country. In his place, Parliament invited his daughter Mary and her husband, William of Orange, both Protestants, to assume the crown. James found sanctuary at the court of Louis XIV of France, who used the "Glorious Revolution" as a pretext to launch against England what was to be grandly named the War of the League of Augsburg.

In 1694, after several years of fighting a country many times its size, England found itself close to bankruptcy. A group of City merchants, all Protestants, many of them French Huguenots only very recently compelled to leave France by Louis XIV's repudiation of tolerance for Protestants, approached the chancellor of the exchequer, Charles Montagu, offering to lend the government £1.2 million in perpetuity at an interest rate of 8 percent. In return, they were to be granted the authority to set up a bank with the right to issue £1.2 million in banknotes—the first officially sanctioned paper currency in England—and to be appointed sole banker to the government. Montagu, desperate for money, jumped at the idea. Before the year was over the new bank opened its doors for business under the name The Governor and Company of the Bank of England.

For its first 150 years, it operated like any other bank, albeit much larger than its competitors, and with certain special privileges, especially its lock on government business, which provided most of its income. Like all the other banks in the country, it issued banknotes and took deposits, maintained its reserves in gold, and discounted bills of exchange—short-term loans to merchants for financing trade and goods in transit.

While the Bank certainly did not see its job as managing the currency, over time, by virtue of its size and stability, it began to acquire a superior status among its fellow banks and its notes became the country's dominant form of paper money. Its smaller competitors began to entrust it with their reserves, and it gradually evolved into a sort of bankers' bank, the City's guardian and nanny, in the process acquiring the affectionate nickname of "The Old Lady of Threadneedle Street." But its powers were never quite formalized and much ambiguity hung about its precise role and responsibilities.

Like so many British institutions of those days, the Bank was run like a club. Control was vested in twenty-six directors of what was quaintly known as the Court of the Bank of England. Its membership was largely drawn from a closed inner circle of City bankers and merchants. They had all gone to the same small selection of schools, preferably Eton or Harrow. Some of them had even attended Oxford or Cambridge. They lived in Kensington or Knightsbridge, belonged to the same clubs, typically White's or Boodle's, and socialized with one another at their gracious but not grand country houses in the areas around London known as the Home Counties. Their daughters occasionally married into the landed aristocracy, but for the most part, they married among themselves. Few societies in the world were as comfortable, confident, and civilized.

Represented on the Court were all the major banking families of the City. There was always a Baring, a Grenfell, and a Goschen. Generally, there was also a partner of Brown Shipley and of Anthony Gibbs. Although the group included the usual smattering of baronets and even the occasional peer, none of the great landed families of Britain were represented—they went into politics. Only once had there been a Jew on the Court of the Bank of England, and that was, of course, Alfred de Rothschild, who had been elected in 1868 and resigned in 1889.

Directors were generally invited to join in their late thirties and were appointed for life, or at least until the onset of senility; many were in their seventies or eighties, and some had been on the Court for over half a century. It was part-time work and not too onerous. They met once a week. In addition, each director had to take his turn on the Committee of Daily Waiting, which required that each day three of the twenty-six directors be physically present at the Bank, responsible for the keys to the vaults, auditing the securities held there, and dining with the commander of the Bank piquet, the Brigade of Guards detachment that marched nightly from its barracks in Knightsbridge to protect the Bank. For these duties, a director received an annual honorarium of the equivalent of $2,500, equivalent to the annual pay of a colonel in the Guards or the stipend of a canon of Westminster.

Among the Court's offices, only the governorship and the deputy governorship were full-time positions. Those who filled those posts were required to take a temporary leave of absence from their own businesses. Each member of the Court was given a chance—indeed was expected—to become deputy governor for two years, and then governor for two years more. To be the governor of the Bank of England in the nineteenth and early twentieth century was therefore not a mark of any particular merit, but merely a sign of the right pedigree, patience, longevity, and the luxury of having a sufficiently profitable business with partners willing to let one take four years' leave. It was the principle of Buggin's turn. At the end of his term—terms were very rarely extended and then only for one year—a retiring governor simply went back to being an ordinary member of the Court until he died or became embarrassingly incoherent.

As Walter Bagehot, the great nineteenth-century editor of the *Economist* who reveled in the quaint paradoxes of English life, described them, members of the Court were generally "quiet serious men . . . (who) have a good deal of leisure." Indeed, he felt it an ominous sign for a private banker to be fully employed. "If such a man is very busy, it is a sign of something wrong. Either he is working at detail, which subordinates would do better and which he had better leave alone or he is engaged in too many speculations . . . and so may be ruined."

These arrangements, according to Bagehot, put the financial stability of London and, as a consequence, the world in the hands of "a shifting executive; a board of directors chosen too young for it to be known whether they are able; a committee of management in which seniority is the necessary qualification, and old age the common result." It was a strange, even eccentric way of doing things—for the most important financial institution in Britain, in fact in the world, to be in the hands of a group of amateurs, men who generally would have preferred to be doing something else but who viewed the years they devoted to steering the Bank as a form of civic duty.*

Though the directors of the Bank were charged with governing the supply of credit in Britain, and by extension around the globe, they did not pretend to know very much about economics, central banking, or monetary policy. An economist of the 1920s once described them as resembling ship captains who not only refused to learn the principles of navigation but believed that these were unnecessary.

To the extent that they did espouse a systematic doctrine of monetary policy, it was the "real bills" theory of credit, that we now consider clearly fallacious. This held that provided banks, including the Bank of England, only made loans to finance inventories of goods—such as bales of cotton, or rolls of paper, truckloads of copper wire or steel girders—rather than for financial speculation in stocks and bonds or for long-term investments then no inflation could result. It is simple to see why this is nonsense. In periods of inflation, as the price of goods in inventory keeps rising, this doctrine would call for banks to keep on expanding credit, thus adding further fuel to the inflationary fire. That this doctrine did not lead to monetary disaster was due to the gold standard, which by keeping prices roughly stable, ensured that the "real bills' doctrine was never given a chance to be applied in an environment of rising prices.

The demands of war finance transformed the Bank. Forced to issue more and more currency notes without gold backing, it became increasingly subordinate to the needs of the UK Treasury. Despite its status as a national institution, the respectable City burghers who ran the Bank had been very careful, over the years, to keep a wary distance from any government. They were clear in their minds that the Bank was not an organ of the state nor did they remotely wish to make it one. An apocryphal story,

---

*That same ethos seems to have extended to the senior employees. Kenneth Grahame, the children's author, joined the Bank of England in 1879 and rose through the ranks, eventually becoming secretary. In 1895, he published *The Golden Age*, a book not about bullion but childhood. In 1907 he retired, after having been shot during an unsuccessful robbery attempt at the Bank, and the following year published *The Wind in the Willows*.

much circulated in the City before the war, best captures that attitude. A governor was asked by the chancellor of the exchequer to testify before a royal commission. When questioned about the Bank's reserves, he was only willing to say that they were "very, very considerable." When pressed to give even an approximate figure, he was supposed to have replied that he would be "very, very reluctant to add to what he said."

As the stresses of raising money for the war mounted, tensions between the Bank and the government escalated, finally coming to a head in 1917. The governor was then Walter Cunliffe, a tall barrel-chested, John Bull sort of character who sported an imposing walrus mustache, was a renowned big game hunter, and looked more like a gentleman farmer than a City grandee. Over the years, he had become increasingly autocratic and erratic in his judgments and had developed an exaggerated sense of his own importance as governor to the point of insisting that his status required him to deal with the government through the prime minister alone, not even through the chancellor of the exchequer.

In 1917, Cunliffe became infuriated by what he believed was the cavalier way he was being treated by officials at the Treasury, among whom the chief culprit was none other than that brilliantly impertinent young upstart Maynard Keynes. Cunliffe was well known in the City as a man of few words and even more limited intelligence, a bully who acted first and thought later. In a fit of temper, without consulting any of his fellow directors, he dispatched a telegram to the Canadian government, then the North American custodian of Britain's gold reserves, forbidding it to accept any further instructions from the Treasury in London. The British government came close to the extremely embarrassing position at the height of the World War of not being able to settle the bills from its American suppliers.

Lloyd George, by now prime minister, and justly furious, summoned Cunliffe to 10 Downing Street, and berated the governor, threatening to "take over the Bank." After some delicate behind-the-scenes negotiations over protocol, the shaken Cunliffe wrote the chancellor of the exchequer as cringing a letter as form would allow, asking him "to accept my unreserved apology for anything I have done to offend you." Cunliffe, who, because of the war and contrary to all tradition, had been appointed for a second two-year term, was not reappointed again.

DURING THE WAR, as the Bank kept expanding its role as chief underwriter and promoter of government debt, its few senior executives found themselves overwhelmed with work and responsibility. In 1915, the deputy governor, Brian Cockayne, invited Montagu Norman to become his adviser. Though this was to be an informal and unpaid position, Norman, then at a loose end after leaving Brown Shipley, jumped at it. He had originally joined the Court of the Bank in 1907, at the age of thirty-six, but had done so largely for tradition's sake—it was customary for a partner at Brown Shipley to be on the Court. Indeed for the first few years, he rarely went into the place and showed little interest in its workings. His associations with the institution, however, went far back. He came from two of the most prominent banking families in the City, that special aristocracy from which the Court of the Bank was drawn, and both of his grandfathers had been long-standing directors of some repute in their time.

His paternal grandfather, George Warde Norman, though not a full-time banker—his own inherited fortune derived from timber and real estate—had acquired a large stake in Martins Bank through marriage and was elected a director in 1821. In 1830, at the age of thirty-seven, George Norman retired from full-time business in order to devote himself to his estate in Kent, indulging his love for literature and history; promoting cricket, a family obsession; and enjoying his brood of seven sons. Nevertheless, he remained a dutiful member of the Court for more than fifty years, although in contrast to the typical member, he developed a great interest and some expertise in monetary economics. Like so many Victorian gentlemen of leisure, he published pamphlets—in his case on monetary theory—and became a leader of the move to codify gold standard rules, which were embodied in the Bank Act of 1844. He further broke with tradition at the Bank by categorically refusing to take his turn as deputy governor and governor. Unable to see any reason why he should tear himself away from the many enjoyments of life to inflict upon himself the unnecessary responsibilities and burdens of office, he claimed that his nerves could not cope with the tensions, a curious hint of the troubles that his grandson would face.

Norman's maternal grandfather, Sir Mark Collet, was very different. A self-made man, he had begun his career as a clerk in a merchant house and moved to New York in 1849. On his return to England two years later, he joined the firm of Brown Shipley, the British arm of the merchant banking house of Brown Brothers of New York and Baltimore, and eventually became senior partner in London. Elected to the Court of the Bank of England in 1866, he dutifully served his turn as governor and was knighted for his services.

Few people were surprised that with this sort of pedigree, Montagu Norman should end up at the Bank. Nevertheless, when he joined in 1915, he had had only a short and not particularly illustrious career as a merchant banker and was not very well known in the City. In his first few weeks, Lord Cunliffe, then governor, was heard to remark, "There goes that queer-looking fish with the ginger beard again. Do you know who he is? I keep seeing him creep about this place like a lost soul with nothing better to do." Few people could then have predicted that the "fish" would accomplish an extraordinary upward swim through the institution. Nothing in his background suggested that he would be well suited to the work of a central banker. Within three years, however, he was elected deputy governor, and two years later became governor, a post he would eventually hold for an unprecedented twenty-four years.

IN GOVERNMENT HANDS

If Britain was the most responsible of the belligerents, its ally France balanced it out by choosing to be the most feckless. The French government spent a total of $30 billion on its war effort. Few nations resisted paying their taxes more vigorously than the people of France—they seemed to view even the slightest official inquiry as to their financial circumstances as an unjustified intrusion by the state "into the most holy recesses of private life" and an infringement of their fundamental rights as citizens. As a result, at least for the first two years of the war, the government balked at raising taxes, not reversing itself until 1916 when it seemed on the verge of financial collapse. In total, France paid for less than 5 percent of its war expenditures out of higher taxation.

The republic was saved from complete economic disaster only by its government's ability to tap two sources: first, the notoriously thrifty French middle classes, which bought $15 billion worth of government bonds; and second, foreign governments, specifically those of Britain and America, which, seeing France bear the brunt of the human cost of the war, lent a total of $10 billion. This still left a substantial gap, which was filled by printing money. While currency in circulation doubled in Britain, in France it tripled.

Drawing on the central bank for money was a much easier process in France than in Britain—in part because the governor of the Banque de France was by tradition not a banker but a high civil servant appointed by the state. Indeed, as far back as 1911 the minister of finance, thinking ahead, had prearranged a line of credit from the Banque to be drawn upon in the event of war. There was a certain irony in this. The Banque de France, like the Bank of England, had been founded in the middle of a war, but unlike its older cousin it had been set up not so much to raise money but to bring order to a chaotic monetary situation.

France in 1799 faced a pressing shortage of currency. Ten years of Revolutionary turmoil had taken their toll. Silver and gold had fled the country, and the failed experiment of the Revolutionary government with the assignats had destroyed any residual confidence in paper money not backed by gold. Two financiers, the Swiss banker Jean-Frédéric Perregaux and the sonorously sounding Jean-Barthélémy Le Couteulx de Canteleu, a rich merchant from Rouen, received the blessings of the first consul of the republic, Napoléon Bonaparte, to create a new bank that would issue currency backed by gold and have a capital of 30 million francs, equivalent to $6 million.*

The Banque opened its doors on January 18, 1800, or according to the calendar of the Revolution then in force, on the 28th day of Nivose, the month of snow, in the year VIII. The bulk of its capital was raised from merchant and banking families, many of them Protestants of Swiss origin. But the glittering arriviste circles surrounding the first consul were also keen to buy into a venture that promised much profit. Napoléon himself took thirty shares, each valued at 1,000 francs; Louis-Antoine Fauvelet de Bourrienne, his secretary, who would later be dismissed for corruption and betray Napoléon by rallying to Louis XVIII, took five; Joachim Murat, Napoleon's brother-in-law and a future king of Naples, nine; Hortense de Beauharnais, Napoleon's stepdaughter, his sister-in-law-to-be, and a future queen of Holland, five; Napoléon's older brother Joseph, a future king of Spain, just one. To encourage investors, the Banque was made as independent of the government as the Bank of England and, in 1803, was granted a monopoly over note issuance in Paris.

In 1805, immediately following the naval disaster at Trafalgar and just as Napoléon was launching his latest campaign against the Austro-Russian alliance, a panic among the merchants of Paris precipitated a run on the still infant Banque and almost forced it into liquidation. It was saved when news arrived in the capital of Napoléon's brilliant victory at Austerlitz. While confidence was quickly reestablished in the new Banque, lubricated by large indemnity from the Austrians, Napoléon remained enraged by the feeble-heartedness of his bankers.

On his return from Austria, he summoned his council of ministers and, in one of his imperial tantrums, fired his minister of finance. To the Banque's three-man management committee he offered the choice between prison or a fine of 87 million francs. They chose the fine. Determined

---

*By comparison, the Bank of the United States, the primary bank of issue for a country with one-sixth of France's population, was capitalized at $10 million.

never again to be held hostage by moneymen, Napoleon changed the Banque's statutes so that henceforth the governor and the two deputy governors would be appointed directly by the government, which at that time meant Napoléon himself. He declared at the time, "The Banque does not belong only to its shareholders, but also to the state.... I want the Banque to be sufficiently in government hands without being too much so."

FOR ÉMILE MOREAU the war meant a continuation of his exile at the head of the Banque d'Algérie. In 1914, after Henriette Caillaux's acquittal, he must have secretly harbored some hope of returning to the Ministry of Finance on his mentor Caillaux's coattails. But this was quickly squashed with the outbreak of war, for Caillaux, always viewed as soft on Germany, was not invited into the war government.

Indeed, Caillaux made things even worse for himself during the war. With his characteristic bad judgment, he became embroiled in 1916 with a shady bunch of characters who were trying to negotiate a back-channel settlement with Germany. One of these, Paul Bolo-Pasha, a confidence trickster in the joint service of the Egyptian khedive and German intelligence, was arrested in 1917, tried, and shot for espionage. In the ensuing spy mania that seethed through France, Caillaux himself was accused of treason. Deprived of his parliamentary immunity, he was jailed in early 1918. He would finally be brought to trial before the Senate, sitting as a high court of justice, in 1920. Though acquitted of treason, a capital offense, he would be found guilty of "imprudent conversations" with the enemy and condemned to three years imprisonment; five years deprivation of civil rights; and a peculiarly French punishment, *interdiction de séjour*—banishment from Paris, a somewhat archaic penalty usually reserved for drug addicts, white slavers, and thugs.

Watching the tragic, almost comical, antics of his old leader, there must have been times when Moreau felt that he had been cursed in his choice of mentors. Though the Banque d'Algérie was called upon to play a modest role in financing the war effort—it supplied some $200 million in loans to the government—this was small compared to the $4 billion provided by its larger and more prestigious sibling, the Banque de France. By 1919, Moreau had almost reconciled himself to serving out his time until retirement in the backwaters of the Banque d'Algérie.

OBEDIENCE AND SUBORDINATION

Germany's strategy for paying for its military effort was dominated by the absolute conviction of the men around the kaiser that the war would be short, that the Reich would prevail, and that it would then present the bill to the vanquished. The German government raised barely 10 percent of the $47 billion it spent on the war from taxes. And because Germany lacked Britain's sophisticated financial market, France's great reserve army of middle-class savers, or a rich ally across the ocean willing to lend it vast amounts of money, it had to resort to an unusually high degree of inflationary finance. Whereas during the war, money in circulation doubled in Britain and tripled in France, in Germany it went up fourfold.

The architects of this disastrous policy were paradoxically two of the most competent financial officials in all Europe: Karl Helfferich, the secretary of the Reich Treasury Office, the imperial German equivalent of minister of finance, and Rudolph von Havenstein, the aristocratic head of the Reichsbank. Helfferich, the most famous economist in Germany, was a professor who before the war had written one of the best works anywhere on monetary economics, *Das Geld*, which had been through six editions and had been translated into numerous languages, including Japanese.

Von Havenstein, a lawyer by training, did not have the same background but was universally acknowledged to be one of the most dedicated, upstanding, and loyal officials in the entire Reich. With his piercing eyes, long and luxuriant, well-waxed whiskers, and pointed beard, he looked like the impresario of a Victorian music hall. In fact, like his two predecessors as president of the Reichsbank, he was a typical product of the higher reaches of the imperial civil service. Born into the Prussian gentry in 1857, of a landowning family from Brandenburg, he studied law and became a county court judge. In 1890, he joined the Prussian Finance Ministry and was appointed president of the Reichsbank in 1908.

Service to the kaiser was the cornerstone of Wilhelmine Germany and both men allowed themselves to be blinded by their loyalty to the emperor, all the easier in Hellferich's case because he was an extreme right-wing nationalist and a fervent believer in the glorious destiny of the German people and the historic mission of their leader.

Von Havenstein was a civil servant of the old school and believed strongly in the paramount virtue of duty. As one banker wrote, "Obedience and subordination [were] part of his flesh and blood." While the Reichsbank was legally owned by private shareholders, Von Havenstein and all his top officials were responsible to a board comprised of politicians: the imperial chancellor and four members representing the federal German states. The structure had been put in place by the founder of the Reichsbank, Count Otto von Bismarck, a man who above all understood power. Aside from the accumulation of an enormous personal fortune, Bismarck showed little interest in economics. However, when the Reichsbank was being formed in 1871, his own private banker and confidant, Gershon Bleichröder, warned him that there would be occasions when political considerations would have to override purely economic judgments and at such times too independent a central bank would be a nuisance.

Thus, even though the German money supply ballooned during the war, and prices more than quadrupled—the inflation rate exceeded 40 percent a year—Von Havenstein became something of a national hero. He was showered with honors and decorations, immensely popular with the public, and the kaiser even affectionately nicknamed him with the engaging pun *der Geld Marschall*, the "Money General."

DESPITE HIS BELIEF that the war had been a mistake, Hjalmar Schacht threw himself into the war effort as energetically as most citizens of imperial Germany. He was severely shortsighted and thus exempted from military service. Convinced like everyone else that German victory was assured, only three weeks after the outbreak he was busy developing a plan for extracting reparations from France. It was a sign of how far off the mark even the most astute observers were to be about the costs of the war that Schacht came up with a working figure of $10 billion. Though ten times the amount France had paid after the Franco-Prussian war of 1870, this would turn out to be only a fifth of the eventual total costs of Germany's war budget.

In October 1914, as the Western Front sank into stalemate, Schacht was offered a job on the staff of the Banking Commission overseeing the finances of occupied Belgium, which was run by the military administration. He soon discovered that he was temperamentally ill suited to the army. He found the rigid hierarchy, the narrowness of the military mind, and the self-importance of the professional officer caste oppressive.

He also seemed to have had an unusual talent for making enemies. Within a short period, he managed to antagonize his superior, Major Karl von Lumm, the banking commissioner, in civilian life a member of the Reichsbank directorate. Schacht, always acutely sensitive when it came to matters of status, asked to join the officers' club then housed in the Brussels casino. Von Lumm, an old bachelor who had been part of the Bavarian reserve before the war and was very proud of his military credentials and uniform, refused, citing Schacht's status as a civilian. Schacht disastrously went over Von Lumm's head to General von der Goltz, the governor general of Occupied Belgium, whom he had known before the war. He was admitted to the club all right, but at the price of Major von Lumm's enduring enmity.

As part of his duties, Schacht organized a system by which the German army, rather than simply commandeering whatever goods it needed, paid for its requisitions with a special occupation currency of "Belgian" francs, which, by design, Germans could buy at a highly favorable exchange rate.

Demand for the Belgian francs was extremely strong, and in February 1915 Schacht allowed the Dresdner Bank, his employer in civilian life, to purchase a large quantity. Von Lumm promptly accused him of having violated the civil service code of ethics and brought Schacht up before an investigating committee. It concluded that while he had done nothing illegal or unethical, Schacht had attempted to cover up his involvement and had come close to perjury by giving "insincere replies to the questions put to him; and when the insincerity was pointed out . . . he attempted to justify himself by a far-fetched explanation of his statements." The matter eventually went up as far as the office of the secretary of state for the interior; Schacht was officially reprimanded and resigned from the Banking Commission rather than risk dismissal.

Von Lumm had undoubtedly made a mountain out of a molehill. But even Schacht was to admit in private years later that while he had not lied during the inquiry, he *had* been highly evasive. The incident, clouded in mystery, would dog his reputation for many years. Rumors circulated that he had embezzled large amounts of money or had personally profited from his access to state secrets.

After war service that had lasted barely nine months, Schacht returned to his banking career. Once again, his overweening ambition got the better of him. Back at the Dresdner Bank, he pressed too hard for promotion to the board, was rebuffed, and had no option but to resign. He moved on to become a director of the Nationalbank, a well-regarded, if sleepy, second-tier firm based in Berlin.

As for so many Germans, the war was a grim time for the Schacht family. He lost two of his brothers—Oluf, from disease, and William, the youngest, at the Battle of the Somme. Food was scarce—they had to grow their own vegetables and acquired a goat, which they learned to milk—and times were hard.

A SCOUTING TRIP

For the United States the war was a windfall. European demand for American materials and supplies soared, setting off an enormous boom. Though these purchases were partly financed by Britain's and France's borrowing some $2 billion a year within the United States, the net effect led to massive influx of gold into America, swelling its bullion reserves from under $2 billion to $4 billion. Because of the operation of the gold standard, the influx of gold created an unusual expansion of credit and the U.S. money supply doubled.

During those first few years of its existence, the Federal Reserve System found itself overwhelmed. It was trying to build up its staff; it had no experience as an institution in monetary affairs, and being the product of countless political compromises, its charter was riddled with contradictions. Benjamin Strong, governor of the Federal Reserve Bank of New York, was quick to exploit the uncertainty about who was in charge. While the New York Fed, as it would come to be called, was on paper merely one among the twelve regional Federal Reserve Banks and theoretically under the supervision of the Federal Reserve Board in Washington, a body made up of political appointees, it was by a long way the largest of the reserve banks, and Strong, not a man to wait upon orders, made himself the chief pilot of the whole system. By virtue of his connections among New York bankers, his background as one of the original architects of the system, and most important, his personality, he came to dominate discussions of monetary and financial policy.

As more and more gold accumulated in the various Federal Reserve banks, Strong had two big fears. One was that at the end of the war, this gold would all pour back to Europe, radically destabilizing the U.S banking system. The other was that the gold would stay, potentially causing a shortage of reserves in Europe and threatening even greater inflation at home. In either case, he recognized that the Fed would be unable to handle the disruptions on its own and would have to coordinate its response with the European central banks. And so in February 1916, he decided to make a "scouting trip" to Europe.

As he arrived, the war, which had been going on for eighteen months, was about to enter its bloodiest year. The actual fighting in Western Europe was restricted to a narrow corridor through Belgium and eastern France, and life in London or Paris, while austere, was not especially dangerous. Since the *Lusitania* had been torpedoed and sunk off the coast of Ireland the year before, drowning almost 1,200 people, 124 of them Americans, the State Department had been warning its citizens not to travel to Europe.

Strong went first to Paris to meet his counterparts at the Banque de France and then to London. It was during this visit to the Bank of England that he first met Norman. Coming from the same generation, they immediately struck up a friendship. Unlike many of his colleagues in the City, Norman, having lived in the United States for two years, liked and admired Americans and he invited Strong to Thorpe Lodge one evening for a quiet dinner. Though Strong was the governor of the New York Fed and Norman a mere adviser to the deputy governor, on his return to the United States in April, Strong started to correspond with Norman. Initially both saw it just as a way to exchange information and views on the narrower aspects of credit policy. But over the months, their letters gradually become less formal and more personal, particularly when Norman took great pains to look after Strong's eldest son, Benjamin, a sophomore at Princeton, who had gone to Europe as a volunteer with the American Ambulance Service in May 1917, after the United States entered the war on the Allied side.

Meanwhile, after Strong returned to the United States from Europe in the summer of 1916, he was buffeted by a series of personal tragedies. His wife, Katharine, still only twenty-eight, left him, taking their two young daughters with her. She moved across the country to Santa Barbara. Their marriage had been on the rocks for a while. They were temperamentally unsuited to each other—he was gregarious and social, she shy and retiring—and their age difference too great. His father-in-law, Edmund Converse, had been against his taking the Fed job from the very beginning, dismissing it as a quasi-government position with no future, and relations between the two men had steadily deteriorated. Katharine for her part had found it difficult to adjust to their diminished financial circumstances. Strong hoped for many years that they might be reconciled and was deeply hurt when in 1921 she filed for divorce without even consulting him. After the summer of 1916, they were never to meet again.

That same summer, as his marriage was falling apart, he also fell ill, developing a nagging cough that became progressively worse. He was soon bringing up blood and experiencing terrible chest pains. That June he was diagnosed with tuberculosis. Then commonly known as consumption, the highly contagious disease, caused by airborne bacteria that attack the membranes of the lungs, was then the most common cause of civilian deaths in both Europe and America, affecting people of all classes, often in the prime of life. Though the incidence of the disease had markedly declined before the war as the poorly ventilated tenements of industrial cities were replaced by better housing, the war had seen a minor resurgence of it in Europe. Strong is likely to have picked up the infection on his visit there.

While the cause of the disease had been isolated in the late nineteenth century, there was still no effective therapy. Half of those who contracted it were dead within five years. At the time, it was thought that the thin dry air in high altitudes helped to contain the infection—with some grounds because its virulence declines in low-oxygen atmospheres. It was also believed—erroneously, it turned out—that total inactivity and complete rest allowed the lungs to rebuild themselves. Luxury sanatoria catering to the rich and the middle class, cut off from the rest of the world, had sprung up in mountain resorts across Europe and America.

Strong's doctors insisted that he take an extended leave of absence from the Fed. In July 1916, he moved to Colorado, where almost a third of the population was then made up of "consumptives" seeking to be cured. He initially checked into a sanatorium in Estes Park, in the heart of the northern Colorado Rockies, but frustrated by this hermetically sealed world where patients spent hours doing nothing but sitting outdoors taking in the mountain air, he moved to Denver that October and set up a small office that allowed him to keep in touch with New York.

Strong was still convalescing in Colorado when the United States entered the war in April 1917. Within six weeks, he was back in New York. For the next eighteen months he threw himself into the task of raising the money to pay for the war. Every other objective of the Fed was now subordinated to this goal. The United States spent in total some $30 billion on the war, a little over $20 billion on its own actual expenditures and another $10 billion in the form of loans to keep other countries going.* Determined to avoid the mistakes that had been made in financing the Civil War, the secretary of the treasury, William McAdoo, who also happened to be the president's son-in-law, launched an aggressive program to induce the American public to purchase war debt. The Fed, as banker to the government, was responsible for selling these so-called Liberty Bonds, which eventually brought in close to $20 billion, about half of this raised by the New York Fed.

Taking the lead in organizing the high-pressure campaigns in New York to stir public enthusiasm for the bonds, Strong suddenly found himself thrust into the limelight. Acting as the master of ceremonies for concerts at Carnegie Hall or at the Metropolitan Opera House, leading great patriotic marches down Fifth Avenue, speaking at rallies featuring such Hollywood celebrities as Mary Pickford and Douglas Fairbanks, he became something of a minor celebrity himself. Publicity stunts were a signature of these campaigns. On one occasion Strong and the other organizers had trenches dug in the Sheep Meadow in Central Park—much to the outrage of conservationists—to show how soldiers were living on the Western Front. To kick off another campaign, they arranged for every air-raid siren, police alarm, tugboat whistle, fire engine bell, and ship foghorn across the city to be turned on for five minutes.

By the time the war drew to a close, the Fed was a transformed institution. While it was not completely immune from the pressures of war finance, unlike so many European central banks, it had resisted purchasing government bonds directly and only indirectly helped to fuel the expansion

---

*By comparison, Britain, with an economy about a third that of the United States, spent a total of $50 billion over a period of four years.

in money supply. It had therefore secured some credibility. More important, the war had irrevocably changed the economic and financial position of the United States in relation to the rest of the world. The Fed, which barely existed in 1914, now sat on the largest reservoir of gold bullion in the world, making it potentially the dominant player if and when the international gold standard was restored.

PART TWO

*

AFTER
THE DELUGE

*

1919-23

7. DEMENTED INSPIRATIONS

GERMAN REPARATIONS

Lenin was certainly right. There is no subtler, no surer means of overturning the existing basis of society than to debauch the currency.

—JOHN MAYNARD KEYNES,
The Economic Consequences of the Peace

ON NOVEMBER 11, 1918, the Great War came to an end as it had begun, as a total surprise. In June 1918, the German army broke through the Allied lines, and came within fifty miles of Paris. The German public, given a distorted picture by its government, fully anticipated victory. A month later, the Allies counterattacked and suddenly the entire German war machine seemed to disintegrate. The German forces, exhausted by that last offensive, withered away; support for the war at home crumbled; civilian morale collapsed; soldiers deserted in droves; the navy, blockaded at Kiel, mutinied; and Germany's allies began to sue secretly for peace. By October, the military, desperate to salvage what it could, turned over power to the civilians. On November 9, the kaiser was forced into exile by his generals, boarding a train for Holland. Early on November 11, in a railway carriage in the forest of Compiègne forty miles outside Paris, an armistice was signed.

Across Europe some 11 million men lay dead, including 2 million Germans, 1.4 million Frenchmen, and 900,000 British. Another 21 million had been wounded, very many maimed for life. Nine million civilians had perished, mostly of hunger, cold, or lowered resistance to the monstrous epidemics. But for all the horrendous human carnage, the actual material destruction of the war was limited to a long but narrow strip of northern France and Belgium. The costs of rebuilding the mines, farms, and factories destroyed on the Western Front amounted to only $7 billion.

Most European economies had contracted—Germany's and France's by 30 percent, Britain by less than 5 percent—as men and capital were siphoned off, as factories diverted to producing arms, and livestock slaughtered. The war had been a boon for the United States. Entering late, it had suffered fewer casualties, while the massive expansion in exports of foodstuffs, raw materials, and war supplies to its allies had provided a gigantic boost to its economy. Before the war, its GDP of $40 billion per annum was roughly the equivalent of that of Britain, France, and Germany combined. By 1919, it was more than 50 percent larger.

The most pernicious and insidious economic legacy of the war was the mountain of debt in Europe. In four years of constant and obsessive battle, the governments of Europe had spent some $200 billion, consuming almost half of their nations' GDP in mutual destruction. To pay for this, they had raised taxes, borrowed gigantic amounts of money both from their own citizens and from the Americans, and simply printed more and more currency. By the end of the war, Europe was awash with the stuff—the money supply in Britain doubled, in France it tripled, and in Germany, the worst culprit, it quadrupled. Though the U.S. money supply also doubled, this was less because of inflationary war finance, which it relied upon to a much smaller extent than the Europeans, and more because of the massive influx of gold. This set the pattern of the next decade: Europe struggling with the legacies and burdens of the past, the United States wrestling with the excess bonuses of its good fortune.

· · ·

ON THE DAY the kaiser fled Germany, Schacht was in Berlin. That morning, although the kaiser had not actually abdicated—and would only formally do so two weeks later from his sanctuary in Holland—the chancellor, Prince Max of Baden, a distant cousin of the kaiser's, announced preemptively that the emperor had gone. The city was like an armed camp, with barbed-wire entanglements and overturned vehicles blocking the streets. Revolution was in the air. A general strike had been declared, and thousands of workers and soldiers paraded through the center of town demanding a republic.

Coming out of the Hotel Esplanade near the Potsdammerplatz at about noon, Schacht was confronted by a convoy of Red soldiers packed in the back of trucks driving across the square. At the station, a machine-gun company was positioned for action. No one seemed to be in charge. To find out what was going on, and to avoid being caught in the mob, Schacht and his companion headed north toward the Reichstag, which they found deserted. A little while before, Philipp Scheidemann, a leader of the Social Democrats, had given history a push by coming out onto the balcony and proclaiming a republic to the crowds below, although no such measure had been passed by the Reichstag. Thus was born the new Republic of Germany. The mobs had then headed off to the emperor's abandoned palace, the Berliner Schloss.

Schacht would remark later that there was a certain distinctively German order amid all the chaos of that dramatic day. The imperial dynasty might have fallen and the political system of Germany overturned, but ordinary people went about their everyday business, trying to ignore the demonstrations. The trams did not stop running; electricity, water, and gas supplies were not interrupted; and almost no one was killed—the casualties that day amounted to fewer than fifteen dead. Even when shots were randomly fired near the palace, the fleeing crowds remained so instinctively law abiding that they obeyed the signs to keep off the grass.

Across the country, workers' and soldiers' councils sprang up and took over the functions of the local authorities. On November 10, Schacht was elected, much to his amusement, to his local community council. After issuing a proclamation welcoming the revolution, it met precisely once more.

The next few weeks were a time of terrible turmoil. Although the November revolution was largely peaceful, by the first weeks of January, violence had broken out and Berlin was wracked by strikes, demonstrations, and fierce street fighting between the Spartacist revolutionaries and the army. It seemed to Schacht then, as to very many others, that Germany was the front line in a grand battle across Europe against the forces of Bolshevism. Going home through the darkened city, he could hear the rattle of machine guns. On one occasion, he was stuck in the Hotel Kaiserhof as a gang of Spartacist demonstrators clashed with a group of government supporters outside. A hand grenade burst among the crowd, scattering it in all directions and leaving one man dead in the street below. The "fate of Germany hung by a thread," he recalled many years later.

It was also, however, a time of opportunity for middle-class men of talent like Schacht. The collapse of empire and an army in defeat shattered the old order. Within forty-eight hours of the kaiser's flight, twenty-five dynasties had abdicated within Germany. The Junkers who had dominated the country were discredited, their power swept away.

Initially Schacht thought he might find his opportunity in politics. Before the war, he had been a member of the Young Liberal Association, an arm of the National Liberals, a nationalistic though not very liberal party, which had enthusiastically supported the kaiser's expansionist policies. In 1901, he had even declined an offer from the party to stand for election to the Reichstag, knowing that power in the Kaiserreich was reserved for the nobility, especially the Prussian nobility, and that a man of his background could not aspire to political office of any consequence. But with the new president of the republic himself a former saddler and the new chancellor a former journalist, it seemed that the old caste system had now disintegrated.

On November 10, the republic only a day old, Schacht was invited to a meeting and asked to help found a new moderate party, the Deutsche Demokratische Partei (DDP), which would oppose alike the socialism of the left and the nationalism of the right. The DDP itself would briefly do very well, becoming a party of academics, journalists, and businessmen, many of them Jewish, and attracting such luminaries as Max Weber and Albert Einstein. In the 1919 election, it vaulted into third place in the Reichstag, after the Socialists and the Catholic Centrum Party.

But Schacht's brief flirtation with democratic politics was not destined to be very successful. With his financial and business connections, he played an important role in raising funds for the DDP, and helped write the party platform. But lacking the common touch that appealed to voters and too proud to forge the necessary personal alliances, he was never able to persuade a constituency to select him as a candidate. He was also viewed with some suspicion within the leadership, whose leading light, Theodor Woolf, editor of the *Berliner Tageblatt,* regarded him as just one more opportunist trying to hitch a ride on the cause of democracy, with little commitment to the new republic.

For his part, Schacht would become steadily disillusioned with the party, formally breaking with it in 1925, when it voted to support the elimination of privy purses to the deposed ruling families. In the late 1920s, the DDP, like all German centrist parties, would shrink into insignificance, squeezed from both ends of the political spectrum, particularly from the right. By then, though, Schacht had moved on to bigger things.

It was perhaps not surprising that he had such little success in electoral politics. He was simply a hard man to like. People found him cold and unemotional, overly calculating and shrewd. By his own admission, he came across as "hard . . . callous . . . and buttoned down." It was partly his appearance. One acquaintance remarked, "He managed to look like a compound of a Prussian reserve officer and a budding Prussian judge who is trying to copy the officer." His physically distinctive characteristics—the crew cut, the rigid bearing, the stiffly upright posture, the perpetual aggressive scowl—would, after he had become famous, make him a popular target for cartoonists.* But more than his appearance, it was his character traits—his extreme vanity, his tendency to talk about himself and his achievements, his inflexibility, his caustic wit laced with cynicism—that put people off.

He displayed an astounding self-confidence. This was not a façade, but a reflection of his astonishing sense of innate superiority. He was in many ways a classic lower-middle-class overachiever. Having grown up poor, in a society where class and family background were still overwhelming factors, he had learned the hard way that in a hostile world he could rely only on himself. Whatever success he had achieved, he owed to himself alone—his own formidable intelligence and impressive capacity for hard work. "Nothing seems sacred to him except his belief in himself, and this is so overwhelming as no longer to seem personal. He makes the most exaggeratedly egotistical statements without his hearer being aware of any personal boasting," wrote one observer. And unlike some men on the make, who cloak their cynicism behind a veneer of charm, he displayed no particular desire to be liked. Much later, when his true colors had been revealed, one politician would write, "He was a man apart, unique, solitary, without followers or any coterie of partisans. He had no friends, only enemies." But no one could dispute his self-discipline, energy, and unrelenting drive.

THE PROBLEM OF German reparations—that is, how much of the cost of the war the victors, particularly Britain and France, could demand from Germany—was to haunt the financial landscape of Europe for the next twenty years. The war may have ended, but the conflicts did not stop. At the Paris Peace Conference, which opened in January 1919, no other issue "caused more trouble, contention, hard feeling, and delay," recalled Thomas Lamont, one of the American negotiators.

---

* He was sufficiently flattered by the attention from cartoonists that, in 1937, he had a collection of cartoons privately published to commemorate his sixtieth birthday.

Everyone arrived in Paris expecting France, which had suffered the worst civilian damage and heaviest casualties, to be the strongest advocate of punitive reparations against Germany. Instead, it turned out to be Britain. A strong liberal contingent within the British Treasury had developed peace plans based on a moderate settlement. But in the months leading up to the Peace Conference, the press, led by the *Times* and the *Daily Mail*, launched a cheap jingoistic campaign in favor of a harsh settlement and, during the December 1918 election campaign, the slogan that the Allies should "squeeze Germany until the pips squeak"* struck a chord with the electorate.

The British prime minister, David Lloyd George, pandering to public opinion, appointed to the British delegation to the Reparations Commission in Paris three of the most hard-line advocates of a punitive settlement: William Hughes, the doggedly aggressive prime minister of Australia; Lord Sumner, a law lord with a reputation for being "stony-hearted"; and Lord Cunliffe, the boorish and irascible former governor of the Bank of England.

Cunliffe was supposed to be the financial brains of this trio. Although he had been a successful banker and even governor of the Bank of England, he retained his ignorance of the most basic rudiments of economics. In the weeks before departing for Paris, he recommended that Germany be required to pay $100 billion in reparations. It was an astounding figure. Germany's annual GDP before the war had been around $12 billion. To burden it with a debt eight times its annual income would have been the height of madness. The interest on that debt alone would have consumed 40 percent of its GDP. Though Cunliffe was willing to admit that the basis for the calculation was "little more than a shot in the dark," which he had been pressed to arrive at "between a Saturday and a Monday," he speculated that perhaps he had even underestimated Germany's capacity to pay,

---

*The actual phrase was coined by Sir Eric Geddes, first lord of the admiralty, who while campaigning in Cambridge on December 9, announced that "Germany was going to pay restitution, reparation and indemnity and . . . they would get everything out of her that you could squeeze from a lemon, and a bit more."

and that if anyone argued that Germany could pay $200 billion, he "would not disbelieve him."

France's desire for reparations arose from its own sense of vulnerability. Twice invaded by Germany in the last fifty years, France was consumed by the fear of a German revival. Germany was more aggressive, more successful, younger, richer, and more dynamic. It was also 50 percent larger—sixty million Germans versus forty million Frenchmen. Though the French prime minister, George Clemenceau, never actually made the statement attributed to him by German propaganda, that the fundamental problem was that there were twenty million too many Germans, it was clearly in his mind. France was therefore determined to weaken Germany by every means possible—by disarmament, by slicing off as many parts of its neighbor as it could, and by extracting reparations.

During the negotiations in Paris, it became apparent that to the French, money was subsidiary to security. While the French finance minister, Lucien Klotz, kept pushing for high reparations, Clemenceau, the head of the French delegation, treated him with contempt, calling him "the only Jew who knows nothing about money" and marginalizing him along with all the other French cabinet members in the negotiations.* Clemenceau tried to be flexible on reparations as a bargaining chip with the Americans in return for security guarantees along their border with Germany. Only when the guarantees proved to be inadequate did he revert to demanding high reparations.

It fell to the American delegation, which included the famous stock market speculator Bernard Baruch; Thomas Lamont of J. P. Morgan and Co.; and a young aide, the thirty-one-year-old John Foster Dulles, to act as the advocates for moderation. They adopted the position that a large reparations bill was incompatible with the initial terms of the armistice agreement under which Germany had laid down its arms. Moreover, they argued that punitive reparations would act as a millstone, not simply around Germany's neck but around that of all Europe.

---

*In July 1929, he was jailed for passing dud checks and died in prison a year later.

The negotiations over reparations dragged on for ten weeks. By the end of March, they were still at an impasse. The British delegation on the Reparations Commission, led by Lord Cunliffe and Lord Sumner, who were by then nicknamed "The Heavenly Twins" because they were always together and insisted on such outrageously high figures, would not agree to a settlement of less than $55 billion.

The Americans preferred a settlement in the region of $10 to $12 billion and would go no higher than $24 billion. Although President Wilson was, for the most part, outnegotiated and outfoxed by the other leaders in Paris, on this point the American delegation stuck to their guns and refused to agree to reparations that exceeded these limits.

Several attempts were made to break the deadlock. Lloyd George himself applied his considerable political skills, but Cunliffe and Sumner refused to budge. Lloyd George's maxim was never to enter into "costly frontal attacks, either in war or politics, if there was a way round" and he had originally appointed them in the hopes of bamboozling them into endorsing a moderate settlement. Now he found himself captive to their intransigence. His solution was to do an end run around them by proposing, at the last minute, that the Peace Conference defer the assessing of reparations to a later date, delegating it to a specially appointed body, which would be required to make its recommendation no later than May 31, 1921. He hoped that by that time, passions would have cooled, the political climate in Britain would have changed, and a more reasonable settlement could be arranged.

IN THE FIRST few months of 1919, as the Peace Conference was getting under way, Schacht, lulled like many other Germans by the high-minded pronouncements of Woodrow Wilson, still expected a generous peace. He believed that the real problem would be the overhang of debt after the war, which would lead to a general European bankruptcy. He talked naively of a grand plan for reconstruction. The great natural resources of Russia would be opened up for exploitation by a unique partnership between

Great Britain and Germany, Britain providing the leadership and capital, Germany the manpower and engineering skills.

In May 1919, when the terms of the peace treaty were finally unveiled to Germany, the whole country exploded in shock and anger. It was to lose one-eighth of its territory. Alsace and Lorraine were to revert to France; the Saar coal mines were also ceded to France; North Schleswig was to be subject to a plebiscite as to whether it wished to become part of Denmark; Upper Silesia, Posen, and West Prussia went to Poland. Both banks of the Rhine were to be permanently demilitarized; the army was to be cut to no more than one hundred thousand men, the navy was to be dismantled, and the merchant marine distributed to the Allies. Though the Allies had delayed fixing the size of reparations, it was widely known that the amounts being mooted were gigantic. In the interim, Germany was required to pay an initial $5 billion before May 1, 1921. A new Reparations Commission, to be based in Paris, was created specifically to determine Germany's liability and to supervise its collection. The worst humiliation was Article 231, the "article of shame," which branded Germany as solely responsible for the war.

The reaction within Germany to the peace treaty reached a pitch of hysteria. All forms of public entertainment were suspended for a week as a sign of protest. Flags across the country were lowered to half-mast. The chancellor, Philipp Scheidemann, characterized the terms as "unbearable, unrealizable, and unacceptable," and proclaimed that it would make the Germans "slaves and helots . . . doing forced labor behind barbed wire and prison bars." The Germans were given a deadline of five days to agree to the terms or face a resumption of hostilities. Scheidemann resigned rather than put his signature on the document, of which he said, "What hand would not wither which placed this chain upon itself and upon us?" On the day that Germany accepted the terms, its Protestant churches declared a day of national mourning.

Behind all the divisions that were to wrack Germany for the next few years, the one single factor that united every class and every political party—democrats and royalists, liberals and Socialists, Catholics and Protestants, northerners and southerners, Prussians, Bavarians, Saxons, and Hessians—was the injustice of the peace treaty, or as it was called the Diktat. And of all the various penalties heaped on Germany by the treaty—disarmament, dismemberment, occupation, and reparations—it was reparations that would become the single most consuming obsession of German foreign policy. Germany had meekly agreed to reduce its military machine to a shadow of its former power, thus leaving it impotent to do anything about the loss of territory or of its colonies. Only on reparations did Germany seem able to fight back. It discovered what every large debtor at some point discovers: that when one owes a large amount of money, threatening to default can give one the upper hand.

Schacht's first introduction to the issue of reparations came in the fall of 1919. He was asked to join a group of industrialists and businessmen sent to The Hague to negotiate with the Allied commission on the delivery of goods in kind as part of the interim settlement. The German delegation was subjected to a litany of petty humiliations: they were forced to stay at the worst hotel, given bad food, their movements restricted, and they were openly followed. Finally, during the negotiations themselves, they were not even provided with chairs but were required to stand. When Schacht complained, he was told, "You seem to forget that your country lost the war." It was Schacht's first encounter with what he was to call the "medieval arrogance" of the victors.

IRONICALLY, IT WAS not a German but an Englishman who launched the most devastating attack on reparations. In November 1919, John Maynard Keynes, the young Cambridge don, published *The Economic Consequences of the Peace*. In the book Keynes argued that in order for Germany to earn the money to pay the Allies, it would have to sell more goods than it bought, and its trade partners would have to be willing to absorb this large influx of goods, with potentially crippling consequences for their own industries. It was therefore in the Allies' own self-interest to moderate their demands. As he put it, "If Germany is to be milked, she must not first of all be ruined." He concluded that the most Germany could afford to pay, without causing a massive disruption of world trade, was around $6 billion.

The book became an immediate best seller; over one hundred thousand copies were bought worldwide in its first six months alone. It was serialized in the United States in the *New Republic* and in France by *La Nouvelle Revue Française* and translated into French, German, Dutch, Flemish, Danish, Swedish, Italian, Spanish, Romanian, Russian, Japanese, and Chinese. At the age of thirty-six, Keynes's brilliant pen had carried him to fame, not merely in Britain but across the world.

From an early age, people had remarked on young Maynard's intellect, which had been carefully nurtured from his childhood. Born in 1883, in Cambridge, England, he spent most of his life in and around Cambridge University. His father, John Neville Keynes, was a don, a philosopher, and logician of great early promise but little ambition who had drifted into university administration. Maynard spent four years at Eton, where he was one of those golden boys known both for their extraordinary academic achievement and their social popularity, and in 1902 he entered King's College, Cambridge, to read mathematics. He was soon elected to that elite intellectual society nicknamed "the Apostles," which already included G. E. Moore, Bertrand Russell, and Lytton Strachey. He spent his years at Cambridge absorbed in a hothouse combination of high-minded philosophical debate and homoerotic entanglements with his fellow Apostles. Even Bertrand Russell, rarely impressed by other people's brainpower, wrote that Keynes' intellect was "the sharpest and clearest that I have ever known."

After graduating in 1904, Keynes briefly tried to escape the university by joining the India Office as a "clerk"—he had only come second in the civil service exams and missed being selected for the Treasury, though he would characteristically insist that it was because "I evidently knew more about economics than my examiners." Within a year of going to the India Office, he resigned. Even though the hours were not at all taxing—he worked from 11:00 a.m to 5:00 p.m. on weekdays, 11:00 a.m. to 1:00 p.m.

on Saturdays, and had eight weeks' vacation a year plus Derby Day—he had found that he did not have enough to do. His assignments included organizing the shipment of ten Ayrshire bulls to Bombay and preparing an annual report to Parliament, "The Moral and Material Progress of India." Amused by the Victorian pomposity of the whole exercise, he joked to Lytton Strachey that he planned to include "an illustrated appendix on Sodomy." Bored with the work and finding it difficult to restrain his natural irreverence toward authority, he returned to Cambridge.

While he almost immediately gained a lectureship in economics at the university, his first love had always been philosophy. In 1909, he began work on a book on the philosophical foundations of probability, which he hoped would change the way philosophers thought about uncertainty. The themes of the book—that nothing can be known with certainty, that it is hard to define what is a rational course of action when the future is so indeterminate, that intuition rather than analysis provides the ultimate basis for action in these circumstances—were to color much of his later economic thinking and his almost equally remarkable ability to make money from speculating.

But for all his passion for abstract ideas and philosophical discussions, Keynes also had wider and worldlier ambitions. In addition to his teaching duties and the book on probability, he spent the years before the war as a member of the Royal Commission on Indian Currency and Finance, even publishing a book on the subject; he took over the investment portfolio of his college; wrote occasional pieces on financial matters for the *Morning Post* and the *Economist*; and became the editor of the *Economic Journal*, to which he also contributed articles and reviews. Then there were his hobbies—the magnificent collections of old books and modern paintings, his golf, his passion for the ballet—and his many remarkable and varied friends. Indeed, there were times when he almost seemed to have too many interests.

To accommodate all these activities, he would spend a couple of days every week in London, where he shared a house at 38 Brunswick Square with some of his Bloomsbury friends—among them Adrian Stephen and

Adrian's sister Virginia and her husband Leonard Woolf—many of whom he had met as an undergraduate at Cambridge. But while his bohemian comrades viewed the world of money and power as somehow tainted, he very much wanted to be part of it.

His chance to return to government came with the war. On Sunday, August 2, he was in Cambridge when he received a letter from an old colleague at the UK Treasury, Basil Blackett. "I tried to get hold of you yesterday but found that you were not in town. I wanted to pick your brains for your country's benefit and thought you might enjoy the process. If by chance you could spare time to see me on Monday, I should be grateful, but I fear the decisions will all have been taken by then." Such an invitation from a man he respected, offering access to the center of world affairs, was irresistible. Unwilling to wait for the next train up to London, he persuaded his brother-in-law, A. V. Hill,* to take him up to London in the sidecar of his motorcycle. By the end of the day, Keynes was ensconced in the Treasury Building in Whitehall, busy drafting a note for the chancellor on whether Britain should follow the rest of Europe into abandoning the gold standard. Within a few months, he had a job as a junior economic adviser within the Treasury.

He quickly rose within its rank. In early 1917, he became chief of the external finance division responsible for securing enough dollars on reasonable terms to pay for the war effort and keep the UK economy afloat. It was perhaps the most critical economic issue confronting Britain during the war, and put Keynes at the heart of economic policy making.

He became completely absorbed in the heady atmosphere of life as an establishment mandarin, thrown into the highest social and political circles. He was invited for country weekends by the prime minister and his wife, played bridge at No. 10 Downing Street, spent the weekend at the home of the chancellor of the exchequer, dined with the Duke of Connaught and the Princess of Monaco. He was, in the words of the society

---

*Hill, a physiologist and a fellow of Trinity College, would win a Nobel Prize before he was forty.

hostess Ottoline Morrell, "greedy for work, fame, influence, domination, admiration."

That combination of success and cleverness could at times make him insufferable. His Bloomsbury friends, who inhabited a rarified world of art and literature and ideas, were able to tease him about his newfound connections in high places. They were even willing to tolerate his irritating cocksureness. He was redeemed in their eyes by the subversive pleasure he took in challenging authority. No one was immune from his witty and biting ripostes. Within just a few months of joining the Treasury, he told no less than Lloyd George, the chancellor of the exchequer, during a meeting, "With the utmost respect, I must, if asked my opinion, tell you that I regard your account as rubbish." But to the many other people to whom he was rude or insulting, he was simply an arrogant young man with an overblown sense of his own intellectual superiority.

One would not have guessed at all of this by looking at him. He looked so very ordinary—receding chin, thinning hair, feeble military mustache— and he dressed so conventionally—dark three-piece suits and a homburg, or sometimes a bowler. At first glance he might have been a modestly successful City drone—an insurance broker maybe—or possibly a minor civil servant.

Beneath that superior façade he actually harbored some profound insecurities—especially about his looks. "I have always suffered and I suppose always will from a most unalterable obsession that I am so physically repulsive that I've no business to hurl my body on anyone else's," he once confessed to his friend Lytton Strachey. But most of those who were close to him agreed that he could be the most attractive and charming of companions, his conversation sparkling, brilliant, and witty. He was "gay and whimsical and civilized" with "that gift of amusing and surprising, with which very clever people, and only very clever people, can by conversation give a peculiar relish to life," remembered the art critic Clive Bell.

Most of Keynes's Bloomsbury crowd were conscientious objectors. As the war dragged on, he himself became increasingly disillusioned with its terrible waste, the relentless loss of lives, the refusal of the politicians to contemplate a negotiated settlement, and the steady erosion of Britain's financial standing. In 1917, he wrote to his mother that the continuation of the war "probably means the disappearance of the social order we have known hitherto. With some regrets I think I am not on the whole sorry. The abolition of the rich will be rather a comfort and serve them right anyhow. What frightens me is the prospect of general impoverishment. . . . I reflect with a good deal of satisfaction that because our rulers are as incompetent as they are mad and wicked, one particular era of a particular kind of civilization is very nearly over."

When the war ended, Keynes was appointed the principal Treasury representative at the Paris Peace Conference. Though his official titles included deputy to the chancellor of the exchequer on the Supreme Economic Council, chairman of the Inter-Allied Financial Delegates in the Armistice negotiations, and representative of the British Empire on the Financial Committee, he soon found himself completely excluded from the most important economic negotiations at Paris, those on reparations. He had to watch impotently from the sidelines as the "nightmare" of the Peace Conference was played out. As he later wrote, "a sense of impending catastrophe overhung the frivolous scene." When the terms of the treaty were finally announced in the middle of May, exhausted and disgusted, he felt he had no alternative but to resign. He wrote to Lloyd George, "The battle is lost. I leave the Twins [Sumner and Cunliffe] to gloat over the devastation of Europe."

THE ECONOMIC CONSEQUENCES OF THE PEACE was a strange book to have sold so well. Two-thirds of it comprised a detailed, often technical, polemic against reparations. At the time and even after, the whole debate over reparations was obfuscated by the enormous figures involved. They were simply too large and abstract for most people, including politicians and many bankers, to comprehend, particularly in an era when few people knew what the GDP of Germany or Britain was or even what the term

meant. Keynes was able to pierce through all of this confusion and translate the tens of billions of dollars that were being bandied about so readily
into something more tangible for the average man to grasp.

A book replete with figures and tables on the value of the housing stock
of France and Belgium, the composition of German exports and imports
in 1914, and estimates of the size of the German railway rolling stock may
have been unlikely material for a best seller. But the sheer physicality of
the technical details served as a chilling reminder that behind all of the
abstract figures, this was an argument about the concrete things necessary
to sustain standards of living.

Its success was partly due to the artfully mordant portraits he drew of
the Big Three at Paris: Clemenceau, "dry in soul and empty of hope, very
old and tired"; Wilson, "his thought and his temperament . . . essentially
theological not intellectual"; "his mind . . . slow and unadaptable"; and
Lloyd George, "with six or seven senses not available to ordinary men,
judging character, motive and subconscious impulse, perceiving what each
was thinking and even what each was going to say next." Keynes was persuaded by several people, including his mother, to omit some of the best
but most inflammatory descriptions—especially the portrait of Lloyd
George, "rooted in nothing; he is void and without content . . . one catches
in his company the flavor of final purposelessness, inner irresponsibility,
existence outside or away from our Saxon good and evil, mixed with cunning, remorselessness, love of power."

What seemed to have captured the public imagination was the outline
of the world economy that Keynes was able to draw. In bold broad strokes,
he described the workings of the prewar Edwardian world, the fragile
foundations on which it had been built, and the mutilation to its financial
fabric left by the war. He gave a foreboding picture of the future as the
forces that had sustained the old economic order began to come asunder.
Sounding at times like an Old Testament jeremiad, the book spoke of
"civilization under threat," of "men driven by starvation to the nervous
instability of hysteria and mad despair." The tone of impending doom

may seem overwrought to our ears, but to a generation that had just emerged from the most horrendous and apparently pointless apocalypse, it rang true.

THE ECONOMIC CONSEQUENCES had an enormous impact on thinking about reparations throughout the world. The biggest change occurred in Britain. Even before the Peace Conference had adjourned in June 1919, Lloyd George had already begun to have second thoughts about the treaty. At the eleventh hour, he even tried to convince the other two leaders that perhaps they should soften the terms, but Wilson had adamantly refused, saying that the prime minister "ought to have been rational to begin with, and then would not have needed to have funked at the end." It was not simply Lloyd George's guilty conscience that led to the British change of heart. Britain, that nation of shopkeepers keen to get back to business, rediscovered the economic centrality of Germany. As foreign minister, Lord Curzon announced to the cabinet, Germany "is to us the most important country in Europe." France, however, clung resolutely to its implacable hostility to its ancient enemy, and with the United States out of the European picture and Britain increasingly sympathetic to Germany, it found itself isolated.

In the four years after the Peace Conference, from early 1919 until the end of 1922, Europe was treated to the spectacle of one international gathering after another devoted to reparations. With governments in both France and Germany constantly falling—during those four years France went through five and Germany six—the one constant fixture at all these gatherings was the British prime minister, Lloyd George. As if trying to make up for his failure in Paris, he threw himself into the process. By one calculation, he attended thirty-three different international conferences in those few years. So many of them were held in the gambling resorts and spas of Europe—at San Remo in April 1920, in Boulogne in June, at Wiesbaden in October 1921, at Cannes in January 1922, and the final "circus" at Genoa in April 1922—that the French prime minister, Raymond Poincaré, dismissed them as *"la politique des casinos."*

For all the magnificent and luxurious settings, these gatherings were painful affairs, not least because the French were so unclear in their own minds what they wanted. As Poincaré said in June 1922, "As far as I am concerned it would pain me if Germany were to pay; then we should have to evacuate the Rhineland. Which do you regard as better, obtaining cash or acquiring new territory? I for my part prefer occupation and conquest to the money of reparations." Or as Lloyd George more pithily put it, "France could not decide whether it wanted to make beef-stew or milk the German cow."

All the age-old animosities between the British and the French, buried for a decade under the common purpose of confronting Germany, resurfaced. The old stereotypes of the French—those "vainglorious, quarrelsome, restless and over-sensitive" people—on which previous generations of Englishmen had been reared, were revived. Foreign Minister Curzon complained of the French proclivity for "the gratification of private, generally monetary, and often sordid interests or ambitions, only too frequently pursued with a disregard of ordinary rules of straightforward and loyal dealing which is repugnant and offensive to normal British instincts." At one point, in 1922, he became so frustrated in a confrontation with French Prime Minister Poincaré that he collapsed in tears, crying, "I can't bear him."

Dealing with Germany was no easier. Before the war, an American journalist had remarked on that "uneasy vanity, that touchiness that has made Germany the despair of all the diplomats all over the world." The initial outrage over the Versailles Diktat had now curdled into frustration, bitterness, and resentment, which only made the defeated nation more difficult to deal with. From that first moment in May 1919, when the German foreign minister, Ulrich Graf von Brockdorff-Rantzau had insulted the Allied statesmen at Versailles by refusing to stand while addressing them, the Germans caused offense by their arrogant demeanor.

It was not simply their bad manners. They calculated, very correctly, that the longer they could string out the bargaining over reparations, the less they would end up paying. Their whole strategy was therefore to negotiate in bad faith. In the first two years after signing the treaty, Germany desperately scraped together what it could, and paid $2 billion out of the $5 billion of interim payments due.

Meanwhile, the Reparations Commission, established in Paris in mid-1920, finally put a figure of $33 billion on the table as its estimate of the amount Germany should pay. The Germans responded by subjecting this figure to a series of adjustments to take into account what they had already paid—so transparently bogus as to embarrass even its own representatives in Paris—and concluded this meant they now owed the Allies just $7.5 billion, provoking Lloyd George to say that if the discussions continued any further in this vein, Germany would soon be claiming reparations from the Allies.

In May 1921, British Treasury officials developed a proposal that they believed to be so reasonable that Germany would find it difficult to turn down. The reparations bill was to be set at the equivalent of $12.5 billion, roughly 100 percent of the German prewar GDP. To meet the annual interest and principal repayments on this new debt, Germany was required to pay between $600 million and $800 million, a little over 5 percent of its annual GDP.

In May 1921, the British proposal was accepted at a conference in London. It seemed as if agreement had finally been reached. The German delegation, led by Foreign Minister Walter Rathenau, made much of the new departure in policy. Henceforth Germany would abandon its resistance to the terms of the treaty, and instead would adopt a policy of "fulfillment."

The problem was that the Germans never really believed that they could meet even this commitment. Despite the fact that the new reparations bill was now closer to the amounts originally proposed by liberal commentators such as Keynes, German officials remained convinced that even $12.5 billion of reparations would prove an intolerable burden. As a consequence, they made no real effort to meet the terms of the London schedule. They paid on schedule just once. Within six months of the London settlement, they were in arrears and back before the Reparations Commission, pleading for a moratorium. Of the $1.2 billion that Germany owed during the first eighteen months of the schedule, it paid little more than half.

WHILE GERMANY WAS grimly trying to negotiate relief from the burden of reparations, its domestic economic policy, bad as it had been during the war, became worse. The country was in perpetual turmoil, constantly on the brink of revolution, run by a series of weak coalition governments, and was quite unable to control its finances. In addition to large residual expenses from the war—pensions to veterans and war widows, compensation for those who had lost private property in the territories forfeited under the Treaty of Versailles—the governments took on enormous new social obligations: an eight-hour day for workers, insurance for the unemployed, health and welfare payments for the sick and the poor. Germany's financial problems were mostly self-inflicted. Nevertheless, reparation payments made what was already a difficult fiscal situation impossible. To finance the gap, the various governments of Germany resorted to the Reichsbank to print the money.

In 1914, the mark stood at 4.2 to the dollar, meaning that a mark was worth a little under 24 cents. By the beginning of 1920, after the full effects of the inflationary war finance had worked through the system, there were 65 marks to the dollar—the mark was now worth only 1.5 cents—and the price level stood at nine times its 1914 level. Over the next eighteen months, despite an enormous budget deficit and a 50 percent increase in the amount of currency outstanding, inflation actually slowed down and the mark even stabilized. Foreign private speculators, betting that the mark had fallen too far, moved some $2 billion into the country. After all, this was Germany, not unjustly viewed before the war as the epitome of discipline, orderliness, and organization. It seemed inconceivable that it would allow itself to sink into an orgy of monetary self-abasement and give up on restoring order.

"Nothing like this has been known in the history of speculation," wrote Maynard Keynes. "Bankers and servant girls have been equally involved. Everyone in Europe and America has bought mark notes. They have been hawked . . . in the streets of the capitals and handled by barbers' assistants in the remotest townships of Spain and South America."

A series of events, however, in the middle of 1921—French inflexibility over reparations, a campaign of political murder by right-wing death squads—broke the public's confidence that Germany's problems were soluble. It abandoned the mark in droves. The foreign speculators who had bought marks the previous two years also bailed out, losing most of the $2 billion they had pumped in. A visitor in the late 1920s to the game rooms of Milwaukee or Chicago would find the walls papered with German currency and bonds that had become worthless.

As the mark plummeted, Germany became caught in an ever-deepening downward spiral. On June 24, 1922, the architect of fulfillment, Foreign Minister Walter Rathenau, one of the most attractive political figures in Germany—cultured, rich, scion of a great industrial family—was gunned down in his car by yet another group of crazed reactionaries. Panic set in. Prices rose fortyfold during 1922 and the mark correspondingly fell from 190 to 7,600 to the dollar.

In early 1923, when Germany was late in meeting a reparations payment for that year—the precipitating incident was the failure to deliver one hundred thousand telephone poles to France—forty thousand French and Belgian troops invaded Germany and occupied the Ruhr valley, its industrial heartland. The chancellor, Wilhelm Cuno, powerless in every other way, launched a campaign of passive resistance. The budget deficit almost doubled, to around $1.5 billion. To finance this shortfall required the printing of ever-increasing amounts of ever more worthless paper marks. In 1922, around 1 trillion marks of additional currency was issued; in the first six months of 1923 it was 17 trillion marks.

Wrote one observer: "In the whole course of history, no dog has run after its own tail with the speed of the Reichsbank. The discredit the Germans throw on their own notes increases even faster than the volumes of notes in circulation. The effect is greater than the cause. The tail goes faster than the dog."

The task of keeping Germany adequately supplied with currency notes became a major logistical operation involving "133 printing works with 1783 machines . . . and more than 30 paper mills." By 1923, the inflation had acquired a momentum of its own, creating an ever-accelerating appetite for currency that the Reichsbank, even after conscripting private printers, could not meet. In a country already flooded with paper, there were even complaints of a shortage of money in municipalities, so towns and private companies began to print their own notes.

Over the next few months, Germany experienced the single greatest destruction of monetary value in human history. By August 1923, a dollar was worth 620,000 marks and by early November 1923, 630 billion.*

Basic necessities were now priced in the billions—a kilo of butter cost 250 billion; a kilo of bacon 180 billion; a simple ride on a Berlin street car, which had cost 1 mark before the war, was now set at 15 billion. Even though currency notes were available in denominations of up to 100 billion marks, it took whole sheaves to pay for anything. The country was awash with currency notes, carried around in bags, in wheelbarrows, in laundry baskets and hampers, even in baby carriages.

It was not simply the extraordinary numbers involved; it was the dizzying speed at which prices were now soaring. In the last three weeks of October, they rose ten thousandfold, doubling every couple of days. In the time that it took to drink a cup of coffee in one of Berlin's many cafés the price might have doubled. Money received at the beginning of the week lost nine-tenths of its buying power by the end of the week.

It became meaningless to talk about the price of anything, because the numbers changed so fast. Economic existence became a race. Workers,

---

*There have been other bad episodes of inflation. Hungary in 1945–46 was worse. The Zimbabwean inflation is as of the writing of this book equally bad—on July 31, 2008, the *Financial Times* reported that the exchange rate of the Zimbabwean dollar reached 500 billion to the U.S. dollar. But Hungary in 1945 and Zimbabwe in 2008 were tiny economies. Germany in the 1920s was the third largest economy in the world.

once paid weekly, were now paid daily with large stacks of notes. Every morning big trucks loaded with laundry baskets full of notes rolled out of the Reichsbank printing offices and drove from factory to factory, where someone would clamber aboard to pitch great bundles to the sullen crowds of workers, who would then be given half an hour off to rush out and buy something before the money became worthless. They grabbed almost anything in the shop to barter later on for necessities in the flea markets, which had sprung up around the city.

Having to calculate and recalculate prices in the billions and trillions made any sort of reasonable commercial calculations almost impossible. German physicians even diagnosed a strange malady that swept the country, which they named "cipher stroke." Those afflicted were apparently normal in every respect except, according to the *New York Times*, "for a desire to write endless rows of ciphers and engage in computations more involved than the most difficult problems in logarithms." Perfectly sensible people would say they were ten billion years old or had forty trillion children. Apparently cashiers, bookkeepers, and bankers were particularly prone to this bizarre disease. Most people simply turned to barter or to using foreign currency. Every middle-class housewife knew up to the latest hour the exchange rate for the mark against the dollar. At every street corner, in shops and tobacconists, even in apartment blocks, minute *bureaux de change* sprang up, with blackboards outside, advertising the latest exchange rates.

With the mark falling faster than domestic prices were rising, foreigners were able to live grotesquely well. Berlin apartments worth $10,000 before the war could be bought for as little as $500. Malcolm Cowley, an American literary critic then living in Paris, in Berlin to visit his friend the journalist Matthew Josephson, wrote, "For a salary of a hundred dollars a month, Josephson lived in a duplex apartment with two maids, riding lessons for his wife, dinners only in the most expensive restaurants, tips to the orchestra, pictures collected, charities to struggling German writers— it was an insane life for foreigners in Berlin and nobody could be happy there." For one hundred dollars, a Texan hired the full Berlin Philharmonic for an evening. The contrast between the extravagance of foreigners, many of them French or British, but also Poles, Czechs, and Swiss, and the daily struggles of the average German to make a living only fed the resentment against the Versailles settlement further.

Inflation transformed the class structure of Germany far more than any revolution might have done. The rich industrialists did well. Their large holdings of real assets—factories, land, stocks of goods—soared in value while inflation wiped away their debts. Workers, particularly the unionized, also did surprisingly well. Until 1922, their wages kept up with inflation and jobs were plentiful. It was only in the last stages, from the end of 1922 into 1923, when the implosion of confidence caused the monetary system to seize up and the economy reverted to barter, that men were thrown out of work.

Those who made up the backbone of Germany—the civil servants, doctors, teachers, and professors—were hit the worst. Their investments in government bonds and bank deposits, carefully accumulated after a lifetime of prudence and discipline, were suddenly worthless. Forced to scrape by on meager pensions and salaries, which were decimated by inflation, they had to abandon their last vestiges of dignity. Imperial officers took jobs as bank clerks, middle-class families took in lodgers, professors begged on the streets, and young ladies from respectable families became prostitutes.

The people who truly raked it in were the speculators. By buying up assets—houses, jewelry, paintings, furniture—at throwaway prices from middle-class families desperate for cash, by cornering the market in goods that were in scarce supply, profiteering in imported commodities and gambling on a further collapse in the currency, they enriched themselves beyond their wildest dreams.

As German society was overturned, the traditional values that had made it so conservative and ordered a community were jettisoned. Stefan Zweig, the writer, tried to capture the mood of that time in his autobiography: "How wild, anarchic, and unreal were those years, years in which, with the dwindling value of money, all other values in Austria and Germany began to slip. It was an epoch of high ecstasy and ugly scheming, a singular mixture of unrest and fanaticism. Every extravagant idea . . . reaped a gold harvest."

THE OFFICIAL MOST responsible for the reckless policy of inflation was none other than Rudolf von Havenstein, the sober and dedicated president of the Reichsbank who had so disastrously overseen Germany's wartime finances. When the war ended in disaster, Von Havenstein fully expected to lose his job. A Prussian official closely identified with the imperial administration, he did not conceal his lack of sympathy for the new government led by the Social Democrats. Nevertheless, during the revolution of 1918, he went out of his way to cooperate with it, even allowing one of the new workers' and soldiers' councils to form within the Reichsbank. During those days of violence and turmoil, he also used a squad of revolutionary sailors to guard the Reichsbank's gold reserves to convey the message that it was the "people" who controlled the nation's treasure, though the word was that he had secretly booby-trapped the safes with poison gas just in case the sailors' loyalty wore thin.

Having successfully maneuvered to keep his job, Von Havenstein found himself in the classic dilemma of the dutiful civil servant. He was now working for a government for which he had little liking, one that was pursuing a social agenda he did not believe in and thought Germany could ill afford. Worst of all, the government had decided to make its best efforts to pay the Allies' demands—the so-called policy of fulfillment. Nevertheless, despite these fundamental disagreements, Von Havenstein acceded to the government's requests and allowed the Reichsbank to print money to finance the budget gap.

Why did Von Havenstein submit without any apparent effort to resist? Two very conflicting pictures have been drawn of his motives: that he deliberately engineered the whole monetary explosion as a way of destroying the financial fabric of Germany, a collective self-immolation designed to prove to the Allies that reparations were uncollectible, or alternatively, that his conduct reflects nothing subtler than sheer economic ignorance. Trained as a lawyer, he had learned the banking business during the gold standard era, when the rules of monetary policy were dictated by the requirement that the Reichsmark be kept convertible at a fixed gold equivalent, and was completely at sea in a world not hitched to gold.

The truth seems to be more complex than either explanation. Von Havenstein faced a very real dilemma. Were he to refuse to print the money necessary to finance the deficit, he risked causing a sharp rise in interest rates as the government scrambled to borrow from every source. The mass unemployment that would ensue, he believed, would bring on a domestic economic and political crisis, which in Germany's current fragile state might precipitate a real political convulsion. As the prominent Hamburg banker Max Warburg, a member of the Reichsbank's board of directors, put it, the dilemma was "whether one wished to stop the inflation and trigger the revolution" or continue to print money. Loyal servant of the state that he was, Von Havenstein had no wish to destroy the last vestiges of the old order.

Alternatively, if by standing firm against the government he forced it to raise taxes or cut domestic expenditures, he would be accused, particularly by his nationalist friends on the right, of being a tool of the bloodsucking Allies, who all along had been insisting that Germany could pay reparations if it would only cut its domestic expenditures and raise taxes. In effect, Von Havenstein would be in the position of doing the Allies' dirty work—he just could not bring himself to act as the collection agent for his country's enemies.

Faced with these confusing and competing considerations, Von Havenstein decided to play for time, supplying the government with whatever money it needed. Contrary to popular myth, he was perfectly aware that printing money to finance the deficit would bring on inflation. But he hoped that it would be modest, and that in the meantime, something would turn up to induce the Allies to lower their demands or at least agree to a moratorium on actual payments, giving Germany some breathing space.

It was a total miscalculation. Von Havenstein failed to recognize that experimenting with the currency was like walking a knife-edge. A moderate degree of inflation does not remain moderate for long. At some point the public loses confidence in the authority's power to maintain the value of money, and deserts the currency in panic. Germany passed this tipping point in the middle of 1921.

Instead of admitting that he had made a terrible mistake, Von Havenstein, with his dogged Prussian sense of duty, dug in his heels, refusing to change any of his policies and continuing to print as much money as the government "needed." The inflation had initially been beneficial to private business because it had the effect of wiping out their debts. By 1923, however, the crisis had moved to a new stage, and without a functioning currency, commerce became impossible. Unemployment, which had hovered around 3 percent suddenly shot up to 20 percent in the fall of 1923. In order to maintain some illusion of solvency, Von Havenstein began to pump Reichsbank money directly to private businesses. He hid behind the claim that, but for reparations, there would be no inflation in Germany and therefore put the blame for the inflation on the rapacious demands of foreigners. He began arguing that the inflation had nothing to do with him, that he was a passive bystander to the whole process, that his task was simply to make enough money available to grease the wheels of commerce, and if business required a trillion more marks, then it was his job to make sure they were run off the presses and efficiently distributed around the country.

On August 17, 1923, he delivered his annual report on economic conditions before the Council of State:

> The Reichsbank today issues 20,000 milliard marks of new
> money daily, of which 5,000 milliards are in large
> denominations. In the next week the bank will have
> increased this to 46,000 milliards daily, of which 18,000
> milliards will be in large denominations. The total issue at
> present amounts to 63,000 milliards. In a few days we shall

therefore be able to issue in one day two-thirds of the total circulation.

Here was the president of the Reichsbank, whose principal obligation was supposed be the preservation of the value of the currency, proudly proclaiming to a group of parliamentarians that he now had the capacity to expand the money supply by over 60 percent in a single day and flood the country with even more paper. For many people, it was just one more sign that German finance had entered an Alice-in-Wonderland phantasmagoria.

"No-one could anticipate such an ingenious revelation of extreme folly to which ignorance and false theory could lead . . . The Reichbank's own demented inspirations give stabilization no chance," wrote the British ambassador, Lord d'Abernon, an expert on state bankruptcies who had thought that he surely had to have witnessed the worst financial excesses in the lunacies of the Egyptian khedives and the Ottoman Turks, only to find them almost Swiss in their rectitude compared to the Germany of 1923. "It appears almost impossible to hope for the recovery of a country where such things are possible. It is certainly vain to hope for it unless power is taken entirely from the lunatics presently in charge."

WHEN THE WAR ENDED, Hjalmar Schacht was just a modestly successful banker, not yet especially distinguished or rich. It was the opportunities thrown up by inflation that would make him powerful and wealthy. He certainly did not make money by speculating himself—having grown up poor, he was very conservative and took few risks with his own savings. He was, however, lucky.

In 1918, he recruited a thirty-six-year-old stockbroker, Jacob Goldschmidt, to join the Nationalbank. Goldschmidt was talented, cultivated, and charming, very different from the traditional conservative bankers of Berlin, a self-made millionaire who had built a successful stock exchange trading firm. Once at the Nationalbank, Goldschmidt began playing the market with large amounts of the bank's capital, and by engineering a series of astute mergers, he transformed the bank, now named the Danatbank, into the third largest banking conglomerate in Germany. By 1923, Schacht had suddenly been vaulted into the upper reaches of the Berlin banking establishment.

In the summer of 1923, he stood at his office window contemplating the scene below. While most of the other large Berlin banks were housed along the Behrenstrasse in somber gray buildings with great rusticated stone walls and massive pillars and pilasters, the Danatbank had chosen for its headquarters a charming red sandstone building overlooking a quiet square on the banks of the Spree. His own office commanded a perfect view of the square below, in the center of which stood a small bronze statue of Karl Friedrich Schinkel, the architect who had designed so much of Berlin—a strangely tranquil scene, he reflected, far removed from the fever gripping the rest of the city.

A constant reminder of what had happened to Germany loomed eastward across the canal: the Berliner Schloss, for almost five centuries the home of the Hohenzollern kings. The vast imperial palace of over 1,200 rooms, its grand dome dominating the landscape for miles, now stood empty, its contents looted and ransacked, its beautiful balconies splintered and shattered, its Baroque façade disfigured by large pallid patches where artillery shells had struck during the 1918 revolution.

Schacht had become increasingly ambivalent about the new republican Germany. In no way nostalgic about the past, he felt no regret at the passing of empire, with its "old style Prussian militarism" that sought to impose a "permanent order of society." But proud and nationalistic as he was, he did look back to the times before the war when Germany had been a nation of order and discipline, the economic powerhouse of Europe. The country was, in his view, now destroying itself pointlessly. The republic had betrayed the professional middle classes, which had once made Germany so strong. The Fatherland had become a "hell's kitchen."

Though he now had the money and position he had so long scrambled to acquire, Schacht felt frustrated. At the Danatbank, he had been sidelined by the more successful Goldschmidt. By writing articles in the *Berliner Tageblatt* and the *Vossische Zeitung*, he had developed something of a reputation as an expert on reparations, arguing that Germany could and should pay no more than $200 million a year, equivalent to a total reparations settlement of $4 billion, a third of what had been agreed to in London in 1921. It was an amount that at the time would have been completely unacceptable to France. He tried to have it both ways. At the same time he was taking a hard line on the level of reparations that Germany could pay, he would urge the government to be more pragmatic, to open negotiations with the French, abandon the failed policy of passive resistance in the Ruhr, and cease printing money.

Had he been honest with himself, he would have had to admit that he was lucky not to have been involved. Over the last three years, as the country had sunk into economic chaos, reparations had been a no-win issue for any German politician or official.

8. UNCLE SHYLOCK

War Debts

Neither a borrower, nor a lender be; for loan oft loses
both itself and friend.

—WILLIAM SHAKESPEARE, *Hamlet*

THE PROBLEM OF collecting reparations from Germany was made infinitely more complex by that of war debts owed to the United States. Britain had gone to war as "the world's banker," controlling over $20 billion in
foreign investments. No other financial center—neither Berlin nor Paris,
certainly not New York—came close to matching London's standing as the
hub of international finance. Through it passed two-thirds of the trade
credit that kept goods flowing around the globe and half the world's long-
term investments—over $500 million a year. Meanwhile, France, though
never so dominant a financial power, had its own overseas portfolio of $9
billion, of which an astounding $5 billion was invested in Russia.

To pay for the four long, destructive years just past, every country in
Europe had tried to borrow as much as it could from wherever it could.
The effect was to create a seismic shift in the flow of capital around the
world. Both Britain and France were forced to liquidate a huge proportion
of their holdings abroad to pay for essential imports of raw materials, and
both eventually resorted to large-scale borrowing from the United States.
By the end of the war, the European allied powers—sixteen countries in

all—owed the United States about $12 billion, of which a little under $5 billion was due from Britain and $4 billion from France. In its own turn, Britain was owed some $11 billion by seventeen countries, $3 billion of it by France and $2.5 billion by Russia, a debt essentially uncollectible after the Bolshevik revolution.

At an early stage of the Paris Peace Conference, both the British and the French tried to link reparations to their war debts, indicating that they might be prepared to moderate their demands for reparations if the United States would forgive some of what they owed America. The United States reacted strongly, insisting that the two issues were separate. Its delegates, many of them lawyers, including the secretary of state, Robert Lansing, made a clear moral and legal distinction between reparations, which resembled a fine and were intended to be punitive, and war debts, which were contractual liabilities voluntarily entered into by the European Allies. The Europeans, less wedded to legal modes of thought, failed to see either the moral or the practical distinction between their obligations to the United States and Germany's obligations to them. Both would be burdensome and both would require material sacrifice for several generations.

As the Peace Conference was winding to its end, Maynard Keynes, distressed at how the negotiations were going, decided on his own initiative to put together a comprehensive plan for the financial reconstruction of Europe. Reparations should be fixed at $5 billion, to be paid by Germany in the form of long-term bonds issued to the Allies, which they would in turn assign to pay their war debts to the U.S government. All other obligations were to be forgiven. It was a clever scheme. The U.S. government would be functionally lending Germany money, which in turn would go to pay reparations to the Allies, who in turn would use those proceeds to settle their loans. The money would start in a United States flush with gold, and eventually return there full circle.

Keynes passed the plan on to the chancellor of the exchequer, Austen Chamberlain, who in turn recommended it to Lloyd George. The prime minister received Keynes's plan just as he was beginning to realize the extent of his tactical errors over reparations and, in a short burst of enthusiasm, submitted it to President Wilson. It was rejected out of hand by the American delegates, who continued to insist that war debts must not be linked to reparations and that the former could not be forgiven on such a scale. And thus the problem of reparations and war debts would be allowed to fester over the maimed economic body of Europe.

TEN DAYS AFTER the armistice of November 11, 1918, Benjamin Strong wrote to Montagu Norman, "The principal danger now ahead of us . . . is not social and political unrest" but that the coming peace negotiations would "develop along lines of economic strife" that would lead to "a period of economic barbarism which will menace our prosperity." "There is no doubt," he continued, "that much of the world's happiness in the future will depend upon the relations now being established between your country and ours." Over the next decade that compact between Britain and the United States—or rather between the Bank of England and the Federal Reserve—built upon the friendship between Norman and Strong, would be one of the fixed points of the world's financial architecture.

The two of them came to that compact from very different directions. For Norman, it was a matter of simple necessity. The war had devastated Britain economically; and, he believed, only by acting in conjunction with the Americans could Britain hope to regain its old financial influence. For Strong, the calculation was a little more complicated. As a banker from the Morgan fold, he was naturally an internationalist. The war had brought a new recognition among U.S. financiers that the fate of their country was inextricably linked to that of Europe. Now, with the arrival of peace, he believed that it was in its own interest for the United States to use some of its huge resources to "help to rebuild a devastated Europe."

There was also a moral imperative to Strong's internationalism. He was part of that generation of Americans who, having begun their careers under Theodore Roosevelt and having reached maturity under Woodrow Wilson, viewed themselves and their country as now uniquely qualified and positioned, by virtue of money and ideas, to transform the conduct of

international affairs. He was, of course, not so naive that he did not recognize that many Europeans remained cynical about U.S. motives—accusing it, for example, of having deliberately waited until Europe had come
close to bankruptcy before entering the war. He, however, was one of those
who believed that now that the war was over, his nation had a unique opportunity to show that it was truly, in his own words, an unusually "unself-
ish, generous people."

He was especially influenced in his sense of high purpose about America's world mission by a group of young men with whom he had become
friends who went by the mysterious name "The Family." Based in Washington, The Family was an exclusive private club, which he had been invited
to join before the war. It had no official name, was indeed not really a club
at all—no officers, no charter, no formal membership roll. It had come into
being in 1902 when three young army officers, captains Frank McCoy,
Sherwood Cheney, and James Logan, all in their early thirties, attracted to
Washington by Theodore Roosevelt's "call to youth," decided to rent a
house together at 1718 H Street. This soon became a gathering spot for
ambitious young diplomats and service officers, all similarly inspired by
Roosevelt's vision of a muscular U.S. foreign policy. In the absence of a
formal name, it came to be known as the 1718 Club or The Family.*

The membership progressively widened to include a more eclectic
circle, including journalists, such as Arthur Page, editor of the popular
monthly *The World's Work;* politicians, like Congressman Andrew Peters,
who would become mayor of Boston; and bankers, such as Strong. Over
the years, though, The Family had remained an extraordinarily tight-knit
group who kept in close touch with one another, particularly during the
war. When the fighting finally stopped, many members found themselves
thrown into the peace negotiations.

No one was more emblematic of the ethos of The Family than Willard
Straight, a flamboyant charmer whose life reads like something out of a

---

* The Family eventually acquired the house at 1718 H Street and established a tradition
that only bachelors could stay the night on the premises.

boy's adventure novel. Early orphaned, Straight had graduated from Cornell, gone out to China, where he learned Mandarin, served as a reporter during the Russo-Japanese war of 1904, become secretary to the American legation in Korea, been appointed consul general in Manchuria, and joined a Morgan-led bank in China, all by the age of thirty. Thereafter he had married an heiress, Dorothy Whitney; helped found the *New Republic;* seen army service in France; and with the armistice, joined the advance team in Paris to prepare for the forthcoming Peace Conference. Tragically, he contracted influenza during the 1918 pandemic and died suddenly in December 1918, at the age of thirty-eight.

Another member, Joseph Grew, had been in Germany as the number two in the embassy during the first years of the war, had gone on to become the State Department's desk officer for Germany, and was now leading the advance team in Paris. William Phillips, who came from a rich family and had rejected a "pallid career" in business to become a career foreign service officer, became a Far Eastern specialist after assignment to Peking. Subsequently posted to London, he was now an assistant secretary of state. Another foreign service hand, Basil Miles, a particularly close friend of Strong's, had taken his degree at Oxford, been posted to Petrograd in 1914, and was now State's prime expert on Russia.

James Logan, one of the founders of this dedicated brotherhood, had stayed in the army, rising to the rank of lieutenant colonel, and had been posted to France in 1914 as chief of the American observer military mission. An overweight *bon viveur,* he had become a fixture in Paris. Once the United States joined the war, he was given a high staff position in the American Expeditionary Force and was now working for Herbert Hoover in the Relief Administration.

With so many fellow members of The Family in Paris in the war's immediate aftermath, Strong decided that he should see for himself what needed to be done in Europe. But as happened so often over the next few years, his body gave out on him. Worn out by the demands of war finance, he suffered a minor recurrence of tuberculosis and was forced to take another leave of absence during the first few months of 1919.

By the summer, he was back on his feet and ready to go to Europe. The Peace Conference had just finished, and as he left the United States the country was still in the full flush of jubilation and optimism over the signing of the peace treaty. Strong arrived in England on July 21, aboard R.M.S. *Baltic*, as Britain's official peace celebrations were winding down. There had been parades and ceremonies across the country from the tiniest villages to the biggest cities. In London a million people had come out to watch a huge parade, including American and French contingents led by General John Joseph "Black Jack" Pershing and Marshal Ferdinand Foch, march past the king and queen and members of the government. The capital was still decked out with flags, and the troops who had taken part were still camped out in Kensington Gardens as Strong's train rolled into the city.

Although the statesmen in Paris had failed to come up with some grand initiative to reconstruct Europe, he arrived full of great expectations, still convinced, for all the failures of the treaty, that the United States would eventually adopt a "constructive policy towards the restoration of Europe," by postponing the repayment of war debts and providing direct aid for reconstruction.

For all the celebrations, he found the city's mood ominously changed. In contrast to America, Britain was only slowly readjusting to peace. Tobacco restrictions had been removed in January and most food rationing in May. But bread was still obtainable only with ration coupons, as was sugar. The initial optimism, which had gripped Britain and all the European victors immediately after the war, was now wearing off as the grim realities of Britain's underlying position were becoming steadily more apparent. The war had changed the balance of financial power, and Strong kept encountering a festering resentment against the United States, especially over war debts.

Few people in those days thought in terms of a "special relationship" between Britain and the United States—indeed, the phrase was only coined in 1945 by Winston Churchill. Before the war, most London bankers viewed their counterparts in the United States with that superciliousness reserved for unsophisticated kinsmen, too rich for their own good.

Within the United States, certain circles—the House of Morgan, the partners at Brown Brothers—were natural Anglophiles. Elsewhere, Britain was generally regarded with suspicion and cynicism. But during the war and after, British arrogance had given way to resentment. London bankers worried that the United States, with its newly acquired financial muscle, was getting ready to elbow its way into the role of banker to the world. During Strong's visit to London in March 1916, he attended a speech made by Sir Edward Holden, chairman of the London City and Midland Bank, "in which [Sir Edward] referred to efforts of American bankers to undermine Lombard Street's supremacy and . . . was so overcome by the mere thought that the old man broke down and wept."

Strong now found British bankers and politicians fervently convinced "that the Allies have made the greatest and most vital sacrifice in the war" while the U.S. sacrifices had "been slight, and our profits immense and that existence of this great debt is a sword of Damocles hanging over their heads." There was considerable bitterness at how long the United States had sat out the war, many of Strong's English acquaintances believing that America had deliberately waited for Europe to wear itself out before stepping in to pick up the pieces. Now those same people argued that the U.S. government was morally obliged to forgive part of their European Allies' war debts. This was especially true in Britain, which had borrowed some $5 billion from the United States but had itself lent $11 billion to France, Russia, and other countries—in effect, simply acting as a conduit for the loans. And though his friend Norman tried to reassure him that people were allowing "their hearts to rule their heads," that Britain's credit was still strong, and that it was still good for its debts, Strong was undoubtedly shaken by the pessimism that hung over the City of London.

Not only had Britain's place in the world changed, but British society had also been transformed by the war. The aristocracy that had ruled Britain for much of the previous century had been badly damaged—as one contemporary author wrote, albeit with some exaggeration, "In the useless slaughter of the Guards on the Somme, or of the Rifle Brigade in Hooge Wood, half the great families, heirs of large estates and wealth, perished without a cry." After enduring savage losses in the fighting—the casualty rate had been three times heavier among junior officers, many of them aristocrats, than among enlisted men—the old elite had also been hurt by the wartime inflation and was now being decimated by postwar economic dislocations. Land prices had collapsed and many large estates been put up for auction. In place of the old and confident ruling class, a whole new breed—"hard-faced men who had looked as if they had done well out of the war," as one eminent politician described his new colleagues in the House of Commons—had come to power.

At the end of July, Strong went on to Paris and, for the next few weeks, used the Ritz Hotel on the Place Vendome as his base while traveling around Europe. He visited Brussels—liberated only a few months before—Antwerp, and Amsterdam, establishing connections with the heads of European central banks but also taking a melancholy motoring trip through the giant cemeteries of the Western Front.

The view from Paris was even more foreboding than from London. The city was dark by 10:00 p.m. for want of coal to generate electricity. The Peace Conference was still officially in session, limping through the final negotiations with the smaller Central Powers and successor states: Austria, Hungary, Bulgaria, and Turkey. But the big delegations had all departed and with them the accompanying train of ten thousand other assorted people: the advisers, the wives, the mistresses, the cooks, drivers, messengers, secretaries, and journalists. The hotels had reverted to their normal business—at the end of July, the Majestic, headquarters of the British delegation during the conference, and the Crillon, that of the American delegation, both reopened for commercial business. The radical journalist Lincoln Steffens, who had come to Paris with the American delegation and stayed on after the conference, best captured the city's bitter mood of disillusionment during those months, "The consequences of the peace were visible from Paris. There were wars, revolutions, distress everywhere."

Over the summer, the political threats to Europe had actually begun to recede. Though civil war still ravaged Russia, the risk of Bolshevik revolution in Germany had diminished. A Communist uprising in Berlin and an attempted revolution in Bavaria had both been crushed. From Strong's point of view, the main danger was now economic. The two largest countries, France and Germany, both urgently needed food from abroad. Continental Europe was desperately short of capital to rebuild itself. Most disturbingly, he found a complete "lack of leadership" in Europe, with "people in authority . . . exhausted."

While Strong was in Paris, it became apparent that the United States was beginning its retreat from European affairs. The peace treaty had run into trouble in the Senate and seemed headed for defeat. Though the president had announced his intention to appeal directly to the people, the mood of the country was clearly turning isolationist.

Strong could not hide his disgust at this betrayal. At the end of August he warned Russell Leffingwell, undersecretary of the treasury and soon to be a Morgan partner, that if the United States were to "desert Europe and leave these new governments to their fate," this could only result in "prolonged disorder and suffering. It would be an act of cowardice for which we would be despised." He returned to the United States in late September. A few days before, on September 25, the president had collapsed with a stroke on his western campaign to drum up support for the treaty, and for the next year was to lie incapacitated in the White House. On November 19 the Senate rejected the treaty by a vote of 55 to 39.

As so often seemed to happen when he got back from Europe, Strong suffered yet another relapse of his tuberculosis. The doctors again insisted that he take a leave of absence, and the directors of the New York Fed released him for a year. Initially he went out to Arizona for the elevation and dry climate and by the following spring seemed well on the way to recovery. In March he set off on horseback across the Arizona desert accompanied by an unusual troop of companions: a mule skinner cum cook; a Pima Indian guide cum horse wrangler whose name was either Frank, Francisco, Pancho, or Juan—no one was quite sure which—a Russian wolfhound named Peter; and Strong's old friend from The Family, Basil Miles. As this entourage trekked across the wilderness, breathing "the most wonderful air," seeing "the most gorgeous sunsets," and sleeping under the stars, the problems of European reconstruction and currency chaos must have seemed far away.

After Arizona, Strong decided to take advantage of his year off by traveling around the world. Accompanied by his eldest son, Ben, and his friend Miles, he left San Francisco in early April for Japan. They went on to China, the Philippines, Java, Sumatra, Ceylon, India, finally arriving at Marseilles in winter 1920. There Strong found a letter from Montagu Norman awaiting him. "Whenever you do come to London, let me remind you of your hotel, of which the address is 'Thorpe Lodge, Campden Hill, W.8.' The Booking Clerk tells me that an hour's notice will be enough to get your room ready, or, if you are in a hurry, this can be done after you have arrived." While Strong had been traveling, Norman had been elevated to the governorship of the Bank of England. It was the beginning of a true partnership.

IF REPARATIONS POISONED the relations among European countries, war debts did the same to the relations between the United States and its erstwhile associates, Britain and France. However hard the Americans tried to separate war debts from reparations, in the minds of most Europeans they remained inextricably linked. Indeed, in the middle of 1922, the British government made the connection explicit in a note drafted by Arthur Balfour, then acting foreign secretary, that Britain would collect no more on its loans to its Continental allies and on its share of reparations from Germany than the United States collected from it as payments on its own war debts.

The Balfour Note provoked an outcry in the United States. Balfour, an aristocrat and philosopher of some repute—in 1895 he had published a work of great subtlety entitled *The Foundations of Belief*—was the elder statesman of British politics, having been prime minister before the war and foreign secretary under Lloyd George. Many were charmed by his urbane gracious manners and his air of bemused detachment—at the Peace

Conference a British diplomat remarked that he "makes the whole of Paris seem vulgar." In the United States, however, he was viewed as a "top-hatted frock-coated personification of British decadence," and the tone of condescension and moral superiority adopted in the Note infuriated the Americans. "Lord Balfour seems to think that he can call us sheep thieves in language so elegant that we shall not understand it," wrote one American. According to the *Philadelphia Inquirer*, "In the Balfour Note John Bull is depicted as the liberal, magnanimous and sympathetic creditor whose heart bleeds for his debtors' sufferings, and who is willing and anxious to relieve them of a burden which he perceives is beyond their ability to bear; Uncle Sam is portrayed as a ruthless, relentless, hard-hearted Shylock, who is making it impossible for John Bull to follow his altruistic and benevolent instincts by stubbornly insisting upon the letter of his bond."

To make matters even worse, Congress had decided to get into the act. In March 1922, Congress created the five-man World War Foreign Debt Commission, which was chaired by the secretary of the treasury, Andrew Mellon, and included the secretary of state, Charles Evans Hughes; the secretary of commerce, Herbert Hoover; Senator Reed Smoot of Utah; and Representative Theodore Burton of Ohio. The commission was to negotiate the terms on which American loans were to be repaid. Concerned that the administration might be too lenient on the debtors, Congress imposed a floor on any settlement—the commission would not be permitted to accept anything less than 90 cents on the dollar.

The congressional stipulations on war debts provided the Europeans their turn to express outrage. "Has America which but yesterday we acclaimed for her generosity and her idealism fallen to the role of a Shylock?" exclaimed a French senator in *L'Éclair*. Throughout Europe, newspapers began referring to Uncle Sam openly as "Uncle Shylock." Even the *Economist*, by no stretch a populist newspaper, printed a letter signed "Portia" that accused the United States of attempting to "lay a tribute upon those who saved Kansas and Kentucky from the German peril."

In October 1922, Lloyd George's government precipitously fell and a new Conservative government under Andrew Bonar Law took office in

Britain. The incoming chancellor of the exchequer, Stanley Baldwin, was a practical and sensible businessman who believed strongly in settling one's debts—he was so firm an advocate of this principle that in 1919 he had anonymously donated $700,000 of his own money, a fifth of his net worth, to the government as his contribution to paying off the national debt after the war.*

With the rhetoric on both sides of the Atlantic becoming increasingly overheated, Baldwin decided to open negotiations for a settlement with the Americans, telling them he wanted "to approach the discussion as business men seeking a business solution of what fundamentally is a business problem."

A British delegation, led by Baldwin himself and including as its principal adviser, the governor of the Bank of England, Montagu Norman, set sail for the United States on December 30 aboard the *Majestic*. Norman was convinced that it was essential to settle with the Americans if Britain was to reestablish its credit, and reclaim London's position as the world's premier financial center. He had visited the United States in August 1921 and May 1922 to make the rounds of senior administration officials in Washington with Strong, including a secret meeting with the president, Warren Harding, to convince them that the United States should remain engaged in European finance. As a result of this groundwork, of all the British financial officials, Norman had the best firsthand knowledge of U.S. politics and the situation in Washington.

On the stormy Atlantic crossing, which took twice as long as normal because of rough seas, gale-force winds, and fog, Baldwin and Norman became fast friends. Norman was usually suspicious of politicians, claiming somewhat disingenuously to have no political views himself—he bragged that he had never voted. The stolid uncharismatic Baldwin was the quintessential nonpolitician. They would remain lifelong friends, sharing a common taste for the pleasures of silence, of country walks and string quartets. Sir Percy Grigg, a high Treasury official who knew both well, described

---

*This is roughly equivalent to $9 million today.

how "they seemed to understand each other and to communicate without having to exchange more than a few monosyllables."

The American negotiating team was led by Secretary Andrew Mellon. Then in his late sixties, Mellon had been born into a wealthy Pittsburgh family and by the age of forty had independently amassed a fortune of some $500 million, making him the third richest man in America, after John D. Rockefeller and Henry Ford. Taciturn, cold, and reclusive—his son Paul would compare him to the money-obsessed Soames Forsythe of John Galsworthy's *Forsyte Saga*—Mellon's riches had brought him little happiness. In his forties, he had married a frivolous young English girl of nineteen, who within a few years left him for a social-climbing con artist, dragging him through a scandalous divorce in the process. He now lived in an opulently furnished six-bedroom apartment at 1785 Massachusetts Avenue, a block east of Dupont Circle, where his daughter Ailsa, a self-involved and sickly young lady prone to all sorts of psychosomatic ailments, acted as hostess.

The discussions were conducted in great secrecy, some sessions even taking place in Mellon's apartment, surrounded by old masters. There were lunches and dinners—to one such event Vice President Calvin Coolidge, "Silent Cal," was invited and did not utter a word to either of his neighbors during the entire meal. He would later famously dismiss the problem of war debts by exclaiming, "They hired the money, didn't they?" Despite Prohibition, the British delegation was surprised to find an abundance of liquor in private homes.

Before leaving London, they had been given to believe by the American ambassador that they should be able to reach an adjustment of 60 cents on the dollar and the cabinet had not given them the authority to go any higher. Arriving in Washington, they discovered that while the U.S. administration was keen to settle, it was limited by what Congress would accept. After two weeks of negotiations, the best that the Americans could offer was 80 cents on the dollar.

While Baldwin was frustrated by America's lack of generosity—at one

point saying that he would like to ship them replicas of the golden calf—
Norman pressed him to agree to the terms. In his view, the willingness of
the Debt Commission to go beyond the limits set by Congress reflected "a
newly found desire on the part of Americans to come into Europe again,"
and even a stiff settlement was a small price to pay for getting the United
States back into European affairs.

On the way home, the British team passed through New York. Strong
and the Morgan partners advised them that they would not get a better
deal by waiting and urged them to settle. Arriving in Southampton on
January 27, 1923, Baldwin made the foolish mistake of revealing the terms
to the press, even before he had had a chance to present them to the
cabinet, and in the belief that his remarks were off the record, declared that
he was for acceptance. He then dug himself in deeper by telling the gathered reporters that any deal would have to satisfy Congress, many of whose
representatives came from the West, where they "merely sell wheat and
other products and take no further interest in the international debt or
international trade." The headlines the next day announced that the British chancellor of the exchequer considered the average senator "a hick from
way back."

The prime minister was furious. Having lost two of his sons in the war,
Bonar Law had been all along deeply offended by the American view of
war debts as just another commercial transaction. "I should be the most
cursed Prime Minister that ever held office in England if I accepted those
terms," he told Baldwin. On January 30, Baldwin made a strong plea in
the cabinet for accepting the deal. He admitted that the Americans could
have been more generous, that they had made great fortunes out of the
war, that they worshipped the "God Almighty Dollar" but this was best
that Britain was going to get.

Bonar Law spoke for rejecting the American offer. He had consulted
Maynard Keynes, who counseled him to hold out, arguing that Britain
should refuse the American offer "in order to give them [the Americans]
time to discover that they are just as completely at our mercy as we are at

France's and France at Germany's. It is the debtor who has the last word in these cases."

But Bonar Law was cornered—to disavow his chancellor who had so publicly endorsed the deal would create a crisis in the government. Outvoted in the cabinet, he accepted defeat, but did take the opportunity to let off steam in the traditional British manner—by writing an anonymous letter to the correspondence columns of the *Times* in which he vigorously attacked his own government's decision to accede to the American terms.

Watching Britain strike such a poor bargain for itself, France chose to wait it out. It would eventually settle its war debts in 1926, when it reluctantly conceded to pay 40 cents on the dollar—even then the arrangement was not ratified by the National Assembly until 1929. Italy did even better. When it settled, also in 1926, it would only agree to pay 24 cents on the dollar. As usual Keynes had been right—holding out would have given Britain a better deal.

As the decade went on, and the Americans insisted on extracting these payments, they were shocked to discover how intensely disliked they were in Europe. Journalists sent home articles dissecting the various sources of American unpopularity under such titles as "Europe Scowls at Rich America" or "Does Europe Hate the U.S. and Why?" or even "Uncle Shylock in Europe." One informal poll revealed that 60 percent of the French regarded the United States as their least favorite nation. The *New York Times* correspondent in Paris reported that "ninety out of a hundred regard Uncle Sam as selfish, as heartless, as grasping." Visiting Britain, the veteran American foreign correspondent Frank Simonds discovered that "the great majority of the British people have made up their minds that American policy is selfish, sordid and contemptible."

But the really pernicious effect of war debts was that they made it hard, if not impossible, for Britain to forgo collecting its own debts from France and Germany, made France all the more obstinate in its efforts to collect reparations from Germany, and led Europe into a self-defeating vicious cycle of financial claims and counterclaims.

. . .

IN DECEMBER 1922, as Norman set out for Washington, the *Times* of London profiled him: "Mr. Montagu Collet Norman, D.S.O., the Governor of the Bank of England . . . certainly one of the most interesting, as well as one of the most able men who have occupied the Chair for a generation or more."

"In appearance he recalls the early Victorian statesmen," it went on, "Aristocratic in manner and temperament . . . his Shakespearian type of head sets well upon his tall, silent and dignified figure. A lover of music, poetry and books, Mr. Norman also possesses a collection of rare and beautiful woods. Many of those who come into contact with him feel that there is an indefinable touch of mystery about him. He has the keen sensitiveness of an 'intellectual.' "

It was remarkable how enormous was the change that had come over Norman since August 1914. Then he had been a pathetic figure, unsure of himself and uncertain about his future, wracked by neuroses, his less than illustrious career cut short by mental illness. Now he was generally recognized as the most prominent and powerful banker in all Europe, if not the world.

From the very start of his tenure at the Bank, Norman had made a point of breaking the mold. Whereas his predecessors had been driven to work, resplendent in top hat and frock coat, he turned up in a business suit by way of the Underground—the Central Line from Notting Hill—with the ticket jauntily protruding from his hatband. His whole persona seemed to have been transformed. Almost everyone remarked on his graciousness, his courtly old-world manners, and most of all, the charm with which he was "singularly gifted." As one of his fellow directors put it, "He never made jokes or anything of that kind. He was just amusing. A continual bubble of wit."

In those five years, he had also acquired something of a mystique in the public mind. Before Norman, the governor of the Bank had generally been a figure of relative obscurity, known to only a few insiders within the

Square Mile. But Norman's personality seemed to exert a powerful fascination on the press, which lauded him as a financial genius of great originality. All those traits, once viewed as the harmless eccentricities of a "strange old man"—his flamboyant way of dressing, his slouch hats, his artistic interests, his knowledge of Eastern philosophy—were now invested with great significance as signs of unusual creativity. His unorthodox appearance, his air of aloof amused amiability, perhaps above all his apparent lack of interest in money, for all his place at the very center of its mysteries, all contributed to the image of austere power, half patrician, half priestly.

This aura was reinforced by his policy of avoiding public appearances. He was rarely seen at the social events of the City, never made any speeches apart from the annual Mansion House toast required by tradition of the governor, and never submitted to newspaper interviews on the record.

It was during those early years that Norman got into the habit of traveling under pseudonyms, which became so much a part of his myth and mystique. It was the high point in the era of the transatlantic liner. The *Times* of London and the *New York Times* regularly ran features listing the most notable passengers on the ocean liners scheduled to leave each week—generally extensions of the social pages heavily populated by ambassadors, film stars, and European nobility.

News that the governor of the Bank of England was traveling to the United States inevitably gave rise to rumors: a settlement of war debts was imminent! Or Britain might return to the gold standard that week! To avoid all this unfounded speculation, Norman's secretary, Edward Skinner, began booking Norman's passage under his own surname.

At some point in Norman's travels across the Atlantic, plain old Skinner became Professor Clarence Skinner. The story goes—one among many—that during one such trip, a Professor Clarence Skinner, professor of applied christianity at Tufts College in Medford, Massachusetts, and a well-known Universalist who had actively campaigned to repeal the statutes prohibiting blasphemy, happened to be traveling on the same liner. The reporters, hovering at the West Side piers of Manhattan for a dockside interview, mistook Norman, with his professorial demeanor, for Professor Clarence Skinner. Norman did nothing to disabuse them of their misconception. Nor did the real professor, who, it seems, was quite amused. The whole incident so appealed to Norman's characteristically quirky sense of the absurd that, thereafter, he always traveled under the pseudonym, Professor Clarence Skinner. Over time, his alias was unmasked by the press. Nevertheless, he continued the practice, and talk of Professor Skinner and his travels became something of an in-joke among the cognoscenti.

Norman's dislike of any sort of press coverage and his attempts to conceal his activities from reporters only further fed their curiosity. Even the most ordinary incidents of his daily life were magnified and nourished speculation. The results could be comic and at times absurd.

Take a typical incident in March 1923, only days after France had occupied the Ruhr: Norman had left for his annual month's vacation in the south of France, where he generally stayed either with his half uncle at Costabelle, near Hyères, or at the Hermitage Hotel in Nice. On this occasion, he decided to stop off in Paris for a few days of meetings with his counterparts at the Banque de France. Making no attempt to keep his trip a secret, he stayed at the prominent and well-known Hôtel Crillon, on the Place de La Concorde. Nevertheless, because the Crillon had mistakenly registered him under the name Norman Montagu, the papers claimed that he was attempting to visit Paris incognito. When his valet was seen buying train tickets from a source other than the hotel's bureau, and was rumored to have been overheard asking the concierge about trains to Berlin, a wire report speculated that Norman was preparing to travel to Germany, and furthermore was attempting single-handedly to negotiate a settlement to the problem of reparations. The story ran in half the London press, and was picked up by many American papers, including the *New York Times,* the *Washington Post,* and the *Chicago Tribune.* In fact, after a few days in Paris, he left for Nice as usual.

Winston Churchill, who would come to know Norman all too well for his liking over the next few years, would later portray him in the *Sunday Pictorial*: "Mr. Norman's dislike of publicity in any form has enshrouded him with an air of mystery, which has led to ordinary and casual incidents of his daily life being scrutinized and magnified by the money markets of the world. . . . The more he seeks privacy, the more significant his acts become. He travels under an assumed name, and is instantly identified. He remains in seclusion in his country home, and the United States is searched to make sure that he is not there. Indeed the very process of self-effacement has proved—to his added disgust—the most subtle and effective form of advertisement. . . . It may well be that a little more plain speech . . . would have served his real purpose better than so much silence and precaution."

Not everyone was taken by his charm or his personality. Hating arguments or direct confrontations, he got his way by going around opponents and consequently developed a reputation for subterfuge. Some people retained a suspicion that Norman's attempts to cloak himself in mystery were simply a more subtle and sophisticated form of showmanship. Lord Vansitartt, head of the British diplomatic service between the wars, dismissed him as a "poseur."

And while Norman's public persona may have changed dramatically, he still carried within him many of the same private demons that had beset him before the war. He was by nature a pessimist, prone to bouts of despair, unfortunate traits in a central banker confronted with the task of nursing a crippled economy back to health. During that first grim year in office, as he struggled with a weak pound and the depths of a recession, he wrote of his "sensation of being as it were tossed about on a sea in which I can hardly swim."

Francis Williams, then city editor of the left-wing *Daily Herald*, considered that though Norman was able to exert a strange fascination over the City, he was "secretive, egotistic, suspicious of intellectual ability, and almost incapable of normal human relationships." Lord Cunliffe may have got the best measure of him when he confided that he thought Norman, "a brilliant neurotic personality [who] is certain to cause trouble. . . ." He added, "He's not an ordinary personality. . . . He needs the power just to keep going and he won't give it up until it's too late."

. . .

DURING THE EARLY 1920s, Norman would often talk of creating a league of central bankers to take responsibility for stabilizing European finances and promoting world economic recovery. No government seemed capable of doing it and he thought—a little grandiosely—that his guild could somehow fill the vacuum left by politicians. He liked to envisage himself and the other members of his small brotherhood as elite tribunes, standing above the fray of politics, national resentments, and amateur nostrums. Though Norman "delighted in appearing unconventional," his views about society were very much "those of an old Etonian." Still an Edwardian, he clung to the belief in aristocratic government.

In March 1922, he wrote to Strong in that elliptical way of his, "Only lately have the countries of the world started to clear up after the war, two years having been wasted in building castles in the air and pulling them down again. Such is the way of democracies it seems, though a 'few aristocrats' in all countries realized from the start what must be the inevitable result of hastily conceived remedies for such serious ills." He obviously thought that the "few aristocrats" were bankers like himself.

At this stage, though, he was the one building castles in the air. His notion that the world's central bankers would not be subject to the same nationalistic pressures to which politicians were also responding was curiously naive. His vision of a league of the lords of world finance was at this stage largely a pipe dream. He could not even get Strong to support him fully. After the Genoa Economic Conference of 1922, he floated the idea of a grand conclave of central bankers. But Strong resisted the idea, fearing that the United States, as the world's major creditor, would be ambushed by a concert of its European debtors, all clamoring for America with its vast gold reserves to refloat them. As he wrote to Norman, "Anything in the nature of a league or alliance, with world conditions as they are, is necessarily filled with peril." It would, he feared, be like "handing a blank check to some of the impoverished nations of the world, or to their banks of issue, and especially to those whose finances are in complete disorder and quite beyond control."

By 1923, Norman's club consisted essentially of himself and Strong, commiserating with each other over their respective health problems and the economic anarchy that seemed to surround them. Their friendship, however, had blossomed.

After Norman's three trips to the United States in 1921 and 1922, they did not see each other again for almost eighteen months. Falling ill once more, Strong had to take a leave of absence for most of 1923. Thereafter, they agreed to meet at least twice a year, alternating generally between Europe in the summer and New York in the winter. They wrote to each other every few weeks—a combination of financial gossip and views about economic policy. Despite their closeness, they usually addressed each other, in the quaintly formal style of the day, as "Dear Strong" or "Dear Norman," although letting their hair down on occasion with "Dear Strongy," "Dear Old Man," or "Dear old [sic] Monty." They furnished each other with advice, often revealing confidential details to which even their own colleagues were not privy. Occasionally they scolded each other. When Norman operated too much on his own and failed to consult his own directors, Strong admonished him, "You are a dear queer old duck and one of my duties seems to be to lecture you now and then."

It was not all about work. They often ribbed each other affectionately. On one occasion, Norman, who had just returned from a visit to Strong in New York and discovered that he had packed one of Strong's jackets by mistake, wrote:

> Dear Ben,
>   Since I wrote on the steamer, a further crime has been discovered. The second evening I was home, as usual I changed clothes in the evening and on going downstairs discovered myself in the disguise of a gentleman, if not a dude! This was due to velvet jacket of good style, fit and

> finish: In other words, Ben, I can only look respectable
> with the help of your wardrobe!

At times, they sounded like a couple of harmless old bachelors who took great pleasure in joshing each other—whether over an oil portrait of Strong upon which Norman had stumbled in the pages of *Town and Country*, or Norman's irritability when Thorpe Lodge was under repair, or his engagement with the philosophy of Spinoza.

Norman, by nature the more emotional, could be gushing and sentimental and fussed over his friend's health. "Let me beg you to care for yourself more than you seem to be doing. You belong to others quite as much as to yourself," he wrote after a 1921 visit to New York. He lectured Strong about smoking too many Camels and insisted on details about "what is happening to your pulse & sleep & pins & breathing . . . not a word have I heard for 4 weeks." The more aloof Strong, with a large family of his own, had less need to confide. But each was the other's closest friend. In 1927 after a visit from Norman while he was down with pneumonia, Strong too would write, "To have a sympathetic person to talk over matters is helpful anyway, but when it is a best friend, it is more than that."

By 1923, they were seriously fearing for the future. The first few years of peace, begun so hopefully, had turned out to be a time of great frustration and disappointment for both. The United States had washed its hands of European affairs and retreated into isolation. Currencies in Europe remained unstable. Neither of them could do much about the failures of economic policy in Germany or France, both paralyzed by reparations: Germany refusing to do anything to stabilize its economy until a fairer settlement was established, France in its turn insisting that it could make no concessions until a deal was reached on its war debts to Britain and America.

Norman saw "the Civilization of Europe" at stake. But all he could do was watch gloomily from the sidelines as matters continued to deteriorate. He became increasingly pro-German and anti-French. French obstinacy during the reparations dispute only served to reinforce his private prejudices, particularly against the French political class, which in his view was uniformly venal, underhanded, corrupt, and dishonorable. "The black spot of Europe and the world continues to be on the Rhine," he wrote to Strong after the occupation of the Ruhr. "There you have all the conditions of war except that one side is unarmed. How long can Germany continue thus?"

For Strong the frustrations were more personal. Though he remained financially comfortable, over the years he had to adjust his lifestyle drastically. The contrast between his relatively modest way of living and those of his old colleagues in the private sector could not have been more apparent. Following his separation and divorce, he lived in a series of small apartments, initially in a suite at the Plaza Hotel, and from mid-1922, in a small two-bedroom apartment in midtown Manhattan. Harry Davison had the benefit of a mansion on Park Avenue, a sixty-acre estate on the North Shore of Long Island, and a plantation estate in Georgia, until he died suddenly of a brain tumor in May 1922. Meanwhile Thomas Lamont, the embodiment to Strong of the road not taken, lived in a large town house at Seventieth Street and Park Avenue, continued to use his property in Englewood during the spring, and summered on his estate in North Haven, Maine.

Strong continued to be plagued by illness. In February 1923, the tuberculosis spread to his larynx, forcing him to take yet another extended leave of absence in Colorado—his fourth in seven years—from which he returned to work in October, and then only part time. Since he had first contracted the disease in 1916, he had spent almost half the time away from his desk. Even when he was nominally at work, he was often incapacitated, "afflicted by the generous use of morphine," to control the terrible pain. He had aged enormously. Compelled to give up tennis and other vigorous exercise, he had put on weight and was losing his hair. He looked haggard and overworked, almost unrecognizable from the tall, slim, confident, good-looking young man of ten years earlier.

In those days, even after his first wife's death, he had always been very social and clubby. Now he rarely went out at night and was never seen at the theater or the opera. His job was his anodyne, his evenings devoted to quiet working dinners with other bankers and officials.

In early 1924, with both his sons talking of getting married, he wrote to Norman: "The temptation is constantly before me to wind up my work and quit, do some traveling, a little writing, and take things easy." Neither of them foresaw that after four years of frustration they were on the verge of achieving their goals.

Maynard Keynes's Wedding, 1925

9. A BARBAROUS RELIC

THE GOLD STANDARD

Time will run back and fetch the age of gold.
—JOHN MILTON, *On the Morning of
Christ's Nativity*

AFTER THE WAR, there was a universal consensus among bankers that the world must return to the gold standard as quickly as possible. The almost theological belief in gold as the foundation for money was so embedded in their thinking, so much a part of their mental equipment for framing the world, that few could see any other way to organize the international monetary system. Leading that quest were Montagu Norman and Benjamin Strong.

The biggest obstacle to such a return was the mountain of paper currency issued by the central banks of the belligerent powers during the war. Take Britain, for example. In 1913, the total amount of money circulating in the country—gold and silver coins; notes issued by the Bank of England and by the large commercial banks; and the largest category, bank deposits—amounted to the equivalent of $5 billion. This supply of money, in all its various forms, was backed in aggregate by the country's $800 million of gold, surprisingly only $150 million of which was held in the vaults of the Bank of England, the remainder consisting of gold coins in circulation or bullion held by the commercial banks, such as Barclays or Midland. By 1920, the Bank of England had lent so much money to the government to help pay for the war effort that the total money supply had ballooned to the equivalent of $12 billion, which in turn had driven prices up by two and a half times. Britain's gold reserves meanwhile remained roughly the same. Thus, whereas in 1913, there had been 15 cents worth of gold within the country for every $1 dollar in money, in 1920 each $1 of money was backed by less than 7 cents. The Bank of England made every effort to economize on gold, for example, by replacing gold coins with paper currency, and by concentrating the bullion originally held by commercial banks into its own holdings. Nevertheless, at war's end it was clear that the country's reserves would not provide enough of a monetary cushion for Britain to contemplate returning to gold at the old 1914 exchange rate.

Every nation involved in the war, even the United States, faced the same dilemma. For all had resorted to inflationary finance to a greater or lesser degree. There were essentially only two ways to restore the past balance between the value of gold reserves and the total money supply. One was to put the whole process of inflation into reverse and deflate the monetary bubble by actually contracting the amount of currency in circulation. This was the path of redemption. But it was painful. For it inescapably involved a period of dramatically tight credit and high interest rates, a move that was almost bound to lead to recession and unemployment, at least until prices were forced down.

The alternative was to accept that past mistakes were now irreversible, and reestablish monetary balance with a sweep of the pen by reducing the value of the domestic currency in terms of gold—in other words, formally devalue the currency. This sounds painless. But to a generation reared on the certainties of the gold standard, devaluation was viewed as a disguised form of expropriation, a way of cheating investors and creditors out of the true value of their savings—which to some degree it was. Moreover, it was not completely costless. Central banks that resorted to devaluation as a way of cleaning up a past monetary mess were viewed as the financial equivalent of reformed alcoholics—it was hard to clear the stain on their reputations for financial discipline, and as a consequence, they generally had to pay up to borrow.

A simple analogy of the choice between deflation and devaluation might be that of the man who has put on weight and is having a hard time fitting into his clothes. He can either choose to lose the weight—that is, deflate—or alternatively accept that his larger waistline is now irreversible and have his clothes altered—that is, devalue. Whether to deflate or devalue became the central economic decision for every country after the war. The burden of deflation fell on workers, businesses, and borrowers, that of devaluation on savers. The fate of the world economy would hinge over the next two decades on which path each country took. The United States and Britain took the route of deflation, Germany and France that of devaluation.

Of all the belligerents, the United States, having come late to the war and having spent the least of any of the major powers, was in the best financial shape. Though it, too, had allowed its currency to expand by 250 percent during the war, and prices to double, it also had seen its gold reserves more than double as the enormous European purchases of war materials and the massive flight of European capital seeking safety across the Atlantic, carried over $2 billion worth of gold into the United States. By 1920, the country held close to $4 billion in gold. Even allowing for war inflation, therefore, it still had a comfortable reserve of bullion to back its expanded currency base, and was able to return to the gold standard almost immediately after hostilities ceased.

Even in the United States, the return to gold and monetary stability was not completely painless. In 1919 and 1920, after the years of wartime austerity, consumers let rip and went on a buying binge; inflation began to accelerate and for a brief moment, seemed about to spin out of control. Strong reacted forcefully, leading a move by the Fed to tighten credit policy dramatically by raising interest rates to 7 percent and keeping them there for a full year. This constriction was accompanied by a similar move by the federal government to bring its budget into balance. The economy plunged into recession. Over two and a half million men lost their jobs.

Bankruptcies soared. But by the end of 1921, with prices down by almost a third, the economy once again began to recover. During the next seven years, the U.S. economy, led by new technologies such as automobiles and communications, would experience an unprecedented period of strong growth and low inflation.

At the opposite end of the spectrum from the United States was Germany, which had taken the path of least resistance during the war and expanded its money supply by 400 percent. By the end of 1920, German prices stood at ten times their 1913 level. Germany had issued so much currency that it had no hope of being able to reverse the process, and when the war ended, seemed clearly headed for a massive devaluation. In retrospect, that would have been a blessing. But instead of trying to rebuild its finances, the German government adopted a policy of systematic inflation, in part to meet reparations, and thus launched itself on that voyage of fantasy into the outer realms of the monetary universe.

Britain and France lay somewhere in between. During the war, France

FIGURE I

Consumer Prices: 1913–24
1914 = 100

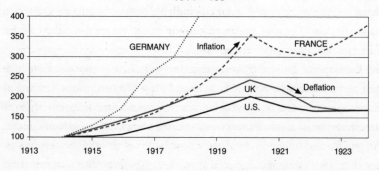

After World War I was over, Germany and France chose
inflation and devaluation, the United States
and the UK chose deflation.

had expanded its currency by 350 percent, pushing up prices equivalently. After the war, the Banque de France avoided German-style hyperinflation and currency collapse by putting a lid on the issue of new currency. However, France continued to flirt with disaster by running budget deficits of $500 million and was saved once again only by the remarkable thriftiness of its people. While there was a group within the Banque who harbored the fantasy of reversing the more than threefold price increase and returning the franc to gold at its prewar parity, most rational observers agreed that when France returned to the gold standard, it would have to be at a radically lower exchange rate—and even that still seemed many years away.

Britain was therefore the only major country that truly faced the choice between devaluation and deflation. To a modern observer, less wedded to the principle that currency rates are sacrosanct, some measure of devaluation would have made sense. After all, Britain was finding it harder to compete in the postwar world economy and, having liquidated vast amounts of its holdings abroad, could only draw upon a much reduced foreign income to cushion the blow. Its exchange rate should have been allowed to fall as a means of making its goods cheaper on world markets.

However, Norman and his generation lived in a different mental world. They saw devaluation not as an adjustment to a new reality but as something more, a symptom of financial indiscipline that might precipitate a collective loss of confidence in all currencies. When people talked of the City of London as banker to the world, this was no mere figure of speech—the City operated literally like a gigantic bank, taking deposits from one part of the world and lending to another. While gold was the international currency par excellence, the pound sterling was viewed as its closest substitute, and most trading nations—the United States, Russia, Japan, India, Argentina—even kept part of their cash reserves in sterling deposits in London. The pound had a special status in the gold standard constellation and its devaluation would have rocked the financial world.

In the last months of the war, the British government set up a commission, chaired by the ubiquitous Lord Cunliffe, only recently departed from the Bank of England, and including Sir John Bradbury of the UK Treasury; A. C. Pigou, professor of political economy at Cambridge; and ten bankers from the City, to review postwar currency arrangements. Twenty-three parties gave evidence before the commission, every one of them, with not a single note of dissent, in favor of a return to gold at the prewar rate. To a man, they believed the restoration of the traditional parity was essential if Britain was to retain its position at the hub of the world's banking system.

The model they had in mind, which was especially seared into the collective memory of the Bank of England, was Britain's experience a century earlier after the Napoleonic Wars. In 1797, four years into the Revolutionary war with France, there was a run on the Bank of England, provoked by rumors that a French army had landed in Wales. The Bank, which had begun the war with gold reserves of £9 million, saw them shrink to £1 million, and was forced, as it would be in 1914, to abandon the gold standard. Under the pressures of war finance, Bank of England notes, which formed the basis for paper money in the country, increased over the next fifteen years from £10 million to over £22 million, doubling prices.

In 1810, a parliamentary inquiry known as the Bullion Committee was formed to examine the whole issue. The committee included Henry Thornton, a banker, parliamentarian, brother to a director of the Bank of England, and the most creative monetary economist of the nineteenth century, whose insights would unfortunately be lost by succeeding generations in charge at the Bank. The committee recommended that the Bank resume gold payments as soon as possible, and in order to achieve this goal, begin to contract its credits to banks and merchants and shrink the supply of paper money by withdrawing its notes from circulation. The Bank wisely waited until 1815, when a defeated Napoléon was safely in exile on St. Helena, before taking this advice. Over the next six years, it almost halved the supply of paper money in Britain, driving down prices by 50 percent. And though those years from 1815 to 1821 had been years of riots and agricultural distress, Britain went back on gold in 1821. Over the subsequent half century, it transformed itself into the world's largest economic power. Many believed that the "resumption" of 1821 had been the single most important defining decision in its financial history. That the Bank had been willing to inflict the pain of a 50 percent fall in prices in order to restore the gold value of the pound had set sterling apart from every other currency in Europe, and made it the world's premier store of value.

Inspired by this example—and in complete contrast to every other European country—in 1920, the Bank of England chose the path of deflation, matching the Fed and raising interest rates to 7 percent. The budget was balanced. The economy plunged into sharp recession, two million men were thrown out of work. Nevertheless, by the end of 1922, the Bank had succeeded in bringing prices down by 50 percent, and the pound, which had fallen as low as $3.20 in the foreign exchange market on the fear that Britain was headed for devaluation, climbed back to within 10 percent of its prewar parity of $4.86.

But whereas the U.S. economy, more dynamic and unhampered by a large internal debt, was quickly able to bounce back from the recession, Britain remained stuck. The number of unemployed would not fall below one million for the next twenty years. It soon became apparent that Britain had sustained terrible damage as an economic power during the war. Industries such as cotton, coal, and shipbuilding, in which it had once led the world, had failed to modernize and the traditional markets had been lost to competitors. Labor costs had risen as unions negotiated shorter working hours.

Norman now faced the uneasy prospect that the only way to follow the example set by his forerunners—his grandfather joined the Court the year of "resumption"—was by keeping unemployment high. But while before the war it might have been politically acceptable to create unemployment deliberately in order to support the currency, in the charged climate after the war—with Lloyd George promising the electorate "a land fit for heroes"—Norman would find himself constantly under pressure to find an alternative.

· · ·

THE PROBLEM OF resurrecting the gold standard went much deeper than selecting new exchange rates for the key currencies, for the war had brought about such a tectonic shift in the distribution of gold reserves that it seemed to threaten the very viability of a monetary system resting on gold.

Before the war, the four largest economies—the United States, Britain, Germany, and France—had operated their monetary systems with about $5 billion worth of gold among them. The amount of new gold mined during the war was small, and by 1923, monetary gold had increased only to $6 billion. Meanwhile, prices in the United States and the UK, even after the postwar deflation, were still 50 percent higher than before the war, which meant that in effect the real purchasing power of gold reserves had contracted by almost 25 percent.

FIGURE 2

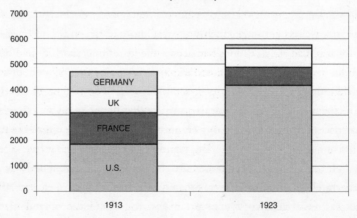

Gold Reserves: 1913–23
($ million)

After the war, the United States acquired
much of the world's gold reserves.

In 1922, Norman worked with officials at the British Treasury to develop a plan whereby some of the European central banks would, as did
many countries in the British Empire, hold pounds rather than gold as
their reserve asset—in much the same way that many central banks hold
dollars nowadays. He argued that substituting pounds for gold would allow
the world to economize on the precious metal and thus reduce the risk of
worldwide shortage. Few people failed to notice that by creating a captive
source of demand for sterling, the plan would add to its privileged position
in the constellation of currencies and greatly ease his job of returning the
pound to gold. The plan never really did take off, except in a few minor
Central European countries.

The bigger concern among bankers after the war was not so much that
the world was short of gold, but that too much of the gold was concentrated in the United States. Before the war, there had been some parity
among the major economic powers between the amount of gold in each
banking system and the size of its economy. For example, the United
States, with a GDP of $40 billion, accounted for about half the output of
the four great economic powers and held about $2 billion in gold, a little
less than half of the total gold of these four countries. The balance was
only rough and ready—France held proportionately more and Britain
less—but the system worked with remarkable smoothness.

By 1923, the United States had accumulated close to $4.5 billion of the
$6 billion in gold reserves of the four major economic powers, far in excess
of what it needed to sustain its economy. About $400 million circulated
in the form of coins; the remainder consisted of ingots, small bars the size
of a quart of milk, each weighing about twenty-five pounds, stored in the
vaults of the Federal Reserve Banks and the Treasury. The largest hoard
lay under lower Manhattan, about $1.5 billion in the Treasury repository
at the legendary intersection of Broad and Wall Streets, and at the New
York Fed. The remainder was scattered among the eleven other Federal
Reserve Banks across the country.* By one estimate, excess gold reserves

---

* Fort Knox, where the Treasury gold is now held, was not constructed until 1936.

in the United States amounted to about a third of its holdings, roughly $1.5 billion.

While the U.S. monetary system was swamped by this enormous surplus, Europe, particularly Britain and Germany, suffered a chronic shortage. The three big European economies, which had operated before the war on $3 billion worth of gold, were left with barely half that. Faced with constant demands to pay out gold, European central banks had resorted to a complex of measures, the most important being to withdraw gold coins from circulation. All those solid talismans of turn-of-the-century middle-class prosperity had gradually disappeared from Europe's pockets, to be replaced by shabby pieces of paper. By the mid-1920s, the United States was the only large country where one could still find gold coins.

The concentration of the world's key precious metal in the United States had left the rest of the world with insufficient reserves to grease the machinery of trade. The world of the international gold standard had become like a poker table at which one player has accumulated all the chips, and the game simply cannot get back into play.

ONE MAN WHO had no difficulty liberating himself from the strictures of the gold standard was John Maynard Keynes. After the Peace Conference, he had gone back to teaching at Cambridge. But following the resounding success of *The Economic Consequences of the Peace*, he reduced his involvement with the university and became increasingly caught up on the grander stage of world affairs. He joined the board of an insurance company and became chairman of the weekly British magazine the *Nation*, for which he wrote regular pieces, as he did for the *Manchester Guardian*, articles that were syndicated around the world, including in the U.S. weekly the *New Republic*. And he began making his fortune as a currency speculator.

In 1919, it was a novel way of making money. Before 1914, currencies had been fixed, and opportunities to profit from the instability of exchange rates had been almost nonexistent. In the aftermath of the war, as exchange rates of the major currencies lurched up and down, it became possible to make large returns—and also lose equally large amounts—by betting on the direction of such moves. In the latter half of 1919, convinced that the inflationary consequences of the war would undermine the currencies of the main belligerents, Keynes went short on the French franc, the German Reichsmark, and the Italian lira, buying the currencies of countries that had sat out most of the war: the Norwegian and the Danish kroner, the U.S. dollar, and interestingly enough, the Indian rupee. He made $30,000 in the first few months. In early 1920, he set up a syndicate, with his brother, some of the Bloomsbury circle, and a financier friend from the City of London. By the end of April 1920, they had made a further $80,000. Then suddenly, in the space of four weeks, a spasm of optimism about Germany briefly drove the declining European currencies back up, wiping out their entire capital. Keynes found himself on the verge of bankruptcy and had to be bailed out by his tolerant father. Nevertheless, propped up by his indulgent family and by a loan from the coolly acute financier Sir Ernest Cassel, he persevered in his speculations—built for the most part around the view that the German and Central European currencies were headed for disaster. By the end of 1922, he had amassed a modest nest egg of close to $120,000.

But by far the most important development in his life was that he had fallen in love—this time with a woman, Lydia Lopokova, a married Russian émigrée ballerina, no less. The daughter of a Russian father, an usher at the Imperial Alexandrinsky Theater, and a Scottish-German mother, Lydia came from a family of dancers—her two brothers and a sister had also gone to the Imperial Ballet School in St. Petersburg. When Maynard met her in 1918, she was traveling with the Diaghilev Ballet, having spent seven years in the United States as a cabaret artist, model, and vaudeville performer, and was married to the business manager of the company, Randolfo Barrochi. After her marriage broke down, she disappeared into Russia, then in the thick of civil war, with a mysterious White Russian general, but reappeared in Keynes's life at the end of 1921.

Though they would not get married until 1925 when her divorce finally came through, they began living together in 1923. They made an unlikely couple—he a brilliant and all too cerebral intellectual with a genius for exposition, she an unpredictable artist with a risqué past, a flighty and vivacious chatterbox with an equal skill for stumbling into the most memorable malapropisms. She once complained that she "disliked being in the country in August, because my legs get so bitten by barristers." On another occasion, after visiting an aviary, she remarked on her hostess's "ovary." And though the rest of Bloomsbury looked down on her, Keynes was to remain completely enchanted with her for the rest of his life.

In December 1923, Keynes published a short monograph, *A Tract on Monetary Reform*, much of which had already appeared as a series of articles in the *Manchester Guardian* during 1922 and early 1923—his first systematic attempt to unravel the sources and consequences of the chronic monetary instability that plagued the postwar world. Like his earlier book, *A Tract* was a strange hybrid, this time a half-theoretical treatise—with sections on "The Theory of Purchasing Power Parity" and "The Forward Market in Exchanges" and half pamphlet for the laity. It was, however, very different in tone from *The Economic Consequences*. That had been an angry, passionate work, written in the heat of debate and controversy. This one had a lighter touch, a "tentative almost diffident tone," as if the author himself were searching for the answer to the quest for monetary stability.

Before the war, however much he had enjoyed challenging conventional nostrums about morality, conduct, and society, in economics Keynes had fully embraced the liberal orthodoxy that dominated his still nascent profession. He believed in free trade, in the unfettered mobility of capital, and in the virtues of the gold standard.

There were times when, like so many other economists, he might speculate whether gold was the right foundation for money. But those had been largely theoretical ruminations; and ultimately, when it came down to it, there seemed no other practical basis so tried and tested upon which to organize the world's currencies. Asked at the height of the 1914 crisis to brief the chancellor of the exchequer as to whether the pound should remain tied to gold, he had come down very strongly in favor of maintaining the link: "London's position as a monetary center depends *very directly* on complete confidence in London's unwavering readiness" to meet its obligations in gold and would be severely damaged if "at the *first* sign of emergency" that commitment was suspended.

Even during the first years after the war, he was still advocating a return to gold. But the shift in the world's economic landscape was beginning to give him doubts. He still believed that the prime goal of central bank policy should be to keep prices broadly stable. But whereas before the war he had thought that the best way to achieve this was to ensure that currencies such as the pound be fully convertible to gold at a fixed value, he had now come to believe that there was no reason why linking money supply and credit to gold should necessarily result in stable prices.

The gold standard had only worked in the late nineteenth century because new mining discoveries had fortuitously kept pace with economic growth. There was no guarantee that this accident of history would continue. Moreover, while the original rationale for a gold standard—the commitment that paper money could be converted into something unequivocally tangible—might have been necessary to instill confidence at some point in history, this was no longer the case. Attitudes toward paper money had evolved and it was not necessary to allow the supply of precious metals to regulate the creation of credit in a sophisticated modern economy. Central banks were perfectly capable of managing their countries' monetary affairs rationally and responsibly, he argued, without any need to shackle themselves to this "barbarous relic."

Though the *Tract* was a technical monograph, the Cambridge undergraduate in Keynes could not resist lacing the book with the playful sarcasms that had made *The Economic Consequences* such a success. He flippantly dedicated the book, "humbly and without permission, to the Governors and the Court of the Bank of England," knowing very well that the members of that august body would disagree with almost everything he had to say. He poked fun at the self-importance of those "conservative bankers" who "regard it as more consonant with their cloth, and also as economizing on thought, to shift public discussion of financial topics off the logical on to an alleged moral plane, which means a realm of thought where vested interest can be triumphant over the common good without further debate." And he peppered it with the sort of bons mots—the most famous being "in the long run we are all dead"—that made him so scintillating a conversationalist.

But more than anything else it was Keynes's ability to strip away the surface of monetary phenomena and reveal some of its deeper realities and its connections to the society at large that has made the *Tract* such an enduring classic. For example, by tracing through the consequences of rising prices on different classes in a stylized picture of the economy—what economists today might call a model—he showed that inflation was much more than simply prices going up, but also a subtle mechanism for transferring wealth between social groups—from savers, creditors, and wage earners to the government, debtors, and businessmen. He thus highlighted the fact that the postwar inflation in countries such as France and Germany was not just the result of an error in monetary policy. Rather, it was a symptom of the fundamental disagreement that had wracked European society since the war about how to share the accumulated financial burden of that terrible conflict.

In contrast to *The Economic Consequences,* the new book had almost no practical impact. At a time when the currencies of Central Europe had completely collapsed and the franc was perilously close to the edge, few people could be convinced to entrust the management of national moneys and currency values to the discretion of treasury mandarins, politicians, or central bankers. There were too many examples to point to—Germany, Austria, Hungary, admittedly some of them pathologically extreme—of what could happen when the discipline of gold was removed. But the experience of the next decade would, in the words of one of Keynes's biographers, win for the *Tract* "the allegiance of half the world."

NORMAN'S RESPONSE TO the *Tract* was predictably to dismiss it as the froth of a clever dilettante. As he wrote to Strong, "For the moment Mr. Keynes seems to have rather outdone himself, a fact that perhaps comes from his trying to combine the position of financial mentor to this and other countries with that of a high-class speculator."

What separated Norman from Keynes had less to do with economics and more to do with philosophy and worldview. For Norman, the gold standard was not simply a convenient mechanism for regulating the money supply, the efficiency of which was an empirical question. He thought about it in much more existential terms. It was one of the pillars of a free society, like property rights or habeas corpus, which had evolved in the Western liberal world to limit the power of government—in this case its power to debase money. Without such a discipline to protect them, central banks would inevitably come under constant pressure to help finance their governments in much the same way that they had done during the war with all the inflationary consequences that were still all too apparent. The link with gold was the only sure defense against such a downward spiral in the value of money.

His reaction to the *Tract* was colored by his personal dealings with Keynes. After the war, Norman, agreeing with much of Keynes's argument on reparations, had consulted him at the height of the German hyperinflation. But Keynes's vocal opposition to the war-debt settlement with the United States, which Norman had been responsible for engineering, created a rift. Norman, acutely sensitive to public criticism, harbored grudges for a long time—"the most vindictive man I have ever known," according to one close friend. Thereafter, though their social circles overlapped somewhat and though Keynes, for all his youthful iconoclasm, was already widely recognized as the most brilliant monetary economist of his generation, Norman studiously ignored him professionally, and refused ever to invite him to advise the Bank.

Strong's reactions were on the surface similar to Norman's. He had never met Keynes, but given his puritan background, he would have vehemently disapproved of the Bloomsbury irreverence and mockery of authority. When *The Economic Consequences* came out, he had written of Keynes, "He is a brilliant but, I fear, somewhat erratic chap, with great power for good and, unfortunately . . . some capacity for harm." Many in his circle had taken offense at Keynes's merciless lampooning of Woodrow Wilson at the Peace Conference. He echoed this again in his reaction to the *Tract*. "Keynes' little book arrived safely and I am just now reading it," he wrote to Norman on January 4, 1924, from the Arizona desert. "I have a great respect for his ability and the freshness and versatility of his mind, but I am much afraid of some of his more erratic ideas, which impressed me as being the product of a vivid imagination without very much practical experience."

The hidden irony was that every one of Keynes's main recommendations—that the link between gold balances and the creation of credit be severed, that the automatic mechanism of the gold standard be replaced with a system of managed money, that credit policy be geared toward domestic price stability—corresponded precisely to the policies Strong had instituted in the United States.

During the war, the flow of gold into the United States had pushed up prices by 60 percent. When the fighting ended, but turmoil in Europe continued and the gold still kept arriving, Strong decided that it was time to abandon the conventional rules of the gold standard and insulate the U.S. economy from the flood of bullion. The system was being swamped by so much excess gold that to have followed the traditional dictates of the gold standard would have led to a massive expansion of domestic credit, which inevitably would have led to very high rates of inflation—Strong calculated that it would cause prices to double. It made no sense to him for the United States to import, in effect, the inflationary policies of Europe and destabilize its own monetary system just because the Old World had been hit by political and financial disaster. The Fed therefore began to short-circuit the effects of additional gold on the money supply by contracting the amount of credit that it supplied to banks, thus offsetting any liquidity from gold inflows.

Having jettisoned the simple operating procedures of the gold standard, which linked credit creation solely to gold reserves, Strong began to improvise an alternative set of principles to guide monetary policy. The Fed's primary goal should be, he believed, to try to stabilize domestic prices. But he thought that it should also respond to fluctuations in business activity—in other words, the Fed should try to fine-tune the economy by opening the spigot of credit when commercial conditions were weakening and closing it as the economy strengthened.

This new set of principles, somewhat cobbled together on the fly, represented a quiet, indeed carefully unheralded, revolution in monetary policy. Until then central bankers had seen their primary task as protecting the currency and confined their responsibilities to ensuring that the gold standard was given free rein, only stepping in at times of crisis or panic. The credit policy of every industrial country had been driven by one factor alone: gold reserves. The United States was, however, now so flush with gold that the solidity of its currency was assured. Led by Strong, the Fed had undertaken a totally new responsibility—that of promoting internal economic stability.

It was Strong more than anyone else who invented the modern central banker. When we watch Ben Bernanke or, before him, Alan Greenspan or Jean-Claude Trichet or Mervyn King describe how they are seeking to strike the right balance between economic growth and price stability, it is the ghost of Benjamin Strong who hovers above him. It all sounds quite prosaically obvious now, but in 1922 it was a radical departure from more than two hundred years of central banking history.

Strong's policy of offsetting the impact of gold inflows on domestic credit conditions meant that as bullion came into the United States, it was, in effect, withdrawn from circulation. It was as if all this treasure that had been so painfully mined from the depths of the earth was being reburied.

Strong's policy contained a fundamental contradiction. On the one hand, he advocated a worldwide return to the international gold standard. On the other, he was doing things that not only undermined the doctrine he claimed most to believe in, but also, by preventing the gold from being recycled to Europe, he was making it all the more difficult for Europe to contemplate rejoining America on the gold standard. It was a dilemma he was never able to resolve.

European bankers argued that the massive bullion imbalance between their countries and the United States was a fundamental problem for the world and pressed for some mechanism to recycle some of this gold. "I do not intend another quarter to pass," wrote Norman to Strong in January 1924, "without seeing you face to face, and asking you how in the name of heaven the Federal Reserve System and the United States Treasury are going to use their gold reserves."

KEYNES WAS THE first to recognize and articulate that, for all the public rhetoric about reinstating the gold standard, the new arrangements were in fact very different from the hallowed and automatic prewar mechanism. As he put it in the *Tract*, "A dollar standard was set up on the pedestal of the Golden Calf. For the past two years, the US has pretended to maintain a gold standard. In fact it has established a dollar standard."

It meant, in effect, that the Federal Reserve was so flush with gold that it had gone from being the central bank of the United States to being the central bank of the entire industrial world. Keynes's main concern was that Britain and other major European countries would find themselves being dictated to by a Fed that focused primarily on the needs of the domestic U.S. economy, yoking the gold-starved Europeans to U.S. credit policy. Strong was in the process of constructing a one-legged gold standard, whose European limb would be firmly tied to classical rules while the American limb would be run by the Fed according to its own set of goals and constraints.

Keynes would have been even more horrified had he probed further into how the Fed operated and the character of the men who ran it. The Federal Reserve Act of 1913 had been a political compromise. Decisions about the level of interest rates and credit conditions were vested in the hands of the twelve banker-dominated regional reserve banks. This network was overseen by an eight-member central Board of Governors, all presidential appointees based in Washington. Broadly speaking, only the reserve banks could initiate policies, but these policies had to be approved by the Board.

It was not surprising that there should have been a certain amount of jockeying for control within the system. The precise locus of authority was ambiguous, and too many big egos—twelve governors of the reserve banks; the six political appointees on the Federal Reserve Board; the secretary of the treasury and the comptroller of the currency, both ex-officio members of the Board—were jostling for power.

From the start, the Board in Washington was an organization of unclear purpose and mandate. When it was created in 1913, Wilson conceived of it as a regulatory agency standing as a watchdog over the various regional reserve banks. He believed, therefore, that it should be comprised of individuals from outside banking. But he was unwilling to give it much stature. When the first governors of the Board complained to the president that the State Department expert on protocol had decided that as the most recently created of the government agencies, they should come last in social precedence, Wilson had replied that as far as he was concerned, "they might come right after the fire department."

The Board did not even have its own quarters but operated from a dark and dreary suite of offices on the top floor of the Treasury Building, from which its long and narrow boardroom overlooked the grimy interior court. Members salaries were typical of the civil service, considerably lower than private sector compensation and even much less than the pay of the governors of the regional Federal Reserve banks. Not surprisingly, the Board found it hard to attract good people—on one occasion six different candidates turned down an offer of a position before someone could be induced to accept.

As a result, the Board was, in J. K. Galbraith's description, "a body of startling incompetence." In 1923, the chairman was Daniel Crissinger. Born in a log cabin in Marion, Ohio, he was a local eminence, a lawyer and banker who had risen to the position of general counsel of the Marion Steam Shovel Company and had twice run for Congress, albeit unsuccessfully. He also had the fortune to have been one of Warren Harding's boyhood chums and, though by all accounts "utterly devoid of global or economic banking sense," was appointed comptroller of the currency in 1922 after his old friend had become president. The following year the president elevated him to the chair of the Board.

Besides its chairman and its two ex-officio members, the Board comprised five other governors, carefully selected not for their expertise but to ensure due representation for the different regions of the country. From Memphis, Tennessee, came George Roosa James, a dry goods merchant, a man of great energy, something of a diamond in the rough. His economic ideas, however, ran on the eccentric side. Firmly rooted in the past, he held that the basic foundation of the economy lay with the horse, the mule, and hay, and that the decay of the nation had begun with the advent of the automobile.

From Iowa came Edward Cunningham, who had started life as a dirt farmer and gone on to become Speaker of the Iowa legislature; from Poughkeepsie, New York, came Edmund Platt, a local newspaper publisher, who had entered politics as a member of the town's board of water commissioners and gone on to serve as its three-term Republican congressman. Boston furnished George Hamlin, longest serving of the governors, having been appointed chairman by Woodrow Wilson in 1914. By profession a lawyer, he had run unsuccessfully for governor of Massachusetts in 1902 and 1910—a failed political career, it seems, was not an impediment, indeed was almost a qualification, for Board membership.

One member, however, who could legitimately claim some relevant expertise was Dr. Adolph Miller. Having studied economics at Harvard, he had been a professor at the University of California at Berkeley for twenty-five years. A deeply insecure man, he resented that his qualifications were not fully appreciated by his colleagues—they in turn tended to dismiss him as an ivory-tower theoretician with no practical experience. He liked to argue, and when his colleagues grew weary of the interminable wrangling, would begin to argue with himself. Not surprisingly, he was often confused and indecisive, with a tendency to adopt extremely dogmatic but contradictory positions on many topics. He had also developed a particular animus against Strong, resenting the younger man's influence and authority.

It did not help that Miller had learned his economics at a time when monetary economics, as a discipline, was very much in its infancy, thus leading him to espouse a series of outmoded beliefs about the way monetary policy was supposed to work. Among these was the now defunct doctrine of "real bills," that as long as the Federal Reserve and commercial banks restricted themselves to providing only short-term credit to finance inventories, nothing much could go wrong.

Faced with overseers such as this, it was not surprising that Strong was able to step into the vacuum of leadership and dominate the institution. Unlike his nominal superiors, he made a concerted attempt—particularly during those many trips to Europe—to educate himself about central banking. It was he, for example, who was most responsible for introducing the biggest innovation in the way the Fed operated—so-called open market operations. When the Fed was conceived, it was assumed that it would primarily influence credit conditions by changes in its discount rate, the interest rate it charged on loans to member banks. By the early 1920s, this technique was proving to be too passive, depending, as it did, for its impact on how much or how little bankers were willing to borrow at the discount window. Strong recognized that by buying or selling government securities from its portfolio, the Fed could directly and immediately alter the quantity of money flowing through the banking system.

It was inevitable that control of open market operations should become the object of an intense power struggle. The purchase and sale of securities out of their portfolios had initially been left to the reserve banks; but in 1923, the Board, recognizing the potency of the new tool, tried to take charge by requiring the committee that made these decisions to operate under its umbrella. Strong was away in Colorado at the time, recuperating from his bout of tuberculosis of the throat. He was furious. "I'll see them damned before I'd be dismissed by that timid bunch!" he wrote to one of his fellow governors. Eventually, though, he did acquiesce in giving the

Board oversight over such operations. But as the most knowledgeable official on the new open market committee, he was easily able to call the shots on virtually all decisions.

In the process he stepped on a lot of toes, not concealing his impatience with the members of the Board. Some complained that he had an overblown sense of his own abilities, that he was too confrontational, that he lacked judgment, particularly about people. But as the intellectual leader of the Federal Reserve, he had acquired a large following within the organization and was "worshipped" by the younger men.

If there was one problem with this whole process of making monetary policy, it was that it all depended too heavily on Strong—on his judgment, his skill, and his insight. He was too autocratic, operated on his own too much, and did not spend the time to build a consensus through the whole system. As a result, the rationale for many of his decisions was misinterpreted and his motives were constantly questioned. His failure to institutionalize policies and the thinking behind them meant that once he was no longer around, the Fed would become paralyzed by internal conflicts.

Keynes once compared the role of the Bank of England under the prewar system to that of the "conductor of an orchestra." Even though the Bank had then been administered by a club of old and established City patricians, the gold standard had been managed well, in part because circumstances were so favorable, in part because the directors of the Bank, however dull and unimaginative, were solid. After the war, as the world struggled to emerge from economic chaos, with currencies still in turmoil and gold in short supply everywhere outside America, it did not bode well that the new "conductor of the orchestra," the Federal Reserve, was a deeply divided organization that did not fully realize the role that had been thrust upon it and, but for Strong, would have been in the hands of a motley crew of small-town businessmen and minor-league political hacks with little expertise in finance or central banking.

PART THREE

*

SOWING
A NEW WIND

*

1923-28

10. A BRIDGE BETWEEN CHAOS AND HOPE

GERMANY: 1923

*Let me issue and control a nation's money and I
care not who writes the laws.*

—MAYER AMSCHEL ROTHSCHILD (1744–1812),
founder of the House of Rothschild

AT 10:00 P.M. on November 8, 1923, two men could have been seen arriving at the Hotel Continental in Berlin for an intimate dinner in one of its private dining rooms. Each was in his own way a caricature of a type of German and could almost have come from central casting. The tall, thin figure with the clipped military mustache, hair cut short and parted very precisely in the center, was Hjalmar Schacht, now one of the most prominent bankers in Berlin, a director and board member of the Danatbank, third largest in Germany.

The other was short and fat, with an enormous head, his bloated face pasty from overindulgence and lack of exercise. With his easy smile and gregarious manner, he looked like a classic lower-class Berliner, crude, brash, but good-hearted. This was Gustav Stresemann, who just three months before had become chancellor of Germany. He was indeed what he appeared to be: a Berliner from the lower middle classes, son of an innkeeper and beer distributor, though he had himself received a doctorate in economics from the University of Berlin, and had been a professional politician and corporate lobbyist since the age of twenty-two.

November 9, the next day, was the fifth anniversary of the flight of the kaiser. The night before, the Soviet embassy had hosted a grand party to celebrate the joint anniversaries of its own revolution and that of Germany, but Stresemann had excused himself on the grounds of state business. For the last two days, he had been locked in conference with members of his cabinet trying to find a way of averting the country's imminent bankruptcy.

On November 5, the price of a two-kilo loaf of bread had soared from 20 billion marks to 140 billion, sparking off nationwide riots. In Berlin, thousands of men and women had paraded the streets, shouting "Bread and work!" Over a thousand shops—bakeries, butchers, and even clothing stores—had been looted. Even in the city's chic west end, cars had been held up and the occupants robbed. In the heavily Jewish areas to the east around the Alexanderplatz, anyone who was known to be Jewish or "looked Jewish" had been attacked by gangs of young hoodlums. The worst violence was directed at Galician Jews, many of whom had their distinctive beards scissored off or their clothes ripped away. The Börse, the stock exchange, had come under siege by a mob shouting, "Kill the Börse Jews."

But by the evening of November 8, the streets were at last quiet, the mobs dispersed at bayonet point by military police. Heavily armed Prussian State Police in green uniforms now patrolled the city. After an abnormally hot Indian summer, the weather had turned extremely cold. That night, it had begun to rain, making life even more difficult for those innumerable Berliners forced to queue up outside the municipal food kitchens and public feeding stations spread across the city.

The Hotel Continental was located in the center of Berlin, just off the tree-lined boulevard of Unter den Linden. Though not one of the major hotels, it was conveniently close to the Reichstag and sufficiently discreet and unobtrusive for Schacht and Stresemann to meet without drawing too much attention to themselves. Neither would have wished to be seen at one of the great fashionable meeting places, the Adlon on Pariserplatz or the Bristol on Unter den Linden, among all the nouveaux riches—the so-called Raffkes and Schiebers, fat, coarse men who had made their money from profiteering during those last few feverish years and who could always be found in the big hotels, drinking champagne and gorging on oysters and caviar.

Despite the riots and the rain, the infamously louche and tawdry night-life of Berlin—that new "Babylon of the world"—continued unabated. On the Friedrichstrasse and along Kurfürstendamm, the bars and dance halls were, as always, full. As on every night, hordes of prostitutes of both sexes—there were said to be a hundred thousand of them in Berlin alone—paraded outside in the strangest and most exotic costumes. "A kind of madness" had taken hold of the city, unhinging the whole society. Fortunes were made overnight and as quickly lost or dissipated. Those with money, desperate to be rid of it before it became worthless, indulged in giddy frenzies of spending, while those without sold what few possessions remained to them, including their bodies, in the struggle to survive. A quarter of the city's schoolchildren suffered from malnutrition.

Berlin had never been an elegant city. Before the war, people thought that it was too close a reflection of the personality of its emperor—brash, self-important, and vulgar—the "German Chicago," Mark Twain had called it. But it had rightly prided itself on being the cleanest and most modern metropolis in Europe. Now it was shabby and going to seed, faded and run down like a "stone-grey corpse," infested by "beggars, whores, invalids and fat-necked speculators," its streets crowded by "legless war veterans riding the sidewalks on rolling planks" and by stunted, bowlegged children bent out of shape by rickets.

STRESEMANN HAD BEEN called upon to form a government that August, when the previous coalition had collapsed, the sixth to fall in five years. He was thought to be the one man politically skillful enough to be able to bring together all the democratic parties—the Socialists, the Catholics, the liberals of the center—into a "Great Coalition" that could try to come to grips with a Germany on the verge of disintegration.

He had had not one but two improbable political careers. Before the war, despite his lower-middle-class background—which twice led the kaiser to snub him conspicuously by publicly refusing to shake hands—he had been an ardent monarchist, a fervent militarist and, as head of the National Liberal Party in the Reichstag, a blind supporter of the military during the war. Known as "Ludendorff's young man" because of his loyalty to the Imperial High Command, he had been an advocate of the whole nationalist agenda—annexation, German expansion, and the campaign of unrestricted submarine warfare that had so angered the Americans. When the military broke down at the end of the war, Stresemann had been left, like so many other politicians of the imperial era, humiliated and discredited. Though he was still only forty years old, his political career seemed to be over. But in the five years since the revolution, he had steadily rebuilt his political image, transforming himself from a jingoistic warmonger to a trusted pillar of the new democracy, though many believed that his conversion was a sham.

Stresemann took over a country in deep crisis. The year 1923 had seen an oppressively hot summer of riots and strikes across a Germany genuinely close to breaking apart. In Saxony, the Communists had threatened to secede as an independent state, while in the south, the Bavarian government was being assailed from the right.

Despite his genial and sentimental exterior, Stresemann was a realist who had come to power determined to end the nightmare. In his first few weeks in office, he had the Reichstag approve an act empowering him to govern by decree; suspended the campaign of passive resistance in the Ruhr, which was costing the government $10 million a day; and declared a state of emergency that gave the army the necessary authority to act against secessionist states.

Recognizing that the political breakdown had its roots in the dislocations and chaos of rampant hyperinflation, Stresemann then turned his attention to the monetary questions. Tax revenues at the time accounted for less than 10 percent of government expenditures, and the gap was being filled by printing money.

Stresemann had invited Schacht to dinner that night to try to persuade him to accept the position of currency commissioner, a new post with responsibility for reforming the whole German currency. It would make Schacht the financial czar of Germany, with more power than even the minister of finance.

The two had known each other for more than twenty years. They socialized in the same circles and were both members of the Berliner Mittwochgesellschaft, the Wednesday Society, a select discussion club restricted to eighty-five members and founded in 1915. Stresemann, who thought highly of Schacht, had been trying to find a position for him in the new administration for some weeks. The previous month, during his first cabinet reshuffle, he had even tried to appoint Schacht minister of finance; but the night before he was to submit his new list of ministers to President Friedrich Ebert, he had received a letter from a high official in the ministry expressing grave doubts about Schacht's suitability for the position, raising the old questions about Schacht's wartime record and hinting at ethical improprieties and corruption. At the last minute, Stresemann had been compelled to drop Schacht's name from his proposed cabinet.

For Schacht, the new opportunity could not have come at a better time. Now independently wealthy, he was eager to enter public life. Though he owed much of his fortune to Jacob Goldschmidt, he viewed his young associate's deal making as dangerous. Increasingly sidelined within Danatbank, he had begun looking for a new challenge.*

He would later describe life that summer as "living on the edge of a volcano." The biggest danger in his view was a Bolshevik revolution. But as the political crisis began to reach a crescendo, he remained convinced that some great opportunity would present itself to him.

---

*His premonition would eventually prove to be right. In 1931, as the Depression in Germany reached its nadir, the Danatbank would collapse, a victim of Goldschmidt's risky business strategy. Goldschmidt himself would become a favorite target of Nazi propaganda about the "unwarranted power" and "sinister influence" of Jewish bankers.

At the end of the summer, he sent his wife, Luise; his twenty-year-old daughter, Inge; and his thirteen-year-old son, Jens, to the safety of Switzerland. He had been hoping that the new government would offer him a position and he wanted to be able to take decisions without, as he put it, being "hindered by personal considerations were I to be drawn into the whirlpool." He knew that Luise, a fervent nationalist and right-wing radical with a "narrow Prussian outlook," was unlikely to be particularly welcoming to the left-wingers and democrats with whom he would have to associate.

At 11:30 p.m., as the two men were finishing dinner and Schacht, a chain-smoker, had lit up, one of Stresemann's aides burst in. For weeks there had been rumors that the right-wing groups in Bavaria, one led by the local army and police commander, the other by a thirty-four-year-old ex-corporal named Adolf Hitler, were planning to seize power. They had now struck. Hitler, apparently working with the fallen general Erich Ludendorff, had taken over a Munich beer hall, drafted local political leaders to back him, and proclaiming the Berlin government deposed, was preparing to march on "that sink of iniquity." Reports were even filtering in that some army units in Munich had gone over to the rebels. Cutting short the dinner, Stresemann raced back to an emergency cabinet meeting at the Chancellery.

THE FOLLOWING MONDAY, November 12, Schacht received a call at his office on the Schinkelplatz from Hans Luther, minister of finance, summoning him to the ministry, located in one of those grim official buildings on the Wilhelmstrasse. Hitler's attempt to seize power—the Beer Hall Putsch, as it was already being called—had collapsed within twenty-four hours, and the Stresemann government was getting back to business.

Short, fat, and completely bald, Luther had become a national hero when as mayor of the city of Essen in the Ruhr valley, he had defied occupying French and Belgian troops. But for all his exploits as a doughty little burgomaster, Luther was a cold, colorless, straitlaced figure, suspicious of Schacht's reputation for sailing too close to the wind. He had initially opposed Schacht's nomination, but when the two other bankers whom he first approached turned him down, he felt he had little choice.

That morning Luther formally offered Schacht the position of currency commissioner. Though Schacht pretended that he needed time to think the matter over, when Luther demanded an immediate reply, he accepted with, as one historian describes it, "an enthusiasm suitable to the as-yet-to-be revealed dimensions of his ambition."

Schacht came to the job with an array of qualifications. He was well known and admired in foreign banking circles, an attribute that would become very important when Germany had to go through its next cycle of wrangling over reparations. He was supported by the center and the left. In addition, it was rumored that Jacob Goldschmidt, powerful in Democratic Party circles and keen to oust Schacht from the Danatbank, was actively lobbying to kick him upstairs.

The post he assumed carried with it unprecedented powers. He was given cabinet rank; was to be invited to all its meetings; and most important, had the right of veto over any measures that had implications for the currency, a veto that could only be overridden by a majority of the cabinet.

Less grandly, for his office he was provided with a room in the back of the Finance Ministry that had once been a broom closet. It was dark, confined, and bare except for a writing table and a telephone. He agreed to take no salary, insisting that his $100 a month go to supplement the meager official $50 a month of his secretary, Fräulein Steffeck, whom he had brought over from the Danatbank and who was his single direct employee.

The plan was to introduce a totally new currency, the Rentenmark, to be backed not by gold but by land. The bank issuing the new currency was granted a "mortgage" on all agricultural and industrial property, on which it could impose an annual levy of 5 percent—in effect, a tax on commercial real estate.

Despite his new position, Schacht was as skeptical about the new plan's chances of success as almost everyone else in Germany. From the very first, he had scoffed at the idea of a land-based currency as a pure confidence trick; currencies had to be backed by a highly liquid, easily transferable, internationally acceptable asset, such as gold. He found it hard to believe that someone being paid in the new currency would derive any comfort from the theoretical promise that those currency notes were ultimately convertible into some slab of inaccessible Thuringian woodland or Bavarian pasture or perhaps of a Communist-riddled Saar factory.

During the debate on the various currency reform plans, Schacht had forthrightly argued for gold as the foundation for a new currency. While no one could challenge the theoretical basis of his logic, the fatal difficulty had been that Germany simply did not have enough gold for the job. Before the war, the country had had a circulating currency of $1.5 billion, backed by just under $1 billion in gold. After five years of reparations and currency collapse, less than $150 million in gold remained. Moreover, the modest amount Germany did possess was in the hands of the Reichsbank, whose president, Rudolf von Havenstein, had been adamant that he would not part with an ounce to support something over which he had no control. While Schacht, usually a realist, had suggested that Germany try to build up its gold reserves by borrowing abroad, few people believed that a country that had defaulted on reparations the previous year and was now partly occupied by foreign troops would get even a hearing from international bankers.

The most important, perhaps the defining, characteristic of the new currency was not that it theoretically rested on land, but that the amount to be issued was to be rigidly fixed at 2.4 billion Rentenmarks, equivalent to around $600 million. Grasping that the key to its credibility was to keep it sufficiently scarce, Schacht was determined to ensure that the amount in circulation did not exceed its statutory ceiling under any circumstances. And though he encountered considerable political pressure to relent, including from his cabinet colleagues, he stuck to his position. He was obstinate, almost brutal, about turning down loan requests from everyone—government agencies, municipalities, banks, or big industrialists.

Fräulein Steffeck has left a vivid picture of Schacht in those first few days:

> He sat on his chair and smoked in his little dark room at
> the Ministry of Finance, which still smelled of old floor
> cloths. Did he read letters? No, he read no letters. Did he
> write letters? No, he wrote no letters. But he telephoned a
> great deal—he telephoned in every direction and to every
> German and international place that had anything to with
> money and foreign exchange. And he smoked. We did not
> eat much during that time. We usually went home late,
> often by the last suburban train, traveling third class. Apart
> from that he did nothing.

He took great pride in this portrait, which he never tired of repeating. He relished the image it evoked of the maverick financial genius operating masterfully on his own where established bankers had failed.

FOR VON HAVENSTEIN, the news of Schacht's appointment was the final humiliation. Though for the last five years he had presided over the single greatest debasement of a currency in history, he still refused to accept responsibility for the debacle. He kept insisting that it was not his fault but the result of government mismanagement and the Allies' extortionary demands.

When Stresemann came to power in August 1923, he tried to persuade Von Havenstein to go of his own accord, arguing that the public had lost all confidence in the currency, and that to reverse this required not just a new medium of exchange but a new president of the Reichsbank. Von Havenstein had categorically refused. By November, the chorus of demands that he resign had spread all the way across the political spectrum—everyone except the furthest-right nationalists. Only a few days earlier the leading industrialists had branded him the "father of the inflation." But the Reichsbank Autonomy Law of July 1922—ironically enacted at the insistence of the British, who hoped, by making the Reichsbank independent of the government, to curb inflation—had given the chief architect of inflation tenure for life.

No one could understand why Von Havenstein, who prided himself on his sense of service, clung so desperately and so humiliatingly to office in the face of such clamor. But he kept repeating that if he went, things would only get worse—how, very few people could see. In many ways it was precisely his pride as a public official that prevented him from resigning and thus acknowledging responsibility for the destruction of the mark and, with it, the savings of so many God-fearing Germans like himself. The most he would concede was that he might resign after a decent interval of several months so as to "preserve his honor."

Saddled with Von Havenstein, Stresemann had simply bypassed him by creating the independent Currency Commissionership outside of the Reichsbank. And so, when the new currency was introduced on November 15, 1923, Germany found itself in the curious position of having two official currencies—the old Reichsmark and the new Rentenmark—circulating side by side, issued by two uniquely parallel central banks. At one end of town was Schacht, operating from his converted broom closet; at the other, Von Havenstein, holed up and increasingly isolated and irrelevant in the Reichsbank's imposing red sandstone building on Jagerstrasse. Although the Reichsbank had now stopped providing money to the government, its printing presses still continued to roll out trillions of Reichsmarks to private businesses.

Neither Schacht nor Von Havenstein made any attempt to communicate with the other. The contrast between the two could not have been greater—Von Havenstein, a true gentleman of the old school, kind, courteous, but completely out of his depth; and Schacht, the arrogant upstart, quite prepared to confront the financial establishment, and not caring on whose toes he trod.

The whole justification for the new currency was to provide a stable alternative to the collapsed Reichsmark. The question immediately arose:

At what rate could people convert their Reichsmarks into Rentenmarks? On November 12, the Reichsmark was trading at 630 billion to the dollar. Some argued that the rate of conversion should be fixed at that point, but Schacht decided to wait. The black market price was still falling, and he wished to allow the selling to exhaust itself before he committed to a rate of conversion. Every day the Reichsmark plunged further, and every day he insisted on holding back. On November 14, when it fell to 1.3 trillion, he did nothing. A day later, it was at 2.5 trillion and still he sat on his hands. Finally, on November 20, when the Reichsmark stood, if that is the word, at 4.2 trillion to the dollar, he fixed the conversion rate at 1 trillion Reichsmarks to a Rentenmark.

The decision to wait those extra days, allowing the old currency to sink by another 80 percent, was a brilliant tactical move. The Reichsmark be-came so worthless that the government was able to buy back its many trillions of debt, valued at $30 billion when first issued, for only 190 million Rentenmarks, equivalent to about $45 million.*

For the next few days, marks, both new and old, continued to fall on the black market. On November 26, the Reichsmark was trading at 11 tril-lion to the dollar in Cologne. Then the strangest thing began to happen. The exchange rate began to reverse itself. By December 10, it was back at 4.2 trillion to the dollar. Within a few days prices stabilized.

When prices were so insanely rising, the average German had done everything he could to get rid of any cash he received as fast as possible. Now this spiral reversed itself. As prices began to hold and then fall, it became profitable to hang on to cash. Farmers, their confidence in money restored, began bringing produce to market, food reappeared in the shops, and those interminable queues began to melt away. Lord d'Abernon, the British ambassador, wrote of the "astonishing appeasement and relief brought about by a touch of the magical wand of "Currency Stability. . . .

---

* There was, in addition, a highly potent symbolism to the rate selected. The Rentenmark would now have an exchange rate of 4.2 to the dollar, the rate that had prevailed under the gold standard before the war. This was designed to send a signal to the public, and to the world, that the new currency was to be as stable as the mark had been before the war.

The economic détente has brought in its train political pacification—dictatorships and putsches are no longer discussed, and even the extreme parties have ceased, for the moment, from troubling."

Not all of this was Schacht's doing. Stresemann and his cabinet colleagues backed the Rentenmark with a series of budgetary measures, suspending all subsidy payments to workers in the Ruhr, firing a quarter of the government workforce, and indexing all taxes to inflation, thus eliminating the incentive for taxpayers to delay payment. By January 1924, the budget was balanced. But it was Schacht who received the prime credit, feted in the press as "The Wizard" or the "Miracle Man."

MAX WARBURG ONCE remarked that he supported Schacht because "he always had good luck." That good fortune once more manifested itself. In early November, Von Havenstein took a few days' leave of absence, in order to get out of Berlin during the humiliation of Schacht's appointment; but he was also known to be seriously ill. In mid-November, he returned to his official apartment on the top floor of the Reichsbank. On November 20, the day that Schacht fixed the conversion value of the new currency, Von Havenstein after a late evening meeting with his board, suddenly collapsed and died of a heart attack at 3:30 a.m. He was sixty-six.

There was something terribly tragic about this deeply well-intentioned man. Not simply a dutiful bureaucrat, he was by all accounts a wonderful human being, to Max Warburg "an extraordinarily sympathetic personality, with an unbending sense of duty and honorable character." He was universally admired, kind, principled, and considerate, always living up to the highest virtues of his class. During the war, while most households supplemented their rations by buying under the counter, Von Havenstein not only refused to use the black market, but even donated some of his own paltry bread and meat ration stamps to the poor. In the last year, however, he seemed to have lost his grip on reality—some said that the pressure he was under had made him prematurely senile—and few mourned his passing.

While Schacht was Von Havenstein's logical successor, his unusual gift for making enemies continued to dog him. The strongest opposition came from within the Reichsbank board, which considered him an unprincipled interloper. The whole Belgian episode resurfaced all over again. The only rival candidate, however, was Karl Helfferich, who as wartime secretary of the treasury had been responsible for the disastrous policies that had left Germany so buried under debt. Helfferich's political views, allied to a taste for polemics, had propelled him into the vanguard of the right-wing nationalists. Because of his vicious ad hominem attacks on democratic politicians, he was blamed for instigating the wave of assassinations by paramilitary vigilantes. Whatever reservations politicians of the center and left who formed the backbone of the government might have held about Schacht, he was infinitely better than Helfferich. On December 20, Schacht was appointed president of the Reichsbank.

But despite the early success of the currency reform, Schacht was acutely aware that Germany's problems would not be solved by its efforts alone. Monetary stability was sustainable only while Germany could stall paying reparations. Ultimately, it would have to strike a deal with the Allies and resume some payments; and at that point, the mark would begin to plummet again.

Schacht believed, moreover, that the Rentenmark, based as it was on the fictional security of land, could only offer a temporary solution, "a bridge between chaos and hope," as he called it. Ultimately any stable German currency would have to be backed by gold. Since the Reichsbank held less than $100 million of the metal, wholly insufficient as the basis for an economy the size of Germany's, he would have to find some way of borrowing from abroad to bring the gold backing to an adequate level.

The United States was the obvious place to go—of all the powers after the war, it was the only one with surplus capital. But for the past three years it had withdrawn from European affairs, though there were some signs that it was waking up to the need to reengage. During his first few days in office, Schacht received some encouraging signals through many intermediaries, such as Gerard Vissering, the governor of the Nederlandische Bank, that Montagu Norman at the Bank of England was keen to find some way of bringing Germany back into the world economy. Norman had to be one of the keys to reestablishing Germany's credit abroad. No major bank, in either London or New York, would think of lending money to Germany without a nod from him. Schacht's first action after taking over at the Reichsbank was to bring his family back from Switzerland; the second was to arrange a meeting with Norman in London.

11. THE DAWES OPENING

GERMANY: 1924

Be extremely subtle, even to the point of formlessness.
Be extremely mysterious, even to the point of sound-
lessness. Thereby you can be director of the
opponent's fate.

—SUN TZU, *The Art of War*

SCHACHT ARRIVED at Liverpool Street Station in London on the boat train from Berlin at 10:00 p.m. on New Year's Eve, 1923. London café society was back in full swing after the war, the streets crowded with revelers. Schacht had arranged to be met by the economic counselor at the German embassy, Albert Dufour-Feronce. As he stepped off the train, he also found waiting "a tall man with a pointed grayish beard and shrewd discerning eyes" who, much to Schacht's surprise, introduced himself as Montagu Norman. "I do hope we shall be friends," Norman said confidingly in his soft voice as he led Schacht to a cab. Before they parted, Norman insisted that they meet at Threadneedle Street the following morning—even though it was not a holiday, most of the City would take the day off.

Schacht was taken aback by the warmth of his welcome and was even more bemused when he learned from Dufour-Feronce how keen the governor had seemed to establish a personal bond with his German counterpart, insisting, "I want to get on well with him."

Schacht was more than flattered that Norman would turn out to welcome him on a cold and foggy December evening when most people were celebrating. After all, he was the supplicant come to enlist help with the German economic crisis. He was also touched by the graciousness of the gesture. After the war, loathing of things German had run high across Europe, and Schacht had become accustomed to slights and petty insults by Allied officials when he traveled abroad.

The next day Norman collected Schacht from the Carlton Hotel in Mayfair and they made their way to the Bank through the empty streets. Covering a full block at the corner of Threadneedle and Princess streets in the heart of the City, the Bank, surrounded by a forty-foot windowless wall topped by balustrades, looked like some medieval citadel. One entered this fortress through two great bronze doors, behind which, hidden from public view, lay a labyrinth of colonnaded courtyards and domed banking halls. By the entrance rose a giant rotunda modeled on the Pantheon in Rome, and next to it was a beautiful private garden with a fountain and a lime tree, planted in the spring with hundreds of flower bulbs. It was a most unusual setting for the headquarters of a central bank and very unlike the stern official-looking building from which Schacht now operated.

After the enormous wartime expansion of the Bank's activities, the halls and courtyards would normally have been as bustling and overcrowded as a bazaar with young clerks, bill brokers, and top-hatted bankers from the discount houses scurrying between the Bank and the investment firms located in the nearby streets and lanes. But that day the warren was silent and deserted, like some vast disused stage set. The governor's room was on the ground floor, overlooking a private courtyard. Norman, with his unbankerly taste for solitude and no family to hold him at home, could often be found here on weekends and holidays. Decorated in a neoclassical style, with paneled walls and a magnificent fireplace, the room was dominated by a large square mahogany table in the center. Instead of using a desk, the governor worked from this table, which was clear—no papers, just two phones. As the two men settled down for the day, they might have been sitting in the master's study of some historic Oxford college.

After spending much of the morning discussing the German situation, Schacht finally got to his main object in coming to London. Though the Rentenmark was for the moment stable, it was not yet acceptable to foreigners, and hence could not provide the basis for loans to import goods from abroad. True recovery depended on getting international commerce moving again. Schacht proposed that the Bank of England lend a certain amount of capital to a new subsidiary of the Reichsbank to build up its sterling reserves and funds. He was asking for a mere $25 million, which, supplemented by a further $25 million that he hoped to raise from capital held abroad by German banks, would be enough to give the new subsidiary access to the London market and provide the nucleus for as much as $200 million in loans.

This was a typically bold Schacht proposal—given the circumstances, almost outrageous. Germany was essentially bankrupt. It had destroyed its own currency, owed the Allies over $12 billion in reparations—and had defaulted on these—was partially occupied by French and Belgian troops and now on the verge of disintegration. Schacht himself had barely been in office for two weeks; had been appointed in the teeth of fierce opposition, especially from within his own institution; and had yet to put his stamp on the place. For the Bank to lend money to Germany and a deeply divided Reichsbank in the current circumstances would be almost foolhardy. Norman could not help being impressed with the audacity of his new acquaintance.

Both men knew that a loan at this moment from an institution with the authority and prestige of the Bank of England would represent a dramatic gesture of support for Germany, and for Schacht personally. There could be no better seal of approval anywhere in the banking world, one that might in itself set in train a self-reinforcing migration of money back into the country.

Norman had been trying over the years to find a way to help Germany.

He had been shocked by the extent of the collapse of the German currency. In 1922, Von Havenstein had come to see him for help. Though he had found his visitor to be "quiet, modest, convincing, and [a] very attractive man: but so sad. . . (with) an attitude of almost hopelessness," he had declined to get involved, believing that the old president was not up to the task.

One element in Schacht's plan was specifically designed to appeal to Norman: the proposal to base the new bank on the pound sterling. Not only was its capital to be denominated in sterling, it would make loans in sterling, and perhaps issue bank notes in pounds to circulate in Germany. Norman had been working to strengthen the pound by having other European central banks hold some of their reserves in sterling rather than gold. He had so far had some modest success with the idea. Austria and Hungary, like Germany ravaged by postwar inflation, had both pegged their currencies to the pound. But they were small nations of little economic significance. To bring a country such as Germany, despite its troubles still the largest economy within Europe, into the ambit of the pound would enormously bolster sterling's faltering position.

Schacht's grasp of the multiple dimensions of the situation, his virtuosity in matters of finances, and his determination clearly impressed Norman, who agreed to the German plan after a single night's reflection. During the next few days he shepherded Schacht around the City to introduce him to the directors of the Bank. Few took to Schacht, finding him to be a pompous blowhard. But for these two polar opposites—the German parvenu, with a direct and aggressive style, and his English guide, with his old-fashioned manners and elliptical ways of thinking and talking—it was the beginning of a genuine and enduring friendship.

For four years, Norman had stood on the sidelines and watched powerlessly as the situation in Germany had progressively deteriorated. With Schacht's arrival on the scene, however, he had found reason for hope. On January 7, three days after Schacht left London, he wrote to Strong, "You know, of course, how precarious the position of Germany has been. . . . None the less we are disposed to believe that there is now a chance, and probably the last chance, of preventing a complete collapse. The new President of the Reichsbank has been here for several days. He seems to know the situation from A to Z and to have, temporarily, more control of it than I should have believed possible: he is acting more resolutely than his predecessor, Havenstein."

WHILE SCHACHT AND Norman were concocting their scheme, a team of American "experts," with even greater ambitions to resolve the problems of German finances, was in mid-Atlantic steaming toward Europe on board a liner. Over the years, Germany had had no shortage of foreign "experts" willing to tell it how to stabilize its currency. The British ambassador, Viscount d'Abernon, himself a currency expert, remarked that on arriving in Berlin, these advisers would be invited to "entertainments after dinner—like actresses with doubtful pasts," thereafter generally to meet a "sad fate. During life, they empty every room in which they hold forth, and death finds them in madhouses." The monetary technicians had universally failed because it was not intellectual but financial help that Germany needed. This time, however, the "experts" were Americans, coming with the blessing of the U.S. government and the promise, so everyone hoped, of American money.

Though the United States, frustrated by Europe and its quarrels, had withdrawn from active involvement in world affairs, there remained a faction within the administration, led by Herbert Hoover, the secretary of commerce, and Charles Evans Hughes, the secretary of state, who had continued to push for some degree of engagement in the belief that European recovery was essential to American prosperity. In October 1923, Hughes took advantage of a Europe-wide mood of exhaustion with the issue of reparations to propose the creation of a new committee of experts. It was to include some prominent Americans, although in deference to the country's isolationist state of mind, they were not to have any official standing but were to act as concerned private citizens.

Even Raymond Poincaré, the French prime minister, recognized that by invading the Ruhr, he had overplayed his hand and that France was for the present a spent force within Europe. He consented to the proposal subject to one firm condition: under no circumstances was the committee to reconsider the total amount of reparations agreed to by all parties. The word *reparations* was not even to appear in the committee's remit. It was only to be asked to consider "the means of balancing the budget and the measures to be taken to stabilize the currency," though no one could quite fathom how it was to accomplish these tasks without addressing the unmentionable issue.

On November 30, 1923, the Reparations Commission announced the appointment of two international committees of experts—the first to consider how to balance the German budget and stabilize the currency, the second to investigate how much German capital had been exported. The first and more important was to be composed of ten men, two each from the United States, Britain, France, Belgium, and Italy. All Europe now awaited the arrival of the Americans.

The leader of that delegation was Charles Gates Dawes, a Chicago banker, who had risen to the rank of brigadier general while serving in France with the American Expeditionary Force and had gone on to become the director of the budget in the Harding administration. He was a straight-talking midwesterner with a long basset hound face who smoked an underslung Sherlock Holmes–style pipe and peppered his conversation with picturesque swearwords.* Asked by reporters, as he was preparing to embark, whether he was hopeful that reparations would ever be paid, he replied, "None of your damned business. It's no use you fellows getting brain fag by thinking up conundrums to put to me before the ship sails, because I do not intend to answer them. I can tell you that I am paying my own fare to France, and am not receiving any pay for my services on the committee." When the reporters kept pressing him, he roared back, "Hell and Maria, go away from me, I am about to lose my temper."

---

*He was also a self-taught composer. In 1911, he composed a piece entitled "Melody in A Major," which, set to words in the 1950s, became the popular hit song "It's All in the Game."

His fellow expert was Owen D. Young, a farm boy from upstate New York who at the age of forty had become president and chairman of the board of the General Electric Company, the tenth largest company in America, and was now also the president of the Radio Corporation of America, the darling of Wall Street. Young, tall, and lanky, with thinning black hair and the "hollow deep-set eyes of an ascetic," was a contrast to the garrulous Dawes, a man of few but well-chosen words. Both he and Dawes were wealthy men who not only refused to accept any compensation for the assignment but also insisted on paying their own expenses.

Though the American party was eagerly awaited in Europe, few people gave the committees much chance of success. The gap between the Germans and the French seemed unbridgeable. The Germans argued that the collapse of the mark was proof enough of their bankruptcy and that for them to pay reparations was impossible. The French, by contrast, saw the collapse of the mark as evidence of capital flight from Germany. How could it claim to be bankrupt when so many rich Germans seemed to be wandering around Europe? Every newspaper was filled with stories of German nouveaux riches flaunting their newly acquired wealth in foreign watering holes, calling attention to themselves by their bad manners and flagrantly conspicuous consumption. The British were caught in the middle. Since the occupation of the Ruhr, public opinion had shifted decisively in favor of Germany, which the French were seen to be trying to dismember, using reparations as an excuse. The British government argued that reparations had to be scaled back.

It was hard to see how a committee of technical experts, even if it did include some prominent Americans, could get the various parties to agree. After all, the premiers of Germany, France, Britain, Belgium, and Italy had met at least a dozen times—at Spa, at San Remo, at Cannes, and several times at conferences in Paris and London—without being able to find common ground, leaving a trail of failed negotiations, torn-up agreements, and bitter ill feeling.

Moreover, with the passage of time, the issue had become hopelessly entangled and complicated. The commission itself had held some four hundred sessions since its creation in 1919. The two Americans were amateurs who knew very little about the technical details, but each represented that new and distinctively American breed, the businessman-turned-political-troubleshooter who was much like his cousin, the Wall Street–lawyer-turned-diplomat. They were down-to-earth practical men who, though they might know little about the precise problem at hand, prided themselves on their ability to cut through rhetoric and obfuscation, and come up with a solution by applying simple old-fashioned American common sense.

On the transatlantic voyage, the American team—General Dawes; his brother Rufus, who was to be the committee's chief of staff; Owen Young; and various aides seconded from government departments in Washington—debated their strategy. Some argued that the committee should cut through the confusion and go directly to the heart of the matter—explicitly recognize that Germany simply could not pay what was demanded of it, estimate what it could come up with, and recommend that figure as what it should pay.

Young took the position that the simple and direct approach would not work. The total figure for reparations, $12.5 billion, was too politically charged a number, particularly in France. Tampering with it would inevitably lead to confrontation. To challenge the French at this stage of the negotiations would bog them down in the sort of wrangling that had produced no results for the last three years. Instead, Young proposed that the committee focus on the very limited but achievable goal of reducing the amount Germany would have to pay in the immediate future to a more manageable level.

The committee should jettison the whole concept of "capacity to pay," he argued. It was impossible to know what this number was. Too many imponderables entered into the calculation, involving such questions as: How much could taxes be raised without triggering mass protest? How tightly could imports be squeezed without precipitating a collapse in production? How far could wages be reduced without provoking labor unrest?

No one could agree on the answers to such cosmic questions. What was needed was a completely new approach to the problem.

In its place, he proposed an alternative criterion: the German public should be required to shoulder the same tax burden as British and French taxpayers. Britain and France had to tap their tax revenues to pay interest on their own internal debts. Germany had inflated away its internal public debt—the Germans, therefore, had a natural surplus from which they could afford to pay reparations. Here was a principle that was easily quantifiable, would be viewed as fair in the court of world public opinion, and would be hard for Germany to argue against. It injected "both the element of novelty and a defensible moral principle" into the whole discussion.

Landing at Le Havre on January 7, the Americans traveled by train to Paris, where they checked into the Ritz. On January 14, the ten-man expert committee held its first meeting at the offices of the Reparations Commission, housed in the Hotel Astoria, a Belle Époque *hotel de luxe* situated at the top of the Champs-Élysées by the Arc de Triomphe. Before the war, the hotel had been popular with rich visiting shoppers. But its conveniently central location and wonderful view of the Arc doomed it to spend the next thirty years under constant requisition by whichever government happened to be in power. The German invasion plans of 1914 had it earmarked for the kaiser's Paris headquarters. In August 1914, it had been shut down by the French authorities because the owner was suspected of being a German spy. In 1919, it had provided one of the homes of the two-hundred-strong British delegation to the Peace Conference. In 1921, while all the other great hotels were profiting from the enormous influx of tourists drawn to Paris by the cheap franc, the Astoria was taken over by the reparations commission.*

Though the Europeans were the most knowledgeable on the technical

---

* In 1940, during the German occupation of Paris, the Astoria would be commandeered by the occupation forces. Subsequently, when the city was liberated in 1944 by the Allies, it would be taken over as General Eisenhower's Paris headquarters. Torn down in the 1950s, its successor building became famous to visitors to Paris in the 1960s as Le Drugstore.

details about reparations, the Americans came to dominate the proceedings. Dawes neither possessed, nor pretended to, the financial expertise to unravel the tangle of claims and counterclaims. He was the cheerleader of the committee, its public face, who used an extensive network of friends within France accumulated during the war to smooth relations with the prickly French. The press loved him. With his quaint pipe and his picturesque language—he called the German nationalists "those foul and carrion-loving vultures" and derided economic experts for their "impenetrable and colossal fog-bank" of opinion—he made great copy.

Young was the brains of the operation. He and Dawes were joined by a third American, Colonel James Logan, Strong's fraternity mate from The Family, who had first come to Paris in 1914 and stayed on after the war and was now the U.S. observer to the Reparations Commission. Through a combination of charm and force of personality, he had become a figure of some renown in Parisian social and diplomatic circles, entertaining so frequently at Voisins, the famous three-star restaurant on the Rue Saint Honoré that it was nicknamed "Logies" by visiting American diplomats. Though only an observer, without any official status, Logan had done more than almost anyone else to keep the United States engaged in Continental affairs and was viewed as the unofficial U.S. ambassador to Europe.

As the committee began its deliberations, it found itself facing two tasks. The first was to persuade the French to accede to a lower payment schedule, at least temporarily, to which they would only agree if stringent foreign controls were imposed on the management of German finances. The French saw German hyperinflation as part of a deliberate campaign by its officials to wreck their own economy and thus prevent reparations from being paid. Some mechanism for preventing any future sabotage of Germany's finances had to be put in place. The second task was therefore to persuade the Germans to accept such an imposition.

The first task became much easier when within a week of the delegation's arrival, France was plunged into its own financial crisis. French finances since the war had been a cross between those of Germany and of

Britain. The war had cost it dearly—in blood and money. In the immediate aftermath it was forced to spend $4 billion on reconstructing the liberated territories. Still unreconciled to its enormous sacrifices, the French government refused to raise taxes to pay for this, stubbornly clinging to the illusion that the costs would eventually be recouped from Germany. "*Les Boches paieront*" "The Krauts will pay"—was the refrain. Like Germany, therefore, France had been slow to bring its deficits under control; five years after the war, the government was still borrowing $1 billion a year.

The French financial situation was exacerbated by a hopelessly primitive system of public accounts. Despite its much vaunted corps of *inspecteurs des finances*, there were huge gaps in its books and no one seemed to know precisely how much had been spent during the war, on what and by whom. It was even hard to reckon the total amount of borrowings—in 1922, an audit discovered that the volume of National Defense Bonds issued had been overestimated by the equivalent of $500 million. Controls over money flowing in and out of the treasury were so rudimentary that during the coming crisis, in a swindle that was never to be solved, $150 million of National Defense Bonds that were generally issued in bearer form and therefore untraceable, disappeared mysteriously from the treasury—in relative terms the equivalent today would be a fraud of $30 billion.

But unlike its German counterpart, the Banque de France was determined to reassert its independence after the war and refused to float the government any longer. Though the French government was able to borrow in the open market because of the high savings rate of its citizens, most of the debt was short term, had to be constantly rolled over, and the government was forced to live a sort of hand-to-mouth existence, always nervous that suddenly its creditors would get fed up and go on a lending strike.

Before the war, there had been just over 5 French francs to the dollar. By the early 1920s, following the wartime trebling of French prices, the franc had stabilized at about a third of its prewar level, about 15 to the dollar. During the latter half of 1923, it became apparent that the invasion of the Ruhr had been a failure and the likelihood of France being able to cover its budget deficit from reparations was increasingly remote. By the beginning of 1924, the exchange rate had fallen to 20 francs to the dollar.

On January 14, the day the Dawes Committee, as it was now being called, began its deliberations, the exchange value of the franc plunged by around 10 percent in a single day. Though it appeared to steady during the next few weeks, it began falling again after mid-February and in two days, March 6 and 7, lost another 10 percent, reaching 27 francs to the dollar on March 8. There were scenes of pandemonium in the Salle des Banquiers at the Bourse as a wildly gesticulating crowd of currency brokers and bankers' agents frantically tried to unload their francs.

The authorities were adamant that foreign speculators, orchestrated in a grand conspiracy by the German government, were to blame. Convinced that finance had become war by other means, officials resorted to military analogies. Prime Minister Poincaré declared in the National Assembly that he had in his possession a secret document outlining a "plan for an offensive against the franc," which Stresemann was supposed to have circulated to a conclave of German bankers at the Hotel Adlon. The "attack" was to be "launched" from Amsterdam, where German business houses had allegedly accumulated a reserve fund of 13 billion francs. It was reported in a U.S. newspaper that the Lutheran pastors of America had received a letter suggesting that they urge their flock to dump francs in order to "assist in bringing France to her knees." The French were then, and would remain for many decades, obsessed with the specter of foreign speculators. Keynes described their attitude in the preface specially written for the French edition the *Tract on Monetary Reform:* "Each time the franc loses value, the Minister of Finance is convinced that the fact arises from everything but economic causes. He attributes it to the presence of a foreigner in the neighborhood of the Bourse or to the mysterious and malignant influences of speculation. This is not far removed intellectually from an African witch doctor's ascription of cattle disease to the 'evil eye' of a bystander and of bad weather to the unsatisfied appetites of an idol."

On March 13, the French government announced that J. P. Morgan & Co. had lent it $100 million on the security of its gold reserves. The conditions attached were made public, including the usual clauses about the government taking steps to balance its budget, reduce expenditures, and float no new loans. But it was also rumored that Morgans, normally considered one of the most pro-French of all American investment houses, had also secretly insisted that the French government bind itself to accepting whatever plan the Dawes Committee might issue. Just the announcement of the loan was enough to turn things around and the franc rebounded from 29 to 18 to the dollar, an appreciation of more than 60 percent in two weeks.

As for Germany, the Dawes Committee quickly recognized that much had changed in the month since it had been appointed. The economic situation had been transformed: the currency was stabilized and the budget was swinging back into balance. Meanwhile, everyone was acclaiming Schacht "the miracle worker."

In the middle of January 1924, Schacht, by now back in Berlin, received an invitation—he called it a "summons"—to appear before the committee in Paris. Arriving on Saturday, January 19, he made the first of his many presentations to the experts at the Hotel Astoria that same afternoon. As he sat on a "stool of repentance" in the middle of the room, like a prisoner in the dock, with the experts ranked before him like hanging judges, it was hard for him to hide his resentment at his country's future being determined in a converted hotel dining room in Paris.

On Monday, January 21, he appeared again for three hours, and testified the next day as well. Although he grumbled that all these presentations were taking him away from the important business of getting the German currency into shape, he clearly relished the spotlight. Speaking without notes, he described the situation in Germany in 1919, "drained dry by the war": the impact of reparations and inflation, the currency reform, the workings of the new Rentenmark, and the plans for the new gold discount bank he was putting together. As he responded in fluent French or English to the committee's questions, he found it hard to keep that inevitable note of self-congratulation out of his replies. "His pride is equaled only by his ability and desire for domination," wrote Dawes in his journal that evening. Nevertheless, the committee could not help being impressed by his grasp of the situation.

Alerted from the start to the size of Schacht's ego—Dawes noting that the most "remarkable revelation of character" came when Schacht baldly told the commission, "As long he was President [of the Reichsbank], he was the Bank"—the committee went out of its way to court him and involve him at every stage in their deliberations.

It decided that it was essential to get Schacht on board in any scheme of foreign supervision of German monetary policy. It dared not risk a confrontation that might undermine or derail his very successful efforts to stabilize the currency, thus provoking a flight of capital that would only compound its difficulties; but it also feared that if it allowed him to get too far ahead of it in his own plans, it might later prove difficult to rein him in.

In the space of only two months, Schacht had gone from being a relatively obscure banker to becoming the key German official to deal with, the man who could deliver. Alexandre Millerand, the president of the republic, invited him to the Élysée. It was even strongly suggested that he call on the germanophobe Poincaré, instigator of the Ruhr invasion. When Schacht declared that he was open to such an invitation, he was told that protocol required that he take the initiative by requesting an audience. He duly complied, presenting himself punctually at 5:00 p.m. one evening at Poincaré's offices on the Quai d'Orsay; but when the prime minister kept him waiting for thirty minutes, Schacht, prickly as ever, stormed out and had to be coaxed back by a group of alarmed functionaries.

On January 31, the committee of experts traveled to Berlin by special train, the first train to go directly from Paris to Berlin since the war, to see for itself the hardships wrought thus far by reparations. German officials, keen to ensure that the visitors obtain enough of an impression of their people's privations, arranged for the electricity in the hotels housing the commission to be deliberately shut off early.

In dealing with the committee, Schacht faced a real dilemma. On the one hand, he was enough of a realist to recognize that while it needed him, he could not afford to alienate it. He could only go so far on his own. Only a group of foreign experts would have the stature to negotiate lower reparations or make it possible to mobilize a foreign loan. Typically, though, one of his biggest concerns seems to have been that the foreigners might try to take the credit for his achievements.

On the other hand, he remained convinced that Germany could not afford to pay anywhere close to the reparations envisaged by the London schedule. He believed that the Dawes approach of not tampering with the total amount of obligations was fundamentally flawed. For the moment, however, he held his peace. Over the next few weeks, Schacht became the critical German interlocutor for the committee when it came to financial reform and the Reichsbank. Although mutual interest kept both parties scrupulously polite to each other, there nevertheless remained an undercurrent of tension in their dealings.

On April 9, the committee issued its plan. As Young had insisted, it very deliberately avoided pronouncing either on the total amount of reparations that Germany should owe or the period over which they should be paid, but focused purely on what should be paid over the next few years. It proposed that Germany begin at $250 million in the first year, and progressively increase the amount to $600 million a year by the end of the decade. By one calculation, using some plausible assumptions about the total period over which Germany might remain obligated, the practical effect of the Dawes Plan was to reduce Germany's debt from $12.5 billion to around $8 to $10 billion.

But the plan's most novel feature was to put in place an ingenious mechanism to ensure that reparations could not undermine the mark as they had in 1922–23. The money to pay reparations was to be raised initially in marks by the German government and paid into a special escrow account in the Reichsbank, where it would fall under the control of an agent-general for reparations who would be responsible for deciding whether these funds could be safely transferred abroad without disrupting the value of the mark. The power was vested in this new office to decide how these funds should be put to use—whether to be paid out abroad, used to buy German goods, or even to provide credit to local businesses. The agent-general would be in a remarkably strong position, a sort of economic pro-consul or viceroy. To make his impartiality completely transparent, the committee recommended that he be an American.

A second and ultimately the central feature of the Dawes Plan was that a loan of $200 million be raised abroad to help pay the first year of repara-tions, to recapitalize the Reichsbank and build up enough gold reserves to jump-start the domestic economy.

Although the French pressed to move the Reichsbank totally out of Germany, possibly to Amsterdam, the rest of the committee recognized that this would be the ultimate humiliation, putting Germany on the same footing as the indigent nations of Egypt and Turkey—in the words of one participant, it would "turkify" the German economy. Instead, the commit-tee managed to persuade all parties, even the French and the Germans, that the Reichsbank should be kept in Berlin but placed under the control of a fourteen-member board, seven foreigners and seven Germans, one of whom would of course be Schacht.

IN JULY 1924, the allies convened a conference in London on how to implement the Dawes Plan. It was the greatest gathering of statesmen since the Paris Peace Conference of 1919. Ramsay MacDonald, the first Socialist prime minister of Britain, who doubled as his own foreign secre-tary, presided. Among his guests were Édouard Herriot, the new Radical prime minister of France, the prime ministers of Belgium and of Italy, and the ambassador of Japan. The United States had initially planned not to attend, for fear of being tainted by too close an association with repara-tions, then viewed as a horrible European disease. However, when the British government allowed its official invitation to the United States to be leaked, the Coolidge administration, which had played such an impor-tant part in getting the Dawes Plan started, felt that it could not refuse without undermining its own efforts, and decided on a public show of support. Frank Kellogg, the white-haired U.S. ambassador to Great Britain, was assigned to lead the U.S. delegation.

Such was the interest within the administration in the outcome of the Dawes Plan, that several cabinet members contrived to find excuses to be in London. Charles Evans Hughes, the secretary of state, arrived ostensibly to attend the annual meeting of the American Bar Association, while Andrew Mellon, the secretary of the treasury, decided that this was an opportune moment to pass through London for some grouse shooting and possibly to see his Savile Row tailor.

Despite all these political luminaries, the central figures in the negotiations were to be two bankers: Montagu Norman and Thomas Lamont of J. P. Morgan & Co. Norman had been at first skeptical of the Dawes Committee. Asked by the prime minister to be one of the British delegates, he had begged off with the excuse that he was too busy at the Bank. If past experience was anything to go by, any committee appointed by the Reparations Commission was bound to get bogged down in political wrangling and would end up deadlocked. As he wrote to Strong, "It looks to me as if that Committee will be finding themselves in great difficulties . . . it is clear that there are as many angles of vision as there are members on that committee."

But during February and March, as the nature of the Dawes Committee's recommendations gradually filtered out, he had begun to change his mind. The heart of the plan, and the reparations settlement it envisaged, was the international loan, over whose terms, Norman realized, he was in a position to exert enormous leverage.

The business of lending to foreign governments was historically one of the more glamorous aspects of banking. Before the war, lending had been firmly in the hands of two British banks with long and storied histories—Baring Brothers and Rothschilds.

Barings was the oldest merchant bank in London—the male descendants of all five of the sons of the original founder, Thomas Baring, now sat in the House of Lords. In 1802, it had helped the U.S. government finance the purchase of the Louisiana Territory from a Napoléon desperate for cash. So great was its authority at one time, that the Duc de Richelieu in 1817 spoke of the "six main powers in Europe; Britain, France, Austria-Hungary, Russia, Prussia and Baring Brothers."

Rothschilds had had an even more eventful history. The family had made its fortune during the Napoleonic Wars. With five branches of the family spread across Europe—in London, Paris, Frankfurt, Vienna, and Naples—it had the most extensive network of contacts of any bank, and its sources of information were legendary. One story was that the family had learned, by homing pigeon, of Napoléon's defeat at Waterloo a day before the rest of London, including before the government itself, and had made an enormous fortune by buying up government bonds. The story was, in fact, seriously wrong—although Rothschilds did learn of the victory before anyone else in London, it actually lost money from betting that the war would still go on for a while by having large amounts of gold bullion in stock—but the myth remained. So great was the Rothschild mystique that the economist J. A. Hobson, echoing a widely shared opinion, wrote in 1902 that no great war could be "undertaken by any European state . . . if the house of Rothschild and its connections set their face against it."

But after the war, with London itself short of capital, the Bank of England had had to impose an unofficial embargo on foreign loans by British houses, and both banks were shadows of their former selves. The mantle of "Banker to the World" shifted from Britain to the United States, though American money, unused to the vagaries of international politics, flowed in fits and starts. The three American firms that had come to dominate the sovereign loan market were the National City Bank, Kuhn Loeb, and—not the largest but the most prestigious—J. P. Morgan & Co.

The House of Morgan had been powerful before the war, helping to finance and restructure the steel, railway, and shipping industries; it had even bailed out the U.S. government in 1895 and saved the banking system in 1907. But its business had been largely domestic. Pierpont Morgan himself had indeed been a well-known figure in Europe, and his father, Junius

Morgan, had helped the French government raise money to pay the indemnity after the Franco-Prussian war of 1870; but in international ranking, J. P. Morgan & Co. had been a second-tier house.

The war had transformed its position. Chosen as the sole purchasing agent of both the British and the French governments in 1914, it had become a power unto itself. Its fourteen partners, who sat together in a large gloomy common office where they could overhear one another's conversations, now supposedly earned an average of $2 million a year. When the war ended, Morgans became the natural conduit of American money into Europe. Its status as one of the great powers to be reckoned with was confirmed in July 1920, when a group of anarchists, instead of targeting a head of state or government as it might have done before the war, chose to place a bomb outside the offices of J. P. Morgan & Co. at 23 Wall Street.* The partners were unscathed, but thirty-eight bystanders were killed and another four hundred injured.

No one exemplified the new role of banker-statesman better than Thomas Lamont, by 1924 the most senior partner after Jack Morgan. The urbane and ever-charming Lamont seemed to have been born under a lucky star. The son of an austere Methodist minister, young Thomas had spent his youth growing up in New England village parsonages, brought up to believe that dancing, playing cards, and even leisurely Sunday strolls were sinful. He attended Phillips Exeter Academy and Harvard on scholarship, and became a financial reporter for the *New York Tribune*, but finding it hard to raise a family on a journalist's salary, he entered the food distribution business. Like Benjamin Strong, a resident of Englewood, New Jersey, he had been plucked from obscurity by Henry Davison, whom he encountered one evening on the commuter train from New York and who is supposed to have recruited him then and there as secretary-treasurer at Bankers Trust.

In 1911, following in Davison's footsteps, Lamont was offered a partner-

---

*Between 1894 and 1914, six heads of state were assassinated by terrorists. See Barbara Tuchman, *The Proud Tower* (New York: Bantam Books, 1966), p. 72.

ship by Pierpont Morgan—then the most prestigious and lucrative job on Wall Street. Lamont initially declined, saying that he wished to have the freedom to travel for three months a year. But Mr. Morgan insisted and Lamont unsurprisingly gave way.

His involvement, as a Morgan partner, in the wartime finances of Britain and France brought him a place on the U.S. reparations team at the Peace Conference. After the war, though a Republican, he broke with the isolationist wing of his party and became a committed internationalist. In those early postwar years, he was the financial emissary par excellence. In 1920, he was in China and Japan; in 1921, in Mexico City as chairman of the International Committee of Bankers for Mexico; in early 1923, in Europe planning a loan to Austria and advising the Italian government. Everywhere he went he was received with the pomp and the deference due to a head of state. In May 1922, when Davison suddenly died of cancer, Lamont stepped into his shoes.

His outside activities not only reinforced the impression that here was a man of the new aristocracy, they also added to his aura of effortless grace. He acquired Alexander Hamilton's old newspaper the *New York Evening Post* and helped start and finance the *Saturday Review of Literature*. He had friends who were writers—at his dinner table one might find H. G. Wells or André Maurois or John Masefield.

Just before the conference was to open, Lamont was dispatched to London with a watching brief for the House of Morgan during the negotiations. He quickly fell under the spell of Norman, who seemed to have an uncanny ability to take visiting American bankers under his wing and fashion them to his own ends. Though Norman suddenly collapsed from "nervous exhaustion" just as the conference was about to open and lay bedridden for a week, by July 15, he was back in the thick of the action.

At the invitation of Prime Minister MacDonald, the two bankers set forth the main conditions that investors would demand before lending money under the Dawes Plan. Recognizing that those who would provide the capital had enormous leverage, Norman insisted that neither British nor American bankers touch the loan "until the French are out of the Ruhr bag and baggage"; and to preclude any further such preemptive and uni-lateral military actions by France, the right to declare Germany in default of its payments was to be vested, not in the Reparations Commission, dominated as it was by the French, but in an independent agency to be run by a neutral American.

For the next four weeks the negotiations centered on these two points. Every time the politicians seemed about to stitch together a compromise, and to paper over their differences, the two bankers—led largely by Nor-man, although Lamont was the spokesman—would return insistently to these core proposals, which, they kept reiterating, were not political dic-tates set by some hidden money power but simply the most elementary conditions that any investors would require as security before committing capital to Germany.

Prime Minister MacDonald, a Socialist and erstwhile pacifist, with a jaundiced view of bankers and their motives, tried to bully the pair with denunciations of their meddling in politics. Owen Young tried to browbeat them into softening their conditions, threatening to go around Morgans and arrange a loan though Dillon Read. All to no avail.

The leader of the French delegation, Prime Minister Herriot, by back-ground a historian more at home in the Left Bank literary salons of Paris than laboring over financial minutiae in a conference room, came to the negotiating table radically unprepared and found himself outfoxed at every turn. A passionate and emotional intellectual, he injected a certain operatic quality into the proceedings by more than once publicly bursting into tears of frustration. He was constantly at odds with his forty-man team, a mot-ley crew of cabinet colleagues, Socialist deputies, and provincial Radical committee presidents, a "swarming, gesticulating, vociferous horde" of amateur diplomats, who turned the lobby of the French embassy in Lon-don into "a public meeting hall without a chairman to arbitrate disputes and without police to throw out the disorderly." At one point, Herriot and his minister of war, General Charles Nollet, got into such a long alterca-tion at an evening meeting at 10 Downing Street that MacDonald declared an adjournment and went to bed. Even then, the two Frenchmen continued to harangue each other as they left the building, and stood screaming insults at each other in the middle of Downing Street.

Herriot called upon Lamont at his residence in Audley Square to plead with him, reminding him of the historic ties between France and the House of Morgan, but Lamont refused to make any concessions. Instead, over the next few weeks, Lamont tightened the screws by making it clear that unless the French became more amenable, Morgans might find it extremely difficult to roll over the loan it had raised for them earlier in the year.

The humiliating spectacle of Anglo-Saxon bankers dictating to their politicians infuriated French public opinion. The Parisian paper *Le Petit Bleu* declared that "Europe shall not become a vast field of exploitation with its only government a vast bankers' combine." Edwin James of the *New York Times* reported that many Frenchmen were convinced that "America's only purpose is to make some more money out of Europe's misfortunes, and that instead of helping France get reparations, the Americans are working on Shylock lines for the preliminary loan." In the United States, as highly respected a newspaper as the Springfield *Republican* commented, "In the lean years that follow an exhausting war, financiers outrank generals. . . . No loan, no Dawes plan. No Dawes plan, no settlement. No settlement, no peace in Europe. . . ."

By the beginning of August the bankers had won. The only concession the French were able to extract was to delay their withdrawal from the Ruhr by a year. Germany was invited to send a delegation to finalize the arrangements. On August 3, the German delegation, led by Chancellor Marx and including Gustav Stresemann, now foreign minister; Finance Minister Hans Luther; Secretary of State Schubert; and Schacht, arrived at the London Ritz. The first plenary session took place on August 5—the first formal meeting between the respective heads of the German and French governments since the Franco-Prussian war of 1870. For the next ten days, as the interminable wrangling began, the conference staggered from one crisis to another, constantly verging on the edge of collapse.

The procedure for declaring a default specified that sanctions could be imposed only in the event of a "flagrant" failure on the part of Germany to fulfill its obligations. The Germans demanded a definition of *flagrant*. That bickering consumed a day. The French had agreed to withdraw from the Ruhr after a year. The Germans wanted to know when the year would begin, and further demanded that the evacuation be completed within a year.

Finally, on August 14, the definitive terms were submitted to the German delegation, who were granted the night to accept or reject them. The Germans gathered in one of the rooms at the Ritz for an all-night session. Each of them spoke his mind. As dawn arrived, the chancellor went around the room with a last poll. All voted for acceptance, except for Schacht, who said, in his harsh Frisian accent, "We cannot accept the terms—we can never fulfill them." He insisted that the Dawes Plan's failure to reduce the total level of reparations was its fatal flaw. But it was Stresemann who had the final word. "We must get the French out of the Ruhr. We must free the Rhineland. We must accept."

ON THE SURFACE, the Dawes Plan appeared to be the turning point for Europe. The wrangling over reparations, which had consumed the energy of officials for the last five years, seemed to be over. In September, the loan that formed the basis of the plan was successfully floated in New York and London. It started a boom in lending to Germany by American banks that was to fuel a recovery in its economy for the next several years and bring stability to the new currency.

Young, the true architect of the plan, had believed that in the climate of bitterness and recrimination prevailing in 1924, Europe would be able to improvise its way toward an eventual solution only by avoiding confronting its problems head-on. The plan had therefore very deliberately swept a whole series of issues under the carpet. The total bill for reparations remained unspecified. As a result, resentment within Germany continued to fester just below the surface. Moreover, the new German prosperity depended on what Keynes described as " a great circular flow of paper" across the Atlantic: "The United States lends money to Germany, Germany transfers its equivalent to the Allies, the Allies pay it back to the United States government. Nothing real passes—no one is a penny the worse. The engravers' dies, the printers' forms are busier. But no one eats less, no one works more." No one was willing to predict what would happen once the music stopped.

Nevertheless, the initial fanfare associated with the plan did catapult Charles Dawes, hitherto a relatively obscure financier, to fame and fortune. In the summer of 1924, Coolidge selected him to be his running mate; Dawes was elected vice president of the United States that autumn. For having bought time for Europe and at least created the illusion that the Continent's battles over money were finally over, he was awarded the 1925 Nobel Prize for peace.

12. THE GOLDEN CHANCELLOR

BRITAIN: 1925

"I never knew a man who had better motives for all the trouble he caused."

—GRAHAM GREENE, *The Quiet American*

By 1924, London had shaken off the grim austerity of the war years and was basking happily and prosperously, as Robert Graves put it, "in the full sunshine of Peace." The shops were crowded, the theaters and cinemas filled to capacity, the streets jammed with traffic. Regent Street had been made over and transformed into a broad thoroughfare, its refurbished buildings gleaming.

Whereas in Germany, a demobilized army officer might find his calling in a right-wing death squad, his counterpart in Britain had plunged into commercial life—it was said that most of the fleets of motor buses that jammed the streets of London were owned and operated by syndicates of former army officers. There was a new freedom in the air. At night, in the West End, the bright young things who set the pace for London society had discovered dancing: the jog-trot, the vampire, the camel-walk, the shimmy, and most infamous of all, the Charleston. That, and a modest relaxation in the wartime liquor-licensing laws, had fueled an explosion in the number of nightclubs. On Bond Street was the Embassy Club, a favorite haunt of the Prince of Wales and the smart set. In the Haymarket was the fashionable Kit-Kat Club, which boasted a dance floor for four hundred and was where Edwina and Dickie Mountbatten could be found most evenings. At 43 Gerard Street was the more raffish and bohemian "43" Club, frequented by, among others, the crown prince of Sweden, Prince Nicholas of Romania, Tallulah Bankhead, Augustus John, and Joseph Conrad. In April 1924, in a scandal that shook all London society, it was raided by the police and one of its members, the well-known London restaurateur "Brilliant" Chang, was arrested for running a cocaine ring.

But while London and the Southeast were celebrating the return of peace and prosperity, not more than a hundred miles north of the capital was another country. The industrial heartland of Britain—the Midlands and the North—was struggling while London danced. The great traditional industries—the cotton mills of Lancashire, the coal mines of Nottinghamshire and South Wales, and the shipbuilding yards along the Tyne—once the engines of the Victorian boom, but now priced out of world markets, had fallen into a severe slump. Textile exports were half of what they had been in 1913, and it was the same with coal. Over a million and a quarter men were unemployed and another million were on part-time work. In some places—the dreary colliery districts of Yorkshire or the blighted ship-building town of Jarrow—one man out of every two was on the dole.

The irony was that Britain's economic troubles were not the result of ineptitude or the wages of financial sin but the unfortunate side effect of a high degree of financial piety and rectitude. The decision to deflate the economy in 1920 and 1921 to reverse wartime inflation had partially succeeded. Prices came down by 50 percent from their postwar peak and the weakness in the currency was reversed—the pound, which had touched $3.20, had rebounded fitfully and erratically to $4.30. But the price of financial orthodoxy had been stiff. While Britain had recovered from the recession of 1921, the rebound had been muted. The City of London, finding it difficult to compete with New York for funds, had been forced to impose a regime of high interest rates, and unemployment remained stubbornly stuck above 10 percent.

The comparison between Britain and France was striking. Solid conservative Britain had pursued the most orthodox and prudent financial policies of any European power, refusing to inflate its way out of debt or to allow its currency to collapse, and had been rewarded with the highest unemployment rate in Europe and a limping economy. By contrast, France had been invaded during the war, suffered the highest ratio of casualties of any country other than Serbia, and seen large tracts of its most productive land leveled and destroyed. After the war, the French had resorted to inflation to lighten the burden of debt and to a weak franc to steal a march on the British by cheapening their goods. Though the government had continuously staggered on the edge of insolvency since the war, the overall economy had done well; exports had boomed. The number of unemployed in France was a fraction of that in Britain. As one contemporary journalist summarized it, "While England is financially sound and economically sick, France is economically sound and financially sick."

All of this self-inflicted pain might have been worthwhile if in the process Britain had been able to achieve its overriding postwar economic objective: the restoration of the pound to its prewar pedestal. But even here the rewards of virtue proved to be elusive

By the fall of 1924, the pound was stuck. Having floated at around $4.35 for two years, it seemed unable to rise any further. Despite mass unemployment and high interest rates, prices in Britain still remained stubbornly elevated compared to the United States. Even if by most calculations the discrepancy was only 10 percent, that last 10 percent was proving to be the hardest.

Facing an economy in poor shape, prices that were too high, and a currency apparently stuck some 15 percent below its prewar parity, one school of economists argued that the authorities should abandon their dogged attempt to depress prices further and with it the goal of restoring the prewar exchange rate. Any attempt in the current circumstances to return to gold

FIGURE 3

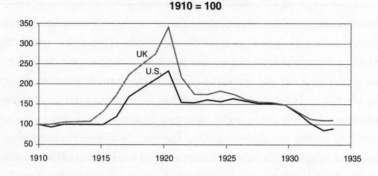

U.S. and UK Wholesale Prices: 1910–33
1910 = 100

In 1925, prices in the UK were still 10 percent too high.

at the old parity would just throw hundreds of thousands more people out of work. They argued that a new level for the pound should be selected that reflected the realities of postwar Britain: the changed international environment, the new competition, Britain's higher cost structure, and the transformation in its international balance sheet brought about by war.

To Norman and the purists within the Bank of England, this was unacceptable. They continued to press for a return to the old gold rate of $4.86, seeing it as a moral commitment on the part of the British nation to those around the world who had placed their assets, their confidence, and their trust in Britain and its currency.

Even the most orthodox among them—like Norman, who in 1918 had wanted to return to gold the moment the guns stopped firing—conceded that the time was not right. The Cunliffe committee of 1918 had originally estimated that it might take as much as a decade for Britain to return to the gold standard. In 1924, another committee, under the chairmanship of Austen Chamberlain, also recommended a delay of some years. Britain's economy was still not in shape to withstand the harsh medicine of a rise in its currency and the strictures of the gold standard.

The success of the Dawes Plan had been seen as a giant step in restoring financial order to continental Europe. The spotlight now shifted to Britain and the pound. With the mark stabilized and now fixed against gold, the universal question was: When would sterling follow? It was an uncomfortable position for Norman. He hated the prospect of having to operate under the white light of publicity. As he complained to Strong, "You know how controversial a subject it is—and how it is everybody's business."

He did worry that Britain was being left behind. Germany, Sweden, Poland, Austria, and Hungary had already returned to gold, while the Netherlands, Canada, Australia, New Zealand, and South Africa were all making plans to do so in the near future. Once all these currencies were stabilized, it would be hard to retain the pound's financial and trading preeminence. Merchants and investors would soon begin looking for an alternative. His fears that the newly stabilized mark might become the strongest on the Continent and supplant the pound were echoed by others in the City who warned that further delay would "hand over to Germany the financial scepter in Europe." Even Strong began kidding him that sterling was "rather far behind in the procession."

In November 1924, the political situation changed suddenly and dramatically. Since the war, Britain had faced an unusual series of fragile coalition and minority governments. The immediate postwar coalition of Conservatives and Lloyd George Liberals was followed in 1922 by a Conservative government, initially led by the dying Bonar Law, and six months later by Stanley Baldwin. In January 1924, a minority Labor government under Ramsay MacDonald took over, but that November, a wave of anticommunist sentiment, fueled by the publication of a fraudulent letter linking the Labor Party to the Soviet Union, led to a Conservative landslide. Norman's close friend Stanley Baldwin resumed the reins of power.

To everyone's surprise, Winston Churchill was appointed chancellor of the exchequer, the second most powerful position in government.

. . . .

No ONE WAS more taken aback by the appointment than Churchill himself. He was then a few days shy of fifty. After a spectacular early career—home secretary at the age of thirty-five and first lord of the admiralty in 1911—he had fallen on hard times. The debacle at Gallipoli in 1915 had been a turning point. Politically damaged, he had gone off to fight on the Western Front, continued to deliver his brilliant speeches, and had become a follower of Lloyd George; when the "Welsh Wizard" was ousted in 1922, Churchill had lost his seat in Parliament and spent the next two years trying to rehabilitate himself.

It was a daunting task. Within political circles, he was almost universally distrusted as a man who had changed parties not just once, but twice. In 1903, after the Tories had split over free trade and their political fortunes seemed bleak, he had crossed the floor to join the Liberals, becoming a junior minister in barely two years. Now again, in 1924, as the Liberals were being shunted into the political wilderness, he had abandoned them—although for the sake of form he did not formally join the Conservatives for several more years. Many people thought that vaulting ambition and poor judgment were hereditary traits of the Churchills, echoing Gladstone's verdict, "There never was a Churchill, from John Marlborough down, that had either morals or principles."

When Baldwin first offered him the chancellorship, Churchill himself was caught so much by surprise that, for a moment, he thought he was being offered the position of chancellor of the Duchy of Lancaster, a sine-cure office that served (and still serves) as a general utility post for junior ministers. So keen was he to return to power that he even toyed with the idea of accepting this position, which he had held a decade earlier in the aftermath of the Gallipoli disaster and had resigned in despair. When his appointment as chancellor was finally announced, there was outrage in the Conservative ranks, one minister complaining that he could not understand "how anybody can put their faith in a man who changes sides, just when he thinks it is to his own personal advantage to do so," and lamenting that the "turbulent pushing busybody Winston will split the party." But Baldwin was willing to weather the reaction of his many diehards, because, it was said, he wanted Churchill inside the government where he could keep an eye on him rather than outside, where he could only cause mischief.

Though everyone acknowledged his talents—formidable energy, exuberance, and restless imagination—many, particularly the more reactionary Tories, viewed Churchill as a pushy, self-promoting, ambitious political adventurer. The louche circle of friends with which he surrounded himself during those years only intensified doubts about his judgment. His three great cronies were Max Aitken, Lord Beaverbrook, the charming and manipulative press lord and a master of political intrigue; F. E. Smith, Lord Birkenhead, a dazzlingly clever lawyer, witty and articulate, who might have become the leader of the Conservative Party had he not been an alcoholic with a proclivity for seducing teenage girls; and Brendan Bracken, MP, an Australian-Irish rogue who fed the rumor that he was Churchill's illegitimate son.

Despite Norman's natural conservatism and his friendship with Baldwin, he did not particularly welcome the new Conservative government, fearing that it would allow its economic policies to fall into the hands of "traders and manufacturers, who, while they profess a remote affection for gold and a real affection for stability, always want a tot of brandy (in the shape of inflation)." And he naturally distrusted flamboyant characters like Churchill. The previous chancellor in the minority Labor government had been Philip Snowden, an intensely moralistic teetotaler, crippled by tuberculosis of the spine, who could only get around supported by two walking sticks. With his thin lips, icy eyes and bloodless skeletal face, his black suit and black Turkish cigarettes, he looked like an undertaker in a horror movie. But despite Snowden's fervent belief that capitalism was doomed and his suspicion of bankers, he had espoused the cause of orthodox finance and the gold standard with all the fervor of the old puritan radical stock from which he sprang and had developed an exceptionally close relationship with Norman.

Churchill and Norman could not have been more different. Churchill avidly sought publicity and had a terrible reputation for grandstanding. Norman chose to wrap himself in enigma, and shunned the limelight. Churchill courted the press lords. Norman considered them part of the vanguard of a new barbarism that preyed on the emotions of the expanded electorate. Churchill was naturally gregarious, loved company, and hated to be alone. Norman rarely socialized, buried himself in his work, and claimed that the Bank of England was "his only mistress." Churchill liked to argue and debate. Norman was reserved and uncommunicative, oddly inarticulate in public, and when confronted by opposition, he retreated into a shell of sullenness.

Their personal habits were also poles apart. Churchill was addicted to high living. He had a Rolls-Royce and a chauffeur and by his own admission had never been on a bus or on the Underground.* He kept an enormous retinue of twenty-four servants, and pampered himself with the finer things of life—silk underwear, champagne at every meal, Havana cigars, strings of polo ponies, and bouts at the gaming tables of Monte Carlo and Biarritz—and was predictably in perpetual debt. Norman, despite his inherited wealth and his grand house in Holland Park, lived an existence of almost monkish simplicity, sleeping on a plain iron bed in a bare room with paintings propped up against the wall and taking the Underground to work every day.

About the only things the two men shared was a common disdain for the parochial "Little Englanders," who would see Britain retreat from its role in the world, and a particular sympathy for the United States, an unusual trait among upper-class Englishmen who had reached maturity in the high noon of Edwardian England.

IN THE LAST few months of 1924, the pound began to rise, buoyed by speculators betting that the new Conservative government would return

---

*According to his wife, Clementine, the first time Churchill ever resorted to public transport was when he took the Underground during the 1926 general strike.

to gold. But the fundamental discrepancy between British prices and American prices remained, and Norman was still unsure whether to press for an early return to gold. Nothing was more symbolic of the change in Britain's financial position than that before he could even think about doing so, he first had to go to New York to consult with Strong.

He arrived in New York aboard the S.S. *Carania* on December 28, having managed to slip out of Britain "undetected, like a shadow in the dead of night," as one magazine put it. But he was quickly unmasked by reporters, provoking the usual speculation. One story had it that he was there to renegotiate the war debt; another hinted that he was on a secret but unspecified mission for the British government. One rumor even had him preparing U.S. bankers for the imminent return of sterling to gold. When pushed by the press for a statement, the bank's official spokesman expressed complete astonishment at his chief's appearance in New York, but glossed over it with the observation that because Norman was in the habit of taking a vacation at this time of year, his absence had gone "unremarked."

The embassy in Washington was more inventive. Two months earlier, the New York Fed had moved into new headquarters on Liberty Street, which boasted not only a giant vault for the bank's very considerable gold reserves, carved out of the solid bedrock of Manhattan and protected by doors ten feet thick and weighing 230 tons each, but also new mechanized coin-handling machines that sorted the twenty tons of nickels, dimes, quarters, and half dollars that clinked in every day. Because the Bank of England was itself about to embark on a construction project to expand its venerable London headquarters, Norman had obviously come to the United States to pick up points.

Norman had not been in the United States for two years. Buoyed by new industries such as automobiles, radios, household appliances, electrical machinery, and plastics, the U.S. economy was just embarking on the spectacular boom of the 1920s. The physical transformation of the city was remarkable. Most noticeable was the number of cars on the road, which had doubled since he was last there—there were now as many on the streets of New York City alone as there were in the whole German republic. Despite the introduction of traffic signals in Manhattan earlier that year, there were still constant jams and everyone complained about the congestion. It was not only the automobile. There had been a dizzying revolution in the types of goods available— household appliances such as washing machines and vacuum cleaners, new materials such as rayon and cellophane, radios and talking movies—that were changing the whole texture of life. The contrast between the gaudy prosperity of the United States, where a typical worker was earning close to $6 a day, with the dingy poverty of postwar Europe, where workers earned less than $2 a day, was another reminder of the terrible price exacted by the war.

Strong was waiting enthusiastically at the pier. He was the U.S. official with the deepest understanding of international financial issues, the widest network of friends and contacts in European banking circles, and the strongest commitment to European reconstruction. Nevertheless, a combination of his ill health and the administration's official hands-off toward European financial affairs had left him relegated to the sidelines. In 1922, he had tried to involve himself in crafting a solution to German hyperinflation but had been expressly warned off by the secretary of state. For much of 1923 he had been ill. Then, earlier in 1924, he had again been excluded from the Dawes Plan negotiations by administration officials, except for a few informal discussions on a brief spring visit to London and Paris. He had fallen ill again on his return and had to spend part of the fall once more recuperating in Colorado.

But he remained convinced that given the importance of the pound to world trade, a global return to the gold standard would only be possible if Britain took the lead: "The great problem is sterling, the others will come along easily if sterling could be dealt with," he kept telling his colleagues.

Strong, who had just moved into a more spacious residence in the Maguery, an elegant apartment hotel located at Forty-eighth and Park Avenue, insisted that Norman stay with him. Over the next two weeks, during the day and in the evenings, Norman was subjected to an intense campaign by the Americans, especially by Strong and the Morgan bankers, to get the pound back on gold as soon as possible.

Strong did not have to persuade Norman of the consequences should Britain not return to gold. They agreed that this could only lead to "a long period of unsettled conditions too serious to contemplate. It would mean violent fluctuations in the exchanges, with probably progressive deterioration in the values of foreign currencies vis-a vis-the dollar; it would prove an incentive to all those who were advancing novel ideas for nostrums and expedients other than the gold standard to sell their wares; and incentives to governments at times to undertake various types of paper money expedients and inflation; it might indeed result in the United States draining the world of gold." It could but end, they believed, "with a terrible period of "hardship, and suffering, and . . . social and political disorder," culminating in some kind of "monetary crisis."

Strong stressed that the British had only a few weeks, at best months, to act. The pound was for the moment supported by the positive political developments at home; American capital was currently very optimistic about Europe in the wake of the Dawes Plan, and the Fed had been able to help Britain out by easing U.S. credit conditions in mid-1924. He warned that this narrow window would soon close, as Britain commenced war-debt payments, an outflow that was certain to weaken sterling. The Fed's easing of credit during 1924 had suited America's own domestic needs—the U.S. economy having suffered a mild and short-lived recession in the summer. But the time was fast approaching when the Fed would be forced to tighten credit for domestic reasons, making it difficult and more expensive for Britain to attract capital to support its currency. There were already murmurs within the corridors of the Fed that Strong was too greatly influenced by his friends in London.

He was acutely aware that British prices were still 10 percent too high, and that further deflation to cut them would bring further hardship. But he had become increasingly convinced that the British needed to be pushed into making the big decision—*force majeure*, he called it. The shock therapy of forcing Britain to compete in world markets, while painful, would bring about the necessary realignment in prices more efficiently than a long drawn-out policy of protracted tight credit.

The Americans recognized that if Britain did go back to gold, it was imperative that the link not snap at the first signs of trouble. Otherwise, the credibility of the whole system might be called into question, throwing all the world's currencies into turmoil. The government of the United States was in no position to lend money to any country—it had had enough of government-to-government lending during the war and was now saddled with renegotiating the terms of those loans. To ensure that Britain had adequate reserves to draw upon, Strong promised $200 million from the New York Fed. From the partners of J. P. Morgan came a further tentative commitment of $300 million.

Strong did impose one important condition: not, as might be supposed, a restriction on the economic policy of the Bank of England—how much credit it could provide or the level of interest rates it could set. The sole condition was that this loan would be available only while Norman remained governor.

As Norman set off homeward, perhaps because of the half-billion-dollar commitment that he metaphorically carried in his coat pocket, perhaps because of the powerful vote of confidence that he personally had received from the Americans, he was in an unusually sentimental mood. From on board the S.S. *France* he scribbled Strong a note:

> My dear Ben,
>
> You won't be expecting me to write you a letter. This beast of a ship rolls so much that I can hardly sit on a chair—much less write at a table. But whatever this year may bring forth for us, I am glad to have begun it with you: it is always true to say that we don't meet often enough. . . . We ought indeed to get together once a quarter if we are to keep together all the year; that much we shall hardly manage; I guess once in 6 months is more

> probable. At least we have made good beginning for
> 1925. . . . And you know, Ben, I am grateful for all your
> welcome and hospitality: and for all you do for me and
> are to me. God bless you.

NORMAN GOT BACK to London in the middle of January to find resistance building against any early return to gold. Even some of his closest allies at the Bank were beginning to resent the American pressure tactics, fearing that Britain might be borrowing too much money for an uncertain payoff.

The most articulate critic of resumption continued to be Maynard Keynes, who railed at those in charge at Threadneedle Street for acting like "the Louis XVI of the monetary revolution," and for "attacking the problems of the post-war world with unmodified pre-war views and ideas." But his own proposals for a managed currency, outlined in the *Tract*, had been largely ignored or disparaged. Recognizing that no one was taking his idea of managed money seriously, he beat a tactical retreat and began urging instead that any return to the gold standard be at least delayed until the discrepancy between British and American costs had narrowed.

His main point was that under current arrangements, given that U.S. gold reserves were so dominant, to tie the pound to gold in effect meant tying it to the dollar and the British economy to that of the United States—and by implication, to Wall Street. He did not attempt to conceal his distaste for what he, and all Bloomsbury with him, considered the crass materialism of the United States or for the prospect of having Britain's economic future determined by the needs of an America, imprisoned in its own insularity. "We should run the risk of having to curtail . . . credit to our industries," he wrote in one article, "merely because an investment boom in Wall Street had gone too far, or because of a sudden change in fashion amongst Americans towards foreign bond issues, or because banks in the Middle West had got tied up with their farmers or because of the horrid fact that every American had ten motor-cars and a wireless set in every room of every house had become known to manufacturers of these articles."

In article after article he returned to the same theme—that Britain, suffering from a slow rate of growth, exhausted finances, and "faults in her economic structure," was simply too weak to tether itself to a United States that seemed to "live in a vast and unceasing crescendo." The United States, with all its strength and dynamism, could "suffer industrial and financial tempests in the years to come, and they will scarcely matter to her; but England if she shares them, may almost drown." Few people, however, paid much attention to such gloomy prognostications.

Much more significant than Keynes's polemics was the opposition of Lord Beaverbrook. This elflike man with a larger-than-life personality was at the time the most dominant and successful newspaper proprietor in England. A Scots-Canadian by birth and a minister's son, though one might not have guessed it, he was a self-made millionaire many times over by the age of thirty-one, when he moved to England, in 1910. Seeing in the power of the press his path to the top, he acquired the *Daily Express*, a small loss-making newspaper with a circulation of some 200,000. By giving the public what it wanted—a bold and simply written paper full of gossip, sports, women's features, and articles about spiritualism and other social trends—he won it the largest circulation in the country with close to 1.5 million subscribers. Beaverbrook was an outsider to Britain, and like his paper, which appealed to all classes, he transcended the British class system. But as a Canadian, he retained a certain suspicion of the United States, and believed that a British return to gold would represent surrender to the Americans, who, according to him, were "pressing the return to the gold standard in order to mobilize the useless gold hordes [sic] of the United States." His view of the gold standard was incisive in its simplicity: "It is an absurd and silly notion that international credit must be limited to the quantity of gold dug up out of the ground. Was there ever such mumbo-jumbo among sensible and reasonable men?"

Beaverbrook and Churchill were both adventurers who, though the best of friends, rarely agreed.* On January 28, 1925, Beaverbrook came to see Churchill and his advisers, only to have his arguments casually dismissed by the Treasury officials. The following day he launched a front-page campaign against the gold standard in the *Daily Express*.

In reaction, Churchill decided one evening to compose a memorandum titled "The Return to Gold." He had found that one of the best ways for him to get his arms around a subject was to debate his own way through the issues. The chancellorship had been a mixed blessing. By his own admission, Churchill never had much interest in finance or economics and knew little about the subjects. He cheerfully liked to recount how his father, Lord Randolph Churchill, chancellor for six months in 1886, when confronted with a report full of figures with decimal points, declared he "never could make out what those damned dots mean." Winston himself, once chancellor, complained about the mandarins at the Treasury, "If they were soldiers or generals, I would understand what they were talking about. As it is they all talk Persian."

His memorandum, patronizingly nicknamed "Mr. Churchill's Exercise" within the Treasury, was a brilliant testament to his talent for self-education that should have put to rest the accusation that he was out of his depth when it came to finance. Circulated among senior Treasury officials and to Norman, it argued that the use of gold as the prime reserve was a "survival of a rudimentary and transitional stage in the evolution of finance and credit." Though the United States seemed "singularly anxious to help" the British return to the gold standard, the source of this "generosity is not perhaps remarkable when we consider her own position. She has by her hard treatment of her Allies, accumulated . . . probably nearly three quarters of the public gold in the world. She is now suffering from that glut of Gold," a large part of which was "lying idle in American vaults, playing no

---

*In old age, Churchill would remark that the only great issue on which they had agreed had been in support of Edward VIII during the abdication crisis and that perhaps they were both wrong that time.

part whatever in the economic life of the United States." Naturally, the Americans, so laden with the metal, had an incentive to ensure that it continued to play "as powerful and dominant a part" in world finance as possible. Churchill, however, questioned whether this was also to Britain's advantage and worried that while the return to gold was in the interest of City financiers, it might not be equally in the interest of the rest of Britain: "the merchant, the manufacturer, the workman, and the consumer." It was a document that could almost have been written by Maynard Keynes.

Norman tended to treat Churchill as one of those clever but erratic forces of nature who has to be carefully managed. Teddy Grenfell, the head of Morgan Grenfell, the House of Morgan's London arm, and a director of the Bank of England, summed it up the best: "We, and especially Norman, feel that the new Chancellor's cleverness, his almost uncanny brilliance, is a danger. At present he is a willing pupil but the moment he thinks he can stand on his own legs and believes that he understands economic questions he may, by some indiscretion, land us in trouble."

Norman's response to the memorandum was characteristic—a point-by-point analysis of the pros and cons of a policy was just not his style. Instead, he wrote to Churchill, "The Gold Standard is the best 'Governor' that can be devised for a world that is still human rather than divine." He warned the chancellor that if he were to choose to return to gold he might be "abused by the ignorant, the gamblers and the antiquated Industrialists," but if he were to choose against it, he "will be abused by the instructed and by posterity."

But Churchill had endured too hard a career in politics to be so easily intimidated by slogans. Over the next few days he zeroed in on the key social and political issue: that for all its benefits, gold, if restored, would end up exacting a heavy cost for those thrown out of work in British industries priced out of world markets. "The Governor of the Bank of England shows himself perfectly happy with the spectacle of Britain possessing the finest credit in the world simultaneously with a million and a quarter unemployed," he growled to his advisers.

Norman had never believed much in the benefits of economic policy analysis—he would later famously instruct the Bank of England's chief economist, "You are not here to tell us what to do, but to explain to us why we have done it"—and was now beginning to find the protracted debate irritating. Feeling "so weary and done up" that he "had to go to bed for 8 days," Norman chose this critical moment to take two weeks off in the south of France. Sometimes his behavior could be frustrating to even his closest friends. As Teddy Grenfell wrote, "Norman elaborates his own schemes by himself and does not take anyone into his counsel unless he is obliged to do so in order to combat opposition. . . . Monty works in his own peculiar way. He is masterful and very secretive."

Meanwhile, Churchill, who, if anything, could usually be counted on to act too hastily, was uncharacteristically having trouble reaching a decision. Both sides in the debate had marshaled a bewildering accumulation of data and arguments. "None of the witch doctors can see eye to eye and Winston cannot make up his mind from day-to day," wrote Otto Niemeyer, his principal adviser. The advice he was getting from within the Treasury and the Bank of England was, however, all one way. He must have been aware that opposing the return to gold would put him in direct confrontation with Norman, whose close friendship with Stanley Baldwin was no secret—Norman often stopped by 10 Downing Street at the end of the day for a quiet chat and was a frequent weekend visitor to Chequers, the prime minister's new official country residence. For the moment, Baldwin had kept out of the gold debate, but Churchill feared that Norman might go around him directly to the prime minister, whom he neither wanted nor was in a position to take on. Nevertheless, the criticisms raised by Beaverbrook and Keynes had a certain unsettling resonance.

Finally, on March 17, Churchill decided to convene a sort of brain trust. His wife, Clementine, was away in the south of France, and so, because he did his best thinking late at night over port, brandy, and cigars, he organized an intimate dinner at his official residence, 11 Downing Street. Norman, just back from the Riviera, was not invited. He was known to dislike these debates and would have just sat there silent and chilling. To represent orthodoxy, Churchill invited his two principal advisers at the Treasury,

Otto Niemeyer and John Bradbury, both men well established in the Norman camp. The case against gold was to be represented by Reginald McKenna, himself a former Liberal chancellor of the exchequer, now chairman of the Midland Bank, and Maynard Keynes.

Dinner began at 8:30 p.m. The small group seated around the table in the intimate oak-paneled dining room on the first floor of 11 Downing Street were all old acquaintances with a long association with one another. When Keynes had been a young Treasury official during the war, McKenna had been chancellor of the exchequer in the first coalition government, with Bradbury as his permanent secretary. Niemeyer, at the age of forty-two, was the controller of the Treasury, its second most powerful official, and the chancellor's chief adviser on matters of domestic and international finance. Behind his disheveled exterior lay a formidable intelligence. Of German Jewish extraction, he had earned a double first at Balliol College, Oxford, and had taken the civil service entrance exams in 1906, the same year as Maynard Keynes, whom he had beaten into second place. As a result, he had joined the Treasury while Keynes had had to settle for the India Office.

As the evening wore on and the alcohol flowed—Churchill was known for his ability to consume prodigious amounts without any apparent impairment of his faculties—the discussion went round and round. The same old arguments echoed off the vaulted ceilings and across the room. Keynes was not on his best form or at his most persuasive. He and McKenna kept returning to the argument that with prices in Britain still 10 percent too high, a return to gold would inevitably involve a great deal of pain, unemployment, and industrial unrest. Sir John Bradbury kept pressing the point that the virtue of the gold standard was that it was "knave-proof. It could not be rigged for political . . . reasons." Returning to the gold standard would prevent Britain from "living in a fool's paradise of false prosperity."

No one changed his mind that night. There was considerable agreement about the facts. All accepted that British prices were too high and that to bring them down would involve some pain, although they disagreed about its extent. All acknowledged that tying Britain to the gold standard would mean tethering it to the United States, with all the risks that entailed. But whereas the "gold bugs" believed that the costs were worth bearing in order to reinstate the automatic mechanism of the gold standard, Keynes and McKenna thought otherwise. There were too many imponderables for anyone to be sure of the answer. Both parties were making a leap of faith. In that sense, the debate that evening, though dressed up as a technical discussion among experts, reflected, at bottom, a philosophical divide between those who believed that governments could be trusted with discretionary power to manage the economy and those who insisted that government was fallible and therefore had to be circumscribed with strict rules.

Finally, as the dinner stretched into the early hours of the morning, Churchill turned to McKenna: "You have been a politician. Given the situation as it is, what decision would you make?"

To Keynes's disgust, McKenna replied, "There is no escape. You will have to go back; but it will be hell."

The gold bugs had won.

After a few more days of agonizing, Churchill decided for the gold standard. Orthodox economic opinion and the country's banking establishment were so strongly in favor that for once in his life, he lacked the necessary confidence in his own judgment to risk another policy. On his way to stay with the prime minister at Chequers one weekend, Norman dropped in at Chartwell, Churchill's country house in Kent, and tried to reassure him, "I will make you the golden Chancellor."

BUDGET DAY WAS until recently something of an occasion in the British parliamentary calendar. The event was traditionally surrounded with its own rituals—the buildup of suspense about the contents, the press speculation, the picture on the actual day of the chancellor emerging from No. 11 Downing Street, conspicuously brandishing the battered red dispatch box, the grand and excessively long speeches in Parliament about the minutiae of taxation and spending.* It was, in short, a perfect opportunity for Churchill to display his talent for playing to the gallery.

On April 28, he rose before the Commons at 4:00 p.m. to great applause. Everyone knew what he was about to say, but there were nevertheless tremendous cheers when, in the first few minutes of his speech, he announced the return to gold. Ever the showman, at one point during his two-hour speech, he paused, declaring, "It is imperative that I should fortify the revenue, and I shall now, with the permission of the Commons, proceed to do so," and proceeded to pour himself a glass of "an amber-coloured liquid," that from the press gallery appeared to be stronger than water.

For all his ambivalence about the decision to return to gold, Churchill put on a great show. He seems to have been most swayed in his decision by the fear that not to return now would be seen as a very public admission of Britain's diminished position in world affairs. Almost every other country was either now on gold—the United States, Germany, Sweden, Canada, Austria, and Hungary—or about to be—Holland, Australia, and South Africa—and "like ships in harbor whose gangways are joined together and who rise and fall together with the tide," they were all linked by a common standard of value. As he would articulate a few days later in committee, "If the English pound is not to be the standard which everyone knows and trusts, the business not only of the British Empire but also of Europe as well might have to be transacted in dollars instead of pounds sterling. I think that would be a great misfortune."

While Churchill was speaking, Norman sat in the distinguished strangers' gallery of the House of Commons, savoring what all London saw as his personal triumph. As Churchill himself would later put it, it was Norman's "greatest achievement . . . the final step without which all those efforts and sufferings [that is, the years since 1920] would have gone for naught."

The decision was received with resounding applause both in the City

---

*Gladstone held the record for the longest speech at four hours and forty-five minutes, in 1853.

and in the press, the *Times* commenting that it was "a signal triumph for those who have controlled and shaped our monetary policy, notably the Governor of the Bank." The *Economist* described it as "the crowning achievement of Mr. Montagu Norman." Only Beaverbrook's chain of papers dissented.

For a few months, McKenna's ominous prediction proved to be wrong. The initial consequences of the move were relatively benign. Britain, with its higher interest rates, attracted enough money that the credits provided by the Federal Reserve and J. P. Morgan were never needed. Britain's gold reserves actually increased during 1925.

For Keynes, borrowing hot money from foreigners was only a way for Britain to buy time. In a three-part series of articles, initially published in late July in Beaverbrook's *Evening Standard,* and later issued as a pamphlet, *The Economic Consequences of Mr. Churchill,* Keynes reminded his readers that Britain would have to "use the breathing space to effect what are euphemistically called the 'fundamental adjustments'" in the economic life of the nation. At its new exchange rate, the pound was overvalued by more than 10 percent. To remedy this would require cuts in wages and prices across the economy that could be achieved "in no other way than by the deliberate intensification of unemployment" through a policy of tight credit and higher interest rates. It seemed perverse to him to institute a regime of credit restrictions at a time when unemployment stood already above one million. "The proper object of dear money is to check an incipient boom. Woe to those whose faith leads them to use it to aggravate a depression!"

Though Keynes could not resist a typically malicious poke at Churchill—"because he has no instinctive judgment to prevent him from making mistakes . . . [and] because, lacking this instinctive judgment he was deafened by the clamorous voices of conventional finance"—the pamphlet was more an attack on the Bank of England and the Treasury.

Certainly, Churchill seems to have seen it that way. In 1927, he invited Keynes to become a member of The Other Club, a private and highly exclusive dining society started by him and Birkenhead in 1911. Its mem-

bers, restricted to no more than fifty, had to be both "estimable and entertaining." It had twelve rules, which were read aloud at the beginning of
each meeting, held every alternate Thursday while Parliament was in session. Churchill and Birkenhead determined who was to be invited to join.
Rule 12 read, "Nothing in the rules or intercourse of the Club shall interfere with the rancour or asperity of party politics." Its members read like
a Who's Who of British history between the wars and included all of
Churchill's pals—Birkenhead, Beaverbrook, and Bracken—but also such
diverse figures as Lord Jellicoe, H. G. Wells, Arnold Bennett, P. G. Wode-
house, and Edwin Lutyens.

By the late summer, the rise in the exchange rate began taking its toll
on the staple export industries of coal, steel, and shipbuilding. Particularly
hard hit was the weakest of these, coal, much of which was threatened with
bankruptcy after the resumption of production in the Ruhr and the squeeze
on prices from the rise in the exchange rate. The owners demanded a cut
in wages and an increase in hours from the coal miners. In *The Economic
Consequences of Mr. Churchill*, Keynes had railed against the social injustice
of a policy where miners were being asked to be "the victims of the economic Juggernaut." They were representatives "in the flesh [of] the fundamental adjustments engineered by the Treasury and the Bank of England
to satisfy impatience of the City fathers to bridge the moderate gap between $4.40 and $4.86."

A national strike was averted only when the government at the last
minute agreed to give the coal industry a massive subsidy of over $100
million. But this could only be a stopgap measure. By 1926, attempts to cut
costs led to a long and bitter strike in the coal industry, and in May 1926,
boiled over into a countrywide ten-day general strike. That this did not
lead to a flight of capital from Britain and a crisis in the exchange market
was only because the underlying weakness of Britain's international position was masked by continued inflows of capital taking advantage of high
interest rates in the London market and escaping the escalating crisis in
France.

The return to gold proved to be a costly error. That the money attracted by the high interest rates was speculative—"hot"—and not a source of permanent investment left a constant threat hanging over the currency. Just to prevent it from flooding back out again, interest rates had to be kept significantly higher than that in other countries for the balance of the decade. With prices falling at around 5 percent per annum, the burden of these charges on borrowers was heavy. Meanwhile, British manufacturing, hobbled in world markets by its high prices, limped painfully along for the next few years while elsewhere in the world industry boomed.

Though Churchill remained chancellor until 1929, by 1927 he had come to realize that the return to gold at the old prewar exchange rate had been a misjudgment. But by then there was little he could do about it except fulminate in private about the evil effects of the gold standard. In later life, he would claim that it was "the biggest blunder in his life." He blamed it on the bad advice he had received. In an unpublished draft of his memoirs, he wrote that he had been "misled by the Governor of the Bank of England [and] by the experts of the Treasury. . . . I had no special comprehension of the currency problem and therefore fell into the hands of the experts, as I never did later where military matters were concerned." He reserved his greatest venom for Norman. It took only the slightest provocation for him to begin to rant on about "that man Skinner," as he disparagingly referred to the governor. In a cabinet meeting in June 1928, one of his colleagues remembered him "to everyone's surprise exploding on Montagu Norman and deflation."

In his speech before Parliament during the debate on the Gold Standard Bill, Churchill had claimed that the move would "shackle Britain to reality." And a shackle it did prove to be, but not so much to reality as to an outmoded way of thinking and to a hopelessly obsolete mechanism for controlling the international finances of the country. As Keynes had written in May 1925:

> The gold standard party have had behind them much that
> is not only respectable but worthy of respect. The state of
> mind that likes to stick to the straight old-fashioned

course, rather regardless of the pleasure or the pain ... is
not to be despised. ... Like other orthodoxies it stands for
what is jejeune and intellectually sterile; and since it has
prejudice on its side, it can use claptrap with impunity.

The most damaging consequence was that in a futile attempt to retain
the primacy of the Bank of England and the City of London, Britain had
now tied itself irretrievably to the United States. During Norman's visit to
New York in January 1925, Strong had warned him, "In a new country such
as ours with an enthusiastic, energetic and optimistic population, where
enterprise at times was highly stimulated and returns upon capital much
greater than in other countries, there would be times when speculative
tendencies would make it necessary for the Federal Reserve Banks to exercise restraint by increased discount rates, and possibly rather high money
rates in the market. Should such times arise, domestic considerations
would likely outweigh foreign sympathies." Norman cannot have realized
how prescient those words were and how cruelly one day they would come
back to haunt him.

13. LA BATAILLE

FRANCE: 1926

*Only peril can bring the French together. One can't
impose unity out of the blue on a country that has
265 different kinds of cheese.*

—CHARLES DE GAULLE

APRIL 1925 might have been a good month for Governor Norman and the Bank of England, but in Paris, Governor Georges Robineau and the Banque de France were being simultaneously vilified and mocked in the press. Earlier that month, the French public had learned that for the past year, senior officials at the French central bank had conspired with their opposite numbers at the French treasury to cook the Banque's books.

The deception had begun as far back as March 1924. The government, finding it difficult to attract new buyers for its short-term debt, was forced to ask the Banque for an advance to cover some of its maturing bonds. But the amount of currency that the Banque could issue was limited by law and, in the embattled climate of the time, the government did not wish to face the political embarrassment of asking the National Assembly to raise the ceiling. Obliging officials at the Banque had found a way of issuing extra currency but disguising the fact with an accounting ruse, at first a technical, almost trivial adjustment, which no doubt those involved thought a temporary and justifiable expedient. But the scope of the operation had

Strong, Strong's daughter Katherine, and Norman at Biarritz, 1925

progressively grown and by April 1925, the "fake balances"—*les faux bilans*—amounted to some 2 billion francs, equivalent to 5 percent of the currency in circulation.

The doctored accounts were first discovered in October 1924 by the Banque's deputy governor, who promptly informed Governor Robineau; the minister of finance, Étienne Clémentel; and the prime minister, Édouard Herriot. Although the governor kept pressing the government to correct the situation by repaying the Banque some of what it owed, the ministers vacillated and did nothing for six months, hoping against hope that public finances might turn around. When news of the falsified statements finally leaked out, the government was forced to go to the National Assembly to ask for an increase in the legal limit. Though the nationalist press called for the prosecution of Governor Robineau, he managed to hang on to his job because at least he had resisted the ensuing cover-up; but the humiliated government fell to a vote of no confidence after a debate in the Senate that was unusually bitter even by the rancorous standards of French political discourse of the time.

The drama hit the headlines at a particularly sensitive moment. France was finally beginning to get its finances in order. The reconstruction of the war-ravaged departments of northeastern France had cost a total of $4 billion, but was now largely complete and the budget deficit had been cut from the equivalent of $1 billion in 1923, over 10 percent of GDP, to under $50 million, less than 0.5 percent. After the Dawes Plan, the government had also become much more realistic in its budgeting of how much it could truly hope to recover in reparations. And since the war, the Banque had been firm about restricting government borrowing from it. The currency ceiling of 41 billion francs established in 1920, a powerful symbol of the Banque's independence, had been scrupulously respected for four whole years.

But French finances balanced on a knife-edge. A large part of the public debt was short-term in nature, which made its refinancing an annual ordeal for the franc as French savers underwent an agonizing reappraisal of their government's solvency. The fact that the Banque de France, of all institutions, should now have fallen from grace and was implicated in this sordid scandal, albeit one in which no individual seemed to have profited financially, provoked a minor crisis of confidence among French investors.

FOR MUCH OF the nineteenth century, the Banque de France had been by far the most conservative financial institution in all Europe, far more cautious, for example, than its cousin the Bank of England. Although it was not legally bound, as was the English central bank, to hold a minimum amount of gold, it had adopted the practice of retaining an unusually large gold reserve to back its currency notes—in 1914, the largest in Europe, totaling over $1 billion. On a number of occasions it had even been asked to come to the aid of the Bank of England—for example, during the crises of 1825 and 1837; in 1890, when Barings Brothers faced bankruptcy over its ill-considered loans in South America, and finally, during the panic of 1907. In effect, the Banque played the role of backstop to the Bank of England.

While the Bank of England was a solidly bourgeois institution, egalitarian in the way that an exclusive men's club is democratic among its members, the Banque de France was from its birth an aristocratic place, even if the aristocracy was only a few years old. Among its first few governors were the comte Jaubert, the comte de Gaudin, the duc de Gaete, the comte Apollinaire d'Argout, and the baron Davillier. Even after 1875, when the republic was brought into being for the third and final time and the French aristocracy abandoned political life, the Banque de France continued to be a haven for the nobility.

The Banque itself remained a private institution owned by shareholders. Though the governor and deputy governors by this time tended to be drawn from the ranks of the higher civil service, they were still ultimately responsible to the twelve-man Council of Regents. In addition, the governor, though appointed by the government, was also required to own one hundred shares, which in the 1920s cost the franc equivalent of $100,000.

Since few government officials, even the very highest, had that much free capital, the purchase money was lent by the regents, making the average governor very much their agent.

In 1811, the Banque moved into the magnificently flamboyant Hôtel de la Vrillière, just north of the Louvre near the Palais Royal. It had once been the town palace of the comte de Toulouse, bastard son of Louis XIV and Madame de Maintenon. Every year at 12:30 in the afternoon, on the last Thursday of January, the pinnacle of French society would gather there for the Banque's Annual General Assembly. Though it had more than forty thousand shareholders, only the top two hundred were eligible to attend the meeting and choose the regents. The conclave was held in the Galerie Dorée, the long rococo hall running down the center of the hotel. There, beneath the gorgeous paintings on the vaulted ceiling, the carved and sumptuously gilded woodwork, the opulent wall mirrors, seated in alphabetical order would be some of the oldest and most aristocratic families in France: Clérel de Tocqueville, La Rochefoucauld, Noailles, Talleyrand-Périgord.

To be invited to this gathering was one of the most highly coveted emblems of social standing in France. Noblemen, who might otherwise care nothing about banking, treasured their family holdings in the Banque, valued typically at several hundred thousand francs, equivalent then to about a hundred thousand dollars, and held for generations as a prized part of their patrimony.

With an electorate of two hundred of the richest and grandest families in France, it was not surprising that seats on the Council of Regents came to be almost hereditary. Five out of the twelve elected regents were descendants of the original founders and a disproportionately large number were Protestants of Swiss extraction. In 1926, the twelve included Baron Ernest Mallet, Baron Édouard de Rothschild, Baron Jean de Neuflize, Baron Maurice Davillier, M. Felix Vernes, and M. François de Wendel. The Mallet family, Protestant bankers originally from Geneva, proprietors of a concern bearing their name, had the distinction of having sat on the council continuously for four generations, since it was first convened in 1800. The

Rothschilds, the only Jewish family on the council, had sat there since 1855, when Baron Alphonse de Rothschild, managing partner of Rothschild Frères, the French arm of the banking empire, had been chosen. On his death in 1905, his seat had been passed to his son Baron Édouard.

The Davilliers, like so many other regent families elevated to the baronage under Napoléon, were primarily industrialists, although they also operated an eponymous private bank. Baron Maurice Davillier was the fourth member of his family to serve on the council. Although Baron Jean de Neuflize was the first member of his clan to be elected, the Neuflizes, who owned one more eponymous bank, had been ennobled by Louis XV. Baron Jean, an avid sportsman who had represented France as an equestrian at the 1900 Olympics, was president of the Society of Steeplechasers and the even more exclusive Casting Club of France; his daughter was married to the wonderfully named English grandee Vere Brabazon Ponsonby, ninth Earl of Bessborough.

Over the 120 years since the Banque's foundation, France itself had experienced no fewer than three revolutions; transformed its political system five times; had had seventeen different heads of state, including one emperor, three kings, twelve presidents, and a president who then made himself emperor; and had changed governments on the average of at least once a year. Meanwhile, the Banque and the same few families that wielded power within its council had remained unmolested. So great was the institution's authority that it had continued to function unhindered during the Paris Commune and had met the currency needs of both sides—not only of the legitimate government at Versailles but of the Commune itself. "The hardest thing to understand," wrote Friedrich Engels, amazed at the deference of those first Communists, "is the holy awe with which they remained standing outside the gates of the Banque de France." The mystique attached to the regents and the top two hundred shareholders would give rise in the 1930s to the legend that France was controlled by a financial oligarchy of *les deux cents familles*, a potent myth that would become a rallying cry for the left.

When war broke out in 1914 and the very survival of the nation was threatened, the Banque, like all the other European central banks, voluntarily subordinated itself to its government, and obligingly printed whatever money was needed to finance the colossal effort. But unlike the Reichsbank, within a few months of the end of the war, it reasserted its independence and refused to go on filling the gap between government spending and tax revenues. In April 1919, the National Assembly fixed a limit on its advances to the state and in September 1920, imposed a ceiling of 41 billion francs on the Banque's note circulation. There things stood until the crisis of 1925.

In 1925, Émile Moreau, now fifty-seven, was in his twentieth year at the Banque d'Algérie and his fourteenth as its director general. He was proud of his achievements: his role in providing credit to the Moroccan economy, in stimulating the development of industry in Algeria after the war, and in launching a campaign against usury in Tunisia. For his services, he had accumulated a large array of decorations, including the czarist Russian Order of Saint Anne, the Spanish Order of Isabella the Catholic, and the Belgian Order of Leopold II, in addition to being a Commandeur de la Légion d'Honneur. But for all of these accolades, he had never been able to shake off the conviction that his assignment remained a form of professional banishment.

For many years, he had harbored the faint hope of one day returning to the mainstream of the civil service, maintaining, for example, his status as a member on leave of absence of the elite Inspectorat des Finances. But as the years had gone by and no new assignment had come his way, he had finally reconciled himself to his lot. In 1922, he had resigned from the higher civil service, though he continued to hold his position as the head of the Banque d'Algérie.

He and his wife had no children, and he was at an age when he could begin to look forward to more time for his other interests—he had assembled an extensive collection of Islamic coins, was an avid bibliophile, and also an active member of the Touring Club France, periodically taking off on long automobile trips through the countryside. And after twenty-two years, he was still a very dedicated mayor of his tiny home commune of Saint Léomer, only two hundred miles from Paris, which allowed him to get back to the old village as often as he wished.

Then suddenly in April 1925, when the Herriot government fell over the scandal at the Banque de France, it seemed that Moreau's star was about to turn. Paul Painlevé* formed a new left-wing coalition government and named as his finance minister a man whose four previous tours in the office had gained him a legendary reputation in the field of public finance: Moreau's old mentor, Joseph Caillaux.

In a country infamous for political instability, few men had had as stormy a career as Caillaux. In 1920, he had been sentenced to three years imprisonment for damaging the security of the state. But having already spent two years at La Santé prison awaiting trial, he had the remainder of his sentence commuted. Legally banished from Paris, Caillaux and his wife, Henriette, retired to the little town of Mamers in the Loire valley. For the next four years they lived quietly. Though he wrote an account of his years in prison that became a best seller, with the shadows of her trial for murder and his conviction for treason hanging over them, they found themselves outcasts, not only shunned in society, but dogged by petty humiliations—turned out of hotels, refused service in restaurants, insulted in cafés and on the streets. Caillaux was even once attacked by a gang armed with clubs and bricks.

But as France headed toward bankruptcy, more and more people could not help remembering Caillaux's warnings at the height of the war that both victors and vanquished would be ruined and increasingly he came to be seen as a victim of wartime hysteria. What had then been looked down upon as defeatism on his part now began to be viewed as prescience. In December 1924, his supporters in the National Assembly voted to abrogate

---

*Like so many politicians from the left, Painlevé was an intellectual, a brilliant mathematician from the Sorbonne with a particular expertise in nonlinear second-order differential equations.

his sentence. His return to the Ministry of Finance with a reputation, according to one French senator, as "a kind of Treasury magician, capable of turning dry leaves into bank notes," was the final vindication for this remarkable man.

Not everyone had forgiven or forgotten, however. As he strode into the Chamber of Deputies on April 21, 1925, to take his place on the government bench, his domed bald head gleaming, a monocle fixed firmly in his right eye, there was hissing and booing and shouts of "traitor" and "deserter." One ardent Nationalist got up and cried, "Have we reached the point where we must chose between bankruptcy and M. Caillaux? Bankruptcy would be better." An American newsmagazine reported that it was as if Benedict Arnold, instead of being condemned to death, had been barred from Philadelphia, exiled to the country, then pardoned, and appointed secretary of war.

Over the years, even during Caillaux's long banishment into the political wilderness, Moreau had assiduously maintained his friendship with the brilliant and erratic politician. For all of Caillaux's many faults—the indiscretions, the abysmal judgment, the disreputable friends with whom he surrounded himself, the terrible thirst for power, his essential "frivolity"—Moreau had never wavered in his belief that Caillaux was one of the best financial brains France had produced and that had he been minister of finance during the war, France would not have been in its present shape.

The situation confronting the new minister was grave. The franc was the only major currency still "off gold" and fluctuating on the exchanges, its ups and downs serving as a barometer of confidence in French financial management. In the spring of 1924, during the Dawes negotiations, it had briefly sunk to 25 to the dollar. Thereafter it had recovered somewhat, remaining reasonably stable for a year at about 18 to 19 to the dollar, 25 percent of its prewar level. But the affair of the *faux bilans* damaged that fragile equilibrium, and by the end of June, it was wavering at around 22 to the dollar.

Caillaux threw himself into the task of saving France from insolvency with characteristic energy. Immediately upon assuming office, he tried to fire Governor Robineau from the Banque de France and replace him with his old friend Émile Moreau. A housecleaning at the Banque would have helped to reestablish its credibility abroad. But fearing such a move would irretrievably compromise the Banque's reputation, the president of the republic killed the idea. Moreau saw his hopes of redemption dashed yet again.

Caillaux succeeded on some fronts. He managed to negotiate a budget deal that, for the first time since 1913, promised to balance the government's accounts. At the same time, he squashed the proposal for a capital levy, a form of wealth tax much enamored by the Socialists, the threat of which was provoking a flight of capital. In July, he went to London and struck a bargain with Winston Churchill to restructure the French war debt to the British at 40 cents on the dollar, effectively cutting it from $3 billion to $1.2 billion.

But the combination of France's financial problems and its political logjam were too great even for a man of Caillaux's abilities as financier and politician. He traveled to Washington to negotiate a similar write-down of the $4 billion debt owed to America but came back empty-handed. And while his appointment may have inspired confidence "in elegant social circles and the higher reaches of the Ministry of Finance," he was less successful in generating the same enthusiasm among those average French investors who held short-term government bonds. He became embroiled in a confrontation with the regents of the Banque de France, who, finding the government unable to meet all of its short-term obligations, tried to push Caillaux to impose some sort of debt moratorium—in effect for the government to admit that it was insolvent. So frustrated was Caillaux by the Banque's attitude that at one point he burst out how much he "regretted not having thrown the management of the Banque out of the window the minute he had assumed power."

In November, Caillaux was ousted, one more victim of the vendettas and personal intrigue that pervaded French political life. As he left, the franc touched 25 to the dollar. In his seven months in office, the cost of living had risen by 10 percent. During the following eight months, France had five different finance ministers, each with his own pet solution—a wealth tax, a moratorium on certain maturing debts, more vigorous collection of taxes, an increase in the turnover tax. Each failed to stem the collapse in confidence. French investors continued to pull their money out of the country.

In April 1926, France and the United States finally negotiated a war-debt settlement at 40 cents on the dollar. The budget was at last fully balanced. Still the franc kept falling. By May, the exchange rate stood at over 30 to the dollar.

With a currency in free fall, prices now rising at 2 percent a month, over 25 percent a year, and the government apparently impotent, everyone made the obvious comparison with the situation in Germany four years earlier. In fact, there was no real parallel. Germany in 1922 had lost all control of its budget deficit and in that single year expanded the money supply tenfold. By contrast, the French had largely solved their fiscal problems and its money supply was under control.

The main trouble was the fear that the deep divisions between the right and the left had made France ungovernable. The specter of chronic political chaos associated with revolving-door governments and finance ministers was exacerbated by the uncertainty over the government's ability to fund itself, given the overhang of more than $10 billion in short-term debt.

It was this psychology of fear—a generalized loss of nerve—that seemed to have gripped French investors and was driving the downward spiral of the franc. The risk was that international speculators, those traditional bugaboos of the left, would create a self-fulfilling meltdown as they shorted the currency in the hope of repurchasing it later at a lower price, thereby compounding the very downward trend that they were trying to exploit. It was the obverse of a bubble, where excessive optimism translates into rising prices, which then induces even more buying. Now excessive pessimism was translating into falling prices, which were inducing even more selling.

In the face of this all-embracing miasma of gloom, neither the politicians nor the financial establishment seemed to have any clue what to do. In early 1926, the budget minister, Georges Bonnet, invited the regents of the Banque de France to his office to seek their advice. He was struck by how extremely old they seemed to be—one of them could only walk leaning on two canes; another entered on the arm of his valet, who had to assist him into his chair. During the meeting, the panel, which represented the collective financial wisdom of France, seemed only to be able to offer one platitude after another about the need to restore confidence. When asked how to achieve this, they fell back on the usual military metaphors that were de rigueur at times of French financial crisis. One of the regents proclaimed vehemently that "we are the soldiers of the franc and we will die in the trenches for the franc." That winter and spring, there was much in the press about the "battle of the franc," "monetary Marnes," and the "Verdun of the currency."

At one point, the government decided it had to do more than just rely on a lot of military-sounding talk. Marshal Joffre, the "Hero of the Marne," was summoned out of retirement and placed in charge of the "Save the Franc Fund." It managed to raise all of 19 million francs, rather less than $1 million, including 1 million francs from Sir Basil Zaharoff, the noted European arms merchant, and 100,000 francs from the *New York Herald*, the precursor of today's *International Herald Tribune*.

The authorities still had one weapon in reserve to break the downward spiral—the more than $1 billion in gold holdings of the Banque de France, some $700 million parked in its vaults on the Rue de la Vrillière, and a further $300 million held abroad with the Bank of England.

For much of modern history, including well into the latter half of the twentieth century, gold has occupied a hallowed place in the French psyche. So revered was it that during these years of financial turmoil, the regents could never quite bring themselves to actually draw upon their reserves. At one point during the war, the British had tried to persuade the Banque de France to utilize some of its gold for the war effort. What was the point, they asked, of building up a reserve if not to use at times of crisis? But the Banque had insisted that its reserves had to be preserved so that when the troubles were all over, and France was in a position to resume its rightful place in the economic order, the gold would be there to back its currency. The French gold reserves were like family heirlooms or jewels, "which must never be brought out and never be touched; to lie idle, as it were, under a glass case."

In early 1926, the government, its finances now restored but its currency still inexorably and inexplicably falling, tried to persuade the Banque that now was the time to redeem its pledge by supporting the franc with foreign currencies borrowed against the security of the gold. The Banque refused. Its behavior during the whole crisis—its reluctance to help and its lack of cooperation with the government—would later give rise to the accusation that the plutocrats at the apex of the French banking system had been determined from the very start to bring the left-wing coalition to its knees. *Le mur d'argent*—the wall of money—it was called, joining *les deux cents familles* as the twin rallying cries of the left in France.

In May 1926, the government, spurned by its own central bank, sought frantically to obtain credit abroad. But the scandal of *les faux bilans* had confirmed the universal prejudice among British and American bankers that French institutions—government, politicians, press, and now even the central bank—were decadent, corrupt, and dysfunctional. A French delegation came to see Benjamin Strong, then in London, to beg for a $100 million loan from the New York Fed and was firmly turned down—he could not lend to the French government by statute and would not lend to the Banque de France until all the groups involved—government, opposition, the Banque itself, and the most important French bankers—"[laid] down their squabbles" and agreed to cooperate. At a further meeting in Paris later in May, when French officials again pressed for a loan, Strong told them that when, as he quite expected, they would be unable to pay, the Americans would have to physically take the pledged gold reserves from the vaults of the Banque, for which they would be "excoriated from one end of France to another." Rejected by the Federal Reserve, the French approached every investment house they could—Morgans, Kuhn Loeb, and Dillon Read. Every house demurred.

On June 15, the "Ballet of Ministries" came around full circle, and Joseph Caillaux returned as minister of finance, his fifth time in that position. This time he finally succeeded in firing Robineau, and Émile Moreau was invited to take over from him. Caillaux was set on making a clean sweep of the Banque's entire upper management, replacing it with men who were more pragmatic and less ideologically opposed to the government. The deputy governor, Ernest Picard, was packed off to the Banque d'Algérie, a convenient and proven place of exile for unwanted civil servants, and replaced by Charles Rist, a professor of law at the Sorbonne, a well-known specialist in monetary economics. Albert Aupetit, as secretary general of the Banque the primary architect of *les faux bilans*, was also shunted aside. When a group of regents threatened to resign en masse in outrage at the government interference in their internal affairs, Caillaux and Moreau called their bluff. All of them stayed.

On June 24, Moreau, fifty-eight years old, vindicated at last, assumed the governorship. That day, the currency stood at 35 francs to the dollar, having bounced modestly from its low of 37 to the dollar. A friend to whom he confided of his elevation to the new position told him that he pitied him. In his diary that evening, Moreau wrote, "Am I to become the liquidator of the national bankruptcy? This has to be feared or at least expected. . . . My wife is very unhappy."

COINCIDENTALLY, AS THE financial crisis in France was reaching a sort of crescendo, Norman and Strong were enjoying their annual vacation together, this year on the French Riviera. They had developed the practice of meeting twice a year, combining business and pleasure—in New York during the winter and in Europe during the summer.

The previous summer, Strong had spent a full three months in Europe. After going to London, Strong, who was accompanied by his eldest daughter, Katherine, had gone on to Berlin with Norman to meet with Schacht, then to Paris and then for a month to the Palace Hotel at Biarritz.

Come 1926, Strong proposed that they go to the south of France. The

Côte d'Azur was one of Norman's favorite vacation spots—he had been a regular visitor since 1902, when he had spent several months in Hyères recuperating after the Boer War. But like most of the other English people who frequented the Riviera in those years, he preferred to be there in the winter and the early spring. "My doubt is only about the heat: I like to be warm but not grilled," he groused when Strong first came up with the idea. But the inducement of being able to sit down with his friend and "ooze out whatever questions are in my head" persuaded him to go along.

They chose to stay at the Hôtel du Cap Eden-Roc. Before the war, the Hôtel du Cap, secluded in twenty-five acres of ornamental gardens at the tip of Cap d'Antibes, had been a favorite watering hole of European royalty. Like most resort hotels on the Riviera, it used to shut between May and September. However, in 1923, a rich young American couple, the Murphys,* persuaded the owner to keep it open and took over the whole hotel for the summer. Thus was born the summer season in the south of France. In the three years since the Murphys had first commandeered the Hôtel du Cap, it had become the most fashionable summer resort hotel on the Côte d'Azur.

In the last week of June, Strong and Norman and the other guests found themselves besieged by newspapermen. It seemed too much of a coincidence that the world's two most important central bankers should happen to be in France at the very moment its currency crisis was reaching some sort of denouement. Rumors were rife that a meeting of the world's great financiers, to be held in Antibes, of all places, was in the offing; that Schacht was on his way; that Andrew Mellon, the U.S. secretary of the treasury, would soon arrive; that Moreau was already in daily contact.

The two bankers did manage to elude the escort of reporters one evening, but were soon discovered dining at the Colombe d'Or, a small restaurant at St. Paul-de-Vence, twenty miles away. Another intrepid

---

*Gerald and Sara Murphy were the models for Dick and Nicole Diver in F. Scott Fitzgerald's book *Tender Is the Night*. They were introduced to the south of France in 1922 by their friends Cole and Linda Porter.

journalist managed to talk his way into the hotel grounds and reported encountering Norman perched acrobatically on a sort of surfboard being dragged through the waves by a small motor dinghy. The hotel management became so irritated with the inconvenience to its other guests caused by the press barrage that its employees were given strict instructions not to deliver messages to the two men. In fact, while Norman and Strong followed the events in Paris avidly, they knew that at this stage it was premature to enter into any sort of discussions with the French authorities.

At the end of July, Norman returned to England. Strong went to Paris, arriving on July 20. Three days before, the latest French government, having lasted all of four weeks, collapsed. It was followed by another left-wing coalition that survived only seventy-two hours. There was talk of revolution or a coup d'état. The streets outside the National Assembly were daily thronged with protesters. Strong found his French banking correspondents so fearful that they had begun sending their families to safety in the provinces, while the American officials he knew were preparing for violent anti-American demonstrations.

Since the founding of their republic, Americans had had a love affair with France and especially with Paris. In the early twenties, with the franc at a quarter of its prewar level, that romance had suddenly become accessible to any American with a couple of hundred dollars to spare. A tourist-class passage across the Atlantic could be had for as little as $80 and the cost of living in France was astoundingly cheap for anyone with dollars. By 1926, an estimated forty-five thousand Americans were living in Paris and every summer another two hundred thousand tourists arrived to enjoy the combination of culture, gracious living, and a risqué nightlife that made Paris, even then, the most visited city in the world.

Unfortunately, the affection of Americans for all things French was increasingly unrequited. The French press had for a while expressed its indignation at the spectacle of rich Americans taking advantage of the low franc to buy up the choicest French property on the Côte d'Azur and Côte Basque, along the Loire valley, and on the Champs de Mars in Paris. The newspaper *Le Midi* had taken to referring to Americans as "destructive grasshoppers."

One incident in particular had been a lightning rod for bad feeling. In March 1924, at the height of the currency crisis, the U.S. ambassador, Myron Herrick, bought out of his own pocket a grand mansion at Two Avenue d'Iéna to house the embassy. Built in the late nineteenth century at a cost of 5 million francs, equivalent at the time to about $1 million, the mansion was now selling for 5,400,000 francs.* Herrick astutely chose to exchange his dollars for francs on March 11, 1924, the very day that panic selling on the Bourse drove the exchange rate down to 27 francs to the dollar, which gave him the house for only $200,000. As ambassador from 1912 to 1914 Herrick had won the affection of the French for his decision to stay in the city when it seemed about to fall to the Germans. The affection was great enough that he had been asked to return as ambassador in 1921. But when the newspapers discovered that the American ambassador himself had cut a sweet deal from the franc's collapse, there was outrage.

The tough stance adopted by the U.S. government, particularly Congress, over repayments of war debts had aroused much bitterness in France. Casualties of Frenchmen during the war had been twenty times that of Americans. Coolidge's infamous remark—"They hired the money, didn't they?"—had displayed a remarkable indifference to the human sacrifice of Britain and France that all Europeans found chilling. The deal over the French war debts agreed to by Victor Henri Berenger and Andrew Mellon in April 1926 did nothing to bridge that chasm but only intensified the resentment further. Americans thought they had been extraordinarily generous by reducing their claim by 60 percent. The French, on the other hand, viewed the American decision to collect at all on a debt, the liquidation of which would take sixty-two years, as simply rapacious.

On July 11, in a dramatic protest, twenty thousand *mutilés*—maimed

---

*The mansion belonged to the family of the French politician Daniel Wilson, the son-in-law of President Grévy, who had been accused in 1887 of selling decorations, including nominations to the Légion d'Honneur, from his office in the Elysée Palace.

war veterans—the legless in wheelchairs, the blind led by nurses, marched in silent protest up the Champs-Élysées to the Place d'Iéna overlooking the U.S. embassy, where they laid a wreath at the foot of the equestrian statue of George Washington.

On July 19, the night before Strong arrived in Paris, a bus carrying American tourists was attacked by a rabble in Montmartre. Two days later a few hundred demonstrators surrounded some Paris-by-night tourist buses near the Opéra and prevented them from taking sightseers through the more insalubrious parts of the city. Several thousand locals soon gathered around and began jeering and hurling epithets. A couple of days later another party of American tourists responded by plastering the partitions of their railway compartment with French money, and conspicuously lighting cigars with fifty- and hundred-franc notes as a mark of their contempt for the currency.

Relations between American visitors and their reluctant hosts had so deteriorated that the *New York World* felt compelled to proffer the following dos and don'ts to tourists planning to visit France that summer:

> Don't boast in cafes that American currency is the only
> real honest-to-God money in the world. It isn't. Besides
> such bursts of financial patriotism are annoying to people
> who did not spend the years 1914 to 1916 accumulating
> world credit by selling munitions, cotton and wheat to
> other nations which were busy with a war. . . .
>   Don't confide to your fellow passengers on railway
> trains that America is the most generous of creditors
> because America has cancelled all that part of debts, which
> nobody can collect. Talk instead of our prowess in
> tennis, golf or Prohibition. It comes with better grace.

It was against this backdrop that Moreau came to see Strong at his hotel in Versailles. They were to meet several times during the next days—always at Strong's hotel, because he did not wish to be seen visiting the

Banque and even requested that the mere fact of their meetings be kept a secret. He was facing severe political opposition at home to any Federal Reserve involvement in the finances of France: "Xenophobic displays in Paris," he explained, "have produced the worst possible impression" on the American public.

The two men got on well. Moreau found Strong "friendly but reserved." Nevertheless, the latter was noncommittal about a loan. For one, it would require some signal that the French government would respect the Banque's independence. For another, the National Assembly would have to ratify the April deal on war debts.

On the morning of July 29, it was Norman's turn to meet with the Banque's new leadership. He came to call on Moreau at his office on the first floor of the Hôtel du Toulouse. The governor's suite at the Banque was a marked contrast to the classical simplicity of his own office on Threadneedle Street. The rooms had once been the private apartments of the princess de Lamballe, granddaughter-in-law of the comte de Toulouse, a close confidante of Marie Antoinette who had often entertained the queen there.* The floor was covered by a floral Savonnerie carpet, the governor's desk faced a painting by Boucher, the anteroom boasted a beautiful Fragonard park scene.

The meeting of the two governors—Norman, tall, distinguished, and cosmopolitan, with his trimmed beard and his well-cut dandyish clothes; Moreau, short, squat, and bald, looking like a provincial notary out of a novel by Flaubert—immediately got off on the wrong foot. For once, Norman's infamous charm seemed to desert him. He was gratuitously patronizing, and despite being fluent in French, insisted on speaking to Moreau, who spoke no foreign languages, in English throughout that first encounter.

---

*When the royal family was imprisoned at the Temple, the princess de Lamballe had accompanied them. She met a gruesome end in September 1791, when she was handed over to a lynch mob, who stripped her naked, gang-raped her in the streets, then mutilated her body before finally impaling her head upon a pike and parading it in front of Marie Antoinette's prison window.

"Mr. Norman arrived at eleven o'clock," Moreau wrote in his diary. "At first sight he is very likeable. He appears to have stepped out of a van Dyck painting, elongated figure, pointed beard, a big hat: he has the bearing of a companion of the Stuarts. It is said that Israelite blood flows in his veins. I know nothing of this, but Mr. Norman seemed, perhaps because of it, full of contempt for the Jews about whom he spoke in very bad terms. He does not like the French. He told me literally: 'I want very much to help the Bank of France. But I detest your Government and your Treasury. For them I will do nothing at all.' On the other hand he seems to feel the deepest sympathy for the Germans. He is very close to Dr. Schacht. They see other often and hatch secret plans. . . . Nevertheless Mr. Norman is above all profoundly English and this makes him very creditable. He is an imperialist seeking the domination of the world for his country which he loves passionately. . . . He adores the Bank of England. He told me: 'The Bank of England is my only mistress. I think only of her and I have given her my life.' He is not a friend to us French. Very mysterious, extremely complicated, one never knows the depths of his thoughts. Even so he is very amiable when he wants to be. . . . Norman spares nothing in his efforts to flatter [Strong] or gain influence over him. He went to spend several days at Antibes, only because Strong was staying there."

A Bank of England official accompanying Norman wrote later that Moreau left the impression of being "stupid, obstinate, devoid of imagination and generally of understanding but a magnificent fighter for narrow and greedy ends."

Norman essentially reiterated the conditions that Strong had set down for assistance: a change in the statutes to give the governor of the Banque security of tenure and the ratification of both the British and American war-debt settlements. Moreau did try to make both men see the political difficulties of each measure, particularly of trying to change the Banque's statutes in such politically fractured times. Many politicians were bitter at the Banque for sitting on its remaining gold reserves when the currency collapsed that year.

Moreau had received a quick lesson in the ways of international capital markets—financial assistance was "a commodity" that his fellow central bankers were "only ready to sell . . . at a stiff price." He would not forget. In his own mind, he blamed the sinister machinations of Norman and his malice toward the French for the failure of central bankers to come to France's aid.

On July 21, Raymond Poincaré was asked to form a ministry. He was then the most illustrious and experienced politician in France, had been in politics for more than forty years—twice prime minister, from 1912–13 and 1922–24, and president of the republic during the fateful years of crisis and war, from 1913–20. Though not formally associated with a party, he was a man of the center who in many ways stood above the political fray. And while he had been the architect of the disastrous and expensive decision in 1923 to occupy the Ruhr, which had left France isolated and weak, he had been equally responsible for setting in motion the Dawes Plan; and his anti-German stance had mellowed considerably in the previous three years. Within two days, he announced a national unity government that encompassed the full spectrum of political opinion, except for the Socialists, and included six former prime ministers.

What happened over the next few days illustrates the overwhelming power that psychological factors had come to exercise over the currency market. On the day that Poincaré became prime minister, the franc touched 50 to the dollar. But even before he had had a chance to outline his financial program or introduce any new tax measures, his presence alone seemed to reassure investors. Within the space of two days, the franc had rebounded to 43 to the dollar and by the following week, it was back at 35, a rise of more than 40 percent. This astonishing recovery seems to confirm the thesis that in the last stages of its collapse, the currency had lost all connection to economic reality and was being driven downward by speculators.

The franc found as much comfort in Poincaré's personality as in his political stature. The most uncharismatic politician in all France—cold, withdrawn, and antisocial*—he made up for it by his prodigious appetite for work, married to a photographic memory, and a meticulous attention to detail. Most of all, in an era when French politicians seemed to have only the vaguest comprehension of the boundary between public obligation and private gain, he was scrupulously honest. He had a well-publicized provincial suspicion of all cosmopolitan Parisians, particularly bankers. The average French investor—the small shopkeeper from Picardy; the thrifty farmer in the Auvergne; the eminently practical village doctor from Normandy; and, of course, the glass manufacturer of Poincaré's native Lorraine—recognized themselves in him and took comfort in his stewardship of their finances.

As the franc surged upward on the exchanges, the prices of imported goods and the cost-of-living index began falling. That summer the papers were full of the comings and goings of American financiers in Europe. On July 24, Secretary of the Treasury Andrew Mellon arrived in Paris. In the first week of August, Strong was discovered in The Hague conferring with Schacht. On August 20, Strong and Mellon surfaced in Evian with Parker Gilbert, the agent-general for German reparations. What could all these prominent American moneymen be talking about if not the problem of the franc? In fact, while the mysterious peregrination of bankers across Europe was wonderful fodder for financial gossipmongers, it proved to be largely a sideshow. Mellon, it turned out, had come to

---

*He made up for his apparent coldness by an obsessive love of animals. He and his wife, Henriette, had no children and lavished their affection on their pet cats and dogs. Poincaré is supposed to have been heartbroken both when his sheepdog Nino died in 1926 and when his favorite Siamese cat, Gris-gris, passed away in 1929.

Europe mainly to see his sick daughter in Rome and take her to Evian for the waters.

The capital that had fled France during the past two years began to wash back irresistibly, largely obviating the need for American or British financial assistance. In any case, Poincaré, confronted by enormous resistance to the war-debt agreements within the National Assembly, delayed submitting them for ratification. Without these agreements, there could be no loans from abroad.

Moreau himself was initially unsure how to respond to the rebound in the franc. His initial inclination was to let it run. He was by training an old school civil servant; and though he had considerable experience in banking, his understanding of monetary economics was quite rudimentary and at times confused. The truth is that at that time, very few bankers could claim to understand fully the situation of France in 1926, particularly the complicated dynamics between the inflow of money and its effect on the exchange rate and domestic prices and, in turn, their impact on the overall economy. Moreau was lucky enough in his two subordinates, Charles Rist and Pierre Quesnay, to have stumbled across two of the few men who did.

Rist, aged fifty-two, had been an academic all his life, and was best known for the classic tome *History of Economic Doctrines from the Physiocrats to the Present Age*, coauthored with his fellow professor Charles Gide, the uncle of the writer. According to Moreau, Rist was something of a "slave to the books he has written and the lectures he has delivered." In 1924, he had come to the attention of the finance bureaucracy with a short but highly influential monograph *Deflation in Practice*, which argued, like Keynes's *A Tract on Monetary Reform*, that attempts to force down prices would impose an excessive cost on the economy and society. He had been very reluctant to escape the comforts of academia when first approached about coming to the Banque and had only been persuaded when Caillaux, at their initial interview, exclaimed, "You are not going to remain a grammarian for the rest of your life!"

Pierre Quesnay was only thirty-one years old, a former student of Rist's who, after being demobilized in 1919, had joined the financial service of the League of Nations. Moreau brought him in as his chief of staff, appointing him as the Banque's director of economic research a month later.*

During the fall, the inflow of money turned into a flood, and as it carried the franc irresistibly upward, breaching 30 to the dollar, Rist and Quesnay began to worry that France might repeat the British mistake: an exchange rate that was too high, making exports chronically overpriced and uncompetitive. In mid-December, as the franc reached 25 francs to the dollar, Moreau's two colleagues, determined to prevent the French economy from slipping into British-like stagnation, began to agitate for the Banque to intervene to cap its rise. At one point, they even threatened to resign unless Moreau persuaded the prime minister to go along.

While Quesnay and Rist provided the Banque's intellectual horsepower, Moreau was the political strategist. He recognized that the choice of the exchange rate ultimately determined how the financial burden of the war was to be shared. It was Maynard Keynes who had first articulated the political dimension to exchange rate policy in the *Tract*, back in 1923: "The level of the franc is going to be settled, not by speculation or the balance of trade, or even the outcome of the Ruhr adventure, but by the proportion of his earned income which the French taxpayer will permit to be taken from him to pay the claims of the French rentier." The higher the Banque de France let the franc rise, the higher would be the value of the government debt, the better for the French rentier and the worse for the taxpayer. As Moreau put it, fixing the exchange rate was a matter of balancing "the sacrifices demanded of the different social classes in the population."

Every country in Europe to emerge from the war had faced the same set of issues. Britain had chosen one extreme: to impose most of the burden on its taxpayers and to protect its savers. Germany had chosen the opposite extreme: the way of pathological inflation, which had wiped away

---

*Pierre Quesnay became a close friend of Moreau's. He drowned in 1937 in a swimming accident in a lake on the grounds of La Frissonaire while staying with Moreau.

its internal debts at the price of annihilating the savings of its middle classes. Moreau was set on finding a middle way.

Poincaré's natural inclination was to savor the benefits to his reputation of the strengthening currency and let the franc keep rising. He was understandably reluctant to go down in history as the man who had formally acceded to an 80 percent reduction in the value of his nation's money. But he also recognized that by allowing it to rise too far, he risked driving the economy into recession. Like many with a genius for detail, Poincaré was by nature indecisive and vacillating, one day in favor of capping the rise, the next day against.

The principle of opposition to capping the franc's recovery did not come from the prime minister but from within Moreau's very own institution. A faction within the Banque's directorate, led by the two most powerful regents, Baron Édouard de Rothschild and François de Wendel, saw in the decline of the franc the decline of France. True diehards, they considered it their moral obligation to defend the interests of all those who had invested in French bonds during the war.

No one better symbolized the power of *les deux cents familles* and *le mur d'argent* than these two men. Rothschild was the epitome of the French aristocrat. Tall and slender, always fastidiously dressed in his old-fashioned banker's uniform of frock coat and top hat, he had become the senior partner at Rothschild Frères at the age of thirty-seven. Beneath his haughty demeanor, he was shy, almost withdrawn; cautious and old-fashioned, he was a true conservative. The family bank matched his character, a place where, according to his son Guy, "The past clung to everything and everyone" and whose main purpose was in "gently prolonging the nineteenth century."

A familiar figure in the best Parisian clubs, Rothschild had been an intimate friend of Edward VII's, and was known as a great philanthropist, being especially generous to Jewish charities. To the public he was above all famous for his racehorses; during the season he was a fixture at Longchamps. More than just another wealthy breeder and owner of thoroughbreds, he was a skilled equestrian in his own right who had even represented France at polo at the 1900 Olympics.

In the world of banking the Rothschild name and the family's great wealth evoked both awe and resentment. There was much anti-Semitic innuendo about their political influence. One exaggerated account has it that between 1920 and 1940, "No cabinet was formed without Édouard de Rothschild being consulted." Édouard had been a young man of twenty-five when the Dreyfus affair broke in 1894. As Dreyfus was being publicly degraded from his rank, an enraged mob had howled, "*A Mort les Juifs!*"— "Death to the Jews!" He was determined thereafter that the Rothschilds should keep a low profile, keep out of the papers, and guard their privacy—though justly enraged by an anti-Semitic slur, he did once challenge a man to a duel.*

If Édouard de Rothschild was the glamorous face on the "wall of money," Francois de Wendel was, in the public mind, its more sinister visage. The Wendels were one of the great arms manufacturers of Europe, armorers from Lorraine for more than 250 years, who had supplied weapons to, among others, Napoléon Bonaparte. Under the Second Empire, they had diversified, building one of the largest steel empires in Europe so that by 1914 the Wendel name in France had become as synonymous with steel as that of Carnegie was in the United States.

In the French edition of *Who's Who*, François de Wendel listed his profession simply as "Maître de Forges"—ironmaster. He did not look the part. His receding chin gave him the appearance of "a tall friendly duck." He lived discreetly in a mansion at 10 Rue de Clichy, not the most elegant or fashionable quartier of the capital, and liked to spend his weekends at

---

*Édouard's efforts to keep his family firmly out of the papers except for the society columns were not helped when his cousin Maurice, a flamboyant womanizer and the black sheep of the family, took it into his head to enter politics, ran for the National Assembly, and in early 1926, was found guilty of having bought his seat by offering his constituents cash handouts, ranging from twenty to a thousand francs. Expelled from parliament, he insisted on running again and won.

his private game reserve just outside Paris, where he was said to be an enthusiastic but not very talented shot.

Unusually for a regent of the Banque de France, Wendel was an elected member of the National Assembly, leaving his two brothers to run the vast steel empire. In 1918, he became president of the Comité des Forges, the very powerful industry association of iron, steel, and armament manufacturers.

It required a certain obstinacy and tenacity of purpose for Moreau to take on the most powerful of his own regents. But over a thirty-year career in the higher civil service, he had acquired the remarkable skill in operating within the machinery of government. He certainly did not rely on diplomatic skills or charm—he had neither. Furthermore, after years on the periphery of power and of avoiding the salons of Paris, he had a limited network of political allies. His one great mentor, Caillaux, who might have helped him through the labyrinth of the French power structure, was gone within a few weeks of his appointment. It did not help that Poincaré was a long-standing enemy of Caillaux's, and from the very start viewed Moreau with some hostility and suspicion as a holdover.

But Moreau proved to be unusually adept at bureaucratic infighting. In his diaries, he displays a natural talent for the give-and-take of policy formulation, knowing when to concede and when to push, when to bluff, when to threaten and when to fold, and considerable insight into the motivations and character of those he was up against.

On December 21, the Banque began to purchase foreign exchange and sell its own currency to prevent the franc from rising above 25 to the dollar. For the next two years, with Poincaré's blessing, Moreau pursued a policy of intervening in the currency market to keep it pegged there.

Meanwhile, Rothschild and Wendel waged a guerrilla campaign against Moreau within the halls of the Banque and the corridors of power of the finance ministry on the Rue de Rivoli. Few institutions were more riddled with byzantine intrigue than the Banque. Moreau had had his first taste of it soon after joining—in August 1926, to his great surprise, he discovered that all incoming and outgoing calls including those from the governor's office were being wiretapped. He had the taps dismantled.

Unable to secure a majority within the Council of Regents, Rothschild and Wendel employed every possible tactic to undermine Moreau. They lobbied the prime minister. They breached a long-standing tradition of discretion among the regents by making public pronouncements on currency policy, hoping thereby to lure such a flood of money into the country that Moreau would be forced to remove the cap. At one point, Rothschild ordered the Chemin de Fer du Nord, the largest railway company in France—of which he was president—to buy francs in order to push the exchange rate higher, risking the accusation that a regent of the Banque de France was engaged in inside trading in the currency market.

By the middle of 1927, it was clear that Moreau had won. Waves of French capital that had fled to London or New York had washed back home, allowing the Banque to accumulate a foreign exchange war chest of $500 million, most of it in pounds. Despite the pressure from the diehards among the Regents, Poincaré had been won over. Moreau kept urging him not to look to France's past but to its future. At 25 francs to the dollar, French goods were among the most competitive in the world; exports were booming, while prices were stable. It seemed as if, thanks to Moreau, France, of all the European countries, had finally hit upon the right recipe for dealing with the financial legacy of the war, avoiding the two extremes of German-style inflation and British-style deflation.

Moreau's mistake was to assume that the value of the currency of a major economic power such as France, the fourth largest industrial economy, was a matter for that country alone. Exchange rates, by their very nature, involve more than one side and are therefore a reflection of a multilateral system. Though it may have been very difficult in 1926 to know the exact ramifications of the franc's exchange rate on surrounding countries, Moreau seems to have deliberately closed his eyes to the impact of his decision on the wider system. Perhaps he was irritated at an international regime that he felt had done so little to support France in its time of trouble. Perhaps he resented that the structure was dominated by an Anglo-American combine led by Norman—or so he believed. Whatever the reason, his decision to fix the franc at an undervalued rate would eventually help to undermine the stability of the very standard to which he had now hitched his currency.

14. THE FIRST SQUALLS

1926-27

Circumstances rule men; men do not rule circumstances.

—HERODOTUS, *Histories*

ORGY OF SPECULATION

No other issue would create more debate, disagreement, feuds, and confusion within the Federal Reserve System than what to do about the stock market. Wall Street had always loomed large in the American national psyche. Charles Dickens, visiting the United States in 1842, had been struck by the local taste for speculation and the desire "to make a fortune out of nothing." After the 1884 panic on the New York Stock Exchange, the London magazine *The Spectator* commented, "The English, however speculative, fear poverty. The Frenchman shoots himself to avoid it. The American with a million speculates to win ten, and if he takes losses takes a clerkship with equanimity. This freedom from sordidness is commendable, but it makes a nation of the most degenerate gamesters in the world."

Surprisingly, despite this national proclivity for betting on stocks, the U.S. market had never been especially large. In 1913, the total value of common stocks was some $15 billion, roughly the same size as the British stock market, which rested upon an economy about a third the size of that of the United States. From the beginning of the century until the outbreak of war, the stock market had essentially gone nowhere. The "merger" bull market from 1900 to 1902 had been cut short by the "rich man's panic" of 1903, which was followed by the "Roosevelt" bull market, then the "1907 panic," and finally the "recovery" bull market. As a consequence, the Dow had fluctuated for a decade and a half in an irregular wavelike movement between 50 and 100 without breaking in either direction.*

When war came, the U.S. economy experienced a boom and profits shot up dramatically for a couple of years as America became the arms supplier and financier to the Allies. But few investors were convinced that European Armageddon could be good for stocks in the long run, and so despite the profit surge, the market remained firmly range bound. Wisely so, for once the United States did enter the fray, labor shortages emerged, the war effort consumed great chunks of the national product, and profits suffered. By the end of 1920, the Dow stood at 72, almost at the midpoint of its range for the last twenty years—though after taking wartime infla-tion into account, this represented half the 1913 level in real terms.

But once the initial postwar adjustment pains had died away, the mar-ket began to take off. From 1922 onward, the Fed, under the leadership of Benjamin Strong, did a remarkable job in stabilizing prices. With inflation thus effectively at zero, it was able to keep interest rates low. This allowed the economy, boosted by the dynamic new industries of automobiles and radios, to surge ahead. While overall economic growth was exceptionally strong, even stronger and more exceptional was the rise in profits. Powered by new forms of organization and by a surge in factory mechanization, productivity accelerated in the 1920s while hourly wages grew only mod-estly. Most of the benefits, therefore, of the "new era" flowed to the corpo-

---

*In this book I have chosen to use the Dow Jones Industrial Average as a measure of the average level of the stock market, for all its many deficiencies, the oldest and best known stock average. Introduced by the founder of the *Wall Street Journal,* Charles Dow, in 1896, it then comprised the average of twelve industrial stocks. The list was expanded to twenty in 1916 and to thirty in 1928. The only index of comparable repute is the S&P, but that was not introduced until 1923 and remained relatively obscure until after the war.

rate bottom line—by 1925, earnings were double their level in 1913. As a result, the Dow, after hitting a low of 67 in the summer of 1921, more than doubled to above 150 during the subsequent four years. By 1925, after the reelection of Calvin Coolidge as president, this last upward ride even acquired its own moniker: the Coolidge bull market.

No company better exemplified the booming economy and provided a better window into the rising stock market than General Motors. It had been founded in 1908 by William Crapo Durant, grandson of H. H. Crapo, the Civil War governor of Michigan. Young Billy Durant grew up in Flint, Michigan, and after dropping out of high school, drifted through a series of nondescript jobs, including grocery boy, drugstore attendant, traveling medicine man, insurance promoter, and tobacco shop manager. The bantam-sized Durant was a natural salesman, charming, soft-spoken but determined, with a winning smile, an infectious attitude of irrepressible

FIGURE 4

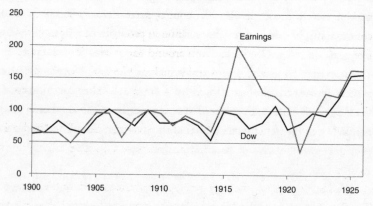

**U.S. Stock Prices and Corporate Profits:
1900–26**

**From 1900–1926, except during the war,
stock prices followed profits.**

optimism, and an unusual talent for persuading people. After building one of the largest buggy businesses in the country, in 1903 he acquired the Buick Motor Company, one of the several hundred car companies then in America, and during the next eight years steadily acquired a whole series of small automobile firms—among them Oldsmobile, Cadillac, and Pontiac—whose names have become so familiar that they are now almost part of the language.

In 1910, after overexpanding and going too deeply into debt, Durant lost control of General Motors to his bankers. Instead of giving up, the indefatigable Durant went on to form a new car company with Louis Chevrolet, a racing driver, and was so successful that in 1915, he was able to reacquire his old company, General Motors, which had gone public, in a takeover raid. But in 1920, the postwar recession once again found him overextended and he lost control of the company for a second time, on this go-around to the Du Pont family.

When the Du Ponts acquired their stake in General Motors, the company was producing 250,000 cars a year, had just earned some $30 million in profit, and was valued at a little over $200 million. Under its new professional management, General Motors went on to become the most successful company in the country and the darling of Wall Street. By 1925, it was making over 800,000 cars a year, about 25 percent of all those sold in the country and generating over $110 million in profit. Its stock price in those five years quadrupled in value, from around $25 to over $100 a share.

Supported by growing companies such as General Motors, the stock market ballooned into something of a financial behemoth during the Coolidge bull market. By the mid-1920s, about $1 billion was being raised annually for new investments, the number of corporations listed had quintupled, and the total value of stocks had increased from $15 billion in 1913 to over $30 billion in 1925.

Wall Street was not the only beneficiary of the growth in the economy. The buoyant stock market was accompanied by a real estate boom in Florida. Since the war, Florida had been swamped by an enormous migration of people attracted by the climate—in five years, the population of Miami had more than doubled. All the money flooding into the state had driven real estate prices into a frenzy. Lured by brochures, which promised graceful palm trees, golden beaches, sun-kissed skies, and whispering breezes, but somehow omitted to mention the hurricanes and the mangrove swamps, the public began buying land indiscriminately. New developments such as Coral Gables and Hollywood-by-the-Sea sprang up overnight. From Palm Beach to Miami and across to the cities of the Gulf Coast, prices skyrocketed. A strip of land on Palm Beach worth a quarter of a million dollars before the boom was priced, by early 1925, at close to $5 million; vacant lots that had once gone for a few hundred dollars were being sold for as much as $50,000.

Watching other people become rich is not much fun, especially if they do it overnight and without any effort. It was therefore inevitable that all this frenetic activity—the thriving stock market, the new issues, the ballyhoo about a new era, the buying and selling of Florida real estate—provoked a chorus of voices demanding that the Fed do something to stop the "orgy of speculation," a phrase that would become so commonplace over the next few years as to lose all meaning.

Leading the charge was the ever disputatious Adolph Miller. His hostility to the rise in the stock market rested, like so many of his arguments, upon several misconceptions. There was the erroneous notion that a rising stock market "absorbs" money from the rest of the economy. This is sheer nonsense, because for every buyer of stocks there is a seller and whatever money flows into the stock market flows immediately out.

In the fall of 1925, Miller had also become particularly alarmed by the data on so-called brokers' loans. These were loans provided by banks to stock brokers who used the money to finance their own inventories of securities or to lend to their own customers to buy equities on margins. Typically such margin investors only paid 20 to 25 percent of the value of stocks with their own money and borrowed the rest. The total volume of such brokers' loans, which had averaged around $1 billion in the early years of the decade, had suddenly ballooned to $2.2 billion at the end of 1924 and looked likely to reach $3.5 billion by the end of 1925. Miller saw these loans as a symptom of speculation, and he was firmly convinced that it was somehow more "inflationary" for banks to finance stock market purchases than for them to finance other activities. Again, we now know this to be fallacious—the inflationary consequences of easy credit have much more to do with the total amount the public borrows and very little to do with the purposes for which it does so.

Miller's campaign was given an added boost one quiet Sunday afternoon in November 1925, when he was sitting in the study of his house on S Street in Washington, going through one of the many Board reports he took home with him, and the doorbell rang. "Before the butler could move," Miller's neighbor from two doors down pushed his way into the house unannounced, "bounded up the stairs, taking them two at a time," and barged in, demanding, "Are you as worried about this speculation as I am?"

Miller's unusually energetic neighbor was none other than the "boy wonder," Herbert Hoover, secretary of commerce. Hoover, a Quaker orphan from Iowa, was an engineer by profession who had graduated in the very first class from Stanford and had made a fortune in the first decade of the century as a promoter of mining ventures in every corner of the globe— from China to the Transvaal, from Siberia to the Yukon, from the Malay peninsula to Tierra del Fuego. He had come to national prominence by accident as the man in charge of evacuating Americans from Europe in 1914, then as the War Food Administrator in the Wilson administration and as the head of Belgian Relief, "the only man who emerged from the ordeal of Paris with an enhanced reputation," according to Maynard Keynes. Appointed to the cabinet by Harding, he had distinguished himself from his do-nothing colleagues by his superb organizational ability, his belief in himself, and the constant flurry of activity that always surrounded him.

In the fall of 1925, Hoover, not shy about interfering in his cabinet colleagues' business—Parker Gilbert called him the "Secretary of Commerce and the Under-Secretary of all other departments"—decided to launch a campaign against the pervasive atmosphere of speculation that he claimed was infecting the country, from Florida real estate to the stock market.

For both Miller and Hoover, the culprit behind this speculative fever was Benjamin Strong. They believed that his policy of keeping interest rates artificially low to help European currencies was responsible for fueling the incipient bubble. Hoover had once been a prime supporter of American engagement in European affairs following the war, and had counted Strong a good friend. But he was now convinced that the policy of propping up Europe with artificially cheap credit had been taken too far. In his words, Strong had become "a mental annex to Europe."

Like every other financial official at the time, Strong was taken aback by the surprising strength of the stock market and was himself also worried about a potential bubble. His letters to Norman are filled with misgivings about the rise in prices on Wall Street. Though he had a somewhat jaundiced view of the stock market, dominated as it was by its motley crew of outsiders—its plungers and pool operators, all of whom were very much at the bottom of the Wall Street social ladder—he was acutely aware of its power to cause trouble. Stock market crashes and banking panics had always been closely linked in the pre-Fed world and many of the country's past financial crises had emerged from Wall Street: 1837, 1857, 1896, and 1907. In his early days as a stockbroker, he himself had been a witness firsthand to the crash of 1896, and had been an active participant in restoring order after the panic of 1907.

But as an experienced Wall Street hand, he was quite aware of how difficult it was to identify a market bubble—to distinguish between an advance in stock prices warranted by higher profits and a rise driven purely by market psychology. Almost by definition, there were always people who believed that the market has gone too high—the stock market depended on a diversity of opinion and for every buyer dreaming of riches in 1925, there was a seller who thought the whole thing had gone too far. Strong recognized his own highly fallible judgment about stocks was a very thin reed on which to conduct the country's monetary policy. Even though his initial reaction was that the market might have gone too far, he asked himself, "May it not be the case the world is now entering upon a period where business developments will follow the recovery of confidence, so long lost as a result of the war? Nobody knows and I will not dare prophesy." Given so much uncertainty, he was convinced that the Federal Reserve should not try to make itself an arbiter of equity prices.

Moreover, even if he was sure that the market had entered a speculative bubble, he was conscious that the Fed had many other objectives to worry about apart from the level of the market. He feared that if he added yet another goal—preventing stock market bubbles—to the list he would overload the system. Drawing a rather stretched analogy between the Federal Reserve and its various and conflicting objectives for the economy and a family burdened by many children, he ruminated, "Must we accept parenthood for every economic development in the country? That is a hard thing for us to do. We would have a large family of children. Every time one of them misbehaved, we might have to spank them all." He wanted the Fed to focus on stabilizing the overall economy and was reluctant to allow its policies to be dominated by the need to regulate the "affairs of gamblers" who thronged the tip of Manhattan.

In Strong's view, something about the American character—the exuberance, the driving optimism, the naive embrace of fads—lent itself to periods of speculative excess. "It seems a shame that the best sort of plans can be handicapped by a speculative orgy," he mused almost philosophically to Norman at the end of 1925, "and yet the temper of the people of this country is such that these situations cannot be avoided."

Despite the agitation from Hoover and Miller in late 1925, Strong concluded that with absolutely no signs of domestic inflation, the pound having only just returned to gold and the European currency situation still fragile, this was not the time to tighten credit. For the moment he would just have to ignore the stock market.

Even in combination there was little that Hoover and Miller were able to do to force his hand. As secretary of commerce, Hoover had no remit to interfere in the deliberations of an independent agency like the Fed. Miller was in a minority on the Board. And while the two of them campaigned to change the Fed's policy by co-opting allies in Congress, senators and congressmen are rarely informed enough to be persuasive advocates for changes in monetary policy.

It helped Strong enormously that the Fed's charter had an inherent bias toward inaction. Under the then law, only the reserve banks could initiate changes in policy. While the Board had the power to approve or disapprove such changes, it could not force the reserve banks to act. It was a recipe for the worst sort of stalemate. Checks and balances may work well in politics, but they are a disaster for any organization—the military is one example; central banks are another—required to act quickly and decisively. But in 1925 and 1926, with Hoover and Miller pushing to tighten credit policy, Strong was able to hide behind the Fed's charter and do nothing.

Nothing illustrates the dilemmas posed for monetary policy by the stock market than the push to tighten in 1925. It turned out that Hoover and Miller had raised a false alarm. There was no bubble. Stock prices took a breather in the spring of 1926, falling by about 10 percent, and then resumed a steady but not yet spectacular rise. By the middle of 1927, the Dow stood at 168. Meanwhile, profits grew strongly and the price-earnings ratio, one measure of market valuation, remained around 11, well below the danger level of 20 that is often considered a sign of overvaluation.* The Florida real estate bubble burst of its own weightlessness, helped by a devastating hurricane in 1926, and though there was much local disruption, its impact on the national economy was minor. Meanwhile, consumer prices remained almost completely flat.

In retrospect, Strong made the right decision in resisting the pressure from Miller and Hoover to tighten credit in late 1925 and 1926. In their enthusiasm to save the country from overspeculation, they had fallen into the first trap of financial officials dealing with complex markets—an excessive level of confidence in their own judgments. Miller, the academic economist, and Hoover, the engineer, were both insulated from doubt by

---

*By comparison, during the great boom years from 1890 to 1910, it oscillated between 15 and 20. In 1929, it reached a peak of 32; at the height of the Internet bubble, it soared to 45.

their ignorance of the way markets operate. In their zeal to burst a bubble that did not exist, they would have damaged the economy without any tangible benefit.

There is no better way to understand the stock market of those years than to return to the story of General Motors. Between 1925 and 1927 the profits of General Motors went up almost two and a half times. With earnings of almost $250 million a year, it overtook U.S. Steel to become the most profitable company in America. Though its stock price quadrupled in those two years, and by the middle of 1927 the company was valued at close to $2 billion, with a price-earnings ratio of less than 9, it was still considered to be reasonably priced.

What of Billy Durant? If General Motors was the emblematic story of the 1920s boom, its founder came to symbolize the other face of that frenetic decade. Although the company he had started had gone on to become the most successful corporation in America, he refused to look back after losing control of it for the second time in 1920. At his peak, he had been worth $100 million. In 1920, the roughly $40 million he received for his stock in General Motors had largely gone to pay off his personal loans, and he had emerged with barely a couple of million dollars.

He was, however, obsessed with the stock market. He formed a consortium of multimillionaires—many of whom were also from Detroit and had made their money in the automobile industry—to play the market. Within four years, he had rebuilt his fortune. By 1927, he was running a fund of over $1 billion, and had indirect control of another $2 to $3 billion that friends would invest alongside him. It was as if Bill Gates had been forced out of Microsoft, only to reappear on Wall Street as one of the largest hedge fund managers.

THIS CHIMERA

Central bankers can be likened to the Greek mythological character Sisyphus. He was condemned by the gods to roll a huge boulder up a steep hill, only to watch it roll down again and have to repeat the task for all eternity. The men in charge of central banks seem to face a similar unfortunate fate—although not for eternity—of watching their successes dissolve in failure. Their goal is a strong economy and stable prices. This is, however, the very environment that breeds the sort of overoptimism and speculation that eventually ends up destabilizing the economy. In the United States during the second half of the 1920s, the destabilizing force was to be the soaring stock market. In Germany it was to be foreign borrowing.

By the beginning of 1927, Germany seemed to have fully recovered from the nightmare years of hyperinflation. Schacht was in a position of unassailable power at the Reichsbank. After the Dawes Plan, he had been appointed to a four-year term during which, by the new bank law, he enjoyed complete security of tenure and independence of the government. He had consolidated his position within the Reichsbank by getting rid of the old guard from the Von Havenstein era, who had opposed his appointment, and putting his own people in charge. Moreover, though a General Council consisting of six German bankers and seven foreigners was supposed to oversee him, it met only quarterly, leaving him to operate unhampered. As one senior German politician of the time remembered, he employed the "tactic of consulting everyone and then doing exactly what he pleases."

By virtue of position and personality, he dominated most discussions of economic policy within Germany. The liberal economist Moritz Bonn, an adviser to the Reichsbank, wrote of Schacht in those years, "He looked upon the world as Hjalmar Schacht's particular oyster, and was very sensitive to public criticism. Having clashed with many strong and ambitious personalities in the German banking and business world, he was full of resentment against colleagues who had at some time outdistanced him. Once he arrived at the head of the central bank, he gloried in being their boss."

To the public, Schacht remained "the Wizard," the savior of the mark. The visit by Strong and Norman in June 1925, his own trip to the United States that fall, and his acceptance as the third member of the central

banking triumvirate running the world's finances had enormously enhanced his prestige. In the three years since their first meeting, he had
developed a very strong personal bond with Norman—they met five times
in 1924, three times in 1925, and four times in 1926. Norman admitted that
Schacht could be difficult to work with, that among his peculiarities was
a love of publicity and the habit of making too many speeches. But it was
"a joy to talk finance" with Schacht, he used to say. His admiration for the
German was so great that Sir Robert Vansittart, later head of the British
diplomatic service, complained that Norman was "infatuated by Dr.
Schacht."

Strong, however, had not taken to Schacht to the same degree. "He is
undoubtedly an exceedingly vain man. This does not so much take the
form of boastfulness as it does a certain naïve self assurance," wrote the
American. Nevertheless, he was impressed by the way Schacht handled
the Reichsbank. "He runs his part of the show with an iron hand. He does
it openly, frankly, and courageously, and seems to have the support of his
Government but it certainly would not do in America. . . . He doesn't gloss
things over; he seems actually to relish the difficulties. . . ."

Power seemed to suit Schacht. The family had moved out of their villa
in Zehlendorf into the official residence of the Reichsbank president on
the top floor of its headquarters on Jägerstrasse. Financially he had little
to worry about—his salary was the equivalent of $50,000 and he drew a
further $75,000 from the pension that he had wrung from the Danatbank.
To show he had arrived, he bought a grand country house some forty miles
north of Berlin, which had been the hunting lodge and estate of Count
Friedrich Eulenberg.

When in town, the Schachts entertained frequently. With his "ugly
clown mask of a face, curiously alive and attractive," Schacht, always sport-
ing a big cigar and accompanied by his matronly wife, Luise, who kept a
"vigilant watch" on him—he was said to have a wandering eye—became
something of a fixture on the social circuit. He had a pompous habit of
wearing his culture conspicuously on his sleeve, which some found irritating, while others ridiculed him behind his back for his arriviste preten-

sions—one acquaintance remarked that "he dresses with the taste of a socially ambitious clerk." Nevertheless, he was a popular guest, something of a catch celebrated for his "cutting and devastating humor." The Aga Khan remembered the Schacht of those years as one of the most charming of dinner companions, who could hold "a whole table enthralled" with his sparkling conversation. Priding himself as something of a poet, he would compose amusing little pieces of doggerel to entertain his fellow guests.

Before the war, social life in Berlin had been especially stultifying. Under the oppressive hierarchy imposed by the Junker elite around the court, there had been little interaction between the various circles in the city. However, the overthrow of the old Prussian nobility and the destruction of the middle class by inflation had transformed Berlin into a rootless society of politicians and profiteers, former aristocrats and foreign diplomats. It would have been an arid soulless sort of place but for its demimonde of artists. With its past swept away, the city had an unhinged nervous energy, an edge to it, that no other city in Europe could match, and it had attracted the best of the European avant-garde: writers, painters, architects, musicians, and playwrights. William Shirer, the journalist who would chronicle the rise of Nazism, first came to Berlin during those years and was captivated. "Life seemed more free, more modern and more exciting than in any place I had ever seen."

But for all its "jewel-like sparkle," the city was wrapped in an atmosphere of impending doom. Norman sensed it when visiting Schacht in late 1926: "You feel all the time that politically as well as economically Germany is still not far from a precipice." After the fiasco of the Beer Hall Putsch, most people treated Hitler as a laughingstock. Nevertheless, there were ominous undercurrents of the convulsions to come. On March 21, 1927, a band of six hundred Nazi brownshirt storm troopers of the *Sturmabteilung*, the SA, beat up a group of Communists in eastern Berlin and marched into the center of the city, attacking anyone on the Kurfürstendamm who looked Jewish. The city authorities responded by banning Nazi activity from Berlin for a year.

But the economy was booming. Over the three years since the mark had been stabilized, output rose close to 50 percent and exports by over 75 percent. The GDP had surpassed its prewar level by a good 20 percent, unemployment was now at a modest 6 percent, and prices were steady. The recovery was reflected in the stock market. During the hyperinflation, few people had believed that capitalism would even survive in Germany and equities had become dirt cheap, having fallen to less than 15 percent of their 1913 inflation-adjusted value—the whole of the Daimler-Benz motor company, for example, could have been bought for the price of 227 of its cars. By 1927, however, the market had quadrupled in value from its low point in 1922.

The Dawes Plan had been an enormous success. In fact it had worked almost too well. American bankers, assured under the plan of being repaid first ahead of reparations owed to France and Britain, had fallen over one another in their enthusiasm to lend to Germany. In the two years since the plan, $1.5 billion flowed into the country, giving Germany the $500 million due for reparations and still leaving it an enormous surplus of foreign cash. Some of this money had gone to finance the reconstruction of industry; but a very large amount had been taken up by the newly empowered states, cities, and municipalities of the budding democracy to build swimming pools, theaters, sports stadiums, and even opera houses. The zeal with which foreign bankers promoted their wares led to a great many imprudent investments and a lot of waste—one small town in Bavaria, having decided to borrow $125,000, was persuaded by its investment banks to increase the amount to $3 million.

With so much foreign money coming in, imports ballooned and the pressure on the government to lighten up on the austerity of 1924 and 1925 became irresistible. By 1926, the national government itself was back to running deficits. These were, however, modest—only $200 million, or less than 1.5 percent of GDP—compared to the giant shortfalls of the hyperinflation years, and financed as they were by hard currency from abroad, did not lead to inflation.

By every indication, Schacht, as one of the architects of this authentic economic miracle, should have been a happy man. Instead, he continued to be obsessed with reparations. Even at the time of the Dawes Plan, he had never been fully convinced that Germany could or even should pay the amounts envisaged. Nevertheless, he had grudgingly supported the plan and the foreign loans that came with it. He had hoped that as the credits from the United States built up and began to rival reparations as a claim on Germany's foreign exchange, they would create a powerful lobby of American bankers, who would share a common interest with the German authorities in getting future payments to the Allies reduced.

But Germany was now borrowing too much abroad. Schacht worried that the foreign debt buildup was becoming so large that when the day came for it to be repaid, it would precipitate a gigantic payments crisis and national bankruptcy. It made no sense to him for Germany to be borrowing dollars to build wonderfully modern urban amenities, such as opera houses, which could never generate the foreign currency to repay the loans. Moreover, Germany was so awash with foreign capital, and was being driven by so conspicuous a boom, that it was getting progressively harder for him to argue that the republic could not afford to meet its reparations obligations. The artificial boom was giving everyone at home and abroad a false sense of prosperity—a "chimera," as he called it.

His problem was that there was very little he could do about the situation. If he tried to tighten credit to curb the domestic boom, he would simply end up encouraging borrowers to look abroad for cheaper loans and thus exacerbate the already excessive foreign borrowing.

He was not a man to agonize too long over dilemmas. In many ways, for someone with the reputation of being a calculating opportunist, he was oddly impulsive. On Thursday, May 12, 1927, he made his move. The Reichsbank instructed every bank in Germany to cut its loans for stock trading by 25 percent immediately. The next day, nicknamed "Black Friday" by the Berlin press, stock prices fell by over 10 percent. Over the next six months, they would slide by another 20 percent.

By going after the stock speculators, Schacht was hoping to crack the atmosphere of overconfidence and curb inflows of foreign money into Germany. This proved to be a serious miscalculation. Even though stocks had gone up a lot in the last five years, this represented a recovery from the brink of disaster. The market was by no means overpriced—in early 1927, its total capitalization was only around $7 billion, less than 50 percent of GDP, still only 60 percent of its prewar level. More important, German municipalities, which were immune to stock market fluctuations, kept on borrowing abroad. All that Schacht had achieved with this hasty maneuver was unnecessary damage to business confidence.

Having thus failed to dam the inflow of foreign loans with his broadside against the stock market, Schacht now began to talk about doing something dramatic over reparations. A New York Fed official, Pierre Jay, passing through Berlin in June 1927, remarked that Schacht did "not wish to have things seem too good in Germany for fear that it will help the execution of the [Dawes] Plan," and speculated that he might take some other action deliberately to undermine Germany's fragile prosperity in order to prove that reparations were too burdensome. Parker Gilbert, the American agent-general for reparations, who was as close to Schacht as anyone, observed that he had begun "openly and actively working for a breakdown" of the Dawes agreement, and described him during this period as "changeable and moody," "temperamental and mercurial."

No one was quite sure what he had in mind. Berlin was rife with rumors that he might deliberately engineer a new crisis. It was the beginning of what one historian has described as Schacht's descent into "irresponsibility and unpredictability." His tendency to "extreme and erratic" behavior seemed to be a deliberate ploy to keep friends and enemies alike guessing. It certainly unnerved his counterparts, Norman and Strong. They feared that consumed as he was by reparations, he might try some reckless and foolhardy gamble to sabotage the Dawes settlement, which would not only plunge Germany into chaos and undermine its fragile new democracy, but might capsize the international monetary structure, which they had so painstakingly put together over the last few years.

They had always worried about Schacht's tendency to embroil himself in highly visible political conflicts. Never much of a diplomat, he had always been very open in his criticisms of government budgetary policy, particularly of the states and municipalities borrowing so much abroad. Back in 1925 during the central bankers' visit to Berlin, Strong had remarked on Schacht's tendency to "get into political matters which would be [better] left alone by the head of the Reichsbank," and Norman had gently tried to warn him to be more discreet. But it always seemed that Schacht had enough of an instinct for survival to avoid rocking the political boat too hard. Now, however, he became increasingly indiscreet and strident in his remarks.

One episode in particular brought his confrontation with the government to a head. At a cabinet meeting in June, Schacht launched into a vituperative attack, which left the ministers speechless with outrage. It was typical of the man that having insulted the cabinet, he was not content to leave ill enough alone. He was overhead bragging to the other guests at a private dinner that evening about how he had taken on the politicians. He revealed confidential details of the whole cabinet debate, made insulting comments about individual ministers, dismissed the finance minister as incompetent, and called for his resignation. Even his old supporter Stresemann agreed that Schacht's behavior was a problem and that his constant and naked self-aggrandizement was becoming intolerable. It was but a small harbinger of things to come.

IMPERIALIST DREAMS

The miracle of the franc's recovery may have been good for France but imposed its own financial strains upon Europe. The money drawn back to the franc on Poincaré's coattails continued to flow in throughout the spring and early summer of 1927, mostly out of sterling. The Banque de France, in an effort to prevent this flood from pushing the franc to uncompetitive levels, kept buying foreign currencies, and by the end of May, had accumulated a foreign exchange war chest totaling $700 million, half of which was in pounds.

The rebound in the financial position of the Banque took Norman completely by surprise. He had never made a secret of his disdain for the

French and their way of doing things—the constant intrigue and infighting, the chronic instability of governments, the overweening role of the state. During 1924, and especially 1925 after Britain had gone back to the gold standard, he had indulged in a certain schadenfreude at France's financial travails. As the franc plunged, he confessed to Strong that the position of France, held up since the war as an example of the advantages of unorthodox financial management, made him "smile."

Moreau, for his part, reciprocated the enmity. From his very first few days in office, he had been irritated by the presumption of Anglo-Saxon bankers that the French would be unable to stabilize the franc without their help. Much of his animosity was specifically directed against Norman, a reflection of a wider and more pervasive suspicion toward the governor of the Bank of England throughout Europe, except in Germany. Strong had picked up on it in the summer of 1926, noting that Continental financial officials "seem to be afraid of him and somewhat distrust him."

With the Banque flush with hard currency and the franc stable, Moreau was determined to use his newfound independence to reestablish French financial prestige. He had not forgotten that before the war Paris had been the second most important money center in the world.

His first opportunity to assert himself on the international stage came in connection with a loan to Poland, which had regained its independence after the war and was historically seen as a partner of France in containing German power. In late 1926, a consortium of central banks, including the Federal Reserve, the Bank of England, the Reichsbank, and now the Banque de France, put together a financial package to help stabilize the Polish zloty. When Norman tried to grab the lead role, the French objected strongly to what they saw as a British attempt to muscle in on France's traditional sphere of influence in Eastern Europe. For Moreau it was one more example of Norman's "imperialist dreams."

In February 1927, the Banque also tried to renegotiate terms on a loan from the Bank of England dating back to 1916 and secured by French gold. As usual when it came to the French, Norman was unhelpful, putting numerous obstacles in the way. Frustrated by Norman's obstructionism, the

Banque surprised the Bank of England in May by announcing that it would pay off the loan and take back the $90 million of gold reserves pledged as security. The next month, without even consulting the British, the Banque issued instructions that $100 million of its sterling balances be converted into gold. The effect would have been to drain almost $200 million of gold out of the Bank of England's reserves. Both actions came as a shock to Norman. Moreau's demands were "capricious" and would "menace the gold standard," he complained to Strong.

Norman and Moreau met repeatedly during the first few months of 1927—in Paris in February, in London in March, and at the Terminus Hotel in Calais in early April—to try to resolve some of these issues. Though the tensions between them never quite broke into open conflict—they were careful to maintain a frosty politeness in all their dealings—their mutual dislike and mistrust were apparent. Moreau had clearly not forgotten how unwilling Norman had been to come to the aid of France at the height of the previous year's crisis, a sharp contrast to the way the Englishman had bent over backward to help Schacht and the Germans in 1924.

The gold standard did offer a traditional safety valve for dealing with shifts in gold holdings. The shrinkage of reserves in the country losing bullion was supposed to lead to an automatic contraction in credit and a rise in interest rates, which would thereby shrink its buying power, while attracting money from abroad. Meanwhile, the country gaining gold would find its credit expanding and its capacity to spend increasing. These "rules of the game," as Keynes called them, were designed to set in train automatic gyroscopic forces to balance out the shifting tides of gold among countries.

But in early 1927, the Bank of England and the Banque de France could not agree how to apply these rules. A conference was arranged and on May 27, Norman revisited the Banque. It was a very different meeting from that first disastrous encounter a year earlier. Now it was Norman's turn to plead for help. He claimed that it would be politically impossible to tighten credit in Britain, that "he could not do so without provoking a riot." Arguing that most of the money flowing into France came from speculators betting that the franc would have to appreciate, he pressed Moreau to cut interest rates.*

Moreau, on the other hand, had just weathered a decade of high inflation, which he did not wish to risk repeating by easing credit. He insisted that under the rules of the gold standard, he had the complete right to convert his sterling holdings into bullion, and should this put Britain's reserves under pressure, the Bank of England could always raise rates.

Quite aware that too precipitate an action by the Banque de France would threaten the Bank's ability to keep the pound on gold, he tried to reassure Norman that he had no intention of destabilizing the gold standard or trying to undermine sterling, declaring melodramatically, "I do not want to trample on the pound." Both parties claimed to be committed to the game, but each was adamant that it was the other who was not following the rules.

The British were not completely on the defensive. They did point out that while France held some $350 million in sterling that it could convert into gold, the British government held $3 billion of French war debts on which it could theoretically demand immediate repayment. The meeting closed in an inconclusive truce. In the following weeks, both sides somewhat halfheartedly backed down, the Bank of England allowing rates in Britain to rise modestly and the Banque de France engineering a fall in its rates. For the moment, outright financial conflict had been averted.

---

*He also argued that while the franc had been stabilized de facto but not de jure at 25 francs to the dollar, speculators could still harbor the hope that the franc would eventually be fixed at a higher exchange rate, providing those who held francs with windfall gains. Norman insisted that the only way to combat this form of destabilizing speculation was for the French government to fix its rate de jure. It finally did so in June 1928.

Schacht, Strong, Norman, and Rist on the Terrace at the New York Fed, July 1927

15. UN PETIT COUP DE WHISKY

1927–28

Not every mistake is a foolish one.

—CICERO

BY THE END of 1926, this quartet of central bankers had already begun to worry about three of the factors—the U.S. stock market bubble, excessive foreign borrowing by Germany, and an increasingly dysfunctional gold standard—that would eventually lead to the economic upheaval at the end of the decade. None of them, however, yet anticipated the scale of the coming storm. Hjalmar Schacht was locked in combat with his own government; Montagu Norman and Émile Moreau were squabbling with each other; and Benjamin Strong was, as always, battling on two fronts—with his health and with his colleagues within the Federal Reserve System.

In 1926, after almost two years without an attack of tuberculosis, Strong developed pneumonia on his return from his summer in Europe. While lying sick with the new disease, at one point close to death, he was again scarred by personal tragedy, this one carrying with it a hint of scandal.

Confined to the Cragmore Sanatorium at Colorado Springs in 1923, he had struck up a friendship with another tubercular patient, Dorothy Smoller, a twenty-two-year-old actress from Tennessee. She had once been a dancer with Anna Pavlova's ballet company, had had several parts on

Broadway, and had even had a bit part in a movie. After a few months in the sanatorium, her money had run out and Strong and some other rich patients stepped in to support her. In November 1926, she resurfaced in New York, to be treated by Dr. James Miller, a Park Avenue physician and Strong's personal doctor—like most tuberculosis patients, she had not fully shaken off the disease. She had just landed a part in another Broadway play when on the morning of December 9, after receiving a mysterious letter that reportedly distressed her, she killed herself by drinking a bottle of liquid shoe polish.

By her bedside were three letters, one for her mother in Long Beach, California, one for a friend, and one for Strong. She left instructions that the photograph of Strong in her possession be returned to him. No one can know whether she and Strong were romantically involved. Perhaps she was just a lost and unhappy young woman, a victim of the Broadway version of the boulevard of broken dreams, who had developed a fixation upon a distinguished and kindly man who had helped her. Whatever the case, her suicide, with its echoes of his wife's death twenty years earlier, must have shaken him profoundly.

In December, he again left New York to recuperate, for a few weeks at the Broadmoor Hotel in Colorado Springs and thereafter in North Carolina. He returned to work six months later, in May 1927, to find the strains and stresses within Europe again building. The quarrel between Moreau and Norman was threatening to derail the pound, and had the potential to undermine the stability of the entire structure of the worldwide gold standard. Meanwhile, Schacht was beginning to clamor for some sort of international initiative to control the flow of foreign money into Germany, which, he feared, would never be able to repay all of its various accumulating debts.

Strong had always hoped that once the other major countries were back on gold, the lopsided maldistribution, which had left so much of the world's gold stock in the United States, would correct itself. But that had not happened. Sterling had returned to gold at an unrealistically high exchange rate, leaving British goods expensive and difficult to sell in the world market. France, on the other hand, had done exactly the opposite. By pegging the franc at 25 to the dollar, the Banque de France had kept French goods very cheap. France was therefore in a position to steal a competitive edge over its European trading partners, particularly Britain. While this discrepancy between British and French prices persisted, the tensions could only fester. There was a natural tendency for money to move from overpriced Britain to underpriced France. To correct the situation, either prices had to fall further in Britain—which the authorities were trying to bring about without much success—or rise in France—which the Banque de France would not permit. The only alternative was to change the gold parity of sterling. But everyone feared that such a devaluation would so shock the banking world as to undermine any hope of order in international finances and even destroy the gold standard.

The Germans had avoided the British mistake. At the exchange rate of 4.2 marks to the dollar set by Schacht back in late 1923, German goods were cheap. Germany had a different problem. It had been denuded of gold during the nightmare years of the early 1920s and was now spending so much on reconstruction and reparations that, despite its large foreign borrowing, it was unable to build up new reserves. Thus, of all the countries in Europe, only France had enjoyed any success in attracting gold, although even this had been done, not so much by drawing gold from America as by weakening the position of Britain.

There was one way for the Fed to help Europe out of these dilemmas, or at least buy it some time. It could lower its interest rates further. In addition to giving Britain some breathing room, there were good domestic reasons to justify such a cut. Prices around the world were falling—not precipitously, but very gradually and very steadily. Since 1925, U.S. wholesale prices had fallen 10 percent, and consumer prices 2 percent. The United States had also entered a mild recession in late 1926, brought on in part by the changeover at Ford from the Model T to the Model A. The two main domestic indicators that Strong had come to rely on to guide his credit decisions—the trend in prices and the level of business activity—argued that the Fed should ease. But interest rates at 4 percent were already unusually low.

Ever since the early 1920s when he had embarked on his policy of keeping interest rates low to help Europe, a faction within the Fed, led by Miller, had argued that Strong was too influenced by international considerations and especially by Norman. During Britain's return to gold in 1925, he had been accused by some members of the Board of having exceeded his authority in providing the line of credit to the Bank of England. But at the time, there had been so much support within U.S. financial circles for Britain's return to gold, and when the British did not even have to draw on the line of credit, the dissenting voices had died away. In 1926, while Strong was in France, he was again criticized by Board members for freelancing and acting too much on his own initiative. He responded that unless they were willing to come to Europe as frequently as he did, and familiarize themselves with the people and the situation, they would just have to trust him. While he did not shy away from conflict—quite the contrary, according to one colleague he seemed to "thoroughly enjoy getting into a fight and coming out on top"—the constant sniping over international policy became so wearing that he even threatened to resign.

The same faction that had opposed him on Europe had pressed him to tighten in 1925 and 1926 to bring down equity prices. While they had then sounded a false alarm on a bubble in stocks, with the market still strong— the Dow was hovering close to 170—he knew that were he now to loosen monetary policy to bail out the pound, he risked severely splitting the Fed.

In the summer of 1927, still weak from his recent illness, Strong decided that rather than go to Europe as he usually did, he would invite Norman, Schacht, and Moreau to the United States.* Before the war, when the gold standard had worked automatically, the system had simply required all

---

* The Banco d'Italia, which had stabilized the lira in December 1926, only six months after the franc, somehow got the impression that it, too, would be asked to attend, and was much disappointed when no invitation arrived.

central banks, operating independently, to follow the rules of the game. Collaboration had not needed to go beyond occasionally lending one another gold.

Ever since the war, as the gold standard had been rebuilt and evolved into a sort of dollar standard with the Federal Reserve acting as the central bank of the industrial world, Strong had found it useful to consult frequently with his colleagues—he generally used his summers in Europe as an occasion to meet all of his European counterparts. This had begun with his getting together with Norman very informally and with minimum publicity once or twice a year—meetings of two friends who agreed on most essentials. After the stabilization of the mark in 1924, Schacht had joined the club, and the three of them convened in Berlin in 1925 and at The Hague in 1926. He now proposed a meeting of all four central banks, including the French.

Moreau, who spoke no English and feared being excluded from the most important discussions, decided to send his deputy governor, Charles Rist, in his place. Norman and Schacht traveled across the Atlantic together on the *Mauretania*, arriving on June 30. They took the usual precautions—their names did not appear on the passenger list and even their baggage was unmarked. But news of the meeting had leaked well in advance and the usual posse of reporters was waiting for them at dockside. Norman, nervous that Rist had arrived two days earlier and might have stolen a march on him, insisted on going straight from the ship to the downtown offices of the New York Fed.

Over the years, each of the central banks had acquired its distinctive architectural signature, somehow expressive of the institution's character. While the Bank of England, for example, looked like a medieval citadel, the Banque de France like an aristocrat's palace, the Reichsbank like a government ministry, for some reason—perhaps in a salute to those first international bankers, the merchant princes of Renaissance Italy—the New York Federal Reserve had chosen to dress itself up as a Florentine palazzo. With its ground-floor arches, heavy sandstone and limestone walls pierced with rows of small rectangular windows, and loggia gracing the twelfth floor, it was an almost exact imitation, on a grander and more epic scale, of the Pitti or the Riccardi palaces in Florence.

It was on the twelfth floor of this faux Italian palace that the four great banking powers of the world first convened. That weekend, however, desperate to get away from the prying eyes of the press, they moved in great secrecy to an undisclosed location out of the city. Strong had chosen for their clandestine meeting the summer home of Ogden L. Mills, undersecretary of the treasury. In an administration whose secretary of the treasury, Andrew Mellon, was the third richest man in the United States, it was in keeping that his deputy should be the heir to a robber baron fortune. Ogden Mills was, however, by the standards of third-generation wealth, a serious man with a law degree from Harvard who had made a career with a respectable white-shoe New York law firm.

But he had not completely given up on the privileges of inherited wealth.* His estate lay on the North Shore of Long Island, now buried under suburban sprawl and, to present eyes, an unlikely setting for a secret conclave of central bankers. But in the 1920s, this was the "Gold Coast," a Gatsby-esque world, now long gone, of mansions with gilded ceilings, of grand formal gardens and marble pavilions, of racing stables, foxhunts, and polo fields, boasting castles larger than those of Scotland and châteaus grander than along the Loire. Among those who summered there were J. P. Morgan, Otto Hermann Kahn of Kuhn Loeb, and Daniel Guggenheim, the copper king.

Its mere twenty rooms made the Mills house, a discreet and elegant neo-Georgian brick mansion with vine-covered walls, located on the Jericho Turnpike in the town of Woodbury, New York, a modest residence by the standards of some of its neighbors. A few hundred yards farther up the turnpike stood Woodlands, a thirty-two-room estate that Andrew Mellon had just bought for his daughter Ailsa as a wedding gift. Half a mile down

---

*With his sister, Gladys Livingstone Mills Phipps and his polo-playing brother-in-law, Henry Carnegie Phipps, he owned the Wheatley Stable, which bred the legendary racehorse Seabiscuit.

the road stood Oheka, the second largest house in the United States, a mock chateau of 127 rooms owned by Kahn.

The four men remained in seclusion for five days, No official record of the discussions was kept. Although they socialized and had meals together, they rarely gathered as a group, relying instead upon bilateral meetings. Strong and Norman in particular spent hours "closeted together." The discussions were almost entirely devoted to the problem of strengthening Europe's gold reserves and to finding ways to encourage the flow of gold from the United States to Europe.

Norman dominated the proceedings, seated at one end of the conference room in a fan-backed oriental chair. In spite of the warm weather, he insisted on wearing his velvet-collared cape, which only added to the picturesque figure he evoked. He made it clear that his gold reserves were critically low. Any further erosion would force him to put up rates. The link between the pound and gold was seriously in peril. Moreover, he argued, the on-going worldwide decline in wholesale prices was a symptom of a mounting global shortage of gold as countries returning to the standard built up their reserves.* And so it was imperative that countries with large reserves ease credit to spread the bullion around.

Rist, on the other hand, argued that the question of European gold was largely a British problem. Having made the mistake of fixing sterling at too high an exchange rate, Britain had no alternative but to continue its policy of deflation, however painful that might be.

Schacht proved to be more of an observer than a key participant. His main goal was to curb the flow of hot money into Germany, which the others saw as largely a side issue. He did warn that this was but one symptom of a wider problem—that Germany was getting too heavily into debt and that a breakdown over reparations would soon occur, with damaging consequences for the whole world. While Strong and Norman had some

---

*For most goods, when a shortage emerges and demand exceeds supply, the price rises. Because under the gold standard, the price of gold was fixed in dollar terms, the first symptom of a gold shortage was not a rise in its price—that by definition could not happen—but a fall in the price of all other commodities.

sympathy for Schacht's desire to renegotiate reparations once more, they warned him to be patient, that nothing could be done till after the American, French, and British elections in 1928. Nevertheless, Strong was sufficiently concerned by Schacht's gloomy forecast that after the meeting, he asked Seymour Parker Gilbert, the agent-general for reparations, to begin work on a new deal on reparations.

Strong, though increasingly sympathetic to the French point of view—much to Norman's discomfort—had arrived at the conference with his mind already made up. The only way to reduce selling pressure on the pound in the short run would be to cut U.S. interest rates. It helped that the domestic indicators he relied upon—price trends and economic activity—also justified a cut. And though he recognized that the stock market was a big stumbling block—he ruefully predicted to Charles Rist as the meeting got under way that a cut would give the market *"un petit coup de whisky"*—it was a risk he was willing to take.

Strong had very deliberately not invited any members of the Federal Reserve Board to the Mills house. After the meeting was over, on July 7, the four did go down to Washington for a day, during which they paid "courtesy calls" on members of the Board and had a "social" lunch at the Willard Hotel. They were all very careful to remain quite tight-lipped with officials in the capital. Before departing the United States, the Europeans had a final meeting in New York, to which Chairman Crissinger was invited, but none of the other members were even informed. Strong, bitter at the constant obstructionism he had met with over the years, was firmly set on keeping them out of the loop—a churlish decision that served no purpose but to irritate the Board and accumulate more enemies against him.

A few days after the European central bankers left, the New York Fed and eight of the other reserve banks voted to cut interest rates by 0.5 percent to 3.5 percent. It was a move that split the system. Four reserve banks—Chicago, San Francisco, Minneapolis, and Philadelphia—insisting that such a move would only fuel stock market speculation, refused to follow. Until then the Board had adopted the view that while it could veto reserve banks' decisions, it could not force them to change policy. Now, in a closely argued decision that also split the Board down the middle, it ruled that it did indeed possess the statutory authority to compel Chicago and the other intransigents to follow the majority. In the recriminations that followed, Crissinger resigned.

The two most vocal of Strong's critics happened to be out of town when the Fed decided to cut rates. Miller had left in the middle of July for two months' vacation in California, although he tried to exert every influence against the decision from afar. Hoover was in the South, managing relief operations to deal with the great Mississippi flood of that year. Returning in August, he submitted a stern memorandum to the Board, arguing that "inflation of credit is not the answer to European difficulties," and that "this speculation . . . can only land us on the shores of depression." He urged both the president and Secretary Mellon to act to forestall the Fed move. Coolidge, who had elevated inaction into a philosophical principle, had become increasingly irritated by his secretary of commerce's constant insistence not only that something must be done about everything but that he, Hoover, knew exactly what was needed. Coolidge would later complain, "That man has offered me unsolicited advice for six years, all of it bad!" Fobbing Hoover off with the excuse that the Fed was an independent agency, the president refused to intervene.

When Strong flippantly spoke to Rist of giving the stock market that *petit coup de whisky*, in his wildest imagination he could not have foreseen the extent of the drunken ride that was to come. In 1925, he had kept money easy to help sterling, betting successfully that the stock market would remain under control. He was now trying the same gamble a second time. This time he was badly wrong. In August, following the Fed cut in rates, the market immediately took off. By the end of the year, the Dow had risen over 20 percent, breaking 200. In January 1928, the Fed revealed that the volume of broker loans had risen to a record $4.4 billion from $3.3 billion the previous year.

By early 1928, the calls on the Fed to do something about the market had become a clamor. The United States had come out of its brief recession, and for the first time since the war, gold was flowing into Europe. Even the pound seemed in better shape. In February 1928, Strong, recognizing that the cut might have been a mistake, bowed to pressure and agreed to reverse course. Over the next three months, the Fed raised its rates from 3.5 percent to 5 percent.

In 1931, Adolph Miller would testify before the Congress that the easing of credit in the middle of 1927 was "the greatest and boldest operation ever undertaken by the Federal Reserve System, . . . [resulting] in one of the most costly errors committed by it or any other banking system in the last years." Some historians, echoing the views of Hoover and Miller, see the meeting on Long Island as the pivotal moment, the turning point that set in train the fateful sequence of events that would eventually lead the world into depression. They argue that by artificially depressing interest rates in the United States to prop up the pound, the Fed helped fuel the stock bubble that subsequently led to the crash two years later.

It is hard to dismiss this view. Though the cut was small—only 0.5 percent off the level of interest rates—and short lived—reversed within six months—the fact that the market should begin the dizzying phase of its rally in the very same month, August 1927, that the easing took place has to be more than mere coincidence. The Fed's move was the spark that lit the forest fire.

As NORMAN TRAVELED back to England, he had every reason to be satisfied with the outcome on Long Island. He had achieved his primary goal of getting the Federal Reserve to support the pound by easing credit. Nevertheless, he had an uneasy feeling. It was clear that Strong was increasingly sympathetic to the French. Sounding like a jealous suitor vying for the attentions of a popular girl, Norman lamented that Strong "takes great interest in the Banque de France and has much personal liking and sympathy" for Charles Rist, which put Norman himself at "a disadvantage." But it was not simply that the Banque de France was beginning to supplant the Bank of England in the affections of the New York Fed. More important in Norman's mind was the central bankers' failure, as prices kept falling, to counter deflationary forces around the world. They had to find more permanent ways to keep "gold out of New York," and redistribute reserves more efficiently.

The summer of 1927 would prove to be the high point of Norman's influence. The modest Fed easing in August brought a temporary reprieve. Gold flowed into Britain. But he still faced the same old problems with France. In February 1928, Norman and Moreau clashed yet again. Romania, one of the last Central European economies to get its house in order, approached the club of central bankers for a loan. Norman assumed that the Bank of England would take charge of the operation, much as it had in the case of Austria and Hungary. But with French finances now strong, Moreau could see no reason why France should not resume its old position of authority in Central Europe. After all, before the war, Romania had been part of the traditional French sphere of influence. On February 6, 1928, as the power struggle over monetary leadership in Eastern Europe reached its head, he wrote in his diary,

> I had an important conversation with M. Poincaré over the issue of the Bank of England's imperialism.
>
> I explained to the Prime Minister that since England was the first European country to recover a stable and reliable currency after the war, it had used this advantage to build the foundation for a veritable financial domination of Europe. . . .
>
> England has thus managed to install itself completely in Austria, Hungary, Belgium, Norway and Italy. It will implant itself next in Greece and Portugal. It is attempting to get a foothold in Yugoslavia and it is fighting us on the sly in Rumania.
>
> We now possess powerful means of exerting pressure on the Bank of England. Would it not be in order to have a serious discussion with Mr. Norman and attempt to di-

vide Europe into two spheres of financial influence assigned respectively to France and England?

On February 21, Moreau, irritated by the British "intrigues to prevent
France from playing the dominant role" in Romania, arrived in London,
declaring that he was going to "ask Norman to choose between peace and
war." Norman, who hated outright confrontations, feigned illness at the
last minute and begged off the meeting, leaving his directors to deal with
the now doubly irritated Frenchman.

The Romanian issue, exacerbated by pettiness on both sides, threatened
to escalate into a major diplomatic incident between the two great banks.
Strong initially tried to act as a mediator but eventually came down on the
side of the Banque de France. He was especially irritated by reports in
European banking and political circles that his friend Norman was trying
"to establish some sort of dictatorship over the central banks of Europe"
and that Strong "was collaborating with him in such a program and supporting him." Norman had obviously taken advantage of their friendship
to give everyone the impression that he had the Fed in his pocket.

By now, he had begun to regret his support for the doctrine that central
banks be encouraged to hold pounds as a substitute for gold. The policy
had allowed Britain to buoy its international position by using its status as
a pivotal currency to postpone some hard choices. By avoiding an immediate crisis, the policy had set the stage for an even greater crisis in the future.
As money continued to pour into France, the Banque had accumulated
over a billion dollars worth of pounds, which at some point it would want
to cash in for gold. Strong had some sympathy for its dilemma. The gold
standard demanded that a central bank should allow all comers to switch
their currency holdings freely into bullion. But unless Britain's position was
to improve, such a move would completely drain the Bank of England's
reserves and threaten the very viability of the gold standard.

He also began to realize that his policy of keeping U.S. interest rates
low to bolster sterling had failed to solve the fundamental problem of the
British economy—that its prices were too high and its currency overval-

ued. Furthermore, he had unintentionally provided the impetus for the growing bubble on Wall Street. And it had exposed him to constant criticism at home over his excessive focus on international affairs. That summer the *Chicago Tribune* denounced him for creating "speculation on the stock market that was growing . . . like a snowball rolling down a hill" and called for his resignation.

He was by now exhausted and disillusioned, particularly with the quarrelsome Europeans. His doctors warned him that if he wished to live, he could not continue to work. His lungs were failing. He was hit by a bout of shingles that covered his face, temporarily blinding him in one eye and leaving only partial sight in the other. The virus brought on a severe case of neuritis and the massive doses of morphine that cut back the pain sufficiently for him to work had destroyed his digestive system. The tuberculosis had come back in his left lung and, once more, he developed bronchial pneumonia.

In May 1928, Strong sailed for Europe. He had already decided to submit his resignation. Ironically, he seemed on the verge of finding some personal happiness. In 1926, his ex-wife Katharine had written to him, regretting her past mistakes and asking for reconciliation. He wrote back to say that would not be feasible, citing his illness as the reason. By 1928, however, he had begun a relationship with a much younger woman, an opera singer whom he intended to marry.

Deliberately avoiding London, he arrived at Cherbourg in the third week of May. Norman rushed over to see him. That last meeting was a difficult one. Losing his temper, Strong tried to make Norman see that he was his own worst enemy. He reminded his friend, in the "most vehement language" that Moreau's hoard of sterling was a "sword of Damocles" over the Bank of England, making it "stupid beyond understanding" for Norman to pick a quarrel with the French when he was so "completely dependent upon the good will of the Bank of France." They parted on bad terms. Though Strong did write a letter over the summer to make up, he still grumbled to friends about Norman's obsessive scheming for power within Europe.

The strain of the quarrel with Strong and the tensions with the French had begun to tell on Norman's nerves. As the stresses grew, he withdrew more and more into himself, refusing to take his colleagues into his confidence. At one point, several frustrated senior directors of the Bank launched a campaign of noncooperation by pointedly refusing to speak at the weekly meetings of the Committee of the Treasury, the Court's policymaking group. Everyone remarked on the increased volatility of the governor's mood swings. "One moment he would be sunny and all smiles, the next, for no apparent reason his face would be like a thundercloud," recalled one colleague. He threw tantrums at the staff—in a fit of temper, he once flung an ink pot at Sir Ernest Harvey, the comptroller—and his bouts of "nervous exhaustion" seemed to become more frequent. In mid-February 1928, he collapsed and was bedridden for a few days. A week later, it happened again. In the middle of March he was forced to take three weeks off to recuperate in Madeira. A few weeks after that last difficult meeting at Cherbourg, he left for a three-month complete rest in South Africa and did not return to work until early September.

Strong spent a melancholy summer in France. After a few weeks in Paris, he went on to Evian and Grasse, in the south of France. In July, he wrote to Norman of his decision to resign. "How hard and how cruel life is." Norman wrote back, "But what a stage ours has been over these ten or twelve years. . . . Your early dreams set a goal before a world, which was then so distracted as to be blind and incredulous. Now your dreams have come true."

After Strong returned to New York, on October 15, he underwent an operation to stem intestinal bleeding. The next day, he died in the hospital of a severe secondary hemorrhage. He was only fifty-five.

Norman took the blow very badly. "I am desolate and lonesome at Ben's sudden death," he wrote to a friend. They had been close for barely seven years. But in that time the friendship had become central to each of their lives. He would soon discover that Strong's death had not only robbed him of his best friend, but also of much of his power.

PART FOUR

REAPING ANOTHER
WHIRLWIND

*

1928-33

16. INTO THE VORTEX

1928–29

At particular times a great deal of stupid people
have a great deal of stupid money. . . . At intervals
. . . . the money of these people—the blind capital, as
we call it, of the country—is particularly large and
craving; it seeks for someone to devour it, and there
is a "plethora"; it finds someone, and there is "specu-
lation"; it is devoured, and there is "panic."

—WALTER BAGEHOT

THE GREAT BEAR of Wall Street legend, Jesse Livermore, once observed that "stocks could be beat, but that no one could beat the stock market." By that he meant that while it was possible to predict the factors that caused any given stock to rise or fall, the overall market was driven by the ebb and flow of confidence, a force so intangible and elusive that it was not readily discernible to most people. There would be no better evidence of this than the stock market bubble of the late 1920s and the crash that followed it.*

---

*Livermore's own career belied his own statement. Sensing that the boom in 1907 was going to turn into a spectacular bust, he made his first millions by shorting the market just before the panic of that year. He reputedly made another fortune the same way in 1929— he would make and lose several such fortunes in his lifetime. In 1940, he shot himself in

The bubble began, like all such bubbles, with a conventional bull market, firmly rooted in economic reality and led by the growth of profits. From 1922 to 1927, profits went up 75 percent and the market rose commensurately with them. Not every stock went up in the rise. From the very start, the 1920s market had been as bifurcated as the underlying economy—the "old economy" of textiles, coal, and railroads struggling, as coal lost out to oil and electricity, and the new business of trucking bypassing the railways while the "new economy" of automobiles and radio and consumer appliances grew exponentially. Of the thousand or so companies listed on the New York Stock Exchange, as many went down as went up.

The first signs that other, more psychological, factors might be at play emerged in the middle of 1927 with the Fed easing after the Long Island meeting. The dynamic between market prices and earnings seemed to change. During the second half of the year, despite a weakening in profits, the Dow leaped from 150 to around 200, a rise of about 30 percent. It was still not clear that this was a bubble, for it was possible to argue that the fall in earnings was temporary—a consequence of the modest recession associated with Ford's shutdown to retool for the change from the Model T to the Model A—and that stocks were being unusually prescient in anticipating a rebound in earnings the following year. The market was still well behaved, rising steadily with only a few stumbles, and without the slightly crazed erratic moves and frenetic trading that were to come.

It was in the early summer of 1928, with the Dow at around 200, that the market truly seemed to break free of its anchor to economic reality and began its flight into the outer reaches of make-believe. During the next fifteen months, the Dow went from 200 to a peak of 380, almost doubling in value.

That it was so obviously a bubble was apparent not simply from the fact that stock prices were now rising out of all proportion to the rise in corporate earnings—for while stock values were doubling, profits main-

---

the cloakroom of the Sherry Netherlands Hotel in New York City. He had $5 million in his bank account.

FIGURE 5

U.S. Stock Prices and Corporate Profits: 1922–36

The bubble began in the fall of 1927.

tained their steady advance of 10 percent per year. The market displayed every classic symptom of a mania: the progressive narrowing in the number of stocks going up, the nationwide fascination with the activities of Wall Street, the faddish invocations of a new era, the suspension of every conventional standard of financial rationality, and the rabble enlistment of an army of amateur and ill-informed speculators betting on the basis of rumors and tip sheets.

By 1929, anywhere from two to three million households, one out of every ten in the country, had money invested in and were engaged with the market. Trading stocks had become more than a national pastime—it had become a national obsession. These punters were derisively described by professionals like Jesse Livermore as "minnows." But while the bubble lasted, it was the people who were the least informed who were the ones making the most money. As the *New York Times* described it, "The old-timers, who usually play the market by note, are behind the times and wrong," while the "new crop of speculators who play entirely by ear are right."

The city that was most obsessed was New York, although Detroit, home to so many newly enriched "motor millionaires," came a close second, followed by two other new-money towns, Miami and Palm Beach. The infatuation with the market took over the life of New York City, sucking everything into its maw. As Claud Cockburn, a British journalist newly arrived in America, observed, "You could talk about Prohibition, or Hemingway, or air conditioning, or music, or horses, but in the end you had to talk about the stock market, and that was when the conversation became serious." Anyone trying to throw doubt on the reality of this Promised Land found himself being attacked as if he had blasphemed about a religious faith or love of country.

As the crowd piling into the market grew, brokerage house offices more than doubled—from 700 in 1925 to over 1,600 in 1929—mushrooming across the country into such places as Steubenville, Ohio; Independence, Kansas; Amarillo, Texas; Gastonia, North Carolina; Storm Lake, Iowa; Chickasha, Oklahoma, and Shabbona, Illinois. These "board rooms" became substitutes for the bars shut down by Prohibition—the same swing doors, darkened windows, and smoke-filled rooms furnished with mahogany chairs and packed with all sorts of nondescript folk from every walk of life hanging around to follow the projected ticker tape flickering on the big screen at the front of the office. The grail was to discover the next General Motors, which had risen twentyfold during the decade, or the next RCA, which had gone up seventyfold. The newspapers were full of articles about amateur investors who had made fortunes overnight.

The old crowd on Wall Street had a rule that a bull market was not in full stampede until it was being played by "bootblacks, household servants, and clerks." By the spring of 1928, every type of person was opening a brokerage account—according to one contemporary account, "school teachers, seamstresses, barbers, machinists, necktie salesmen, gas fitters, motormen, family cooks, and lexicographers." Bernard Baruch, the stock speculator who had settled down to a life of respectability as a presidential adviser, reminisced, "Taxi drivers told you what to buy. The shoeshine boy could give you a summary of the day's financial news as he worked with rag and polish. An old beggar, who regularly patrolled the street in front of my office, now gave me tips—and I suppose spent the money, I and others gave him, in the market. My cook had a brokerage account."

The stock pronouncements of shoeshine boys would become forever immortalized as the emblematic symbol of the excesses of that period. Most famously, Joseph Kennedy decided to sell completely out of the market when in July 1929, having already liquidated a large portion of his portfolio, he was accosted by a particularly enthusiastic shoeblack on a trip downtown to Wall Street, who insisted on feeding him some inside tips. "When the time comes that a shoeshine boy knows as much as I do about what is going on in the stock market," concluded Kennedy, "it's time for me to get out."

About a third of the new speculators were female. Articles on investing regularly appeared in women's magazines. Indeed, the seminal manifesto of the time, "Everyone Ought to Be Rich" originally appeared in the August 1929 *Ladies' Home Journal*. Its author, John J. Raskob, recently treasurer of General Motors, now sponsor of the Empire State Building then in its planning stages, made the case that anyone who invested $15 a month and reinvested the dividends would have a fortune of $80,000 after twenty years.

Initially, Wall Street, always a bastion of misogyny, dismissed the new class of speculatrices as "hard losers and naggers . . . stubborn as mules, suspicious as serpents and absolutely hell bent to have their own way." Even the *New York Times* had to have its chuckle about some of the characteristics of these novices—their memory lapses, their superstitions, their gullibility. But women soon became so important to the market that brokerage houses opened up special offices on the Upper East Side on Fifth or Madison or on Broadway in the West Seventies to cater specifically to this ever more substantial clientele.

The new folk heroes of the market were the pool operators, a band of professional speculators analogous to the hedge fund managers of today.

They were typically outsiders, despised by the Wall Street establishment, who accumulated their fortunes—though they would soon enough lose them—by betting on stocks with their own and their friends' money. The seven Fisher brothers who had sold their automobile body company to General Motors for $200 million ran such an enterprise, as did Arthur Cutten, an old hard-of-hearing commodity trader from the Chicago wheat pits; Jesse Livermore, the great bear trader; and Kennedy, who had made his first million investing in the stock of the Hertz Yellow Cab Company and was now making his profits as an investor in the movie industry.

Biggest of them all was Billy Durant, who became the cheerleader for the bull market. Operating from a high-floor office at the corner of Broadway and Fifty-seventh, the exiled creator of General Motors now specialized in ramping stocks—acquiring large blocks in secret, eventually publicizing his positions to drive the price high, then off-loading them as a sadly unsuspecting public piled in. He traded so frequently and in such large amounts that he had to use twenty different brokers, his commissions just to one of whom amounted to $4 million a year. When he went to Europe, his transatlantic phone bills alone were said to be $25,000 a week.

On Wall Street, opinion about the markets was as always split. Charles E. Mitchell, head of the National City, the largest bank in the country, was nicknamed "Sunshine Charlie" for his infectious optimism. He was the carnival salesman of American banking, who had transformed his firm into a giant machine for selling stocks. Paul Warburg, one of the wise men of American banking, the intellectual father of the Federal Reserve System, kept predicting that it would all end in disaster, issuing his most powerful jeremiad on March 8, 1929: "History, which has a painful way of repeating itself, has taught us that speculative overexpansion invariably ends in over-contraction and distress." If the "debauch" on the stock market and the "orgies of unrestrained speculations" continued, he warned, the ultimate collapse in stocks would bring about "a general depression involving the entire country." He was promptly accused of "sandbagging American prosperity."

Even within the same firm opinions were divided. At Morgans, Thomas Lamont was a believer in the New Era. Russell Leffingwell, a former assistant secretary of the treasury, who had become a partner in 1923, blamed the bubble on Norman and Strong. In March 1929, on the very same day that Warburg issued his ominous pronouncement, Leffingwell predicted to Lamont, "Monty and Ben sowed the wind. I expect we shall have to reap the whirlwind.... I think we are going to have a world credit crisis."

The financial press was as much at odds as the men they covered. While the *Journal of Commerce* and the *Commercial and Financial Chronicle* hammered away at the "speculative orgy," the *Wall Street Journal* kept the faith, insisting that, "There are many underlying reasons why the size of the market should be many times what it was a decade ago." There was much editorial head-shaking in the mainstream newspapers. Alexander Dana Noyes, the bespectacled, professorial financial editor of the *New York Times*, who had been watching the market for forty years, warned that "stock speculation has reached an exceedingly dangerous stage," while the *Washington Post* editorialized that "thousands of buyers of stocks are in for serious losses."

The *New York Daily Mirror*, by contrast, was so transported by its vision of the future that it was unable to restrain its soaring flight of rhetoric:

> The prevailing bull market is just America's bet that she
> won't stop expanding, that big ideas aren't petering out,
> that ambition isn't tiring in the wings, that tomorrow is
> twitching with growth pains. Graph hounds, chart wavers
> and statistic quoters may shout their pens hoarse with con-
> trary sentiment—financial Jeremiahs may rave of days of
> doom, but these minority reports are drowned by the hur-
> rahing ticker tape and the swish of skyrocketing securities.
> We're gambling on continued prosperity, full employment,
> and undiminished spending capacity—on freight loadings,
> automobile output, radio expansion—on aviation develop-

ment, crop yields, beef prices—on mail order sales and
sound retailing.

It was from Washington that the bull market faced its greatest hostility. Every senior financial official in the government thought that stocks were now in a speculative bubble—everyone, that is, except the president, Calvin Coolidge. For some reason unfathomable even to members of his own administration, Silent Cal seemed blithely unconcerned about developments on Wall Street. In February 1929, as he prepared to leave the White House, he declared that stocks were "cheap at current prices" and conditions absolutely sound, probably just to irritate his successor, Herbert Hoover.

The new president was so well known to be a fervent opponent of the speculation on Wall Street that in the week of his nomination to the Republican candidacy, the stock market had gone down 7 percent. Like all of Washington, he faced a quandary. While he believed that the market was now living in a world of fantasy, the underlying economy was healthy and doing well. It was almost impossible to craft his comments in such a way as to talk the stock market back to earth without at the same time damaging the economy and laying himself open to accusations of undermining the American dream.

He therefore felt compelled to be extremely circumspect. In the spring of 1929, he did invite the editors of the nation's largest newspapers to Washington to enlist them against the perils of speculation; he sent Henry Robinson, president of the First Security National Bank of Los Angeles, as his personal envoy to Wall Street to warn that the market was unsound; and he continued to press his friend Adolph Miller for the Federal Reserve Board to use its armory of measures to deflate the bubble. All to little avail.

At the Treasury Department, Andrew Mellon was even less successful. By 1929, he had served under three presidents and was being hailed as the "best Treasury Secretary since Alexander Hamilton." Gloomy and gaunt, he was an unlikely figure to have presided over a decade of such economic exuberance. The truth was that most of his public achievements were a matter of luck. In 1921 he had inherited an economy still on the vestiges of a war footing. The peace dividend allowed him to slash public spending almost in half, while at the same time cutting income taxes and paying down the national debt from $24 billion to $16 billion. In international finance, he had left all currency matters to Benjamin Strong. Similarly, though he was a member of the Federal Reserve Board, he usually absented himself from its deliberations; most of the Fed's achievements in monetary policy were Strong's. What contribution the United States had made to solving the problem of reparations was largely the work of private businessmen, such as Dawes and Young. Mellon could claim to have played a key role in restructuring the Allied war debts. But the British part of the deal had been unusually harsh, only agreed to by a Britain eager to resume its place as the linchpin of the gold standard. Even now, the French had yet to ratify their settlement.

The emotionally crippled Mellon, long divorced from his wife and now estranged from his children, seemed to find his main solace in obsessively collecting works of art. By the late 1920s, his avocation had come to dominate his life and he had become oddly disengaged in his role as treasury secretary. For example, when he quite coincidently turned up in Paris in the middle of the French currency crisis in September 1926, he was received by the desperate Émile Moreau, who could not help noticing that Mellon seemed almost bored during their discussions and "displayed some life only in front of the Fragonard" that hung on Moreau's office wall.

Mellon would eventually be accused of having encouraged the market higher out of the crude desire to enlarge his personal fortune. This is unfair. In private, he acknowledged that stocks were in a bubble. But his experience as one of the country's great financiers convinced him that there was little that the Fed or anyone else could do about it, observing to a fellow member of the Federal Reserve Board, "When the American people change their minds, this speculative orgy will stop but not before." Having decided that trying to talk the market down was an impossible task and that he would only look foolish when he failed, he waited for the frenzy to burn itself out, saying as little as possible publicly. In March 1929, he did declare that he thought this was a good time for investors to buy bonds, but this was so coy a pronouncement that those few people who paid any attention poked fun at Mellon's admonition that "gentlemen prefer bonds."

The irrepressible gentlemen on Capitol Hill were not so reticent. In February and March of 1928, the Senate Committee on Banking and Currency held hearings on brokers' loans and, from March to May, its House counterpart opened its own investigation into stock market speculation—overall a spectacle somehow both embarrassing and uplifting. It was painful to watch the good senators flailing around trying to understand the workings of a complicated financial system and hurling foolish questions at the expert witnesses. But there was also something admirable as they voiced the outrage of the common man at the absurdities of Wall Street.

The following exchange captures the quality of the discussion and the mood of the Congress. In the middle of the hearings, Senator Earle Mayfield of Texas suddenly has an inspiration: Why not ban all stock trading?

SENATOR MAYFIELD: Well, instead of urging all these various changes in the law, why do you not prohibit gambling in stocks and bonds on the New York Stock Exchange? In that way you could make a short cut to the proposition. Just stop it.

SENATOR BROOKHART: Well, I do not have any objection to doing that. But Senator Couzens, in discussing the thing, said we needed a market—a legitimate market for stocks and bonds.

SENATOR MAYFIELD: Preserve the legitimate market, but cut out the gambling. . . .

SENATOR EDGE: Does the senator from Texas seriously consider passing a bill prohibiting that?

SENATOR MAYFIELD: There are millions of dollars of stocks and bonds sold every day by people who do not own them and have no idea of owning them. Purely gambling on the market.

SENATOR BROOKHART: There is no trouble at all in stopping the gambling. . . . We have a law against poker gambling, and we can have a law against stock gambling.

The discussion during the hearings continued in an attempt to refine the distinction between investing and gambling. Finally, Senator Carter Glass, one of the architects of the Federal Reserve System and secretary of the treasury during the last two years of the Wilson administration, thought he had it figured out. A stock he had bought only the previous January at 108 was now selling on the market at 69. "Now what is that but gambling?" he exclaimed.

It was great theater, put on, according to *Time* magazine, with that combination of "oratory, ethics and provincialism" at which the U.S. Congress is so good: a reenactment of an old morality play that had divided the republic since its founding—between those, like Hamilton, who believed that great wealth was the reward for taking risks and those, like Jefferson, who believed that prosperity should be the reward for hard work and thrift.

The strongest calls to do something came from senators representing the farm states of the Midwest and the Great Plains: Borah of Idaho, La Follette and Lenroot of Wisconsin, Brookhart of Iowa, Pine of Oklahoma, and Mayfield of Texas. They had their roots in those parts of the country that had always been suspicious of bankers and were ambivalent about the power of money in American life. Their constituents, the farmers, had already been through hard times for most of the decade as commodity prices fell and were now being starved of credit as it was diverted into the stock market. But the senators slowly came to recognize that they would only inflict greater damage upon their people if they pressed for tighter credit to force stock prices down.

And so Congress's efforts to control speculation yielded little except for some gloriously overheated language. In February 1929, Senator Tom Heflin of Alabama introduced a resolution asking the Federal Reserve Board to control speculation, thundering to the Senate: "Wall Street has become the most notorious gambling center in the whole universe . . . the hotbed and breeding place of the worst form of gambling that ever cursed the country." The Louisiana State Lottery "slew its hundreds," he continued, "but the New York State gambling Exchanges slay their hundreds of thousands. . . . The government owes to itself and to its people to put an end to this monstrous evil."

It was thus left to the Fed to wrestle with the conundrum of how to deflate the stock bubble without crippling the economy. Recognizing that the easing of credit policy in the middle of 1927 had been a mistake, it raised rates from 3.5 percent in February 1928 to 5 percent in July 1928. But just as the stock market began its second leg upward in the middle of 1928, the Fed fell silent and disappeared from view, brutally divided about how to react.

Any further measures to bring the market to earth were bound to inflict collateral damage to the economy, especially on farmers. Moreover, capital had once again begun flowing in from abroad, attracted by the returns on Wall Street. Were the Fed to raise interest rates now, it might well pull in even more gold, possibly even forcing sterling off the gold standard.

Strong was still grappling to the very end with these issues. He was willing to concede that it had been a mistake to delay tightening credit so long in early 1928, thus letting the bull market build up such a head of steam. Nevertheless, in the last weeks before he died, he had begun arguing that the Fed should not tighten any further but step aside in the hope that the frenzy would burn itself out.

Strong's successor at the New York Fed was George L. Harrison, a forty-two-year-old lawyer, with impeccable establishment credentials. Born in San Francisco, the son of an army colonel, Harrison had had a peripatetic childhood while his father was posted to various forts across the country. He had been lame from childhood as result of a fall and hobbled around with a heavy walking stick. He had gone to Yale, where he had run with "right crowd" and had become a member of Skull and Bones, the elite secret society for seniors that supposedly serves as an entrée into the upper echelons of business and government. His Yale roommate and close friend was Robert Taft, the son of President William Taft, and they had gone on to Harvard Law School together. Graduating close to the top of his class, Harrison was offered a clerkship on the Supreme Court with Justice Oliver Wendell Holmes, a position in which he would be followed by Harvey Bundy, father of the Bundy brothers, William and McGeorge, and by Alger Hiss, the senior State Department official later accused of being a Soviet spy.

Harrison had joined the Federal Reserve Board as assistant general counsel in 1914 soon after it opened and in 1920 had been persuaded by Strong to come to the New York Fed as his deputy. A scholarly-looking man with a big head of wavy hair, friendly blue eyes, and a warm and genial manner, he was a committed bachelor, lived in a small suite at the Yale Club, and liked to spend his evenings playing poker with his friends. Having been groomed for the job, he was the obvious choice to succeed Strong. He shared his mentor's international outlook and as the deputy governor responsible for the day-to-day's dealings with European central banks, he had developed close working relationships with both Norman and Moreau.

Nevertheless, filling Strong's shoes was a daunting task. As Russell Leffingwell, the Morgan partner, put it, Harrison had the double disadvantage of "being young and new," while as Strong's protégé he "had inherited all the antagonisms that poor Ben left behind him." Harrison also had a very different personality from his predecessor's. Where Strong was forceful and aggressive, the affable and easygoing Harrison was cautious and diplomatic. Strong had a terrible temper and was impatient with incompetence in his subordinates. Harrison by contrast found it hard to fire anyone. There was never much doubt where Strong stood on an issue and he did not shy from confrontation, while Harrison believed in keeping his cards close to his chest.

Strong's death had left a political vacuum within the system as a whole. The chairman of the Board, Roy Young, who had taken over from Daniel Crissinger in late 1927, was a florid-faced glad-handing banker from Minnesota who loved to regale people with his stories. With Strong dead,

Young very consciously set out to reclaim leadership, to reassert Washington's control over the decision-making process, and in his words, "raise the prestige of the Board within the system."

A majority of the Board in Washington, among them Young, Miller, and Hamlin, the same governors who had been so strongly in favor of raising interest rates to curb speculation as the bull market built up, had now changed their minds. Fearful that increasing the price of money at this stage would harm the economy without checking the orgy on Wall Street, they now began to press for "direct action" against speculators.

By early 1929, the bubble was not simply a problem for the Fed but for almost every European central bank as well. New York was sucking in capital from abroad at a time when Europe was still very dependent on American money. The weakest links were Germany and the other Central European countries. But the Bank of England was losing gold as well. While in early 1928, it held over $830 million in reserves, the highest since the war, by early 1929, these had fallen below $700 million and were still going down. In the old days, when his gold reserves came under strain, Norman's first reaction would have been to press his friend Strong to ease Fed policy. Now grimly aware that with Wall Street on a roll, no one would dance to that tune, he thought out a very different strategy.

He arrived in New York on January 27 armed with his new proposal. Meeting with Harrison at the New York Fed, Norman now surprised everyone by arguing for a sharp rise in U.S. rates, possibly by 1 percent, even by 2 percent, taking the discount rate to 7 percent. The Fed should try to break "the spirit of speculation," "prostrating" the market by a forceful tightening of credit. Once a change in psychology had been achieved, interest rates could be then brought down again and capital flows to Europe would resume. For some reason Norman thought the Fed could pierce the bubble with a surgical incision that would bring it back to earth, without harming the economy. It was a completely absurd idea. Monetary policy does not work like a scalpel but more like a sledgehammer. Norman could neither be sure how high rates would have to go to check the market boom nor predict with any certainty what this would do to the U.S. economy.

Nevertheless, such was his power that Harrison embraced the idea. He did, however, warn Norman that since Strong had died, things had changed within the Fed. The conflict between the Board and the New York Fed had become even greater than in the past. There was now general agreement that the United States was faced with a stock market bubble. But the system was deeply divided about how to respond. While the reserve banks wanted to raise rates, it was now the Board that was resisting, and it had become more aggressive about getting its way. Harrison himself had just emerged from a collision with the Board over issues of jurisdiction, Chairman Young warning him that he and the other Board members did not "any longer intend to be a rubber stamp." Harrison urged Norman to visit Washington—which he had till now ignored—and begin building a relationship with the Board if he wanted to continue to influence U.S. credit policy.

On February 5, Harrison, fortified by his discussions with Norman, himself went down to Washington and proposed exactly the Norman strategy to Young. He rejected the idea that his old chief, Strong, had been advocating in his last few months—that the Fed should passively sit by and "let the situation go along until it corrects itself." Instead, he now pressed for "sharp incisive action," a rise in rates of 1 percent. He had come to the conclusion, as he would put in later, that it would be better "to have the stock market fall out of the tenth story, instead of the twentieth later on." Once the speculative fever had been broken, rates could be brought down again. The next day, Norman also turned up in Washington, bearing the same message. Members of the Board could not help but remark on the almost sinister influence that he seemed to exert over the New York Fed, originally upon Strong and now upon Harrison. One governor would later comment that Harrison "lived and breathed for Norman."

While Harrison and Norman were pressing for rate hikes, the Board continued its campaign for direct action. On February 2, it issued a directive to all its member banks that they should not borrow from the Fed "for the purpose of making speculative loans or for the purpose of maintaining speculative loans." Four days later, it made the directive public. The Dow fell 20 points over the next three days, but quickly recovered and by the end of the week was back at the highs. The market's attitude was best summarized by an editorial in the Hearst newspapers. "If buying and selling stocks is wrong, the Government should close the Stock Exchange. If not, the Federal Reserve Board should mind its own business."

Norman left for home in the middle of February shaken by his trip. In the old days, during his visits to the United States, there had been an easy camaraderie and his friend Strong had always exercised a calming influence over him. This time he returned to Britain as anxious as when he had set out. It had been "the hardest time in America that he had ever had," he reported to his colleagues. He had found the American central bankers paralyzed by indecision; there was "no leader"; within the Federal Reserve System, they were "at odds with one another, drifting and not knowing what to do." In a circular letter sent to several heads of European central banks, he wrote that he had set off in the hope of getting a clearer view of what was going on in the United States only to return with "an even deeper feeling of confusion and obscurity."

Meanwhile, back in the United States the struggle between the Board and the New York Fed was intensifying. On February 11, the directors of the New York Fed voted unanimously to raise rates by 1 percent to 6 percent. Harrison called Young in Washington to inform him of the decision, acknowledging the Board's right to override it. Young asked for time to consider the initiative, but Harrison insisted on a definitive answer that day. After three hours of calls back and forth in which Young unsuccessfully tried to persuade Harrison not to force a showdown, he eventually called to say that the Board had voted to disallow the hike. Over the next three months, the directors in New York voted ten times to raise rates and each time were overridden by Washington.

The Fed was now paralyzed by this standoff between its two principal arms. The Board kept insisting that the right way to deflate the bubble was through "direct action": credit controls, particularly of brokers' loans. New York was equally insistent that such a policy could not work, that it was impossible to control the application of credit once it left the doors of the Federal Reserve. Meanwhile, the pace of speculation was accelerating.

It did not help that the Fed seemed incapable of even exerting its control over leading bankers, let alone over the crowd psychology of investors. At the end of March, it was announced that total broker loans had increased to almost $7 billion, and the market swooned. The fear that some drastic action from the Fed to curtail the amount of credit going into the stock market was imminent drove the rate on brokers' loans to over 20 percent. Instead, Charlie Mitchell of National City Bank, himself a director of the New York Fed, defied the Board by calling a press conference and announcing that his bank would pump an extra $25 million into brokers' loans to support the stock market. After that, what little credibility the Fed possessed was irretrievably lost.

It is too easy to mock the Fed for entangling itself in a bureaucratic turf feud and fiddling while Rome was burning. Both parties to the debate were in fact right. The Board was undoubtedly correct that with the demand for money on Wall Street so strong, call money averaging over 10 percent, sometimes spiking as high as 20 percent, and speculators counting on gains of 25 percent a year and more, a hike in the Fed's discount rate from 5 percent to 6 percent or even 7 percent at this stage of the game was going to have almost no effect. To be sure of pricking the bubble would have required raising interest rates higher, perhaps to 10 or 15 percent, which would have caused massive cutbacks in business investment and would have plunged the economy into depression.

But the New York Fed also happened to be right. All the jawboning about reducing credit for speculators proved to be pointless. It did in fact succeed in curbing the amount of money going into brokers' loans from banks—between early 1928, when the Board first declared war on brokers' loans, and October 1929, banks cut their loans to brokers from $2.6 billion to $1.9 billion. Meanwhile, other sources of credit—U.S. corporations with excess cash, British stockbrokers, European bankers flush with liquidity, even some Oriental potentates—more than made up for the decline by increasing their funding of brokers' loans from $1.8 billion to $6.6 billion. It was these players, all of them outside the Fed's control, who were by far the most important factor supporting leveraged positions in the stock market.

Even Adolph Miller, the most vocal opponent of speculation in general and brokers' loans in particular, could not resist the temptation to earn 12 percent on his own savings. In 1928, Fed officials discovered that he had invested $300,000 of his own money in the call market through a New York banker, personally helping to feed the very speculation that he so vociferously opposed at the Board.

One is led to the inescapable but unsatisfying conclusion that the bull market of 1929 was so violent and intense and driven by passions so strong that the Fed could do nothing about it. Every official had tried to talk it down. The president was against it, Congress too; even the normally reticent secretary of the treasury had spoken out. But it was remarkable how difficult it was to kill it. All that the Fed could do, it seemed, was to step aside and let the frenzy burn itself out. By trying to stand up to the market and then failing, it simply made itself look as impotent as everybody else.

PERHAPS THE MOST perverse consequence of the bubble was that by the strange mechanics of international money, it helped to tip Germany over the edge into recession. For five years, hordes of American bankers had descended on Berlin to press loans upon German companies and municipalities. However much Schacht had tried to wean his country from this dependence on foreign capital, there was little he was able to do about it. Over the five years between 1924 and 1928, Germany borrowed some $600 million a year, of which half went to reparations, the remainder to sustain the rebound in consumption after the years of austerity.

In fact, Germany's appetite for foreign exchange was so great that even the deluge of long-term loans from U.S. bankers was not enough, and it was forced to supplement this with short-term borrowings in international markets closer to home. Out of the total of $3 billion for which German institutions signed up in those years, a little less than $2 billion came in the form of stable long-term loans. But more than $1 billion was "hot money," short-term deposits attracted to German banks by high interest rates—7 percent in Berlin compared to 5 percent in New York—and subject to being pulled at any time. In late 1928, as the U.S. stock market kept climbing and call money rates on Wall Street skyrocketed, American bankers mesmerized by the phenomenal returns at home suddenly stopped coming to Berlin.

It was the combination of the drying up of foreign credit due to high interest rates induced by the U.S. stock bubble and the residual lack of confidence among German businessmen following Schacht's ill-fated strike against the stock market in 1927 that drove Germany into recession in early 1929. Moreover, as long-term American loans stopped, Germany was forced to rely more and more on hot money, some raised from London, but much from French banks, then flush with all the excess gold that had been sucked into their country. Germany therefore found itself slipping into recession just as its foreign position was becoming increasingly vulnerable. A British Treasury official, recalling how much money France had pumped into Russia before the war, could not help remarking with cynical detachment, "The French have always had a sure instinct for investing in bankrupt countries."

The collapse in foreign loans and the recession could not have come at a worse time for Germany. Under the Dawes Plan schedule, Germany was to have fully recovered by now, and was due to ramp up its reparations payments in 1929 to the full $625 million a year, about 5 percent of its GDP. This would not have been an intolerable burden by historical standards. But Schacht, for that matter most of the German leadership, had always been resolute that with its new constitution still fragile, its body politic still divided, its people still bitter over the defeat, and its middle classes decimated by the ravages of the inflation years, Germany simply could not pay this amount.

As 1929 and the scheduled rise in payments approached, Schacht was of two minds about what to do. He often spoke about simply waiting for the economic crash that so many financial experts were predicting. It was a common view in Britain, held, for example, by Frederick Leith-Ross, the top Treasury official responsible for reparations, that the world was headed for a massive payments crisis in which several European countries would default on their debts, setting the stage for a general restructuring of all international commitments arising from the war. Europe could then wipe the slate clean of both reparations and war debts and start over again. Occasionally, Schacht even talked almost too glibly about provoking such an upheaval himself.

The alternative was to reopen negotiations before the jury-rigged payments system broke down. During the Long Island central bankers' meeting of 1927, Schacht had made enough of a stir about Germany's foreign debt problem as to convince Strong and Norman that something had to be done soon, to the point that Strong in turn pressed Agent-General Seymour Parker Gilbert to strike a deal before the whole thing blew up in their faces.

Gilbert, effectively Allied economic proconsul for Germany for the last four years, was even then all of thirty-six years old. A precocious genius, he had graduated from Rutgers at the age of nineteen, from Harvard Law School at twenty-two, had become one of the four assistant secretaries at the U.S. Treasury at the age of twenty-five, and been promoted to under-secretary, the second most powerful official in the department at the age of twenty-eight. In 1924, at the tender age of thirty-two he had been appointed agent-general for reparations, responsible for managing Germany's payments, and most important, for deciding how much it could afford to transfer into dollars every year. In the hands of this tall, shy, boyish, sandy-haired young man from New Jersey lay the immediate fate of the world's third largest economy.

There was little doubt that they were very capable hands. Reserved, bookish, and taciturn, Gilbert was uncomfortable around people, speaking "with a mixture of awkwardness and arrogance, mumbling the words so that one could hardly understand his English." But his intellectual power and capacity for work were legendary. At the Treasury, he had usually been at his desk till two or three o'clock in the morning, seven days a week. Living in Berlin for five years, he did not socialize, never learned German, did "nothing but work without interruption," according to the German finance minister, Heinrich Kohler. "No theater, no concert, no other cultural events intruded into his life…."

That so young an American should have such enormous sway over the life of their country was greatly resented by most Germans. Government officials also suspected the staff in his office of being espionage agents, sent to report on Germany's attempts to cheat on the limitations imposed on its armed forces by the Versailles Treaty. In February 1928, a right-wing group staged a mock coronation attended by ten thousand people in which Gilbert's effigy was crowned "the new German Kaiser who rules with a top hat for a crown and a coupon clipper for scepter." Schacht, always attuned to the locus of power, was one of the few German officials to befriend Gilbert.

Apart from his power to determine transfer payments, Gilbert's most potent weapon was his annual report. Generally viewed as the best independent assessment of Germany's economic policy and overall situation, it was always eagerly awaited by Germany's creditors. Though successive ministers of finance may have resented being lectured for overspending by this absurdly young whippersnapper of an American, no German politician dared challenge him because of the influence he carried abroad.

In his 1927 report released in December, Gilbert declared that the time had come for Germany to take control over her own economic destiny "on her own responsibility without foreign supervision and without transfer protection." Germany should be told once and for all exactly how much she owed and for how long. Moreover, the transfer protection clause embodied in the Dawes Plan, while useful in 1924 for restarting foreign lending, was now creating its own perverse incentives—what we now refer to as moral hazard. By providing an escape clause in the event of a payments crunch, the plan encouraged foreign bankers to be too cavalier in their lending and allowed Germany to be too lax about the consequences of accumulating so much debt "without the normal incentive to do things and carry through reforms that would clearly be in the country's own interests." Though Gilbert thus announced his intention of working himself out of one of the most powerful economic positions in the world, it did help that he had just received the highly lucrative offer to join J. P. Morgan & Co. as a partner.

There were many on the British side, and even among the Germans, who thought that it was still premature for a final reckoning. The bitterness between France and Germany had yet to subside; more time was needed until the German economy had truly revived before the amount of foreign payments it could sustain could definitively be settled.

By late 1928, however, Gilbert had been successful in persuading the Allies to convene a conference in Paris in February 1929 to do just that. He had even convinced the powers in Berlin that though the current situation—no new foreign loans coming in, large debts to nervous French depositors in German banks, and rising domestic unemployment—did not provide the ideal backdrop against which to reopen negotiations, it was best to try to strike a deal now while at least the rest of the world was booming.

Gilbert and the German leadership, Schacht included, were operating, however, from two completely different assumptions about what such a deal might look like. During his campaign to get a new round of negotiations started, the Allies had very explicitly told Gilbert that any further concessions would have to be small. Receipts from Germany had to cover payments on war debts to the United States and provide France and Belgium something beyond this to cover some of the costs of reconstruction. The lowest figure that the Allies could concede was an aggregate payment of $500 million a year. In his enthusiasm to get the parties to the table, Gilbert convinced himself and told everyone on the Allied side that the Germans would be willing to accept such a settlement as the price for getting France out of the Rhineland and regaining economic sovereignty.

Meanwhile, Schacht believed that American bankers had now committed so much money to Germany—they had provided some $1.5 billion of the $3 billion it had borrowed—that they represented an effective lobby for reduction and would bring enough political pressure on the creditor governments for Germany to swing a settlement of $250 million a year. Schacht, having by now broken with the German Democratic Party (DDP), which he had helped found, was beginning to flirt with the right-wing reactionaries of the DNVP, the German Nationalist People Party. At one point, he even bragged to his new friends that he could get reparations below $200 million a year. Gilbert tried his best to disabuse the Germans of such excessive optimism and they in turn tried to convince him that Germany "was dancing on a volcano" and could not afford $500 million a year. But the two parties ended up talking past each other.

Thus as the delegations began to descend on Paris in February 1929 for yet one more summit devoted to reparations, none of the participants realized how wide the chasm of disagreement between the various sides remained. It came as an ill omen when, just as the conference convened, a massive cold front descended across Europe, bringing with it the coldest temperatures for almost a century. Temperatures in Berlin fell to their lowest level in two hundred years; in Silesia it was 49 degrees below zero, the coldest day since records had begun in 1690. Europe was icebound. Across the continent, trains were immobilized, ships lay frozen in the Baltic and on the Danube, and many rural communities, particularly in Eastern Europe, faced actual famine. The newspapers carried chilling reports evoking the Dark Ages, of packs of starving wolves attacking isolated villages in Albania and Romania and of a whole band of gypsies found frozen to death in Poland.

The German delegation, weighed down with twenty-seven boxes of files, arrived by train from Berlin on February 8. Paris had escaped the worst of the cold—the temperature was only 10 degrees below zero. Nevertheless, the city authorities had lined the streets with braziers. But for all the chill, in contrast to Central and Eastern Europe, the French capital was visibly booming. The local economy, fueled by soaring exports, high savings, and large capital inflows, was expanding at 9 percent a year, making it the fastest growing major country. In the last two years, the French stock market had enjoyed the best performance in the world, beating even

Wall Street's—having gone up 150 percent since the end of 1926, while the Dow had risen 100 percent. With the good times had come a renewed self-confidence, even arrogance, and this being Paris, scandals. As the delegates arrived, the city was still abuzz with L'Affaire Hanau.

Marthe Hanau was a forty-two-year-old divorcée who in 1925 had started a stock tip sheet, *La Gazette du Franc*. By 1928, she had a following of hundreds of thousands of investors. Taking advantage of the gullibility and cupidity of the small-town savers who were her clients—local priests, retired soldiers, schoolteachers, and shopkeepers—she promoted stocks that were often little more than paper companies. When her success brought her to the attention of the authorities, Hanau, nicknamed by the press "La Grande Catherine de Finance," kept investigators at bay by bribing politicians. The archbishop of Paris was one of her clients. But eventually her extravagance—she always traveled in a convoy of two limousines, in case one of them broke down; regularly splurged $100,000 on diamonds; and periodically spent the weekend at the Monte Carlo gaming tables—caught up with her. In December 1928, she was arrested and forced into bankruptcy, owing $25 million. Now in prison, she was awaiting trial threatening to name names.*

The Germans were put up at the Royal Monceau, a new luxury hotel near the Arc de Triomphe, and furnished with four new limousines by Mercedes-Benz for the duration. This was the first conference at which they felt themselves treated as equals rather than as the enemy. They were even invited to the opening lunch at the Banque de France on Saturday, February 9, hosted by the head of the French delegation, Émile Moreau. Representing the United States were Owen Young and Jack Morgan, with Thomas Lamont as Morgan's alternate; from Britain came Sir Josiah Stamp, one of the original members of the Reparations Commission of

---

*She went on a hunger strike in jail, became a national folk heroine when she escaped the prison hospital by climbing down a rope made of bedsheets, was recaptured, and at her trial revealed the names of politicians she had bribed. She committed suicide in prison in 1935.

1921, and Lord Revelstoke, one of the five peers in the Barings family and chairman of the bank; the industrialist Alberto Pirelli, one of the richest men in Italy, and the banker Émile Francqui, the richest man in Belgium, represented their countries. Also attending was a delegation from Japan. It was a reunion for many of the men, who like Young and Stamp, had been on the Dawes negotiating teams.

Over a six-course lunch—Huîtres d'Ostend washed down with a 1921 Chablis, Homard à l'Américain with a 1919 Pouilly, Rôti de Venaison accompanied by an 1881 Château Lafite-Rothschild, Faisans Lucullus with a 1921 Clos de Vougeot, Salade d'Asperge with a 1910 Château d'Yquem, a 1910 Grand Fine Champagne with desserts, and finally a bottle of the 1820 Cognac Napoléon over coffee—the delegates selected Owen Young, with his perfect diplomatic skills, as their chairman.

On February 11, the Young Conference—as it would come to be called but was for the moment referred to as the Second Dawes Conference—opened in the Blue Room at the Hotel George V. During the previous decade Paris had been the scene of so many international gatherings that every other grand hotel—the Crillon on the Place de la Concorde, the Bristol on the Rue Saint Honoré, the Majestic on the Avenue Kléber, and the Astoria on the Champs-Élysées—carried in its faded corridors and meeting rooms the echoes of some gathering of statesmen that had ended in acrimony. It seemed only fitting, a sort of rite of passage, for the George V only recently opened for business to host this new meeting before it could claim its place in the ranks as a true Parisian *hôtel-de-luxe*.

On the second day, seated around the horseshoe table, Schacht made his opening offer—$250 million a year for the next thirty-seven years. Moreau conveyed to Young that France would accept nothing less than $600 million a year for the full sixty-two years and might even demand as much as $1 billion. Young was shocked at the huge gap between the main protagonists. Being the consummate financial diplomat, and recognizing that a premature discussion of numbers on reparations would merely lead to an early breakdown in negotiations, he arranged for all the delegates to be tied up in subcommittees for the next six weeks talking around the subject, while he used the time in back-channel shuttle diplomacy between the Germans and the French.

As the conference stretched into its sixth week, a sour and cynical mood began to pervade its halls. Lord Revelstoke complained in his diary that the sessions were "lengthy, tiresome and far from satisfactory. Schacht resumes his most negative attitude, is unhelpful to the last degree." One of the journalists present described Schacht, storming out of meetings with threats to abort the talks, as "a vehement, intolerant man; excitable and dogmatic; . . . the most tactless, the most aggressive and the most irascible person I ever have seen in public life." He alienated all the other delegates with his "tantrums and exhibitionism." Revelstoke thought that with his "hatchet, Teuton face and burly neck and badly fitting collar" he looked like a "sea lion at the Zoo."

Moreau by contrast sat there obstinate and ill-tempered, his mouth shut, Revelstoke observed, "like a steel trap when Schacht pleads poverty and inability to pay." As Moreau watched the Germans become more isolated, he tried to keep quiet and let them dig their own graves. But eventually, unable to restrain himself, he exploded and publicly accused Schacht of negotiating in bad faith. Jack Morgan, bored with the sort of details he generally left to underlings and shaken by his one attempt to try to reason with Schacht, left for a cruise on his yacht around the Adriatic and the Aegean with the archbishop of Canterbury, complaining that, "If Hell is anything like Paris and an International Conference combined, it has many terrors and I shall try to avoid them."

The German delegates found the atmosphere in Paris menacing. They were not being paranoid. The French secret police were tapping their phones. All communications with their government had to be conducted by courier or by cipher telegrams, with each of the twenty-eight participants assigned a code name. The three senior representatives, Schacht included, took turns traveling back to Berlin by train every two weeks in order to brief the cabinet.

Finally, in early April, Young felt ready to allow the Allies to unveil their proposal. Germany would have to make annual payments of $525 million for the first thirty-seven years and, in order to match exactly the Allied war debts to the United States, $400 million a year for the subsequent twenty-one years. The Allies made it clear that the only reason they were saddling two generations of Germans with reparations was that they themselves were in debt to the Americans for the same length of time. On hearing the Allied proposal, Schacht turned pale and, in a voice trembling in anger, declared the session terminated.

By now he realized how totally he had miscalculated. The American bankers' power to pressure the Allies had foundered on the U.S. government's unwillingness to contemplate any further reduction in war debts. Without such an easing, the Allies would not reduce their claims on Germany. Schacht was now caught between letting the conference collapse thus very likely provoking a financial crisis in Germany for which he would be blamed, or settling for the terms on offer, for which he feared he would be equally vilified.

Schacht had always been a gambler. In a desperate effort to win more options, he decided to change the German offer radically. He had always believed that one of the greatest injustices of Versailles had been the seizure of Germany's colonies—an odd collection of territories that Germany, late to the scramble for empire, had accumulated, including most of Samoa, part of New Guinea, Togoland, German South-West Africa, the Cameroons, and Tanganyika—which Schacht implausibly claimed had been worth $20 billion to Germany, an amount that overshadowed even the bill for reparations. He now argued that Germany would be unable to meet the victors' demands unless its former colonies were restored. Even more provocatively, he demanded that the Danzig corridor, the most contentious strip of land in all Europe, taken from Germany to give Poland access to the sea, should also be returned.

In seeking to tack what amounted to a territorial revision of Versailles upon what was supposed to have been a purely financial negotiation, Schacht had gone out on a limb, and without the permission, or even the knowledge, of his own government. The détente between Germany and the Allies, so painstakingly achieved since the withdrawal from the Ruhr five years before, had rested on the principle that Germany would not seek to overturn the political or territorial clauses of the 1919 settlement. Here was Schacht in one stroke trying to undermine the whole fragile basis of European peace.

It has always been something of a mystery what Schacht was hoping to achieve. He did have a habit of shaking things up without quite knowing where it would all end. But he must have known that no one at the Young Conference had the authority to renegotiate crucial parts of the Treaty of Versailles, that the gambit was bound to end in failure. Some thought he was just grandstanding for domestic consumption to prepare for a political career on his return to Germany, others that he was just trying to provoke a crisis to give himself a smoke screen to avoid taking the blame for the poor deal for Germany.

Schacht's proposal was initially received in stunned silence. Once the other delegates had had time to absorb his demands—and he had made them sound like an ultimatum—the table dissolved into an uproar, with cries of astonishment and outrage. Moreau was so furious that he pounded the table and, in a rage, flung his ink blotter across the room.

With the conference now close to collapse, Pierre Quesnay of the Banque de France told one of the Americans that evening that French depositors would withdraw $200 million from German banks by noon the next day. It was unclear whether this was intended as a threat or a prediction. In any case, Germany suddenly began to lose gold at an accelerating pace—$100 million over the next ten days, forcing the Reichsbank to raise rates to 7.5 percent, despite Germany's being deep in recession, with two million unemployed.

Seeing this as the first salvo in an economic war, Schacht accused the Banque de France of having secretly orchestrated the withdrawals to force his hand and threatened that if Germany's reserves continued to fall, he would have no option but to invoke the transfer clause of the Dawes Plan to default on all further reparations. At that moment, such a move would have set off a global financial meltdown. German banks, municipalities, and corporations owed money to everybody—$500 million to British banks, several hundred million to French banks, and some $1.5 billion to American lenders. Had it defaulted on reparations at that point, every financial institution with exposure to Germany would have tried to pull what money it could out of the country. Germany would have had to suspend payments on all its commercial loans, creating a domino effect across the globe. Half the London banks would have gone under. Britain, its reserves already depleted, would have been flung off the gold standard. The financial chaos would have been catastrophic.

The Banque de France had in fact considered launching such a preemptive financial strike against Germany but rejected the idea as too risky. Moreau did not want to be blamed for a world economic collapse. Some French banks undoubtedly did pull some deposits home but this was mere commercial prudence in the light of the deteriorating turn of events. Meanwhile, in an effort to forestall a breakdown in world finances, Norman and George Harrison of the New York Fed had begun mobilizing money to support the Reichsbank.

At this point, with a financial crisis looming, Lord Revelstoke saved the day by suddenly dropping dead. The consequent suspension of the proceedings forced the parties to catch their breath for a few days and step away from the brink. Schacht left with the German delegation for consultations in Berlin. There he found the cabinet up in arms. He had clearly overreached. The foreign minister, Stresemann, who had repeatedly tried to warn Schacht not to overstep his authority, feared that he might have jeopardized Germany's still very delicate political position. Other ministers were alarmed about the domestic economic ramifications. Not only had unemployment already reached two million, but a wave of strikes was now threatening to put another million men out of work. Schacht's gamble threatened to plunge Germany into even deeper recession.

Schacht fought back. He blamed Gilbert for having misled him. He even turned on his erstwhile patron Stresemann, whom he accused of having undercut him by caving in to the Allies behind his back even before the conference had started and of now making him the scapegoat for the political fallout at home.

While Schacht, even at this stage, would have been willing to go for broke and risk a global banking crisis, his government was not. Fearing that Germany would once again become a pariah nation, the cabinet disavowed his position, forced him to recant, and insisted that he return to Paris and resume negotiations on the basis of the last Allied proposal. He reluctantly agreed, provided the cabinet gave him political cover by publicly accepting final responsibility for any settlement. Schacht had no intention of ending up as the fall guy for what nationalists were bound to see as a sellout.

The German delegation returned to the table. In the middle of May, negotiations were again suspended for few days—though this time it was so that Moreau could return to fight the mayoral elections in his tiny hamlet of Saint Léomer. A few weeks later a compromise was reached. Germany would pay a little under $500 million for the next thirty-six years and $375 million a year for the twenty-two after that to cover the Allies debt to the United States. A new bank, the Bank of International Settlements (BIS), jointly owned by all the major central banks, would be set up to administer and where possible to "commercialize"—the modern term is securitize—these future payments, that is, to issue bonds against them. Any profits generated by the Bank were to accrue to Germany to help defray the burden. All foreign control over German economic policy was to be removed—Gilbert could pack his bags and join Morgans. The transfer protection clause was eliminated, although a small safety valve was retained whereby should Germany get into economic trouble, it could postpone two-thirds of its payments for two years.

In the circumstances, this was truly the best deal that Schacht could get. As the delegates gathered for the signing ceremony in the meeting room of the George V, the curtains suddenly burst into flame—the photographers lights had caused them to overheat. Schacht saw it as an omen. He had been humiliated in the negotiations and, on his return to Germany, was criticized from all sides—from the left, for having risked the future of Germany on a gamble that had gone badly wrong, and from the right, for having put his signature to a bill that would "shackle" the next two generations. Even his wife greeted him at the station with the words, "You ought never to have signed." And though he publicly supported the Young Plan, in private he painted a much darker picture of the future. "The crisis may have been postponed for another two years, but it will arrive with the same certainty and with even greater severity." In the ensuing financial chaos, he foresaw that "Germany will be cut off from all foreign capital for a long time, maybe two to three years. For all segments of the German people this will mean managing without, longer working hours, lower wages." An ominous prediction, accurate to the year.

THAT OTHER GREAT pessimist on reparations, Maynard Keynes, shared Schacht's view of the new arrangements. Believing that Germany would find it difficult to keep borrowing its way out of its hole, Keynes responded to the new plan by proclaiming, "My prophecy would be that the Young Plan will not prove practicable for even a short period . . . and I should not be surprised to see some sort of crisis in 1930."

Marriage had mellowed Keynes. Confounding all the clever predictions of his sophisticated friends, he and Lydia had settled into a blissfully happy union. He commuted between the London apartment in Gordon Square, where they lived during the week; his bachelor rooms in college at Kings on the weekends; and their country house at Tilton in Kent, during the holidays. Though less prolific with articles on current affairs, he had not completely retired from his position as the premier gadfly of economic orthodoxy.

But for the last four years, he had been hard at work on a new book. After *The Economic Consequences of the Peace* and *A Tract on Monetary Reform*, both monographs devoted to the immediate and practical concerns of the chaotic postwar world, he was now struggling with a more ambitious work, a theoretical treatise on the interactions between the monetary sphere—the world of banks and other financial institutions—and the underlying real economy—the world of stores and factories and farms. He had begun this line of thought in the *Tract*, but that had been built on a very simple picture, almost a cartoon, of the economy. In this new book, he was trying to paint a richer portrait of the paths along which money flowed in order to understand better the fundamental source of the instability he believed to be inherent in the credit system of modern capitalism.

He also remained an active speculator, an exhausting and dangerous pastime in that turbulent decade. As the bursar of Kings, he managed a pool of money for the college; he was chairman of the board of the National Mutual Insurance Company; and he had set up several investment companies with his friend, Oswald Falk, head of the London stockbroking firm of Buckmaster and Moore. In addition, he continued to manage his own money very actively, usually from the vantage point of his bed in the morning. Buying and selling on margin, he was able to leverage his positions substantially and his portfolio could be very volatile. He began 1923 with about $125,000, the profits of those first forays into the foreign exchange markets. During the next five years, he doubled his money, making most of it trading commodities and currencies, rather than stocks.

Despite his reputation as a Cassandra, by early 1928, his view of the future, as reflected in his investment portfolio, was uncharacteristically sanguine. He avoided the U.S. market, but made substantial investments in the shares of British motor companies, particularly Austin and Leyland. His largest bet, however, was a very substantial complex of long positions in commodities—especially rubber, but also corn, cotton, and tin—a strategy heavily influenced by his perception of Fed policy. He thought that the American central bank under Strong had done a remarkable job, a "triumph" he called it. The Fed, while hiding behind the smoke screen of adhering to the gold standard, had managed very successfully to stabilize U.S. prices, and Keynes believed that with Strong at the helm, it could and would continue to do so.

But as 1928 progressed, his portfolio began to unravel. He sustained substantial losses in April when rubber prices collapsed by 50 percent as the world cartel broke down, forcing him to liquidate large holdings at a loss to meet margin requirements. The Fed's tightening of early 1928 to cap the stock market took Keynes by surprise. After all, he argued, U.S. prices were stable and there was "nothing which can be called inflation yet in sight." In September 1928, with the Dow at 240, he circulated a short note among friends titled "Is there Inflation in the U.S.?" which predicted that "stocks would not slump severely [that is,] . . . unless the market was discounting a business depression," which the Fed "would do all in its power to avoid."

His big error was a failure to take into account the deflationary forces that had begun to sweep the world. After Strong's death in October and as the Fed initiated its campaign of words against the exuberance of the market, he began slowly to realize that the risk had now shifted "on the side of business depression and a deflation." But by his own admission, even in early 1929, he still did not comprehend the impact that the scarcity of gold would have on central banks. He had thought that over time they would liberate themselves from the hold of the "barbarous relic." He completely failed to foresee the sort of scramble for gold that emerged in 1929. "I was forgetting that gold is a fetish," he confessed.

The price for being a speculator was that all these miscalculations wrought havoc on his net worth. By the middle of 1929, he had lost almost three-quarters of his money. The only saving grace was that in order to meet his margin payments, he was forced to liquidate much of his stock portfolio and entered the turmoil of 1929 only modestly invested in the market.

The role of Cassandra was instead taken over by Montagu Norman. Of all the various flashpoints ready to detonate in the world economy that fateful spring and summer—Germany teetering on the brink of default, the shortage of gold, falling commodity prices, the madness on the U.S. exchanges, a chronically weak sterling held hostage by the Banque de France—he found it hard to tell which was the most combustible.

In April 1929, with the negotiations in Paris deadlocked, Norman wrote, "Picture to yourself that at one and the same time a committee is laboriously discussing the whole question of German reparations in Paris: that the rate of interest was yesterday 20% in New York, where the Reserve System is not functioning and where the stock market is playing ducks and drakes with their own and other people's money; that three of the central banks in Europe have raised their rates within the last month, perhaps only as a beginning." The world, it seemed to him, was sleepwalking toward a precipice.

Germany, now locked out of the American market, grabbed at any and every source of credit on which it could lay its hands. In May 1929, the Swiss banker Felix Somary, nicknamed by his American colleagues the "Raven of Zurich" for his unremitting dark "croakings" of a crash to come, received a frantic call from the German finance minister, Rudolf Hilferding, desperate to borrow $20 million to pay public employees. Somary flew to Paris to finalize the necessary arrangements with Schacht, reporting back to the president of the Swiss National Bank, "Almost all the great powers have been negotiating for months about how many billions a year should be paid until 1966, and thereafter until 1988, by a country that is not even in a position to pay its own civil servants' salaries the next day."

Germany was so hard up that it even began loan negotiations with the mysterious Ivar Kreuger, one of that handful of shadowy figures, like Calouste Gulbenkian and Sir Basil Zaharoff, who hovered over the European financial scene in the interwar years, making fortunes in suspicious deals with governments. Kreuger himself was said to be worth several hundred million dollars, and maintained six or seven residences, including his three summer mansions in Sweden, his permanent suite at the Carlton in London, apartments in Berlin, on Park Avenue in Manhattan, and on the Avenue Victor Emmanuel III in Paris, where he had installed a string of mistresses—ex-chorus girls, students, shop assistants, even the occasional streetwalker—on whom he lavished presents.

Whereas Gulbenkian, nicknamed "Mr. Five Percent," dealt in Middle East oil rights and Zaharoff in arms, Kreuger manufactured nothing grander or more threatening than plain little matches. Given the scale of his empire, however—he then controlled three-quarters of the world's match manufacturing—he could borrow money in New York on finer terms than most European governments. Exploiting this financial muscle, he floated bonds on Wall Street and used the proceeds to shore up the finances of the less creditworthy governments across the globe, exacting in return match monopolies in the countries to which he lent. He had concluded such deals with Poland, Peru, Greece, Ecuador, Hungary, Estonia, Yugoslavia, Romania, and Latvia. He had even provided $75 million to the French government during the stabilization of the franc in return for a quasi monopoly in France. Now he offered the German government $145 million in return for a ban on all imports of cheap Russian matches.

As interest rates rose in the United States and New York functioned as a magnet, drawing money from all corners of the globe, every country in Europe, except France, struggled to prevent its gold from escaping across the Atlantic. Interest rates, as Keynes put it, "even in countries thousands of miles away from Wall Street," ratcheted upward, propelled by the scramble for gold. In February 1929, the Bank of England raised its rates a full percentage point to 5.5 percent, despite unemployment above 1.5 million. In March, Italy and the Netherlands followed suit. Germany was already deep in recession, but after the raid on its reserves during the Young Plan negotiations, had also been forced to hike its rates to 7.5 percent. Austria and Hungary more than matched the Reichsbank, taking their rates to over 8 percent. In July, Belgium joined the column.

With the steady erosion in commodity prices, the effect of the rate hikes was to raise the real cost of money in many places to over 10 percent, bringing with it the first signs of worldwide economic slowdown. This had begun in 1928 in the big commodity producers: Australia, Canada, and Argentina. By early 1929, Germany and Central Europe were also in recession.

The U.S. stock market meanwhile refused to pay attention to either the rising cost of money around the world or the first signs of slowdown abroad. In June, it broke out on the upside. As reports of outstanding corporate earnings poured in, the Dow kept going up. In June it rose 34 points and another 16 in July.

The character of the market had by now become almost completely speculative. As trading turned feverish, action increasingly concentrated in an ever narrower roster of companies and was no longer led by those that were making sustained large profits—the General Motors corporations of the world. Instead, it was frantically pursuing glamour stocks—Montgomery Ward, General Electric, and the most dazzling of them all, Radio Corporation of America. Thus, while the market averages continued to race up, reaching their peak in September, most individual stocks had hit their highs in late 1928 or at best in early 1929. Indeed, on September 3, 1929, the day the Dow topped out, only 19 of the 826 stocks on the New York Exchange attained all-time highs. Almost a third had fallen at least 20 percent from their highest points.

It was during these months that most of the large stock traders sold their positions. Claims by speculators about what they did in 1929 and when they did it need to be taken with some grains of salt. People rarely tell the complete truth either about their amorous exploits or their stock portfolios, the latter being especially true for professional investors whose reputations hinge on appearing to be prescient about the market.

In February, Owen Young, alarmed by the feverish level of stock prices and the Fed's war of words, sold his entire portfolio of $2.2 million, some of it held on margin. David Sarnoff, Young's vice president at RCA and a member of the U.S. delegation to the Paris conference, got out in June. John J. Raskob, the man who sincerely wanted everyone to be rich and was touting stocks as a long-term investment in the *Ladies' Home Journal*, had apparently liquidated most of his portfolio before his article appeared. Joe Kennedy, catching the last rally, sold in July 1929. Bernard Baruch claims, in his autobiography, to have had an epiphany on the Scottish moors in September of 1929, rushed home and dumped everything by the end of the month. Even Thomas Lamont, the inveterate optimist, sold substantial amounts of his portfolio during the spring and summer.

Even the greatest cheerleader of them all, that most determined of bulls, Billy Durant, got rid of his positions. In April 1929, he had some friends arrange for him to meet secretly with the president. He slipped out of New York, careful not to inform even his secretary of his destination, took a train down to Washington, hopped anonymously into a taxi, and arrived at the White House at 9:30 in the evening, when he was ushered into the president's study. He told Hoover that unless the Fed eased up its assault against the stock market, there would be a financial catastrophe. It is not clear whether Durant understood that he was wasting his breath, that Hoover was fully behind the Fed's campaign. He does seem to have realized soon after the meeting that his warnings had gone nowhere. On April 17, he set sail for Europe aboard the *Aquitania*, and a few weeks later, he and most of his crowd began liquidating their positions.

But behind the scenes, the Board of the Federal Reserve was finally ready to concede that its attempts at "direct action" were a failure. On August 8, after the market had closed, the New York Fed announced that it was raising its discount rate from 5 percent to 6 percent. The next day the Dow plunged 15 points in frantic trading, the largest daily decline in the index's history. The market suddenly realized, however, that speculators had been comfortably making large profits while paying much higher rates in the brokers' loan market. Within a day, all the losses were recouped.

Over the next three weeks, the Dow went up another 30 points. Among investors there reigned, as one commentator described it, the sort of "panic which keeps people at roulette tables, the insidious propaganda against quitting a winner, the fear of being taunted by those who held on." It was symptomatic of the market's reach when on August 14, the New York Stock Exchange firm of Saint-Phalle and Co. announced that it had opened direct ship-to-shore service aboard the transatlantic liner *Ile de France,* to be followed a few days later by M. J. Meehan and Co, opening a similar service on the *Berengaria* and the *Leviathan.*

Even Europe was drawn into the frenzy. "Scores of thousands of American shares are bought everyday in London alone and Paris, Berlin, Brussels and Amsterdam are pouring money into New York as fast as the cable can carry it," complained Viscount Rothermere in one of his newspapers, the *Sunday Pictorial.* "Wall Street has become a colossal suction pump, which is draining the world of capital and the suction is fast producing a vacuum over here. That is why bank rates are rising throughout Europe. That is the reason of the steady withdrawal of gold from the Bank of England. That is the explanation of the frequent visits which the governor of the bank, Mr. Montagu Norman, pays to New York and Washington."

In July, Norman made his second trip of the year to the United States. He spent most of his weeks of holiday with his old friend Mrs. Markoe at Bar Harbor in Maine but did go to see Harrison in New York. He came back even more pessimistic than after his February trip. He was now convinced that some sort of stock market crash in the United States was inevitable. No one could be sure what might set it off or how bad it would be. The longer the bubble continued, the more unavoidable would be the breakdown. And though the Fed was finally beginning to act, it had left things very late and still remained a bitterly divided institution.

Throughout the summer of 1929, Britain's reserves came under siege. By the end of July, the Bank of England had already lost $100 million of its $800 million of gold and in August and September, it lost a further $45 million, mainly into the United States. There were also signs that the Banque de France had resumed converting its pounds. Since 1927, the flow of money into France had continued unabated, although now most of it was in the form of gold rather than sterling. By the middle of 1929, the Banque de France had accumulated $1.2 billion in gold and another $1.2 billion in foreign exchange, giving it an extraordinary hold on the world financial situation.

During the two years since Norman and Moreau had first fallen out, the Banque de France, recognizing that it had the power to destabilize the world currency situation, had actually been very restrained in handling its sterling. But the Young Plan negotiations put a new strain on Anglo-French relations. Having made some concessions to Germany on reparations, the former Allies fell out on how to divide the burden.

In June 1929, Britain went to the polls. After four years of high unemployment under Conservative rule, the Tories were voted out of office and a minority Labor government took power. Churchill was replaced at the Exchequer by Philip Snowden, a long and bitter opponent of France and

French policy on reparations. At a conference at The Hague in August 1929 to wrap up some of the details of the Young Plan, he entered into a particularly heated exchange with his French counterpart, Henri Chéron, in the course of which he described the French finance minister's arguments as "ridiculous and grotesque." The translation into French, *"ridicule et grotesque"* has a much harsher connotation, implying bad faith and utter stupidity. As the economic historian Charles Kindleberger put it, the English expression could be used in the House of Commons, the French expression would not be allowed in the Chambre des Députés. Chéron, a "fat excitable man" whose enormous girth had made him the constant victim of jokes and who was, consequently, unusually sensitive, took offense at Snowden's remarks, and sent his seconds to demand an apology—the French were only just weaning themselves off the practice of dueling.

Though he was eventually induced to return to the negotiating table, relations between Britain and France were severely strained. At one meeting during the same negotiations, Pierre Quesnay of the Banque de France is said to have threatened to convert France's holdings of sterling into gold unless the British conceded. Though the evidence is murky, this was not mere saber rattling and Britain's gold continued to come under attack.

On August 19, *Time* magazine ran a cover story on Norman, the "Palladin of Gold," as it called him. The article described how within Europe "invisibly the battle of gold was on." In late August, as Britain's reserves hit a postwar low, Norman warned his fellow directors that unless something were to change, large parts of Europe, including Britain, would be driven off gold and that they should begin to prepare for the impending havoc. But first another cataclysm was to blindside the world economy.

Wall Street, Black Tuesday, October 29, 1929

17. PURGING THE ROTTENNESS

1929-30

If stupidity got us into this mess, then why can't it get us out?

—WILL ROGERS

THERE IS an old stock trader's adage: "Nobody rings a bell at the top of the market." As Wall Street returned to work after Labor Day on Tuesday, September 3, few people thought that this might be the end of the bull market. The weekend had been unusually hot, and the journey home from the beach was marred by terrible traffic jams and long delays at train stations. Congestion on the New Jersey highways was so bad that thousands of people had parked their cars and finished the journey home to Manhattan by subway.

As bankers assessed the market after the summer, they were assisted by a fresh new voice to add to the blithe new-era optimism of the *Wall Street Journal* and the dark mutterings about "portents" and "misgivings" from Alexander Dana Noyes, financial columnist of the *New York Times*. That week, the premiere issue of *BusinessWeek* hit the newsstands. It sought to bring the successful *Time* magazine formula of snappy and vivid writing to the corporate world. From the very first issue, the editors expressed their skepticism about the bull market. "For five years at least," they wrote,

"American business has been in the grips of an apocalyptic, holy-rolling exaltation over the unparalleled prosperity of the 'new era' upon which we, or it, or somebody has entered." It had carried the country "into a cloud-land of fantasy." "As the fall begins," they warned, "there is a tenseness in Wall Street . . . a general feeling that something is going to happen during the present season. . . . Stock prices are generally out of line with safe earnings expectations, and the market is now almost wholly 'psychological.'"

The market had become inured to such prognostications on the way up and continued to ignore them on the first day of trading. On September 3, 1929, the Dow traded up a single point to close at a record high of 381. For the next day and a half, it clung to that peak.

At two o'clock on the afternoon of September 5, the newswires reported that the Massachusetts economist and statistician Roger Babson had announced at his annual National Business Conference in Wellesley, Massachusetts, "I repeat what I said at this time last year and the year before that sooner or later a crash is coming . . . and it may be terrific. . . . The Federal Reserve System has put banks in a strong position but it has not changed human nature." Observing further that "a detailed study of the market shows that the group of advancing stocks is continually becoming narrower and smaller," he predicted that the Dow would probably drop 60 to 80 points—15 to 20 percent—and that "factories will shut down . . . men will be thrown out of work . . . the vicious circle will get in full swing and the result will be a serious business depression." That afternoon the Dow fell 10 points, roughly 3 percent.

Babson was a well-known market seer, the founder of the Babson Statistical Organization, the country's largest purveyor of investment analysis and business forecasts. Every month the company mailed out reams of charts and tables, dissecting the behavior of individual stocks, the overall market, and the economy. Babson had built his forecasting method around two somewhat antithetical notions: that the "ups and downs" of the economy "operate according to definite laws" derivable from Newton's third law of motion and that emotions were "the most important factor in causing the business cycle."

Babson had some other quirkier ideas. Having suffered a bout of tuberculosis as a youth, he believed in the benefits of fresh air and insisted on keeping all the windows in his office wide open. In winter, his secretaries, wrapped in woolen overcoats, sheepskin boots, and thick mittens, had to type by striking the keys with a little rubber hammer that Babson had himself expressly invented. He was a strict Prohibitionist, believed that the gravity of Newtonian physics was a malevolent force, and had published a pamphlet entitled *Gravity—Our Enemy Number One*.* He had been predicting a market crash for the past two years and until now had been completely ignored.

After Babson's gloomy forecast, the *New York Times* sought a rejoinder from Irving Fisher, professor of economics at Yale, and the most prominent economist of the time. Originally a mathematician who had gone on to make major contributions to the theory of money and of interest rates, Fisher was quite as odd a bird as Babson. Having also suffered from tuberculosis—although in his case at the age of thirty-one—he had emerged from the sanatorium a committed vegetarian. He suffered from terrible insomnia and, to cope with it, had designed a bizarre electrical contraption that he hooked up to his bed and was convinced helped him to fall asleep. He was also a proponent of selective breeding and was secretary of the American Eugenics Society; he believed that mental illness originated from infections of the roots of the teeth and of the bowels and, like Babson, was a fervent advocate of Prohibition—by 1929, he had even written two books on the economic benefits of Prohibition. Again like Babson, he was a wealthy man, having invented a machine for storing index cards—a precursor of the Rolodex—the patent of which he sold to Remington Rand in 1925 for several million dollars. By 1929, he was worth some $10 million, all of it invested in the stock market.

---

*He was the founder of no less than three business colleges: Babson College in Massachusetts, Webber College in Florida, and the now defunct Utopia College in Eureka, Kansas. In 1940, he ran for president of the United States as the Prohibition Party's candidate, receiving 57,800 votes In 1948, he formed the Gravity Research Foundation, an organization dedicated to combating the effects of gravity, including the quest for antigravity matter.

Prefacing his remarks with the concession that "none of us are infallible," Professor Fisher declared, "Stock prices are not too high, and Wall Street will not experience anything in the nature of a crash." A noted "student" of the market, he based his assessment on the assumption that the future would be much like the recent past, that profits would continue to grow at over 10 percent as they had done over the previous five years. It was an early example of the pitfalls of placing too much faith in the abilities of mathematicians, with their flawed models, to beat the market. Simple commonsense techniques for valuing equities such as those Babson relied on—for example, positing that prices should move in tandem with dividends—indicated that stocks were some 30 to 40 percent overvalued.

Though the market initially fell sharply on the day of Babson's prediction, the next day, deciding that it preferred Fisher's sweet elixir to Babson's harsh medicine, it rebounded. Babson, the "prophet of loss," as he was now nicknamed, was derided up and down Wall Street, mocked even by *Business-Week* for his "Babsonmindedness." During the month of September, these two New England cranks—Babson and Fisher—battled for the soul of the market. Every time one was quoted, the newspapers obtained a rebuttal from the other.

The official chronicler of business cycles in the United States, the National Bureau of Economic Research, a not-for-profit group founded in 1920, would declare, though many months later, that a recession had set in that August. But in September, no one was aware of it. There were the odd signs of economic slowdown, especially in some of the more interest-rate-sensitive sectors—automobile sales had peaked and construction had been down all year, but most short-term indicators, for example, steel production or railroad freight car loadings, remained exceptionally strong.

By the middle of the month, the market was back at its highs and Babson's forecast of a crash had been thoroughly discredited. The broader indices even set new records—for example, the most widely used measure of the market, the *New York Times* index of common stocks, reached its all time peak on September 19—though the Dow never did get quite back to 381.

Even the usually bearish Alexander Dana Noyes of the *New York Times* was skeptical of the forecast of a market collapse. It is "not perhaps surprising that the idea of an utterly disastrous and paralyzing crash . . . should have found few believers," he wrote; after all, in contrast to previous episodes, the country now has "the power and protective resources of the Federal Reserve," while the market was "guarded against the convulsions of old-time panics . . . by the country's accumulation of gold." Previous crashes had all been preceded by an extraneous shock of some sort, which broke the herd psychology. The crash of 1873 had been foreshadowed by the bankruptcy of Jay Cooke and Company. In 1893, it had been the failure of the National Cordage Company, while in 1907, it was the collapse of the Knickerbocker Trust Company. Noyes took comfort in the fact that no such event seemed remotely on hand.

He spoke too soon. On Friday, September 19, the empire of the British financier Clarence Hatry suddenly collapsed, leaving investors with close to $70 million in losses. Hatry, the son of a prosperous Jewish silk merchant, had attended St. Paul's School in London, immediately thereafter had taken over his father's business and, by the age of twenty-five, was bankrupt. By thirty-five, however, he was a rich man again, having recouped his fortune by speculating in oil stocks and promoting industrial conglomerates in the heady postwar merger boom. Throughout the 1920s, he had led a roller-coaster career as an entrepreneur, with some spectacular successes and equally dramatic failures. By the latter part of the decade, he had a finger in almost every corner of the British economy. He made a fortune by building a retail conglomerate, the Drapery Trust, and then selling it to Debenhams, the department store; he engineered the merger of the London bus corporations into the London General Omnibus Company, ran a stockbroking firm specializing in municipal bonds, and was the head of an interlocking series of investment trusts that played the stock market. His latest ventures were the Photomaton Parent Company, which operated a countrywide chain of photographic booths, and the Associated Automatic Machine Corporation, which owned vending machines on railway platforms.

A small, sallow, birdlike man with a close-cropped mustache, Hatry was so flamboyant it was said that he even had the bottoms of his shoes polished. He lived in a garishly ornate mansion in Stanhope Gate, off Park Lane, around whose rooftop swimming pool he held lavish parties. He ran the requisite string of racehorses, entertained at his country house in Sussex, and owned the largest yacht in British waters, with a crew of forty. Needless to say, he did not endear himself to traditional British society by this vulgarly extravagant Hollywood lifestyle.

The City financial establishment kept a wary distance. "Mr. Hatry is very clever, and one or two of the people we know who have had business relations with him have always told us that they have nothing against him," wrote Morgan Grenfell to its corresponding partners J. P. Morgan & Co. But the letter continued, "He is a Jew. His standing here [in London] is by no means good. We should ourselves not think of doing business with him." Nevertheless, with his enormous apparent wealth, he was able to induce some of the grandest names in the country to join his boards—for example, the Marquess of Winchester, who could trace his title back to the time of Henry VIII and was holder of the oldest marquessate in the country, was chairman of one of his companies—and no one questioned his financial situation.

In 1929, with grand plans to rationalize the British steel industry, he acquired a major manufacturer, United Steel Limited, for $40 million in what would today be called a leveraged buyout. In June, his bankers withdrew their financing at the last moment. He spent the next few weeks scrambling for cash, even approaching Montagu Norman, for Bank of England help. Needless to say, Norman, who would have found a man like Hatry highly distasteful, refused, telling him that he had paid too much for United Steel. Having borrowed as much as he could against all of his companies, Hatry eventually resorted to petty fraud: forging a million dollars worth of municipal bonds to post as collateral against additional loans.

Early in September, as rumors circulated that he was massively overextended, his companies' shares plunged, and his bankers called in their loans. Recognizing that the game was up, Hatry went under in true British fashion. On September 18, he called upon his accountant, Sir Gilbert Garney, and told him of the forgery. After hearing him out, Sir Gilbert telephoned his old friend Sir Archibald Bodkin, the director of public prosecutions, to say that he had a group of City men who wished to come in to confess to fraud of a "stupendous" magnitude. Sir Archibald, after hearing that the sum involved was as high as $120 million—equivalent as a percentage of the British economy to the Enron imbroglio of 2001 in the United States—arranged for them to turn themselves in at his office at ten o'clock the next morning. Hatry duly arrived the following day, confessed to his crimes, and was remanded in custody.

When New York opened on Friday, September 20, the market faltered, losing 8 points to close at 362. The following week the Bank of England, fearing that sterling might be imperiled by Hatry's collapse, raised interest rates to 7.5 percent and the market tumbled a further 17 points.

Because the many British investors who had lost money with Hatry were forced to liquidate their U.S. stock positions and began pulling their money out of the New York brokers' loan market, the Dow came under mounting pressure, falling another 20 points over the week of September 30 to 325. In the space of two weeks, it had given up the gains of the previous two months. However, so far the market crack, while vicious, was not out of the ordinary. Indeed in the week of October 7 it surprised everyone by rallying 27 points. The Dow thus began the week of October 14 at around 350, a little less than 10 percent below its all-time highs.

On Tuesday, October 15, economist and market pundit Irving Fisher, in a speech that would go down in history for its spectacularly bad timing, threw his normal caution to the winds, with the declaration, "Stocks have reached what looks like a permanently high plateau." Among the reasons he would later cite for this optimistic forecast were the "increased prosperity from less unstable money, new mergers, new scientific management, new inventions" and finally, Fisher being Fisher, he could not resist adding, on account of the benefits of "prohibition." The market began to sag once again—dropping 20 points the next week and another 18 points in the first three days of the week after. It was by now back to 305, having lost about 20 percent of its value since the September peak. So far, however, there had been no real reason to panic.

Another victim of bad timing was Thomas Lamont of J. P. Morgan & Co., who chose the weekend of October 19 to send Hoover an eighteen-page letter. "There is a great deal of exaggeration in current gossip about speculation," he warned the president. Indeed, he suggested that a certain amount of speculation was a healthy way of engaging the American public in the benefits of owning stocks, in the same way that "a jaded appetite was sometimes stimulated by a cocktail to the enjoyment of a hearty meal." "The future appears brilliant," he wrote, and vigorously urged the president not to intervene. The letter is now in the presidential archives with the phrase "This document is fairly amazing" scribbled by Hoover across the top.

On Wednesday, October 23, quite out of the blue, a sudden avalanche of sell orders, the origin of which was a complete mystery, knocked the market down by 20 points in the last two hours of trading. The next day, soon to be known as Black Thursday, saw the first true panic. The market opened steady with little change in prices; but at about 11:00 a.m, it was blindsided by a flood of large sell orders from all around the country, rattling out of such diverse places as Boston, Bridgeport, Memphis, Tulsa, and Fresno. Prices of major stocks started gapping lower. During the next hour, the major indices fell 20 percent, while the bellwether of speculation, RCA, plunged more than 35 percent. Adding further to the panic, communications across the country were disrupted by storms, and telephone lines were so clogged that many thousands of investors could not get through to their brokers.

Rumors of the turmoil spread quickly through the city, and by noon, a crowd of ten thousand sightseers, attracted by the reek of calamity, had gathered at the corner of Broad and Wall, just opposite the stock exchange. Police Commissioner Grover Whalen dispatched an extra six hundred policemen, including a mounted detail, to keep order and rope off the crowd from the entrance to the stock exchange. A gaggle of newspaper photographers and film cameramen collected on the steps of the Subtreasury Building to document the scene.

A little after noon, the barons of Wall Street—Charles Mitchell of National City Bank, Albert Wiggin of Chase, William Potter of Guaranty Trust, Seward Prosser of Bankers Trust, and George Baker of First National—were seen pushing their way through the crowd into the front door of J. P. Morgan & Co. at 23 Wall Street. After a mere twenty minutes, they emerged grim faced and left without speaking to reporters. A few minutes later, Thomas Lamont appeared and held an impromptu press conference in Morgan's marble lobby.

Looking "grave" and "gesturing idly with his pince-nez as he spoke," he began by announcing, "There has been a little distress selling on the Stock Exchange." Though he was only trying to steady the market's nerves, this was a remark that would go down in history as a classic, forever mocked as an embodiment of Wall Street's capacity for self-delusion and obfuscation. "Air holes" caused by a "technical condition" had developed in the market, asserted Lamont. The situation, he assured his listeners, was "susceptible of betterment."

What he did not announce was that the six bankers had agreed to contribute to a pool that would provide a "cushion" of buying power to support stock prices. At 1:30 p.m., Richard Whitney, president of the stock exchange—brother of Morgan partner George Whitney and himself stockbroker for the company—strode confidently onto the crowded floor of the exchange and placed an order for ten thousand shares of U.S. Steel at 205, 5 points above the price of its last sale. He then went from one post to the other, sprinkling similarly huge orders for blue chips—at a total cost of between $20 and $30 million. To the accompaniment of a chorus of cheers and whistles from the floor, the market rallied dramatically and by the end of the day was off a mere 6 points. Though stocks had taken comfort from the rescue operation, even as the market was rallying that afternoon, Lamont was closeted with the governors of the exchange to warn them that the bankers' support was limited: "There is no man or group of men who can buy all the stocks that the American public can sell."

While the private bankers were throwing the market this life buoy, the central bank, the Federal Reserve, was paralyzed by dissension. To try to ease conditions that morning, the directors of the New York Fed had voted to cut its lending rate from 6 percent to 5.5 percent, only to have the decision vetoed from Washington by the Federal Reserve Board. The latter spent the day closeted in meetings at its offices in the Treasury Building, next door to the White House. At 3:00 p.m., Secretary of the Treasury Andrew Mellon joined the conference, which broke up at 5:00 p.m. with no official announcement. A "senior" Treasury official did speak, however, to reporters off the record, expressing the view that the market had broken under the stress of "undue speculation" and that the harm done, after all, only constituted "paper losses," which would not prove "disastrous to business and the prosperity of the country."

The newspapers reported next day that heroic action on the part of the bankers had successfully halted the panic. The *Wall Street Journal* carried the headline "Bankers Halt Stock Debacle: 2 Hour Selling Deluge Stopped After Conference at Morgan's Office: $1,000,000,000 For Support."

Though the amount committed by the Morgan-led consortium was nowhere near that amount, the market was buoyed by the apparent success of the "organized support" and stabilized over the next two days, though trading remained heavy. Rumors circulated that the bankers felt sufficiently confident to begin disposing of the stocks they had acquired on Thursday at a small profit. But late on Saturday, the market began to fall again.

The "second hurricane of liquidation" roared in on Monday, October 28—Black Monday. It came from every direction: demoralized individual investors, pool operators liquidating, Europeans throwing in the towel, speculators forced to sell by margin calls, banks dumping collateral. Investors, who had originally bought stocks only because they saw prices rising, now sold them because they saw prices falling. By the end of the day, 9 million shares had changed hands and the Dow was down 40 points, roughly 14 percent, the largest percentage fall in a single day in the market's history—$14 billion wiped off the value of U.S. stocks.

Reporters, remembering all the various times in history that the U.S.

banking system had been saved from the Morgan offices, were camped out in front of 23 Wall Street. At 1:10 p.m. Mitchell of the National City Bank was seen entering the building. The market immediately rallied. But there was no sign of the other bankers or any evidence of any further "organized support." It would later turn out that Mitchell was personally overextended and, desperate for cash, had gone in to negotiate a private loan for himself.

The press was so fascinated by the very conspicuous comings and goings of bankers to and from "No. 23" that they failed to recognize that the true locus of power no longer lay with Morgan but had shifted three blocks north to the offices of the New York Federal Reserve at 33 Liberty Street. The real hero of the day was not one of those bankers shuttling in and out of Morgan's offices but George Harrison of the New York Fed.

Stock market crashes during the nineteenth and early twentieth century had invariably been associated with banking crises. The market and the banking system were too interconnected. Because the big New York City banks held their reserves in the form of call loans to stockbrokers, a collapse in stocks inevitably raised concerns about the safety of one bank or the other, often leading to a run on the system, which in turn led to a withdrawal of liquidity from the market, which in turn drove the market down further. The Fed had been created in part to break that nexus and Harrison was determined to prevent the market turmoil from widening into a full-scale financial crisis. He spent the whole day in close contact with the heads of the city's major banks.

The country's money center banks were confronted with a potentially life-threatening hit. Many of the largest traders on Wall Street, especially the pool operators, held gigantic leveraged positions in the stock market that had been financed by brokers' loans—in some cases as much as $50 million, some of which had come from banks. The danger was that as the market fell, brokers, frantic to recoup their loans, would be forced to dump the stocks they held as collateral, creating further declines in the market and intensifying the vicious cycle of selling.

Rebuffed the previous Thursday by the Federal Reserve Board, Harrison now took matters into his own hands. That night, Wall Street bankers were invited to a dinner in honor of Winston Churchill at the Fifth Avenue home of Bernard Baruch. Despite the days' events, the general consensus among the financiers was that stocks were now undervalued. Mitchell even managed to raise a laugh when in his toast to the British visitor he addressed the company as "friends and former millionaires."

Down on Wall Street the lights in the skyscrapers glowed far into the early hours as exhausted clerks and bookkeepers tried to tally their records after a day of unprecedented trading. Meanwhile, at the Fed's offices on Liberty Street, Harrison and his staff were developing a plan to inject large amounts of cash into the banking system by buying government securities. Fortunately, there was no time to consult the Board in Washington. He barely managed to reach two of his own directors, and then only at 3:00 a.m., to secure their approval. Early the next morning, even before the market had opened, the New York Fed injected $50 million.

That day, which came somewhat unoriginally to be christened Black Tuesday, saw no letup in selling. The crowd of ten thousand that again gathered that morning stood in hushed awe, fully aware that they were "participating in the making of history," and that they were unlikely ever again to witness such scenes. The *New York Times* man on the spot described Wall Street that morning as a street of "vanished hopes, of curiously silent apprehension, and of a paralyzed hypnosis." Churchill chose that day to visit the stock exchange and was invited inside to witness the scene. Though he was heavily invested in the market and lost over $50,000, most of his savings, in the collapse, he seems to have responded to his change in fortunes quite philosophically—"No one who has gazed on such a scene could doubt that this financial disaster, huge as it is, cruel as it is to thousands, is only a passing episode. . . ." Commissioner Whalen himself kept a close eye on the market, and the minute he saw prices sagging, had dispatched an extra squad of policemen downtown. The financial district looked like a city under siege.

The bankers' consortium gathered twice that day. Lamont struck a noticeably less confident note at his next press conference. Their objective was not to support prices, he told the reporters, but to maintain an orderly market. Toward the end of the day, after over 16 million shares had changed hands and the Dow had fallen more than 80 points—it had now lost 180 points, or close to 50 percent of its value in less than six weeks—it seemed as if the selling had begun to burn itself out. In the last fifteen minutes of trading, the market made a vigorous rally of 40 points.

During the day, the New York Fed had injected a further $65 million. The Board, especially Roy Young, was greatly irritated when it found out later that day about Harrison's show of independence and initiative; his failure to get Washington's approval first was a clear defiance of established protocol. In response to Young's rebuke, Harrison shot back that there had never been such an emergency, that the world was "on fire" and that his actions were "done and can't be undone." The Board tried to pass a regulation prohibiting the New York Fed from making any further independent transfusions of cash, but questions arose about whether it had the legal authority to do so. During the next few days, there was considerable legal wrangling over the precise jurisdictions of the Board and the New York Fed. Harrison eventually proposed that they postpone the bureaucratic argument over powers and procedures until the crisis was over, agreeing in the meantime not to act unilaterally provided the Board gave him the authority to buy as much as $200 million more in government securities—an arrangement which allowed him to draw on the whole Federal Reserve System rather than the resources of the New York Fed alone.

That evening a somewhat larger group of bankers once again gathered in the library of Jack Morgan's house at Madison Avenue and Thirty-fifth Street, the scene of his father's legendary rescue of the New York banking system in 1907. Among them was George Harrison.

With stocks now in free fall, all those who had pumped money into the brokers' loan market—the corporations with excess cash, foreigners drawn by high rates of interest, small banks around the country—were rushing for the exits. In the days since Black Thursday over $2 billion, about one-quarter of all brokers' loans, had been or was about to be pulled out. This was creating massive additional selling and a scramble for cash that risked toppling the entire financial structure of brokers and banks on Wall Street. In order to forestall this financial fire stampede, with everyone heading for the doors at the same time, some of the bankers proposed to close down the stock exchange as had been done at the outbreak of war in 1914.

The meeting went on till 2:00 a.m. Harrison was adamant. "The Stock Exchange should stay open at all costs," he told the gathering. Closing the stock market would not solve the problem, only postpone it and, by preventing transactions, might possibly prolong it and force even more bankruptcies. He proposed instead that the New York banks take over a good portion of brokers' loans from those trying to pull out of the market. By thus stepping into the breach, they would head off panic selling and a complete meltdown. "I am ready to provide all the reserve funds that may be needed," he reassured the bankers.

Over the next few days, as the Fed did just that, New York City banks took over $1 billion in brokers' loan portfolios. It was an operation that did not receive the publicity of the Morgan consortium, but there is little doubt that by acting quickly and without hesitation, Harrison prevented not only an even worse stock collapse but most certainly forestalled a banking crisis. Though the crash of October 1929 was by one count the eleventh panic to grip the stock market since the Black Friday of 1869 and was by almost any measure the most severe, it was the first to occur without a major bank or business failure.

The market traded up for the last couple of days of October. It then fell back again, revisiting the lows of Black Tuesday on November 13. By the last weeks of November, the Dow had settled at around 240—a 40 percent retreat over the eight weeks since late September. The bubble that had begun in early 1928 had lasted little more than a year and a half. By all indications, the effect of the October crash had merely been to squeeze out all the froth and return the stock market closer to its fair value.

IN THE WEEKS that followed the Great Crash, the dazed financial press struggled to make sense of what had happened. Despite the magnitude of the losses—$50 billion wiped off the value of stocks, equivalent to about 50 percent of GNP—and the ferocity of the decline, many papers were surprisingly sanguine, calling it the "prosperity panic." The *New York Evening World* even argued that the panic had only occurred because "underlying conditions [had] been so good," that speculators had "an excuse for going clean crazy," creating a bubble and thus setting the stage for it to burst.

The *New York Sun* made the case that the crash would have a minimal impact on the economy, that Main Street could be decoupled from Wall Street. "No Iowa Farmer will tear up his mail order blank because Sears Roebuck stock slumped. No Manhattan housewife took the kettle off the stove because Consolidated Gas went down to 100. Nobody put his car up for the winter because General Motors sold 40 points below the year's high."

Indeed, *Business Week*, which had been one of the most vocal critics of the speculation on the way up, went one step further, insisting that the economy would be in even better shape now that the distracting bubble had burst. "For six years, American business has been diverting a substantial part of its attention, its energies and its resources on the speculative game. . . . Now that irrelevant, alien, and hazardous adventure is over. Business has come home again, back to its job, providentially unscathed, sound in wind and limb, financially stronger than ever before."

The consensus, however, was that the crash would cause a transitory and mild business recession, particularly in luxury goods. B. C. Forbes, founder of *Forbes* magazine, thought that "just as the stock market profits stimulated the buying of all kinds of comforts and luxuries, so will the stock market losses inevitably have an opposite effect."

The immediate impact on the United States in fact proved to be much greater that anyone expected. Industrial production fell 5 percent in October and another 5 percent in November. Unemployment, which during the summer of 1929 had hovered at around 1.5 million, 3 percent of the workforce, shot up to close to 3 million by the spring of 1930. The country had become so emotionally invested in the vagaries of Wall Street that the psychological impact of the collapse turned out to be profound, particularly in consumer demand for expensive goods: the automobiles, radios, refrigerators, and other new products that had been at the heart of the boom. Car registrations across the country plummeted by 25 percent and radio sales in New York were said to have fallen by half.

The editor of the *Economist*, Francis Hirst, who had fallen ill on a trip to the United States and was convalescing in Atlantic City at year's end, captured the mood. "Rich people who have not sold their stocks *feel* much poorer. . . . The first result therefore, has been a heavy decline in luxury buying of all sorts and also a large amount of selling of such things as motor cars and fur coats, which can now be bought secondhand at surprisingly low prices. The favored health resorts have suffered enormously . . . a very great number of servants, including butlers and chauffeurs, have been dismissed."

Immediately after the crash, Hoover, who liked nothing better than emergencies, threw himself into action. He was one of the hardest-working presidents in the history of the office, at his desk by 8:30 a.m and still there into the early hours of the next morning. Within a month, his administration had pushed through an expansion in public works construction and submitted a proposal to Congress to cut the income tax rate by a flat 1.0 percent. The federal government, however, was then tiny—total expenditures amounted to $2.5 billion, only 2.5 percent of GDP—and the effect of the fiscal measures was to inject barely a few hundred million dollars, less than 0.5 of 1.0 percent of GDP into the economy.

Hoover had, therefore, to content himself with playing the part of chief economic cheerleader. Unfortunately, it was a role for which he was poorly suited. Shy, insecure, and stiff, he was ill at ease with people and surrounded himself with yes-men. He was also "constitutionally gloomy," according to William Allen White, "a congenital pessimist who always saw the doleful side of any situation." Unable to inspire confidence or optimism, he resorted, according to the *Nation* magazine, to "trying to conjure up the genie of prosperity by invocations" that things were about to get better.

On December 14, 1929, barely six weeks after the crash, he declared that the volume of shopping indicated that country was "back to normal." On March 7, 1930, he predicted that the worst effects would be over "during the next sixty days." Sixty days later he announced, "We have passed the worst."

To some degree he was caught in a dilemma that all political leaders face when they pronounce upon the economic situation. What they have to say about the economy affects its outcome—an analogue to Heisenberg's principle. As a consequence, they have little choice but to restrict themselves to making fatuously positive statements which should never be taken seriously as forecasts.

The task of trying to talk the economy up was complicated by the fact that it did not go down in a straight line. At several points along the way it seemed to stabilize. After falling in the last few months of 1929, it found a footing in the early months of 1930. The stock market even rallied back above 290, a rebound of 20 percent. And the Harvard Economic Society, which was one of the few outfits to have predicted the recession, now argued that the worst had passed. Clutching at whatever straws he could find, Hoover seized upon these brief interludes of good news, not realizing they were head fakes. In June 1930, when a delegation from the National Catholic Welfare Council came to see him to request an expansion in public works programs, he announced, "Gentlemen, you have come sixty days too late. The depression is over." That very month the economy began another down leg.

Eventually, when the facts refused to obey Hoover's forecasts, he started to make them up. He frequently claimed in press conferences that employment was on the rise when clearly it was not. The Census Bureau and the Labor Department, which were responsible for data on unemployment, found themselves under constant pressure to fudge their numbers. One expert quit in disgust over attempts by the administration to fix the figures. Finally, even the chief of the Bureau of Labor Statistics was forced into retirement when he publicly disagreed with the administration's official statements on unemployment.

In contrast to Hoover, Treasury Secretary Mellon refused even to make a show of joining the cheerleading. His view was that speculators who had lost money "deserved it" and should pay for their reckless behavior; the U.S. economy was fundamentally sound and would rebound of its own accord. In the meantime, he argued that the best policy was to "liquidate labor, liquidate stocks, liquidate the farmers, liquidate real estate. . . . It will purge the rottenness out of the system . . . . People will work harder, live a more moral life. Values will be adjusted, and enterprising people will pick up the wrecks from less competent people."

One group who seemed to have taken Mellon's advice on liquidation to heart was the Russians. In 1930, desperately in need of foreign exchange, the Soviet government secretly decided to put its most treasured art works up for sale to its capitalist enemies. For Mellon, it was a once-in-a-lifetime opportunity to purchase a unique collection of art at throw-away prices, and he did not let it pass. Following a series of clandestine negotiations through art dealers in Berlin, London, and New York, Mellon arranged to purchase a total of twenty pieces. Each was a cloak-and-dagger operation. The money was wired to a dealer in Berlin, who placed it in a blocked account and paid out 10 percent to the Russians. Meanwhile, the pictures were surreptitiously removed from the Hermitage, in Saint Petersburg, the surrounding paintings repositioned to disguise the disappearance. They were then handed over at a secret rendezvous and shipped to Berlin for transport to the United States. In this way, during 1930 and into the early months of 1931, the secretary of the treasury spent almost $7 million of his money buying up half of the Hermitage's greatest paintings. Among the paintings he bought were the *Madonna of the House of Alba* by Raphael, the *Venus with the Mirror* by Titian, the *Adoration of the Magi* by Botticelli, and *The Turk* by Rembrandt as well as several works by Van Eyck, Van Dyck, and Frans Hals.

It was probably the greatest single art purchase of the century. Leaving mundane matters of economic policy to his deputy, Ogden Mills, Mellon became consumed by the whole transaction. On one occasion in September 1930, he was so engrossed in a discussion with one of his art dealers that he kept a group of bankers waiting for two hours.

With the federal government unable and unwilling to act—or in Mellon's case, perhaps otherwise occupied—the task of managing the declining economy fell almost entirely on the Fed. Between November 1929 and June 1930 the Fed eased monetary policy dramatically. It injected close to $500 million in cash into the banking system and cut rates from 6.0 percent to 2.5 percent—mostly the work of Harrison in New York. The Board in Washington only grudgingly registered the full force of what had happened. Not only did Harrison have to deal with its constant delaying tactics, but he also faced outright resistance from the majority of his fellow governors of the regional reserve banks—seven out of the twelve of them, from Boston, Philadelphia, Chicago, Kansas City, Minneapolis, Dallas, and San Francisco, opposed his attempts at a vigorous easing.

Most governors feared that "artificial" attempts to stimulate the economy by injecting liquidity into the banking system would not jump-start business activity, but just touch off another bout of speculation. Too much cheap credit had created the original bubble in the first place. Now that it had been pricked and stock prices were falling to more reasonable levels, why short-circuit the process, they asked, by making credit too cheap once again. As one argued, further easing would only result in a replay of the "1927 experiment, now quite generally . . . admitted to have been disastrous." The recession was a direct consequence of the past overspeculation, during which money had been thrown down absurd and uneconomic avenues. The only way to return to a healthy economy was to allow it to suffer for a while, a form of penance for the excesses of the last few years.

Because the notion of an active monetary policy to combat the business cycle was so novel and the knowledge of how the economy worked so primitive, debates among the various factions within the Fed became highly confused and at times even incomprehensible. In September 1930, Governor Norris, an otherwise highly competent and respected banker, found himself arguing at a Fed meeting that by easing interest rates, they had their policy backward. "We have been putting out credit, in a period of depression, when it was not wanted and could not be used, and will have to withdraw credit when it is wanted and can be used." He failed to recognize that the logic of his premise would have led him to the oddly perverse recommendation that the Fed should contract credit in a depression so that it might supply lots of it during a boom.

Without a common vocabulary for expressing ideas, Fed officials resorted to analogies. One of the governors likened any attempt by the Fed to revive the economy to a band desperately trying to keep the music going at a "marathon dance." On another occasion, he compared it to a physician's trying to bring a dead patient "back to life through the use of artificial respiration or injections of adrenalin."

In the early summer, the Fed stopped easing. It proved to be a mistake. For just as it went on hold, the economy embarked on a second down leg, industrial production falling by almost 10 percent between June and October. There is some debate about Harrison's reasons. Some argue that he thought he had done enough. Having staved off catastrophe by pumping a large amount of money into the system and cutting rates to an unprecedented low level, he believed that he had been as aggressive as he could. Others argue that he was operating with what might be called a faulty speedometer for gauging monetary policy. The usual indicators that he relied upon suggested that conditions were very easy—short-term rates were truly low and banks flush with excess cash. The problem was that some of these measures were now giving off the wrong signals. For example, when banks overflowed with surplus cash, this was generally an index, in a more stable and settled economic environment, the Fed had pushed more than enough reserves into the system to restart it. In 1930, however, in the wake of the crash, banks had begun carrying larger cash balances as a precaution against further disasters, and excess bank reserves were more a symptom of how gun-shy banks had become and less how easy the Fed had been.

. . .

IN SEPTEMBER 1930, Roy Young resigned as chairman of the Federal Reserve Board to become the head of the Boston Fed, a position that not only paid two and a half times as much—$30,000 as compared to $12,000—but also carried some executive authority. Finding replacements on the Board had never been easy; in the middle of a growing depression, it was doubly hard. Luckily Hoover had exactly the right candidate and promptly phoned his old friend, the noted banker and government financier Eugene Meyer, to offer him the job, saying, "I won't take no for an answer," and hung up without even waiting for a reply. He did not have to. He knew his man.

Few people were more enthusiastic or better prepared to take on the task of running the Federal Reserve than Meyer, a complete contrast to the second-rate figures who had so far inhabited the Board. A successful financier, he had accumulated a large fortune by the age of thirty-five, had run not one but two government-backed financial institutions, and unlike most bankers, believed very strongly in activist government policy and a more expansionary Fed policy to reverse the slide in the economy and halt deflation.

Meyer had been born in California, the son of Marc Meyer, a self-made man who had become a partner in the investment house of Lazard Frères. After graduating from Yale in 1895, he, too, went to work at Lazards, but quit in 1901, embarking on his own as a Wall Street speculator. He cleaned up during the 1907 panic, and by 1916 had amassed a fortune of $40 to $50 million.

He came to Washington in 1917 as a dollar-a-year man working for Woodrow Wilson, and had stayed on, becoming director of the War Finance Corporation and then head of the Federal Farm Loan Board. A larger-than-life figure, he commuted between a grand house on Crescent Place off Sixteenth Street, full of Cézannes and Monets and Ming vases; a seven-hundred-acre estate in Mount Kisco in New York; a six-hundred-acre cattle farm in Jackson Hole, Wyoming; and a plantation in Virginia. His wife, Agnes, a difficult egocentric woman who put him through a rocky and unhappy marriage, ran the most fashionable salon in Washington, where poets, painters, and musicians might mingle with politicians and bankers.*

Meyer's was not an uncontroversial nomination—Huey Long, the populist governor of Louisiana, declared he was nothing but "an ordinary tin-pot bucket shop operator up in Wall Street . . . not even a legitimate banker." His confirmation hearings proved to be difficult. Senator Brookhart of Iowa came out against him, calling him a "Judas Iscariot . . . one who has worked the Shylock game for the interests of big business"— for all his wealth, he had had to struggle with anti-Semitism throughout his career.

If there was anyone who seemed capable of reversing the paralysis of the Fed, it was Meyer. Yet, even he was soon overwhelmed. He found a Board racked by petty intrigues and feuds. Adolph Miller was at war with Charles James. Some of the old guard, such as Hamlin, resented Meyer and thought that he was too closely identified with the president.

The system of decision making and authority within the Fed, complex as it had been, had become even more byzantine. During Strong's time, decisions about how much to inject into the banking system through open market purchases of government securities had been taken by the five-member Open Market Investment Committee (OMIC), comprising the governors of the Federal Reserve Banks of Boston, New York, Philadelphia, Chicago, and Cleveland. Strong, therefore, had to persuade only two others to get a majority vote his way.

In January 1930, policy decisions for open market operations were shifted to a new twelve-man Open Market Policy Conference (OPMC), consisting of all the governors of the reserve banks. Each of these, of

---

*Meyer remained a Washington figure of some repute. After he retired from the Fed in 1933, he bought the near bankrupt *Washington Post*, which he successfully turned around. He was the father of the late Katharine Graham.

course, had to refer to his own nine-member board of directors. The old five-member committee (OMIC), renamed the Executive Committee of the OPMC, retained responsibility for execution. Now three separate groups were jockeying for power—one body, the OPMC, could initiate policy but could not execute; another, the Board, had to approve policy decisions but could not initiate them; and a third, the Executive Committee of the OPMC, implemented decisions within certain discretionary limits. At each stage policy could be vetoed or stymied. As a consequence, even though the two most prominent members of the Fed, Harrison and Meyer, both believed that it should be more aggressive, they were defeated by the system.

THE GREAT CRASH was greeted in Europe with a combination of schadenfreude and relief. According to the *New York Times*, Black Thursday's "panicky selling left London's City in a comfortable position saying, 'I told you so.'" Contacted by the *New York Evening Post* that same day, Maynard Keynes commented that "we in Great Britain can't help heaving a big sigh of relief at what seems like the removal of an incubus which has been lying heavily on the business life of the whole world outside America." The Wall Street collapse was, according to one French authority, like the bursting of an "abscess." The hope was that all the European capital that had been sucked into Wall Street would return home, alleviating the pressure on European gold reserves, and allowing such countries as Britain and Germany to ease credit and restart their economies.

Much to his delight, Émile Moreau had not had to miss the fall hunting season in Saint Léomer that year. By the last week of October 1929, he and Hjalmar Schacht were at the Black Forest spa of Baden-Baden attending an international bankers' conference to finalize the Young Plan and draw up the by-laws of the newly created Bank for International Settlements. Schacht learned of the events on Wall Street when he happened to notice the American delegation looking especially glum on the morning of October 29 and could hardly contain his glee when he discovered the reason. To a visiting Swiss banker, he announced that he hoped that the coming chaos would finally put an end to reparations.

But of all the central bankers in Europe, Montagu Norman was the most relieved. The crash had arrived just in time to rescue sterling. Convinced that it had been the rise in British interest rates on September 26 that finally burst the bubble, he started claiming credit for the collapse. So relaxed was he about the events on Wall Street, that on the morning of October 29, Black Tuesday, while the financial world was falling apart, he kept his usual appointment for a sitting with artist Augustus John, who had been commissioned by the Bank of England to paint his portrait.

During the last week of October and the first weeks of November, George Harrison kept him in touch with developments on Wall Street by cable and transatlantic telephone, his voice drifting in and out under the usual atmospherics. On October 31, Harrison called to announce cheerfully that the market had pretty much completed its fall; the bubble had been pricked without a single bank failure.

For the first few months, things went according to plan. European stock markets dropped in sympathy with Wall Street, but not having gone up so much, they fell much less precipitously. While the U.S. market slid almost 40 percent, Britain's went down 16 percent, Germany's 14 percent, and France's only 11 percent. Though the size of the British stock market was comparable as a percentage of GDP to that in the United States, the average British person preferred to bet on sports and left the stock market to the City bigwigs, while in France and Germany the size of the stock markets was tiny. Thus the crash did not exert the same hold on the psychology of European consumers and investors, and the effect on their economies was correspondingly less traumatic. Moreover, as credit conditions eased in the United States, foreign lending revived. Money suddenly became more freely available. Central banks across Europe, no longer having to defend their gold reserves against the pull of New York, were able to follow the Federal Reserve in cutting interest rates. By June 1930, with U.S. rates at their postwar low of 2.5 percent, the Bank of England was down to 3.5 percent, the Reichsbank to 4.5 percent, and the Banque de France to 2.5 percent.

Just as the threat of having to fight off an attack on sterling receded, Norman found himself harassed from another, and completely unexpected, quarter. In November 1929, a few weeks after the crash, the new British Labor government responded to criticisms about the endemically poor performance of the British economy by appointing a select committee under an eminent judge, Lord Macmillan, to investigate the workings of the British banking system. Half of its fourteen members were bankers; the remainder, an assortment of economists, journalists, industrialists, among them three of the staunchest critics of the gold standard: Maynard Keynes, Reginald McKenna, and Ernest Bevin of the Transport and General Workers Union, the country's most formidable trade union leader.

In setting up this committee, the allegedly radical government had made it clear that the issue of whether Britain should remain on the gold standard should be kept off the table. Even Keynes, the unremitting critic of the mechanism and the strains it had imposed on the British economy, was ready to concede that it was a fait accompli and that departing from gold at this stage would be just too disruptive.

Nevertheless, the Bank of England—and especially Norman—approached the committee with great suspicion. Within the City, it had always been said that the motto of the Bank of England was "Never explain, never apologize." That he and the Bank were now to be subject to the spotlight of public scrutiny filled him with dread. The committee began its hearings on November 28; Norman was to appear as one of the first witnesses, on December 5. As the date approached, his nervous ailments reappeared, and two days before he was due to testify, he predictably collapsed. His doctors recommended a short leave of absence and Norman duly departed for the next two months on an extended cruise around the Mediterranean, ending up in Egypt.

In place of Norman, the deputy governor, Sir Ernest Harvey, appeared. Even without its chief, the Bank found its habits of secrecy just too ingrained to abandon lightly. Consider this exchange between Keynes and Harvey:

KEYNES: "Arising from Professor Gregory's questions, is it a practice of the Bank of England never to explain what its policy is?"

HARVEY: "Well, I think it has been our practice to leave our actions to explain our policy."

KEYNES: "Or the reasons for its policy?"

HARVEY: "It is a dangerous thing to start to give reasons."

KEYNES: "Or to defend itself against criticism?"

HARVEY: "As regards criticism, I am afraid, though the Committee may not all agree, we do not admit there is need for defense; to defend ourselves is somewhat akin to a lady starting to defend her virtue."

Norman finally returned in England in February 1930 and agreed to provide evidence to the select committee. He was not a good witness. Witty and articulate in private, he became sullen and defensive in public settings, replying to the questions, which in deference to his position were never aggressive, in curt sentences and sometimes even in monosyllables. Unaccustomed to having to articulate his thought processes or justify himself, he said things that he did not mean or could not possibly believe, insisting, at one point, that there was no connection between the Bank's credit policies and the level of unemployment. He appeared to be callous and indifferent to the plight of the unemployed, reinforcing the stereotype of bankers among the Socialists of the new government and the voting public who were getting their first glimpse of this man. Confronted with Keynes's coldly precise questions, Norman seemed to be dull and slow, retreating behind platitudes.

Finally asked by the chairman what the reasons were for a particular policy decision, he initially said nothing but simply tapped the side of his nose three times. When pressed, he replied, "Reasons, Mr. Chairman? I don't have reasons. I have instincts."

The chairman patiently tried to probe further, "We understand that, of course, Mr. Governor, nevertheless you must have had some reasons."

"Well, if I had I have forgotten them."

Keynes would later describe Norman as looking like "an artist, sitting with his cloak round him hunched up, saying, 'I can't remember,' thus evading all questions." Norman testified for only two days—the bank's senior staff realized that he was doing more harm than good, and the remainder of the testimony was passed back to the deputy governor. But the damage to Norman's standing had been done. In the aftermath, one banker confided to his colleagues that the governor "grows more and more temperamental, freakish, and paradoxical."

18. MAGNETO TROUBLE

1930-31

To what extremes won't you compel our hearts,
you accursed lust for gold?

—VIRGIL, *The Aeneid*

IN DECEMBER 1930, Maynard Keynes published an article titled "The Great Slump of 1930," in which he described the world as living in "the shadow of one of the greatest economic catastrophes of modern history." During the previous year, industrial production had fallen 30 percent in the United States, 25 percent in Germany, and 20 percent in Britain. Over 5 million men were looking for work in the United States, another 4.5 million in Germany, and 2 million in Britain. Commodity prices across the world had collapsed—coffee, cotton, rubber, and wheat prices having fallen by more than 50 percent since the stock market crash. Three of the largest primary producing countries, Brazil, Argentina, and Australia, had left the gold standard and let their currencies devalue. In the industrial world, wholesale prices had fallen by 15 percent and consumer prices by 7 percent.

Despite all this bad news, at this stage Keynes was uncharacteristically sanguine. "We have involved ourselves in a colossal muddle, having blundered in the control of a delicate machine, the working of which we do not understand," he wrote. Comparing the economy to a stalled car, he declared it was a simple matter of some "magneto trouble" (a magneto was a device then commonly in use for creating an electric spark in the ignition system of automobiles), trouble that could be easily cured by "resolute action" by the central banks to "start the machine again."

There were in fact reasonable grounds for optimism. The downturn that had hit the United States in 1930 in the wake of the stock market crash had indeed been deep, but the U.S. economy had faced a similarly sharp decline in prices and production in 1921 and had bounced back. There had been as yet no major financial disaster or bankruptcy.

Keynes did recognize that it was hard for any single central bank to act alone. To jump-start the economy, a central bank had to have enough gold, the underlying raw material for credit creation under the gold standard. The international monetary system was now operating, however, in a very perverse way. Because of investor fear, capital in search of security was flowing into those countries with already large gold reserves—such as the United States and France—and out of countries with only modest reserves—such as Britain and Germany.

As it had been during the 1920s, the United States was a major haven for gold flows. Far more damaging than the effect of the protectionist Smoot-Hawley Act was the collapse in capital flows. After a brief revival early in 1930, U.S. foreign investment into Europe suddenly dried to a trickle. American bankers became risk averse and cautious and, claiming that it was hard to find creditworthy borrowers, pulled in their horns. With American capital bottled up at home and U.S. demand for European goods shrinking—a result of the weak U.S. economy and of higher import tariffs imposed in June 1930 by the Smoot-Hawley Act—Europe could only pay for its imports and service its debts in gold. During 1930, a total of $300 million in bullion was shipped across the Atlantic into the vaults of the Federal Reserve system.*

---

*Many popular accounts of the Great Depression attribute a large weight to the protectionist Smoot-Hawley Act as a cause of the economic collapse. Tariffs shift demand from imports to domestic goods, so if anything, it should have had an expansionary effect. Retaliation by foreigners did hurt the U.S. economy, but exports were a small percentage of

Even more disruptive to international stability, however, was the flow of gold into France, the one country in Europe that had somehow remained immune from the world economic storm. Émile Moreau's strategy of keeping the franc pegged at a low rate had meant that French goods remained attractively priced. As a result the economy held up very well in 1929 and 1930, and capital, in search of safety, started flooding into France: a total of $500 million of gold during 1930. It was one of the startling ironies of that whole period that France, viewed by bankers in the years after the war as irresponsible and suspect, had now become the world's financial safe haven. By the end of 1930, the Banque de France, in addition to the $1 billion it held in sterling and dollar deposits, had accumulated a gold reserve mountain of over $2 billion, three times that of the Bank of England. French officials, who only a few years before had been quick to blame their woes on the work of international currency "speculators," now began touting the superior wisdom of these selfsame "investors" for the votes of confidence they had cast on French economic management.

While everywhere else in the global economy consumers and businesses were cutting back and slashing their budgets, in France, money remained easily available and people continued to spend. French commentators were calling their country L'Île Heureuse. In the summer of 1930, Paris was still full of tourists, and business at Au Printemps, the famed Parisian department store, was booming. The contrast with its neighbors could not have been greater. While in Germany 4.5 million men were on the dole and in Britain 2 million, in France only 190,000 men were collecting unemployment benefits. And while prices across the rest of the world were dropping like stones, in France they continued to rise.

Quite without knowing what it was doing, France had backed into the position of the strongest economy in Europe. After a decade of suffering an inferiority complex created by the combination of "the war . . . fear of Germany [and] the franc's fall," it responded to its unexpected good for-

GDP—less than 4 percent—so the total effect would have been small. Changes in capital flows dwarfed the impact of trade.

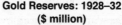

FIGURE 6

**Gold Reserves: 1928–32
($ million)**

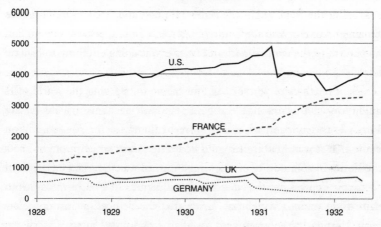

After 1929, France accumulated enormous reserves of gold.

tune with an outburst of self-congratulation. According to the prime minister, André Tardieu, France, having successfully navigated the economic storm, was admired by the whole for its "harmonious economic structure . . . the natural prudence of the French people, their ability to adapt, their modernity and their courage." Tardieu, with his bejeweled pince-nez and his gold cigarette holder, his boulevardier taste in silk hats and fancy waistcoats, his fondness for raffish company, his involvement before the age of thirty-five in at least two financial scandals, was the embodiment of all that the British despised about French politicians. That this "glittering new embodiment of Gallic self confidence" could now lecture the world about prudence and indulge in his nation's habit of attributing its successes to the innate and inestimable advantages of French civilization profoundly irritated France's neighbors.

British commentators, unable to understand why commodity prices kept falling, why, despite the massive cuts in interest rates, production in their own country kept dropping and unemployment rising, blamed the operation of the gold standard as the primary cause of world depression, especially the role played by the Federal Reserve and the Banque de France. By the end of the year, the United States and France, between them, held 60 percent of the world's gold, and neither was doing anything to recirculate it.

The French came in especially for blame for starving the world of liquidity by short-circuiting the gold standard mechanism. Paul Einzig, author of the influential Lombard Street column for the *Financial News,* wrote that it was "the French gold hoarding policy which brought about the slump in commodity prices, which in turn was the main cause of the economic depression; that it is the unwillingness of France to cooperate with other nations which has aggravated the depression into a violent crisis." Similarly, the prominent Swedish economist, Gustav Cassell, the primary exponent of the view that world deflation in commodity prices reflected insufficient circulation of gold, argued, "The Banque de France has consistently and unnecessarily acquired enormous amounts of gold without troubling in the least about the consequences that such a procedure is bound to have on the rest of the world, and therefore on the world economic position."

By the end of 1930, the Banque de France had begun to understand that this accumulation of gold was harming the rest of the world by starving it of reserves. It was especially damaging because of the idiosyncrasies of the French banking system. In most countries, banks worked to make every dollar of gold support a multiple of that amount in currency and credit. The French banking system, however, was unusually inefficient in putting its bullion to use. As a result, the newly arrived $500 million of gold was translated into less than $250 million in circulating currency.

French officials claimed that there was little they could do about this buildup, that the high demand for gold in France was a consequence of the rural character of the country or the innate thriftiness and risk aversion of its citizenry. In fact, it was clear that during 1930, the Banque under Émile

Moreau had been very consciously and deliberately offsetting—the technical term was *sterilizing*—the natural tendency of an influx of gold to expand the currency, lest it lead to inflation. With prices around the world collapsing, this may sound strange, but it was a symptom of how badly scarred he and other French officials had been by the currency crises of 1924 and 1926.

Unknown to most people, much of the gold that had supposedly flown into France was actually sitting in London. Bullion was so heavy—a seventeen-inch cube weighs about a ton—that instead of shipping crates of it across hundreds of miles from one country to another and paying high insurance costs, central banks had taken to "earmarking" the metal, that is, keeping it in the same vault but simply re-registering its ownership. Thus the decline in Britain's gold reserves and their accumulation in France and the United States was accomplished by a group of men descending into the vaults of the Bank of England, loading some bars of bullion onto a low wooden truck with small rubber tires, trundling them thirty feet across the room to the other wall, and offloading them, though not before attaching some white name tags indicating that the gold now belonged to the Banque de France or the Federal Reserve Bank.* That the world was being subject to a progressively tightening squeeze on credit just because there happened to be too much gold on one side of the vault and not enough on the other provoked Lord d'Abernon, Britain's ambassador to Germany after the war and now an elder statesmen-economist, to exclaim, "This depression is the stupidest and most gratuitous in history."

As the French hoard kept piling up during the summer and fall of 1930—and with it tensions between Britain and France—the French went through the motions of proposing remedies. The return of French gold policy to the forefront of economic debate was too much for Norman. He

---

*Schacht liked to tell the story of how when he came to New York in the mid-1920s, Strong had taken him down into the vaults of the New York Fed to show him where the Reichsbank's gold was stored. Much to Strong's embarrassment, Fed officials were unable to find the pallet of bullion that had been specifically earmarked for the Reichsbank. See Hjalmar Schacht, *My First Seventy-six Years* (London: Allan Wingate, 1955), page 264.

was happy to deal with the Americans, but having had his fingers burned by his experience with Moreau in 1927, he absolutely refused to have anything to do with French officialdom.

Instead, he wisely left it up to the British Treasury to try to negotiate with their counterparts in the Ministry of Finance. These conversations led nowhere. Indeed, they brought out the worst in the characters of both countries. The British insisted upon patronizing lectures on the primitive nature and deficiencies of the French banking system, without any sense that they themselves would have found such advice from abroad intrusive and insulting.

It soon became clear that France was motivated not so much by economic arguments but by strategic calculations. French officials tried to use their financial muscle to extract political concessions—money to them not being its own reward. Even the French Military High Command became involved. General Réquin, a senior adviser to Minister of Defense André Maginot, wrote to General Weygand, chief of the General Staff, urging that France "lean on England while the pound is at our mercy. . . . We can make her understand . . . that if she wants our help as a lender, other questions must first be settled."

In September 1930, it was suddenly announced that Moreau was resigning. This had been rumored in Paris for months, but it still came as a great shock in British banking circles. Initially the talk was that he was being forced out by British pressure and that his departure might foreshadow a change in French policy.

In fact, having presided over the recovery of the franc, he had just been decorated as Grand Officier de la Légion d'Honneur and decided himself that it would be a good time to go. He was simply following the age-old practice in France whereby senior civil servants, unusually poorly paid by international standards, move to the private sector to build up a nest egg. He had accepted the position of vice president of the Banque de Paris et Pays-Bas, the most prominent of the private *banques d'affaires,* a distinctively French type of banking house that combined security underwriting with direct investments in industry. Indeed, he had already moved out of the official apartment assigned to him as governor, which despite its "sumptuous trimmings" was lit by kerosene lamps, had especially "antiquated heating," and smelled of "a miser's snuggery," into a magnificent *hôtel particulier,* a large town house on the Rue de Constantine opposite Les Invalides.

He was succeeded by his deputy, Clément Moret, like Moreau a graduate in law, who had then gone on to Sciences Po, and also on to the Ministry of Finance—Moret, however, was not part of the elite Inspectorat des Finances. Instead, the self-effacing Moret had spent twenty-five years clambering up the Ministry of Finance hierarchy. Plucked from obscurity by Poincaré, who described him as "abnormally honest," Moret had become a director general within the ministry and in 1928 had been assigned to the Banque as deputy governor.

He was of a different generation—at the age of forty-five the youngest man to be appointed governor. And in contrast to Moreau, who had been blunt to the point of rudeness, Moret was courteous and thoughtful. But though there was a change in style at the Banque, there was to be no change in the substance of policy. Indeed, Moret thought of himself, even more than had Moreau, as a civil servant and the Banque de France as essentially an arm of the state. He did propose that if the goal was to redirect gold reserves from France to Britain, the British government should borrow directly in France. Of course, lacking any assurance that the pound would remain stable, such a loan would have to be denominated in francs. For Norman, who thought that it was contrary to the "prestige" of London even to appear to "ask favors from the French," this would have been the ultimate humiliation. And so, as a combination of British pride and heavy-handedness locked horns with French selfishness and arrogance, the French gold mountain kept growing.

Norman instead latched onto a grandiose plan that, it was claimed, would provide a "blood transfusion" to cure the Depression. An international bank, a sort of forerunner of the World Bank, was to be set up and headquartered in a neutral country, Switzerland or the Netherlands, with capital of $250 million. It would be able to borrow another $750 million primarily in gold-rich France and America, which would be channeled to governments and businesses around the world in need of capital. Norman rolled it out at the February 1931 monthly meeting in Basel of the BIS, which had become a sort of club for central bankers. They would gather there on a Sunday night, have an informal and private dinner together, and spend the next day in meetings. Even before the wining and dining was over—for the monthly meetings at Basel would become a byword for good food—it was clear that the plan would go nowhere. Neither the French nor the Americans were willing to hand over large amounts of money to an internationally run organization likely to be dominated by Englishmen.

The following month Norman sailed for the United States, which he had not visited since the summer of 1929. It was obvious that in the intervening two years the American press had greatly missed him. From the very start, following the suddenly announced mission of what the *New York Times* called "England's elusive master banker" and "man of mystery," vaguely hinting that some great initiative to solve the world Depression was in the offing, they would not leave Norman alone. From his departure aboard the *Berengaria* on March 21, he was followed everywhere on his "secret mission" and his movements—his meetings at the New York Fed, attended by even the secretary of state, Henry Stimson; his trip to Washington; his visit to the White House; lunch with Secretary of the Treasury Mellon—were all examined in minute detail. He put on a wonderful performance, hamming it up for the crowd of reporters that pursued him. Looking more like "an orchestra leader than a banker of such eminence," he wished them "better luck next time" when they tried to extract the purpose of his visit. When they begged him for some tidbit of insight into the world financial situation, he teased them by gravely announcing that he thought the recent departure of King Alfonso of Spain into exile would have no effect on international finance. But for all the frenetic schedule of meetings, even his most devoted followers among the press had the suspicion that there was much less there than met the eye.

Even before Norman had arrived in the United States, J. P. Morgan & Co., usually his biggest supporter, had signaled that it had no intention of backing an "artificial" agency or any "form of international organization of credit." The New York Fed had cabled that it thought the whole scheme too "visionary and inflationary."

Norman tried to convince his American hosts of the "very gloomy situation" of Europe. The only hope for Britain now was a savage reduction in wages. In Eastern and Central Europe the position was even more desperate. "Russia was the very greatest of dangers," he told Stimson. Germany and Eastern Europe were not receiving enough "help from the capitalist system to stand the expense of remaining capitalist . . . and all the time while they wobbled and wavered Russia was beckoning to them to come over to her system." The specter of communism, which would persuade a later generation of Americans to pour vast amounts of money into Europe, did not have the same potency in 1931.

The United States was in a depression of its own, had over the previous seventeen years already committed some $15 billion to Europe, including war loans, and was eager to avoid any further entanglements across the Atlantic. Norman returned empty-handed. In May, when Thomas Lamont was passing through London, Norman complained to him that the "U.S. was blind and taking no steps to save the world and the gold standard."

It was becoming apparent to most commentators that the continued flow of gold into France would eventually create a breakdown in the mechanism of international payments. As usual, Keynes put it the most graphically, "Almost throughout the world, gold has been withdrawn from circulation. It no longer passes from hand to hand, and the touch of the metal has been taken from men's greedy palms. The little household gods, who dwelt in purses and stockings and tin boxes, have been swallowed by a single golden image in each country, which lives underground and is not seen. Gold is out of sight—gone back into the soil. But when the gods are no longer seen in a yellow panoply walking the earth, we begin to rationalize them; and it is not long before there is nothing left." The bullion reserves that backed the credit systems of the world, buried as they were in underground vaults—or in the case of the Banque de France, underwater, because its vaults lay below a subterranean aquifer—were invisible to the public eye. They had acquired an almost metaphysical existence. Keynes thought that perhaps gold, its usefulness now outlived, might become less important. He compared the situation to the transition in government from absolute to constitutional monarchy. He would eventually be proved right but not before a wrenching upheaval.

IN EARLY 1931, a similar insidious process of paralysis also began to affect the U.S. banking system. It originated in the most unlikely of places—the Bronx, one of the outer boroughs of New York City—with the strangely named Bank of United States (BUS), which despite its official-sounding title bore no relationship to the U.S. government but traced its very modest roots to the garment industry on the Lower East Side of Manhattan.

On the morning of December 10, 1930, a small merchant from the Morrisania section of the Bronx went to his local branch of the Bank of United States on the corner of Freeman Street and Southern Boulevard and asked that the bank buy back his modest holdings of its stock. This was not as strange a request as it sounds. In the middle of 1929, the bank had set out to support the value of its shares by selling them to its own depositors. As an inducement, investors were given informal assurances that they could sell the stock back to the bank at the original purchase price—around $200 a share. If this sounds too good to be true, it was; but in the middle of 1929, people were willing to believe anything. By the fall of 1930, after the collapse on Wall Street and amid mounting concerns about the economic situation of New York, shares were trading at around $40.

Officials at the Bronx branch tried to convince the exigent depositor that he should hold on to his stock, that even at current prices it remained an excellent investment. No doubt irritated at this obvious attempt to renege on a clear promise, he stormed out and began reporting that the bank was in trouble. By the afternoon, a small horde of depositors had begun lining up outside the branch's tiny neoclassical limestone building to withdraw their savings before closing time. Until now, despite the Depression, there had been no bank runs in New York, and soon a crowd of twenty thousand curious bystanders had gathered to watch. As the anxious depositors became restless, a squad of mounted police had to be sent in to control them and several customers were arrested; and when the mob became frantic, the police charged the crowd with their horses.

The Bank of United States had fifty-seven branches across the four larger boroughs of New York, and over four hundred thousand individual depositors, more than any other bank in the country. Rumors of the trouble quickly swept the city and similar scenes were enacted that afternoon at many other branches, with armored trucks being called in to deliver extra cash.

The bank had been founded in 1913 by Joseph S. Marcus, a Russian Jewish immigrant who had come to the United States in 1879, and having begun as a garment worker on Canal Street, had made good as a manufacturer of clothing and then as a local banker. The first branch of his bank, located on the corner of Orchard and Delancey Street, catered to the neighborhood's mostly Jewish garment workers and merchants. As a result of Marcus's reputation among the Lower East Side traders for honesty and fair dealing, the bank had done well, although it was undoubtedly helped by the name, which gave many of its Yiddish-speaking clients the impression that it was somehow backed by the full faith and credit of the national government. By the time the older Marcus died in 1927, the bank had grown into an institution with $100 million in assets, a head office at 320 Fifth Avenue, and seven branches across the city. But its officers and its clientele remained predominantly Jewish, and it was snidely nicknamed "The Pants Pressers' Bank."

When Joseph Marcus died, the bank was taken over by his son Bernard Marcus, a brilliant but flamboyant businessman with a taste for conspicuous consumption far removed from his father's modest ways. When, for instance, Bernard went to Europe, he traveled with thirty pieces of luggage and always insisted on occupying the grandest suite on board ship. Over the next two years, he expanded his base through a series of mergers so that by 1929 it had grown to $250 million in assets.

Marcus resorted to a series of practices considered shady, even by the lax standards of the time. The bank lent some $16 million, a third of its capital, to officers of the company and their relatives to allow them to buy its stock. To finance its headlong growth—the bank more than doubled in size in two years—Marcus issued large slabs of equity, which he committed to buy back at the original price of $200. When the price began to fall in the spring and summer of 1929, many investors held Marcus to his guarantees. In order to take up all the stock coming on the market, he created a series of affiliate companies—in today's parlance, off-balance-sheet special-purpose vehicles—that repurchased the equity with money borrowed from the bank itself. Marcus was in effect using depositors' money to support the shares of his bank.

In its lending policy, the bank made a big bet on the value of New York City real estate. Half its loan portfolio, double that of comparable firms, went into real estate finance, though again the true exposure was hidden by channeling money through affiliate companies. When the crash hit, the bank was committed to two big projects on Central Park West: $5 million for the Beresford, a twenty-story building at Eighty-second Street with over 170 apartments and another $4 million for the San Remo on Seventy-fourth with 120. Though it was rumored that Marcus himself owned these two developments, his interest in them was disguised through dummy corporations, and every single penny for their construction came from the bank.

Thus by the middle of 1930, while the official books gave the impression of a bank that had $250 million in deposits, $300 million in good quality assets and $50 million in equity, the operational reality behind these numbers was quite different. The true value of assets was worth no more than $220 million, all its equity had been wiped out, and the bank was $30 million in the hole.

In the fall of 1930, as rumors that the BUS might be in trouble circulated through the higher financial circles of New York, the Fed tried to engineer a merger with some of the other Jewish majority-owned banks in the city: the Manufacturers Trust, the Public National Bank, and the International Trust Company. The deal would have required the resignations of Marcus and his cronies who had presided over its mismanagement. But suspicion of Marcus within the financial community was so great that no one could bring themselves to trust the accounts, and the deal fell through at the last minute.

On the evening after the run began on December 10, all of the familiar Wall Street barons—George Harrison of the New York Fed, Thomas Lamont of J. P. Morgan, Albert Wiggin of Chase, Charles Mitchell of National City, and another half dozen of the city's top bankers—gathered on the twelfth floor of the New York Fed to try to put together a rescue package. By 8:30 that evening they were close to striking a deal and Harrison had even begun preparing his press statement. To save the bank, they would collectively have to be willing to pump in $30 million. At the last moment, however, several key bankers balked.

These men had all been reared on Walter Bagehot's nineteenth-century classic *Lombard Street,* which described how the Bank of England, then the financial center of the world, handled financial crises and panics. Bagehot argued that during normal times a central bank should follow the gold standard rule book, allowing credit to expand and contract in line with bullion reserves. But in a financial crisis, it should throw away the rule book and "lend freely, boldly, and so that the public may feel you mean to go on." As he put it, "A panic . . . is a species of neuralgia, and according to the rules of science you must not starve it." In other words, a central bank had to be willing to inject as much money as was necessary to satisfy the public demand for cash and safe assets.

But Bagehot did inject one caveat. Though he argued that in a panic the central bank should lend without hesitation or question, it should do so only to banks facing a temporary squeeze on liquidity and never to those actually insolvent. The problem this time was that the BUS was not just temporarily short of funds, it was insolvent and could not hope to cover its obligations.

There was another element involved in the decision not to bail out the Bank of United States, though it was unspoken. Marcus was a Jew and, moreover, a Jew of the wrong sort. There had always been a divide between the WASP houses and the Jewish houses on Wall Street. But firms such as Kuhn Loeb, Lehman Brothers, and J. W. Seligman represented "Our Crowd," the German Jewish elite, and for all the anti-Semitic bigotries of old dinosaurs like Jack Morgan, these firms were held in very high regard and viewed as reputable and very prestigious institutions. But the Wall Street patricians gathering on the evening of December 10 would have found it hard to hide their distaste for bailing out a Jew like Marcus, an ex-garment manufacturer from the Lower East Side who was running a bank that, according to Thomas Lamont's son, Tommy, was patronized largely by "foreigners and Jews." Russell Leffingwell, the Morgan partner, described it as a bank "with a large clientele among our Jewish population of small merchants, and persons of small means and small education, from whom all the management were drawn."

When Joseph Broderick, the New York State superintendent of banks, learned of the decision, he insisted on coming to address the meeting. After being pointedly kept waiting until 1:00 a.m., he was finally admitted. He would testify later that "I told them that the Bank of United States occupied a rather unique position in New York City, that in point of people served it was probably the largest bank in the city and that its closing might affect a large number of smaller banks and that I was afraid that it would be the spark that would ignite the whole city." Broderick reminded the grandees that only two or three weeks before "they had rescued two of the largest private bankers in the city." One of them was Kidder Peabody, an investment bank run by Boston Brahmins, founded in 1865, which as result of the crash and of subsequent withdrawals of deposits by, among others, the government of Italy, had had to be bailed out in 1930 with $15 million from J. P. Morgan and Chase.

Though the meeting continued into the early hours of the morning, he was unable to persuade the few recalcitrants to change their mind. The Fed, believing that it could throw a ring fence around the BUS and prevent its troubles from spreading, decided to close the bank's doors the next morning. "I warned them that they were making the most colossal mistake in the banking history of New York," Broderick would later testify at a trial. Marcus and one of his lieutenants were tried, convicted, and sentenced to three years' imprisonment. Broderick was separately indicted for alleged negligence in not closing the bank earlier. The case ended in a mistrial; after a second trial, he was acquitted.

Dramatic as it was, the failure of the Bank of United States was in fact not that unusual. The United States had historically always suffered from an unstable banking system—the consequence of having no central bank compounded by an astoundingly fragmented banking structure. The creation of the Fed in 1913 had more or less solved the first problem, but did nothing to change the organization of banking in the country. During the 1920s, the United States was still populated with some 25,000 banks, many of them so tiny, undiversified, and dependent on the economic conditions of their localities that every year roughly 500 went under. In the first nine months of 1930, as a result of the deepening hard times, 700 had closed their doors. That October, two months before the BUS crisis, the terrible drought across the Midwest and South led to the collapse of the Tennessee investment bank, Caldwell and Company, which controlled the largest chain of banks in the South, leaving a string of failures in its wake—120 in all across Tennessee, Kentucky, Arkansas, and North Carolina.

After closing the BUS, the Fed did successfully manage to avoid a chain reaction among local banks. December 1930 and January 1931 saw a brief spike in bank runs in New York and Pennsylvania, but the sense of panic quickly died down. However, the failure of the BUS did mark a profound change in public sentiment toward banks.

Shaken by such a high-profile failure, depositors started becoming more cautious about where they placed their money. Unable to tell whether a bank was sound or not, they began pulling their cash indiscriminately out of all banks, good and bad. At first it was a mere ripple—in the months after the twin failures a total of $450 million dollars left the banking system, less than 1 percent of total deposits.

Because of the way banking works, however, such withdrawals had a negative multiplier effect. In an effort to maintain a prudent balance between their own liquidity and their loan portfolios, banks had to call in three or four dollars of loans for each dollar in cash withdrawn. Moreover, as their loans were called, borrowers in turn withdrew their deposits from other banks. The effect was to spread the scramble for liquidity right across the system. In this climate, all banks felt the need to protect themselves by building up cash reserves and thus called in even more loans. By the middle of 1931, bank credit had shrunk by almost $5 billion, equivalent to 10 percent of outstanding loans and investments.

After a lull during the spring, in May 1931, the bank runs resumed. A real estate bubble in the Chicago suburbs collapsed, and thirty Chicago banks with $60 million in deposits were swept away. Over the summer, the virus spread to Toledo—every large bank but one was shut down; the remaining one being saved only when, at the last minute, trucks from the Federal Reserve Bank of Cleveland drew up at its doors laden with $11

FIGURE 7

U.S. Bank Credit: 1922–36
($ billion)

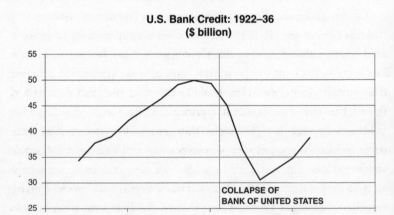

The U.S. credit crunch began in 1931.

million in crisp new currency notes. Seventy percent of the city's deposits were frozen, retail business came to a standstill, and even the Inverness Golf Club, scene of the most recent U.S. Open, was closed.

Within the Fed, officials were fully aware of the strains on the financial system—the hoarding of currency, the growing problem of bank failures, the reluctance of banks to lend, prices falling at a rate of 20 percent per annum. Somehow they were unable to put all these pieces of the jigsaw puzzle together. At the Federal Reserve Board, Meyer pressed for a more aggressive policy and even Adolph Miller, who with his natural contrarian streak seemed to end up so often in the minority, joined him. But the Board was legally powerless to initiate action.

Meanwhile, the governors of the various Federal Reserve banks, who could have taken the initiative, refused to act. A large number of the banks in trouble, particularly the small ones, were not members of the Federal Reserve System—only half of the twenty-five thousand banks in the country had joined the system, although they accounted for about three-quarters of all deposits. The regional bank governors did not feel any responsibility for these nonmember banks, despite their impact on the nation's overall supply of credit.

The real issue for the governors was that many of the banks closing their doors—by one estimate close to half—had sustained such large losses on their loans that they were, like the BUS, insolvent. Determined to follow Bagehot's rule of only lending to "sound" institutions and believing that propping up failing banks would be throwing good money after bad, the regional governors made it a principle to let them go under. They failed to recognize that by doing so they were undermining public confidence in banks as a repository of savings and were causing the U.S. credit system to freeze up.

Strangely enough in the first quarter of 1931, as the world banking system was having to cope on one side with the hoarding of currency by a frightened American public and on the other by the piling up of gold bullion at the Fed and the Banque de France, the economy went through one of its little rebounds, both in the United States and across Europe. If the banking system can be compared, as it often is, to the plumbing of the world's economy, then the double drain of cash was like two invisible leaks. Their effects were not immediate and would only become apparent gradually.

It was during the spring of 1931 after Norman had returned from the United States that he wrote his infamous letter to Moret, foreseeing the wreck of "the capitalist system throughout the civilized world" within a year and asking that his prediction "be filed for future reference."* He could sense that the world's credit supply was beginning to dry up. But he and his fellow central bankers had been unable to agree among themselves on what to do. Norman found himself increasingly without influence and powerless to act. The letter, a poor substitute for action, was undoubtedly shrugged off within the Banque de France as only old Montagu Norman going on about the end of Western civilization for the umpteenth time.

---

*See page 5 above.

19. A LOOSE CANNON ON THE DECK OF THE WORLD

1931

Money has no motherland; financiers are without patriotism and without decency; their sole object is gain.

— Napoléon Bonaparte

In the spring of 1931, the one major country most weighed down by a sense of collective despair and individual hopelessness was Germany. The official figures indicated that 4.7 million people, close to 25 percent of the workforce, double that in the United States, were without jobs. And this did not include another 2 million forced into part-time work. Pawnshops multiplied as did astrologers, numerologists, and other charlatans. Even before Hoovervilles had become common in cities across America, shantytowns of tents and packing cases had sprung up in the parks and forests around Berlin. These camps, displaying the German gift for organization, soon had their own "mayors," "town councils," and community kitchens where women cooked turnips.

But then Germany, burdened by the twin problems of foreign debt and reparations, had been in a constant state of feverish turmoil ever since the

Norman and Schacht, 1935

middle of 1929. No sooner had the Young Plan been signed in Paris in July of that year, than the campaign to repudiate it had gone into high gear. A national committee led by Dr. Alfred Hugenberg, chairman of the right-wing German Nationalist Party—third largest in the Reichstag, where it held 73 seats out of a total of 491—was formed to organize a referendum on the plan. Known as the German Randolph Hearst, Hugenberg, a former chairman of the famed arms manufacturer Krupps, had branched out into the news business after the war and now controlled some of the country's largest papers, including *Der Tag*, the biggest movie production company, and the largest independent telegraph agency.

Among those whom Hugenberg enlisted was Adolf Hitler, then still regarded as something of a joke, a minor figure from a fringe far-right group with an embarrassing past as the leader of the 1923 "beer cellar *Putsch*." In the previous year's national elections, the Nazis had won a bare 2.6 percent of the vote and only twelve seats in the Reichstag. They did, however, add their own distinctive brand of venom to the referendum campaign. Arguing that the Young Plan would submit Germany to "three generations of forced labor," they branded it a "Jewish machination" and a "a product of the Jewish spirit." The referendum, which would have required the government to renegotiate the repeal of the hated War Guilt clause, suspend all payments on reparations, and to make it a crime for any official to enter into any further agreement thereon, received 4,135,000 votes, a sign of the growing popular disenchantment with the policy of fulfillment.

No one provided a better weather vane for the shifting political winds than Hjalmar Schacht. The Young Plan negotiations left him disappointed and bitter. In the late 1920s, he and his old protector Gustav Stresemann had allowed Germany to borrow vast amounts of money from U.S. banks in the hope of forcing American involvement in the reparations question. Their strategy of binding the German republic to American money had, however, not paid off. In Schacht's view, the American bankers had failed to deliver. He and Stresemann had clearly exaggerated the power and influence of Wall Street to impose a resolution of the reparations issue.

In October 1929, three weeks before the Wall Street crash, Stresemann died suddenly of a stroke at only fifty-one, a victim of stress and overwork. After the grim letdown of the Young Plan negotiations and Stresemann's death, Schacht lost any remaining faith in the American solution.

He was now in a quandary. Disillusioned with the Americans, he was more willing to explore alternatives, including the unilateral repudiation being advanced by the nationalist right. But it was hard for him to jettison the Young Plan at this stage—after all, the document bore his signature—without looking like a shameless opportunist.

In November, during negotiations at The Hague, the German government agreed to modest adjustments to the Young Plan terms. In return, the Allies agreed to advance the date for withdrawing their remaining troops from the Rhineland, and reached a settlement on the status of German citizens in lands previously part of East Prussia but ceded to Poland at Versailles. The effect of all these modifications was to add some 4 to 5 percent to the Young Plan payments, amounting to about $25 million a year. The economic significance was trivial—nevertheless, it provided Schacht with just the excuse he needed to break with the government.

Moreover, as the German unemployment rolls kept rising, the cost of unemployment benefits mounted with them and the budget deficit kept increasing. The government, a grand coalition of all democratic parties led by the Socialist Hermann Müller, proposed to finance itself by more borrowing abroad. For Schacht, who had been on a campaign against excessive foreign debt since 1927, this was one more sign that a coalition that included the Socialists was incapable of governing Germany. Having failed to control either its spending or borrowing abroad during the good times, it was now repeating the mistake as times turned bad. He feared that Germany was heading for national bankruptcy.

On December 5, he dropped his bombshell on Berlin. Without warning he issued a public statement in which he accused the government in inflammatory language of "twisting" the Young Plan and failing to take the necessary steps to control its own finances. Declaring that it would be "self-deception" for the German people to believe that the nation could pay a pfennig more than it had agreed to in Paris, he publicly repudiated the plan's latest revisions. A few weeks later, he sabotaged the government's attempt to raise a loan in New York through the American investment house of Dillon Read.

Such an open declaration of war on the government by the head of the central bank in the middle of an economic crisis threatened to plunge the country into chaos. The government was barely able to survive financially and then only by tapping the loan from the munificent Ivar Kreuger.

The following weeks were a time of terrible stress for Schacht. While the ultimate severity of the coming Depression could not yet be foreseen, he could tell that after the Wall Street crash Germany was headed for a catastrophe and wished to avoid being buried by the coming disaster. And yet, if he resigned now, he would be giving up the most powerful economic position in Germany and stalking off into the political wilderness with no apparent way back. Having already alienated the right wing by signing the Young Plan, he was now falling out with the left and center by challenging the coalition's financial policy.

The tension of having to juggle all these competing considerations, some opportunistic, others heartfelt, began to tell. He seemed at times to be close to a breakdown. One foreign banker, meeting him in January 1930, described his paranoia as he ranted about how "he was about to be crucified by a gang of corrupt politicians." His old friend Parker Gilbert, increasingly baffled at such erratic behavior, could only say that he thought Schacht had gone "crazy."

The final and dramatic denouement occurred at an intergovernmental conference on the Young Plan that opened at The Hague in early January. Shaken by the demagoguery of the German Nationalist right and by Schacht's repudiation of the plan, the French revived the issue of what to do should Germany cease payment by introducing a new clause that in the event that Germany was held by the International Court at The Hague to have willfully defaulted on its obligations, the creditor powers would "recover full liberty of action" as envisaged by the Treaty of Versailles, a proposal that evoked memories of the occupation of the Ruhr in 1923, of French soldiers marching back into Germany.

Schacht had promised the government that though he had broken with it, he would do nothing to embarrass Germany in an international forum. Once more his impulsiveness got the better of him. The new sanctions clause was a slap in Germany's face, representing a radical change in the "spirit" of the Young Plan. Though the Reichsbank was powerless to prevent the revised plan from going into effect, in order to register his protest "on the highest moral grounds," Schacht announced that it would refuse to subscribe a pfennig to the new Bank for International Settlements, declaring melodramatically that he "would stick to his position until he died."

The German delegation, led by the new foreign minister Julius Curtius, was furious. At a stormy closed-door meeting, Schacht was accused of fomenting "mutiny before the enemy," of grandstanding on an issue of no material importance, of using the issue as a political gambit aimed at rebuilding his credibility with the right—a rumor was circulating in Berlin that Schacht was contemplating a run for the presidency when Von Hindenburg, who was pushing eighty-five, retired in early 1932. It was, said the *Times* of London, an example of the sort of "flamboyant political moves which are expected of him." The left-leaning *Die Welt* accused him of being "the head not only of a state within the State, but of a state above the State."

The next day, however, he found himself outmaneuvered when the German delegation kept its nerve and proposed that if the Reichsbank refused to sign, the government would find a consortium of other German banks to subscribe the capital. Schacht's tendency to overplay his hand now undid him. He negotiated a face-saving formula under which the government would pass a law requiring the Reichsbank to subscribe, thus allowing him to declare that while he still thought the Young Plan an "immoral agreement," he was obliged as a good citizen to obey the "German law or else emigrate." Nevertheless, his histrionics at The Hague had put him in an untenable position. Back in Berlin, on March 7, he announced his resignation. "I will now become a country squire and raise pigs," he declared at a turbulent press conference where he lost his temper more than once at the journalists who questioned his motives for resigning a little too closely. One correspondent asked bewilderedly, "Dr. Schacht, is there any particular point to your resignation?" "My act has nothing to do with politics," replied an agitated Schacht. "It is merely the moral act of a self-respecting man."

The *Vossische Zeitung*, the German national paper of record, equivalent to the *Times* or *Le Monde*, expressed the general sense of puzzlement in Berlin when it asked, "What is the actual reason for his resignation? Nobody knows." Nevertheless, alert as ever to his own self-interest, Schacht did negotiate an attractive severance arrangement, waiving his annual pension for a lump sum of $250,000.

SCHACHT LEFT OFFICE believing that the Socialist-dominated coalition would lead Germany to financial disaster, precipitated by what he judged to be an inescapable foreign debt crisis. At this stage he still viewed Germany's problems through the prism of the 1920s; for him the central issue was that the country had profligately saddled itself with far too much foreign debt. The solution, he thought, was to curb government expenditure and avoid borrowing abroad. His recommendations were still very orthodox, designed to prevent an exchange crisis rather than to address the growing problem of unemployment.

Three weeks later, the government with which he had broken split over the unemployment question and fell, the Socialists wanting to finance an expansion in unemployment benefits by more foreign borrowing, the center parties to cut the budget deficit. A new center-right coalition, excluding the Socialists, took office and was led by a new chancellor, Heinrich Brüning, a dour Catholic, former army officer, and staunch monarchist.

Unable to get anything through a divided parliament, Brüning was forced to rule by decree, moving Germany in a more authoritarian direction by his reliance on the constitution's provisions for emergency powers. Defeated in the Reichstag, he had Von Hindenburg dissolve it and hold new elections in September 1930, two years early. The results came as an ugly shock. In a campaign dominated by the deteriorating economy, Hitler appealed across class lines, promising to reunite the nation, rebuild its prosperity, restore its position in the world, and purge the country of profiteers. He put a lid on some of his more extreme anti-Jewish rhetoric. Speaking at giant open-air rallies, many in sports stadiums lit by arrays of blazing torches, he mesmerized the tens of thousands who attended these events with his oratory. Meanwhile in the streets, his jack-booted paramilitary thugs, armed with truncheons and knuckledusters, clashed violently with Communists and Socialists. The Nazis won 6.4 million votes, and vaulted into second place in the Reichstag with 107 seats.

The election panicked the financial markets; an estimated $380 million, about half of Germany's reserves, bolted. To halt the flight, the Reichsbank was forced to raise its rates, so that while in New York and Paris these stood at 2 percent, and in London at 3 percent, in Germany they went up to 5 percent. With prices falling at a rate of 7 percent per year, it meant that the effective cost of money had risen to 12 percent, gravely exacerbating the economic weakness.

As the economy lost ground, unemployment climbed, and the budget deficit widened, Brüning focused on balancing the budget. Unemployment benefits were restricted; salaries of all high federal and state officials, including the president's, were slashed by 20 percent. Wages of lower-level officials were cut 6 percent; income taxes were raised, taxes on beer and tobacco increased, and new levies imposed on warehouses and mineral water. All of these measures made the Depression worse.

Germany was unusual in the degree of deflation that the government imposed on the economy. In the United States, the Hoover administration had cut taxes and allowed the budget to go from a surplus of $1 billion in 1929 to a deficit of $2 billion in 1931, 4 percent of GDP. Britain ran a deficit of $600 million in 1931, 2.5 percent of GDP. By contrast in Germany, even though revenues fell as activity faltered, expenditures were cut even more, and the deficit was actually reduced from an already modest $200 million to $100 million, less than 1 percent of GDP.

Brüning, who was now being called the "Hunger Chancellor," would later claim that his austerity measures had been designed to prove to foreigners that Germany could no longer pay reparations, a reprise of the old perverse "hair-shirt" policy attempted in the early 1920s: to inflict so much damage on Germany's economy that her creditors would be forced to reduce their demands.

Historians have debated whether the government had any alternative. Borrowing abroad was not an option. By the middle of 1930, foreign lending throughout the world had collapsed. Moreover, Germany had borrowed so much during the boom years, living by the standards of the time so high on the hog that when bad times finally arrived and it really needed the money, it had exhausted its credit lines and loans were no longer available.

The problem was made much worse by one of the unintended consequences of the Young Plan. Under the Dawes Plan before it, private commercial lenders had priority over reparations at a time of crisis. In effect, Germany's public creditors, principally the governments of France, Belgium, and Britain, had to stand last in line. The Young Plan's elimination of this "transfer protection," which incidentally Schacht had tried to resist, put an end to the guarantee. In the event of a payments crisis, private lenders did not automatically move to the front of the line but had to wait their turn with the big governments. Not surprisingly, private foreign lending to Germany collapsed.

No longer able to borrow abroad, Germany could only have avoided the Brüning austerity package if the government had borrowed from the Reichsbank—in other words, financed its budget deficit by printing money. But memories of the hyperinflation of the early 1920s were too fresh. Moreover, the Dawes and Young plans severely limited the Reichsbank's ability to buy government debt. The only way Germany could have followed such a policy was to cut loose from gold; and almost no one was ready for so drastic a move.

Out of office, Schacht was careful not to criticize Brüning's domestic policies, perhaps in the hope that he might return to power as part of a conservative Nationalist government. At the time, he did not realize how lucky he was. The new government adopted many of the austerity policies that he himself was advocating, with catastrophic results. But he was able to watch from the sidelines while the German economy fell apart, remaining free from any blame.

He could not, however, keep silent about reparations. The idea that the way to escape them was to inflict a terrible recession on Germany was to him completely absurd. Though he spent the first few months of his retirement at his estate at Gühlen, he quickly became frustrated at his confinement. In the summer of 1930, he embarked on a worldwide speaking tour, beginning in Bucharest, and thence to Berne, Copenhagen, and Stockholm. In September, he departed for two months to the United States.

He made something of a splash in America. With his pince-nez and his distinctive hair *en brosse,* the "Iron Man" of Germany, as *Time* magazine labeled him, was immediately identifiable. He was certainly more familiar to the average reader of the London *Times* or the *New York Times* than any of the last few German chancellors. He traveled to over twenty cities, giving almost fifty talks to audiences of college students and professors, bankers and business associations, at private clubs and in public meetings.

Mostly he spoke about reparations, seeking to make his audiences understand German bitterness over the issue: "You must not think that if you treat people for ten years as the German people have been treated they will continue to smile." Germany, with its GDP of $16 billion, exports of $3 billion, and an overhang of private foreign debt now amounting to $6 billion, simply could not afford to pay $500 million a year to France and Britain. In Cincinnati, he declared, "Reparations are the real cause of the world-wide economic depression." Everywhere he went he was asked about the recent elections and Hitler. "If the German people are going to starve, there are going to be many more Hitlers," he would reply. Back in Europe, when a Swedish journalist asked him, "What would you do if you were to become Chancellor tomorrow?" Schacht replied with no hesitation, "I would stop making payments of reparations that very day."

In January 1931, he took his first tragic steps down the Faustian path. In December 1930, he had been introduced to Hermann Göring. Until then, despite his dealings with the Nationalist leader Hugenberg, he had had very little contact with the Nazis, whom he would later claim to have dismissed as a fringe group of rabble mongers. Nevertheless, Schacht's wife was well known to hero-worship Hitler and was a devoted supporter of the party. In her diary, Bella Fromm, the diplomatic columnist of the *Vossische Zeitung*, recounts how she encountered the Schachts in February 1930 at the silver wedding reception of a prominent Berlin banker. Frau Schacht wore an expensive swastika of rubies and diamonds on her ample bosom and Fromm recorded the rumor that Schacht himself was "not above using the swastika as his insignia whenever he thinks it will suit his purpose." That night he even told her, "Why not give the National Socialists a break? They seem pretty smart to me."

The conversation during his evening with Göring focused on the "economic situation, the rise in unemployment figures, the timidity of German foreign policy," and Schacht took to this "pleasant, urbane" man. On January 5, Göring invited Schacht, along with Fritz Thyssen, chairman of the giant United Steel Works, to meet Hitler at his modest apartment in a middle-class neighborhood of Berlin—Göring did not yet have access to the government money that would allow him to become the corrupt voluptuary of later years. The Nazi leader arrived after dinner dressed in the yellow and brown uniform of his paramilitary forces; Joseph Goebbels also showed up. Schacht admitted to being impressed. Hitler was surprisingly modest and unpretentious, especially for the leader of the second largest party in the country. During the next two hours, Hitler, "in spite of a hoarse, somewhat broken and not infrequently croaking voice," dominated the discussion, doing 95 percent of the talking—about the restoration of Germany's position in the world, about the need to get the six and a half million unemployed back to work, and how this could only be done by state intervention. Hitler was articulate, speaking without any "propagandist pathos," but obviously "a born agitator." It was a fateful encounter for the fascinated banker.

. . .

ARNOLD TOYNBEE, IN his magisterial review of the year's events on behalf of the Royal Institute of International Affairs, would later compare the events of the summer of 1931 to the summer of 1914. Both began with relatively minor events far from the hub of the world that nevertheless set in train a cascade that plunged out of all control and brought down an entire world order. In 1914, it was the assassination of the Austrian heir presumptive, the archduke Franz Ferdinand, at Sarajevo. In 1931, it was the failure of the Credit Anstalt, the oldest and largest bank in Austria.

On Friday, May 8, the Credit Anstalt, based in Vienna and founded in 1855 by the Rothschilds, with total assets of $250 million and 50 percent of the Austrian bank deposits, informed the government that it had been forced to book a loss of $20 million in its 1930 accounts, wiping out most of its equity. Not only was it Austria's biggest bank, it was the most reputable—its board, presided over by Baron Louis de Rothschild of the Vienna branch of the family, included representatives of the Bank of England, the Guaranty Trust Company of New York, and M. M. Warburg and Co. of Hamburg. After a frantic weekend of secret meetings, the government made the problem public on Monday, May 11, at the same time announcing a rescue package of $15 million, which it would borrow through the BIS.

Austria was a small country, about a tenth the size of Germany, with a population of fewer than seven million and a GDP of $1.5 billion. Nevertheless, the news burst like a bombshell upon the City of London and the Bank of England. By an odd coincidence, Schacht was staying with Norman at Thorpe Lodge when the story broke. Harry Siepmann, one of the governor's principal senior advisers, knowing something of the scope of the tangled mess that lay behind the headlines, announced, "This, I think, is it, and it may well bring down the whole house of cards in which we have been living."

Like many German banks, the Credit Anstalt made direct investments in industry, similar to those of a modern private equity firm. It was, however, especially vulnerable not only because it borrowed short-term money to finance what were long-term, highly illiquid, investments but also because it had an unusually large amount of foreign borrowing on its books—some $75 million out of a total deposit base of $250 million.

It had grown over the last decade by absorbing a series of failing small banks and, in 1929, had been further "persuaded" by the Austrian National Bank to take over the Bodencreditanstalt, its next largest rival, whose losses turned out to be gigantic. In order to compensate Credit Anstalt for saving the Austrian banking system by taking on the burden of a such a large bankrupt institution, the Austrian central bank had been funneling money secretly to it through London banks, a fact of which the Bank of England was well aware.

The announcement of the rescue package failed to stabilize the situation, perhaps because more people knew how deep the problems went than the government realized—when Credit Anstalt was finally wound up two years later, the accumulated losses amounted to $150 million. Over the next four days a run developed, not only on the Credit Anstalt but on all Austrian banks, which lost some $50 million in deposits, about 10 percent of the total. In an attempt to shore up its banking system, the Austrian National Bank followed Bagehot's principle and lent freely, injecting an extra $50 million, which caused an overnight jump of 20 percent in the national money supply.

Norman had a soft spot for Austria. After the war, he had provided it with the first loan to stabilize its currency—for his services to the country he had been awarded the Grosse Goldene Ehrenzeichen (Grand Decoration of Honor in Gold) from the Austrian ambassador to the Court of Saint James, Baron Georg von und zu Franckenstein. For the next several days, having now discovered the remarkable advantages of international telephone calls, he was constantly on the line to Harrison in New York and Luther in Berlin. Fearing that a monetary breakdown in Austria would spread to neighboring countries, he was determined to mount an international rescue effort.

None of the central bankers had faced an international financial crisis before; they therefore had to make things up as they went along. In so doing they made two mistakes. Given the scale of the problem, they came up with far too little money; and believing that it was necessary to put together as international a consortium as possible, they did not act quickly enough. For all the frantic telephone calls, it took them three weeks to drum up the money, and then only came up with $15 million.

By the time the loans had been agreed to, the promised money had already been used up and the run on Austrian banks had become a run on the Austrian currency. The National Bank lost $40 million of its $110 million of gold reserves. Faced now with both a banking system under threat and a currency under siege, it now pleaded for another $20 million.

The crisis was made immeasurably more complicated by the politics of the situation. In March 1930, Germany and Austria had announced that they would form a customs union. Germany's neighbors, in particular the French and the Czechs, remembering that the nineteenth-century Zollverein, the historic customs union among the states of the German Confederation, had been a prelude to German unification, and fearing that this might be the first step to *Anschluss*, union between Austria and Germany, had been agitating to block the move.

The French government now saw its opportunity. Indeed it helped to create it by secretly encouraging French banks to pull money out of Austria. By June 16, the situation was becoming more desperate by the hour. The cabinet, fearing the breakdown of law and order in Vienna, was on the verge of imposing a bank holiday. Austria was still waiting anxiously for the second loan when it received word that France had offered to provide it—but only if Austria would abandon the customs union. As if in an ultimatum, the Austrian government was given three hours to respond.

With its back to the wall, Austria might have accepted. In London, however, Norman was outraged at this blatant abuse of French monetary power in such a delicate financial situation and cabled that the Bank of England would provide the loan on its own. But if he thought he had succeeded in pricking the panic in its bud, he was mistaken.

. . .

ON JUNE 5, at 2.30 in the afternoon, Thomas Lamont put a call through to President Hoover. As soon as the Austrian crisis had broken, Germany had also begun to lose gold reserves. The contagion was not so much because Germany had a large amount of capital tied up in Austria, rather it was largely a matter of psychology. The world, which had never drawn much of a distinction between the banking situation in Berlin and that in Vienna, jumped to the conclusion that if the main Austrian bank was in such serious trouble, it was very possible that a German bank might soon follow. As money started escaping Germany, rumors circulated that Berlin might soon request a suspension of reparations. Lamont feared that to cope with the political turmoil and flight of capital that would ensue, Germany might impose exchange controls. With American institutions holding about a billion dollars in short-term credits to Germany, such a move could threaten the solvency of more than one U.S. bank.

Saying that he was about to make a suggestion that the president would "more than likely throw out of the window," Lamont proposed that Hoover unilaterally declare a holiday on all payments on war debt and reparations. No European country could advance the idea, for it would immediately call into question its own credit, signaling to its creditors as he put it that "the jig is up." Only the United States was in a position to take the lead. Hoover was initially unconvinced. "I will think about the matter" he told Lamont, "but politically it is quite impossible. Sitting in New York as you do, you have no idea what the sentiment of the country at large is on these intergovernmental debts. . . . Congress sees France piling up lots of gold, increasing armaments. . . ."

Lamont tried to convince Hoover that it would actually help him politically. There were "a lot of people whispering about the 1932 convention," he warned, and such a dramatic move would quiet doubts about the beleaguered president's leadership. He signed off with the casual authority that went with being a senior partner at J. P Morgan & Co: "One last thing, Mr. President, if anything by any chance ever comes out of this suggestion, we should wish to be forgotten in the matter. This is your plan and nobody else's."

In response to Lamont's call, that same afternoon Hoover summoned his trio of senior advisers—Secretary of State Henry Stimson; Secretary of the Treasury Andrew Mellon; and Mellon's undersecretary, Ogden Mills—to work out a moratorium along Lamont's lines. Mellon declared his "unqualified disapproval" of such a move but left on vacation the very next day for Europe.

Stimson, however, was enthusiastic. A true American aristocrat, born into a wealthy New York family, a graduate of Phillips Academy in Andover, Yale and Harvard Law School, a member of Skull and Bones, and a partner in the white-shoe Manhattan law firm of Root and Clark, Stimson was the first of that breed of Wall Street wise men. He brought to the State Department a Victorian sense of propriety—he and his wife, for example, refused to receive divorced people in their home—and a strongly anti-isolationist international perspective. So committed was he to promoting goodwill among nations that when, in 1929, he discovered that the State Department's "Black Chamber" had been routinely breaking the coded communications between foreign embassies and their home governments, he immediately closed down the practice, arguing later that "gentlemen do not read each other's mail." Relying on his fellow Bonesman and internationalist, George Harrison of the New York Fed, to feed him advice on world finance, he had ever since taking office been an advocate of forgiving war debts.

On the very day that Hoover was proposing a moratorium to his cabinet colleagues, Chancellor Brüning had launched his own initiative. On June 5, he unveiled a new package of austerity moves that included a further lowering of civil servants' salaries, a cut in unemployment assistance, and new taxes. In order to sweeten the pill, Brüning accompanied the measures with a manifesto. Sensational and provocative in tone, the German proclamation announced that "the limit of privations that we can impose on the nation have been reached." The economic assumptions on which the Young Plan had been based had proved to be wrong, and thus "Germany had to be relieved of "the intolerable reparation obligations" and "tributary payments" to which it was subject.

That very weekend, Brüning was in London on a long-planned visit to the British prime minister, Ramsay MacDonald. The German delegation was spending the weekend at the prime minister's official country house, Chequers, in the Kent countryside, where Norman joined the party on Sunday, June 7. After a leisurely lunch for nineteen, which included such guests as John Galsworthy and George Bernard Shaw, both authors very popular in Germany, the officials withdrew to discuss financial issues. Brüning described the terrible situation in Germany. That year, when the Reichswehr needed six thousand new recruits, eighty thousand men applied, half of them undernourished. People were in despair. The social fabric was unraveling. The menace of Nazi and Communist agitation was growing by the day.

While Brüning was holding forth, several frantic telegrams arrived from the British ambassador in Washington, who had just heard from Stimson, who was infuriated by the manifesto's confrontational tone. On no account, warned the secretary of state, should the Germans take any unilateral action, which could only trigger a massive flight of short-term funds out of Germany that would rob Hoover's planned moratorium, which was still a secret, of much of its benefit. The telegrams threw the British into shock. It was the first they had even heard of the manifesto, which had not even been published in the British newspapers. Their guests had omitted mentioning it, for it was a document designed for internal consumption and Brüning had no real plans to renegotiate reparations at least until the fall.

Any German move to suspend reparations now would be disastrous, Norman told the shaken table. Any more surprises like this to European confidence and we will soon be "conducting a post-mortem" on the corpse of Europe, he declared.

It was now a race. Could Hoover gather enough support for his initiative before Germany ran out of gold? In Washington, the temperature reached 102 as the teams at Treasury and State toiled eighteen-hour days to work out the details in offices that had no air-conditioning. They were besieged by New York bankers who "came crying down . . . and said they were busted," according to Stimson's economic adviser. Ogden Mills, acting as head of the Treasury in Mellon's absence, shuttled back and forth through the underground passage that linked the Treasury Building to the White House to brief the president. Hoover himself was racked by doubts. The constant press criticism and the cynical jokes about his unpopularity had taken their toll. When H. G. Wells visited the White House later that fall, he found "a sickly, overworked and overwhelmed man." A siege mentality had taken over at the Executive Mansion. The president's gloom was so oppressive that Stimson complained that meeting with him in his room was "like sitting in a bath of ink."

Meanwhile during the first three weeks of June, Germany lost some $350 million, over half its gold reserves. In London, Norman spent the time cajoling British bankers not to pull their money out of Germany as currency and banking crises spilled across Europe into Hungary, Romania, Poland, and Spain.

On Saturday, June 20, Hoover's plan was publicly announced. The United States would forgo one year's principal and interest of $245 million on the war debts due from Britain, France, Italy, and some of the smaller European powers, provided, and only provided, that the Allies themselves suspend $385 million in reparations due from Germany. The effect was electric. The following Monday, the German stock market jumped 25 percent in a single day.

Hoover had tried to consult everyone possible in the lead-up to his announcement—he was said to have already enlisted the support of twenty-one senators before publicly revealing the plan. Senator Arthur Vandenberg of Michigan, off junketing in Canada, was connected by phone to the president from a Toronto drugstore. Several senators and representatives had even been invited to spend the night at the White House. The secretary of state got up one morning at 5:30 a.m. to put a call through to Prime Minister MacDonald.

The administration had consulted everyone—everyone, that is, except the French. In the most astoundingly inept piece of diplomacy of his whole presidency, the one party Hoover neglected to prepare not only happened to be Germany's largest creditor but was at the moment the dominant financial power in Europe. The French government reacted with astonishment and then fury.

The U.S. ambassador, Walter Edge, was due to spend the afternoon with the rest of the diplomatic corps at the Longchamps races as a guest of the president of the republic. He had spent his two years trying to dispel the suspicion within French government circles that "we [the Americans] and the British had been plotting against France." France had the world's largest standing army; with the second highest gold reserves in the world after the United States, it was financially the strongest country in Europe; its economy had weathered the global Depression better than almost any other. And yet, complained the men who ran France, the Anglo-Saxons still treated it as a mere second-rate power.

In the president's box at the races, Edge was peppered with questions by a phalanx of steaming French politicians. It was fine for the United States to forgive its debtors; but how could the United States unilaterally suspend Germany's debts to France without even bothering to consult France herself? She was being treated as a "stepchild." Pierre Laval, the prime minister, former Socialist now turned nationalist, demanded to know what guarantee the United States could provide that payments would resume after a year. Another minister launched into a highly colorful and sarcastic diatribe—France was being asked to pay the bill for the "reconciliation feast" in honor of the "prodigal Reich," while Wall Street and the City of London rejoiced over "the killing of the fatted calf." The foreign minister, Aristide Briand, called in Edge the next day to subject him to a tirade, singling out the Bank of England as the mainspring of the whole plot—he cited Norman's visit to the United States a few weeks earlier as inescapable confirmation of an Anglo-Saxon bankers' conspiracy.

The following Monday, the French press universally condemned any notion of a moratorium. The *Journal des Débats*, the organ of French industry, said in a fume that "the more one reflects, the more one is stupefied by the initiative of Mr. Hoover."

In Washington, the president decided that Mellon, then in Britain to attend his son Paul's graduation ceremony from King's College, Cambridge, and to receive an honorary degree himself, his fifteenth, should be dispatched to Paris to bring the French around. For all that a world financial crisis was raging, Mellon had arrived in London and very deliberately avoided contacting any UK Treasury or Bank of England officials, believing that his vacation time was sacrosanct. When Norman tried to get in touch with him through his secretary in Washington, he was fobbed off with the excuse that Mellon was on a private visit and incommunicado. Finally, Norman got hold of young Mellon at Cambridge and tracked his father down at Claridge's. After some persuading, Mellon reluctantly agreed to suspend his impending holiday at Cap Ferrat and go to Paris.

He arrived on June 25, to be greeted at the Gare du Nord by Robert Lacour-Gayet of the Banque de France. When asked, "Are you glad to be in Paris, Mr. Mellon?" the secretary of the treasury replied noncommittally with a barely perceptible smile, "M. Lacour-Gayet, we are here." Obviously unhappy, he kept reminding reporters that he had come to Europe planning on a pleasure trip in the Riviera with his daughter, Ailsa, and her husband, the young diplomat David Bruce.

For the next couple of weeks, Mellon engaged in a protracted bout of negotiation. Every day he would dutifully troop off with Ambassador Edge to the ancient and musty building that housed the Ministry of the Interior and was also home to the French secret police. Mellon, who generally preferred a club sandwich at his desk, had to sit through the eight-course meals, each with its own wine, that were a customary part of French diplomacy.

The French team, who negotiated by day and had to sit through all-night sessions in the National Assembly, was led by Prime Minister Laval. He was a protégé of Tardieu, who had been compelled to resign in December, after becoming caught up in yet another banking scandal. At forty-six, Laval was the youngest premier in the history of the Third Republic. Born of peasant stock in the south of France, with his dark skin, straight black hair, and scraggly mustache, he looked "dopey in appearance, like an overworked headwaiter on his day off." He liked to wear dingy white bow ties and a straw boater.

Mellon tried to convince the French that in return for giving up about $200 million a year in reparations, they would avoid having to pay $115 million in war debts—at a net cost to them of "only" $85 million a year. The Americans, on the other hand, would be conceding a total of $260 million a year. Laval was implacable. For two weeks the negotiations dragged on.

The seventy-six-year-old Mellon had to work both Washington and Paris hours. Statesmen had just discovered the advantages of the telephone. Every evening and sometimes two or three times a day Mellon would place a call to the White House from the U.S. ambassador's residence. The French phone system was being revamped and there were only two phones working: one in the concierge's room in the basement and the other in the bedroom of the ambassador's wife. The soft-spoken Mellon could often barely be heard.

Tempers began to fray. Growing more irritated by the day, Hoover vented against the French and accused Mellon of being soft on France. Meanwhile, Germany's gold reserves continued to hemorrhage. Central bankers provided a loan of $100 million on June 24. Within ten days, it was gone. Berlin was being "bled to death" while the French and the Americans were busy arguing, complained Norman on what had become one of his regular calls to Harrison in New York. The British prime minister put it more pungently in his diary: "France has been playing its usual small minded and selfish game over the Hoover proposal. . . . To do a good thing for its own sake is not in line with France's official nature. So Germany cracks while France bargains."

The negotiations were finally concluded on July 7, the Americans conceding that Germany would only suspend payments on a portion of its reparations, the French, however, agreeing to lend the remaining reparations they did receive straight back to Germany. Both sides could claim victory. "Now, Monsieur Mellon, you can take up your interrupted vacation," said the French prime minister sarcastically. The secretary of the treasury promptly set off for the Riviera.

It was too late. On June 17, the Norddeutsche Wolkkammerei—"Der Nordwolle," a large German wool combine—declared bankruptcy, revealing losses amounting to $50 million, which it had managed to conceal by transferring its inventory at bloated prices to its Dutch subsidiary. The Nordwolle had not lost all this money in the production of blankets and comforters—it seems that its management had speculated on a rise in wool prices by building up its inventories and buying in the forward market, a bet that had gone badly wrong.

On July 5, a Basel newspaper stated that an unnamed German bank was in trouble. As Berlin swirled with rumors, on July 6, the day before the negotiations on the moratorium were concluded, the Danatbank, Schacht's old employer, the third largest in Germany, issued a denial that it was having difficulties. A bank cannot survive without confidence; when it is forced to deny rumors that it is in trouble, it is by definition in serious trouble. Two days later, the head of the Danatbank, Jacob Goldschmidt, Schacht's old colleague and nemesis, informed the Reichsbank that his bank could not meet its liabilities.

Schacht's successor at the Reichsbank was Hans Luther, who as minister of finance in 1923 at the height of the hyperinflation had originally and reluctantly appointed Schacht currency commissioner. Luther, though not a member of the Reichstag and "a politician without party," had been chancellor for eighteen months in 1925 but had been humiliatingly forced out when his government had instructed German consulates and diplomatic offices to fly, in addition to the republican flag (black, red, and gold), the flag of the merchant marine, which looked suspiciously like the banned imperial flag (black, white, and red). He was not a good choice for the Reichsbank. Though a competent administrator, he had made his reputation as a stolid municipal official and simply lacked what it took to run a central bank, especially the understanding of the psychological dimension to the crisis and the importance of restoring confidence.

On July 8, Luther called Norman. The Reichsbank was in a desperate situation. It had lost a huge slice of its gold reserves. If it tried to bail out the Danatbank, it would fall below the minimum reserve threshold it was required to maintain by law which, in the current environment, was bound to provoke a run on its currency. It therefore faced a terrible dilemma: support its currency and let the Danatbank fail or try to support its domestic banking system and watch what reserves it had left fly out of the country. It was one of those situations in which there are no good options—only the choice between a bad outcome and a disastrous one.

Luther's only solution was to borrow abroad. He needed $1 billion, he told Norman. On July 9, Luther, his "round face deep lined with anxiety," boarded a private plane in Berlin—the first such resort by a desperate central banker. In Amsterdam he met with the governor of the Dutch central bank for two hours, then took off for Britain. He was received at Croydon Aerodrome by Norman and the British foreign secretary, Arthur Henderson. The party drove up to London, where Luther briefly met with the chancellor of the exchequer Philip Snowden. Norman was due in Basel for the monthly board meeting of the BIS and Luther decided to accompany him on the boat train as far as Calais.

It was on that journey, as Luther described the deteriorating situation in Germany, that it finally dawned on Norman that the game was up. The German economic position was now irretrievable. As a central banker, all he could do was provide a temporary loan to buy a little more time. Germany was now in deep water and sinking. The numbers would not add up. It had a GDP now of $13 billion that was shrinking by the month, reparation debts of $9 billion, and foreign private obligations of $6 billion, $3.5 billion of it short-term that could be pulled at any moment. Over the last year, $500 million in capital had fled the country. Barely $250 million in gold reserves remained. Harrison and Norman had been pushing Luther to restrict credit yet more rigorously in order to curb the outflow of capital. But with the banking system on the verge of collapse, he had run out of room. His only hope, Norman told him, lay in a long-term loan from France, the one European nation with sufficient gold reserves to bail out

Germany. But he warned that French money would only come with draconian political conditions. Luther and Norman separated at Calais, Norman to go on to Basel, Luther to Paris.

Luther was received at the Gare du Nord by Governor Moret of the Banque de France. On Friday, July 10, he lunched at the Banque with the regents, the two most powerful of whom, François de Wendel and Baron Edouard de Rothschild, both resolutely anti-German, turned down the idea of a credit from the Banque and told Luther that his only hope was a loan from the government. That afternoon and into the evening, the Reichsbank president shuttled back and forth from ministry to ministry, missing one train after another for Berlin. The French government informed him that it might be prepared to lend as much as $300 million, provided that Germany abandon the customs union with Austria, suspend the construction of two new pocket battleships, raise interest rates sharply to halt the flight of capital abroad, and "orient itself definitely towards a policy of democracy and pacifism" by banning public demonstrations by Nationalist organizations.

Merely president of the Reichsbank, Luther did not have the authority to agree to these terms. On Saturday, July 11, he boarded an airplane at Le Bourget for Berlin. "Not since those days of July 1914 when the World War was brewing have potent rumors been so thick," wrote *Time* magazine of that weekend. The German cabinet convened at 8:00 p.m. and debated into the early hours of the morning. Every major German newspaper fulminated against French "political blackmail" and warned that this would only increase the "bitterness of the German people" toward France. Rumors circulated that President Hindenburg would resign if the government knuckled under. An even more startling rumor came over the wires. The cabinet was considering nationalizing all private industry, banks, shipping, and trade.

That Sunday, the German cabinet announced that it was rejecting the French offer. The French cabinet, which had dispersed for the long Bastille Day weekend—Laval to his country cottage, Foreign Minister Briand fishing on his farm at Cocherel, Finance Minister Flandin at the beach in

Brittany—was summoned back to Paris. They heard an impassioned plea for reconsideration from the German ambassador, Dr. Leopold von Hoesch. Did they really want to provoke a revolution in Germany? Though Laval agreed that "they had come to a decisive point in world history," he was unwilling to offer anything new.* Paul Einzig captured the view of many in Europe at that point when he later wrote, "On the ruins of the wealth, prosperity, and stability of other nations, France has succeeded in establishing her much desired politico-financial hegemony over Europe."

The American ambassador in Berlin, Frederick Sackett, cabled to Washington that unless Germany received $300 million immediately, it would declare national bankruptcy and default on the $3 billion it owed American banks and investors. George Harrison convened an emergency meeting at the New York Fed with Under Secretary Mills and the two most knowledgeable men on Germany, Owen Young and Parker Gilbert. They concluded it would be throwing good money after bad, when the United States had already contributed $300 million by its moratorium on war debts.

Another long Cabinet meeting in Berlin ensued that evening. To the surprise of most attending, Schacht was invited and seated next to the chancellor. By a strange quirk of fate, the English and American editions of his book *The End of Reparations* were to be published in London and New York the very next day. The book was a long assault on reparations, the policy as Schacht described it of "bleeding Germany white" and "destroying Germany's credit." One excerpt in particular was heavily quoted in British and American newspapers: "Never has the incapacity of the economic leaders of the capitalist world so glaringly demonstrated as today. . . . A capitalism which cannot feed the workers of the world has no right to exist. The guilt of the capitalist system lies in its alliance with the

---

* It was a turning point with especially tragic consequences for Laval himself. Following the defeat of France in 1940, he joined the Vichy government and became one of the most active French collaborators with the Nazis. He was tried for treason after the war, and following a botched suicide attempt with cyanide, he was executed by firing squad, half conscious and vomiting, in October 1945.

violent policies of imperialism and militarism. . . . The ruling classes of the world today have as completely failed in political leadership as in economic." Such criticism from "the head of one of the world's most powerful capitalist organizations" was somewhat unusual, commented the *New York Times*.

Speaking with his usual self-assurance, Schacht urged the cabinet to suspend payments to the foreign creditors of Danatbank, forcing them to bear the consequences of their foolhardy and unsound lending practices. The government, believing that this would completely destroy any hope of a rescue from abroad, decided not to take his advice.

The cabinet meeting finished at 2:00 a.m. Later that morning Luther boarded yet another plane, this time for Basel, to make one last desperate plea to the central bankers gathered at the BIS. After being closeted in conference for twelve hours, they emerged to announce that no new credits would be forthcoming. At 11:20 p.m. Basel time, Harrison got through to Norman. The Englishman sounded "tired, disgruntled and discouraged." The problem was just "too big for the central banks," he reported. The only solution was for the whole structure of war debts and reparations that had weighed down the world for the last dozen years to be swept away.

On the morning of Monday, July 13, as Luther was setting off for Basel, the Danatbank had failed to open. On the locked doors of all its branches was posted a government decree guaranteeing its deposits. At a press conference, Jacob Goldschmidt revealed that the bank had lost 40 percent, some $240 million, in deposits over the last three months, about half of which were to foreigners. He blamed the run on wild rumors fueled by anti-Semitic agitation in the Nationalist press.

The Reichsbank, hoping that the impact might be contained, kept the rest of the banking system open that day. By lunchtime, branches of every bank in the country were besieged. The leading banks restricted withdrawals to no more than 10 percent of a depositor's balance. In the Berlin suburbs, savings banks were so overwhelmed that that they closed under heavy police guard. In Hamburg, sporadic riots were blamed on Communist agitators. That evening President Hindenburg proclaimed a two-day bank holiday. The authorities hoped that a short breathing space would allow people to come to their senses. In the event, banks throughout Germany remained closed—except for the most essential business of paying wages and taxes—for another two weeks, during which commercial life in the country was brought to a virtual standstill.

All the banks in Hungary were closed for three days. In Vienna, another of the large banks shut its doors. In Danzig and Riga, in Poland, Yugoslavia, and Czechoslovakia, banks were suspended. German tourists across Europe, even in fashionable sophisticated cure resorts like Marienbad and Carlsbad, were stranded when no hotels or shops would accept their marks. The German government issued one decree after another. Despite the massive unemployment, interest rates were hiked to 15 percent just to keep money in the country. All payments on Germany's short-term foreign debt were suspended. All foreign exchange had to be turned over to the Reichsbank and all movements of money out of Germany were tightly regulated, the practical equivalent to going off gold.

For the second time in less than eight years, Germany faced economic disaster. Despite the chaos, the country remained surprisingly peaceful, save for a few small riots in Leipzig and Dresden, Düsseldorf and Koblenz. There was an atmosphere of "resigned passivity born of a weary submission to the inevitable," wrote the *New York Times*, the consequence of a decade of economic turmoil. The British ambassador, returning after a few weeks' absence, noted that he was "much struck by the emptiness of the streets and the unnatural silence hanging over the city, and particularly by an atmosphere of extreme tension similar in many respects to that which I observed in Berlin in the critical days immediately preceding the war . . . an almost oriental lethargy and fatalism."

"In such circumstances," he continued, "Dr Schacht's financial reputation has revived and he has reappeared on the stage . . . there are small but widening circles which feel that Dr. Schacht, if only he could overcome his unpopularity abroad, and especially in the U.S.A. and with Social Democrats at home, might yet be the man to save Germany." The government did try to induce Schacht to return to power, offering him the position of the banking czar with responsibility for sorting out the whole mess caused by the meltdown. Fearing he was being offered a poisoned chalice, he refused and returned to his country estate to wait upon events.

The collapse of the German banking system in the summer of 1931 sent the economy lurching downward once again. Over the next six months production fell by another 20 percent. By early 1932, the industrial production index reached 60 percent of its 1928 level. Nearly six million men—a third of the labor force—were without work.

In October 1931, the parties of the right collectively staged a rally in the little mountain spa of Bad Harzburg, one of the few places where the wearing of brownshirt Nazi uniforms had not been banned. It was a reunion of everyone who was or had ever been against democracy in Germany. The town was festooned with banners in the old imperial colors. Aged generals and admirals from the previous war turned out, as did two of the sons of the ex-kaiser, the princes Eitel Friedrich and August Wilhelm, rubbing shoulders with an assorted collection of industrialists, politicians, and five thousand goose-stepping paramilitary militia and storm troopers from various factions. The event was kicked off by an invocation for divine guidance by a Lutheran pastor and a Catholic priest. The star of the occasion was Hitler, who hogged the spotlight with his impromptu speeches.

An equally big stir occurred, however, when Schacht, in his first public appearance as an associate of the Nazis, ascended the stage to speak. He accused the government of misleading the country on the amount of foreign debts and gold reserves. As to the economic policies of the opposition, he was obscurely vague, saying only that "the program to be executed by a national government rests on a very few fundamental ideas identical to those of Frederick the Great after the Seven Years War."

The speech provoked outrage in the Reichstag and within the government. For the ex-president of the Reichsbank to declare publicly that the country was bankrupt—though this was essentially true—was viewed as an act of vindictive irresponsibility and betrayal that could only add to the economic turmoil. That most of the foreign debt had been amassed on

Schacht's watch only added to the anger. There were even calls in parliament and in the press for his prosecution on a charge of high treason. Schacht had long since broken with the left. He had now estranged himself from the democratic center. His only home was with the Nazis. And though the struggle against reparations was now essentially over, the fight for the future of Germany was still to enter its last act.

20. GOLD FETTERS

1931-33

Lo! thy dread empire Chaos! is restored:
Light dies before thy uncreating word;
Thy hand, great Anarch! lets the curtain fall,
And universal darkness buries all.

—ALEXANDER POPE, *The Dunciad*

ON JULY 14, Norman returned from Basel to find the crisis now spreading to Britain. That evening Robert Kindersley, a director of the Bank of England and head of the London arm of the great investment house of Lazards, asked to see him in private and told him that Lazards itself was in serious trouble. Ironically enough it had little to do with the crisis ravaging Central and Eastern Europe. In the midtwenties, a rogue trader in the Brussels branch of the bank had made a wild bet on the collapse of the French franc and lost $30 million, almost double the bank's capital. He had managed to cover up the loss for years with the connivance of several members of the Brussels office, by issuing IOUs on behalf of Lazards to its counterparts. The extent of the problem had only recently come to light when these obligations were finally presented. When confronted with the evidence, the trader in question, a Czech, confessed, then suddenly pulled out a gun in the office and shot himself. Fearing that the failure of a merchant bank of Lazards' standing would set off a panic in the City, the Bank of England agreed to bail it out. The following week two other British merchant banks, Kleinworts and Schroders, informed Norman that they, too, were in trouble. Unable to prop up everyone, the Bank arranged for them to be rescued by loans from the commercial banks.

Meanwhile, on the heels of the closure of banks in Germany, a "blizzard" swept through the world's financial system. A bank holiday was imposed in Hungary, major financial institutions failed in Romania, Latvia, and Poland. In Cairo and Alexandria, a run began on the German-owned Deustche Orientbank and police had to be called in to protect the management. Istanbul saw runs on the local branches of the Deutsche Bank, and the Banque Turque pour le Commerce et l'Industrie was closed.

The world economic crisis had already engulfed large tracts of South America—Bolivia had defaulted in January and Peru in March. In the last two weeks of July, the contagion extended to other Latin countries. On July 16, the government of Chile suspended payments on its foreign debt. Five days later, it fell and the head of the central bank took over as premier. He lasted barely three days. Over the next twenty-four hours, three different premiers were sworn in, until, fed up with the turmoil, the military took over. On July 25, the Mexican government announced that gold was no longer legal tender and that instead it was shifting to silver. The currency dropped 36 percent and after days of confusion a leading bank, the Credito Español de Mexico, was forced to close its doors.

As the world financial system ground to halt, the City of London, with tentacles that stretched into every corner of the globe, found itself especially vulnerable. On July 13, as the German crisis reached its denouement, the Macmillan Committee on the workings of the British banking system issued its report. Considering all that was going on in Europe, the press paid little attention to it. Nevertheless, hidden in the report was a set of figures that shook the City.

During London's heyday as a financial center, British industry and British banking had complemented each other. The large export surpluses generated by what was then "the workshop of the world" had provided the funds to finance Britain's long-term global investments and underpinned London's status as banker to the world. After the war and the return to the gold standard, Britain's manufacturing capacity had stagnated. Throughout the 1920s, however, London, determined to maintain its primacy in global finance, continued to lend $500 million a year to foreign governments and companies. But because Britain was unable to generate the same export surpluses as before the war, the City had to finance its long-term loans by relying more and more on short-term deposits. While everyone was dimly aware of this growing mismatch between liabilities and assets, no one had any idea of its magnitude.

The Macmillan Report now revealed that the City's short-term liabilities to foreigners came close to $2 billion. This was viewed as a shocking number even though it eventually turned out to be a gross underestimate—the true figure was closer to $3 billion.

Furthermore, after the imposition of German exchange controls, a good percentage of the loans made with these deposits were now frozen—British banks had an estimated $500 million tied up in Germany and several hundred million more in Central Europe and Latin America. Suddenly, confronted with the previously unthinkable prospect that London houses, weighed down by bad loans, might fail to meet their obligations, investors around the world started withdrawing funds from the City.

In the last two weeks of July, the Bank of England lost $250 million—almost half its gold reserves. It reacted by raising interest rates modestly from 2.5 percent to 4.25 percent in the hopes of inducing capital not to desert sterling. Norman resisted further hikes, fearing that they would only create more unemployment and by intensifying the domestic depression, might even reinforce the speculative attack on the pound. Since he did not know what else to do, he acted as if the crisis were a temporary bout of nerves and arranged to borrow $250 million from the New York Fed and from the Banque de France to tide the Bank of England through.

Norman had now been dealing with one emergency after another for ten weeks and the "steady drip of the unseen pressure" was beginning to tell on his fragile constitution. He was easily distraught, changed his mind frequently, and at times seemed paralyzed by indecision—bouts of "nervous dyspepsia," as one of his fellow directors described it. As the prospect of a break from gold loomed, he would portray the consequences in apocalyptic terms—an evaporation of confidence in money such as had occurred during the German hyperinflation, a collapse in currency values, spiraling prices, food shortages, strikes, rationing, and riots. So exaggerated and gloomy was the portrait he painted that Russell Leffingwell, a partner in the House of Morgan, where he was usually treated with enormous deference, finally complained, "Can't he be persuaded to quit his panicky talk?"

Finally, on Wednesday, July 29, Norman left work early, noting meticulously in his diary, "Feeling queer." That evening he collapsed and was confined to his house under doctors' orders to take a complete rest. His colleagues at the Bank, fearing that his erratic moods and impaired judgment would only complicate their efforts to deal with the impending crisis, urged him to go abroad to recuperate. Jack Morgan, possibly prompted by one of the Bank directors, even generously offered his yacht, the *Corsair IV*, with its crew of fifty. Instead, on August 15, Norman set sail for Canada aboard the *Duchess of York*.

On July 31, as Parliament rose for its summer recess and politicians and bankers left London for the country, yet another official committee—the May Committee—submitted its report. As the Depression in Britain had deepened, the budget had slipped into deficit and was running around $600 million, 2.5 percent of GDP—a modest gap in the circumstances. The May Committee formed to consider economy measures, exaggerated the size and significance of the deficit out of a combination, in the words of historian A. J. P. Taylor, of "prejudice, ignorance, and panic," which, in the middle of a run on sterling, created only even more alarm. The May Committee proposed that the government seek to reverse the budgetary slide by cutting its expenditures by $500 million—including a 20 percent reduction in unemployment benefits—and raise an extra $100 million from higher taxes. In the light of what we now know about the way the economy works, it was completely absurd for the committee to propose that the solution to Britain's economic problems, with 2.5 million men out of work, production down by 20 percent, and prices falling at a rate of 7 percent a year, was to cut unemployment benefits and raise taxes. But at the time, the prevailing orthodoxy held that budget deficits were always bad, even in a depression. Maynard Keynes called the May report "the most foolish document I have ever had the misfortune to read."

The committee's recommendations split the cabinet. The majority, led by the prime minister, Ramsay MacDonald, and the chancellor, Philip Snowden, though all fervent and committed Socialists, were wedded to the belief that the budget must be balanced, no matter that Britain was in depression.

Meanwhile, the $250 million loan from the New York Fed and the Banque de France had already been used up—the Bank of England had now paid out a total of $500 million in gold and still the drain continued. Bank officials, taken aback by the immensity of the outflow but convinced that raising interest rates was not the answer, could only propose more borrowing—this time not by the Bank itself, whose credit lines were running out, but by the government. At the beginning of August, the government requested that the Bank put out informal feelers to ascertain the conditions that American bankers might attach to such a loan. The New York Fed, itself precluded by statute from lending directly to foreign governments, passed the inquiry on to J. P. Morgan & Co.

Bankers confronted with a country in need of money almost instinctively reach for budget cuts, preferably achieved by slashing public expenditure, as the right solution for almost any problem. During the following couple of weeks, as the conditions were being hammered out, the government, the Bank of England, and the House of Morgan threw up an intricate smoke screen around their discussions. Morgans certainly did not want its fingerprints on any evidence that it had imposed "political conditions" on a sovereign British government. Nor did the Labor prime minister want it known, not even within his own cabinet, that he had sought the permission of foreign bankers before acting. The chancellor put together a package of measures cutting $350 million in expenditures, including a 10 percent reduction in the dole, and raising taxes by $300 million and submitted it, through back channels at the Bank of England, for Morgan's consideration.

By the weekend of August 22, as gold losses mounted, a sense of crisis pervaded London. The king suddenly and mysteriously cut short his three-week holiday at Balmoral to return to Buckingham Palace. The cabinet remained in session over the weekend, the first time since the war. For all the prime minister's efforts at keeping the negotiations under wrap, the whole country, it seemed, awaited the telegram from New York signaling Morgan's approval. "It certainly is a tragically comical situation," wrote Beatrice Webb, wife of Sidney Webb, one of the recalcitrant minority in the cabinet against the budget cuts, "that the financiers who have landed the British people in this gigantic muddle should decide who should bear the burden, the dictatorship of the capitalist with a vengeance!"

On Saturday, August 22, the Morgan partners assembled at the house of F. D. Bartow in Glen Cove, Long Island, and after a long weekend of debate, gave the budget their blessing on Sunday afternoon. A telegram signaling their approval, its language suitably camouflaged to hide any hint that the budget had been submitted to the American bankers for vetting, was dispatched to Sir Ernest Harvey, deputy governor of the Bank of England, anxiously waiting at his City office. It arrived at 8:45 p.m. London time. He rushed it over personally to 10 Downing Street, outside which a large crowd had gathered as it always did at a time of national emergency—the street was littered with cigarette boxes, burned matches, paper bags, and newspapers. It was a balmy summer evening and the cabinet members were in the garden, nervously pacing around. When Harvey arrived, the prime minister snatched the telegram from his hands and rushed toward the Cabinet Room. Minutes later, the sound of angry voices emerged. To Harvey it seemed that "pandemonium had broken loose."

Despite the promise of Morgan money, the cabinet remained split over the cuts in unemployment benefits, and that evening the prime minister went to Buckingham Palace to tender his government's resignation. Two days later, the *Daily Herald*, official organ of the Labor Party, believing erroneously that the telegram had come from the Fed and not from Morgan, carried a photograph of George Harrison on its front page under the headline "Banker's Ramp," a ramp being a fraudulent move by financiers to manipulate the market. Within Britain, it remained an article of faith among left-wingers that the Labor government had been deliberately undermined by American fat-cat bankers opposed to socialism.

Within three days, a new National government, a coalition of fragments of Labor and the Liberals with a united Conservative Party, assumed office led by MacDonald and introduced much the same budget package that had split the previous ministry. In addition to cutting the dole by 10 percent, at the king's insistence his Civil List, the provision by the state for his expenses, a total of $2.25 million a year, was also reduced by 10 percent. Other members of the royal family copied his example, the Prince of Wales even returning $50,000 of his income of $300,000 from the Duchy of Cornwall. No one knows whether the next time George V and his friend Jack Morgan went out shooting, the topic of the loan and the king's economies ever came up in conversation.

On August 28, the British government received a $200 million loan from a consortium of American banks led by Morgans and a further $200 million from a group of French banks. It was gone within three weeks. The budget cuts did no good, largely because they were beside the point. A reporter for the British left-wing magazine *New Statesman and Nation* tried to describe the issue in the simplest of terms, as follows:

> What the City did in fact was to borrow from the French at 3% in order to lend to the Germans at 6% or 8%. Then came the crash in Vienna; the Bank [of England] lent money. Next the crash in Berlin, and again the Bank [of England] lent money. The French thereupon had a vision: they saw the various banks. Austrian, German, and English tied together like Alpine climbers above the abyss. Two of them had tumbled over; might they not drag the

> third with them? Acting on this vision they started a run
> on the Bank of England; in plain words they called in their
> deposits. . . . The "dole" has nothing to do with it.

In other words, Britain's problem was not its budget deficit, but rather that it had clung to the role of banker to the world without any longer having the money or the resources to do so and at a time when most of the world was a damn poor risk.

It was by now increasingly obvious to most observers that Britain would have to cut loose from gold. Back from America on July 18, Maynard Keynes, in a private letter, warned the prime minister, "It is now clearly certain that we shall go off the existing parity at no distant date . . . when doubts as to the prosperity of a currency, such as now exist about sterling, have come into existence, the game's up." In a series of magazine articles he argued that the deflationary budget cuts would only make the situation worse, describing them in a meeting with parliamentarians as "the most wrong and foolish things which Parliament has deliberately perpetrated in my lifetime." Even though he made an effort to be restrained in his public criticism of the Bank of England, recognizing that it would only add to the currency's problems, on August 10, Harry Siepmann invited him to the Bank to persuade him to tone down his writings. In fact, by now even such Bank men as Siepmann were losing faith. According to one visiting New York Fed official, Bank officers "admit quite frankly that the way out is for England and most of the other European countries to go off the gold standard temporarily, leave France and the United States high and dry, and then return to gold at a lower level."

The UK Treasury became the last bastion of the diehards. When a journalist even raised the question at a press conference there of whether Britain could or should remain on a gold standard that had become un-workable, required Britain to borrow gigantic amounts of money to sustain it, and was imposing intolerable sacrifices on the great mass of people, Sir Warren Fisher, head of the civil service and permanent secretary to the treasury, "rose to his feet, his eyes flashing, his face flushed with passion," and berated the journalists as if he had caught them "exchanging obscenities." "Gentlemen, I hope no one will repeat such sentiments outside this room," he scolded. "I am sure all those of you who know the British people will agree with me that to make such a suggestion is an affront to the national honor and would be felt as a attack on their personal honor by every man and woman in the country. It is quite unthinkable." Meanwhile, the flight from sterling continued unabated.

Among the new government's economy measures were pay cuts for all public employees, including the military. Within the navy, a flat shilling a day was taken from the pay of all ranks from admirals to ordinary seamen. Not surprisingly, this provoked enormous resentment among the lower decks at the unfairness of the differential burden so imposed. On September 14, a group of sailors of the Atlantic Fleet at Invergordon refused to muster and put to sea. It was a minor incident of no great significance but was reported in the foreign press as a mutiny, conjuring up the image that Britain was on the verge of revolution and that that last bastion of empire, the Royal Navy, was falling apart.

By now the Bank was losing $25 million of gold a day. Ministers kept leaking the figures on reserves to their cronies on the backbenches, who promptly passed them along to City speculators. On Thursday, September 17, the losses rose to over $80 million and similarly the following day. Since the crisis had begun, the Bank had watched $1 billion fly out of the window.

On Saturday, September 19, the British government made a last desperate plea to the Hoover administration for help. An emotional Stimson, a great Anglophile, called the British ambassador to the White House, to explain that every possible avenue for helping Britain had been explored, including further reductions in war debt, but that the United States was helpless. That weekend, the prime minister, after meeting with the officials of the Bank of England, took the decision to suspend gold payments.

A telegram was dispatched to Norman, then in mid-Atlantic aboard the HMS *Duchess of Bedford*, on his way home from Canada but still two days from shore. He had not taken his codebook and the radio message had to be sent on an open line. There is a wonderful but apocryphal story that to disguise the message, the deputy governor wrote, "Old Lady goes off on Monday." Puzzled by this cryptic note, Norman assumed that it referred to his mother's plans to go on holiday and thought nothing further of it.

The real story is almost as good. The cable in fact read, "Sorry we have to go off tomorrow and cannot wait to see you before doing so." Norman assumed that it meant Harvey was going to be away on the day of his return to Britain. He only discovered the truth when he landed at Liverpool on Wednesday, September 23. After meeting with the prime minister, he departed for a long weekend in the country to get over the shock. As his friend Baldwin put it indelicately, "Going off the gold standard was for him as though a daughter should lose her virginity." But, for all his anger, it is hard to see what he would or could have done differently had he been around.

The initial public reaction that week was one of alarm and astonishment. Few people understood what it meant. Most newspapers lamented it as the end of an epoch. Only the *Daily Express,* organ of that clear-sighted financial adventurer Lord Beaverbrook, called it a victory for common sense. "Nothing more heartening has happened in years . . . we are rid of the gold standard, rid of it for good and all, and the end of the gold standard is the beginning of real recovery in trade," he beamed.

The *Sunday Chronicle* of September 20 carried a profile of Montagu Norman by Winston Churchill, as part of a commissioned series on contemporary figures. Since leaving office in June 1929, Churchill had quarreled with his Conservative colleagues over Indian self-rule and, now isolated and out of favor, felt free to express his disillusionment with the gold standard orthodoxy openly. The problem was not so much the standard itself, he argued, but the way it had been allowed to operate. It was the hoarding of gold by the United States and France and the resulting shortage in the rest of the world that had brought on the Depression. He had begun to sound almost like Keynes—in a speech to Parliament the week before he had described how gold "is dug up out of a hole in Africa and put down in another hole that is even more inaccessible in Europe and America."

That weekend Churchill had the star of *The Gold Rush*, Charlie Chaplin, as a guest at Chartwell, his country house in Kent—they had met in Hollywood when Churchill was visiting the United States in October 1929 at the time of the crash. Over dinner Chaplin opened the conversation by saying, "You made a great mistake when you went back to the gold standard at the wrong parity of exchange in 1925." Churchill was somewhat taken aback. As the film star proceeded to hold forth at length about the subject with a great deal of knowledge, Churchill, who hated to be reminded of past mistakes, sank into a morose silence, a mood broken only when the comedian picked up two rolls of bread, put two forks in them and did the famous dance from the movie.

The next day, Monday, September 21, the first day off gold, by an odd quirk of fate, Churchill lunched with Maynard Keynes, now an ally and friend. Churchill spent much of the time protesting that he had never been in favor of returning to gold in 1925 and been overridden by Norman and the rest of the City. For Keynes it was a day of celebration and not regret. He could hardly contain his glee, "chuckling like a boy who has just exploded a firework under someone he doesn't like." "There are few Englishmen who do not rejoice at the breaking of the gold fetters," he wrote in an article later that week. "We feel that we have at last a free hand to do what is sensible. . . . I believe that the great events of the last week will open a new chapter in the world's monetary history."

But among bankers, especially European bankers, the British departure from gold was seen as an utterly dishonorable step, a "tragic act of abdication" that "inflicted heavy losses on all those who had trusted" the word of the Bank of England. Within a few days the pound had fallen by almost 25 percent in the foreign exchange markets from $4.86 to $3.75. By December it was a little below $3.50, a drop of 30 percent. Altogether twenty-five countries followed Britain off gold during the next few months, not only the nations of the empire and its satellites Canada, India, Malaya, Palestine, and Egypt, but also the Scandinavians—Sweden, Denmark, Norway, and Finland—and finally those European countries with close commercial ties to Britain: Ireland, Austria, and Portugal.

Though the papers kept telling him that it was the end of an era, for the average Englishman, after a few days of stunned confusion, it was as if nothing had happened. There were no bank runs, no food shortages, no rush to the stores, no hoarding of goods. Indeed, while wholesale prices in the rest of the world would continue to fall, dropping 10 percent over the next year, in Britain deflation came to an end—prices over the next year even rose a modest 2 percent.

The one group who received a big shock was the small number of British people traveling abroad. *Time* magazine recounted how one man in an Old Etonian tie was sufficiently incensed at being offered only $3 for his pounds in New York—a "hold-up," he called it—that he stormed off muttering, "A pound is still a pound in England. I shall carry my pounds home with me."

The recriminations began almost immediately. Snowden in his speech to the Commons on September 20 blamed the debacle on the gold policies of the United States and France. Though Americans came in for their fair share, the greatest vituperation was reserved for the French. Margot Asquith, in a letter to Norman wishing him well on his return, captured the country's mood when she wrote, "France will be heavily punished for her selfish short-sightedness. She has been the curse of Europe. . . ." Ironically, the one institution upon which the devaluation wrought disaster was the Banque de France. For years an urban myth insisted that it had been French selling of the pound that had set off the debacle. In fact, the Banque had hung on to every penny of its $350 million in sterling deposits. So supportive had it been during the crisis that Clément Moret was later named an honorary Knight Commander in the Order of the British Empire. The Banque de France ended up losing close to $125 million, seven times its equity capital. A normal bank would have been driven under.

Other central banks, especially those of Sweden, the Netherlands, and Belgium, that had been persuaded during the 1920s to keep part of their reserves in sterling lost enormous amounts. The Dutch central bank lost all its capital—the bitterness ran particularly deep because a few days before the devaluation, its governor, forgetting that only simpletons ask a central banker about the value of his currency and expect an honest answer, had inquired whether his deposits were safe and had been unequivocally reassured. Norman was so embarrassed by the losses sustained by his fellow central bankers that he contemplated submitting a letter of resignation to the BIS. It would have been a quaintly anachronistic gesture—like an ashamed bankrupt resigning from his club—but he was persuaded that it would be impractical for the institution to operate without a Bank of England presence at its meetings.

No ONE HAD done more to prop up Europe that summer than George Harrison. It must have seemed to him at times that he had spent most of the summer on transatlantic telephone calls—at the height of the Central European crisis he and Norman must have spoken on the phone, not a simple matter in those days, more than twenty-five times. After the first Austrian loan back in May, when few could have foreseen how far the panic would go, the Fed had provided the Reichsbank with $25 million, been ready to throw in a mammoth $500 million for the second loan that never got off the ground, supplied a further $250 million to the Bank of England, and, finally, been instrumental in orchestrating the last $200 million loan from the Morgan consortium to the British government. It had all been to no effect. Europe's problems had proved to be much deeper, and its needs far larger, than the Fed was capable of handling.

After Britain left the gold standard, the financial crisis now spread across the Atlantic. Over the next five weeks, Europeans, fearing that the United States would be next to devalue, converted a massive $750 million of dollar holdings into gold. While some popular accounts attributed the outflow of gold to "panicky millionaires" and speculators hoping to make a buck from such a collapse, it was not private investors who were principally behind the flow but European central banks, the largest single mover of capital being the staid and upright Swiss National Bank, which transferred close to $200 million. The National Bank of Belgium moved $130 million; the already badly burned Netherlands Bank, $77 million; and the Banque de France, $100 million. Having lost its capital seven times over during the sterling devaluation out of a misplaced sense of "solidarity and politeness"—Governor Moret's words—and having been rewarded with a campaign of public vilification in Britain, the Banque de France had learned its lesson. The cost of being a responsible global citizen was just too great.

The outflow of gold came at a particularly crucial juncture for the U.S. banking system, then reeling under the wave of failures that had begun in the spring in Chicago. By September, the panic had swept Ohio and was circling back to Pittsburgh and Philadelphia. A committee of prominent Philadelphians, including the president of the University of Pennsylvania, the cardinal archbishop, and the mayor, published an appeal in the newspapers urging faith in local banks. To no avail—39 banks in the city with over $100 million in deposits were forced to close down. In one month alone after the British departure from gold, 522 American banks went under—by the end of the year, a total of 2,294, one out of every ten in the country, with a total of $1.7 billion in deposits, would suspend operations.

The mounting bank failures intensified hoarding—$500 million in cash was pulled from banks. While most of this was stashed away in traditional hiding places—socks, desks, safes, strongboxes under the bed, deposit vaults—some found its way to very unconventional spots, including, according to a congressional report, "holes in the ground, privies, linings of coats, horse collars, coal piles, hollow trees." Anywhere but bank accounts.

The Fed had begun 1931 with a massive $4.7 billion in gold reserves. Even after the fall outflow, it had more than enough bullion and was never at any risk of being stripped bare as the Bank of England or the Reichsbank had been. Nevertheless, because of a strange technical anomaly in its governing laws, it found itself facing an artificial squeeze on its reserves.

By statute, every $100 in Federal Reserve notes had to be backed by at least $40 in gold, the remaining $60 by so-called eligible paper—that is, prime commercial bills used to finance trade. Even though the Federal Reserve banks were permitted to hold government securities, and the buying and selling of such securities—open market operations—was one of the mechanisms by which the Fed injected money into the system, government paper could not be employed as an asset to back currency. Even when first introduced in the original 1913 legislation setting up the Fed, the restriction had been redundant, since the 40 percent gold requirement was enough to prevent the central bank from being used as an instrument of inflation. By 1931, with no risk of inflation—the country in fact facing a problem of deflation—the restriction served no purpose. Nevertheless, it remained obstinately on the books.

With the Depression and the ensuing stagnation in trade, prime bills were scarce and hard to find. The Fed had to rely on gold to back its currency. Thus, in the fall of 1931, instead of having $2 billion too much gold and being grateful that some of it was finally flowing back to Europe, it found itself scrambling to hold on to its reserves. It was a manufactured problem, the result of an anachronistic regulation that had no basis in economic reality but which tied up a large amount of U.S. gold unnecessarily.

And so early that October, in the midst of the Depression, as bank runs raged across the Midwest, thousands of businesses closed down, and industrial production contracted at an annualized rate of 25 percent, the Fed raised interest rates from 1.5 percent to 3.5 percent. With prices falling by 7 percent a year, this put the effective cost of money above 10 percent. So dominant was the view that abiding by these reserve requirements trumped every other consideration, there was no internal resistance at the Fed to jacking up the cost of credit. Even the two principal expansionists, Meyer and Harrison, went along.

The president still continued to cling to the notion that private sector initiatives were the best way to revive the economy. On the evening of Sunday, October 4, he secretly slipped out of the White House and made his way to Mellon's apartment at 1785 Massachusetts Avenue, where Harrison of the New York Fed had assembled a group of nineteen New York bankers, among them Thomas Lamont and George Whitney of J. P. Morgan & Co., Albert Wiggin of Chase National, William Potter of Guaranty Trust, and Charlie Mitchell of National City—in short, the usual suspects. Amid the Rubenses and Rembrandts, which Mellon had so assiduously collected, the president outlined a plan to try to break the vicious cycle whereby people were pulling cash out of banks and banks were having to cut credit.

Banks were going under in part because the assets they held on their books could not be used as collateral to borrow from the Fed. By the fall of 1931, the neat distinction between liquidity and solvency on which the Fed, following Bagehot, had placed so much emphasis, was becoming meaningless. Many banks experiencing withdrawals would have been fine under normal circumstance, but forced to call in loans and liquidate assets in a falling market at fire-sale prices, they were being driven into insolvency. Hoover proposed that a new fund of $500 million be created by the larger and stronger private banks to lend to smaller banks on collateral that the Federal Reserve was legally unable to accept.

That meeting went on long into the evening. The bankers were dubious about the idea and kept asking why the government or the Fed did not act—had not the Fed after all been created precisely to avoid such banking panics? Hoover returned to the White House after midnight "more depressed than ever before." The next day, prodded by Harrison, the bankers reluctantly agreed to try the plan. Over the next few weeks, the new fund lent a grand total of $100 million and then, paralyzed by its proprietors' ultraconservatism and fear of losing money, folded. The days of the great Pierpont Morgan, when large banks assumed responsibility for propping up smaller ones and for supporting the integrity of the entire financial system, were long gone.

The bank runs, the spike in currency hoarding, and now the rising cost of money imposed a massive and sudden credit crunch upon an already fragile United States. Between September 1931 and June 1932 the total amount of bank credit in the country shrank by 20 percent, from $43 billion to $36 billion. As loans were called in, small businesses were driven into default. Lenders were forced to absorb losses and in turn lost their own cushion of capital, making depositors quite justly fearful for the security of their money and leading to further withdrawals from banks, which in turn forced more loan recalls and thus more defaults. Though depositors and bankers individually behaved quite rationally to protect themselves, collectively their actions imposed a vicious spiral of tightening credit and loan losses on the already depressed U.S. economy.

"If there is one moment in the 1930s that haunts economic historians," writes the economist J. Bradford DeLong, "it is the spring and summer of 1931—for that is when the severe depression in Europe and North America that had started in the summer of 1929 in the United States, and in the fall of 1928 in Germany, turned into *the* Great Depression." The currency and banking convulsions of 1931 changed the nature of the economic collapse. As prices fell and businesses were unable to service their debts, bankruptcies proliferated, further chilling spending and economic activity. A corrosive deflationary psychology set in. Fearing that prices would fall further, consumers and businesses cut spending, adding to the downward spiral in consumption and investment.

Every economic indicator seemed to fall off a cliff—1932 was the deepest year of depression in the United States. Between September 1931 and June 1932, production fell 25 percent; investment dived a stunning 50 percent; and prices dropped another 10 percent, reaching 75 percent of their 1929 level. Unemployment shot up beyond ten million—more than 20 percent of the workforce was now without jobs.

American corporations, which had made almost $10 billion in profits in 1929, collectively lost $3 billion in 1932. On July 8, 1932, the Dow, which had stood at 381 on September, 3, 1929, and was trading around 150 before the European currency crisis, hit a low of 41, a drop of almost 90 percent over the two and a half years since the bubble first broke. General Motors, which had traded at $72 a share in September 1929, was now a little above $7. And RCA, which had peaked at $101 in 1929, hit a low of $2. When, in August 1932, a reporter for the *Saturday Evening Post* asked John Maynard Keynes if there had ever been anything like this before, he replied, "Yes. It was called the Dark Ages, and it lasted four hundred years."

In 1932, Meyer, having uncharacteristically allowed himself to be hamstrung by the Fed bureaucracy for his first year in office, finally took charge. In January, he persuaded the administration that its attempt to have the large banks voluntarily take responsibility for supporting the system had failed. The Reconstruction Finance Corporation (RFC) was established to channel public money—a total of $1.5 billion—into the banking system. Congress would agree to the new agency only if Meyer took on the chairmanship. For six months Meyer held two full-time posts: head of the RFC and chairman of the Federal Reserve Board. Eventually the toll on him became so great that his wife, Agnes, personally lobbied the president for him to resign one of the positions.

In February 1932, he pressed Congress to pass legislation that would make government securities an eligible asset to back currency. At the stroke of a pen the gold shortage was lifted, allowing the Fed to embark on a massive program of open market operations, injecting a total of $1 billion of cash into banks. The two new measures combined—the infusion of additional capital into the banking system and the injection of reserves—allowed the Fed finally to pump money into the system on the scale required. But Meyer had left it too late. A similar measure in late 1930 or in 1931 might have changed the course of history. In 1932 it was like pushing on a string. Banks, shaken by the previous two years, instead of lending out the money used the capital so injected to build up their own reserves. Total bank credit kept shrinking at a rate of 20 percent a year.

Bankers and financiers, the heroes of the previous decade, now became the whipping boys. No one provided a better target than Andrew Mellon. In January 1932, a freshman Democratic congressman from Texas, Wright Patman, opened impeachment hearings for high crimes and misdemeanors against the man once hailed as the "greatest Secretary of the Treasury since Alexander Hamilton." Mellon found himself accused of corruption, of granting illegal tax refunds to companies in which he had an interest, of favoring his own banks and aluminum conglomerate in Treasury decisions, and of violating laws against trading with the Soviet Union. During the ensuing investigations, it turned out that he had used Treasury tax experts to help him find ways to reduce his personal tax bill and that he had made liberal use of fictitious gifts as a tax-dodging device. Being a member of the Federal Reserve Board, he had been required to divest his holdings of bank stock, with which he had duly complied—except that he had transferred the stock to his brother. In February, Hoover, recognizing that Mellon had now become a liability, packed him off as ambassador to London.* His place was taken by his undersecretary, Ogden Mills.

On March 12, 1932, the world learned that Ivar Kreuger, the Swedish match king, who had bailed out so many penniless European countries, had shot himself in his apartment on the Avenue Victor Emmanuel III in Paris. At first it was assumed that he was just another victim of the times— he had recently suffered a nervous breakdown and his physician had warned him about the constant strain of his lifestyle on his heart. Within three weeks it became apparent that his whole enterprise had been a sham. His accounts were riddled with inflated valuations and bogus assets, including $142 million of forged Italian government bonds. When the losses to investors were eventually tallied, they amounted to $400 million.

Bankers were now increasingly viewed as crooks and rogues. In early 1932, the Senate Banking and Currency Committee began hearings on the causes of the 1929 crash. Designed at first to appease a public hungry for scapegoats, the hearings achieved little until, in March 1933, a young assistant district attorney from New York City, Ferdinand Pecora, took over as chief counsel. The public was soon riveted by the tales of financial skullduggery in high places. It learned that Albert Wiggins, president of Chase, had sold the stock of his bank short at the height of the bubble and collected $4 million in profits when it collapsed during the crash; that Charles Mitchell, old "Sunshine Charlie," of the National City Bank had lent $2.4

---

* The accusations of tax dodging resurfaced in 1934 when the Justice Department indicted him for having falsified his 1931 tax returns and sought more than $3 million in back taxes and penalties. He was cleared on appeal, but his estate eventually paid some $600,000 as a settlement.

million to bank officers without any collateral to help them carry their stock after the crash, only 5 percent of which was repaid; that Mitchell himself, despite earning $1 million a year, had avoided all federal income tax by selling his bank stock to members of his family at a loss and then buying it back; that J. P. Morgan had not paid a cent of income taxes in the three years from 1929 to 1931.

"If you steal $25, you're a thief. If you steal $250,000, you're an embezzler. If you steal $2,500,000, you're a financier," wrote the magazine the *Nation*. Few critics went as far or tapped into as strong a vein of popular discontent as Father Charles Coughlin. Pastor of the Shrine of the Little Flower in Royal Oak, Michigan, Coughlin was the originator of right-wing radio. His Sunday afternoon broadcasts delivered in a soothing and intimate voice of mellow richness captivated millions as he held forth on the "banksters," as he called them, who had led the country into the Depression.

He actually did have some understanding of the driving forces in international finance. For example, in a broadcast delivered on February 26, 1933, he explained somewhat cogently that "the so-called depression, with its bank failures, is traceable to the inordinate, impossible debts payable in gold—debts which came into being and were multiplied as a result of the war." But he embellished his radio sermon with one of his fire-and-brimstone rants on "the filthy gold standard which from time immemorial has been the breeder of hate, the fashioner of swords, and the destroyer of mankind," and ended by urging his listeners to rise up "against the Morgans, the Kuhn-Loebs, the Rothschilds, the Dillon-Reads, the Federal Reserve banksters, the Mitchells and the rest of that undeserving group who without either the blood of patriotism or of Christianity flowing in their veins have shackled the lives of men and of nations with the ponderous links of their golden chain."

The 1932 presidential campaign was dominated by the Depression. The Democratic candidate, Franklin Roosevelt, the handsome and attractive, astoundingly self-confident governor of New York, was initially dismissed as a lightweight. But his jaunty optimism—his campaign's signature tune became "Happy Days Are Here Again"—his inspirational speeches, and his promise of vigorous action to restore prosperity made a sharp contrast with the dour and resentful Hoover.

On economics, Roosevelt had a breezy and disconcerting ability to put forward contradictory policies without the slightest embarassment. So while he pledged to increase federal relief for unemployment, supported higher tariffs, government development of power projects, increased regulation of securities markets, and the separation of commercial and investment banking, he also criticized Hoover for fiscal extravagance, accused him of encouraging inflation, and promised to balance the budget and commit himself to "sound money." But voters did not care about consistency, they wanted bold action. In November 1932, Roosevelt got 22.8 million votes against Hoover's 15.7 million, the greatest electoral sweep since Lincoln beat McClellan in 1864.

In the interregnum between the election and inauguration, a new wave of bank failures swept the country—this time starting in the West. On November 1, the governor of Nevada declared a twelve-day bank holiday, after the suspension of a bank chain that accounted for 65 percent of the state's deposits. He was followed by his counterparts in Iowa in January 1933 and Louisiana in early February.

It was, however, the run on the Guardian Trust Company of Detroit, a bank controlled by Edsel Ford, scion of the Ford motor family, that transformed the new crisis into a national one. The Guardian Trust had done well during the 1920s financing consumer purchases of Ford cars. When auto sales dried up in the early 1930s, the bank found itself in serious trouble and had been forced to borrow from the RFC. In early 1933, the RFC balked at providing more money unless the sponsors, who were, after all, the second richest family in the country after the Rockefellers, put in more capital. Patriarch Henry Ford, now in his seventies and increasingly autocratic and unreasonable, refused to bail out his son. He had a long-standing antipathy to bankers and could not quite grasp why banks should be allowed to use the money he deposited for making risky loans— "It's just as if I put my car in a garage and when I came to get it, I found somebody else had borrowed it and run it into a tree," was the way he saw it. Faced with a statewide run on its banking system, on February 14, the governor of Michigan issued a proclamation closing all 550 banks in the state for eight days. The residents of Michigan woke up on Saint Valentine's Day to find that all that they could draw upon was the cash in their pockets.

Across the country, depositors watching the whole monetary system of a major industrial state shut down began pulling their money out of their banks just in case. Governor after governor was forced to follow Michigan and declare a state bank holiday. Indiana closed its banks on the twenty-third of February, Maryland on the twenty-fifth, Arkansas on the twenty-seventh, and Ohio on the twenty-eighth. In early March, the contagion spread into Kentucky and Pennsylvania. During February and the first few days of March, close to $2 billion, a third of all the currency in the country, was withdrawn from banks.

A banking panic on such a scale raised the specter of Central Europe in the summer of 1931 when the sequence of banking crises had forced country after country off the gold standard. The domestic run on the U.S banks now provoked a similar international run on the dollar.

The flight from the dollar was exacerbated by suspicions over the incoming president's currency intentions. Ever since he had been elected, Roosevelt had been floating trial balloons about abandoning gold. In January, he told an emissary from William Randolph Hearst, "If the fall in the price of commodities cannot be checked, we may be forced to an inflation of our currency." On January 31, his secretary-of-agriculture designate, Henry Wallace, was quoted as saying, "England has played us for a bunch of suckers. The smart thing to do would be to go off the gold standard a little further than England has. The British debtor has paid off his debts 50% easier than the U. S. debtor has."

Roosevelt was not alone in his talk of devaluation. At least six bills were circulating through the halls of Congress that involved the emergency issue of currency or a change in the value of the dollar. The Frazier-Sinclair-Patman bill provided for government financing of farm mortgages by the issue of Federal Reserve notes without gold backing; the Campbell bill would have allowed issue of full legal tender Treasury notes backed by municipal bonds. Congress was considering one bill to devalue the dollar against gold by 50 percent and another one to reinstate silver as a monetary metal. The most extreme of the measures, the McFadden bill, called for the abolition of the gold standard and the Federal Reserve System and their replacement by a new monetary system based on units of "human effort."

Hoover had meanwhile convinced himself yet again that the economy had been on the verge of recovery before this last panic hit, which he attributed solely to fears over Roosevelt's inflationary policies. On February 17, Hoover composed a ten-page handwritten letter and had it delivered by Secret Service messenger to Roosevelt. What was needed to restore confidence, he wrote, was a formal statement from the president-elect pledging himself to a balanced budget and eschewing inflation or devaluation. If Hoover was trying to elicit Roosevelt's support for preemptive bipartisan action, this was a clumsy, inept, and transparently self-serving way to go about it. Hoover himself admitted in a private letter that it would have involved Roosevelt abandoning 90 percent of his "so called New Deal" program. The incoming president dismissed the letter as "cheeky" and chose simply to sit on it for a couple of weeks.

Until then, panics had mainly affected the smallest banks in the nation. But as the run took on an international dimension, the most important financial institution in the country, banker to its largest banks, the New York Fed became the center of the storm. In the last two weeks of February, it lost $250 million, almost a quarter of its gold reserves. Though the Federal Reserve System as a whole had more than ample gold reserves, had the New York Fed run out of gold and been compelled to call in its loans to banks and shrink its balance sheet in a hurry, this would have created a disastrous situation for the banking system not only in New York but across the country. Theoretically, it could always have borrowed from other Federal Reserve banks in the system—but with every bank in every region under threat, there was no guarantee that its sister banks would have cooperated. There was a real fear that if it became a situation of every man for himself, even the Federal Reserve System might fall apart.

George Harrison had become convinced as early as mid-February that the only solution to the spreading panic caused by state-by-state bank closures was a nationwide bank holiday. In a visit to the White House, he urged the president to close all banks. Hoover tried to pass the buck back to the Fed, requesting that the Board come up with a set of proposals for saving the banking system short of shutting it down completely. Eugene Meyer had come to a similar conclusion to Harrison. He feared that if the Fed took inadequate measures that then failed, it would only make the situation worse and he would be blamed. So Meyer kicked the ball back to Hoover.

On the afternoon of Thursday, March 2, two days before the new president was to be inaugurated, Harrison called Meyer to inform him that the New York Fed had fallen below its minimum gold reserve ratio.

During the next forty-eight hours, as the nation's banking system unraveled by the hour, the Fed, unwilling to act on its own, tried to find someone else to take responsibility for the situation. But it was caught in the limbo between administrations. That same Thursday afternoon, Harrison called the president, begging him once again to declare a national banking holiday. Hoover replied that he "did not want his last official act in office to be the closing of the banks." Adolph Miller, Hoover's old friend and neighbor, also went to the White House to try to persuade the president. Hoover said he would do nothing unless Roosevelt also signed up.

Roosevelt traveled down to Washington that day, and no sooner had he checked into his suite at the Mayflower Hotel than the phone began ringing. It was Meyer calling to urge him to endorse a national proclamation closing all banks. Roosevelt refused to commit himself to any course of action until he was inaugurated—why box himself in at this stage? he quite justly thought.

On Friday, March 3, the New York Fed lost a total of $350 million—$200 million in wire transfers out of the country and $150 million in actual physical currency withdrawals from banks in the New York area. Now short some $250 million in reserves, it tried to borrow from the Chicago Fed but was turned down—the risk of the Federal Reserve System balkanizing and falling apart was becoming a reality.

March 3 was Hoover's last full day in office, and that afternoon Roosevelt and some of his family—Eleanor, his son James, and his daughter-in-law, Betsy—paid him a courtesy call. After a strained tea party of polite small talk, Hoover asked to see Roosevelt alone. They retired to Hoover's study where they were joined by Meyer; Secretary of Treasury Mills; and Roosevelt's aide, Raymond Moley. Meyer and Mills again tried to persuade the president-elect to join the outgoing Republican administration in some sort of bipartisan action. Roosevelt stood his ground. The sitting president should do what he had to—he himself would do nothing until after his inauguration at noon the next day. Eleanor heard snatches of the conversation through the open door. At one point, Hoover asked, "Will you join me in signing a joint proclamation tonight, closing all the banks?" Roosevelt replied, "Like hell, I will! If you haven't got the guts to do it yourself, I'll wait until I am President to do it!" It was now very obvious that Roosevelt's strategy was to withhold his cooperation in the hope that conditions would deteriorate so badly before he took office that he would get all the credit for any subsequent rebound.

That evening at the Roosevelt suite, the telephone would not stop ringing. Among the callers was Thomas Lamont who was at the New York Fed with sixteen of the most powerful bankers in the city. An old friend of Roosevelt's, Lamont had sent him a letter two weeks earlier warning him against closing the banks, "Urban populations cannot do without money. . . . It would be like cutting off a city's water supply. Pestilence and famine would follow. . . ." Lamont now reiterated this view, telling Roosevelt that he was sure that there would be a change in national psychology after the inauguration that would restore confidence.

The Fed made one last attempt to bridge the gap between Hoover and Roosevelt with Meyer calling Hoover and Miller calling Roosevelt. Hoover and Roosevelt even exchanged several calls, at 8:30 p.m., at 11:30 p.m., and at 1:00 a.m. Neither of them shifted their positions. Finally Roosevelt suggested that they both turn in and get some sleep.

Meyer, having been repeatedly rebuffed by the White House over the last two days and despite knowing that it was futile, decided to make one last effort—perhaps he wanted to protect himself and the Fed from the verdict of history. At 9:15 p.m. on March 3, he assembled his colleagues on the Board for the third time that day. Charles Hamlin was called out of the inaugural concert he was attending and despite the foul weather—it had been sleeting—George James was dragged from his sickbed. The Board drafted a formal request in writing to the president to proclaim a national bank holiday. It was 2:00 a.m before the letter was sent to the White House. The president had gone to bed. No one wanted to wake him up and the letter was slipped under his door. The next morning, he was furious at this ploy by his erstwhile friend, Meyer, to leave him holding the bag.

Having failed with the president, the Federal Reserve Board now focused on getting the governors of the two most important states to close their banks. Governor Horner of Illinois could not be found at first. When tracked down, he refused to move unless New York governor Herbert Lehman of the eponymous banking family acted first. In the middle of the night, Harrison, Lamont, and a group of bankers trooped over to Lehman's Park Avenue apartment. Lamont and the private banks tried to persuade Lehman to hold off doing anything while Harrison kept insisting that they had no choice—gold withdrawals had become unbearable, and if they did nothing, on Monday morning the New York Fed would run completely out of reserves. Finally at 2.30 a.m. Lehman relented and proclaimed a three-day bank holiday in New York. An hour later Governor Horner followed his lead. The governors of Massachusetts and New Jersey moved to close their banks early the next morning. Fed officials tried to contact Governor Gifford Pinchot of Pennsylvania, who was in Washington for the inauguration and staying at a private residence, but no one would pick up the telephone. Finally a Fed official volunteered to go by his house to rouse him. He finally issued his proclamation to close the banks in his state as dawn was breaking, noting ruefully that he was only carrying 95 cents in his pocket.

That day as a hundred thousand people stood on the Mall to witness Roosevelt being sworn in on the steps of the Capitol, they were watched over by army machine guns. It was like "a beleaguered capital in wartime," wrote Arthur Krock of the *New York Times*.

Meanwhile, the credit and currency machinery of the country had come to a grinding halt. The banking systems in twenty-eight states of the union were completely closed and in the remaining twenty partially closed. In three years, commercial bank credit had shrunk from $50 billion to $30 billion and a quarter of the country's banks had collapsed. House prices had gone down by 30 percent, leaving almost half of all mortgages in default. With the contraction in credit, mines and factories across the country had to shut down. Steel mills operated at less than 12 percent of their full capacity. Automobile plants, which had once churned out twenty thousand cars a day, were now producing less than two thousand. Industrial output had fallen in half, prices had tumbled 30 percent, and national income had contracted from over $100 billion to $55 billion. A quarter of the workforce—13 million men in all—were without jobs. In the richest nation in the world, 34 million men, women, and children out of a total population of 120 million had no apparent source of income.

More than half a century before, Karl Marx had predicted that as the boom and bust cycles of capitalism became progressively worse, it would eventually destroy itself. That day, it seemed that the back of the system had finally broken in one last stupendous crisis.

PART FIVE

*

AFTERMATH

*

1933-44

21. GOLD STANDARD ON THE BOOZE

1933

In order to arrive at what you do not know
You must go by a way which is the way of ignorance.
—T. S. ELIOT, *Four Quartets*, "East Coker"

ONE DAY into office, the very first action that Roosevelt took was to close every bank in the country. Invoking an obscure provision of the 1917 Trading with the Enemy Act, designed to prevent gold shipments to hostile powers, he imposed a bank holiday until Thursday, March 9. Simultaneously, he suspended the export or private hoarding of all gold in the United States.

To the surprise of many, Americans adapted to life without banks remarkably well—the initial reaction was not chaos but cooperation. Storekeepers liberally extended credit, while doctors, lawyers, and pharmacists continued to provide services in return for personal IOUs. Harvard University allowed its students to obtain meals on credit. Across the country in El Paso, Texas, the First Baptist Church announced that personal promissory notes would be welcome in the Sunday collection plate instead of silver. Even taxi dancers at Manhattan's Roseland dance hall on Broadway agreed to take IOUs for the 11 cents that they charged per dance—provided their customers could produce bankbooks showing evidence of funds.

More than a hundred cities and towns, including Atlanta, Richmond, Knoxville, Nashville, and Philadelphia, issued their own scrip. The Dow Chemical Company coined magnesium into alternative coins. That prominent undergraduate newspaper, the *Daily Princetonian* rose to the occasion by assuming the role of central bank of Princeton and issuing $500 of its own currency, in denominations of 25 cents, which local merchants agreed to accept—a reflection of how adaptable and elastic the notion of money can be.

Other places resorted to barter. In Detroit, the Colonial Department Store agreed to accept farm produce in exchange for goods—a dress went for three barrels of Saginaw Bay herring, three pairs of shoes for a 500-pound sow, and other merchandise went for fifty crates of eggs or 180 pounds of honey. In Manhattan, the promoters of the Golden Globe amateur boxing tournament announced that fans would be admitted in return for anything assessed to be worth 50 cents— that night the box office took in hats, shoes, cigars, combs, soap, chisels, kettles, sacks of potatoes, and foot balm.

There were, of course, some disruptions. In Detroit, now in its fourth week without banks, merchants stopped extending credit, food disappeared from the shelves, and the City of Detroit defaulted on its bonds. In Reno, the divorce industry ground to a halt when women could not pay the filing fees. Tourists and traveling salesmen around the country found themselves stranded. In Florida, the American Express office agreed to cash checks up to a limit of $50 and was besieged by five thousand tourists. The first official task for the new secretary of state, Cordell Hull, was to placate the diplomatic corps in Washington, who argued that their money was entitled to immunity from sequestration and should be immediately released. The movie *King Kong* in its second week played to half-empty theaters—total box office receipts were down almost 50 percent.

The biggest problem was not cash but change. Nickels for use on the subway and on trolley and bus lines were so scarce that an officer of the Irving Trust Company declared that a "nickel famine" was in effect. Suddenly automats, where food was served from coin-operated vending machines and where a lot of coins changed hands, were besieged by women in mink desperate not for a meal, but for loose silver.

On Sunday, March 5, the day after the inauguration, William Woodin, the new secretary of the treasury, began organizing a team of experts to put together a bank rescue package. The diminutive Woodin, who had been the president of the American Car and Foundry Company, was a far cry from the austere Mellon. A Republican who had switched parties to support Roosevelt, he was as multifaceted as Charles Dawes of the Dawes Plan. An accomplished musician, having composed several orchestral pieces, including the *Covered Wagon Suite*, the *Oriental Suite*—and in honor of the inauguration, the "Franklin Delano Roosevelt March"—he liked to unwind at the office by playing the mandolin or strumming his guitar.

Woodin quickly recognized that neither he nor his aides had the knowledge or experience to handle the situation alone. He managed to persuade none other than his predecessor as secretary of the treasury, Ogden Mills, and Mills's deputy, Arthur Ballantine, to lead the bank rescue effort, even though Mills, who owned an estate in the Hudson Valley just five miles north of Roosevelt's home, Hyde Park, was no admirer of the new president—later he would become a very vocal critic of the New Deal. On the very last day of Hoover's presidency and his own tenure in office, Mills had prepared a draft, which now became the foundation of the Roosevelt plan. Even Roosevelt's proclamation closing the banks in the country was based on a draft of a statement that Ballantine had originally prepared for Hoover.

The team's other principal player was George Harrison, who came down to Washington that Sunday. Realizing that any bank plan would have to pass muster with bankers, Woodin wanted someone who could be a bridge to Wall Street, and as a former outside director of the New York Fed, he knew Harrison well. He also very deliberately kept the group of presidential advisers with a reputation for being left-wing—men such as Adolph Berle, Rex Tugwell, and Raymond Moley—well in the background.

During the next few days, as bankers came and went, the Treasury team, led by the trio of Woodin, Mills, and Harrison, considered and rejected numerous proposals. Some people wanted a nationwide issue of scrip—paper currency backed only by a government pledge. Others recommended that all state banks be incorporated into the Federal Reserve System. Yet others believed a federal government guarantee on all bank deposits was the solution. The president himself came up with the zaniest idea—that all government debt, $21 billion, be immediately convertible into currency, in effect doubling the money supply at a stroke.

By Thursday, March 9, the Emergency Banking Act was ready to be submitted to Congress. Most of it was based on the original Mills proposal. Banks in the country were to be gradually reopened, starting with those known to be sound, and progressively moving to the shakier institutions, which would need government support. A whole class of insolvent banks would never be permitted to reopen. The bill also granted the Fed the right to issue additional currency backed not by gold but by bank assets. And it gave the federal government the authority to direct the Fed to provide support to banks. The legislation was supplemented by a commitment from the Treasury to the Fed that the government would indemnify it for any losses incurred in bailing out the banking system. This unprecedented package finally forced the Fed to fulfill its role as lender of last resort to the banking system. But to achieve this, the government was in effect providing an implicit blanket guarantee of the deposits of every bank allowed to reopen.

For Harrison the transformation was almost too much to believe, leaving him constantly beset by doubts. Only a week before he had been dealing with a president who seemed incapable of taking action. He now had to contend with a president who would try anything. As a protégé of Benjamin Strong, Harrison believed fervently in what he called the "separation of the central bank from the state"—the financial equivalent of the separation of the powers in the political sphere. The new legislation would give the president unprecedented control over the Fed. Harrison had also been taught that currency should be backed either by gold or liquid assets readily convertible into cash. The new law expanded the category of assets against which the Fed could lend, compelling it to print money, Harrison agonized, against "all kinds of junk, even the brass spittoons in old-fashioned country banks." But at least the drift was over and something was finally being done.

At ten o'clock on the evening of Sunday, March 12, Roosevelt gave the first of his fireside chats over the radio. "My friends," he began in his easy patrician voice, "I want to talk for few minutes with the people of the United States about banking . . . I want to tell you what has been done in the last few days, why it was done, and what the next steps are going to be." In simple and clear language, he explained to the sixty million people listening in countless homes across the nation, "When you deposit money in a bank, the bank does not put the money in a safe deposit vault. It invests the money, puts it to work." "I know you are worried . . . ," he told them, "I can assure you, my friends, it is safer to keep your money in a reopened bank than under the mattress." The next day the comedian Will Rogers wrote to the *New York Times*, "Our President took such a dry subject as banking . . . [and] he made everyone understand it, even the bankers."

As the first banks prepared to open on Monday, March 13, no one could be sure what would happen. Many feared that after the measures restricting the convertibility of currency into gold, the panic might even continue and indeed become worse. As Harrison put it, "We had closed in the midst of a great bank run, and as far as we knew would reopen under the same conditions."

That morning, long lines of depositors formed outside the reopened banks. But instead of taking their money out, they were putting it back in. The combination of the bank holiday, the rescue plan, and Roosevelt's masterful speech—there is no way of distinguishing which was the more important—created one of those dramatic transformative shifts in public sentiment. As on other similar occasions where a new administration has taken charge in the middle of a crisis and introduced a radically new package of policies—for example, in Germany in November 1923 when hyperinflation was ended or in France in July 1926 when Poincaré stabilized the franc—the mood of the nation changed overnight.

On March 15, when the New York Stock Exchange reopened after being closed for ten days, the Dow jumped 15 percent, the largest move in a single day in its history. By the end of the first week, a total of $1 billion in cash—half of everything that had been pulled out in the previous six weeks—had been redeposited in banks. By the end of March, two-thirds of the banks in the country, twelve thousand in total, had been permitted to resume business and the currency hoard in the hands of the public had dropped by $1.5 billion.

This was one more bitter pill for Hoover to swallow. A bank rescue plan introduced by Roosevelt, a man he despised, drafted by Hoover's own people on principles he had originally proposed, had in the space of a week restored confidence that had eluded poor old Hoover in three years of fighting the Depression.

Raymond Moley would later write of that week, "Capitalism was saved in eight days." He was only half right. The rescue plan may have saved the banking system. But the tasks of getting the factories across the country producing once again and of putting average Americans back to work still remained.

Over the next three months—the celebrated "first hundred days"—Roosevelt bombarded Congress and the country with new legislation. On March 20, Congress passed the Economy Act, which cut the salaries of public employees by 15 percent, slashed department budgets by 25 percent, and cut almost a billion dollars in public expenditures. At the end of March, it approved the creation of the Civilian Conservation Corps to employ young men in flood control, fire prevention, and the building of fences, roads, and bridges in rural areas. In the middle of May came the Emergency Relief Act and that same day Congress passed the Agricultural Adjustment Act, designed to push agricultural prices higher by controlling production and reducing acreage. The Tennessee Valley Authority was set up to build dams and construct public power plants. The National Industrial Recovery Act was passed in the middle of June to permit price fixing. It also authorized $3.5 billion in public works programs. The Glass-Steagall Act, also passed in the middle of June, divorced commercial and investment banking and guaranteed bank deposits up to a maximum of $2,500, while the Truth-in-Securities Act established disclosure provisions to govern the issue of new securities.

The string of measures was a strange mixture of well-meaning steps at social reform, half-baked schemes for quasi-socialist industrial planning, regulation to protect consumers, welfare programs to help the hardest hit, government support for the cartelization of industry, higher wages for some, lower wages for others, on the one hand government pump priming, on the other public economy. Few elements were well thought out, some were contradictory, large parts were ineffectual. While much of the legislation was very laudable, aimed as it was at improving social justice and bringing a modicum of economic security to people who had none, it had little to do with boosting the economy. Tucked away, however, in this whole motley baggage, as a last-minute amendment to the Agricultural Adjustment Act, was one step that succeeded beyond anyone's wildest expectations in getting the economy moving again. This was the temporary abandonment of the gold standard and the devaluation of the dollar.

The rescue of the banks had been brought about by one of the oddest partnerships in the history of economic policy making—between a Democratic treasury secretary and his Republican predecessor. Devaluation involved one of the strangest confrontations in that history. On one side stood the top echelon of presidential economic advisers, a brilliant group of young men, most of them new to government, the "hard money" men, as they were colloquially referred to in the press. At Treasury was Woodin's undersecretary, the polished and urbane forty-year-old Dean Acheson, son of the Protestant Episcopal bishop of Connecticut, a graduate of Groton, Yale, and Harvard Law School, a protégé of Felix Frankfurter and clerk for Justice Louis Brandeis at the Supreme Court. Though he knew little about economics—and with his British colonel's mustache and his tweed bespoke suits, he looked like an old fogy—Acheson had a reputation as an outstanding corporate lawyer, a pragmatist with an incisive brain and a talent for crafting solutions to complex problems.

The adviser to the president on monetary affairs was the thirty-seven-year-old James Warburg, son of Paul Warburg, the father of the Federal Reserve System. After graduating from Harvard, the debonair Warburg embarked upon a stellar career in banking, becoming the youngest chief executive on Wall Street while still finding time to publish his poetry in the *Atlantic Monthly* and write the lyrics to a Broadway musical, *Fine and Dandy*. He had turned down Acheson's job as undersecretary of the treasury, preferring to exert his influence as an unpaid and untitled adviser to the president, who liked to refer to him as "the white sheep of Wall Street."

And finally, the hardest-currency man of them all was the thirty-eight-year-old budget director, Lewis W. Douglas. Scion of an Arizona mining family, Douglas had taught at Amherst and since 1927 had been in Congress, where he had championed the cause of government economy and balanced budgets during the Depression.

The spokesman for Wall Street should have been the head of the Federal Reserve Board, Eugene Meyer. But he found himself completely out of sympathy with the new administration and submitted his resignation at the end of March. As a consequence, Harrison of the New York Fed acted as the primary go-between for bankers and the White House.

Every one of Roosevelt's advisers, including Harrison, believed that having stabilized the banking system, they could rely on the traditional levers—expanding credit, undertaking open market operations—to get the economy moving again. Most important, none of them could see any reason for breaking with gold.

Pitted against this array of economic expertise was one man—the president himself. Roosevelt did not even pretend to grasp fully the subtleties of international finance; but unlike Churchill, he refused to allow himself to be in the least bit intimidated by the subject's technicalities—when told by one of his advisers that something was impossible, his response was "Poppycock!" Instead, he approached the subject with a sort of casual insouciance that his economic advisers found unnerving but which nevertheless allowed him to cut through the complications and go to the heart of the matter.

His simplistic view was that since the Depression had been associated with falling prices, recovery could only come about when prices began going the other way. His advisers patiently tried to explain to him that he had the causality backward—that rising prices would be the result of recovery, not its cause. They were themselves only half right. For in an economy where everything is connected, there is often no clear distinction between cause and effect. True, in the initial stages of the Depression the collapse in economic activity had driven prices downward. But once in motion, falling prices created their own dynamic. By raising the real cost of borrowing, they had discouraged investment and thus caused economic activity to weaken further. Effect became cause and cause became effect. Roosevelt would have been unable to articulate all the linkages very clearly. But he had an intuitive understanding that the key was to reverse the process of deflation and kept insisting that the solution to the Depression was to get prices moving upward.

There still remained a chicken-and-egg problem. How to get prices up without first having to wait for economic recovery? Several years before when Roosevelt needed help with the trees on his estate in Hyde Park, his Hudson Valley neighbor and friend Henry Morgenthau introduced him to an obscure fifty-nine-year-old economist, George Warren, professor of farm management at Cornell, under whom Morgenthau had studied as an undergraduate.

The short and stocky professor, with his owlish spectacles, Quaker-like earnest demeanor and a bunch of pencils protruding from his top pocket, had none of the earthiness that one might associate with an expert in farming. He had in fact grown up herding sheep on a Nebraska ranch and still lived firmly rooted to the soil on a five-hundred-acre working farm outside Ithaca, New York, where he raised cash crops and a large herd of Holstein cows. He had published a variety of books and pamphlets on agriculture, including a monograph titled *Alfalfa* and another, *An Apple Orchard Survey of Wayne and Orleans County, New York*, which exhaustively documented the various techniques for growing apples in upstate New York, down to which manures worked the best; a standard textbook, *Dairy Farming*; and two seminal works, *The Elements of Agriculture* and *Farm Management*. He had also devised a system for inducing chickens to lay more eggs. As a teacher, he was known to be dismissive of theories and made a point of taking his students out to working farms. His quaint pastoral homilies on these visits had become part of the Cornell folklore—"You paint a barn roof to preserve it. You paint a house to sell it. And you paint the sides of barn to look at"—although none of his students were quite sure what they meant.

During the 1920s, as agricultural prices kept falling, this expert on cows, trees, and chickens had also spent a decade researching the determinants of commodity price trends. In 1932, he and a colleague published their work in an exhaustive monograph titled *Wholesale Prices for 213 Years: 1720–1932*, which created enough of a stir that, in 1933, it was issued as a book. Warren was able to document how trends in commodity prices correlated strongly with the balance between the global supply and demand for gold. When large gold discoveries came onto the world market and supply outpaced demand, commodity prices tended to rise. By contrast, when new supply lagged behind, this showed up in declining prices for commodities. It was easy to quibble with some of the details of the thesis—the correlation was not perfect because a variety of other factors, not least of which were wars, intervened to blur the link. Nevertheless, it was hard to argue with the general conclusion. After all, under the gold standard, there was supposed to be a direct connection between bank credit and gold reserves—thus when gold was plentiful, so was credit, which in turn caused prices to rise.

It was Warren's policy conclusions, however, that generated the most controversy. If commodity prices fell because of a shortage of gold, he argued, then one way to raise them was to raise the price of gold—in other words, to devalue the dollar. An increase of 50 percent in the price of bullion was no different in its effects from suddenly discovering 50 percent more of the metal. Both brought about a higher value of gold within the credit system and both would therefore stimulate higher commodity prices.

It sounded simple, but to most of Roosevelt's economic advisers, talk of devaluation was plain blasphemy, smacking of the worst forms of repudiation. How was this different from the practice of clipping and debasing coins adopted by insolvent monarchs in the Middle Ages? Given its vast gold reserves, the United States had little reason to resort to this currency manipulation, which might threaten confidence in the credit standing of the U.S. government and even endanger rather than promote recovery.

During the first few weeks of the administration, following the proclamation suspending gold exports on Roosevelt's first day in office, the currency situation remained in limbo. Secretary Woodin tried to reassure everyone that the United States had not left the gold standard, but the president was not so unequivocal. At his first press conference, on March 8, he joked with reporters, "As long as nobody asks me whether we are off the gold standard or gold basis, that is all right, because nobody knows what the gold basis or gold standard really is."

On the evening of April 18, he gathered his economic advisers in the Red Room at the White House to discuss preparations for the forthcoming World Economic Conference in London. With a chuckle, Roosevelt casually turned to his aides and said "Congratulate me. We are off the gold standard." Displaying the Thomas amendment to the Agricultural Adjustment Act, which gave the president the authority to devalue the dollar against gold by up to 50 percent and to issue $3 billion in greenbacks without gold backing, he announced that he had agreed to support the measure.

"At that moment hell broke lose in the room," remembered Raymond Moley. Herbert Feis, the economic adviser to the State Department, looked as if he were about to throw up. Warburg and Douglas were so horrified that they began to argue with the president, scolding him as if "he were a perverse and particularly backward schoolboy." Warburg declared that the legislation was "completely hare-brained and irresponsible" and would lead to "uncontrolled inflation and complete chaos." Imperturbable as ever, Roosevelt bantered good-naturedly with them, insisting that going off gold was the best way to lift prices and that unless they did something to reflate, Congress would take matters in its own hands.

The discussion continued until midnight. Leaving the White House, a group of aides—Warburg, Douglas, Moley, and William Bullitt, a special assistant to the secretary of state—having just been presented with what many of them viewed as the most fateful step since the war, were unable to sleep and continued the discussion in Moley's hotel room. They talked for half the night, analyzing the impact on the credibility of the whole New Deal program, the value of the dollar, capital flows, and relations with other countries. Finally, Douglas announced, "Well, this is the end of western civilization."

ROOSEVELT'S DECISION TO take the dollar off gold rocked the financial world. Most people could not understand why a country with the largest gold reserves in the world should have to devalue. It seemed so perverse. Indignant bankers lamented the loss of the one anchor that could keep governments honest. Bernard Baruch, the noted financier, went a little overboard though when he said that the move, "can't be defended except as mob rule. Maybe the country doesn't know it yet, but I think we may find that we've been in a revolution more drastic than the French Revolution."

But in the days after the Roosevelt decision, as the dollar fell against gold, the stock market soared by 15 percent. Financial markets gave the move an overwhelming vote of confidence. Even the Morgan bankers, historically among the most staunch defenders of the gold standard, could not resist cheering. "Your action in going off gold saved the country from complete collapse," wrote Russell Leffingwell to the president.

Taking the dollar off gold provided the second leg to the dramatic change in sentiment, which had begun with the bank rescue plan, that coursed through the economy that spring. Harrison, spurred into action by the threat that the government might issue unsecured currency, injected some $400 million into the banking system during the following six months. The combination of the renewed confidence in banks, a newly activist Fed, and a government that seemed intent on driving prices higher broke the psychology of deflation, a change reflected in almost every indicator. During the following three months, wholesale prices jumped by 45 percent and stock prices doubled. With prices rising, the real cost of borrowing money plummeted. New orders for heavy machinery soared by 100 percent, auto sales doubled, and overall industrial production shot up 50 percent.

If the decision to take the dollar off gold split the U.S. banking community, it unified European bankers—provoking another quip from Will Rogers: that it was obviously the best thing to do if both Britain and France were against it.

After the pound had been so humiliatingly ejected from the gold standard, Montagu Norman seemed to lose his bearings. He found himself on a road without familiar guideposts, and all his old certainties had gone. As he confessed at his annual Mansion House Speech in October 1932, "The difficulties are so great, the forces are so unlimited, precedents are so lacking, that I approach the whole subject in ignorance. . . . It is too great for me—I will admit that for the moment the way, to me, is not clear."

Though the press still continued to be oddly fascinated by him, the tone of the coverage had changed—it was now tinged with a hint of mockery. When he came to the United States in August 1932, *Time* magazine described him as "a handsome, fox-bearded gentleman with a black slouch hat and the mysterious manner of the Chief Conspirator in an Italian opera." The *New York Times* scolded him for his "penchant for mysterious comings and goings, his acceptance of the alias 'Professor Clarence Skinner' to mask what purported to be a simple vacation," and "his affectation of the role of international man of mystery."

When, he dropped the pseudonym on his visit to the United States the next year, the *New York Post* could not help poking fun:

> Deport The Blighter:
>
>   We have a bone to pick with Montagu Norman, governor of the Bank of England. He has enjoyed American

hospitality for several summers, and his visits have provided copy for the press during the doldrums. Not because
the American public is interested in the Bank of England
but because Mr. Norman had the bright idea of traveling
incognito as Professor Skinner.

Mr. Norman, governor of the Bank of England, is
worth a paragraph. But Mr. Norman, governor of the Bank
of England, traveling as Professor Skinner, commanded
reams of copy. It suggested plots. It conjured up visions of
international cabals. . . .

We regard "Montagu C. Norman Lands in New York
Under His Own Name" as a threat to an established
American institution. . . . How much longer must we suf-
fer the machinations of international bankers?

Though Norman no longer dominated the stage of international finance, most of his colleagues remarked on how much easier he was to deal
with. The reason was revealed on January 20, 1933. The press uncovered
that he had applied to the Chelsea Registry Office for a marriage license.
The next day, to the great bemusement of all London, he was married at
the age of sixty-one to the thirty-three-year old Priscilla Worsthorne. Born
into an old aristocratic Roman Catholic family, she had been married once
to a rich and indolent Belgian émigré, Alexander Koch de Gooreynd, who
had adopted the anglicized name of Worsthorne. They had two sons but
were now divorced. Norman had hoped for a small private ceremony. Instead the Chelsea Registry Office was mobbed by reporters and the newly
married couple had to make a getaway by the back door and through an
almshouse. Later that afternoon to avoid the paparazzi, they escaped
Thorpe Lodge by climbing over the back garden wall.

The week that Roosevelt took the dollar off gold, Norman was away
in the Mediterranean on a belated honeymoon. On his return to London
the following week, no one could tell him what was going on. Even Har-

rison was able to provide only a little direction, telling Norman on the phone that he had been taken completely by surprise by the dollar devaluation. He himself was having to rely on the newspapers for information on currency policy, which as far as he could tell was being decided by the "whims" of the brain trust in the White House. With the president's hands on the lever, the Fed itself was now "completely in the dark as to what our policy is or is to be." Meanwhile, Meyer had resigned from the Fed Board, which was now hardly functioning, and Morgans was supporting the president's inflation policy.

It was hard for Norman to know how to respond. However much he longed for the certainties of the gold standard, he had to admit that going off gold had worked for Britain. The country had benefited enormously from the 30 percent fall in the pound. The sinking currency had insulated the local economy from the worldwide chaos of late 1931 and 1932—while prices in the rest of the world had fallen 10 percent during 1932, in Britain they actually rose by a couple of percentage points. Moreover, once the need to keep the pound pegged to gold had been removed, Norman had been able to cut interest rates to 2 percent. The combination of the end to deflation, cheap money at home, and a lower pound abroad, making British goods more competitive in world markets, touched off an economic revival. Britain was thus the first major country to lift itself out of depression.

Norman, however, drew a distinction between the situation of Britain, which had been forced off gold by its weak international position, and the situation of the United States, which with its enormous bullion reserves could play the leadership role in the world economy. He feared that the United States was now abdicating that position, that the dollar devaluation might be a first predatory step in a full-scale currency war as countries tried to weaken their exchange rates in order to steal markets from one another and that the world might be entering a period of monetary anarchy.

While Norman was worried about what the dollar move might mean for Britain, he at least shared Roosevelt's belief that falling prices were the cause of the Depression. Clément Moret, the governor of the Banque de France, saw the world in very different terms. For France, the last major power still clinging to gold, the fall in the dollar was a disaster. By undervaluing the franc during the 1920s and thus undercutting its competitors in world markets, France had managed to sidestep the collapse of the world economy in 1929 and 1930. It was now having the tables turned on it. It had been hit hard when sterling was knocked out of the gold standard in 1931. The U.S. devaluation compounded the problem. France now risked being left stranded as the highest cost producer of all the major powers in the world.

Moret, however, refused to subscribe to the view that the solution was to inject more money into the system. For him the source of the world's economic problems was a lack of confidence brought on precisely by too much experimentation with money. Having been scarred so badly by their experience in the early 1920s, French monetary officials believed, with all the fervor and dogmatism of reformed alcoholics, that the path to recovery was a generalized return to the gold standard. In Moret's case, his orthodoxy in economic matters was not mere theorizing. He practiced it in his personal life. After a twenty-five-year career as an official in the Ministry of Finance, he had grown so used to living modestly that in the years since he was appointed governor of the Banque de France, he had ended up saving 85 percent of his $20,000 a year salary. It was all invested in French gold bonds.

Roosevelt's decision to devalue came just a few weeks before a long-planned World Economic Conference was scheduled to open in London. It had originally been conceived under Hoover, who, believing that the Depression originated with international problems, thought that a global conference might be the answer. In the event, the London conference proved to be a complete fiasco, the last of that long line of disastrous summits that had begun in Paris in 1919.

It started with the usual squabbles about the agenda. The British wanted to talk about war debts. The Americans refused, presumably on the principle that one cannot be forced into concessions about something one will not discuss. As a tactic for debt collecting, it did not work. France had already stopped making payments on its war debts. Britain would make a token payment that June, in the middle of the conference, and then also stop paying. The only country that eventually paid the Americans in full was Finland.

After the U.S. break from gold, the only thing that everyone—except the Americans—wanted to talk about was currency stabilization, how to prevent the dollar from falling too low. In the weeks before the meeting, as one foreign leader after another paraded through Washington in preparation for the conference, Roosevelt was his usual obtuse self. The visiting delegations all came away with the impression that the president was open to an arrangement for stabilizing the dollar. Even his own financial advisers reached that conclusion. The problem was that Roosevelt, who disliked open confrontations, had mastered the art of seeming to agree with whomever he was talking to while keeping his own cards close to his chest. He was not exactly being deceitful—he had not decided himself what to do.

The president's true attitude to the conference should have been obvious from his choices for the U.S delegation. Even by the insular standards of the Congress, they were singularly unqualified to represent their country in an international forum. Secretary of State Cordell Hull led the team, accompanied by James M. Cox, former governor of Ohio; Senator James Couzens of Michigan, a noted protectionist; Senator Key Pittman of Nevada, a longtime believer in inflation and advocate of the remonetization of silver; Ralph W. Morrison of Texas, a bigwig in Democratic Party finances; and Samuel D. McReynolds, a congressmen from Tennessee. None of them had ever been to an international conference before, most of them knew little or nothing of economic matters, and three were isolationists convinced that the whole exercise was bound to fail.

The conference opened on June 12 in the Geological Museum in South Kensington. Of the sixty-seven nations invited, all but one accepted—poor little Panama replied that it had insufficient funds to pay for its delegates. Attending the conference were one king—Feisal of Iraq—eight prime ministers, twenty foreign ministers, and eighty other cabinet members and heads of central banks. Even Foreign Commissar Maxim Maximovitch Litvinov of the Soviet Union, which had almost completely cut itself off from the world economy, decided to attend.

While the American delegates may not have matched these luminaries in prestige, they made up for it in colorfulness, Senator Pittman in particular providing great fodder for scandalmongers. At an official reception at Windsor Castle, he broke with all social convention by wearing his raincoat and a pair of bright yellow bulbous-toed shoes while being presented to King George V and Queen Mary, greeting them with the salutation, "King, I'm glad to meet you. And you too Queen." He was usually drunk but even then amazed everyone by his ability to spit tobacco juice into a spittoon from a great distance with remarkable accuracy. One night he was discovered by floor waiters at Claridges sitting stark naked in the sink of the hotel pantry, pretending to be a statue in a fountain. Another night, he amused himself by shooting out the streetlamps on Upper Brook Street with his pistol. Pittman did take one subject seriously—the remonetization of silver, of which Nevada was a major producer—an issue about which he was so passionate that one evening when one of the American experts expressed a contrary opinion on its merits, Pittman pulled out a gun and chased the poor man through the corridors of Claridges. For his part, Congressman McReynolds paid only the most cursory of attention to the business of the conference and rarely attended any meetings. He spent his energies on getting his daughter presented at court, at one point threatening the prime minister's private secretary that the American delegation would pack up and go home unless the desired invitation from the palace arrived.

The first big spat of the conference was over the chairmanship. Before they sailed for Europe, the Americans had been led to believe that they had been promised the chair. In London they discovered that the French finance minister, Georges Bonnet, coveted the post. After all, this was a conference about international money and France was the sole great power still on the gold standard. "With Washington committed to devaluation we cannot have an American as monetary chairman," declared Bonnet.

"With France committed to repudiation," replied James Cox, referring to the French default on war debts, "we cannot have a Frenchman." It was all downhill from there.

In the first few days of the conference as more than a thousand people crammed into the small and poorly ventilated museum, each nation was permitted a fifteen-minute opening statement—which, allowing for translations, occupied four whole days. Supporting the American delegation was a team of financial experts, which included Warburg, Harrison, and Oliver Sprague, professor of economics at Harvard, Roosevelt's old economics teacher, a longtime adviser to the Bank of England and now an adviser to the U.S. Treasury. They had all arrived in London believing—perhaps because they wanted to believe it—that the president had given them a mandate to negotiate an arrangement to stabilize currencies. But recognizing that a debate about key currencies in a forum of a thousand delegates would quickly deteriorate into incoherence, they decided to take the discussion offstage. Led by the three major central bankers of the conference—Harrison of the New York Fed, Norman of the Bank of England, and Moret of the Banque de France—a select band gathered out of the limelight at the Bank of England to hammer out an arrangement for stabilizing currencies. For a few days it looked as if the "Most Exclusive Club in the World" was back in business.

They had almost reached agreement—it would have involved allowing the pound to remain some 30 percent below its original gold standard level, the dollar to be propped up at some 20 percent below its par value, and the franc to remain at parity, thus leaving Britain with a modest cost advantage and setting the floor to currencies, which the French were demanding—when word leaked out. Though they had only agreed to a temporary attempt at currency stability for a period limited to the duration of the conference, New York financial markets, fearing a return to the gold standard and the end of Roosevelt's experiment with inflation, took a tumble. Commodity prices fell 5 percent and the Dow swooned by 10 percent. Roosevelt, who by now had begun taking his cue from the commodity exchanges and stock markets, dispatched a cable to the American delegates curtly reminding them that they were there to focus on plans for economic recovery and were not to be sidetracked by the European obsession with currency stabilization.

Moreover, the White House went out of its way to disavow any knowledge of Harrison's activities, pointedly reminding reporters that he was not a representative of the government but of the New York Fed, an independent entity. With the rug pulled out from underneath him and feeling betrayed, Harrison returned to New York—he told friends that "he felt as if he had been kicked in the face by a mule." It was a lesson that the old days of the "Most Exclusive Club in the World," when central bankers meeting in private could set credit and currency conditions without reference to politicians, were now gone.

The American experts in London still had a hard time getting the message. By the end of June, a new yet more innocuous agreement was negotiated with the British and the French, this time by Warburg and Moley. It committed no one to anything. It merely expressed the intention of the parties to return the pound and the dollar to the gold standard at an unspecified exchange rate and at an unspecified date when the time was right. Again as word of the new agreement came over the wires, New York financial markets expressed their discomfort.

Roosevelt was on his summer yachting holiday with Morgenthau aboard the schooner *Amberjack II* off the coast of New England. As he torpedoed this new agreement, he made sure on this occasion not to mince his words. "I would regard it as a catastrophe amounting to a world tragedy," he cabled from the naval destroyer *Indianapolis*, which had been escorting his boat "if the greatest conference of nations, called to bring about a real and permanent financial stability . . . allowed itself a purely artificial and temporary expedient. . . ." Condemning the "old fetishes of so-called international bankers . . . ," he declared that the current plans for stabilization were based on a "specious fallacy." Though Roosevelt would later concede that his choice of words for a cable to be publicly released to the whole conference was a little too strong, he had at least finally got his point across with brutal clarity. He would not allow international considerations to stand in the way of getting the U.S. economy moving again, and devaluation of the dollar was the key to revival.

Maynard Keynes was among the few economists to applaud Roosevelt's decision. In an article in the *Daily Mail* headlined "President Roosevelt Is Magnificently Right," he hailed the message as an invitation "to explore new paths" and "to achieve something better than the miserable confusion and unutterable waste of opportunity in which an obstinate adherence to ancient rules of thumb has engulfed us."

Thereafter the conference limped to a sad close. A disillusioned Warburg resigned, saying, "We are entering upon waters for which I have no charts and in which I therefore feel myself an utterly incompetent pilot."

Roosevelt was still not finished. By October 1933, though the dollar had fallen by more than 30 percent, commodity prices began to sink again and the economy started to stall once more. Roosevelt decided that it was time for a new initiative. Warren's original proposal to devalue the dollar had been controversial enough. Now the professor recommended that the government give the dollar another nudge downward by itself buying gold in the open market.

On October 22, Roosevelt told the country in another of his fireside chats, "Our dollar is altogether too greatly influenced by the accidents of international trade, by the internal policies of other nations and by political disturbances in other continents. Therefore the United States must take firmly in its own hands the control of the gold value of the dollar." Whereas the first fireside chat had brought clarity to a complex issue, this one was a masterpiece of obfuscation. The following day the government started to buy gold.

Every one of the president's economic advisers was opposed to the policy. Secretary Woodin had fallen fatally ill with cancer and Undersecretary Acheson was acting for him. Though the punctilious Acheson believed that the new policy was in fact against the law, he decided to sit on his objections temporarily in the hope of heading off even worse policies. Even so he was contemplating resigning when Roosevelt, falsely suspecting that he might be the source of newspaper leaks critical of the gold purchases, fired him. In a surprise appointment, Henry Morgenthau, the man who had first brought George Warren to Washington, became acting secretary of the treasury. In the following weeks, Professor Sprague also resigned from the Treasury, no doubt disappointed at his former student's failure to grasp the fundamentals of monetary economics.

Every morning at nine o'clock, Morgenthau; Jesse Jones, the head of the RFC; and George Warren would meet with the president over his breakfast of soft-boiled eggs, to determine the price of gold for that day. They began at $31.36 an ounce. The next morning this increased to $31.54, then $31.76 and $31.82. No one had a clue how they went about setting the price, although everyone presumed that some subtle analyses of the world bullion and foreign exchange markets went into their calculations. In fact, the choice of price was completely random. All they were trying to do was push the price a little higher than the day before. The exercise brought out the juvenile in Roosevelt. One day he picked an increase of 21 cents, and when asked why, replied that it was a lucky number, three times seven.

Everyone wanted to know more about the mysterious "crack-brained" economist of whose theories Roosevelt had become so enamored. Much to the dismay of the publicity-shy Warren, his face appeared on the cover of *Time* magazine. Reporters finally managed to track down the elusive professor who had taken leave from Cornell; he was living at the Cosmos Club in Washington and worked from an office in the Commerce Building with an unlisted phone number. There were no files in the office—he carried all his research in his briefcase and slipped in and out of the White House through one of the side entrances. Anyone knocking at the door would be greeted with a cry, "Not in!"

As the bridge between the government and the markets, it was Harrison at the New York Fed who actually had to buy the gold. Here was a man trained to believe that nothing was more sacrosanct than the value of the currency, a protégé of one of the key architects of the postwar gold standard, being asked to weaken the dollar as an act of policy. It was, as one journalist put it, "like asking a sworn teetotaler to swallow a bottle of gin."

Harrison was by nature a diplomat. With Wall Street mocking the president for allowing currency policy to fall into the hands of an expert on chickenfeed, it required all his tact and diplomatic skills to act as the intermediary between the bankers and a White House that was breaking every monetary convention in the rule book. When Harrison first informed Norman of the new policy, the British central banker "hit the ceiling." "This is the most terrible thing that has happened. The whole world will be put into bankruptcy," he exclaimed. Roosevelt and Morgenthau both roared with laughter at the thought of "old pink whiskers"—Roosevelt's nickname for Norman—and the other "foreign bankers, with everyone of their hairs standing on end with horror."

During November and December 1933, Harrison and the president would talk on the telephone several times a week, sometimes several times a day. Though Harrison thought that Warren's ideas were complete bunkum, he gradually found himself succumbing to Roosevelt's seductive charm, even becoming an honorary associate member of the president's circle. And so while all the other hard-currency men who had come in with the new administration—Warburg, Sprague, Acheson, Moley—resigned or were fired, Harrison hung in there, convinced that if he went, Roosevelt might come up with some even more harebrained scheme; or even worse, that Congress would get into the act. And he feared the inflationists in Congress more than Roosevelt's predilection for wacky ideas.

THE THREE-MONTH interlude in which Roosevelt spent his breakfast hours managing the world's gold price represents one of the more bizarre episodes in the history of currency policy. It undermined the dignity of the office of president and diminished respect for him abroad. Even Maynard Keynes, who was in favor of managed currencies, dismissed the exercise as "the gold standard on the booze." But at least the dollar staggered in the right direction.

By the end of the year, Roosevelt had begun to tire of the game; and in January 1934 he agreed to stabilize gold at $35 to the ounce. The dollar had now been devalued by over 40 percent. And while the high priests of Wall

Street had prophesied chaos, Roosevelt's instincts were vindicated. Devaluation changed the whole dynamic of the economy.

This worked in two ways. First, as Warren had predicted, the fall in the dollar did get prices moving upward—by roughly 10 percent per annum. Once prices began rising, the burden of interest payments and the real cost of money were automatically reduced, making businesses more willing to borrow and consumers more ready to spend. By thus shaking the country out of its funk, the dollar move reversed expectations out of their vicious and self-fulfilling downward spiral into a virtuous circle pointing the other way. For as the economy developed momentum, the recovery fed on itself.

Devaluation not only changed the dynamic of spending, it also supplied the fuel to power those expenditures. In the four years after 1933, the value of gold held by the Fed almost tripled, to $12 billion, in part due to the higher value of the existing stock of gold, in part to new inflows of gold from abroad—over $5 billion of additional bullion arrived in the country. Some of this was drawn from other central banks. But most came from the ground, as the higher price spurred the mining industry—worldwide gold production added almost $1 billion a year to world reserves. A high fraction of this additional liquidity went into building up the reserves of banks, which, scarred by the years from 1931 to 1933, took a long time to regain their nerve. Nevertheless, there was enough money flooding through the system that it percolated through to the rest of the economy.

As a consequence, during Roosevelt's first term, U.S. industrial production doubled and GDP expanded by 40 percent—the largest peacetime increase in economic activity in a presidential term. The expansion did not occur in a straight line and was not uniform. Confidence was still fragile and recovery thus subject to fits and starts. Investment did not rebound as much as consumption—for many of the New Deal policies to support wages hurt both profits and general business confidence. The economic indicator, which took the longest to recover, was employment. Even while production doubled in four years, the number of unemployed remained stubbornly high—by 1936, there were still ten million men without jobs.

Again, many of Roosevelt's measures to boost prices or wages by govern-ment fiat raised the cost of hiring workers and hampered recovery. Because the contraction had gone so deep, it still took ten years for the economy to regain its old trend.

While the rebound was powered by an abundance of money at low interest rates, the Fed found itself ejected from the driving seat. Having made such a mess during the collapse, it had lost whatever prestige it once possessed.

In 1935, Congress passed a banking act designed to reform the Federal Reserve. Authority for all major decisions was now centralized in a restruc-tured Board of Governors. The regional reserve banks were stripped of much of their powers and responsibility for open market operations was now vested in a new committee of twelve, comprising the seven governors and a rotating group of five regional bank heads, renamed presidents. The secretary of the treasury and the comptroller of the currency were removed from the Board, giving it theoretically even greater independence from an administration. While these measures improved the efficiency of the Fed's decision-making machinery, they came ironically enough at a time when there were few decisions to take. In 1934, Marriner Eccles, a Mormon banker from Utah, had taken over as the head of the Federal Reserve Board. Scarred by the experiences of running a bank during the Great Depression, Eccles held to the view that with unemployment still high and confidence still weak, the Fed's prime task should be to keep interest rates as low as possible.

Though the New York Fed lost much of its clout and was now over-shadowed by the Board in Washington, George Harrison soldiered on as its president for another eight years. In 1941, he left to become the chief executive of the New York Life Insurance Company. During World War II, he was asked by his old friend Henry Stimson, now secretary of war, to become his special assistant for matters related to the Manhattan Project. He served on the Interim Committee, a secret high-level group formed in May 1945 to examine problems related to the creation of the atomic bomb and to advise on its use against Japan. On July 16, after the successful detonation of the world's first nuclear device in the New Mexico desert, it was Harrison who was the author of the now-famous cable to Secretary Stimson and President Truman at Potsdam: "Operated on this morning. Diagnosis is not complete but results seem satisfactory and already exceed expectations."

After the war he returned to the New York Life Company. Like so many central bankers, he married late—at the age of fifty-three—to Mrs. Alice Grayson, widow of his old friend Admiral Grayson, who had been Woodrow Wilson's doctor and accompanied him to the Paris Peace Conference. Harrison died in 1958 at the age of seventy-one.

22. THE CARAVANS MOVE ON

1933-44

If a man will begin with certainties, he shall end in doubts; but if he will be content to begin with doubts, he shall end in certainties.

—FRANCIS BACON

BREAKING with the dead hand of the gold standard was the key to economic revival. Britain did so in 1931 and began its recovery that year. The United States followed in March 1933 and that proved to be the low point in its depression. France hung on to its link with gold for the longest. In 1935, Clément Moret was fired as governor of the Banque de France for resisting government measures to utilize its gold reserves to expand credit. Only in the following year did France finally abandon the gold standard. It was thus the last of the major economies to emerge from depression.

The exception to this pattern was Germany. After the summer 1931 crisis, it defaulted on reparations and introduced exchange controls. But it never officially left the gold standard. Still obsessed by an archaic fear of inflation, a carryover from 1923, and despite having no gold reserves, Germany decided to act as if it were still on gold, nailing itself to a sort of shadow standard and thereby forgoing the benefits of a cheap currency.

Schacht with Adolf Hitler

FIGURE 8

Industrial Production: 1925–36
1929 = 100

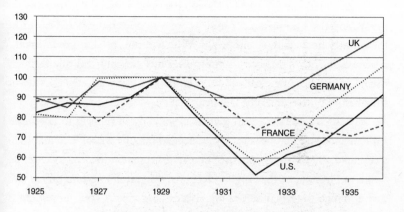

**Recovery in each country only began
after it left the gold standard.**

When Britain devalued the pound in September, German foreign trade completely collapsed.

The continued economic slide in 1932 precipitated even more political turmoil. In May 1932, Brüning was turned out of office by a right-wing cabal. The following month, France and Britain, finally recognizing that it was impossible to squeeze any money out of Germany in the current environment, formally agreed to forgive all reparations. In the fourteen years since these had first been imposed, the Allies, who had once demanded $32 billion, and had settled on $12 billion, had succeeded in collecting a grand total of $4 billion from their old enemy.

Brüning was replaced by Franz von Papen, an ex-cavalry officer from an impoverished aristocratic family who had married into wealth and whose only talent was his horsemanship. In August, he called new elections, in which the Nazis won 230 seats, more than double their previous representation, making them the largest party in the Reichstag. But President Von Hindenburg was not yet ready to invite the "Bohemian Corporal," as he referred to Hitler, to become chancellor.

In 1931, Hjalmar Schacht had been interviewed by the American journalist Dorothy Thompson. "If Hitler comes to power, the Nazis can't run the country financially, economically. Who will run it?" she asked. "I will," replied Schacht. "The Nazis cannot rule, but I can and will rule through them." It had become clear to him even then that it was only a matter of time before Hitler would become chancellor.

Schacht would later claim that he never allowed himself to fall under Hitler's spell and that because Hitler needed him, he was able to maintain a certain degree of independence. This is not apparent in a creepy letter he wrote to Hitler after the August elections, congratulating him on his victory and regretting that he was not already chancellor: "Your movement is carried internally by so strong a truth and necessity that victory in one form or another cannot elude you for long. During the time of the rise of your movement you did not let yourself be led astray by false gods. . . . If you remain the man that you are the success cannot elude you for long." But the main purpose of the letter was to urge Hitler to avoid becoming entangled in economic ideology—for Schacht realized that if he wanted to run Nazi economic policy, he would have to counteract some of the anticapitalist sloganeering of the party's left. At this stage he believed that its virulently anti-Semitic ragings were restricted to a lunatic fringe. He ended by saluting Hitler "with a vigorous Heil."

Over the next few months, as the Nazis maneuvered to undermine successive governments in the Reichstag, Schacht became a prominent supporter of the movement and a major fund-raiser for the party. In November, he was one of twenty-four industrialists, including the steel magnate Fritz Thyssen and the arms manufacturer Gustav Krupp, who signed a public letter urging Von Hindenburg to appoint Hitler chancellor. In an interview carried in newspapers around the world, Schacht declared that Hitler was "the only man fit for the Chancellorship." Finally, in January

1933, the president bowed to necessity and appointed the "Bohemian corporal" as chancellor.

Two months later, on March 16, 1933, Schacht was back at the Reichsbank, after a three-year hiatus. Hitler, who showed little interest in economics, had two overriding objectives—to combat unemployment and to find the money to rearm. The details of how to achieve these goals he left to Schacht, who in those early years was given almost complete control over economic policy—in addition to being president of the Reichsbank, he became minister of the economy in August 1934. Hitler would later confess that he thought Schacht "a man of quite astonishing ability . . . unsurpassed in the art of getting the better of the other party. But it was just his consummate skill in swindling other people which made him indispensable at the time."

Displaying the inventive genius that distinguished him as the most creative central banker of his era, immediately upon taking office, Schacht threw the whole baggage of orthodox economics overboard. He embarked on a massive program of public works financed by borrowing from the central bank and printing money. It was a remarkable experiment in what would come to be known as Keynesian economics even before Maynard Keynes had fully elaborated his ideas. Over the next few years, as the German economy experienced an enormous injection of purchasing power, it underwent a remarkable rebound. Unemployment fell from 6 million at the end of 1932 to 1.5 million four years later. Industrial production doubled over the same period. Schacht also renegotiated the terms of Germany's massive foreign debts, ruthlessly playing off its creditors against one other, particularly the British and the Americans.

The recovery was not quite the miracle that Nazi propagandists made everyone believe it was. Though there were some highly visible achievements—the creation of millions of jobs, the construction of the famed autobahns—the boom remained stunted and lopsided. Much of the increase in production came in arms-related industries, such as autos, chemicals, steel, and aircraft, while such everyday consumer items as clothing, shoes, and furniture stagnated. As a consequence, the standard of living of ordinary Germans rose hardly at all. They had to content themselves with a drab existence of shoddy goods made of ersatz materials—sugar from sawdust, flour made with potato meal, gasoline distilled from wood, margarine from coal, and clothes made out of chemical fibers.

While other European countries let their currencies fall against gold, Schacht, motivated by a combination of concern for prestige and fear of inflation, refused to break officially from gold and devalue the Reichsmark. German goods were overpriced on the world markets and its exports stagnated. In order to cope with the pressures created by this bloated exchange rate, an elaborate system of import controls was put in place and foreign trade was largely based on barter. Under this "Schachtian" system, Germany was reoriented from an open economy integrated with the West to a closed autarkic economy connected to Eastern Europe and the Balkans, a precursor of the inefficient Soviet trade system of the 1950s and 1960s.

Behind the gleaming achievements, therefore—the autobahns, the Volkswagen, the Junker bombers, and the Messerschmitt fighter planes—the Nazi economy was a rickety machine plagued by shortages and relying heavily on rationing to allocate scarce consumer goods.

Schacht, once such a strong believer in an open Germany integrated with the West, justified himself by arguing that he had been driven to the policy of hunkering down and looking inward by a deranged international system: "The whole modern world is crazy. The system of closed national boundaries is suicidal . . . everybody here is crazy. And so am I. Five years ago I would have said it would be impossible to make me so crazy. But I am compelled to be crazy."

When he first came to power, Schacht used to say that he would be willing to make a pact with the devil in order to restore German economic strength. By the late 1930s, he began to fear he had done just that. He never joined the Nazi Party nor did he become a member of Hitler's inner circle. But as the regime's abuse of power mounted, he found himself increasingly at odds with the direction of those who ran it. He had always kept his distance from the other Nazi bigwigs—Himmler, Göring, Goebbels—

often treating them with contempt and relying on Hitler to protect him. Now he came into open conflict with them, especially over corruption.

On the Berlin cocktail circuit the rumor was that Schacht had the banknotes issued to the ministries controlled by Göring, Goebbels, and Himmler marked, thus enabling him to track how much ended up in foreign accounts. He was increasingly heard referring to the Nazis as a bunch of "criminals" and "gangsters," and even calling Hitler a "cheat and a crook."

Schacht was not above exploiting the popular irrational hatred and suspicion of Jews by peppering his speeches with anti-Semitic remarks. Nevertheless, he fought against many of the regime's more extreme policies against Jews not so much on moral grounds as out of the pragmatic fear that they were harming the economy. In 1938, he was one of the architects of a plan to allow four hundred thousand German Jews to emigrate over the coming three-year period, their assets to be expropriated and placed in a trust as collateral for bonds that were to be sold to rich Jews outside Germany. The money so raised was to be used to resettle German Jews and to subsidize German exports—a macabre extortionary scheme in effect to ransom these desperate people. It placed the international Jewish community in a quandary—whether to agree to a plan that implicitly sanctioned seizing Jewish property in Germany and Austria, channeling money to the Nazi regime and setting a precedent for other blackmail elsewhere in Europe, but which had the potential to save lives. Schacht would later defend himself by claiming that his scheme could have saved hundreds of thousands of lives—he seemed conspicuously unaware of the moral dilemmas it posed. In any case, it died for lack of money and of countries willing to accept the refugees.

By 1937, the strains of helter-skelter rearmament and deficit financing began to tell. Shortages began to bite. Schacht tried to push Hitler to go slow on the arms buildup and ease up on consumer austerity. In November 1937, after falling out with Hermann Göring, he was fired by Hitler as minister of the economy and replaced by Walter Funk, an alcoholic homosexual. Two years later, when Schacht tried to resist further central bank

financing of the ever-growing budget deficit, he was also removed from
the Reichsbank, again to be replaced by Funk. Though Hitler gave him
the titular position of minister without portfolio, this was largely window
dressing for foreigners—Schacht was still respected by the international
banking community—and he was now for all intents and purposes a private citizen.

In the years immediately before the war, Schacht took a leading part in
several of the conspiracies by conservative politicians and businessmen to
overthrow Hitler. They involved trying to induce members of the army
high command to stage a coup by convincing them that under the Nazis
Germany would be plunged into a war for which it was ill prepared. The
first took place in 1938 when Hitler tried to take over Czechoslovakia.
Plans for that pustch were aborted at the last minute when British prime
minister Neville Chamberlain and French premier Édouard Daladier
backed away from the brink by making concessions at Munich. A second
occurred in late 1939 in the weeks before the invasion of Poland. This final
conspiracy was overtaken by events before the plotters could act.

After war broke out, Schacht kept a low profile, retiring to his estate in
Gühlen away from the intrigue and paranoia of Berlin. It was ironically a
time of great personal happiness. His first wife died in 1940. They had
become estranged over time and lived apart. The following year, at the age
of sixty-four, he married a woman thirty years his junior, a museum cura-
tor whom he had met at a fashionable Munich nightclub. Over the next
three years, they had two children, both girls.

Though Schacht remained on the fringes of the resistance movement,
he was never trusted enough to be included in the inner circles. But his
name was frequently mooted as a potential successor to Hitler in the event
of a coup. In April 1944, his son-in-law Hilger von Scherpenberg, a German foreign service officer based in Stockholm, was arrested by the Ge-
stapo. Following the failed July 20 plot to assassinate Hitler, Schacht was
also arrested and imprisoned in Berlin—not because of any evidence of his
complicity but because of his potential usefulness as a hostage or an intermediary in future negotiations with the Allies. In April 1945, he was sent

to Dachau. Two weeks later, as the Allied armies advanced into Germany, he was one of a group of high-value prisoners, including Prince Philip of Hesse: the French ex-prime minister Léon Blum and his wife; General Franz Halder, formerly chief of the army staff, and his wife; Fritz Thyssen, the steel baron; and Prince Frederick Leopold of Prussia, who were shipped out—to be traded as potential hostages. They were finally liberated by the Allies from a camp in the southern Tyrol.

Instead of greeting Schacht as a hero, the Americans arrested him, and he was among the twenty-four major figures to be prosecuted at Nuremberg. Furious at being lumped in with the "gangsters" of the Nazi regime, he insisted that he was different, that he had acted only in self-defense to protect Germany against the Allied economic stranglehold and had broken with the führer once he realized war was inevitable. A prison psychologist describes Schacht losing his temper one day and ranting, "Don't forget what desperate straits the Allies drove us into. They hemmed us in from all sides—they fairly strangled us! Just try to imagine what a cultured people like the Germans has to go through to fall for a demagogue like Hitler. . . . All we wanted was some possibility for export, for trade, to live somehow. . . ."

In the lead-up to the trial, each of the defendants was subject to extensive interrogation, a battery of psychiatric interviews, and even an intelligence test—Schacht achieving the highest score, 143. During the ensuing trial, he found it hard to disguise his fury. The novelist John Dos Passos described him as glaring "like an angry walrus" during the whole proceedings. Rebecca West wrote that he sat "twisted in his seat so that his tall body, stiff as a plank, was propped against the side of the dock. Thus he sat at right angles to his fellow defendants and looked past them and over their heads: it was always his argument that he was far superior to Hitler's gang. He was petrified by rage because this court was pretending to have this right. He might have been a corpse frozen by rigor mortis. . . ."

Schacht and Von Papen were acquitted, on the grounds that their involvement with the Nazi regime had ended before war broke out. Three days after being released, he was rearrested by the new government of the

State of Bavaria under its de-Nazification laws. After five different trials, all of which ended without a conviction, he was finally released in 1950.

In the last few days of the war, his only son, Jens, had been captured by the Russians and was never heard of again, one of the countless German soldiers who disappeared in the death march of prisoners on the Eastern front. Destitute at the age of seventy-three, Schacht started a new life and a new career as an independent economic consultant and became an adviser to the governments of Indonesia, Egypt, and Iran. He died, substantially prosperous, in 1970, aged ninety-three. To the end he refused to concede that he had ever done anything wrong.

THE WAR MADE for strange bedfellows. The other member of the quartet, Émile Moreau, had become president of the Banque de Paris et des Pay-Bas after retiring as governor of the Banque de France in October 1930. In 1940, after the fall of France and the German occupation, Moreau was forced out by the Vichy regime for being too sympathetic to Britain—the ultimate irony for a man who at the peak of his career had done his best to undermine British dominance in finance.

Horrified at the social and ideological conflicts by which France was riven in the 1930s, Moreau became progressively more disillusioned with French republican politics and parliamentary democracy. He could not support the left, and the right was becoming more fascist by the day. Instead, he became a royalist—a quixotic commitment. Royalists were a fringe group—one poll found less than 6 percent of the French believed that the monarchy had any role whatever to play in the politics of the country.

In 1935, he took on the position of secretary to the pretender to the throne, Jean d'Orléans, duc de Guise, great-grandson of Louis Philippe, the liberally inclined king of France from 1830 to 1848. The law of exile passed in 1886 prohibited the heirs of former French dynasties from entering France, and Moreau acted as the duke's liaison in France. In 1940, when Jean d'Orléans died, his son Henri, comte de Paris, succeeded as pretender.

After the fall of France that year, Henri tried to provide a bridge between the Free French and the collaborators at Vichy and for a brief moment there was even talk that the monarchy might return. Though Moreau did his best to promote the idea, nothing came of it and the comte de Paris returned to his place on the social pages of *Paris Match*.

In 1950, the law of exile was finally repealed and the comte de Paris was allowed back to France. Moreau lived long enough to receive his beloved sovereign at his home in Paris, which subsequently became the secretariat for the comte's activities. Moreau died that November.

WHILE HJALMAR SCHACHT was propelled back into power during the 1930s, his friend Montagu Norman had to content himself with a much diminished role in British and international financial affairs. In October 1933, he crowned his annual Mansion House speech by quoting an old Arab proverb: "I console myself with this thought, that the dogs bark but the caravan moves on." In the old days it would have been viewed as one of those enigmatic Zen-like pronouncements that evidenced the governor's superior wisdom. Instead, it now provoked an outcry. The implication that his critics were no more than barking dogs unleashed a torrent of indignation directed against the entire banking and financial establishment. "They were wrong about reparations from Germany and its effects. They were wrong when they advised Mr. Churchill about the gold standard, and wrong when they pled in 1931 that the resuspension of the standard would knock the bottom out of civilization." He was increasingly viewed as an "old gentleman complaining that things were not what they were." Despite all this, he was reappointed governor for an additional eleven years—perhaps because with his authority so diminished there was little damage he could do.

In the late 1930s, he became associated with the party of appeasement. Though he was not part of the whole Cliveden set around Nancy Astor, finding the whole atmosphere of political gossip and scandal distasteful, he shared their belief that another war would just be too catastrophic to contemplate and was willing to do almost anything to avoid it. Appeasement was still then a respectable word—it had not yet come to imply cowardice or self-deception. Indeed, it was considered to be not simply a pragmatic policy but a moral one as well. In the wake of the carnage of the First World War, pacifism was much in vogue, and German anger and bitterness at the Treaty of Versailles were viewed as justified. In Norman's case this was reinforced by his preference for the diligent Germans over the treacherous French and for his admiration of Schacht, and during the early years of Nazi rule, even the achievements of Hitler—he is said to have told a Morgan partner that "Hitler and Schacht are the bulwarks of civilization in Germany."

In the last months of 1939, as war seemed increasingly likely, he lamented to the U.S. ambassador in London, Joseph Kennedy, "If this struggle goes on, England as we have known her is through. . . . Without gold or foreign assets, England's trade is going to be forced to narrow itself more and more. . . . The end is likely to be that . . . the Empire will contract in power and size to that of other nations."

During the 1930s, he and Schacht maintained their close friendship—they would meet regularly at the monthly BIS meetings in Basel. In January 1939, he visited Berlin to attend the christening of Schacht's grandson, who was named Norman in his honor. The Foreign Office tried to convince him that, in the circumstances, such a visit was undesirable, but Norman insisted on going. It was to be their last meeting. Once their two countries were at war, they could not communicate, though there were constant rumors even in official circles that they stayed in touch. After the war, while Schacht was in prison, Norman sent him food parcels. But when the German tried to come to Britain in 1950 to visit his old friend, he was denied a visa.

In 1944, during a bad fog, Norman tripped over a large granite stone at his country cottage, and after grazing his leg, developed an infection that spread to his brain. Though he recovered after an operation, his health was now seriously impaired and he was finally persuaded at the age of seventy-three to retire as governor. He was elevated to the peerage that year as Lord

Norman of St. Clere, the name of the village in Kent where his grandfather's house was located and which he had inherited from his uncle. He spent most of his last years there as an invalid. He died in 1950.

Norman himself provided the most poignant assessment of his own career. In 1948, he wrote: "As I look back, it now seems that, with all the thought and work and good intentions, which we provided, we achieved absolutely nothing . . . nothing that I did, and very little that old Ben did, internationally produced any good effect—or indeed any effect at all except that we collected money from a lot of poor devils and gave it over to the four winds."

AFTER 1931, AS Norman's star fell, that of Maynard Keynes rose. Before the breakup of the gold standard Keynes had been the maverick. After the rupture he was increasingly acknowledged to have been right not simply about the gold standard but about almost every one of the battles in which he had been engaged during the previous decade. German reparations had now been canceled; France and Britain had defaulted on war debts; and the two major central banks, the Bank of England and the Fed, had embraced a policy of keeping money deliberately cheap.

With the world economy still stuck in the Depression, Keynes took a step back from public life and began work on a new theoretical book—an attempt to understand the causes of mass unemployment. Some of the driving forces behind the Depression, such as the collapse in Germany, could be explained by country-specific factors, for example, reparations and the overhang of foreign debt. But the United States had suffered none of these problems—it was a creditor country and had ample gold reserves. That it too had been hit by a downturn as deep, in some respects deeper, as that in Europe remained a mystery. Keynes wanted to understand how an economy could get stuck in such a severe slump and what might prevent conventional corrective forces—cuts in interest rates, for example—from working.

He drew on many of the same themes that had informed much of his previous work—the pervasive effects of uncertainty, the ways in which the financial system could short-circuit the normal operations of the economy, the inherent instability caused by fluctuations in confidence. The book was not completed until late 1935, and was published, in February 1936, as *The General Theory of Employment, Interest, and Money*. By the time it came out, Britain, the United States, and Germany were all on the road to recovery and the book itself did not have much impact on immediate government policy. Nevertheless, it was to be Keynes's masterpiece. While it was not universally accepted and indeed remained bitterly disputed for many years, it transformed the understanding of the modern monetary economy and still today provides the foundation for much of the government and central banks' management of the system.

A year after *The General Theory* was published, in the spring of 1937, Keynes suffered the first of his many "heart attacks." He was diagnosed with a chronic cardiac condition caused by a bacterial infection of the heart valves. For the next three years he was almost an invalid. In 1939, he fell into the hands of a Dr. Janos Plesch, a Hungarian Jewish émigré, who, according to Keynes, was a cross between a "genius" and a "quack." In addition to some highly unorthodox protocols—three-hour sessions of ice packs placed on the chest or Dr. Plesch jumping up and down on his patient as he lay in bed—the doctor put Keynes on a course of the newly discovered and much in vogue sulfa drugs, the first and only effective antibiotic in the years before the large-scale use of penicillin. Though his heart condition was not completely cured, under the care of the eccentric Dr. Plesch—whom Lydia nicknamed "The Ogre"—Keynes was at least able to return to work.

During the 1930s, Keynes's speculative activities made him a rich man. After losing 80 percent of his money when commodity prices collapsed after 1928, he had ended 1929 with a portfolio of under $40,000. He shifted his strategy from short-term speculation to long-term investment and at the lows of the Depression put together a concentrated portfolio of a select number of British and American equities. Convinced that Roosevelt would succeed in reviving the U.S. economy, Keynes used margin to leverage his portfolio by as much as two to one. By 1936, his net worth was close to $2.5 million—the equivalent today of $30 million. Though the bear market of 1937 more than halved this, by 1943 it had recovered to $2 million.

By the late 1930s, Keynes was the most famous economist in the world and a pillar of the British establishment. He was elevated to the peerage in 1941, as Lord Keynes of Tilton, and much to the amusement of his bohemian Bloomsbury friends, was to be found regularly in attendance at the House of Lords. He was even invited to be a director of the Bank of England by his old opponent, Montagu Norman. While they continued to disagree—"I do enjoy these lunches at the Bank: Montagu Norman, always absolutely charming, always absolutely wrong," he remarked after one of his regular weekly meetings—it was now Keynes's ideas that were in the ascendancy.

When the Second World War broke out in Europe, Keynes became an unpaid economic adviser to the chancellor of the exchequer. Within a short time he was Britain's principal wartime economic strategist. Determined to avoid a repeat of the mistakes of the First World War, which had largely been financed by printing money, Keynes designed the framework for paying for this war without as much recourse to inflation. He also acted as the principal negotiator for Britain with the Americans over the scope, terms, and conditions of Lend-Lease.

In 1942, he turned his attention to planning for the postwar world. After the First World War, central bankers had tried to re-create the golden age before 1914, to which they looked back so nostalgically. Keynes, in putting together his plan for a new international monetary system, had no such illusions—no one, least of all him, looked back except with horror to the chaos of the twenties and thirties.

In developing his ideas for the postwar world, Keynes sought to create an international financial system based like the gold standard on rules while tempering its rigidity. His plan called for currencies to be "pegged but adjustable." In contrast to the gold standard, under which currency values were supposed to be immutable fixed points, countries would be allowed to alter the value of their currencies when their economic circumstances changed. He was determined to avoid the need for the sort of straitjacket policies of the twenties and thirties when Germany and Britain had been forced to hike interest rates and create mass unemployment to protect currency values that were in any case unsuitable.

A second element of the plan was an international central bank. In order to avoid the chronic shortage of gold reserves that had prevented the global financial system from functioning smoothly between the wars, Keynes proposed creating an institution that would lend money to countries in need on a temporary basis, rather like an overdraft facility at a bank.

Luckily for Keynes, the Americans began working independently on a similar conception. The architect of the U.S. plan was Harry Dexter White, the assistant secretary for international affairs at the U.S. Treasury. White had been born in Boston in 1892 of Lithuanian parents who had fled the czarist pogroms. Educated at Stanford and Harvard, he had eventually joined the Treasury in 1934 as a New Dealer and enjoyed a meteoric rise within the department through a combination of hard work, intelligence, and flattery in the right places.

Short and stocky with a round face, rimless glasses, and fleshy lips topped by a trim mustache, White was an unprepossessing man with few friends. He seemed unable to resist being overbearing and rude in his professional dealings, even to his colleagues, and he has variously been described by those who knew him as "the unpleasantest man in Washington," "a son-of-a bitch," and "an intolerable human being." Keynes, who was remarkably able to put up with people's foibles and idiosyncrasies, wrote that "he has not the faintest conception of how to behave or observe the rules of civilized discourse." But even though White was often overtly anti-British, Keynes grew to develop great respect for his incisive intelligence, his single-mindedness, and his drive.

White also happened to be a Soviet agent, originally recruited in 1935 to the same spy ring that included Whittaker Chambers and Alger Hiss. During the war, along with several colleagues at the Treasury's Division of Monetary Research, whom he talked into the cause, he did much to support the Soviet war effort and beyond. As the principal Treasury representative on interagency committees dealing with international affairs, White handled more pieces of classified information than any other single official in the administration, including the president, and passed on secrets about the whole range of U.S. financial policies to Soviet intelligence, including U.S. strategy on financial aid to the USSR. He helped the Communist cause in China by delaying payments of American aid to Chiang Kai-shek, and arranged for the U.S. government to furnish the Soviets with a duplicate set of printing plates of the currency to be issued under the Allied occupation of Germany—thereby allowing the Soviets to finance their share by printing American money with American-supplied plates. When these activities eventually came to light after the war, he insisted that he had not been a Soviet agent—he was neither a member of the Communist Party nor had he accepted any money from the Soviets—but had only been acting in the best interests of the United States, believing that the United States and the Soviet Union, allies at that time, had closely aligned objectives. But in 1942, no one was yet aware of White's secret life.

As originally conceived, the British and American plans did differ in emphasis. Keynes's plan was more ambitious in size and scope. Remembering the acute lack of liquidity during the 1920s, he wanted something closer to a world central bank with the power to create an international currency; White wanted an institution more like an international credit cooperative that would give countries access to loans, the size of which would be constrained by the amounts paid in by the other member countries. Keynes wanted the fund to be $26 billion, while White, conscious that the United States would be paying much of the bill, wanted to limit it to $5 billion; they finally compromised on $8.5 billion. Keynes also wanted to introduce a mechanism for disciplining countries that unfairly cheapened their currencies and accumulated excessive amounts of the world's reserves without recycling them, as France had done in the twenties and thirties. But the United States, fearing that in the aftermath of the war it might find itself flooded with gold, and thus be accused of underpricing its currency, would not agree.

After two years of negotiations between Keynes and White, the differences were ironed out—largely in favor of the more powerful Americans. By 1944, with much of the design work done and with the two principal Western Allies in a position to present a united front, the United States felt ready to invite some forty-four countries to a conference to discuss reconstructing the postwar international monetary system.

The United States chose to host the gathering at the Mount Washington Hotel at Bretton Woods in the White Mountains of New Hampshire. With its rural seclusion, mild summer weather, and cool high-country air, it was a perfect site for such a meeting. Built in 1902 to cater to rich Bostonians and New Yorkers escaping the summer heat of the East Coast, the hotel looked like a great Spanish castle, with white stucco walls, two large castellated turrets, and a red roof. The interior was decorated in a rich Victorian style with Tiffany stained-glass windows. Though the hotel had fallen upon hard times in the 1930s, a victim of the Depression, it had recently been bought and refurbished by a syndicate of Boston-based investors. Moreover, unlike most large hotels in the White Mountains, which did not allow Jews—inconvenient for a conference hosted by Treasury Secretary Morgenthau, himself Jewish—the Mount Washington had no such restrictions on guests.

The conference opened on June 30, 1944. In contrast to the many international summits of the interwar period, which had been characterized by a corrosive atmosphere of mistrust, Bretton Woods was a collegial, almost jovial, affair. "The flow of alcohol is appalling," wrote Keynes. With 750 delegates, and even more assistants, it was, according to Lydia Keynes, a "madhouse with most people . . . working more than humanly possible." Committees met all day, broke for evening cocktails and rounds of dinner parties, reconvening thereafter till 3:00 a.m., only to resume at 9:30 the next morning.

By the time of the Bretton Woods conference, Keynes's wartime efforts had taken a severe toll on his health. The drugs, which Plesch had prescribed, had not cured the bacterial infections in his heart, and he was now seriously sick. Lydia forbade Keynes to attend the cocktail parties and required him to take his dinner with her in their suite. Nevertheless, she contributed her own part to the madhouse atmosphere by doing ballet exercises late at night in her room and keeping other guests awake, including Mrs. Morgenthau in the suite below.

Much of the negotiating had been done prior to the conference between the Americans and the British. At Bretton Woods, the biggest controversy was over how much money each country would be eligible to borrow from what was now being called the International Monetary Fund. The Russians, who were there in strength though very few of them spoke English, demanded that their borrowing rights reflect not simply economic power but also military strength, and insisted on equality with the British; India wanted to be on a par with China; the Bolivians wanted parity with the Chileans and the Chileans with the Cubans. The United States, as the fund's prime financier, set these quotas in a series of backroom deals orchestrated by White.

On July 22, the conference came to its formal close with a great banquet. Keynes gave a final address. He reminding the participants of the economic chaos that had afflicted the world for almost a generation and paid tribute to the spirit of cooperation that had informed the discussions: "If we can so continue, this nightmare, in which most of us present have spent too much of our lives, will be over. The brotherhood of man will have become more than a phrase." As he left the room, the delegates sang "For He's a Jolly Good Fellow."

Two years later, Keynes's heart finally gave out and he died at the age of sixty-one. White was appointed the U.S. executive director of the International Monetary Fund after the war, but in 1947, under investigation by the FBI, he was forced to resign, citing ill health. The next year, after being publicly named as a Soviet agent by Whittaker Chambers, he was called to testify before the House Committee on Un-American Activities. Three days after his testimony, on August 16, 1948, he, too, collapsed and died of a heart attack at the age of fifty-six.

Nevertheless, the legacy of these two men, the international monetary arrangements known as the Bretton Woods System, fruitfully endured for another thirty years. It provided the foundations for the reconstruction of Europe and Japan after the war, it allowed the global economy to boom through much of the 1950s and 1960s without any of the financial crises that had been so much a part of its history, and it set the stage for one of the longest periods of sustained economic growth the world has ever seen.

23. EPILOGUE

*I have yet to see any problem, however complicated,
which, when looked at in the right way did not become still more complicated.*

—POUL ANDERSON

ANYONE who writes or thinks about the Great Depression cannot avoid the question: Could it happen again? First it is important to remember the scale of the economic meltdown that occurred in 1929 to 1933. During a three-year period, real GDP in the major economies fell by over 25 percent, a quarter of the adult male population was thrown out of work, commodity prices fell in half, consumer prices declined by 30 percent, wages were cut by a third. Bank credit in the United States shrank by 40 percent and in many countries the whole banking system collapsed. Almost every major sovereign debtor among developing countries and in Central and Eastern Europe defaulted, including Germany, the third largest economy in the world. The economic turmoil created hardships in every corner of the globe, from the prairies of Canada to the teeming cities of Asia, from the industrial heartland of America to the smallest village in India. No other period of peace-time economic turmoil since has even come close to approaching the depth and breadth of that cataclysm.

Part of the reason for the extent of the world economic collapse of 1929 to 1933 was that it was not just one crisis but, as I describe, a sequence of crises, ricocheting from one side of the Atlantic to the other, each one feeding off the ones before, starting with the contraction in the German economy that began in 1928, the Great Crash on Wall Street in 1929, the serial bank panics that affected the United States from the end of 1930, and the unraveling of European finances in the summer of 1931. Each of these episodes has an analogue to a contemporary crisis.

The first shock—the sudden halt in the flow of American capital to Europe in 1928 which tipped Germany into recession—has its counterpart in the Mexican peso crisis of 1994. During the early 1990s, Mexico, much like Germany in the 1920s, allowed itself to borrow too much short-term money. When U.S. interest rates rose sharply in 1994, Mexico, like Germany in 1929, found it progressively harder to roll over its loans and was confronted with a similar choice between deflation or default.

There are, of course, differences. Germany in 1928 was much larger compared to the world economy—about three times the relative economic size of Mexico in 1994.* But the biggest difference was to be found in the management of the crisis. The U.S. Treasury under Secretary Robert Rubin forestalled a default by providing Mexico an emergency credit of $50 billion with astonishing rapidity. Germany in 1929 had no such savior. Moreover, in 1994, Mexico could devalue the peso. In 1929, having only just emerged from a terrible bout of hyperinflation, Germany felt bound by gold-standard rules and sacrificed its economy to maintain the parity of the Reichsmark.

The second crisis of the series, the Great Crash, has a very obvious modern-day parallel in the fall of the stock market in 2000. Both followed a frenzied bubble in which stocks completely lost touch with economic reality, becoming grossly overvalued—by most measures 30 to 40 percent. In both cases, after the sell-off it became apparent that much of the rise had been pushed by a rogue's gallery of Wall Streeters and corporate insiders. Both resulted in similar initial losses in wealth expressed as a percent-

*German GDP in the 1920s was $15 billion, one-sixth the size of the U.S. economy. By comparison, Mexico in 1994 had a GDP of $450 billion, a little more than one-eighteenth that of a U.S. economy then of $7.5 trillion.

age of GDP—roughly 40 percent in the first year—and were followed by a sharp contraction in investment. The reaction of the authorities was not that dissimilar—in the first year after the 1929 crash interest rates in the United States were cut from 6 percent to 2 percent; in 2000 they were slashed from 6.5 percent to 2.0 percent.

The 1931–33 sequence of banking panics that started with the failure of the Bank of United States has many of the same characteristics as the current global financial crisis that began in the summer of 2007 and, as I write, is still sweeping through the world's banking system. Both originated with doubts about the safety of financial intermediaries that had sustained large losses. In 1931–33 those fears precipitated a series of bank runs, as depositors pulled their money out of banks and hoarded currency, that over a two-year period spread in waves across the United States. The present turmoil has also led to a mass run on the financial system—this time not by panicked individuals desperate to withdraw their money but by panicked bankers and investors pulling their money out of financial institutions of all stripes, not only commercial banks but investment banks, money market funds, hedge funds, and all those mysterious "off-balance-sheet special-purpose vehicles" that have sprung up over the past decade. Every financial institution that depends on wholesale funding from its peers has been threatened to a greater or lesser degree.

In some respects the current crisis is even more virulent than the banking panics of 1931–33. In the 1930s most depositors had to line up physically outside their bank to get their money. Now massive amounts of money are being siphoned off with the click of a mouse. Moreover, the world's financial system has become both larger compared to GDP and more complex and interconnected. There is much greater leverage, and many more banks rely on short-term wholesale sources of funding that can evaporate overnight. The world's banks are therefore much more vulnerable than they were then. As a result panic has swept through the system faster and more destructively.

Offsetting this has been the response of central banks and financial officials. In 1931–33 the Fed stood passively aside while thousands of banks failed, thus permitting bank credit to contract by 40 percent. In the current crisis, central banks and treasuries around the world, drawing to some degree on the lessons learned during the Great Depression, have reacted with an unprecedented series of moves to inject gigantic amounts of liquidity into the credit market and provide capital to banks. Without these measures, there is little doubt that the world's financial system would have collapsed as dramatically as it did in the 1930s. Though the net impact on credit availability of the present crisis and the remedial actions taken by central banks is still uncertain and won't be known for many months, the authorities seemed to have at least staved off a catastrophe.

Finally, the European financial crisis of 1931 also has its modern-day counterpart in the "emerging markets" crisis of 1997–98. In 1931, the evaporation of confidence in European banks and currencies caused Germany and much of the rest of Central Europe to impose capital controls and default on their debts, leading to a contagion of fear that culminated in forcing Britain off the gold standard.

In 1997, a similar sequence of rolling crises afflicted Asia. South Korea, Thailand, and Indonesia all had to suspend payments on hundreds of billions of dollars of debt. Asian currencies collapsed against the dollar, undermining all confidence in emerging-market securities and eventually setting off the default of Russia in 1998 and of Argentina two years later. But in 1931, that part of Europe affected by the crisis was about half the size of the U.S. economy; in 1997, the GDP of the emerging markets that defaulted represented about a quarter of U.S. GDP.

As with all analogies, the comparisons are never exact. Nevertheless, they illustrate the scale of the economic whirlwind of 1929–32—a crisis equivalent in scope to the combined effects and more of the 1994 Mexican peso crises, the 1997–98 Asian and Russian crises, the 2000 collapse in the stock market bubble, and the 2007/8 world financial crisis, all cascading upon one and other in a single concentrated two-year period. The world has been saved in part from anything approaching the Great Depression because the crises that have buffeted the world economy over the past decade have conveniently struck one by one, with decent intervals in between.

For many years people believed—even today many continue to do so—that an economic cataclysm of the magnitude of the Great Depression could only have been the result of mysterious and inexorable tectonic forces that governments were somehow powerless to resist. Contemporaries frequently described the Depression as an economic earthquake, blizzard, maelstrom, deluge. All these metaphors suggested a world confronting a natural disaster for which no single individual or group could be blamed. To the contrary, in this book I maintain that the Great Depression was not some act of God or the result of some deep-rooted contradictions of capitalism but the direct result of a series of misjudgments by economic policy makers, some made back in the 1920s, others after the first crises set in—by any measure the most dramatic sequence of collective blunders ever made by financial officials.

Who then was to blame? The first culprits were the politicians who presided over the Paris Peace Conference. They burdened a world economy still trying to recover from the effects of war with a gigantic overhang of international debts. Germany began the 1920s owing some $12 billion in reparations to France and Britain; France owed the United States and Britain $7 billion in war debts, while Britain in turn owed $4 billion to the United States. This would be the equivalent today of Germany owing $2.4 trillion, France owing $1.4 trillion, and Britain owing $800 billion. Dealing with these massive claims consumed the energies of financial statesmen for much of the decade and poisoned international relations. More important, the debts left massive fault lines in the world financial system, which cracked at the first pressure.

The second group to blame were the leading central bankers of the era, in particular the four principal characters of this book, Montagu Norman, Benjamin Strong, Hjalmar Schacht, and Émile Moreau. Even though they, especially Schacht and Norman, spent much of the decade struggling to mitigate some of the worst political blunders behind reparations and war

debts, more than anyone else they were responsible for the second fundamental error of economic policy in the 1920s: the decision to take the world
back onto the gold standard.

Gold supplies had not kept up with prices; and the distribution of gold
bullion after the war was badly skewed, with much of it concentrated in
the United States. The result was a dysfunctional gold standard that was
unable to operate as smoothly and automatically as before the war. The
problem of inadequate gold reserves was compounded when Europe went
back to gold at exchange rates that were grossly misaligned, resulting in
constant pressure on the Bank of England, the linchpin of the world's financial system, and a destructive and petty feud between Britain and
France that undermined international cooperation.

The quartet of central bankers did in fact succeed in keeping the world
economy going but they were only able to do so by holding U.S. interest
rates down and by keeping Germany afloat on borrowed money. It was a
system that was bound to come to a crashing end. Indeed, it held the seeds
of its own destruction. Eventually the policy of keeping U.S. interest rates
low to shore up the international exchanges precipitated a bubble in the
U.S. stock market. By 1927, the Fed was thus torn between two conflicting
objectives: to keep propping up Europe or to control speculation on Wall
Street. It tried to do both and achieved neither. Its attempts to curb speculation were too halfhearted to bring stocks back to earth but powerful
enough to cause a collapse in lending to Germany, driving most of central
Europe into depression and setting in train deflationary forces throughout
the rest of the world. Eventually in the last week of October 1929, the
bubble burst, plunging the United States into its own recession. The U.S.
stock market bubble thus had a double effect. On the way up, it created a
squeeze in international credit that drove Germany and other parts of the
world into recession. And on the way down, it shook the U.S. economy.

The stresses and strains of trying to keep the limping gold standard
going may have made some sort of financial shakeout inevitable. It was,
however, not necessary for the crisis to metastasize into a worldwide catastrophe. European central bankers had been dealing with financial crises for

more than a century. They had long absorbed the lesson that while most of the time the economy works very well left in the care of the invisible hand, during panics, that hand seems to lose its grip. Markets, particularly financial markets, became unthinkingly fearful. To reestablish sanity and restore some sort of equilibrium in these circumstances required a very visible head to guide the invisible hand. In a word, it required leadership.

After 1929, responsibility for world monetary affairs ended up in the hands of a group of men who understood none of this, whose ideas about the economy were at best outmoded and at worst plain wrong. Strong died in 1928. His successor, George Harrison, tried his best to fill his shoes but did not have the personality or the stature to assume control. Instead, authority at the Fed shifted to a group of inexperienced and ill-informed timeservers, who believed that the economy would automatically return to an even keel, that there was nothing to be done to counteract deflationary forces except wait them out. They failed to fulfill even the most basic central banker's responsibility: to act as lender of last resort and support the banking system at a time of panic.

Norman and Schacht both understood that a financial system in free-fall requires active central bank intervention. But their two central banks, the Bank of England and the Reichsbank, were both chronically short of gold and had no room for maneuver. As a consequence, for all of Norman's enormous prestige and Schacht's creativity, they were both hamstrung by the dictates of the gold standard and were forced to remain locked in with the United States, deflating as it did.

The only central banker outside the Fed with enough gold to act independently was Moreau at the Banque de France. But having stumbled inadvertently into a position of financial dominance, he seemed more intent on using France's newfound strength for political rather than economic ends. And so what began as modest and corrective recessions in the United States and Germany were transformed by sheer folly and short-sightedness into a worldwide catastrophe.

In 1934, Yale economist Irving Fisher testified before a House committee that when Strong died, "his policies died with him. I have always believed, if he had lived, we would have had a different situation." He was the first of many economists and historians to raise the tantalizing counterfactual that things would have turned out differently if Strong had lived. Though Strong was responsible for many of the errors surrounding the reestablishment of the gold standard, and for the easy money policy that led to the stock market bubble, there is little doubt that in early 1931 he would have acted more vigorously and with greater effect than his successor, George Harrison, to prevent the cascade of bank runs. Moreover, on the international front he was the only member of the quartet with the necessary combination of ability, brains, and vision but also the economic firepower of the Fed's gigantic gold reserves behind him to have assumed the leadership of the world economy and taken steps to counteract the global deflation.

More than anything else, therefore, the Great Depression was caused by a failure of intellectual will, a lack of understanding about how the economy operated. No one struggled harder in the lead-up to the Great Depression and during it to make sense of the forces at work than Maynard Keynes. He believed that if only we could eliminate "muddled" thinking—one of his favorite expressions—in economic matters, then society could allow the management of its material welfare to take a backseat to what he thought were the central questions of existence, to the "problems of life and of human relations, of creation, behavior and religion." That is what he meant when in a speech toward the end of his life he declared that economists are the "trustees, not of civilization, but of the possibility of civilization." There is no greater testament of his legacy to that trusteeship than that in the sixty-odd years since he spoke those words, armed with his insights, the world has avoided an economic catastrophe such as overtook it in the years from 1929–33.

TRANSLATING SUMS OF MONEY

This book is inevitably full of figures—particularly financial figures—in a variety of currencies. To keep things simple and help the reader, I have converted amounts that would normally be expressed in other currencies (for example French francs or German marks) into U.S. dollars—except in those cases where the context clearly requires otherwise.

Understanding the significance of economic numbers from the 1920s and relating them to today's dollars is not a straightforward exercise. Not only have prices risen enormously since then, but the United States and European economies have also grown gigantically.

Financial magnitudes that relate to an individual's economic situation—say Hjalmar Schacht's salary—are best translated by adjusting for changes in the cost of living. As a rule of thumb, to compensate for the effects of inflation, multiply by a factor of 12. Thus Benjamin Strong's salary of $50,000 as governor of the New York Fed in the mid-1920s would be the equivalent today of $600,000. And Keynes's nest egg of $2 million built up over a long career of speculating in financial markets would be the same as $24 million today.

By contrast, in order to grasp the true significance of sums of money that relate to the economic situation of whole countries, such as the size of war debts owed to the United States, it is most useful not simply to make allowances for changes in the cost of living, but instead to adjust for changes in the size of economies. To translate such figures into comparable 2008 magnitudes, multiply by factor of 200.

For example, the bill for German reparations was fixed in 1921 at $12 billion. A similar debt today would be $2.4 trillion.

ACKNOWLEDGMENTS

I have been thinking about this book now for over a decade. In 1999, *Time* magazine featured a cover story entitled "The Committee to Save the World." The cover depicted three men: Alan Greenspan, then chairman of the Federal Reserve Board; Robert Rubin, then secretary of the treasury; and Larry Summers, then deputy secretary of the treasury. The article described how close the world had come to an economic meltdown in 1997 and 1998—the big Asian economies of Korea, Thailand, and Indonesia had had to suspend payments on hundreds of billions of dollars of debt, Asian currencies had collapsed against the dollar, Russia had defaulted on its domestic debt, and the hedge fund, Long-Term Capital Management, had lost $4 billion of its investors' capital, threatening the stability of the entire U.S financial system. The three "economist heroes," as *Time* magazine called them, were able to avert a disaster by acting quickly and aggressively to commit billions of dollars in public funds to stem a panic of proportions not experienced since the 1930s.

While the crisis of 1997 and 1998 was being played out, I was a professional investment manager. In trying to understand the origins of that economic breakdown and the role of central bankers in the drama, I began reading about the history of past upheavals, and in particular about the greatest financial crisis of them all, that which began in 1929 and led to the Great Depression. I discovered that in the 1920s, there was another group of high financial officials, this one dubbed by the press the "Most Exclusive Club in the World," which in its day also sought to manage the international financial system. But, instead of averting a catastrophe and saving the world, the committee from the 1920s ended up presiding over the greatest collapse that the global economy had ever seen. This book is the result of that research.

My biggest debts are to Strobe Talbott and Brooke Shearer. Ever since I began serious work on the book in 2004, they have been mentors, promoters, counselors, and editors, painstakingly reading and commenting on each successive draft. I also owe an enormous debt to Timothy Dickinson. He too read and commented on various drafts. With his astounding knowledge of history and his prodigious memory for facts, quotes, and anecdotes, he has helped me to understand much better the wider social and political context in which the events described here took place.

I would also like to thank all those who helped in various ways in the researching and writing of this book: David Hensler, Peter Bergen, and Michael D'Amato, whom I press-ganged into reading various sections of the book; Derek Leebaert, who guided me through the ways and byways of embarking on such a venture; Lily Sykes, who was so creative in hunting down documents and old newspapers clippings from archives in France and Germany; Felix Koch, who assisted with translations from German; Sarah Millard, Hayley Wilding, and Ben White at the Bank of England, Joseph Komljenovich and Marja Vitti at the Federal Reserve Bank of New York and Fabrice Reuzé at the Banque de France for their help in tracking down letters, documents, and photographs in their collections; and Reva Narula and Jane Cavolina for so efficiently organizing the footnotes. In addition, thanks to those friends who have listened so patiently to me talk about this book and given their support and encouragement: Michael Beschloss, David and Katherine Bradley, Jessica and Bob Einhorn, Michael Greenfield, Philip and Belinda Haas, John Hauge, Margaret Hensler, Homi Kharas, Tom and Marilyn Block, Bahman and Roya Irvani, Robert and Mary Haft, Antoine van Agtmael, Vikram Mehta and Shahid Yusuf.

I would like to express my gratitude to Peregrine Worsthorne for spending an afternoon with me sharing his memories of his stepfather, Montagu Norman.

Over the years, including while researching this book, my whole family and I have benefited from the generosity of Richard and Oonagh Wohanka, who have opened their various homes to us in London, Paris, and most inspiringly Cap d'Antibes—which makes an unlikely but important cameo appearance in this book. Another place in the south of France, Cap Ferrat, shows up in the story. It is therefore fitting that I thank Maryam and Vahid Allaghband. I had few more productive weeks of writing than the one I spent working from the terrace of their villa on Cap Ferrat overlooking the Mediterranean.

I discovered that becoming an author can be a lonely business. I am therefore grateful to all those who have given me an excuse to get away periodically from pouring over old biographies and newspaper articles from the 1920s. I especially want to thank my colleagues at The Rock Creek Group, Afsaneh Beschloss, Sudhir Krishnamurthy, and Siddarth Sudhir and Nick Rohatyn of The Rohatyn Group for allowing me to keep at least one foot in the world of investments.

I had the good fortune to persuade David Kuhn to take me on as a client. He has not simply been my agent but more than anyone else helped give substance to what was at the time only the germ of an idea. I would also like to thank Billy Kingsland.

I have also had the benefit of working with two great editors at Penguin. Scott Moyers provided me with his incisive comments and direction during the early stages and Vanessa Mobley helped shape the book into its final form. I must also thank Ann Godoff for taking a gamble on an unknown and unproven writer. Susan Johnson did a stellar job with the copyediting while the whole team at Penguin, particularly Nicole Hughes and Beena Kamlani, shepherded the book through the production process with great efficiency.

Finally, I would like to thank my family. My constant companion while writing has been our dog Scout, who took over the armchair in my study. My two daughters, Shabnam and Tara, have now flown the coop, but from afar have humored—and also encouraged—their father in his endeavor to transform himself from investment manager to writer. No one has been a greater champion of that change than my darling wife, Meena. For thirty years, she has been my anchor. It is to her that this book is dedicated.

NOTES

XI   "Read no history": Disraeli, *Contarini Fleming*, 141.

INTRODUCTION

1   "I feel I want a rest": "Norman Sails Unexpectedly for a Vacation in Canada," *New York Times*,
      August 16, 1931.

2   "monarch of [an] invisible empire": Kathleen, Woodward. "Montagu Norman: Banker and Leg-
      end," *New York Times*, April 17, 1932.

2   "the citadel of citadels" and "Montagu Norman was the man": Monnet, *Memoirs*, 95.

2   "the most exclusive club": *New York Herald Tribune*, July 10, 1927.

4   "We are today": Keynes, J. M., "An Economic Analysis of Unemployment?" June 22, 1931, in
      Collected Writings, 13: 343.

5   "In 1931, men and women": Toynbee, *Survey of International Affairs*, 1.

5   "Unless drastic measures are taken": "Ein' Feste Burg." *Time*, July 27, 1931, and Howe, *World
      Diary*, 111.

5   It was rumored: Taylor, *English History*, 290.

5   "the wisest man": Letter from Lamont to Norman, December 4, 1946, cited in Schuker, *The End
      of French Predominance in Europe*, 291.

5   "might have stepped out": Snowden, Philip, "The Governor of the Bank of England," *The
      Banker*, February 1926.

6   "Everyone I meet": Hassall, *Edward Marsh*, 570.

9   "second rate people," "the Jew is always a Jew": Chernow, *The House of Morgan*, 215, 310.

11   The pound sterling: There were 480 grains to a troy ounce, a measure of weight some 10 percent
      greater than a conventional ounce.

13   The totality of gold: The total amount of gold mined until 1913 was calculated to be 750 million
      ounces, or 22,500 tons. See Triffin. *The Evolution of the International Monetary System*, Table 17,
      79. Because a cubic foot of gold is estimated to weigh about half a ton, this would amount to
      45,000 cubic feet, equivalent to a cube with sides of about 35 feet.

13   "You came to tell us": Bryan, *The First Battle: A Story of the Campaign of 1896*, 199–206.

I: PROLOGUE

19   "What an extraordinary episode": Keynes, *Collected Writings: The Economic Consequences*, 2: 6.

20   "a magnificent stupid honesty": Wells, *The Work, Wealth, and Happiness of Mankind*, 398.

21   Even Kaiser Wilhelm: "Successful War No Advantage to Victor Says Angell," *New York Times*,
      June 15, 1913.

21   In February 1912: Committee of Imperial Defense, Testimony of Sir John H. Luscombe, Chair-
      man of Lloyds, *Report and Proceedings of the Standing Sub-Committee for the Committee of Impe-
      rial Defense on Trading with the Enemy*, 1912, paragraphs 120–143.

21 "new economic factors," "commercial disaster": Esher, *Journals and Letters*, 211–28 and 229–261, quoted in Tuchman, *Guns of August*, 10.

2: A STRANGE AND LONELY MAN

23 "Anybody who goes": Samuel Goldwyn quote from *Bartlett's Familiar Quotations*, 695

23 "feeling far from well": Letter to Caroline Brown from Boyle, *Montagu Norman*, 98.

27 "I feel a different person": Clay, *Lord Norman*, 44.

28 He would end up embracing: Boyle, *Montagu Norman*, 87.

29 "with tears in his eyes": McEwen, *The Riddell Diaries*, 85.

30 "the coming conflict": Geiss, *July 1914: The Outbreak of the First World War*, Document 162.

30 "acute anxiety": Wilson and Hammerton, *The Great War*, 26.

30 "stood nervously fingering their notes": "London Exchange Closes Its Doors." *New York Times*, August 1, 1914.

31 "although many hundreds of people," "traditionally phlegmatic and cool": *Times*, August 1, 1914.

31 Nevertheless, just in case: "English Bank Act to Be Suspended." *New York Times*, August 2, 1914.

31 "in case of an outbreak": Memorandum by Sir Felix Shuster, director of the Union Bank of London, circulated to the Clearing Bankers' Gold Reserves Committee quoted in Kynaston, *The City of London: Golden Years*, 588.

32 "European prospects very gloomy": Clay, *Lord Norman*, 81.

32 "Financiers in a fright": Lloyd George, *War Memoirs*, 111.

32 "shook his fist": Sayers, *The Bank of England*, 75.

33 "I have been at work": Boyle, *Montagu Norman*, 98.

3: THE YOUNG WIZARD

36 One of those who: Chernow, *The Warburgs*, 153.

36 The famously indiscreet kaiser: Ferguson, *The Pity of War*, 191.

36 There was also talk: Wilson and Hammerton, *The Great War*, 68.

37 "considerably outshone his fellow directors": Somary, *The Raven of Zurich*, 71.

37 "curiously stiff gait": Bonn, *Wandering Scholar*, 303.

38 "a restless wanderer": Schacht, *My First Seventy-six Years*, 24.

38 "sentimental, gay and full of feeling": Goldensohn, *The Nuremberg Interviews*, 231.

41 "Germany's steady advance": Schacht, *My First Seventy-six Years*, 129.

42 a large "howling mob": Tuchman, *The Guns of August*, 129.

42 Bizarre rumors spread: Wolff, *The Eve of 1914*, 524.

43 "The next time": Charles A. Conant, "How Financial Europe Prepared for the Great War," *New York Times*, August 30, 1914.

44 "a tremendous solemnity": Schacht, *My First Seventy-six Years*, 60.

4: A SAFE PAIR OF HANDS

45 "Show me a hero": F. Scott Fitzgerald quote from *The Yale Book of Quotations*, 274.

45 Strong had been elected president: "E. C. Converse Drawing Out," *New York Times*, January 9, 1914.

45 He had left the United States: "Cloud and Rain Mar Berlin Season," *New York Times*, June 14, 1914.

47 Finished from floor to ceiling: "No Morgan Bower atop Bankers Trust," *New York Times*, May 16, 1912.

47 In 1912, during the Pujo Committee hearings: "Five Men Control $368,000,000 Here," *New York Times*, December 11, 1912.

48 Anxious to avoid: "Bankers Here Confer on War," *New York Times*, July 31, 1914.

49 "The credit of all Europe": Chernow, *House of Morgan*, 185.

51 In later years: Nicolson, *Dwight Morrow*, 111.

51 In May 1905: "Mrs. Strong Kills Herself," *New York Times,* May 11, 1905.

53 "And to think": Strouse, *Morgan,* 15.

53 they were exactly the type of young men: Strouse, *Morgan,* 576.

54 Besides Davison himself: The only two participants who wrote about the Jekyll Island meeting were Frank Vanderlip in his autobiography *From Farm Boy to Financier* and Paul Warburg in a communication to Thomas Lamont reproduced in Thomas W. Lamont, *Henry P. Davison,* 97–101. The first contemporary description, though secondhand, appeared in an article by Bertie Charles Forbes, who later founded *Forbes* magazine, in *Current Opinion,* December 1916, 382. An account is also given in Stephenson, *Nelson Aldrich.* Recent descriptions are in West, *Banking Reform and the Federal Reserve,* 222–224; Chernow, *The Warburgs,* 133–134; and Michael A. Whitehouse, "Paul Warburg's Crusade to Establish a Central Bank in the United States" in *The Region,* Federal Reserve Bank of Minneapolis, May 1989.

55 "the highest pitch of intellectual awareness": Vanderlip, *From Farm Boy to Financier,* 216

57 Reports were rife: "Army of Refugees Flees to London," *New York Times,* August 3, 1914.

57 He immediately organized: "Exiles Meet in London," *New York Times,* August 4, 1914.

58 Strong persuaded: "Gold Cruiser to Sail Today," *New York Times,* August 6, 1914.

58 "Wherever he sat": Chandler, *Benjamin Strong,* 48.

58 "Jekyll and Hyde personality": Interviews with Leslie Rounds, *Committee on the History of the Federal Reserve System,* Washington: Brookings Institution, 1954–55

58 If the Aldrich Plan of a single central bank: Interviews with William McChesney Martin Sr., *Committee on the History of the Federal Reserve System,* Washington: Brookings Institution, 1954–55.

59 The salary he would receive: "Bank Head's Pay $30,000," *Chicago Daily Tribune,* October 27, 1914.

59 "Ben is not going to live" : Federal Reserve Bank of New York, "Biography of Benjamin Strong by his Son, Benjamin Strong." 1978

59 Only the year before: Details of Strong's apartment at 903 Park Avenue from "The Real Estate Field," *New York Times,* January 15, 1914.

5: L'INSPECTEUR DES FINANCES

61 "There isn't a bourgeois alive": Gustav Flaubert quote from *Bartlett's Familiar Quotations,* 527

61 It was the latest in a long chain: Berenson, *The Trial of Madame Caillaux,* 2.

63 the École Libre des Sciences Politiques: Zeldin, *French Passions: Intellect and Pride,* 343.

64 His family, minor gentry: Dutron de Bornier from Pierre Lyautey, "Eloge de M. Moreau," *Comptes Rendus Mensuels de L'Académie des Sciences Coloniales, Séance du 15 Octobre 1954,* Paris, 1954. Joseph Marie-François Moreau from "Leur Vacances," *Le Petit Parisien,* September 4, 1927.

64 Although the examination system had made: Zeldin, *French Passions: Ambition and Love,* 118.

65 To be *chef de cabinet*: For role of *cabinets ministériel,* see Keiger, *Raymond Poincaré,* 34.

66 "increased abnormally": Brogan, *France Under the Republic,* 128.

66 "moral collapse": Moreau, *The Golden Franc: Memoirs,* 17–18.

67 Over the next eight years: Moreau's career at Banque d'Algérie from Pierre Lyautey, "Eloge de M. Moreau," *Comptes Rendus Mensuels des L'Académie des Sciences Coloniales, Séance du 15 Octobre 1954,* Paris, 1954.

68 When he thought back: Moreau, *The Golden Franc: Memoirs,*12.

68 It was there: Jacques Rueff. "Preface to the French Edition," in Moreau, *The Golden Franc: Memoirs,* 2.

68 In any other year: Adam, *Paris Sees It Through,* 15.

68 "to keep it exciting": "Leur Vacances," *Le Petit Parisien,* September 4, 1927, and Giscard D'Estaing, Edmond, "Notice sue Emile Moreau," *Comptes Rendus Mensuels de L'Académie des Sciences Coloniales: Séance du 1 Decembre 1950,* Paris, 1950.

69 "Brawls were now breaking": Adam, *Paris Sees It Through,* 12–13.

69   At the first sign: "French Gold Famine," *Times*, July 30, 1914.

69   That afternoon: *Le Figaro*, July 31, 1914

70   "All classes of society": "Vanished Gold," *Times*, August 1, 1914.

70   "immense and perilous duties," "formidable test," "calmness, vigilance, initiative," and "all [his] authority": "Circulaire Bleu" from the Banque de France, *Le Patrimonie*, 423.

71   An hour later: "Paris Has Given Up All Hope of Peace, " *New York Times*, August 2, 1914.

71   Within days of the outbreak: Cronin, *Paris on the Eve*, 441–42, and Adam, *Paris Sees It Through*, 21.

71   The next day, a Sunday: Clarke, *Paris Waits*, 65–67, and "Un Avion Allemand Sur Paris," *Le Figaro*, August 31, 1914.

71   Few people: Lucien Klotz, "Mes Souvenirs du Temps de Guerre," *Le Journal*, December 14, 1922, and Gaston-Breton, *Sauvez L'Or*, 28.

6: MONEY GENERALS

73   "Endless money": Cicero quote from *Bartlett's Familiar Quotations*, 91.

73   "the amounts of coin": Quoted in Blainey, *The Causes of War*, 215.

74   "unlimited issue of paper": Charles A. Conant, "How Financial Europe Prepared for the Great War," *New York Times*, August 30, 1914.

74   Sir Felix Schuster: Stone, *World War One*, 30.

74   "he was quite certain": Ferguson, *The Pity of War*, 319, and Bell, *Old Friends*, 45.

74   That same month: Strachan, *First World War*, 816.

74   The Hungarian finance minister: Stone, *World War One*, 30.

75   By then the five major powers: "Fifty Billions Cost of War Up To Date." *New York Times*, July 30, 1916.

79   "quiet serious men": Bagehot, *Lombard Street*, 156.

79   "a shifting executive": Bagehot, *Lombard Street*, 157.

80   An economist of the 1920s: Hawtrey, *Art of Central Banking*, 246–47.

81   "very, very considerable": Cyril Asquith quoting Keynes in Jackson, *The Oxford Book of Money*, 46.

81   "take over the Bank": Sayers, *The Bank of England*, 105.

81–82 "to accept my unreserved apology": Sayers, *The Bank of England*, 107.

83   "There goes that queer-looking fish": Boyle, *Montagu Norman*, 105.

84   "into the most holy recesses": Brogan, *France Under the Republic*, 115.

85   The Banque opened its doors: Stephane Lausanne. "The Bank of France," *Banker*, August 1926, 93.

86   "The Banque does not belong": Valance, *La Legende du Franc*, 167.

86   Indeed, Caillaux made things: Gunther, *Inside Europe*, 145.

88   "Obedience and subordination": Feldman, *The Great Disorder*, 795.

88   Convinced like everyone else: Hjalmar, Schacht. "Bemerkungen über die Art und Weise der vorassichtlichen Kriegsentschädigung Frankreichs an Deutschland," August 26, 1914, in Bundesarchiv Koblenz, Nachlass Schacht, Nr. 1.

90   "insincere replies to the questions": Mühlen, *Schacht: Hitler's Magician*, 9.

90   But even Schacht: Testimony of Wilhelm Volcke on May 3, 1946, in *Trial of Major War Criminals Before the International Military Tribunal*.

90   Rumors circulated that he had embezzled: For example, the entry for "Schacht, Hjalmar Horace Greeley" in *Current Biography 1944*, 594–97, includes the following passage: "With the endorsement of the military government he issued several millions of counterfeited banknotes to pay for supplies bought from the Belgians but Berlin authorities became suspicious when he never accounted for the bulk of this money. Also accused of having seen to it that his banking connections profited from his knowledge of Government secrets. . . ."

94 On one occasion: "Vote for Trenches in Central Park over Protests," *New York Times*, March 23, 1918.

94 To kick off another campaign: "Wilson to Make War Speech Here in Drive for Loan," *New York Times*, September 26, 1918.

7: DEMENTED INSPIRATIONS

99 "Lenis was certainly right": Keynes, *Collected Writings: The Economic Consequences*, 2: 148. In four years: Hardach, *The First World War*, 153.

100 By the end of the war: Ferguson, *The Pity of War*, 322–31.

102 "fate of Germany": Schacht, *My First Seventy-six Years*, 158.

103 "hard . . . callous . . . and buttoned down": Schacht, *My First Seventy-six Years*, 17.

103 "He managed to look": Bonn, *Wandering Scholar*, 303.

104 "Nothing seems sacred": Roberts, *The House That Hitler Built*, 182.

104 "He was a man": Rauschning, *Men of Chaos*, 117.

104 "caused more trouble": Macmillan, *Peacemaker*, 191.

105 "little more than a shot": Lentin, *Guilt at Versailles*, 21.

106 "twenty million too many: Holborn, *A History of Modern Germany*, 566.

106 "the only Jew": Macmillan, *Peacemaker*, 201.

107 "costly frontal attacks": Taylor, *English History*, 74.

107 The great natural resources: Wolff, *Through Two Decades*, 261.

108 "unbearable, unrealizable, and unacceptable": Eyck, *A History of the Weimar Republic*, 1: 98.

109 "You seem to forget": Schacht, *My First Seventy-six Years*, 161–162.

110 "If Germany is to be": Keynes, "Memorandum by the Treasury on the Indemnity Payable by the Enemy Powers for Reparations and Other Claims," in *Collected Writings*, 16: 375.

110 "the sharpest and clearest": Russell, *Autobiography*, 1: 69.

110 "I evidently knew more": Harrod, *The Life of John Maynard Keynes*, 121.

111 "an illustrated appendix": Skidelsky, *John Maynard Keynes: Hopes Betrayed 1883–1920*, 177.

112 "I tried to get hold": Keynes, "Letter from Basil Blackett," in *Collected Writings*, 16: 3.

113 "greedy for work": Skidelsky, *John Maynard Keynes: Hopes Betrayed*, 304.

113 His Bloomsbury friends: Bell, *Old Friends: Personal Recollections*, 48.

113 "With the utmost respect": Harrod, *The Life of John Maynard Keynes*, 201.

113 But to the many other: Skidelsky et al., *Three Great Economists*, 232, and Harrod, *The Life of John Maynard Keynes*, 31.

113 He looked so very ordinary: Skidelsky et al., *Three Great Economists*, 231.

113 "I have always suffered": Skidelsky, *John Maynard Keynes: Hopes Betrayed*, 67, 169.

113 "gay and whimsical," "that gift of amusing": Bell, *Old Friends: Personal Recollections*, 52, 60.

114 "probably means the disappearance": Skidelsky, *John Maynard Keynes: Hopes Betrayed*, 346.

114 "a sense of impending": Keynes, *Collected Writings: The Economic Consequences*, 2: 2–3.

114 "The battle is lost": Keynes, "Letter to David Lloyd George," June 5, 1919, in *Collected Writings*, 16: 469.

115 "dry in soul": Keynes, *Collected Writings: The Economic Consequences*, 2: 20.

115 "his thought and his temperament": Keynes, *Collected Writings: The Economic Consequences*, 2: 26.

115 "his mind . . . slow": Keynes, *Collected Writings: The Economic Consequences*, 2: 27.

115 "with six or seven senses": Keynes, *Collected Writings: The Economic Consequences*, 2: 26.

115 "rooted in nothing": Keynes, "Lloyd George," in *Collected Writings*, 10: 23–24.

115 "civilization under threat," "men driven by": Keynes, *Collected Writings: The Economic Consequences*, 2: 144.

116 "ought to have been": Trachtenberg, *Reparation in World Politics*, 94.

116 "is to us the most important": Schuker, *End of French Predominance in Europe*, 17.

117 *"la politique des casinos"*: Steiner, *The Lights That Failed*, 183.

117   "As far as I am concerned": Howe, *A World History*, 152.
117   "France could not decide": Garratt, *What Has Happened*, 161.
117   "vainglorious, quarrelsome": Carlyle, 1870 letter to the *Times* quoted in Wilson, the *Victorians*, 345.
117   "the gratification of private": Schuker, *End of French Predominance in Europe*, 17.
117   "I can't bear him": Adamthwaite, *Grandeur and Misery*, 75.
117   "uneasy vanity": Collier, *Germany and the Germans*, 470.
118   The Germans responded: Martin, *France and the Après Guerre*, 75.
120   "Nothing like this": Keynes, "Speculation in the Mark and Germany's Balances Abroad," in *Manchester Guardian Commercial*, September 28, 1922, in *Collected Writings*, 18: 49–50.
120   A visitor in the late 1920s: Kindleberger, *A Financial History*, 310–11.
120   "In the whole course": d'Abernon, *The Diary of an Ambassador*, 2: 124.
121   "133 printing works": Schacht, *The Stabilization of the Mark*, 105.
121   Basic necessities: "Berlin Now Shivering in Sudden Cold Wave," *New York Times*, November 8, 1923.
122   German physicians: "Cipher Stroke a New Disease for Germans Figuring Marks." *New York Times*, December 7, 1923.
122   "For a salary": Cowley, *Exile's Return*, 142.
123   "How wild anarchic": Zweig, *The World of Yesterday*, 301.
124   During those days of violence: Habedank, *Die Reichsbank*, 34.
125   "whether one wished": Warburg Archives, *Jahresbericht 1923*, 43, quoted in Ferguson, *Paper and Iron*, 9.
126   "The Reichsbank today": Ferguson, *When Money Dies*, 169.
127   "No-one could anticipate": D'Abernon communication to Foreign Office, quoted in Ferguson, *When Money Dies*, 169.
127   "It appears almost impossible": d'Abernon, *The Diary of an Ambassador*, 2: 240.
128   "old style Prussian," "permanent order": Schacht, *My First Seventy-six Years*, 161.
128   "hell's kitchen": Schacht. *My First Seventy-six Years*, 177.

8: UNCLE SHYLOCK

132   "The principal danger": Bank of England, letter from Strong to Norman, November 22, 1918.
132   "help to rebuild": "Wilson Stirs Audience," *New York Times*, September 28, 1918.
133   "The Family": Bacevich, "Family Matters" and "Bachelor as Guest Is Sole Occupant of Exclusive Club," *Washington Post*, August 22. 1926.
134   "pallid career": Phillips, *Ventures in Diplomacy*, 6, quoted in Bacevich, "Family Matters," 406.
135   "constructive policy": Letter from Strong to Leffingwell, July 31, 1919, quoted in Chandler, *Benjamin Strong*, 144.
136   "in which [Sir Edward]": Strong to James Brown, September 14, 1916, quoted in Roberts, "Benjamin Strong, the Federal Reserve."
136   "that the Allies," "been slight": Letter from Strong to Leffingwell, July 25, 1919, quoted in Chandler, *Benjamin Strong*, 142.
136   "their hearts to rule": Letter from Strong to Leffingwell, July 31, 1919, quoted in Chandler, *Benjamin Strong*, 143.
136   "In the useless slaughter": Masterton, *England After the War*, 32–33.
137   "The consequences": Steffens, *Autobiography*, 803.
138   "lack of leadership," "people in authority": Letter from Strong to Leffingwell, August 30, 1919, quoted in Chandler, *Benjamin Strong*, 145–46.
138   "desert Europe," "prolonged disorder": Letter from Strong to Leffingwell, August 30, 1919, quoted in Chandler, *Benjamin Strong*, 145–46.
139   "the most wonderful," "the most gorgeous": Bank of England, letter from Strong to Norman, March 1, 1920.
139   "Whenever you do come": Bank of England, letter from Norman to Strong, December 3, 1920.
140   "makes the whole of Paris": Nicolson, *Peacemaking 1919*, 330.

140 "top-hatted frock-coated": Brendon, *Eminent Edwardians*, 115.

140 "Lord Balfour seems": Quoted in Middlemas and Barnes, *Baldwin*, 133.

140 "In the Balfour Note": Quoted in Rhodes, "The Image of Britain," 196.

140 "Has America which but yesterday": "Still Scolding America for Funding Bill," *New York Times*, February 7, 1922.

140 "lay a tribute upon": Garet, Garrett. "Shall Europe Pay Back Our Millions," *New York Times*, November 26, 1922.

141 "to approach the discussion": "British to Pay All, Ask a Square Deal, Debt Board Is Told", *New York Times*, January 9, 1923.

142 "they seemed to understand": Boyle, *Montagu Norman*, 156.

143 "merely sell wheat": "Baldwin Says We Don't Understand Situation on Debt," *New York Times*, January 28, 1923.

143 "a hick": Grigg, *Prejudice and Judgment*, 102.

143 "I should be the most cursed": Blake, *The Unknown Prime Minister*, 492.

143 "in order to give them": Keynes. "Letter to J. C. C. Davidson," January 30, 1923, in *Collected Writings*, 8: 103.

144 As the decade went on: Edwin L. James, "Europe Scowls at Rich America," *New York Times*, July 11, 1926; Frank H. Simonds, "Does Europe Hate the U.S. and Why?" *American Review of Reviews*, September 1926; "Uncle Shylock in Europe," *American Review of Reviews*, January 1927.

145 "Mr. Montagu Collet Norman": "The Mission to America," *Times*, December 27, 1922.

145 "singularly gifted": Charles Addis diary quoted in Kynaston, *The City of London: Illusions of Gold*, 64.

145 "He never made jokes": George Booth quoted in Kynaston, *The City of London: Illusions of Gold*, 66.

146 His unorthodox appearance: Kynaston, *The City of London: Illusions of Gold*, 64–66; "The Governor of the Bank of England," the *Strand Magazine*, April 1939.

146 At some point: "Along the Highways of Finance," *New York Times*, September 4, 1932.

147 Take a typical incident: "Bank of England Head May Be in Berlin," *New York Times*, March 18, 1923; and "Bank of England Governor Settles Problem in Berlin," *Christian Science Monitor*, March 17, 1923; and "France Against Mediation in Ruhr by Outside Power," *Washington Post*, March 17, 1923.

147 "Mr. Norman's dislike": Winston. Churchill, "Montagu Norman," *Sunday Pictorial*, September 20, 1931.

148 "poseur": Vansittart, *The Mist Procession*, 301.

148 "sensation of being": Letter from Norman to Caroline Brown, quoted in Boyle, *Montagu Norman*, 140.

148 "secretive, egotistic": Williams, *A Pattern of Rulers*, 205.

148 "a brilliant neurotic": Boyle, *Montagu Norman*, 129–30.

149 "delighted in appearing," "those of an old": Templewood, *Nine Troubled Years*, 78.

149 Still an Edwardian: Worsthorne, *Democracy Needs Aristocracy*, 26–28.

149 "Only lately have the countries": Bank of England, letter from Norman to Strong, March 22, 1922.

149 "Anything in the nature": Bank of England, letter from Strong to Norman, July 14, 1922. "Dear Strongy": Bank of England, letter from Norman to Strong, May 24, 1922.

150 "Dear Old Man": Bank of England, letter from Norman to Strong, March 27, 1923.

150 "Dear old [sic] Monty": Bank of England, letter from Strong to Norman, May 1, 1927.

150 "You are a dear": Bank of England, letter from Strong to Norman, May 1, 1927.

150 "Dear Ben.": Bank of England, letter from Norman to Strong, January 24, 1925.

151 they sounded like a couple of: Bank of England, letter from Norman to Strong, April 2, 1927, and letters from Strong to Norman, March 25, 1927, and April 14, 1927.

151 "Let me beg you": Bank of England, letter from Norman to Strong, September 15, 1921.

151 "what is happening": Bank of England, letters from Norman to Strong, March 21. 1925, and February 26, 1927.

151   "To have a sympathetic person": Bank of England, letter from Strong to Norman, February 15, 1927.

151   "the Civilization": Bank of England, letter from Norman to Strong, December 18, 1921.

152   "The black spot of Europe": Bank of England, letter from Norman to Strong, April 9, 1923.

152   "afflicted by the generous use": Bank of England, letter from Strong to Norman, February 18, 1922.

152   In those days: "Finance as Recreation," *Gettysburg Times*, November 19, 1928.

153   "The temptation": Bank of England, letter from Strong to Norman, January 4, 1924.

9: A BARBAROUS RELIC

155   *Time will run back*: John Milton quote from *Bartlett's Familiar Quotations*, 258.

165   In the latter half of 1919: Moggridge, *Maynard Keynes*, 349–50.

166   "disliked being in the country": Harrod, *The Life of John Maynard Keynes*, 364.

166   "ovary": Skidelsky, *John Maynard Keynes: Hopes Betrayed*, 211.

166   "tentative almost": Harrod, *The Life of John Maynard Keynes*, 339–40.

167   "London's position": Keynes, "Memorandum Against the Suspension of Gold," August 3, 1914, in *Collected Writings*, 16: 7–15.

167   "humbly and without permission": Keynes, *Collected Writing: A Tract, 4:* xv.

167   "conservative bankers": Keynes, *Collected Writings: A Tract, 4:* 56.

168   "the allegiance of": Harrod, *The Life of John Maynard Keynes*, 339–40.

168   "For the moment": Bank of England, letter from Norman to Strong, January 30, 1924.

169   "the most vindictive man": Kynaston, *The City of London: Illusions of Gold*, 65.

169   "He is a brilliant": Bank of England, letter from Strong to Norman, February 6, 1920.

170   "Keynes's little book": Bank of England, letter from Strong to Norman, January 4, 1924.

170   Having jettisoned : Friedman and Schwartz, *A Monetary History*, 240.

172   "I do not intend": Bank of England, letter from Norman to Strong, January 30, 1924.

172   "A dollar standard": Keynes, *Collected Writing: A Tract*, 4: 155.

173   "they might come": Walworth, *Woodrow Wilson*, 320, n. 12.

173   Not surprisingly, the Board: Norris, *Ended Episodes*, 204.

173   "a body of startling incompetence": Galbraith, *The Great Crash*, 32.

173   "utterly devoid of global": Hoover, *Memoirs*, 9.

174   From Memphis, Tennessee: Interviews with Roy Young and Chester Morrill, *Committee on the History of the Federal Reserve System*, Washington: Brookings Institution, 1954–55.

174   From Iowa came: Interviews with George Harrison, Leslie Rounds, Roy Young, and Chester Morrill, *Committee on the History of the Federal Reserve System*, Washington: Brookings Institution, 1954–55.

175   "I'll see them damned": Letter from Strong to J. H. Case, April 21, 1923, quoted in Chandler, *Benjamin Strong*, 228.

176   In the process: Interview with Leslie Rounds, *Committee on the History of the Federal Reserve System*, Washington: Brookings Institution, 1954–55.

176   "worshipped": Interview with Jay Crane, *Committee on the History of the Federal Reserve System*, Washington: Brookings Institution, 1954–55.

10: A BRIDGE BETWEEN CHAOS AND HOPE

179   At 10:00 p.m. on November 8 1923: Stresemann, *Diaries, Letters and Papers*, 199.

180   On November 5: "Berlin Food Rioters Attack and Beat Jews." *New York Times*, November 6, 1923; "Berlin Now Shivering in Sudden Cold Wave," *New York Times*, November 8, 1923; Feldman, *The Great Disorder*, 780.

181   "Babylon of the world" "A kind of madness": Zweig, *The World of Yesterday*, 238.

181   "German Chicago": Large, *Berlin*, 48.

181   "stone-grey corpse": Quote by George Grosz in Hanser, *Putsch*, 253.

181 "beggars, whores": Sahl, *Memoiren*, 36–37 quoted in Ian Buruma, "Weimar Faces," *New York Review of Books*, November 2, 2006.

183 The previous month: Stresemann, *Diaries, Letters and Papers*, 145–47.

183 "living on the edge": Schacht, *My First Seventy-six Years*, 177.

184 "hindered by personal considerations": Schacht, *My First Seventy-Six Years*,177.

184 "narrow Prussian": Schacht, *My First Seventy-six Years*, 120.

185 "an enthusiasm suitable": Feldman, *The Great Disorder*, 793.

185 Schacht was as skeptical: Schacht, *The Stabilization of the Mark*, 79, and Feldman, *The Great Disorder*, 751.

187 "He sat on his chair": Schacht, *My First Seventy-six Years*, 187.

187–188 "father of the inflation": "Stinnes Would Oust Head of Reichsbank," *New York Times*, November 13, 1923.

188 "preserve his honor": Feldman, *The Great Disorder*, 715.

189 "astonishing appeasement": d'Abernon, *The Diary of an Ambassador*, 2: 283.

190 "he always had good luck": Feldman, *The Great Disorder*, 822.

190 On November 20: "Herr Havenstein Dead," *Times*, November 21, 1923.

190 "an extraordinarily sympathetic personality": Max Warburg Papers, Unpublished Memoirs, 1923, 69, quoted in Feldman, *The Great Disorder*, 795.

190 During the war: Feldman, *The Great Disorder*, 74.

11: THE DAWES OPENING

194 *"Be extremely subtle"*: Sun Tzu quote from *Bartlett's Familiar Quotations*, 83.

194 "a tall man with a pointed grayish beard" "I want to get on": Schacht, *My First Seventy-six Years*, 194.

194 Decorated in a neoclassical: "The Governor of The Bank of England," *Strand Magazine*, April 1939.

196 "quiet, modest": Bank of England, letter from Norman to Strong, October 28, 1921.

196 "You know, of course": Bank of England, letter from Norman to Strong, January 7, 1924.

197 "entertainments," "sad fate": d'Abernon, *The Diary of an Ambassador*, 2: 122–23.

198 "Hell and Maria": "The Committees," *Time*, January 7, 1924.

199 "hollow deep-set eyes": Klingaman, *1929: The Year of the Crash*, 95.

201 "both the element of novelty": Dawes, *The Dawes Plan in the Making*, 34–35.

202 "those foul and carrion-loving," "impenetrable and colossal": "Whirlwind Diplomacy: How Dawes Plays Game," *New York Times*, January 27, 1924.

202 Through a combination of charm: Schuker, *End of French Predominance*, 284.

203 in 1922, an audit: Brogan, *France Under the Republic*, 517.

203 $150 million of National Defense Bonds: Shirer, *The Collapse of the Third Republic*, 161.

204 On January 14: "La Foire aux Devises," *Le Quotidien*, March 12, 1924, cited in Schuker, *End of French Predominance*, 89.

204 Prime Minister Poincaré declared: Jeanneney, *François de Wendel*, 187–88.

204 "assist in bringing France": "The Franc Fighting for Its Life," *The Literary Digest*, March 22, 1924.

204 "Each time the franc loses": Keynes, *Collected Writing: A Tract*, 4: xvi–xvii

205 "stool of repentance": Schacht, *My First Seventy-six Years*, 208.

206 "His pride is equaled": Dawes, *A Journal of Reparations*, 54.

206 "remarkable revelation": Dawes, *A Journal of Reparations*, 54.

209 "It looks to me": Bank of England, letter from Norman to Strong, January 30, 1924.

210 "six main powers": Ziegler, *The Sixth Great Power*, 1.

210 One story was that the family: Ferguson, *The House of Rothschild: Money's Prophets*, 95–98.

210 "undertaken by any European": Hobson, *Imperialism*, 64.

211 The son of an austere Methodist: "Lamont, Thomas William," in *Current Biography*, 1940, 476.

213 "until the French are out": Schuker, *End of French Predominance*, 215.

213 "swarming, gesticulating": Saint-Aulaire, *Confessions*, 718, quoted in Schuker, *End of French Pre-dominance*, 299.

214 "Europe shall not," "America's only purpose,"

214 "In the lean years": Edwin L. James, "French Condemn Our Role in London," *New York Times*, July 26, 1924, and "The 'Money Devil' Mixes in the Reparations Row," *The Literary Digest*, August 9, 1924.

215 "We cannot accept": Klein, *Road to Disaster*, 248.

216 "The United States lends money:" Keynes, "The Progress of the Dawes Scheme," in *The Nation and the Athenaeum*, September 11, 1926, in *Collected Writings*, 18: 281.

12: THE GOLDEN CHANCELLOR

217 *'I never knew a man'*: Greene, *The Quiet American*, 72.

217 "in the full sunshine": Graves and Hodges, *The Long Weekend*, 102.

217 Regent Street had been made over: "England Not Merry Under Labor's Rule," *New York Times*, June 8, 1924.

217 There was a new freedom: Graves and Hodges, *The Long Weekend*, 108–110.

219 "While England is financially sound": Sisley, Huddelston. "Personalities and Politics in France," *Atlantic Monthly*, January 1925, 117.

221 "You know how controversial": Bank of England, letter from Norman to Strong, October 16, 1924.

221 "hand over to Germany": Notes on discussion with Walter Leaf, June 13, 1924. Bank of England quoted in Kynaston, *The City of London: Illusions of Gold*, 109.

221 "rather far behind": Bank of England, letter from Strong to Norman, July 9, 1924.

222 "There never was a Churchill": Quoted in Wilson, *The Victorians*, 485.

222 "how anybody can put their": Letter from William Bridgeman to his wife, quoted in Manchester, *The Last Lion*, 785.

223 F. E. Smith, Lord Birkenhead: Wilson, *After the Victorians*, 248–49

224 "his only mistress" : Moreau, *The Golden Franc*, 51.

224 He had a Rolls-Royce: Manchester, *The Last Lion*, 778–79.

224 Norman, despite his inherited wealth: Lyttelton, *Memoirs of Lord Chandos*, 137.

225 "undetected, like a shadow": "From the 'Old Lady.'" *Time*, January 12, 1925.

225 "unremarked": "Plan to Pay Gold Calls Norman Here" *New York Times*, January 1, 1925. carved out of the solid bedrock: "Federal Bank Vault Carved in Solid Rock." *New York Times*, October 18, 1924.

225 Most noticeable was the number of cars: "One Auto in the City to Each 16 Persons," *New York Times*, May 18, 1924, and "Automobile Census Shows World Has 21,360,779 Cars," *New York Times*, March 8, 1925. For relative wages between the United States and Europe, see "Premium on Dollar Keeps Wages Up," *New York Times*, December 31, 1924.

226 "The great problem is sterling": Strong memorandum to Carl Snyder, April 3, 1922, quoted in Chandler, *Benjamin Strong*, 291.

227 "a long period of unsettled conditions": Strong memorandum, January 11, 1925, quoted in Chandler, *Benjamin Strong*, 309.

228 "My dear Ben": Bank of England, letter from Norman to Strong, January 18, 1925.

229 "the Louis XVI of the monetary revolution": Keynes, "Letter to Sir Charles Addis," July 25, 1924, in *Collected Writings*, 19: 371–72.

229 "We should run the risk": Keynes, "The Problem of the Gold Standard," in *The Nation and Athenaeum*, May 2, 1925, in *Collected Writings*, 19: 337–44.

230 "faults in her economic structure": Keynes, "The Return Towards Gold," in *The Nation and Athenaeum*, February 21, 1925, in *Collected Writings: Essays in Persuasion*, 7: 192–200.

230 "pressing the return to the gold standard": Taylor, *Beaverbrook*, 227.

230 "It is an absurd and silly notion": Taylor, *Beaverbrook*, 319.

231 "he never could make out": Churchill, *Lord Randolph Churchill*, 2: 184.
231 "If they were soldiers": James, *Churchill: A Study in Failure*, 204.
231 "survival of a rudimentary": "Mr. Churchill Exercise," February 29, 1925, U.K. Treasury Papers, quoted in Moggridge, *British Monetary Policy*, 76.
232 "We, and especially Norman, feel": Letter from Edward Grenfell to Jack Morgan, March 23, 1925, quoted in Chernow, *The House of Morgan*, 275–76.
232 "The Gold Standard is the best 'Governor'": Moggridge, *British Monetary Policy*, Appendix 5, 270–72.
232 "The Governor of the Bank": Winston Churchill to Otto Niemeyer, February 22, 1925, U.K. Treasury Papers in Moggridge, *British Monetary Policy*, Appendix 5.
233 "Norman elaborates his own schemes": Letter from Edward Grenfell to Jack Morgan, March 23, 1925, quoted in Chernow, *The House of Morgan*, 274.
233 "None of the witch doctors": Leith-Ross, *Money Talks*, 91.
233 Norman often stopped by: Templewood, *Nine Troubled Years*, 78.
234 "knave-proof," "living in a fool's paradise": Grigg, *Prejudice and Judgment*, 183.
235 "You have been a politician": Grigg, *Prejudice and Judgment*, 184.
235 "I will make you the golden Chancellor": Boyle, *Montagu Norman*, 189.
236 "It is imperative that": Text of Churchill's speech, including remark about fortifying himself, from *Hansard*, House of Commons Debates, 5 Series, vol. 183, cols 49–114.
236 "an amber-coloured liquid": Howe, *A World History*, 290.
236 "If the English pound is not": Churchill, *Complete Speeches*, 4: 3587.
236 "greatest achievement . . .": Winston, Churchill. "Montagu Norman," *Sunday Pictorial*, September 20, 1931.
237 "a signal triumph": *Times*, April 29, 1925.
237 "the crowning achievement": *Economist*, May 2, 1925.
237 "The proper object of dear money": Keynes, "The Economic Consequences of Mr. Churchill," in *Collected Writing: Essays in Persuasion*, 9: 220.
237 "because he has no instinctive judgment": Keynes, "The Economic Consequences of Mr. Churchill," in *Collected Writing: Essays in Persuasion*, 9: 212.
237 In 1927, he invited Keynes: Skidelsky, *John Maynard Keynes: The Economist as Saviour*, 203.
238 "the victims," "in the flesh [of] the fundamental": Keynes, "The Economic Consequences of Mr. Churchill," in *Collected Writing: Essays in Persuasion*. 9: 223.
239 "the biggest blunder": Moran, *Winston Churchill*, 303–304, quoted in Kynaston, *The City of London: Illusions of Gold*, 129.
239 "misled by the Governor": Toye, *Lloyd George and Churchill*, 256.
239 "that man Skinner": Grigg, *Prejudice and Judgment*, 193.
239 "to everyone's surprise": Amery, *Diaries*, 552, quoted in Kynaston, *The City of London: Illusions of Gold*, 129.
239 "The gold standard party": Keynes, "The Gold Standard," in *The Nation and Athenaeum*, May 2, 1925, in *Collected Writings*, 19: 361.
240 "In a new country": Strong Memorandum, January 11, 1925, quoted in Chandler, *Benjamin Strong*, 309.

13: LA BATAILLE
241 *Only peril*: Charles de Gaulle quote from *Bartlett's Familiar Quotations*, 728.
245 Noblemen, who might otherwise: Plessis, *Histoires de la Banque*, 205–10.
246 Over the 120 years: Garratt, *What Has Happened to Europe*, 164–65.
246 "The hardest thing to understand": Quoted in Brogan, *France Under the Republic*, 66.
249 "a kind of Treasury magician": Binion, *Defeated Leaders*, 95.
249 As he strode into the Chamber: "Caillaux's Political Resurrection," *The Literary Digest*, May 2, 1925, and "In Parliament," *Time*, May 4, 1925.

249 "frivolity": Moreau, *The Golden Franc*, 37.

250 "in elegant social circles": Jeanneney, *François de Wendel*, 248.

250 "regretted not having thrown": Jeanneney, *François de Wendel*, 254.

252 "we are the soldiers": Bonnet, *Vingt Ans de Vie Politique*, 101–102, quoted in Jeanneney, *François de Wendel*, 271.

252 "battle of the franc": Sisley, Huddleston. "France Mobilizes to Save the Franc," *New York Times*, May 30, 1926.

252 It managed to raise: "Save the Franc," *Time*, May 3, 1926, and *New York Herald Tribune*, April 21, 1926.

253 "which must never be brought out": Sisley, Huddleston. "France Mobilizes to Save the Franc," *New York Times*, May 30, 1926.

253 "[laid] down their squabbles": Letter from Strong to Peter Jay, May 9, 1926, quoted in Chandler, *Benjamin Strong*, 362.

253 "excoriated from one end": Letter from Strong to George Harrison, May 23, 1926, quoted in Chandler, *Benjamin Strong*, 363.

254 "Am I to become the liquidator": Moreau, *The Golden Franc*, 12.

255 "My doubt is only about": Bank of England, letter from Norman to Strong, June 8, 1926. The two bankers did manage: "Strong Refuses to Discuss Finance," *New York Times*, June 30, 1926, and "Financiers Gather at Antibes," *New York Times*, July 9, 1926.

255–56 Another intrepid journalist: "M. Strong et Sir [sic] Montagu Norman se reposent paisiblement a Antibes," *La Volonté*, July 5, 1926.

256 Strong found his French banking: Leffler, *The Elusive Quest*, 146.

256 By 1926, an estimated forty-five thousand: "Il y a 500,000 Étrangers a Paris," *Le Journal*, February 2, 1925.

256 The French press had: "L'Infiltration des Capitaux Américains dans l'Économie Francaise." *La Vie Financier*, April 26, 1926.

257 "destructive grasshoppers": *Le Midi*, April 17, 1926.

257 On July 11, in a dramatic protest: "Maimed and Blind Lead Paris Parade to Protest on Debt," *New York Times*, July 12, 1926.

258 A couple of days later another party: "Reasonable Resentment," *Washington Post*, July 26, 1926.

258 "Don't boast in cafes": "Our Tourist Troubles in France," *The Literary Digest*, August 14, 1926.

259 "Xenophobic displays": Moreau, *The Golden Franc*, 53.

259 "friendly but reserved": Moreau, *The Golden Franc*, 43.

259 The governor's suite at the bank: "Leur Vacances," *Le Petit Parisien*, September 4, 1927, and Banque de France, *Treasures*.

260 "Mr. Norman arrived at eleven": Moreau, *The Golden Franc*, 51.

260 "stupid, obstinate": H. A. Siepman, "Central Bank Cooperation," quoted in Mouré, *The Gold Standard Illusion*, 156.

261 "a commodity," "only ready to sell": Moreau, *The Golden Franc*, 182.

263 "slave to the books he has written": Moreau, *The Golden Franc*, 124.

263 "You are not going to remain": See the Introduction by Jean-Noël Jeanneney to Rist, *Une Saison Gatée*, 11.

264 "The level of the franc": Keynes, *Collected Writing: A Tract*, 4: 60.

264 "the sacrifices demanded": Boyle, *Montagu Norman*, 226.

265 "The past clung to everything": Ferguson, *The House of Rothschild*, 458.

265 A familiar figure: Obituary in *Le Monde*, July 2, 1949.

266 "No cabinet was formed": Lottman, *The French Rothschilds*, 136.

266 an enraged mob had howled: Chapman, *The Dreyfus Trials*, 52.

266 "Maître de Forges": "'The Iron Master,'" *Time*, January 24, 1949, and "Francs and Frenchman," *Time*, May 18, 1936.

267 Moreau had had his first taste: Moreau, *The Golden Franc,* 73.
268 Rothschild and Wendel employed every: Moreau, *The Golden Franc,* 261, 264, 279; Netter, *Histoire de la Banque de France,* 153.

14: THE FIRST SQUALLS

270 *"Circumstances rule men"*: Herodotus quote from *Bartlett's Familiar Quotations,* 71.
270 "to make a fortune": Fraser, *Every Man a Speculator,* 45.
270 "The English, however speculative": Sobel, *Panic on Wall Street,* 223.
270 In 1913, the total value: Rajan, "The great reversals," Table 3, 15.
271 The "merger" bull market: Leonard P. Ayres, "The Great Bull Market of 1925," *American Review of Reviews,* January 1926.
272 No company better exemplified: Sobel, *The Great Bull Market,* 100–105.
273 The buoyant stock market was accompanied: Allen, *Only Yesterday,* chap. XI.
275 "Before the butler could move": Wueschner, *Charting Twentieth-Century Monetary Policy,* 91.
275 "the only man who emerged": Keynes, *Collected Writings: The Economic Consequences,* 2: 174, n.1.
275 "Secretary of Commerce": Schlesinger Jr. *The Crisis of the Old Order,* 84.
276 "a mental annex": Hoover, *Memoirs,* 9.
276 "May it not be the case": Strong memorandum to Carl Snyder, May 21, 1925, quoted in Chandler, *Benjamin Strong,* 428.
277 "Must we accept parenthood": Strong memorandum to Carl Snyder, May 21, 1925, quoted in Chandler, *Benjamin Strong,* 428.
277 "affairs of gamblers": Letter from Strong to Governor George Norris, August 18, 1927, quoted in Chandler, *Benjamin Strong,* 444.
277 "It seems a shame": Letter from Strong to Norman, November 7, 1925, quoted in Chandler, *Benjamin Strong,* 329.
280 "tactic of consulting everyone": James, *The Reichsbank,* 26.
280 "He looked upon the world": Bonn, *Wandering Scholar,* 303.
281 "infatuated by Dr. Schacht": Bennett, *Germany and the Diplomacy of the Financial Crisis,* 127, and Vansittart, *The Mist Procession,* 301.
281 "He is undoubtedly": Letter from Strong to Peter Jay, July 20, 1926, quoted in Chandler, *Benjamin Strong,* 333.
281 his salary was the equivalent: Kopper, *Hjalmar Schacht,* 86.
281 "ugly clown mask," "vigilant watch": Dodd, *Through Embassy Eyes,* 234.
282 "he dresses with the taste": Johannes, Steel. "The Ambitious Dr. Schacht," *Current History,* June 1934, 285–90.
282 "cutting and devastating humor": Dodd, *Through Embassy Eyes,* 234.
282 "a whole table enthralled": Aga Khan, *Memoirs,* 337.
282 "Life seemed more free": Shirer, *The Rise and Fall of the Third Reich,* 118.
282 "jewel-like sparkle": Large, *Berlin,* 211.
282 "You feel all the time": Boyle, *Montagu Norman,* 167.
283 The recovery was reflected in the stock market: Voth, "With a Bang, Not a Whimper." one small town in Bavaria: Frieden, *Global Capitalism,* 141.
284 He had hoped that: James, *Europe Reborn,* 112. a "chimera": Voth, "With a Bang, Not a Whimper," 72.
285 "not wish to have things seem too good": Letter from Pierre Jay to Strong, June 22, 1927, quoted in McNeil, *American Money and the Weimar Republic,* 152.
285 "changeable and moody": Letter from Parker Gilbert to Strong, September 8, 1927, quoted in McNeil, *American Money and the Weimar Republic,* 174.
285 "irresponsibility and unpredictability," "extreme and erratic": James, *The Reichsbank,* 61, and McNeil, *American Money and the Weimar Republic,* 180.

286 At a cabinet meeting: Stresemann diary entry, June 22, 1927, in Stresemann, *Diaries, Letters and Papers,* 2.

287 made him "smile": Bank of England, letter from Norman to Strong, November 23, 1925.

287 "seem to be afraid of him": Letter from Strong to Pierre Jay, September 15, 1926, quoted in Chandler, *Benjamin Strong,* 348.

287 "imperialist dreams": Moreau, *The Golden Franc,* 220.

288 "capricious," "menace the gold standard": Norman cables to Strong, May 24 and 25, 1927, quoted in Clarke, *Central Bank Cooperation,* 117, n. 25.

289 "he could not do so": Moreau, *The Golden Franc,* 295.

289 "I do not want to trample": Moreau, *The Golden Franc,* 298.

15: UN PETIT COUP DE WHISKY

292 She had just landed a part: "Actress a Suicide by Poison in Hotel," *New York Times,* December 10, 1926, and "Illness Drives 2 Women to Suicide in Hotels," *Washington Post,* December 10, 1926.

294 In 1926, while Strong was in France: Wueschner, *Charting Twentieth-Century Monetary Policy,* 125.

294 "thoroughly enjoy getting into a fight": Interview with Leslie Rounds, *Committee on the History of the Federal Reserve System,* Washington: Brookings Institution, 1954–55.

294 the constant sniping: Wueschner, *Charting Twentieth-Century Monetary Policy,* 123.

295 Over the years, each of the central banks: John, Brooks. "Annals of Finance: In Defense of Sterling," *New Yorker,* May 23, 1968, 44.

297 "closeted together": Sayers, *The Bank of England,* 339.

297 Norman dominated the proceedings: Interview with Mrs. Ogden Mills, *Committee on the History of the Federal Reserve System,* Washington: Brookings Institution, 1954–55.

298 "*un petit coup de whisky*": Banque de France, Charles Rist memorandum "Conversation du 1 au 7 Juillet, 1927 a New York et Washington;" Charles, Rist. "Notice Biographique," *Review D'Économie Politique.* Nov-Dec 1955, 1006; and Sayers, *The Bank of England,* 340.

298 "courtesy calls": Entry for July 7, 1927: Hamlin diary, Volume 14, Library of Congress.

299 "inflation of credit": Hoover, *Memoirs,* 11.

299 "That man has offered me unsolicited advice": Schlesinger Jr., *The Crisis of the Old Order,* 88.

299 Fobbing Hoover off: Hoover, *Memoirs,* 11.

300 "the greatest and boldest operation": Robbins, *The Great Depression,* 53.

300 "takes great interest": "Manuscript Notes by the Governor on Benjamin Strong and on Europe, 3–9 July 1927," reproduced as Appendix 17 in Sayers, *The Bank of England,* 2: 96–100.

301 "I had an important conversation": Moreau, *The Golden Franc,* 430–31.

302 "intrigues to prevent France," "ask Norman to choose": Moreau, *The Golden Franc,* 443, 445. "to establish some sort of dictatorship": Letter from Strong to Walter Stewart, quoted in Clay, *Lord Norman,* 265.

303 "speculation on the stock market": *Chicago Tribune,* July 14, 1928.

303 "most vehement language": "Memorandum on Bank of England—Bank of France Relations," May 24, 1928, quoted in Chandler, *Benjamin Strong,* 417–18.

304 At one point, several frustrated senior directors: Letter from Siepmann to Steward, July 8, 1928, cited in Boyce, *British Capitalism,* 23, n. 69.

304 "One moment he would be sunny": Boyle, *Montagu Norman,* 235.

304 "How hard and how cruel": Chandler, *Benjamin Strong,* 472.

304 "I am desolate and lonesome": Boyle, *Montagu Norman,* 238.

16: INTO THE VORTEX

307 *At particular times*: Bagehot, "Edward Gibbon," *National Review,* January 1856, in *The Collected Works: Literary Essays,* 352.

307 "stocks could be beat": "The Magnet of Dancing Stock Prices," *New York Times,* March 24, 1929.
308 The bubble began: Acampora, *The Fourth Mega-Market,* 129.
309 "The old-timers": "The Magnet of Dancing Stock Prices," *New York Times,* March 24, 1929.
310 "You could talk about Prohibition": Cockburn, *In Time of Trouble,* quoted in Brooks, *Once in Golconda,* 82.
310 Anyone trying to throw doubt: Noyes, *The Market Place,* 322.
310 As the crowd piling into the market: Charles, Merz. "Bull Market," *Harpers Monthly Magazine,* April 1929, 643.
310 "bootblacks, household servants": Charles, Merz. "Bull Market." *Harpers Monthly Magazine,* April 1929, 643.
311 "Taxi drivers told you what to buy": Baruch, *The Public Year,* 220.
311 "When the time comes that a shoeshine boy": Goodwin, *The Fitzgeralds and the Kennedys,* 488.
311 "hard losers and naggers": Patterson, *The Great Boom and Panic,* 18.
311 Even the *New York Times*: "The Army of Women Who Watch the Ticker," *New York Times,* March 31, 1929.
312 Biggest of them was Billy Durant: Sparling, *Mystery Men of Wall Street,* 3–42.
312 "History, which has a painful way": "Warburg Assails Federal Reserve," *New York Times,* March 8, 1929.
312 "sandbagging American prosperity": Galbraith, *The Great Crash,* 77.
313 "Monty and Ben sowed the wind": Chernow, *The House of Morgan,* 313.
313 "speculative orgy," "There are many underlying reasons," "stock speculation," "The prevailing bull market": "The Stock-Speculating Mania," *The Literary Digest,* December 8, 1928.
314 It was from Washington: Ellis, *A Nation in Torment,* 40.
315 "displayed some life": Moreau, *The Golden Franc,* 89.
315 "When the American people": Interview with Roy Young, *Committee on the History of the Federal Reserve System,* Washington: Brookings Institution, 1954–55.
316 The following exchange: *Hearings of Senate Committee on Banking and Currency on Brokers' Loans.* Washington: United States Government Printing Office, 1928, quoted in Lawrence, *Wall Street and Washington.*
317 "oratory, ethics and provincialism": "Federal Reserve versus Speculation," *Time,* February 25, 1929.
317–18 "Wall Street has become the most notorious": "Senate Votes to Ask Reserve Board How to Bar Speculation," *New York Times,* February 12, 1929.
318 Nevertheless, in the last weeks: Letter from Strong to Walter Stewart, August 3, 1928, quoted in Chandler, *Benjamin Strong,* 460–61.
318 Strong's successor: Matthew, Josephson. "Money Men are Different Now," *Saturday Evening Post,* February 26, 1949.
319 "being young and new," "had inherited all antagonisms": Letter from Leffingwell to Edward Grenfell, May 29, 1919, quoted in Kunz, *The Battle for Britain's Gold Standard,* 19.
319 With Strong dead: Interview with Leslie Rounds, *Committee on the History of the Federal Reserve System,* Washington: Brookings Institution, 1954–55.
320 "raise the prestige": "Memorandum on conversation with Governor Young: March 6, 1929," Goldenweiser Papers, Library of Congress, quoted in Clarke, *Central Bank Cooperation,* 156.
321 "any longer intend to be": Bierman, *The Great Myths of 1929,* 78.
321 Harrison urged Norman: Hamlin Diary, February 11, 1929, quoted in Bierman, *The Great Myths of 1929,* 105, n. 11.
321 "to have the stock market fall": Josephson, *Infidel in the Temple,* 22.
321 Once the speculative fever: Harrison Memorandum, "Conversations with Federal Reserve Board: February 5, 1929," quoted in Clarke, *Central Bank Cooperation,* 152.
321 "lived and breathed": Hamlin Diary, March 5, 1929, Library of Congress; "Memorandum on conversation with Governor Young: March 6, 1929," Goldenweiser Papers, Library of Congress, quoted in Clarke, *Central Bank Cooperation,* 157.

322 "If buying and selling stocks": "The War Against Wall Street Speculation," *The Literary Digest,* April 13, 1929.

322 "the hardest time in America": Letter from Peacock to Revelstoke, February 18, 1929, quoted in Kynaston, *The City of London: Illusions of Gold,* 157.

322 "an even deeper feeling": Letter from Norman to European Central Bankers, February 21, 1929, quoted in Clay, *Lord Norman,* 249.

322 Over the next three months: Friedman and Schwartz, *A Monetary History,* 259.

324 Even Adolph Miller: Hamlin Diary, January 3, 1929, quoted in Wueschner, *Charting Twentieth-Century Monetary Policy,* 153.

325 "The French have always had": McNeil, *American Money and the Weimar Republic,* 228.

325 Under the Dawes Plan schedule: Under the Dawes Plan, reparations were supposed to increase according to a "prosperity index," calculated based on trends in foreign trade, the budget, coal production, railway traffic, consumption of sugar, tobacco, and beer and spirit. While the increase in payments was potentially indefinite, most people worked on the calculation that the annual tribute would settle somewhere around $700 million.

326 "with a mixture of awkwardness": McNeil, *American Money and the Weimar Republic,* 228.

327 "nothing but work ": McNeil, *American Money and the Weimar Republic,* 228

327 Government officials: Bennett, *Germany and the Diplomacy of the Financial Crisis,* 5.

327 "the new German Kaiser": "69," *Time,* February 6, 1929.

327 "without the normal incentive": Annual Report of Agent General for Reparations, 1927, quoted in Eyck, *A History of the Weimar Republic,* 2: 174.

329 "was dancing on a volcano": Stresemann Note on Meeting with Parker Gilbert, November 13, 1928, in Stresemann, *Diaries, Letters and Papers,* 2: 406.

329 It came as an ill omen: "Europe's Cold Snap Worst in Centuries," *New York Times,* February 12, 1929; "100 Die in Europe as Cold Holds Grip," *New York Times,* February 13, 1929; "Freezing Europe Faces Cold Famine," *New York Times,* February 14, 1929.

330 Marthe Hanau was a forty-two-year-old: Janet Flanner, "Annals of Finance: The Swindling Presidente," the *New Yorker,* August 26 and September 2, 1939.

332 "lengthy, tiresome": Ziegler, *The Sixth Great Power,* 357.

332 "a vehement, intolerant man": Huddleston, *In My Time,* 256.

332 "tantrums and exhibitionism": Leith-Ross, *Money Talks,* 119.

332 "hatchet, Teuton face," "like a steel trap": Ziegler, *The Sixth Great Power,* 356–57.

332 "If Hell is anything like Paris": Klingaman, *1929: The Year of the Crash,* 163.

332 The German delegates: Kopper, *Hjalmar Schacht,* 146.

334 Schacht's proposal was initially received: Stuart Crocker Memoirs, quoted in Jacobson, *Locarno Diplomacy,* 257.

334 Pierre Quesnay: Stuart Crocker Memoirs, quoted in Jacobson, *Locarno Diplomacy,* 265.

337 "You ought never to have signed": Schacht, *My First Seventy-six Years,* 247.

337 "The crisis may have been": Kopper, *Hjalmar Schacht,* 154.

337 "My prophecy would be": Keynes, "Letter to Andrew Mcfadyean," January 5, 1930, in *Collected Writings,* 18: 346–47.

338 In addition, he continued to manage: Hession, *John Maynard Keynes,* 175.

338 Despite his reputation: Skousen, "Keynes as a Speculator," 161–69.

338 "triumph": Keynes, *Collected Writing: A Tract,* 4: 231.

339 "nothing which can be called inflation": Keynes, "Is There Inflation in the United States?" September 1, 1928, in *Collected Writing,* 13: 52–59

339 "on the side of business depression": Keynes, "Letter to Charles Bullock," October 4, 1928, in *Collected Writings* 13: 70–73.

339 "I was forgetting that gold": Keynes, "Is There Enough Gold? The League of Nations Inquiry," *The Nation and Athenaeum,* January 19, 1929, in *Collected Writing,* 19: 775–80.

339 "Picture to yourself": Kynaston, *The City of London, Illusions of Gold,* 157.

340 "Almost all the great powers": Somary, *The Raven of Zurich,* 155.

341   "even in countries thousands of miles": Keynes, "A British View of the Wall Street Slump," *New York Evening Post*, October 25, 1929, in *Collected Writings*, 20: 2–3.

341   The character of the market: White, "The Stock Market Boom and Crash of 1929 Revisited," 77.

342   Indeed, on September 3, 1929: Paul, Desmond. "An Exploration of the Nature of Bull Market Tops," *Lowry Reports*, 2006.

342   In February, Owen Young: Klingaman, *1929: The Year of the Crash*, 159, 211.

342   Joe Kennedy: Goodwin, *The Fitzgeralds and the Kennedys*, 488.

342   Bernard Baruch claims: Baruch, *The Public Years*, 224–25.

342   Even Thomas Lamont: Lamont, *The Ambassador from Wall Street*, 260.

342   In April 1929, he had some friends: Durant's secret visit to the White House from Sparling, *Mystery Men of Wall Street*, 3–6.

343   "panic which keeps people": Seldes, *The Years of the Locust*, 40.

343   "Scores of thousands: "Europe's 'Wall Street Panic,'" *The Literary Digest*, August 24, 1929.

345   "fat excitable man": Snowden, *Autobiography*, 2: 827.

345   "invisibly the battle of gold": "Palladin of Gold," *Time*, August 19, 1929.

345   In late August, as Britain's reserves hit: Clay, *Lord Norman*, 252.

17: PURGING THE ROTTENNESS

347   "For five years at least": *BusinessWeek*, September 7, 1929

348   "I repeat what I said": "Babson Predicts 'Crash' in Stocks," *New York Times*, September 6, 1929.

349   He was a strict Prohibitionist: Fridson, *It Was a Very Good Year*, 87–88.

350   "none of us are infallible": "Fisher Denies Crash Is Due," *New York Times*, September 6, 1929.

350   Simple commonsense techniques: White, "The Stock Market Boom and Crash of 1929 Revisited," 72–73.

351   "not perhaps surprising": "Financial Markets: Last Week's Reaction in Stocks and the Talk of a Future 'Crash,'" *New York Times*, September 9, 1929.

352   "Mr. Hatry is very clever": Kynaston, *The City of London: Illusions of Gold*, 140.

353   "Stocks have reached what looks like": "Fisher Sees Stocks Permanently High," *New York Times*, October 16, 1929.

353   "increased prosperity": "Says Stock Slump is Only Temporary," *New York Times*, October 24, 1929.

354   "There is a great deal of exaggeration": "Letter from Lamont to Herbert Hoover," October 19, 1929, quoted in Lamont, *The Ambassador from Wall Street*, 266–68.

354   "This document is fairly amazing": Kunz, *The Battle for Britain's Gold Standard*, 55.

354   On Wednesday, October 23: Henry, Lee. "1929: The Crash That Shook the World," *American Mercury*, November 1949.

355   "grave," "gesturing idly": Brooks, *Once in Golconda*, 124.

355   "susceptible of betterment": "Financiers Ease Tension," *New York Times*, October 25, 1929.

355   "There is no man or group": Bell, "Crash: An Account of the Stock Market Crash of 1929."

356   "undue speculation": "Treasury Officials Blame Speculation," *New York Times*, October 25, 1929.

356   "Bankers Halt Stock Debacle": *Wall Street Journal*, October 27, 1929.

358   "friends and former millionaires": Manchester, *The Last Lion*, 826.

358   "participating in the making of history": "Closing Rally Vigorous" and "Crowds See Market History Made," *New York Times*, October 30, 1929.

358   "No one who has gazed": William Manchester, *The Last Lion*, 827.

359   "on fire," "done and can't be undone": Josephson, *The Money Lords*, 82.

359   That evening: Josephson, *The Money Lords*, 82.

360   Though the crash of October 1929: Soule, *Prosperity Decade*, 309.

361   "underlying conditions," "an excuse for going": "What Smashed the Bull Market?" *The Literary Digest*, November 9, 1929.

361   "No Iowa Farmer will tear up his mail order blank": "Wall Street's 'Prosperity Panic,'" *The Literary Digest,* November 9, 1929.

361   "For six years, American business": *BusinessWeek,* November 2, 1929.

361   Industrial production fell: Romer, "The Great Crash and the Onset of the Great Depression," and Galbraith, *The Great Crash,* 142.

362   "Rich people who have not sold": Hirst, *Wall Street and Lombard Street,* 59.

362   "constitutionally gloomy": White, *Autobiography,* 515.

363   "back to normal," "during the next sixty days," "We have passed the worst": Mangold, W. P. "The White House Magicians: Prosperity Invocations," *The Nation,* October 21, 1931, and Allen, *Washington Merry-Go-Round,* 75–76. At several points along the way: Galbraith, *The Great Crash,* 76, 149–51.

363   "Gentlemen, you have come": Schlesinger, *The Crisis of the Old Order,* 231.

363   He frequently claimed in press conferences: Mangold, W. P. "The White House Magicians: Playing with Statistics," *The Nation,* October 28, 1931; "Victory in Maine predicted by Fess," *New York Times,* August 27, 1930; "Labor Commissioner Stewart Quits Post," *New York Times,* July 3, 1932.

364   "liquidate labor, liquidate stocks": Hoover, *Memoirs,* 30.

364   For Mellon, it was a once-in-a-lifetime: Cannadine, *Mellon,* 414–27.

365   Between November 1929 and June 1930: Chandler, *American Monetary Policy,* 144.

365   "1927 experiment": Federal Reserve Board letter from John Calkins, Governor of San Francisco Fed, to George Harrison, January 7, 1930.

366   "We have been putting out credit": Federal Reserve Board, Minutes of the Open Market Policy Committee, September 25, 1930: quoted in Chandler, *American Monetary Policy,* 137.

366   "marathon dance": Federal Reserve Board of Governors, letter from Talley, Governor of Dallas Fed to J. Herbert Case, Chairman of New York Federal Reserve Bank, March 13, 1930.

366   "back to life": Harrison Papers, Letter from Talley to Harrison, July 15, 1930, quoted in Friedman and Schwartz, *A Monetary History,* 372.

367   In September 1930, Roy Young: Pusey, *Eugene Meyer,* 203.

368   "an ordinary tin-pot bucket shop operator," "Judas Iscariot": "Meyer, Eugene" in *Current Biography,* 1941, 575–78.

368   In January 1930, policy decisions: Chandler, *American Monetary Policy,* 133.

369   "panicky selling left London's city": "London Disturbed by Continued Fall," *New York Times,* October 30, 1929.

369   "we in Great Britain": Keynes, "A British View of the Wall Street Slump," *New York Evening Post,* October 25, 1929, in *Collected Writings,* 20: 2–3.

369   like the bursting of an "abscess": Sauvy, *Histoire Economique,* 115.

370   To a visiting Swiss banker: Somary, *The Raven of Zurich,* 157.

370   Convinced that it had been the rise: Sayers, *The Bank of England,* 229, n. 3.

370   During the last week of October: Bank of England, Notes on telephone calls between Harrison and Norman, October 25, October 31, and November 15, 1929.

372   Keynes: "Arising from": HMSO. *Report of Committee on Finance and Industry* (Cmd. 3897), Minutes of Evidence, 1931, 27–31.

372   "Reasons, Mr. Chairman": Boyle, *Montagu Norman,* 327.

373   "an artist, sitting with his cloak": Woolf, *Diary,* 208.

373   "grows more and more temperamental": Papers of Sir Charles Addis, May 7, 1930, quoted in Kynaston, *The City of London, Illusions of Gold,* 202.

18: MAGNETO TROUBLE

374   "To what extremes": Virgil, *The Aeneid,* Book iii, l. 79–81.

374   "the shadow of one of the greatest": Keynes, "The Great Slump of 1930," *Nation and Athenaeum,* December 20 and 27, 1930, in *Collected Writing: Essays in Persuasion,* 9: 126–34.

376–77 "the war . . . fear of Germany": Adamthwaite, *Grandeur and Misery*, 132.

377 "harmonious economic structure": *L'Echo de Paris*, December 7, 1930, cited in Mouré, *Managing the Franc Poincaré*, p. 27.

377 "glittering new embodiment": Brendon, *The Dark Valley*, 132.

378 "the French gold hoarding policy": Einzig, *Behind the Scenes*, vii.

378 "the Banque de France": Howe, *World Diary*, 65.

379 In fact, it was clear that during 1930: Mouré, *Managing the Franc Poincaré*, 143. and Johnson. *Gold, France and The Great Depression*, pp. 152–57.

379 Bullion was so heavy: "Gold: 150 Tons," *Time*, December 26, 1932.

379 "This depression is the stupidest": "D'Abernon on Gold," *Time*, January 5, 1931.

380 "lean on England": General Réquin to General Weygand, February 2, 1931, quoted in Adamthwaite, *Grandeur and Misery*, 138.

381 "sumptuous trimmings: "Tightwad Up and Out," *Time*, January 14, 1935.

381 He was succeeded by his deputy: "Tightwad Up and Out," *Time*, January 14, 1935.

381 Moret thought of himself: Netter, *Histoire de la Banque de France*, 341.

381 "ask favors from the French": Boyce, *British Capitalism*, 296.

382 From his departure aboard the *Berengaria*: "Along The Highways of Finance," *New York Times*, April 12, 1931.

382 "an orchestra leader": "Norman Arrives on Banking Mission," *New York Times*, March 28, 1931.

382 When they begged him: "Norman Goes Home Silent on His Plans," *New York Times*, April 15, 1931.

383 "artificial" agency: Clarke, *Central Bank Cooperation*, 180.

383 "visionary and inflationary": Clarke, *Central Bank Cooperation*, 180.

383 "very gloomy situation": Morison, *Turmoil and Tradition*, 345.

383 "Russia was the very greatest": Stimson Diary, April 8, 1931, quoted in Schmitz, *Henry Stimson*, 85.

383 "U.S. was blind": Lamont Diaries, May 8, 1931, quoted in Kunz, *The Battle for Britain's Gold Standard*, 46.

385 Rumors of the trouble: "False Rumors Lead to Trouble at Bank," *New York Times*, December 11, 1930.

385 The bank had been founded: Werner, *Little Napoleons and Dummy Directors*, 1–12.

385 When, for instance, Bernard went to Europe: Ellis, *A Nation in Torment*, 109.

386 The Bank lent some $16 million: Lucia, "The Failure of the Bank of United States" and Trescott, "The Failure of the Bank of United States, 1930."

386 two big projects on Central Park West: Werner, *Little Napoleons and Dummy Directors*, 125–27.

387 "lend freely, boldly": Bagehot, *Collected Works, Volume 9: Lombard Street*, 79.

387 "A panic . . . is a species": Bagehot, *Collected Works, Volume 9: Lombard Street*, 73.

388 "foreigners and Jews": Letters from Thomas S. Lamont to Edward C. Grenfell, December 13 and 30, 1930, quoted in Chernow, *The House of Morgan*, 326.

388 "with a large clientele": Letter from Russell Leffingwell to Benjamin Joy, January 23, 1931, quoted in Chernow, *The House of Morgan*, 326–27.

388 "I told them": Werner, *Little Napoleons and Dummy Directors*, 206–07.

388 "I warned them": Friedman and Schwartz, *A Monetary History of the United States*, 309n.

389 shaken by such: Friedman and Schwartz, *A Monetary History*, Appendix A.

390 By the middle of 1931: Federal Reserve System, *Banking and Monetary Statistics*, Washington, D.C., 1943, 18. See Bernanke, "Nonmonetary Effects of The Financial Crisis," in *Essays on the Great Depression*, 41–69. in May 1931, the bank runs resumed: "More Bank Trouble," *Time*, August 24, 1931.

391 The real issue for the governors: Gary Richardson, "Bank Distress During the Great Depression: The Illiquidity-Insolvency Debate Revisited" (December 2006), *NBER Working Paper*.

392 "the capitalist system": "Ein' Feste Burg," *Time*, July 27, 1931, and Howe, *World Diary*, 111.

19: A LOOSE CANNON ON THE DECK OF THE WORLD

395 "three generations," "Jewish machination," "a product of the Jewish spirit": Chernow, *The Warburgs*, 323.

396 On December 5, he dropped his bombshell on Berlin: "Schacht Protests Demands on Reich," *New York Times*, December 6, 1929.

397 "he was about to be crucified": Letter from de Sanchez to Lamont, April 28, 1934, quoted in James, *The German Slump*, 59.

397 Schacht had gone "crazy": Kopper, *Hjalmar Schacht*, 171.

398 "on the highest moral grounds": "Success at The Hague," *Time*, January 27, 1930.

398 "flamboyant political moves": The *Times*, January 14, 1930, quoted in Simpson, *Hjalmar Schacht in Perspective*, 52.

398 "immoral agreement": "Schacht to a Piggery," *Time*, March 17, 1930.

399 "What is the actual reason": Quoted in Mühlen, *Schacht: Hitler's Magician*, 28.

401 Historians have debated: Balderston, *Economics and Politics*, 92.

401 unintended consequences of the Young Plan: Ritschl. "Reparations transfers, the Borchardt hypothesis and the Great Depression."

402 "You must not think": "Schacht Blames Reparations for World Slump: Holds Moratorium for Germany Inevitable," *New York Times*, November 22, 1930.

402 "If the German people are going to starve": "Schacht, Here, Sees Warning in Fascism," *New York Times*, October 3, 1930.

402 "I would stop making payments": Schacht, *My First Seventy-six Years*, 277.

403 "not above using the swastika": Fromm, *Blood and Banquets*, 29.

403 "economic situation," "pleasant, urbane" man: Schacht, *My First Seventy-six Years*, 279.

403 On January 5, Göring invited Schacht: Schacht, *My First Seventy-six Years*, 279–280, and Schacht, *Account Settled*, 29–30.

405 It had grown over the last decade: Schubert, *The Credit Anstalt Crisis*, 31–44.

405 to compensate Credit Anstalt: Aguado, "The Creditanstalt Crisis of 1931."

406 The French government: Aguado, "The Creditanstalt Crisis of 1931," and Lewis, *Economic Survey*, 63.

407 "more than likely throw out of the window": Lamont Memorandum to Leffingwell," Debt Suspension Matters," June 5, 1931, quoted in Lamont, *The Ambassador from Wall Street*, 295–96.

408 "gentlemen do not read each other's mail": Stimson and Bundy, *On Active Service*, 188.

409 "conducting a post-mortem": Leith Ross, *Money Talks*, 135.

410 "came crying down . . .": Interview with Herbert Feis, November 4, 1955, quoted in Morrison, *Turmoil and Tradition*, 349.

410 "a sickly, overworked and overwhelmed man": Wells, *Experiment in Autobiography*, 679, quoted in Schlesinger Jr. *The Crisis of the Old Order*, 244.

410 "like sitting in a bath of ink": Stimson diary, June 18, 1931, quoted in Schlesinger, *The Crisis of the Old Order*, 243.

411 "we [the Americans] and the British": Edge, *Jerseyman's Journal*, 156.

411 "the killing of the fatted calf": Edge, *Jerseyman's Journal*, 192.

412 "the more one reflects": Howe, *World Diary*, 105.

412 Norman got hold of young Mellon: Anon, *High Low Washington*, 99.

412 "Are you glad to be in Paris": "Secretary Acts Quickly," *New York Times*, June 26, 1931. Hoover vented against the French: Ferrell, *American Diplomacy*, 114.

413 Berlin was being "bled to death": Federal Reserve Bank of New York, Memorandum on telephone call between Harrison and Norman, July 1, 1931.

413 "France has been playing": Macdonald Diary, July 5, 1931, quoted in Boyce, *British Capitalism*, 336.

414 "Now, Monsieur Mellon": Cannadine, *Mellon*, 438.

415 "round face deep lined": "Beggar No Chooser," *Time*, July 20, 1931.

416 "Not since those days of July 1914": "Beggar No Chooser," *Time*, July 20, 1931.

417 "they had come to a decisive point": Bennett, *Germany and the Diplomacy of the Financial Crisis*, 236.

417   "On the ruins of the wealth": Einzig, *Behind the Scenes of International Finance,* vii.

417   "Never has the incapacity of the economic leaders": "Schacht Arraigns Capitalist Greed," *New York Times,* July 11, 1931.

418   the Danatbank had failed to open: "German Banks Curb Runs by Depositors," *New York Times,* July 14, 1931.

419   "resigned passivity": Guido Enderis, "Berliners Calm in Money Crisis," *New York Times,* July 17, 1931.

419   "much struck by the emptiness," "In such circumstances": E. L. Woodward and R. Butler, eds., *Documents on British Foreign Policy,* 2: 225–26.

420   "the program to be executed": "Hitler Unites Ranks of the Old Germany to War on Brüning," *New York Times,* October 12, 1931.

20: GOLD FETTERS

422   "Lo! thy dread empire Chaos!": Alexander Pope quote from *Bartlett's Familiar Quotations,* 313.

424   Macmillan Report: Williams, "London and the 1931 Financial Crisis."

425   "nervous dyspepsia": Addiss Papers, August 5, 1931, quoted in Kynaston, *The City of London: Illusions of Gold,* 234.

425   "Can't he be persuaded": Letter from Leffingwell to Jack Morgan, July 28. 1931, quoted in Kunz, *The Battle for Britain's Gold Standard,* 107.

425   "Feeling queer": Bank of England, Norman Diary, July 29, 1931.

425   "prejudice, ignorance, and panic": Taylor, *English History,* 288.

427   "It certainly is a tragically comical situation": Webb, *Diary,* 253. 10 Downing Street: Harold Callender, "A Picture of Britain in the Time of Crisis," *New York Times,* August 30, 1931.

427   "pandemonium had broken loose": Boyle, *Montagu Norman,* 272–73.

428   "What the City did": Howe, *World Diary,* 115.

429   "It is now clearly certain": Keynes, "Letter to Ramsay MacDonald," August 5, 1931, in *Collected Writings,* 20: 591–93.

429   "the most wrong and foolish things": Keynes, "Speech to Members of Parliament," September 16, 1931, in *Collected Writings,* 20: 607–11.

429   "admit quite frankly that the way out": Moggridge, *Maynard Keynes,* 525.

430   "rose to his feet, his eyes flashing": Williams, *Nothing So Strange,* 105.

431   "Going off the gold standard": Jones, *Diary, 32–33,* quoted in Brendon, *The Dark Valley,* 164.

431   "Nothing more heartening has happened": "Run," *Time,* September 28, 1931.

432   gold "is dug up out of a hole in Africa": Manchester, *The Last Lion,* 862.

432   Charlie Chaplin, as a guest at Chartwell: Boothby, *Recollections of a Rebel,* 51.

432   "chuckling like a boy": Rolph, *Kingsley,* 164, quoted in Skidelsky, *John Maynard Keynes: The Economist as Saviour,* 397.

432   "There are few Englishmen who do not rejoice": Keynes, "The End of the Gold Standard," in the *Sunday Express,* September 27, 1931, in *Collected Writings: Essays in Persuasion,* 9:245–49.

432   "tragic act of abdication": Bonn, *Wandering Scholar,* 318–19.

433   "A pound is still a pound": "Pound, Dollar and Franc," *Time,* October 5, 1931.

433   "France will be heavily punished": Boyle, *Montagu Norman,* 276.

435   "solidarity and politeness": Letter from Moret to Harrison, October 7, 1931, quoted in Kindelberger, *The World in Depression,* 168.

435   "holes in the ground, privies": *Congressional Record,* 72 Congress, 1 Session, December 9, 1931, 75: 233-6, quoted in Warren, *Herbert Hoover,* 164.

437   "more depressed than ever": Hoover, *Memoirs,* 86.

438   "If there is one moment": J. Bradford DeLong, "The Economic Foundations of Peace" http://econ161.berkeley.edu/Econ_Articles/lal.html

439   "Yes. It was called the Dark Ages": Edwin Lefèvre, "When Is It Safe to Invest?" *Saturday Evening Post,* August 6, 1932.

439   A similar measure in late 1930: Bordo et al., "Was Expansionary Monetary Policy Feasible?"

441 "If you steal $25": *The Nation*, March 8, 1933, quoted in Kennedy, *The Banking Crisis of 1933*, 126.

441 "the so-called depression": "Radio address delivered on February 26, 1933, in Coughlin, *Driving Out the Money Changers*.

442 "It's just as if I put my car": "Close to Bottom," *Time*, March 6, 1933.

443 "If the fall in the price of commodities": Schlesinger Jr., *The Crisis of the Old Order*, 453. "England has played us": "Roosevelt's Ten," *Time*, March 6, 1933.

443 At least six bills were circulating: "Inflation—Curse or Cure?" *The Literary Digest*, February 11, 1933.

444 Hoover composed a ten-page handwritten letter: Schlesinger Jr., *The Crisis of the Old Order*, 477.

445 he "did not want his last official act": Josephson, *The Money Lords*, 120.

445 the New York Fed lost: Wigmore, "Was the Bank Holiday of 1933 Caused by a Run on the Dollar?" Tape 1, 745.

446 "Like hell, I will!": Dorothy Roe Lewis, "What FDR told Hoover, March 3, 1933," *New York Times*, March 13, 1981.

446 "Urban populations cannot do without": "Letter from Lamont to Franklin D. Roosevelt," February 27, 1933, quoted in Lamont, *The Ambassador from Wall Street*, 330.

447 At 9.15 p.m. on March 3: Pusey, *Eugene Meyer*, 235–36.

448 "a beleaguered capital": Arthur, Krock. "100,000 at Inauguration," *New York Times*, March 5, 1933.

21. GOLD STANDARD ON THE BOOZE

451 *"In order to arrive"*: Eliot, *Collected Poems*, 187.

451 To the surprise of many: See William Manchester, "The Great Bank Holiday," *Holiday*, February 1960; "City Awaits Scrip as Cash Dwindles," "Harvard Students Aided," "Divorce Holiday in Reno," and "Scrip at Princeton," *New York Times*, March 7, 1933; "Envoys Lack Cash; Complain to Hull," *New York Times*, March 9, 1933; "Michigan," and "Money and People," *Time*, March 13, 1933. The legislation was supplemented: William L., Silber, "Why Did FDR's Bank Holiday Succeed?"

455 "all kinds of junk": Josephson, *The Money Lords*, 120.

455 the first of his fireside chats: "The President's Speech," *New York Times*, March 13, 1933.

455 "Our President took such a dry subject": "Will Rogers Claps Hands for the President's Speech," *New York Times*, March 14, 1933.

455 "We had closed in the midst": Josephson, *The Money Lords*, 120.

456 "Capitalism was saved in eight days": Moley, *After Seven Years*, 155.

458 "the white sheep of Wall Street": Warburg, *The Long Road Home*, 107.

459 "Poppycock!": Schlesinger Jr., *The Coming of the New Deal*, 195.

459 His simplistic view was: Wicker, "Roosevelt's 1933 Monetary Experiment."

460 "You paint a barn roof": "Teachers and Pupils," *Time*, November 27, 1933; Brooks, *Once in Golconda*, 160–63.

461 "As long as nobody asks me": Schlesinger Jr., *The Coming of the New Deal*, 195.

462 "Well, this is the end of western civilization": Accounts of that meeting are variously provided by Moley, *After Seven Years*, 159–61; Feis, *1933: Characters in Crisis*, 126–30; Warburg, *The Long Road Home*, 119–20; James Warburg, Oral History Project, 492–99, quoted in Schwarz, *1933: Roosevelt's Decision*; and Schlesinger, *The Coming of the New Deal*, 200–201.

462 "can't be defended except as mob rule": Schlesinger Jr., *The Coming of the New Deal*, 202.

462 "Your action in going off gold": Letter from Leffingwell to Roosevelt, October 2, 1933, quoted in Schlesinger, *The Coming of the New Deal*, p. 202.

462 dramatic change in sentiment: Temin and Wigmore, "The end of one big deflation,"

463 "The difficulties are so great": Gunther, *Inside Europe*, 287.

463 "a handsome, fox-bearded gentleman": "Professor Skinner," *Time*, August 29, 1932.

463 "his affectation of the role": "Along the Highways of Finance," *New York Times*, September 4, 1932.

464 "Deport the Blighter": from *Press Time: A Book of Post Classics*, 310–11.

65 "whims" "completely in the dark": Bank of England telephone conversations between Harrison and Norman, April 27, 1933, and May 26, 1933.

66 He practiced it in his personal life: "Tightwad Up and Out," *Time,* January 14, 1935.

68 "King, I'm glad to meet you.": Brooks, *Once in Golconda,* 158; Galbraith, *Money,* 202–203; Warburg, *The Long Road Home,* 128–29.

68 "With Washington committed": "Disgust," *Time,* June 26, 1933.

70 "he felt as if he had been kicked": Josephson, *The Money Lords,* 130.

71 "President Roosevelt is Magnificently Right": Keynes, "President Roosevelt is Magnificently Right," *Daily Mail,* July 4, 1933, in *Collected Writings,* 21: 273–77.

71 "We are entering upon waters": Warburg, *The Long Road Home,* 135–36.

72 "crack-brained" economist: "Teachers and Pupils," *Time,* November 27, 1933; Brooks, *Once in Golconda,* 160–63.

72 "like asking a sworn teetotaler": Josephson, *The Money Lords,* 131.

73 "hit the ceiling": Harrison Diary, October 28, 1933, quoted in Brooks, *Once in Golconda,* 168.

73 "This is the most terrible thing": Henry Morgenthau, Jr., "The Morgenthau Diaries: Part V: The Paradox of Poverty and Plenty," *Colliers,* October 25, 1947.

73 "the gold standard on the booze": Maynard Keynes, "Keynes to Roosevelt: Our Recovery Plan Assailed—An Open Letter," *New York Times,* December 31, 1933, in *Collected Writings,* 21: 289–97.

74 In the four years after 1933, the value of gold: Romer, "What Ended the Great Depression?" and Meltzer, *A History of the Federal Reserve,* 573.

76 "Operated on this morning": Rhodes, *The Making of the Atomic Bomb,* 685–86.

12. THE CARAVANS MOVE ON

77 *If a man will begin:* Francis Bacon quote from *Bartlett's Familiar Quotations,* 166.

77 Breaking with the dead hand of the gold standard: Eichengreen and Sachs, "Exchange Rates and Economic Recovery," and Choudhri and Kochin, "The Exchange Rate and the International Transmission of Business Cycle."

80 "If Hitler comes to power": Gunther, *Inside Europe,* 99; Mühlen, *Schacht: Hitler's Magician,* viii.

80 "Your movement is carried internally": Letter from Schacht to Hitler, August 29, 1932, in Office of the Counsel for Prosecution of Axis Criminality, *Nazi Conspiracy and Aggression,* Vol VII, Washington D.C.: Government Printing Office, 1946, 512–14.

80 "the only man fit": "Hitler Holds Back Decision on Cabinet as Aides Disagree," *New York Times,* November 23, 1932.

81 "a man of quite astonishing ability": Hitler, *Hitler's Secret Conversations,* 350.

81 The recovery was not quite the miracle: This section draws heavily on Tooze, *The Wages of Destruction,* 37–43, and Evans, *The Third Reich in Power,* 322–77.

82 "The whole modern world is crazy": Dodd and Dodd, *Ambassador Dodd's Diary,* 175.

85 "Don't forget what desperate straits": Gilbert, *Nuremburg Diary,* 153–54.

85 In the lead-up to the trial: Overy, *Interrogations,* 73.

85 "like an angry walrus": Dos Passos, *Tour of Duty,* 301.

85 "twisted in his seat": West, *A Train of Powder,* 5.

87 "They were wrong about reparations": Kynaston, *The City of London: Illusions of Gold,* 373–74.

87 "old gentlemen complaining": Williams, *A Pattern of Rulers,* 221.

88 "Hitler and Schacht": Memo from Leffingwell to Lamont, July 25, 1934, quoted in Chernow, *The House of Morgan,* 398.

88 "If this struggle goes on": Goodwin, *The Fitzgeralds and the Kennedys,* 687.

89 "As I look back": Boyle, *Montagu Norman,* 327–28.

90 During the 1930s, Keynes's speculative activities: Skousen, "Keynes as a Speculator," 162, and Moggridge, *Maynard Keynes,* 585.

91 "I do enjoy these lunches": Sayers, *The Bank of England,* 602.

92 "the unpleasantest man in Washington": Skidelsky, *John Maynard Keynes: Fighting for Britain,* p. 260.

492 "he has not the faintest conception": Keynes, Letter to Wilfrid Eady, October 3, 1943, in *Collecte Writings*, Vol. XXV, pp. 352-57.

494 "The flow of alcohol is appalling": Cassidy, John ."The New World Disorder," *New Yorke* October 26, 1998, p 198.

494 "madhouse with most people": Skidelsky, *John Maynard Keynes: Fighting for Britain*, p. 347.

495 "If we can so continue": Skidelsky, *John Maynard Keynes: Fighting for Britain*, p 355.

23: EPILOGUE

497 I have yet to see any problem: Poul Anderson quote from *The Yale Book of Quotations*, 19.

503 "his policies died with him": U.S. House of Representatives, *Banking Act of 1935*, Committee o Banking and Currency, 74 Congress, Ist Sess. 1935.

503 "problems of life": Keynes, "Preface" in *Collected Writings: Essays in Persuasion*. 9: xviii.

503 "trustees, not of civilization": Harrod, *The Life of John Maynard Keynes*, 193-94.

BIBLIOGRAPHY

The bibliography includes not only works referred to in the text but also a selected list of books and articles on the economic history of the period that I have found useful in my research. The interpretation of the causes of the Great Depression set out here is eclectic. Nevertheless, my thinking has been framed by four books in particular: the classic by Milton Friedman and Anna Schwartz, *A Monetary History of the United States 1857–1960*, which highlights the dysfunctional policies and decision making at the Fed; the 1973 book by Charles Kindelberger, *The World in Depression*, one of the early contemporary books to focus on the global dimension of the economic collapse; and the works of Peter Temin and Barry Eichengreen, especially Temin's *Lessons from the Great Depression* and Eichengreen's *Golden Fetters*, which identify the gold standard as the chief culprit for transmitting depression around the world.

ACAMPORA, RALPH. *The Fourth Mega-Market.* New York: Hyperion, 2000.

ADAM, H. PEARL. *Paris Sees It Through: A Diary 1914–1919.* London: Hodder and Stoughton, 1919.

ADAMTHWAITE, ANTHONY. *Grandeur and Misery.* London: Arnold, 1995.

AGUADO, IAGO GIL. "The Creditanstalt Crisis of 1931 and the Failure of the Austro-German Customs Union Project." *The Historical Journal* 44 (2001): 199–221.

ALDCROFT, DEREK H. *From Versailles to Wall Street.* Berkeley: University of California, 1977.

——————— "Currency Stabilization in the 1920s: Success or Failure?" *Economic Issues* 7 (2002): 83–102.

ALLEN, FREDERICK L. *Only Yesterday: An Informal History of the Nineteen-Twenties.* New York: Harper and Row, 1931.

——————— *The Lords of Creation.* New York: Harper and Brothers, 1935.

ALLEN, ROBERT S. *Washington Merry-Go-Round.* New York: Horace Liveright. 1931.

AMERY, LEO. *The Leo Amery Diaries, Volume 1: 1896–1929.* Edited by John Barnes and David Nicholson. London: Hutchinson, 1980.

ANGELL, NORMAN. *The Great Illusion.* New York: G. P. Putnam, 1912.

ANONYMOUS. *High Low Washington.* Philadelphia: J. B. Lipincott, 1932.

ASQUITH, H. H. *Letters to Venetia Stanley.* Edited by Michael Brock and Eleanor Brock. Oxford: Oxford University Press, 1982.

AULD, GEORGE P.. *The Dawes Plan and the New Economics.* Garden City, NJ: Doubleday, 1927.

BACEVICH, ANDREW J. "Family Matters: American Civilian and Military Elites in the Progressive Era." *Armed Forces and Society* 8 (1982): 405–418.

BAGEHOT, WALTER. *The Collected Works of Walter Bagehot. Volume 1: Literary Essays.* Edited by Norman St. John-Stevas. London: The Economist, 1978.

——————— *The Collected Works of Walter Bagehot. Volume 9: Lombard Street.* Edited by Norman St. John-Stevas, London: The Economist, 1978.

BALDERSTON, THEO. "The beginnings of the depression in Germany: investment and the capital market." *Economic History Review* 36 (1983): 395–415.

—————— "War Finance and Inflation in Britain and Germany, 1914-1918." *Economic History Review* 42 (1989): 222-244.

—————— *The Origins and Course of the German Economic Crisis: November 1923 to May 1932.* Berlin: Halder and Spener, 1993.

—————— *Economics and Politics in the Weimar Republic.* Cambridge: Cambridge University Press, 2002.

BANQUE DE FRANCE. *Le Patrimonie de la Banque de France.* Paris: Flohic Édition, 2001.

—————— *Treasures of the Banque de France.* Paris: Éditions Hervas, 1993.

BARTLETT, JOHN, *Bartlett's Familiar Quotations.* Edited by Justin Kaplan. New York: Little Brown, 2002.

BARUCH, BERNARD. *The Public Years: My Own Story.* New York: Holt, Reinhart and Winston, 1960.

BELL, CLIVE. *Old Friends: Personal Recollections.* New York: Harcourt Brace, 1957.

BELL, ELLIOTT V. "Crash: An Account of the Stock Market Crash of 1929," in *We Saw It Happen: The News Behind the News That's Fit to Print.* New York: Simon and Schuster, 1938.

BENNETT, EDWARD W. *Germany and The Diplomacy of the Financial Crisis: 1931.* Cambridge, MA.: Harvard University Press, 1962.

BERENSON, EDWARD. *The Trial of Madame Caillaux.* Berkeley: University of California, 1992.

BERGMAN, CARL. *The History of Reparations.* New York: Houghton Mifflin, 1927.

BERNANKE, BEN S. "The World on a Cross of Gold." *Journal of Monetary Economics* 31 (1993): 251-267.

—————— *Essays on the Great Depression.* Princeton, New Jersey: Princeton University Press, 2000.

BERNSTEIN, PETER L.. *The Power of Gold: The History of an Obsession.* New York: John Wiley and Sons, 2000.

BIERMAN, HAROLD. *The Great Myths of 1929 and the Lessons to Be Learned.* Westport, Connecticut: Glenwood Press, 1991.

—————— *The Causes of the 1929 Stock Market Crash.* Westport, Connecticut: Glenwood Press, 1998.

BINION, RUDOLPH. *Defeated Leaders: The Political Fate of Caillaux, Jouvenel, and Tardieu.* New York: Columbia University Press, 1960.

BLAINEY, GEOFFREY. *The Causes of War.* New York: The Free Press, 1988.

BLAKE, ROBERT. *The Unknown Prime Minister: The Life and Times of Andrew Bonar Law, 1858-1923.* London: Eyre and Spottiswoode, 1955.

BONN, MORITZ J. *Wandering Scholar.* New York: The John Day Co., 1948.

BONNET, GEORGE. *Vingt Ans de Vie Politique 1918-1938: de Clemenceau à Daladier.* Paris: Fayard, 1969.

BOOTHBY, ROBERT. *Recollections of a Rebel.* London: Hutchinson and Co., 1978.

BORDO, MICHAEL D. , EHSAN U. CHOUDHRI, and ANNA J. SCHWARTZ: "Was Expansionary Monetary Policy Feasible During the Great Contraction? An Examination of the Gold Standard Constraint." *Explorations in Economic History,* 39 (2002): 1–28.

BOYCE, ROBERT W. *British Capitalism at the Crossroads 1919-1932.* Cambridge: Cambridge University Press, 1987.

BOYLE, ANDREW. *Montagu Norman.* London: Cassell, 1967.

BRAUN, OTTO. *Von Weimar zu Hitler.* New York: Europa Verlag, 1940.

BRENDON, PIERS. *Eminent Edwardians.* London: Seeker and Warburg, 1979.

—————— *The Dark Valley.* London: Jonathan Cape, 2000.

BROGAN, D. W. *France Under the Republic.* New York: Harper and Brothers, 1940.

BROOKS, JOHN. *Once in Golconda.* New York: John Wiley and Sons, 1999.

BRYAN, WILLIAM J. *The First Battle: A Story of the Campaign of 1896.* Chicago: W. B. Conkey Company, 1896.

CALMORIS, CHARLES W. "Financial Factors in the Great Depression." *The Journal of Economic Perspectives*, 7 (1993): 61–85.

CANNADINE, DAVID. *Aspects of Aristocracy*. New Haven: Yale University Press, 1994.

_____ *The Decline and Fall of the British Aristocracy*. New York: Vintage Books, 1999.

_____ *Mellon: An American Life*. New York: Alfred A Knopf, 2006.

CASSEL, GUSTAV. *The Downfall of the Gold Standard*. Oxford: Clarendon Press, 1936.

CECCO, MARCELLO DE. *The International Gold Standard: Money and Empire*. 1984.

CECCHETTI, STEPHEN G. "Understanding The Great Deflation: Lessons for Current Policy." in *The Economics of the Great Depression*. Edited by Mark Wheeler. Michigan: W.P. Upjohn Institute, 1998.

CHANDLER, LESTER V. *Benjamin Strong: Central Banker*. Washington D.C.: The Brookings Institution, 1958.

_____ *American Monetary Policy: 1928–1941*. New York: Harper and Row, 1971.

CHAPMAN, GUY. *The Dreyfus Trials*. New York: Stein and Day, 1972.

CHERNOW, RON. *The House of Morgan*. New York: Atlantic Monthly Press, 1990.

_____ *The Warburgs*. New York: Random House, 1993.

CHOUDHRI, EHSAN U., and LEVIS A. KOCHIN. "The Exchange Rate and the International Transmission of Business Cycle Disturbances: Some Evidence from the Great Depression." *Journal of Money, Credit and Banking*, 12 (1980): 565-574.

CHURCHILL, WINSTON. *Lord Randolph Churchill*. London: Macmillan and Co., 1906.

_____ *Winston S. Churchill, His Complete Speeches, 1897–1963*. Edited by Robert Rhodes James. London: Chelsea House, 1974.

CLAPHAM, JOHN. *The Bank of England: A History*. Cambridge: Cambridge University Press, 1970.

CLARKE, M. E. *Paris Waits*. London: Smith Elder and Co, 1915.

CLARKE, STEPHEN V. *Central Bank Cooperation*. New York: Federal Reserve Bank of New York, 1967.

_____ *The Reconstruction of the International Monetary System: The Attempts of 1922 and 1933*. Princeton, New Jersey: Princeton University Press, 1973.

CLAY, HENRY. *Lord Norman*. London: Macmillan and Co., 1957.

COCKBURN, CLAUD. *A Discord of Trumpets*. New York: Simon and Schuster, 1956.

_____ *In Time of Trouble*. New York: Simon and Schuster, 1956

COLLIER, PRICE. *Germany and the Germans*. New York: Charles Scribner's Sons, 1913.

COWLEY, MALCOLM. *Exile's Return*. New York: Norton. 1934.

CRONIN, VINCENT. *Paris on the Eve: 1900–1914*. London: William Collins, 1989.

D'ABERNON, VISCOUNT. *The Diary of an Ambassador*. New York: Doubleday, Doran and Company, 1931.

DAWES, CHARLES. *A Journal of Reparations*. London: Macmillan and Co., 1939.

DAWES, RUFUS. *The Dawes Plan in the Making*. Indianapolis: Bobbs-Merrill Company, 1927.

DISRAELI, BENJAMIN. *Contarini Fleming: A Psychological Romance*. London: M. Wally-Dinner, 1904.

DODD, MARTHA. *Through Embassy Eyes*. New York: Harcourt Brace, 1939.

DODD, W. E. Jr. and MARTHA DODD. *Ambassador Dodd's Diary*. New York: Harcourt Brace, 1941

DOS PASSOS, JOHN. *Tour of Duty*. Boston: Houghton Mifflin, 1946.

EDGE, WALTER. *A Jerseyman's Journal: Fifty Years of American Business and Politics*. Princeton: Princeton University Press. 1948

EICHENGREEN, BARRY and PETER TEMIN. "The Gold Standard and The Great Depression." *Contemporary European History*, 9 (2000): 183-207.

EICHENGREEN, BARRY and JEFFREY SACHS. "Exchange Rates and Economic Recovery in the 1930s." *The Journal of Economic History*, 45 (1985): 925–946.

EICHENGREEN, BARRY. "Did Speculation Destabilize the French Franc in the 1920s." *Explorations in Economic History* 19 (1982): 71-100.

_____ "Did International Forces Cause the Great Depression?" *Contemporary Policy Issues 6 (1988):* 90–114.

_____ "The Bank of France and The Sterilization of Gold: 1926-1932." *Elusive Stability: Essays in the History of International Finance: 1919–1939.* Cambridge: Cambridge University Press, 1990.

_____ "The Origins and the Nature of the Great Slump Revisited." *Economic History Review* 45 (1992): 213–239.

_____ *Golden Fetters.* New York: Oxford University Press, 1992.

_____ *Globalizing Capital.* Princeton: Princeton University Press, 1996.

_____ *The Gold Standard in Theory and History.* London: Routledge, 1997.

EINZIG, PAUL. *Behind The Scenes of International Finance.* London: Macmillan and Co., 1932.

ELIOT, T. S. *Collected Poems: 1909–1962.* New York: Harcourt Brace, 1963.

ELLIS, EDWARD ROBB. *A Nation in Torment: The Great American Depression, 1929–1939.* New York: Coward McCann, 1970.

ESHER, VISCOUNT. *Journals and Letters, Volume 3: 1910–1915.* London: Nicolson and Watson, 1938.

EVANS, RICHARD J. *The Coming of the Third Reich.* New York: The Penguin Press, 2003.

_____ *The Third Reich in Power.* New York: Penguin Press, 2005.

EYCK, ERICH. *A History of the Weimar Republic.* Cambridge, MA.: Harvard University Press, 1962.

FEIS, HERBERT. *1933: Characters in Crisis.* New York: Little Brown. 1966.

FELDMAN, GERALD R.. *The Great Disorder.* New York: Oxford University Press, 1997.

FERGUSON, ADAM. *When Money Dies: The Nightmare of the Weimar Collapse.* London: William Kimber and Co., 1975.

FERGUSON, NIALL. *Paper and Iron.* Cambridge: Cambridge University Press, 1995.

_____ *The House of Rothschild: Money's Prophets 1798–1848.* New York: Viking Penguin, 1998.

_____ *The House of Rothschild: The World's Banker 1849–1999.* New York: Viking Penguin, 1999.

_____ *The Pity of War.* London: Penguin Press, 1998.

FERRELL, ROBERT H. *American Diplomacy in the Great Depression: Hoover-Stimson Foreign Policy, 1929–1933.* New Haven: Yale University Press. 1957.

FITZGERALD, F. SCOTT. *The Notebooks of F. Scott Fitzgerald.* Edited by Matthew J. Bruccoli. New York: Harcourt Brace Jovanovich, 1978.

FRASER, STEVE. *Every Man a Speculator: A History of Wall Street in American Life.* New York: HarperCollins, 2006.

FRIDSON, MARTIN. *It Was a Very Good Year: Extraordinary Moments in Stock Market History.* New York: John Wiley & Sons, 1998.

FRIEDEN, JEFFREY. *Global Capitalism: Its Fall and Rise in the Twentieth Century.* New York: W.W. Norton and Co., 2006.

FRIEDMAN, MILTON, and ANNA J. Schwartz. *A Monetary History of the United States 1857–1960.* Princeton, New Jersey: Princeton University Press, 1963.

FRIEDRICH, OTTO. *Before the Deluge.* New York: Harper and Row, 1972.

FROMM, BELLA. *Blood and Banquets: A Berlin Social Diary.* London: Geoffery Bles, 1942.

FRYE, BRUCE. *Liberal Democrats in the Weimar Republic.* Illinois: Southern Illinois University Press, 1985.

GALBRAITH, JOHN K.. *Money: Whence It Came, Where It Went.* New York: Houghton Mifflin, 1975.

_____ *The Great Crash.* New York: Houghton Mifflin, 1997.

GARRATT, GEOFFREY T. *What Has Happened to Europe.* Indianapolis: Bobbs-Merrill Company, 1940.

GARRETT, GARET. *A Bubble That Broke The World.* Boston: Little Brown and Co. 1932.

GASTON-BRETON, TRISTAN. *Sauvez L'Or de la Banque de France.* Paris: Le Cherche Midi, 2002.

GEISS, IMMANUEL. *July 1914: The Outbreak of the First World War.* New York: Charles Scribner's Sons, 1967.

GILBERT, GUSTAVE M. *Nuremburg Diary.* New York: Farrar Straus, 1947.

GILL, ANTON. *A Dance Between Two Flames.* London: John Murray, 1993.

GIUSEPPI, JOHN. *Bank of England: A History from Its Foundation in 1694*. London: Evans Brothers, 1966.

GOLDENSOHN, LEON. *The Nuremberg Interviews*. New York: Alfred A Knopf' 2004.

GOODWIN, DORIS K. *The Fitzgeralds and the Kennedys*. New York: St. Martin's Press, 1988.

GRAVES, ROBERT and ALAN HODGES. *The Long Weekend: A Social History of Great Britain: 1918–1939*. New York: W.W. Norton and Co., 1963.

GREENE, GRAHAM. *The Quiet American*. New York: Modern Library, 1992.

GRIGG, P. J. *Prejudice and Judgment*. London: Jonathan Cape, 1948.

GUNTHER, JOHN. *Inside Europe*. New York: Harper and Brothers, 1937.

GUTTMANN, WILLIAM and PATRICIA MEEHAN. *The Great Inflation : Germany 1919–1923*. London: Westmead, 1975.

HABEDANK, HEINZ. *Die Reichsbank in Der Weimar Republik*. Berlin: Akademie Verlag, 1981.

HALL, THOMAS E. and J. DAVIS FERGUSON. *The Great Depression: An International Disaster of Perverse Economic Policies*. Ann Arbor: University of Michigan Press, 1998.

HAMILTON, JAMES."Monetary Factors in the Great Depression." *Journal of Monetary Economic* 34 (1987): 145-69.

_____ "Role of the International Gold Standard in Propagating the Great Depression." *Contemporary Policy Issues* 6 (1988): 67–89.

HAMMERTON, J. A. and H.W. WILSON. *The Great War*. London: The Amalgamated Press, 1914.

HANSER, RICHARD. *Putsch*. New York: Peter H Wyden, 1970.

HARDACH, GERD. *The First World War 1914–1918*. London: Penguin Press, 1977.

HARGRAVE, J. *Professor Skinner, Alias Montagu Norman*. New York: Greystone Press, 1942.

HARROD, ROY. *The Life of John Maynard Keynes*. London: Macmillan and Co., 1951.

HASSALL, CHRISTOPHER. *A Biography of Edward Marsh*. New York: Harcourt Brace, 1959.

HAWTREY, RALPH G.. *The Art of Central Banking*. London: Longmans Green, 1932.

_____ *The Gold Standard in Theory and Practice*. London: Longmans Green, 1947.

HESSION, CHARLES H. *John Maynard Keynes*. New York: Macmillan, 1984.

HIRST, FRANCIS W. *Wall Street and Lombard Street*. New York: Macmillan and Company, 1931.

HITLER, ADOLF. *Hitler's Secret Conversations: 1941–1944*. New York: Farrar Strauss and Young, 1953.

HOBSBAWM, ERIC. *Age of Empire: 1875–1914*. New York: Vintage, 1989.

HOBSON, JOHN A. *Imperialism, A Study*. London: James Nisbet and Co, 1902.

HOLBORN, HAJO, *A History of Modern Germany: 1840–1945*. New York: A. Knopf, 1969.

HOLTFRERICH, CARL-LUDWIG. "Economic policy options and the end of the Weimar Republic" in *Weimar: Why Did German Democracy Fail*. Edited by Ian Kershaw, London: Weidenfeld and Nicolson, 1990.

HOLTFRERICH, CARL-LUDWIG. *The German Inflation 1914–1923*. New York: Walter de Gruyter, 1986.

HOOVER, HERBERT. *The Memoirs of Herbert Hoover: The Great Depression 1929–1941*. New York: Macmillan and Company, 1952.

HOWE, QUINCY. *World Diary: 1929–1934*. New York: Robert M McBride and Co, 1934.

_____ *A World History of Our Times: The World Between the Wars*. New York: Simon and Schuster, 1953.

HUDDLESTON, SISLEY. *France and the French*. New York: Charles Scribner's Sons, 1925.

_____ *In My Time: An Observer's Record of War and Peace*. New York: E.P.Dutton, 1938.

JACKSON, KEVIN. *The Oxford Book of Money*. Oxford: Oxford University Press, 1995.

JACOBSON, JON. *Locarno Diplomacy: Germany and the West 1925–1929*. Princeton, New Jersey: Princeton University Press, 1972.

JAMES, HAROLD. "The causes of the German banking crisis of 1931." *Economic History Review* 37 (1984): 68-87.

_____ *The Reichsbank and Public Finance in Germany: 1924–1933*. Frankfurt am Main: Knapp, 1985.

_____ *The German Slump: Politics and Economics 1924–1936*. New York: Oxford University Press, 1986.

_____ "Economic Reasons for the Collapse of Weimar" IN *Weimar: Why Did German Democracy Fail.* Edited by Ian Kershaw, London: Weidenfeld and Nicolson, 1990.

_____ *Monetary and Fiscal Unification in 19th Century Germany.* 202. Princeton: Princeton University Press, 1997.

_____ *The End of Globalization: Lessons From the Great Depression.* Cambridge, Ma.: Harvard University Press, 2001.

JAMES, ROBERT RHODES. *Churchill: A Study in Failure 1900-1939.* London: Penguin, 1973.

JEANNENEY, JEAN-NOËL. *François de Wendel en République: L Argent et le Pouvoir.* Paris: Perrin, 200.

JOHNSON, CLARK. *Gold, France and the Great Depression.* New Haven: Yale University Press, 1997.

JOHNSON, ROGER T. *Historical Beginnings: The Federal Reserve.* Boston, MA: Federal Reserve Bank of Boston, 1977.

JONES, THOMAS. *A Diary with Letters: 1931-1950* Oxford: Oxford University Press, 1954.

JOSEPHSON, MATTHEW. *Infidel in the Temple: A Memoir of the Nineteen Thirties.* New York: Alfred A. Knopf, 1967.

_____ *The Money Lords: the Great Finance Capitalists 1925-1950.* New York: Mentor, 197

KAUFFMANN, EUGENE. *La Banque en France.* Paris: Gird et Briere, 1914.

KEEGAN, JOHN. *Winston Churchill.* New York: Viking Penguin, 2002.

KEIGER, J. F.. *Raymond Poincaré.* Cambridge: Cambridge University Press, 1997.

KELLEY, DOUGLAS M. *22 Cells in Nuremberg.* New York: Greenberg, 1947.

KEMMERER, E W. *Gold and The Gold Standard.* New York: McGraw Hill, 1944.

KENNEDY, SUSAN E. *The Banking Crisis of 1933.* Kentucky: University of Kentucky, 1973.

KESSLER, HARRY. *The Diaries of a Cosmopolitan; 1918-1937.* London: Weidenfeld and Nicolson, 1971

KEYNES, JOHN MAYNARD. *Collected Writings of John Maynard Keynes: The Economic Consequences of The Peace.* Vol. II. Edited by Don Moggridge, London: Macmillan and Co., 1971.

_____ *Collected Writings of John Maynard Keynes: A Tract on Monetary Reform.* Vol. IV. Edited by Don Moggridge, London: Macmillan and Co., 1971.

_____ *Collected Writings of John Maynard Keynes: The General Theory of Employment, Interest and Money.* Vol. VII. Edited by Don Moggridge, London: Macmillan and Co., 1971.

_____ *Collected Writings of John Maynard Keynes: Essays in Persuasion.* Vol IX. Edited by Don Moggridge, London: Macmillan and Co., 1971.

_____ *Collected Writings of John Maynard Keynes:Essays in Biography.* Vol. X. Edited by Don Moggridge, London: Macmillan and Co., 1971.

_____ *Collected Writings of John Maynard Keynes: Economic Articles and Correspondence: Academic.* Vol. XI. Edited by Don Moggridge, London: Macmillan and Co., 1971.

_____ *Collected Writings of John Maynard Keynes: The General Theory and After: Part 1, Preparation.* Vol. XIII. Edited by Donald Moggridge, London: Macmillan and Co., 1981.

_____ *Collected Writings of John Maynard Keynes: Activities 1914-1919: The Treasury and Versailles.* Vol. XVI. Edited by Elizabeth Johnson, London: Macmillan and Co., 1971.

_____ *Collected Writings of John Maynard Keynes: Activities 1922-1923: The End of Reparations.* Vol. XVIII. Edited by Elizabeth Johnson, London: Macmillan and Co., 1978.

_____ *Collected Writings of John Maynard Keynes: Activities 1922-1929: The Return to Gold and Industrial Policy.* Vol. XIX. Edited by Don Moggridge, London: Macmillan and Co., 1981.

_____ *Collected Writings of John Maynard Keynes: Activities 1929-1931: Rethinking Employment and Unemployment Policies.* Vol. XX. Edited by Donald Moggridge, London: Macmillan and Co., 1981.

_____ *Collected Writings of John Maynard Keynes Activities 1940-44: Shaping The Post-War World.* Vol. XXV. Edited by Don Moggridge, London: Macmillan and Co., 1981.

KHAN, AGA. *The Memoirs of The Aga Khan: World Enough and Time.* New York: Simon and Schuster, 1954.

KINDELBERGER, CHARLES P. *The World In Depression 1929-1939.* Berkeley: University of California 1973.

_____ *A Financial History of Western Europe.* Oxford: Oxford University Press, 1993.

KIRCHER, R. *Englander*. London: William Collins, 1928.

KLEIN, ERNST. *Road to Disaster*. London: George Allen and Unwin, 1940.

KLEIN, MAURY. *Rainbow's End*. New York: Oxford University Press, 2001.

KLINGAMAN, WILLIAM K.. *1929: The Year of the Crash*. New York: Harper and Row, 1989.

KOPPER, CHRISTOPHER. *Hjalmar Schacht: Aufstieg und Fall von Hitlers machtigstem Bankier*. Munich: Hanser, 2006.

KUNZ, DIANE B. *The Battle for Britain's Gold Standard in 1931*. Beckenham, Kent: Croom Helm Ltd. 1987.

KYNASTON, DAVID. *The City of London: Golden Years 1890–1914*. London: Chatto and Windus, 1995.
_____ *The City of London: Illusions of Gold 1914–1945*. London: Chatto and Windus, 1999.

LAMONT, EDWARD. *The Ambassador from Wall Street*. Landon, MD: Madison Books, 1994.

LAMONT, THOMAS W. *Henry P. Davison*. New York: Harper and Brothers, 1933.

LARGE, DAVID CLAY. *Berlin*. New York: Basic Books, 2000.

LAWRENCE, JOSEPH S. *Wall Street and Washington*. Princeton, New Jersey: Princeton University Press, 1929.

LEAGUE OF NATIONS. *Course and Phases of the World Economic Depression*. Geneva: League of Nations. 1931.

LEFFLER, MELVIN. *The Elusive Quest: America's Pursuit of European Stability and French Security, 1919–1933*. Chapel Hill, NC: University of North Carolina Press, 1979.

LEITH-ROSS, SIR FREDERICK. *Money Talk: Fifty Years of International Finance: The Autobiography of Sir Frederick Leith-Ross*. London: Hutchinson and Co., 1968.

LENTIN, ANTHONY. *Guilt at Versailles: Lloyd George and the Pre-History of Appeasement*. London: Methuen and Co., 1985

LEWIS, W. Arthur. *Economic Survey: 1919–1939*. London: Routledge, 1957.

LLOYD GEORGE, DAVID. *War Memoirs 1914–1918*. New York: Little Brown, 1935.

LOTTMAN, HERBERT. *The French Rothschilds*. New York: Crown Publishers, 1995.

LUCIA, JOSEPH L. "The Failure of the Bank of United States." *Explorations in Economic History* 22 (1985): 402-416.

LYTTELTON, OLIVER. *The Memoirs of Lord Chandos*. London: The Bodley Head, 1962.

McNEIL, WILLIAM C. *American Money and the Weimar Republic*. New York: Columbia University Press, 1986.

MAKINEN, GAIL E. and G. T. WOODWARD. "A Monetary Interpretation of the Poincaré Stabilization of 1926." *Southern Economic Journal* 56 (1989): 205-208.

MANCHESTER, WILLIAM. *The Last Lion*. New York: Little Brown, 1983.

MARQUAND, DAVID. *Ramsay MacDonald*. London: Jonathan Cape, 1977.

MARTIN, BENJAMIN. *France and the Après Guerre 1918–1924*. Baton Rouge: Louisiana State University Press, 1999.

MASTERTON, C.F.G. *England After the War*. London: Hodder and Stoughton, 1922.

McCULLEY, RICHARD T. *Banks and Politics During the Progressive Era: The Origins of the Federal Reserve System 1897–1913*. New York: Garland, 1992.

McEWEN, JOHN M. *The Riddell Diaries 1908–1923*. New Jersey: Athlone Press, 1986.

MACMILLAN, MARGARET. *Peacemakers: The Paris Conference of 1919 and Its Attempt to End War*. London: John Murray, 2001.

MELTZER, ALAN. *A History of the Federal Reserve: Vol.1 1913–1951*. Chicago: University of Chicago Press, 2003.

MIDDLEMAS, K., and J. BARNES. *Baldwin: A Biography*. London: Weidenfeld and Nicholson, 1969.

MILYNARSKI, FELIX. *Gold and Central Banks*. London: Macmillan and Co., 1929.

MOGGRIDGE, DON. *British Monetary Policy 1924–1931: The Norman Conquest of $4.86*. Cambridge: Cambridge University Press, 1972.
_____ *Maynard Keynes: An Economist's Biography*. London: Routledge, 1992.

MOLEY, RAYMOND. *After Seven Years*. New York: Harper and Brothers, 1939.

MONNET, JEAN. *Memoirs*. New York: Doubleday, 1978.

MORAN, LORD. *Winston Churchill: The Struggle for Survival, 1940–1965.* London: Constable, 1966.

MOREAU, EMILE. *The Golden Franc; Memoirs of a Governor of the Bank of France.* trans. Stephen D. Stoller and Trevor C. Roberts. Boulder, Colorado: Westview Press, 1991.

MOTT, T. Bentley. *Myron Herrick; Friend of France,* Garden City New Jersey: Doubleday Doran & Co, 1929.

MOURE, KENNETH. *Managing The Franc Poincaré.* Cambridge: Cambridge University Press, 1991.

——————— "Undervaluing the franc Poincaré". *Economic History Review* 49/1 (1996): 137-153.

——————— *The Gold Standard Illusion.* New York: Oxford University Press, 2002.

MÜHLEN, NORBERT. *Schacht: Hitler's Magician.* New York: Alliance Book Corporation, 1939.

NETTER, MARCEL. *Histoire de la Banque de France entre les deux Guerres.* Pomponne: Monique de Tayrac, 1993.

NICOLSON, HAROLD. *Dwight Morrow.* New York: Harcourt Brace and Co., 1935.

——————— *Peacemaking 1919.* New York: Harcourt Brace and Co., 1939.

NORRIS, GEORGE W. *Ended Episodes.* Philadelphia: John C. Winston. 1937.

NOYES, ALEXANDER D. *The Market Place: Reminiscences of a Financial Editor.* New York: Little Brown, 1938.

NURSKE, RAGNAR. *International Currency Experience.* Geneva: League of Nations, 1944.

OVERY, RICHARD. *Interrogations: The Nazi Elite in Allied Hands, 1945.* London: Penguin, 2001.

PALYI, MELCHIOR. *The Twilight of Gold.* Chicago, IL: Henry Regnery Company, 1972.

PARKER, RANDALL E. *Reflections on The Great Depression.* Cheltenham: Edward Elgar, 2002.

——————— *The Economics of the Great Depression.* Cheltenham: Edward Elgar, 2007.

PATTERSON, ROBERT T. *The Great Boom and Panic 1921–1929.* Chicago: Regency, 1965.

PENTZLIN, HEINZ. *Hjalmar Schacht: Leben und Wirken einer umstrittenen Personlichkeit.* Berlin: Ullstein, 1980.

PETERSON, EDWARD N. *Hjalmar Schacht: For and Against Hitler.* Boston: The Christopher Publishing House, 1954.

PETZINA, D. "Germany and the Great Depression." *Journal of Contemporary History* 4 (1969): 59-71.

PHILLIPS, WILLIAM. *Ventures in Diplomacy.* Privately Published, 1952.

PLESSIS, ALAIN. *Histoires de la Banque de France.* Paris : Albin Michel, 1998.

PRATI, ALESSANDRO. "Poincaré's Stabilization: Stopping a Run on Government Debt." *Journal of Monetary Economics* 27 (1991): 213-39.

PRINGLE, ROBERT AND MARJORIE DEANE. *The Central Banks.* New York: Viking Penguin, 1975.

PUSEY, MERLO J. *Eugene Meyer.* New York: Knopf. 1974.

RAJAN, RAGHURAM G., and LUIGI ZINGALES. "The Great Reversals: The Politics of Financial Development in the Twentieth Century." *Journal of Financial Economics,* 69 (2003): 5-50.

RAUSCHNING, HERMANN. *Men of Chaos.* New York: G.P. Putnam's Sons, 1942.

REES, GORONWY. *The Great Slump: Capitalism in Crisis 1929-1933.* London: Weidenfeld and Nicolson, 1970.

REUTER, FRANZ. *Hjalmar Schacht.* Stuttgart: Stuttgart, 1937.

RHODES, BENJAMIN D. "The Image of Britain in the United States, 1919–1929: A Contentious Relative and Rival" in *Anglo-American Relations in the 1920s: The Struggle for Supremacy.* Edited by B. J. C. McKercher Alberta; The University of Alberta Press. 1990

RHODES, RICHARD. *The Making of the Atomic Bomb.* New York: Simon and Schuster, 1986.

RINGER, FRITZ K. *The German Inflation of 1923.* New York: Oxford University Press, 1969.

RIST, CHARLES. *Une Saison Gatée.* Paris: Fayard, 1983.

RITSCHL, ALBRECHT. "Reparations transfers, the Borchardt hypothesis and the Great Depression in Germany, 1929-1932: A Guided Tour for Hard-headed Keynesians." *European Review of Economic History,* 2 (1998): 49-72.

ROBBINS, LIONEL. *The Great Depression.* London: Macmillan and Co., 1934.

ROBERTS, PRISCILLA. " 'Quis Custodiet Ipsos Custodes': The Federal Reserve's System's Founding Fathers and Allied Finances in the First World War." *Business History Review* 72 (1998): 585-620.

_____ "Benjamin Strong, the Federal Reserve, and the Limits to Interwar American Nationalism." *Economic Quarterly Federal Reserve Bank of Richmond,* 86 (2000): 61-98.

ROBERTS, STEPHEN. *The House That Hitler Built.* London: Methuen, 1937.

ROGERS, WILLIAM. *The Writings of Will Rogers.* Edited by James M. Smallwood, et. al. Stillwater, OK.: Oklahoma State University Press, 1973-1983.

ROLPH, C.H. *Kingsley: The Life Letters and Diaries of Kinsley Martin.* London: Victor Gollancz. 1973.

ROMER, CHRISTINA D. "The Great Crash and the Onset of the Great Depression." *Quarterly Journal of Economics* 105 (1990): 597-624.

_____ "The Nation in Depression," *Journal of Economic Perspectives* 7 (1993): 19-39.

_____ "What Ended the Great Depression?" *The Journal of Economic History,* 52 (1992): 757-784.

ROTHBARD, MURRAY. *A History of Money and Banking in the United States.* Alabama: Ludwig Von Mises Institute, 2002.

RUSSELL, BERTRAND. *Autobiography.* London: George Allen and Unwin, 1967.

SAHL, HANS. *Memoiren eines Moralisten.* Frankfurt:Luchterland,1985.

SAINT-AULAIRE, COMTE DE. *Confessions d'un Vieux Diplomate.* Paris, 1953.

SARGENT, THOMAS. "Stopping Moderate Inflation: The Methods of Poincaré and Thatcher." in *Inflation, Debts and Indexation.* Eds. Rudiger Dornbusch, Mario H. Simonsen, Cambridge, Mass: MIT Press, 1983.

SARGENT, THOMAS. Stopping Moderate Inflation: The Methods of Poincare and Thatcher" in *Rational Expectations and Inflation,* New York: Harper Collins, 1993.

SAUVY, A. *Histoire Economique de la France entre les Deux Guerres.* Paris: Fayard, 1965.

SAYERS, R.S.. *The Bank of England 1891-1944.* Cambridge: Cambridge University Press, 1976.

SCHACHT, HJALMAR. *The Stabilization of the Mark.* London: George Allen and Unwin, 1927.

_____ *The End of Reparations.* New York: Jonathan Cape, 1931.

_____ *Account Settled.* London: George Weidenfeld and Nicholson, 1949.

_____ *My First Seventy-six Years.* London: Allan Wingate, 1955.

SCHEELE, GODFREY. *The Weimar Republic: Overture to the Third Reich.* London: Faber and Faber, 1946.

SCHLESINGER, ARTHUR M. Jr.: *The Age of Roosevelt: The Crisis of the Old Order, 1919-1933.* Boston: Houghton Mifflin Company, 1957.

_____ *The Age of Roosevelt: The Coming of The New Deal.* Boston: Houghton Mifflin and Co. 1988.

SCHMITZ, DAVID F. *Henry Stimson : The First Wise Man.* Wilmington, Delaware: SR Books. 2001.

SCHUBERT, AUREL. *The Credit Anstalt Crisis of 1931.* Cambridge: Cambridge University Press, 1991.

SCHUKER, STEPHEN. *The End of French Predominance in Europe.* Chapel Hill, NC: University of North Carolina Press, 1976.

SCHWARTZ, ANNA J. *A Retrospective on the Classical Gold Standard.* Chicago: University of Chicago Press, 1984.

SCHWARZ, JORDAN. *1933: Roosevelt's Decision, The United States Leaves the Gold Standard.* New York: Chelsea Publishing House, 1969.

SEDILLOT, RENÉ. *Histoire du Franc.* Paris: Recueil Sirey, 1939.

_____ *Les Deux Cents Familles.* Paris: Librarie Academique Perrin, 1988.

SELDES, GILBERT. *The Years of the Locust: America 1929-1932.* Boston: Little Brown, 1933.

SHAPIRO, FRED. (ed.) *The Yale Book of Quotations.* New Haven: Yale University Press, 2006.

SHIRER, WILLIAM L. *The Collapse of the Third Republic.* New York: Simon and Schuster, 1969.

_____ *The Rise and Fall of the Third Reich.* New York: Simon and Schuster, 1990.

SICSIC, PIERRE. "Was the Poincaré Franc Deliberately Undervalued?" *Explorations in Economic History* 29 (1992): 71-74.

SILBER, WILLIAM L., "Why Did FDR's Bank Holiday Succeed?" (August 2007). New York University, Leonard N. Stern School of Business Working Paper.

SIMONDS, FRANK H. *How Europe Made Peace Without America*. Garden City, NJ: Doubleday Page, 1927.

SIMPSON, AMOS E.. *Hjalmar Schacht in Perspective*. New York: Humanities Press, 1969.

SKIDELSKY, ROBERT, DONALD WINCH and D. D. RAPHAEL. *Three Great Economists: Smith. Malthus, Keynes*. Oxford: Oxford University Press, 1997.

SKIDELSKY, ROBERT. *John Maynard Keynes: Hopes Betrayed 1883–1920*. London: Macmillan and Co., 1983.

_____ *John Maynard Keynes: The Economist as Saviour 1920–1937*. London: Macmillan and Co., 1992.

_____ *John Maynard Keynes: Fighting for Britain 1937–1946* . London: Macmillan and Co., 2000.

SKOUSEN, MARK. "Keynes as a Speculator: A Critique of Keynesian Investment Theory" *Dissent on Keynes*. Edited by Mark Skousen. New York: Praeger, 1992

SNOWDEN, PHILIP. *An Autobiography*. London: Ivor Nicholson and Watson, 1934.

SOBEL, ROBERT. *Panic on Wall Street*. New York: E.P.Dutton, 1988.

_____ *The Great Bull Market*. New York: W.W. Norton and Co., 1968.

SOMARY, FELIX. *The Raven of Zurich: The Memoirs of Felix Somary*. New York: St Martins Press. 1986.

SOULE, GEORGE. *Prosperity Decade: From War to Depression: 1917–1929*. New York: Rinehart, 1947.

SPARLING, EARL. *Mystery Men of Wall Street: The Powers Behind the Market*. New York: Greenberg, 1930.

STEFFENS, LINCOLN. *The Autobiography of Lincoln Steffens*. New York: Harcourt, Brace, 1931.

STEINER, ZARA. *The Lights That Failed*. Oxford: Oxford University Press, 2005.

STEPHENSON, NATHANIEL W. *Nelson Aldrich: A Leader in American Politics*. New York: C. Scribner's Sons, 1930.

STIMSON HENRY L. and McGeorge Bundy. *On Active Service In Peace and War*. New York: Harper and Brothers. 1948.

STONE, NORMAN. *World War One: A Short History*. London: Allen Lane, 2007.

STRACHAN, HEW. *The First World War*. New York: Oxford University Press, 2003.

STRESEMANN, GUSTAV. *Gustav Stresemann: His Diaries, Letters and Papers*. ed Eric Sutton, New York: Macmillan and Company, 1935.

STROUSE, JEAN. *Morgan: An American Financier*. New York: Random House, 1999.

TAYLOR, A.J.P. *English History 1914–1945*. Oxford: Oxford University Press, 1965.

_____ *Beaverbrook*. New York: Simon and Schuster, 1972.

TEMIN, PETER. "The beginnings of the Depression in Germany." *Economic History Review* 24 (1971): 240–48.

_____ "Transmission of the Great Depression." *Journal of Economic Perspectives* 7 (1991): 87–102.

_____ *Lessons from the Great Depression*. Cambridge, Mass: MIT Press, 1989.

TEMIN, PETER and BARRIE A. WIGMORE. "The end of one big deflation." *Explorations in Economic History*, 27 (1990): 483–502.

TEMPERLEY, HAROLD AND G.P GOOCH. *British Documents on the Origins of the War* Vol 11. London: HMSO, 1926.

TEMPLEWOOD, VISCOUNT. *Nine Troubled Years*. London: Collins, 1954.

THOMAS, DANA. *The Plungers and the Peacocks*. New York: G.P. Putnam's Sons, 1967.

THOMAS, GORDON and MAX MORGAN-WITTS. *The Day the Bubble Burst*. New York: Doubleday, 1979.

TOOZE, ADAM. *The Wages of Destruction: The Making and Breaking of the Nazi Economy*. New York: Viking Penguin, 2006.

TOYE, RICHARD. *Lloyd George and Churchill: Rivals for Greatness*. London: Pan Books, 2007.

TOYNBEE, ARNOLD. *Survey of International Affairs 1931*. Oxford: Oxford University Press, 1932.

TRACHTENBERG, MARC. *Reparation in World Politics: France and European Economic Diplomacy, 1916–1923* . New York: Columbia University Press, 1980.

TRESCOTT, PAUL. "The Failure of the Bank of United States, 1930." *Journal of Money Credit and Banking* 24 (1992): 384-399.

TRIFFIN, ROBERT. *The Evolution of the International Monetary System: Historical Reappraisal and Future Perspectives.* Princeton, New Jersey: Princeton University Press, 1964.

_____ *Our International Monetary System: Yesterday, Today and Tomorrow.* New York: Random House, 1968.

TUCHMAN, BARBARA. *The Guns of August.* New York: Random House, 1962.

_____ *The Proud Tower.* New York: Macmillan and Co. 1966.

U.S. GOVERNMENT. *Trial of Major War Criminals Before The International Military Tribunal.* Washington D.C.: U.S. Government Printing Office, 1949.

VALANCE, GEORGES. *La Legende du Franc.* Paris: Flammarion, 1996.

VANDERLIP, FRANK A. *From Farm Boy to Financier.* New York: Appleton-Century Co., 1935.

VANSITTART, ROBERT. *The Mist Procession: The Autobiography of Lord Vansittart.* London: Hutchinson and Co., 1958.

VIRGIL. *The Aeneid.* Translated by Robert Fagles. New York: Viking, 2006.

VOTH, HANS-JOACHIM. "Did high wages or high interest rates bring down the Weimar Republic?" *Journal of Economic History* 55 (1995): 801-821.

_____ "With a Bang, not a Whimper: Pricking Germany's Stock Market Bubble in 1927 and the Slide into Depression." *Journal of Economic History* 63 (2005): 65-99

WALWORTH, ARTHUR. *Woodrow Wilson.* New York: W.W. Norton and Co. 1978.

WARBURG, JAMES. *The Long Road Home.* Garden City: Doubleday and Co., 1964.

WARBURG, PAUL. *The Federal Reserve System: Its Origins and Growth.* New York: The Macmillan Company, 1930.

WEBB, BEATRICE. *Diary of Beatrice Webb: The Wheel of Life, 1924-1943, Vol. 4.* Edited by Norman and Jeanne Mackenzie, Cambridge: Harvard University Press. 1985.

WEBB, STEVEN B. *Hyperinflation and Stabilization in Weimar Germany.* New York: Oxford University Press, 1989.

WEITZ, JOHN. *Hitler's Banker.* New York: Little Brown, 1997.

WELLS, H.G.. *The Work, Wealth and Happiness of Mankind.* New York: Doubleday Doran and Company, 1931.

_____ *Experiment in Autobiography.* New York. Macmillan, 1934.

WERNER, M.R. *Little Napoleons and Dummy Directors: The Narrative of the Bank of United States.* New York: Harper and Brothers. 1933.

WEST, REBECCA. *A Train of Powder.* New York: Viking. 1955.

WEST, ROBERT C. *Banking Reform and the Federal Reserve 1863-1923.* Ithaca, N.Y.: Cornell University Press, 1977.

WHEELOCK, DAVID. "Monetary Policy in the Great Depression: What the Fed Did and Why." *Federal Reserve Bank of St. Louis Review,* March 1992, 3-28.

WHITE, EUGENE N. "The Stock Market Boom and Crash of 1929 Revisited." *Journal of Economic Perspectives* 4 (1990): 67-83.

WHITE, WILLIAM ALLEN. *The Autobiography of William Allen White.* New York: Macmillan, 1946.

WICKER, ELMUS. *The Banking Panics of The Great Depression.* Cambridge: Cambridge University Press, 1996.

_____ "Roosevelt's 1933 Monetary Experiment." *The Journal of American History,* 57 (1971): 864-879.

WIGMORE, BARRIE A. "Was the Bank Holiday of 1933 Caused by a Run on the Dollar?" *The Journal of Economic History,* 47 (1987): 739-755.

WILLIAMS, DAVID. "London and the 1931 Financial Crisis." *The Economic History Review,* 15 (1963): 513-528.

WILLIAMS, FRANCIS. *A Pattern of Rulers.* London: Longmans , 1965.

WILSON, A. N.. *The Victorians.* London: Hutchinson and Co., 2002.

_____ *After the Victorians.* London: Hutchinson and Co., 2005.

WINKELMAN, BARNIE F. *Ten Years of Wall Street*. Philadelphia, PA: John C. Winston and Co., 1932.

WOLFF, THEODORE. *The Eve of 1914*. New York: Alfred A Knopf, 1936.

_____ *Through Two Decades*. London: William Heinemann Ltd, 1936.

WOOLF, VIRGINIA. *The Diary of Virginia Woolf*: Vol. 4. Edited by Anne Olivier Bell, London: Hogarth, 1982.

WORSTHORNE, PEREGRINE. *Democracy Needs Aristocracy*. London: HarperCollins, 2004.

WUESCHNER, SILVANO. *Charting Twentieth-Century Monetary Policy: Herbert Hoover and Benjamin Strong 1917–1927*. Westport CT: Greenwood Press, 1999.

YEAGER, LEYLAND B. *International Monetary Relations*. New York: Harper and Row, 1976.

ZELDIN, THEODORE. *A History of French Passions; Volume One: Ambition and Love*. Oxford: Oxford University Press, 1980.

_____ *A History of French Passions: Volume Three: Intellect and Price*. New York: Oxford University Press, 1980.

ZWEIG, STEFAN. *The World of Yesterday*. Nebraska: University of Nebraska Press, 1964.

ZIEGLER, PHILIP. *The Sixth Great Power: Barings, 1762–1929*. London: Collins, 1988.

INDEX